A Philosophy of Mass Art

414/
Conclusion - Passivity vs Accessibly

411 - Ideology + form of Mass Art

p. 405 - Mass Art as often rhetorically fulfilling presuppositions - ideology

I) Carroll to Cultural self Theory

II) Carroll in relationship to Phil.

236 - Cultural Studies + its prejudice in favor of Culture →
8
response to ... Mass Culture
Carroll's response

45 - Good examples
Carroll's reductive

243
Carroll advances repeatedly the problem form / content

372 - Gives up on systematicity of ideology.

373 - Note happening of perspective
tied to capitalism

224 - Opposition AG + Mass Art

193 - Conventionality of Mass Art

2 Benjamin Discussion can't take cognizance of the difference between B's theory of history + orthodox Marxism
— Not progressivist
— Utopia not conceived as greater production

P. 170 Mass Art not AG

184 Theory as non-evaluative

190 - AG vs Mass Art

195 - Ease of understanding / Return to critics

289 Mass Art +
296 Emotion /
Carroll's ideology revealed in the case by case

202 - Hidden politics of Mass Cons.

207 - AG vs. Mass Art

361 Carroll's doubts about ideology

A Philosophy of Mass Art

Noël Carroll

CLARENDON PRESS · OXFORD
1998

Oxford University Press, Great Clarendon Street, Oxford OX2 6DP

Oxford New York

Athens Auckland Bangkok Bogota Bombay
Buenos Aires Calcutta Cape Town Dar es Salaam
Delhi Florence Hong Kong Istanbul Karachi
Kuala Lumpur Madras Madrid Melbourne
Mexico City Nairobi Paris Singapore
Taipei Tokyo Toronto Warsaw

and associated companies in
Berlin Ibadan

Oxford is a trade mark of Oxford University Press

Published in the United States
by Oxford University Press Inc., New York

British Library Cataloguing in Publication Data
Data available

Library of Congress Cataloging in Publication Data

Carroll, Noël (Noël E.)
    A philosophy of mass art / Noël Carroll.
    Includes bibliographical references.
    1. Mass media and the arts.   2. Popular culture.   I. Title.
    NX180.M3C37   1997
    700'.1'03–dc21   97–25934
ISBN 0–19–871129–8
ISBN 0–19–874237–1 (Pbk)

10 9 8 7 6 5 4 3 2 1

Typeset by J&L Composition Ltd, Filey, North Yorkshire
Printed in Great Britain on acid-free paper by
Bookcraft Ltd
Midsomer Norton, Somerset

Dedicated to Arthur Danto

Acknowledgements

This book has been germinating for a long time. The first seeds were planted at Wesleyan University in the mid-80s when a group of us—mostly *habitués* of the Center for Humanities—set about planning the formation of a cultural studies programme. Led by Betsy Traube, Dick Ohmann and Khachig Tololyan, our number included Sally Banes, Hazel Carby, Michael Denning, Len Tennenhouse, Nancy Armstrong, Christina Crosby, Alex Dupuy, Richard Stammelman, Richard Slotkin, Andy Szegedy-Maszak, and Richard Vann, among others. Our initial idea was to produce a statement explaining what cultural studies was to the rest of the campus. I thought that this would take about an afternoon. After a year, it still wasn't finished. For we quickly discovered that each of us had a different idea of what cultural studies was supposed to be. Even a visit from Stuart Hall didn't settle the matter. But the debate was informative for all of us. My approach was to define cultural studies in terms of its object of enquiry, which I thought was obviously mass art. I don't think that anyone agreed with me. And in retrospect, I think that they were probably right. Nevertheless, I had a subject that intrigued me, and I gave up trying to define cultural studies and concentrated on mass art instead.

It was my great luck when I moved from Wesleyan to Cornell that popular culture was an abiding interest of the Society for Humanities there. It was as a fellow of the Society that I taught my first course in mass art. Under the auspices of Jonathan Culler and Dominic LaCapra, the Society enlisted a lively parade of speakers and fellows including David Bathrick, Rachel Bowlby, Laura Mulvey, Karal Ann Marling, Constance Penley, Richard Dyer, Andrew Ross, Linda Williams, and Alexander Doty. Especially pleasant were several conversations with Simon Frith, who gave me useful pointers on popular music, and great gossip. Others on the Cornell campus who offered me useful feedback on my writing were Kwame Anthony Appiah, Carl and Sally Ginet, Cynthia Baughman, Richard Moran, and Peter Lamarque, a visitor from Scotland at the time.

My first paper on mass art was presented at a symposium sponsored by the Volkswagen Stifung at the University of Wurzburg in 1991. There I benefited from thoughtful criticisms and suggestions from Gerhard Hoffman, Alfred Hornung, Herbert Grabes, Lothar Bredella, Hans Bertens, Malcolm Bradbury, Christopher Butler, Paul Levine, David Nye, Herb Blau, and Kathleen Woodward.

Later in 1991, I joined the faculty of the University of Wisconsin. This put me in direct contact with Madison's magnificent department of Communication Arts. This project has profited immensely from comments by David Bordwell, John Fiske, Julie D'Acci, Michele Hilmes, Vance Kepley, Tino Balio, Ben Brewster, Lea Jacobs, Kristin Thompson, Mary Anne Fitzpatrick, Jim Dillard, Don Crafton, J. J. Murphy, and Bill Boddy (who visited for a year). Lewis Leavitt of the History of Medicine, and Pediatrics Departments generously shared with me his penetrating understanding of research on violence in the media.

My own department, Philosophy, has helped me comprehensively—especially by nominating me for a series of grants, fellowships, and finally a named professorship that has supported me in the writing of this treatise. A number of my colleagues have also taken the time and the trouble to provide me with comments on my talks and papers on mass art, and they have made research recommendations that have been important to the production of this book. I would like to note with special thanks the efforts of Elliott Sober, Berent Enc, Dennis Stampe, Alan Sidelle, Harry Brighouse, Ivan Soll, and Andy Levine.

The University of Wisconsin has underwritten the research for this book in a number of ways. I have not only received grants and a named chair with a research budget from the Graduate School in order to pursue this project, but also I have been appointed as a fellow to the Institute for Research in the Humanities for the express purpose of working on mass art. Apart from the benefits in time and money that my appointment to the Institute for Research in the Humanities has provided, it has also given me the opportunity to test my ideas in conversation with other fellows of the Institute, including Paul Boyer, Phillip Harth, David Lindberg, David Bordwell, Klaus Berghahn, David McDonald, Matthew Kramer, and many others.

At Madison, I have had a series of excellent students and teaching assistants who have contributed to my research in diverse ways. Among them are Jeff Dean, Dong Ryul Choo, Sheryl Tuttle Ross, Pat Mooney, Michael Walsh, Randall Blumenstein, Kevin Heffernan, Laura Sizer, and Jinhee Choi.

Quite a large number of aestheticians have read or listened to my work—both formally and informally—and their remarks, arguments, questions, and recommendations have been inestimably important to me. Thus I wish to thank: Philip Alperson, Jim Anderson, Annette Barnes, Ismay Barwell, Margaret Pabst Battin, Peg Brand, John Brown, Lee Brown, Curtis Carter, Allan Casebier, Ted Cohen, Donald Crawford, Gregory Currie, Kendall D'Andrade, Stephen Davies, George Dickie, Denis Dutton, Marcia Eaton, Susan Feagin, Cynthia Freeland, Berys Gaut, Jeffrey Geller, John Gilmour, Jack Glickman, Stan Godlovitch, David Goldblatt, Alan Goldman, Timothy Gould, Theordore Gracyk, Paul Guyer, Karen Hanson, Kathleen Higgins, Thomas Huhn, Gary Iseminger, Matthew Kieran, Peter Kivy, Deborah Knight, Soren Korup, Flo Leibowitz, Jerrold Levinson, Paisley Livington, Antal Lukacs, Joseph Margolis, Patrick Maynard, John Morreall, Mary Mothersill, Alex Neill, David Novitz, Stein Haugom Olsen, Stephanie Ross, Robert Solomon, Goren Sorbom, Richard Shusterman, Anita Silvers, Robert Stecker, Tiffany Sutton, William Taschek, Frank Tillman, Lynne Tirrell, William Tolhurst, Kendall Walton, George Wilson, Tom Wartenberg, and Nicholas Wolterstorff.

Film scholars Richard Allen, Murray Smith, Edward Branigan, Carl Plantinga, Tom Gunning, Tony Pipolo, Douglas Gomery, Joe Anderson, Stuart Liebman, Ed Tan, Lucy Fischer, and Jonathan Buchsbaum have all been willing to discuss my work seriously with me. P. Adams Sitney provided another sort of impetus, challenging me to justify how a supposed aesthetician could be interested in mass art. Julie Hochberg gave me always reliable advice about the psychological literature I needed to master. John Szwed helped me with various musical references, while my brother, Patrick Joseph Carroll, patiently went over the specifics of various sound recording technologies with me. Doug Rosenberg checked my remarks on TV technology. In another vein, Paddy Scannell encouraged me in the conviction that philosophy could be relevant to cultural studies.

I have been invited to speak on mass art in Scandinavia on numerous occasions. Erik Hedling, Torben Grodal, Mariane Marcussen, and Jan Olsson have been among my gracious hosts there. In Moscow, Oleg Krivtsun and Neja Zorkaya, the dean of Russian popular culture studies, sponsored a spirited seminar on my work at the Art Research Institute.

Throughout this project, Annette Michelson has been a constant source of assurance. She has always shown a keen interest in my progress and she has invited me to speak on mass art more than once—both at CASVA and at New York University. She discussed the earlier chapters of this book with me at length as they were developing, and she helped me especially with the sections on Greenberg, Benjamin, and Adorno. I first encountered these authors when I was Annette's student thousands of years ago. Amazingly, however, as I grow older, Annette gets younger—alert, informed, always a step ahead of the moment.

As is his way, David Bordwell took the time out to read my manuscript through several versions, making voluminous comments and suggestions on each pass. Sometimes I feel as though David did more work on this book than I did. I don't know where he found the opportunity or the energy—though I am deeply grateful that he did. His exuberance and productivity seem inexhaustible. Do you think he sleeps?

I have dedicated this book to Arthur Danto. Inasmuch as many university-lifers like me have never left school, I suppose that there is something of the adolescent still in us. We, or, at least, I remain susceptible to academic hero worship, and Arthur Danto has always been my idol. It is not that I envy his brilliance, his wit, and his learning. I am simply always dazzled by them.

My wife, Sally Banes, helped me in every way. She fixed my grammar, my spelling, and my punctuation. She fixed the computer, too, whenever I found some new way to confound it. She vetted mystery novels and Harlequin Romances for me and scouted drugstore book racks for new trends. On the basis of incoherent mumblings, she sang and even danced the rock songs of yesteryear that I could only barely remember. We watched TV reruns together and talked about them till dawn. If one could earn frequent-flyer credits for miles of videotape, Sally could soar around the world for eighty days. But for all the grinding schedule, Sally remained in good cheer—the light and the lightness in my life.

Finally, Andrew Lockett, my editor at Oxford University Press, has been enterprising, enthusiastic, and expeditious. Like everyone else previously mentioned, he has tried to make this a better book. If they have all failed, it is because they have encountered an obstacle.

Me.

Contents

Introduction

This is a book about mass art—about TV, movies, bestselling novels and other sorts of pulp fiction, popular music (both recorded and broadcast), comic books, cartoons, photography, and the like.[1] At present, it is a cliché to say that we live in a world inundated with mass art. The amount of time that the average American household spends in front of the television set seems virtually astronomical. The corporations that specialize in the production and distribution of mass art are significant economic players. And the names of the artists who create mass art are household words. This is true not only of actors and singers, but of writers, directors, and producers. Stephen King and Steven Spielberg are better known than many heads of state.

Clearly this condition is most evident in the industrialized world, where mass art or, if you prefer, mass entertainment, is probably the most pervasive form of aesthetic experience for the largest number of people—people from all classes, races, and walks of life. In the United States, mass art has a genuine claim to providing a substantial portion of what makes up our common culture. Moreover, as is well known, mass art crosses national boundaries easily. In Russian market-places, for example, one can find a Michael Jackson babushka that metamorphoses from a panther into a chimpanzee sitting on a bazaar table alongside matryoshka dolls composed of successively smaller figurines of Bruce Springsteen, Madonna, Boy George, Dave Stewart, and Annie Lennox.[2]

---

[1] Including advertisements of the more creative variety—not ads that address the audience directly, but the ones that employ artistic means, such as montage, collage, juxtaposition, artful composition, and so on.

[2] Benjamin R. Barber, *Jihad vs. McWorld* (New York: Times Books, 1995), pp. 306 and 19 respectively.

If mass art is everywhere in the industrialized West, it is also very widely distributed elsewhere, including the third and fourth worlds. MTV Latino blares 'Chequenos' (Spanlais for 'Check us out') from Mexico to Patagonia.[3] India still produces more films than the United States, and Hong Kong cinema is international fare. Several years ago the most popular TV programme in Russia was a Mexican soap opera. Indeed, Mexico and Brazil have become leading producers and exporters of programmes throughout Latin America.[4] American TV programmes are rerun in South America, and Hollywood film-making has come to depend on the international market as a major source of revenue. A flop stateside can be recuperated overseas.[5]

By the mid-eighties, merely one decade after the VCR became generally available to private households, sixty million units were already in place around the world.[6] Today, one can travel virtually anywhere and find video cassette players. One can visit certain general stores in Bali and find tapes for rental. In 1992, 250 million video cassettes were sold. And, of course, mass art represents the bulk of the software that is played on the VCR hardware. Likewise, the development of direct broadcasting by satellites has not only vastly augmented the distribution of mass art (those legendary five hundred channels), but it has made that process transnational. In short, we live, it seems fair to say, in the age of mass art.

Undoubtedly, it would be hard to fix the date when the age of mass art began. A likely candidate would be somewhere around the invention of the first major or inaugural mass information technology in the West, the printing press, which made possible the emergence of early forms of mass art, such as the novel.[7] Furthermore, the shift from script to print was dramatically accelerated in the nineteenth century by technological innovations like Koenig's steam press and then the rotary press. And since the nineteenth and early twentieth centuries—in concert with the industrial revolution—the means for producing and distributing art on a mass scale have been expanded momentously by the invention of such information technologies as photography, film, radio, sound recording, and TV. Moreover, ever more technologies for the production and distribution of mass

---

[3] Gabriel Escobar and Anne Swardon, 'From Monroe Doctrine to MTV Doctrine', *Washington Post* (National Weekly Edition), 11–17 Sept. 1995, p. 17.

[4] John B. Thompson, *The Media and Modernity: A Social Theory of the Media* (Stanford: Stanford University Press, 1995), 163.   [5] For example, the TV programme *Central Park West*.

[6] Gladys D. Ganley and Oswald H. Ganley, *Global Political Fallout: The VCR's First Decade* (Cambridge, Mass.: Center for Information Policy Research, Harvard University, 1987).

[7] Of course, printing had already existed in China and Korea. For convenience, however, we may date the beginnings of the Western story of mass information technologies at around 1440, when Johann Gutenberg began to experiment with printing. See S. H. Steinberg, *Five Hundred Years of Printing* (Harmondsworth: Penguin, 1974).

art are in the offing, including computers, laser disks, and we know not what. As a result, we may predict that, into the conceivable future, we can expect the production of more and more mass art, rather than less.

Though the term 'mass art' will be defined more precisely in Ch. 3, for the time being, let us say that mass art is popular art produced and distributed by a mass technology. Of course, if by 'technology' we mean that which augments our natural powers, then the question of the relation of art to technology is a perennial one. However, if we have in mind a narrower conception of technology, one that pertains to the use of power technologies—i.e., to the routine, automatic, mass production of multiple instances of the same product (be they cars or shirts)—then the discussion of technologically produced and distributed art becomes a pressing one for our century. For in our century, especially, traffic with artworks has become increasingly mediated by technologies in the narrower (mass production, power technology) sense of the term.

A technology in the broad sense is a prosthetic device that amplifies our powers.[8] In this respect, the technologies that mark the industrial revolution are prostheses of prostheses, enhancing our already augmented productive powers through the automatization of our first-order technologies. Let us call these second-order technologies mass technologies. It is the development of mass communication technologies that has augured in the era of mass art, i.e., an era dominated—at least statistically—by artworks incarnated in multiple instances and disseminated widely across space and time.

Mass art has arisen in the bosom of modern industrial mass society, and it is expressly designed for use by that society, employing as it does the characteristic productive forces of that society—namely, mass technologies—for the purpose of delivering art to enormous consuming populations. Mass art is the art of mass society, and it is intended to serve the purposes of mass society.

Mass society itself begins to emerge gradually with the evolution of capitalism, urbanization, and industrialization, and mass art begins to develop in tandem with the onset of the printing press. As industrialization and the information technologies that are part and parcel of it expanded, photography, motion pictures, radio, telecommunications, sound recording, and now computerization have been added to the arsenal of mass art. Its reach is virtually global. Indeed, it is becoming increasingly difficult, if

---

[8] Patrick Maynard, 'Photo-Opportunity: Photography as Technology', *Canadian Reviews of American Studies*, 22/3 (1991), 305–6.

not effectively impossible, to find people in the world today who have not had at least some exposure to mass art.

And, as already noted, mass art supplies a great many people with their primary access to aesthetic experience. Thus, one would anticipate that mass art would be an important topic for philosophers of art both in the present day and throughout the twentieth century. However, that is not the way that it has been. Most philosophers of art either ignore mass art altogether—preferring to tailor their theories to so-called high art (or avant-garde art)—or, if they do attend to mass art, they do so in order to denigrate it—to explain why it is not really art, or to explain why it is necessarily bad art. Thus, despite the fact that we live in the age of mass art, where most of us, I conjecture, are willing to agree that mass art can be either good or bad, we do not yet have adequate philosophical theories to characterize it. This situation, it seems to me, cries out for rectification. And it is the purpose of this book to make a step in that direction. It is the purpose of this book to contribute to and perhaps even to initiate the philosophy of mass art from the perspective of analytic aesthetics.

I call this book *A Philosophy of Mass Art* rather than *The Philosophy of Mass Art* for several reasons. First, it is hardly definitive. Rather it is at best introductory—not in the sense of being an introductory textbook, but in the sense that it is a first, undeniably lurching, step in the direction of developing what may someday be a better candidate for *The Philosophy of Mass Art*. I have every expectation that other philosophers reading this book will use it as an occasion to do a better job than I have. At the same time, I hope that I have set up a number of philosophical themes, problems, and issues concerning mass art in useful and interesting ways.

Perhaps a better title would be *Prolegomena to the Philosophy of Mass Art*. But that is the sort of title that drives publishers crazy. As that more accurate title suggests, this book is preparatory to the philosophical study of mass art inasmuch as it lays out certain problems in a perspicuous manner. It would be nice if some of the solutions that I suggest hit their mark. But I will be satisfied if the text succeeds in clearing the ground for profitable philosophical dialogue.

Moreover, I say 'prolegomena', rather than 'prolegomenon', and 'a philosophy of mass art' rather than 'the philosophy of mass art' since this book, though it has some systematic aspects, is neither fully systematic with respect to the topics it broaches, nor are the topics it canvasses exhaustive of the questions that philosophers might ask about mass art. The book is a series of introductions to various philosophical problems that, along with others, might become the basis of some future possible book, probably written by someone else, that could be called, unblushingly, *The Systematic Philosophy of Mass Art*. But such a book could only be written at the end of a long discussion of which this book is, at best, a helpful beginning.

This book comprises discussions of a number of sometimes related, sometimes unrelated, philosophical topics concerning mass art. Since I have already claimed that most philosophers of art either ignore or deprecate mass art, the first chapter deals with what I call philosophy's resistance to mass art. In this chapter, I examine a series of important philosophical arguments against mass art, including primarily those of Dwight MacDonald, Clement Greenberg, Robin Collingwood, T. W. Adorno, and Max Horkheimer. I call these arguments philosophical because the arguments in question all rely on some conception of the essential features of mass art. That is, they attempt to show that mass art is never art, or that it is always bad art as a matter of necessity—as a matter of the very nature of mass art.

Most of the first chapter is taken up with refuting these arguments in detail. After that, however, I also go on to speculate about why philosophers of art are so often either oblivious or outright hostile to mass art, despite its claim to being at least one of the most important artistic developments of the twentieth century.

Refuting philosophy's resistance to mass art seems to me to be an unavoidable starting-point for my project, since if there is to be a philosophy of mass *art*, it is necessary to show what is wrong with previous philosophical attempts to demonstrate that it is pseudo or ersatz art. This first chapter does not deal with all of the arguments that philosophers have brought to bear against mass art. Ensuing chapters grapple with additional charges. However, I think the opening chapter does address a number of the most important arguments against the status of mass art *qua* art.

Though I have claimed that in general philosophers have been either stubbornly silent about or aggressively inhospitable toward mass art, there have been a number of exceptions. Thus, the second chapter takes up what I call philosophical celebrations of mass art—philosophical arguments designed to demonstrate that mass art deserves to be considered on a par with other sorts of art. The arguments in this chapter, as in the preceding chapter, are philosophical in the sense that they presuppose notions about the nature of mass art. That is, they attempt to elevate the status of mass art by calling our attention to putatively essential features of mass art (and to the consequences of those features) in a way that recommends mass art to us.

The thinkers whose arguments I examine in the second chapter are Walter Benjamin and Marshall McLuhan. These are two of the most eloquent defenders of mass art. However, though I am allied to them in their suspicion of philosophy's resistance to mass art, ultimately I believe that they try to prove too much on mass art's behalf. Thus, the second chapter of the book turns out to be as critical as the first chapter. I conclude that neither Benjamin nor McLuhan provides a fruitful way in which to initiate a philosophy of mass art. Their claims, examined in the cold light of day, are far too extravagant. Their conceptions of mass art are too charged with enthusiasm. Their characterizations of mass art are overly laden with evaluation and social allegory. If either has a definition of mass art, it is honorific rather than classificatory.

Moreover, since I think that a philosophy of mass art should be grounded in a classificatory definition of the subject, the third chapter of the book sets out to supply just that. Whereas the first two chapters are critical of the theories of other philosophers, the third chapter attempts to construct a positive account of the nature of mass art, including a hypothesis about the ontological status of mass art.

My analysis of mass art is conducted in the style of analytic philosophy. I attempt to develop and defend a series of necessary conditions that are jointly sufficient for calling something a mass artwork. I realize that this sort of search for an analytical definition is often thought to be unrealistic nowadays. However, I persist in the attempt for two reasons: first, we will not know whether it is unrealistic in a specific case until we try it out; and second, because, even if the attempt fails, it is of immense heuristic value for flushing out important theoretical issues. Proceeding as if we might secure a real definition (a definition in terms of necessary conditions that are jointly sufficient) is a highly productive research strategy. Thus, I adopt it even if my conjectures might be subject to future refutations. Of course, at this point in time, I am satisfied with my conjectures. I am only saying that if they are eventually shown to be false I will not be sorry that I attempted to provide a theory of mass art replete with necessary conditions that are jointly sufficient.

Indeed, at least one philosopher, David Novitz, has already attempted to refute my theory of mass art and to field a theory of his own. Consequently, I spend a portion of the third chapter dealing with his criticisms and comparing his theory of mass art to mine. Perhaps needless to say, I argue that mine is superior. However, I do not spend so much time on Novitz's interesting arguments for the sake of oneupmanship, but because I think that dialectically engaging with other theorists provides insight. Novitz's criticisms provide me with the opportunity—in fact, they saddle me with the responsibility—to clarify my own theory in various important ways.

In Chapter 3, I also address several arguments against my conception of mass art that are likely to be directed at it from the field of contemporary inquiry called cultural studies. Since at present cultural studies is the major area in the humanities for discussing what I call mass art, I would be remiss if I did not consider some of its important views.

Outside the environs of philosophy, cultural studies is a hot item. So in the penultimate section of the third chapter I construct a debate between myself and one of the leading international pioneers of cultural studies—John Fiske. If some readers are unhappy that I only deal with Fiske in detail here—rather than a wide array of contemporary cultural theorists—let me remind them that this is a book about the philosophy of mass art and not a book about the philosophy of cultural studies. Such a book on cultural studies could be written. Perhaps it should be written. But if I were to do it, that would have to be somewhere down the road.

After presenting a theory of the nature of mass art, a question arose about what to tackle next. There were many alternatives. The shape of this book has changed more than once. Finally I settled on three topics—mass art and the emotions, mass art and morality, and mass art[9] and ideology. These are the subjects of Chapters 4, 5, and 6 respectively. There might have been different chapters from these; and there might have been more chapters (though not if the publisher had anything to say about it). I chose these because they seemed to be three areas not only of contemporary preoccupation, but also, more importantly, of enduring concern about mass art. The relation of mass art to the emotions is a recurring trope in discussions of mass art, while the relation of mass art to morality is the first and often the sole topic of commentators—from presidential candidates to legislators, religious leaders, journalists, social scientists, and public intellectuals. Perhaps anxieties about the relation of mass art to ideology are less rampant, though it is certainly an obsession with contemporary academics in the humanities. Indeed, it may be the interest in the university with the reception side of things that predisposed me to a selection of these three topics, since they all involve the relation of mass art to its audience.

[9] Richard Rorty has said the 'process of coming to see other human beings as "one of us" rather than as "them" is a matter of detailed description of what unfamiliar people are like and of what we ourselves are like. This is a task not for theory but for genres such as ethnography, the journalist's report, the comic book, the docudrama, and, especially, the novel. . . . That is why the novel, the movie and the TV programme have, gradually but steadily, replaced the sermon and the treatise as the principal vehicles of moral change and progress' *Contingency, Irony and Solidarity* (Cambridge: Cambridge University Press, 1989), p. xvi. In Ch. 5, without concurring with Rorty's demotion of theory, I have tried to provide numerous examples of what he calls the process of coming to see others as 'one of us', or, as I prefer to say, as moral persons.

In each of the last three chapters of the book, one of my primary aims has been to evolve frameworks in which the relation of mass art to the emotions, to morality, and to ideology can be analysed. It is my intention that these frameworks be useful to scholars in the humanities for conducting future research. I have tried to clarify what is at stake in talking about mass art in relation to the emotions, morality, and ideology. In this, I have taken on the philosophical role that Locke dubs the 'underworker' (not that of an undertaker). I have attempted to craft concepts and conceptual frameworks that will be useful to the humane discussion and criticism of mass art. In this, I hope to contribute not only to the philosophical analysis of mass art, but also to make my philosophical results serviceable to scholars in other disciplines.

There is one criticism of my discussions of mass art in relation to the emotions, morality, and ideology that I fear is inevitable. Let me try to head it off at the pass now, though I know this is probably impossible. I already anticipate reviewers raising it again and again. The criticism is this: though I talk about mass art in relation to the emotions, morality, and ideology at length, most of what I say has nothing distinctive to do with mass art. I may use many examples from mass art to illustrate my points, but most of the relations that I identify between mass art and the emotions, morality, and ideology could obtain between this trio of phenomena and what I call esoteric art.

That is, I offer general theories of the relation of art—or, at least, narrative and representational art—to the emotions, morality, and ideology. Though these theories are applicable to mass art, they are applicable elsewhere as well. They are not mass art specific. They are general philosophical theories of narrative and representational art and their relations to the emotions, morality, and ideology. They are not unique to mass art. So why say the book is about the philosophy of mass art when much of it—especially the last three chapters—is about general themes in the philosophy of art as applied to mass art.

This charge is not completely right. It is true that, in the main, I develop somewhat general theories of the relation of narrative and representational art to the emotions, morality, and ideology and then go on to apply these theories to mass art. But it is also true that I try to relate these general theories to what I call, in the third chapter, a central design desideratum of mass art, namely accessibility. That is, I claim that it is a necessary feature of mass art that it is designed to be accessible to masses of people; ultimately, that is why it is called *mass* art. Thus, when it comes to applying general theories of art and the emotions, art and morality, and art and ideology to mass art, I try to show how the applications of the structures in question to mass art involve adapting said structures such that they will be generally accessible to very large audiences, audiences whose composition crosses the boundaries of class, race, ethnicity, gender, nationality, and sometimes even culture.

Having said that much, however, I must also concede the thrust of the observation: my theories are often general theories of art—usually of narrative and representational art—applied to cases of mass art. But I say that unapologetically. There are several reasons for my temerity. First, mass art evolved out of many pre-existing art forms. Therefore, it should come as no surprise that the structures it employs for engaging the emotions, morality, and ideology are on a continuum with structures in already existing art practices that engage the emotions, morality, and ideology. That some of the structures that operate in mass art share essential features with some of the structures in other kinds of art is simply part of the phenomenon under investigation. Of course, my analytic categories will reflect that. If they did not, they would not fit the subject. That is, there would be something wrong with my theories if they only isolated emotional, moral, and ideological structures that pertained to all and only mass art. My theories would, in such a case, be woefully incomplete.

Secondly, I have to confess that I do not think that there are emotional, moral, and ideological structures that are perfectly peculiar to all and only mass art. With respect to these phenomena, I think that mass art is predominantly like other forms of narrative and representational art—at least at a certain level of analytic generality. Thus, my theories reflect this generality.

However, even if there were (as I doubt) some emotional, moral, or ideological structures that are distinctive of all and only mass art, I would still proceed in the manner that I have. For granting, for the sake of argument, some cases like this, even the believer in such essentially mass-art structures would have to agree that they are few and far between. Thus, if we have chosen these topics because of a general concern with the operation of the emotions, morality, and ideology in mass art, and that concern is aimed at a comprehensive account of these phenomena, then my approach seems eminently reasonable, since it covers the largest number of cases. If there are mass-art-specific structures in this neighbourhood (something about which I am extremely sceptical), there are very few. So if we want to account for the general operation of mass art with respect to the emotions, morality, and ideology, one is advised to proceed as I do—working with general theories, rather than putatively mass-art-specific theories. I suspect that many of my colleagues in philosophy will balk at this. But here I stand.

Another criticism of what follows is that many of my theories are best attuned to representational mass art and that the vast majority of what I discuss is narrative mass art, including pulp literature, movies, TV, comic books, songs with stories (or, at least, dramatic personae and implied stories), and so on. That leaves out things like pure instrumental music and sheer visual design. I admit these lacunae are there. That is part of what I meant by acknowledging that my account is not exhaustive. With respect to pure instrumental music, I confess that I did not feel that I had the relevant expertise to speak knowledgeably about it. I leave that task for some other philosopher. Pure visual designs are something I feel more comfortable with and I will attempt to address the topic at a later date. I did not do so here both because I think that most mass art is representational and/or narrative and because I could not figure out how to work in a discussion of pure visual designs without digressing awkwardly from the main lines of argument. These, of course, are excuses, not justifications. Perhaps by saying that the text is only a prolegomena I am attempting to exonerate myself from the brunt of these criticisms.

The style of this book is very argumentative. Logical argumentation and conceptual clarification are its major research tools. There are, in short, a lot of numbered premises and definitions in this book. This, of course, is a reflection of my commitment to the analytic school of philosophy. To readers who are unfamiliar with this approach, much of what follows may seem tiresome, niggling, and obnoxious. In its defence, let me say this much. The argumentation is predicated on a dialectical conception of the acquisition of knowledge; knowledge grows through criticism, if only through the elimination of error. Refuting alternative theories yields insight, if only in the sense of telling you what pitfalls there are to avoid. For the offended reader who hopes that one day I will get my own back and be treated by another philosopher as ruthlessly as I criticize Collingwood, let me say that I hope so too, since whatever progress there is in philosophy depends on criticism.

Readers familiar with some of my other work in the philosophy of art may be surprised at what they find here. Elsewhere I have been very critical of functional theories of the nature of art. But herein I offer what looks like a functional theory of at least mass art. Or, to put the matter differently, when it comes to answering the question 'What is art?' I am on record for defending a historical characterization of art.[10] But, in this book,

---

[10] Noël Carroll, 'Art, Practice and Narrative', *Monist*, 71 (1988), 140–56; id., 'Identifying Art', *Institutions of Art*, ed. Robert Yanal (University Park: Pennsylvania State University Press, 1994), 3–38; id., 'Historical Narratives and the Philosophy of Art', *Journal of Aesthetics and Art Criticism*, 51/3 (1993), 313–26.

there is a major functional component in my account of mass art. Is there an inconsistency here? Can one be a functionalist and a historicist at the same time? Is my general approach to art theory at odds with my theory of mass art?

I don't think so. Despite the similarities between other sorts of art and mass art, there is still a difference between the category of art in general and mass art. I do think that we identify art *simpliciter* historically, but that is compatible with characterizing certain forms of art functionally. Of course, I also claim that mass art is a historically specific form of art. It has not existed for all time. It required the advent of mass information technologies. But if it is historically specific, again the question may arise as to whether it is appropriate to analyse it functionally, especially as I do in the text, where I make reference to the ways in which it frequently engages innate cognitive, perceptual, and emotive capacities.

But once again, I think that there is no tension here. Mass art has a historical provenance. But given its historic purpose—engaging mass audiences—it gravitates to devices that will be accessible to large numbers of people. In order to do this, it may address nearly universal features of people in general. Its devices may be designed to function in just this way. But that it is designed to function in this way does not preclude its historical identity, since it is mass art's purpose for a historically specific culture (or collection of cultures) that explains its exploitation of certain— perhaps transhistorical—possibilities in order to carry out the function that it has inherited historically.

Lastly, I can imagine a reader of this book who worries that it is already irrelevant. My arm-waving at the beginning of this introduction—my importunings after the fashion of an academic, used-car salesman—to the effect that mass art is a worthy subject for research, it might be said, is so much froth. For mass art supposedly will soon be obsolete. The philosophy of mass art does not possess the urgency with which I adorn it, since mass art will turn out to be a mere blip on the radar screen of history. The evolutionary trajectory of communication technology is away from mass art and toward customized art. The consumer of the future will not be part of a mass audience. Consumers in the future will be empowered by new information technologies and they will be able to personalize their own artistic menus, often interactively. Indeed, perhaps we will all become artists in the coming cyber-Utopias—so many da Vincis plugging away at our own personal work stations (oops—entertainment centres).[11]

That is, it may be argued that mass art, as I conceive of it, will be but a

---

[11] For example, see Nicholas Negroponte, *Being Digital* (London: Hodder & Stoughton, 1995).

brief fleeting moment, preceding the glorious emergence of highly individualized technological art consumption (and production). To a limited
extent, the prospects for customized art, it might be said, are already
evident in the existence of cable and satellite channels for specialized
viewers, who may select among cartoon channels, science fiction channels,
comedy channels, history channels, and so on. But this is only a hint of
what is to come. Alleged synergies among telephonic, computer, satellite,
and video technologies promise an era of personalized art consumption
that will create a demand for the production of technological artworks of
an incredibly diverse variety. And when the mass audience disappears,
mass art will disappear with it. Moreover, some would add, that even-
tuality is just around the corner.

Hegel famously writes: 'When philosophy paints its grey in grey, a
shape of life has grown old and it cannot be rejuvenated, but only
recognized, by the grey in grey of philosophy; the owl Minerva begins
its flight only with the onset of dusk.'[12] Hegel's dictum might suggest that
I am ready to write my supposed philosophy of mass art only because
mass art is already near death. I can envision painting mass art with
philosophy's grey in grey only because mass art is on the way out.
Furthermore, if one is really interested in saying something about technological art at this point in time, it could be charged, one should be
anticipating things to come. I should be writing *The Eschatology of Cyber Art*
and not rummaging through the rust belt of mass art.

However, in my opinion, such prophecies are excessively premature.[13]
The kind of 'customization' that we have before us in the form of comedy
channels, cartoon channels, children's channels, and the like is not really
evidence of the passing of mass art, since the choices these channels afford
are merely types or genres of mass art. The structures of the programmes
on the comedy channel and the science fiction channel are not really
different in kind, because they are all mass artworks designed to be
available to the common untutored audience viewer for fast pick-up
with minimum effort. The programmes in question could just as easily
appear on networks that are not dedicated to single genre programming.
They are gathered together on a single channel, but a single channel that is
still devoted to being accessible to large, heterogeneous audiences. Structurally, the programmes on these channels are still examples of mass art.

---

[12] G. W. F. Hegel, *Elements of the Philosophy of Right* (Cambridge: Cambridge University Press, 1991),
23.

[13] Remember all those prophecies about holograms a number of years back? Holograms were going
to change the face of art irrevocably. But where are all those vaunted holograms now? In your wallet on
your credit cards, where they function as little more than commercial insignia.

The editing patterns on *Deep Space Nine* and *Amazing Stories* are formally the same as those employed on *Bewitched*, *The Dick Van Dyke Show*, *The Mary Tyler Moore Show*, *Murphy Brown*, and *The Jeffersons*.

Nor am I convinced that mass art is about to disappear with the advent of technologies that might have the potential to afford a more diversified fare. There are several reasons for this. First, the economies of scale that are available in technological media incline the communication industries toward the production of 'mass-produced, common-denominator, mass-audience media'.[14] These industries are not likely to divest themselves readily of the advantages of these economies of scale nor of the profits they deliver. And, of course, these interests control not only their own mass-art productions, but also many of the relevant mass-media technologies of dissemination and distribution. Be assured, they will not quickly kill the goose that lays the golden eggs.

Furthermore, and of far greater importance, audiences will not change just because technological means alter. A taste for easily accessible art will not evaporate soon, nor will the pleasure to be had from sharing artworks with large numbers of our fellow citizens. For people like to have commerce with the same artworks that their neighbours—far and wide—do. It is part of what Kant called the sociability of art. We enjoy reading, seeing, and listening to the same things, and then talking about them. We enjoy working references and allusions to them into our conversations. That our lovers and co-workers grew up with the same songs and the same TV shows we did is significant to us. It is an important element of possessing a common culture. Certainly mass art can satisfy such social-psychological needs better than the so far only dreamt-of, totally customized arts of cyber-Utopia. And, in any case, it is far from clear that vast majorities of people crave the vaunted capacities for interactivity and selectivity that are putatively just over the horizon.[15] Will there be no couch potatoes in paradise?

Thus, there are economic and psychological counter-pressures that militate against the emergence of the personalized communications panaceas heralded by pundits of the information revolution. Mass art is here to stay for the foreseeable future. And, therefore, it is incumbent upon philosophers of art to start to take account of it theoretically.

Let us begin.

Mass = Easily Accessible

---

[14] W. Russell Newman, *The Future of the Mass Audience* (Cambridge: Cambridge University Press, 1991), 13.

[15] Just because the technology is there provides us with litle reason to predict that people will use it. Think of all those people with unpacked computers. These are hardly the new da Vincis. Whatever psychological and social forces already disincline people to experiment artistically on their own will not disappear simply because of the advent of new technologies.

1 Philosophical Resistance to Mass Art: The Majority Tradition

Introduction

Philosophical aesthetics in the twentieth century has shown a striking inability to come to terms with mass art. In the main, the phenomenon is generally ignored in philosophical treatises on art. Instead, the examples upon which twentieth-century philosophers of art construct their theories are primarily drawn from the realm of what is often called high art. Moreover, when philosophers or philosophically minded art theorists have focused on the topic of mass art, their findings are frequently dismissive and openly hostile. Often their energies are spent in the attempt to show that mass art is not genuine art, but rather something else, sometimes called *kitsch* or pseudo-art. The point of this chapter is to examine some of the leading philosophical arguments against mass art, each one advanced by a significant commentator.[1] Since it is my purpose in this book to show that mass art is a legitimate topic for philosophical aesthetics, I will be at pains to show what is wrong with these arguments. In the following sections, I will critically examine six arguments against mass art. Then I will conclude with a section that offers a conceptual diagnosis of one of the major underlying reasons why most philosophical writing on mass art has been incapable of coming to terms with it.

---

[1] I want to stress that this chapter only examines *some* of the leading philosophical arguments against mass art. There are other important arguments against mass art that I will examine in ensuing chapters. This chapter is meant as an introduction to the theme of philosophy's resistance to mass art. It is not exhaustive in this regard. Thus, other philosophical objections to mass art will crop up as the text proceeds.

Moreover, I should add, that I count an argument against mass art as *philosophical* just in case it is based upon a conception of the *nature* of mass art, of art, or both.

The massification argument

The first argument against mass art that I want to examine comes from Dwight MacDonald's essay 'A Theory of Mass Culture'.[2] Though MacDonald was not a philosopher in the narrow sense of the term, his argument is philosophical in so far as he believes that the problems raised by mass art follow from its very nature. Moreover, MacDonald's argument is of special interest to philosophers of art because he directs his attention to what he takes to be the aesthetic problems of mass art. At the same time, MacDonald's reaction against mass art is symptomatic of a number of the recurrent biases exhibited by American cultural critics through most of the twentieth century with respect to mass art.[3]

For MacDonald, the distinctive or defining feature of mass culture is that it is produced solely and directly for consumption by a mass audience—like 'chewing gum', he says, in order to signal his contempt.[4] He chooses to call the phenomenon *mass culture* rather than *popular culture* because, he notes, works that he regards as high art—such as the writing of Dickens—can be popular, whereas it is not mass culture, i.e., it is not produced *solely* for mass consumption. Rather, MacDonald categorizes it as high art.

But wasn't Dickens's work written for large audiences? Wasn't it serialized in large-circulation periodicals? On what grounds does MacDonald hive off Dickens's work from other contemporary work that appeared in similar mass-market venues? MacDonald is not always forthcoming about this. However, one can glean what he thinks to be the hallmark of high art by attending to the comparison that he draws between Dickens and one of his contemporaries, the novelist G. A. Henty. MacDonald claims that Dickens 'was an artist communicating his individual vision, while Henty

---

[2] Dwight MacDonald, 'A Theory of Mass Culture', from *Mass Culture: The Popular Arts in America*, ed. Bernard Rosenberg and David Manning White (New York: Free Press, 1957), 59–73. The article originally appeared in *Diogenes*, 3 (1953), 1–17. The pagination in my footnotes refers to the version of the article in the book *Mass Culture*.
MacDonald dealt with the problem of mass art in a number of essays besides the one under discussion, notably: 'A Theory of Popular Culture', *Politics*, 1 (February 1944), 20–3; and 'Masscult and Midcult', *Partisan Review* (Spring, Summer 1960), reprinted in Dwight MacDonald, *Against the American Grain* (New York, 1962), 3–75. I have chosen to examine 'A Theory of Mass Culture' because I think that it is the strongest version of his position, philosophically speaking. I will not be concerned with charting the vicissitudes of MacDonald's thinking on mass art, since it is my intention to use him as representative of a position; it is not my purpose to offer an intellectual biography of MacDonald.
[3] See Paul R. Gorman, *Left Intellectuals and Popular Culture in Twentieth Century America* (Chapel-Hill: University of North Carolina Press, 1996), especially ch. 7.
[4] MacDonald, 'A Theory of Mass Culture', 59.

was an impersonal manufacturer of an impersonal commodity for the masses'.[5] That is, the mark of mass art is its impersonality in contrast to the personal expressiveness of high art.

Moreover, this identification of mass art with the impersonal continues throughout 'A Theory of Mass Culture'. MacDonald dismisses Soviet art on the grounds that it is 'manufactured for mass consumption by the ruling class and is not an expression of either the individual artist or the common people themselves.'[6] Likewise, American mass art, such as the products of Hollywood, are, MacDonald maintains, produced by faceless committees of hired technicians.

Mass art contrasts with high art, according to MacDonald, in so far as the former is an impersonal product produced for mass consumption, whereas genuine high art is created by artists possessed of a personal vision. Here, it should be clear that MacDonald is presupposing a version of the expression theory of art as means of challenging the art status of mass art. For MacDonald, distinctive expressivity is a necessary condition of art properly so called.

MacDonald not only contrasts mass art with what he calls high art. He also contrasts it with what he calls folk art. What is the nature of this contrast? Folk art is produced by the people and for the people, whereas mass art is manufactured by industries bent upon making a profit (in capitalist states), or it is made to control the people (in totalitarian states). As MacDonald puts it:

Folk Art grew from below. It was a spontaneous, autochtonous expression of the people, shaped by themselves, pretty much without the benefit of High Culture, to suit their own needs. Mass Culture is imposed from above. It is fabricated by technicians hired by businessmen; its audiences are passive consumers, their participation limited to the choice between buying and not buying. The Lords of *kitsch*, in short, exploit the cultural needs of the masses in order to make a profit and/or to maintain their class rule—in Communist countries, only the second purpose obtains.[7]

As is the case in the contrast he draws between high art and mass art, the contrast between folk art and mass art rests upon the issue of a putative lack of individualized or distinctive expressiveness in mass art.

Folk art articulates the individual ethos or vision of a people from below. It expresses their distinctive mode of being. Mass art, on the other hand, expresses nothing distinctive. It blurs; it homogenizes. And it does this for a reason—namely, so that it will be consumable by the largest

[5] Ibid.   [6] Ibid. 60.   [7] Ibid.

number of people possible. Mass art in the industrial West, MacDonald emphasizes, is a commodity, a commodity designed for a mass audience. So that it will appeal to the largest audience possible, it is intentionally designed for generic use. As such, it lacks both the individualized, personal expressiveness that is putatively the hallmark of high art, on the one hand, and it also lacks the distinctive ethnic (community-based) expressiveness of folk art, on the other hand.

So for MacDonald the terrain of what we call art is partitioned into a number of subdivisions. As we have seen already, there are: high art, folk art, and mass art. But in addition to these, MacDonald also distinguishes two other precincts: avant-garde art and academic art. Avant-garde art is a subcategory of high art that MacDonald characterizes as high art that attempts to withdraw from the world of the market-place and that rejects the reduction of all value to market value. It is difficult, often hermetic art—the art of the intellectual élite. It is art that rebels against the commodification of art—it is art for art's sake, or autonomous art. Baudelaire and Rimbaud represent this art in poetry, while the Cubists and Picasso represent it in painting. Avant-garde art is high art that, in effect, reacts against the emergence of mass art by attempting to sustain the values of so-called high art, most notably the value of personal expression.

Academic art, which might also be called *kitsch* or middlebrow art, is another reaction to the rise of mass art.[8] Whereas avant-garde art supposedly moves away from mass art by becoming less and less accessible to mass audiences, academic art moves toward mass art by becoming more and more accessible. However, the way in which this movement is achieved compromises it. For academic art recycles the high art of yesteryear—most notably in terms of its forms—as if this involved an innovative, personal view. Thus, as a result, academicians, inasmuch as all they do is merely recycle past achievements, are also guilty of impersonality. The academicians attempt to palm off past expressions of personal viewpoints as genuine, original expressions of their own. A suggestive example of this might be the kind of 'impressionist' paintings one finds decorating so many hotels. Here historical impressionism is appropriated to counterfeit the patina of high art.

Though MacDonald's map of the art world was drawn in 1953, it is easy to see how it would apply to the art world today. High art is comprised of two types: the work of the masters, like Rembrandt, and the work of avant-gardists, such as Steve Reich or David Salle or Kathy Acker. Films by

---

[8] The opponents of mass art sometimes use 'kitsch' to refer to middlebrow art, to mass art, or to both. The reader thus must determine which sense is pertinent by means of the context.

Merchant-Ivory arguably fall into the academic category. *The Simpsons* and *Married With Children* are mass art, while break-dancing, at least when it first appeared, was folk art. Moreover, this map also carries implicit evaluations. Only certain high art forms and folk art count as genuine art, for MacDonald, while mass art and academic or middlebrow art are false art or *kitsch*.[9]

So far we've characterized mass art by MacDonald's lights—at least, in the sense that we've situated it on MacDonald's map of the art world. But we haven't yet elucidated the reasons why MacDonald thinks that mass art by its very nature constitutes an aesthetic problem.

MacDonald maintains that it is of the nature of mass art to aim at securing large audiences for the purpose of profit.[10] In order to achieve this end, MacDonald believes that mass art must preclude the sort of expressivity one finds in high art or folk art. Mass art must be impersonal, if it is to succeed on its own terms. Why? Here, it seems that MacDonald is presuming that if an artwork is marked by distinctive expressivity—either in the way of high art or of folk art—its very distinctiveness will alienate large parts of the homogeneous mass audience. Ethnic humour, for example, will be putatively inaccessible to persons lacking the appropriate cultural background references. Thus, for mass art to appeal to a mass audience, it must be impersonal and homogeneous. This is part of the attractiveness of mass art for totalitarian regimes. So among the many problems that mass art raises for MacDonald is that it will erode the resources of individual expression and vision in society.

One of the ways in which this erosion will occur is that mass art will drive high art and folk art from the market-place—just as bad money drives good money from circulation, according to Gresham's law.[11] Also, mass art will tend to promote the degradation of whatever potential for high art remains in the culture. Why? Because the response of artists with pretensions to high art will be perverted into academic or middlebrow art. MacDonald believes that this is likely to occur because in order to compete with mass art, the purveyors of high art will attempt to adapt to the situation by making their works more accessible, and this will incline them toward the recycling of old forms of high art. Thus, through its own agency and

---

[9] NB: in these debates the term *kitsch* is sometimes applied to mass art, sometimes applied to academic art, and sometimes applied to both. I have allowed that ambiguity to stand in my expositions of both MacDonald and Greenberg.

[10] In totalitarian states, as mentioned, MacDonald thinks that mass art also aims at overt ideological control. But since in his essay he concentrates mostly on mass art under capitalism, I will follow him in this when expounding his view in this section.

[11] F. R. Leavis also uses the notion of Gresham's law in *Mass Civilization and Minority Culture* (Cambridge: Gordon Frazer at St John's College, 1930), 9.

through its influence on the development of middlebrow art, mass art will destroy or pervert the sources of individual expression in the culture.

Moreover, MacDonald thinks that these consequences are unavoidable, given the nature of mass art. The essential feature of mass art is its status as a commodity manufactured for mass consumption. This—its nature as a mass-produced commodity—is the essential feature of mass art. And in order to realize its essence—i.e., to accommodate the largest number of consumers—mass art is going to have to aim at the generic or common denominator in terms of taste, sensitivity, and intelligence in its potential audiences. Moreover *ex hypothesi* this common denominator is likely to be very low in terms of standards of expressivity, intelligence, and taste. So if the producers of mass art want to attract the largest audience, they will have to accept, in MacDonald's words, 'any idiocy as long as it is held by a large number of people.'

Thus, by the logic of mass marketing, the products of mass culture will not only homogenize the audience but will homogenize the audience in a downward direction—for in order to cater to the largest audience, the common denominators aimed at by the producers of mass art will be those on the low side of the audience's taste, sensitivity, and intelligence.[12]

For a concrete example of this process, consider what MacDonald calls the infantilization of the audience.[13] In order to secure a larger audience, the producer designs his or her product so that it be consumed not only by adults, but by children. Thus, the intelligence required to engage the artwork is lowered. The adult, MacDonald says, regresses to an infantile or, at least, more childlike state. The adult's broadest potential capacity— in terms of taste, sensitivity, and intelligence—is not fully engaged by the work. In some sense, the capacities of the adult are not challenged and developed as a result. Nor is this, one must concede, a completely para-noid vision. For one recalls similar contemporary arguments when the movie industry releases its blockbusters each summer. Critics, perhaps unconsciously echoing MacDonald's theory, complain that there is nothing here for adults; that the movies are aimed intentionally at an audience comprised of teenage boys.

But whereas these critics speak as though the problem were remediable, MacDonald thinks that something like it is inevitable, given the nature of mass art. MacDonald's observations are not simply critical; they are

---

[12] In this paragraph I have switched from talking about the mass art object as involving a homogeneous address to talking about it homogenizing the audience. In this, I am following a certain looseness in MacDonald's exposition. For, like almost all mass culture critics, he presumes that a homogenized object promotes homogenized taste.

[13] MacDonald, 'A Theory of Mass Culture', 65.

theoretical or philosophical, since MacDonald believes that the damaging effects of mass culture for the aesthetic life of society follow from the very nature of mass art. In this, it is interesting to note that MacDonald stands in a philosophical tradition that begins with Plato, who argued that mimetic art, with all its putative problems of emotional address, was unavoidable, given the demands that the market-place placed on dramatists. That is, Plato maintained in Book 10 of his *Republic*, that the dramatist would have to pander to the masses by means of emotionally provocative representations simply in order to stay in business.

Of course, MacDonald is not as directly concerned with mimesis as Plato was. Thus, the features of mass art upon which he focuses in his deduction are not its representational properties, but its commodity-based properties. As a mass-manufactured commodity, MacDonald argues, the mass artwork is aimed at securing mass audiences. In order to do this, it follows (in a lawlike way) that it must be generic, thereby precluding individual and ethnic (communal) expression, since individualizing expressivity limits the potential audience of the mass artwork.

Furthermore, in order to maximize the scale of the audience, the producers of mass art will aim at the lowest common denominator in audiences, thereby reinforcing very low standards of taste, sensitivity, and intelligence in said audiences. And, in addition to the damage that each mass artwork wreaks directly in its own right, there will be dire, indirect, systematic repercussions as well. For the presence of mass art in the market-place will adversely affect other domains of artistic production. For example, as 'serious' artists respond to the encroachment of mass art, they will attempt to compete with it by producing middlebrow art.

This is an ambitious argument. It attempts to deduce the problematic nature of mass art by means of a reflection on the concept of mass art, supplemented by some putative laws of the art market. In order to appreciate the strength of this argument, it is useful to set it out formally:

1. The mass art object is a mass-manufactured commodity.

That is, *manufactured commodity* is the generic class into which all mass art falls. It is of the nature of mass art to be a commodity. This, presumably, is a premiss that everyone will accept as definitional.

2. All mass-manufactured commodities are designed for mass consumption by the largest number of people possible.

That is, all things being equal, it is the purpose or goal of any mass art object to appeal to the largest number of people possible. This, presumably, for MacDonald, will strike anyone who considers the practice of mass production to be self-evident.

> 3. In order to be suited for mass consumption, the mass art product must be targeted toward what is common for the largest number of people.

If an object is to appeal to a large number of people, the most natural way in which it can perform its function is for it to appeal to what is common to that audience in terms of its interests and abilities. That is, you aim at attracting people in terms of the common, live interests that are shared between the largest number of people. And, at the very least, in order to appeal to large audiences, the mass art object must be accessible to said audiences by establishing some common ground with them. This premiss is apt to be defended as common sense—as a folk-psychological law of the market-place.

> 4. Therefore, the mass art product is targeted at what is common for the largest number of audience members.

> 5. Furthermore, what is common in the audience is not compatible with distinctive expression (neither that of the individual artist nor that of an ethnic, or communal subculture).

That is, mass art is neither high art nor folk art, but generic brand art. This, I suppose, should strike the reader as virtually a corollary of the presupposition that what is common is not distinctive.

> 6. Therefore, mass art is not compatible with distinctive expression.

This conclusion represents the first problem that MacDonald finds with the mass artwork. Since he appears to take distinctive expressivity as a necessary feature of genuine art, this conclusion entails that mass art is not genuine art. So apart from MacDonald's criticism of mass art in terms of cultural degradation, there is also the problem that the mass artwork is at best an artwork *manqué*.

> 7. In order to seek the largest possible audience, the mass art object must gravitate toward the lowest common level of taste, sensitivity, and intelligence in the audience.

The presumption here seems to be that the largest audience will be one that includes those with very low taste, intelligence, and sensitivity. In order to accommodate them and thereby secure the largest audience, the producer of the mass art object will have to pander to them. This appears to rely on an implicit invocation of common sense. If you want to include as many people as possible in your target audience aim low, because there are more potential consumers on the low and middle ends of the scale than there are on either the high end, or the high and middle ends of the scale.

> 8. Therefore, the mass art object gravitates toward the lowest level of taste, sensitivity, and intelligence.

Thus, in addition to the problem that the mass art object is not genuine art, there is a further problem with it, namely, that it tends toward the cheapening of aesthetic stimulation, and, therefore, of taste. Moreover, this is not an accidental feature of mass art; it is mandated by a consideration of what mass art is designed to do—to secure mass audiences. That is, the downward tendency of mass art in terms of taste, intelligence, and sensitivity follows from the nature of mass art, since it is presupposed that in order to command large audiences it is necessary to aim low, given the putative structure of the market-place.

Furthermore, this problem, in MacDonald's estimation, only gets worse with the passage of time. For the tendency of taste to be lowered by mass art is a self-reinforcing process; there is a feedback mechanism in play, so to speak, here. Not only have the so-called masses already been debauched by mass art for generations, but this steadily lowers their standards of taste, sensitivity, and intelligence, so that the common denominator in the audience drops progressively. Thus, there is a downward, descending spiral in taste, sensitivity, and intelligence in the audience. By aiming low, the producers of mass art degrade the audience further, which, in turn, encourages the producers of mass art to aim even lower the next time around. Perhaps an example of what MacDonald has in mind is the progressively escalating grossness—from decade to decade—in mass horror fiction (including pulp fiction, movies, and TV).

Also, in MacDonald's view, mass art not only debauches the audience for mass art, but it also has an impact on the world of high art as well. For as the mass art market expands, high art is forced to compete with mass art. However,

> 9. In order to compete with mass art, high art must also gravitate toward lower levels of taste, sensitivity, and intelligence.

For it is presumably axiomatic that there is no other apparent way in which to compete for a mass audience in a mass market-place. It is an obvious (commonplace) law of that market that one has to compete with mass art on its own terms, if one's aim is to secure comparable audiences.

That is, in order to secure the aim of appealing to a mass audience, the purveyors of high art must adjust their productions downward.

> 10. Therefore, high art gravitates toward lower levels of taste, sensitivity, and intelligence.

Moreover, MacDonald contends that this tendency is already evident in the large-scale proliferation of middlebrow art.

I call this argument the massification argument in honour of the fact that what is said to be problematic about mass art stems from the proposition that such works are by nature mass-manufactured commodities, i.e., objects that are expressly designed, like mass-produced automobiles, to appeal to a mass market. And, from the mass-market nature of the product in question—mass art—MacDonald, with the aid of some putatively commonplace laws of the market-place, deduces three major charges against mass art: first, that it is not genuine art, since it is incompatible with a necessary feature of genuine art (namely, distinctive expressivity); second, that mass art gravitates toward the lowest level of taste, intelligence, and sensitivity (so it is not only art *manqué*, but it is aesthetically bad to boot); and third, in accordance with Gresham's law as applied to art, the emergence of mass art inclines the producers of high art to compete with it in a way that indulges lower levels of taste, sensitivity, and intelligence (thereby, indirectly promoting even more aesthetic awfulness). This is an impressive argument. But is it a sound argument?

The first two premisses of the argument—that the mass art object is a mass-manufactured commodity and that all mass-manufactured commodities are designed for mass consumption—seem fundamentally reasonable, though some minor adjustments are called for. Specifically, MacDonald most frequently speaks of commodities, but since his argument is meant to apply to socialist economies as well as capitalist ones, his language may not be ideal. For it might be argued that commodification requires a market and planned economies are not genuine markets. Nevertheless, it is probably the case that MacDonald could easily rework what he wishes to say in terms of mass-manufactured products rather than mass-manufactured commodities.[14] Moreover, the third premiss in MacDonald's argument seems correct. Ideally a mass-manufactured product is aimed at striking a common chord in a large number of people; the mass art object must be accessible to a mass audience, if it is to succeed, and this requires finding some level of address common to all the potential audience members.

---

[14] I owe this point to Andrew Levine.

However, the fifth premiss of the argument seems problematic. Mac-Donald claims that what is common in the audience is not compatible with distinctive expression, neither that of an individual artist nor that of an ethnic (or folk) community. But this seems false. It is far from clear that what appeals to what is common in a large audience is incompatible with distinctive expressivity. There would appear to be many counter-examples. In film, Charlie Chaplin, Buster Keaton, and Alfred Hitchcock all achieved the highest levels of original expression by any fair accounting. Though there are many problems with the so-called auteur theory, surely it has been established that many film directors possess distinctive, personal visions and original expressive powers. In our own day, Tim Burton is a director with a unique personal vision, as well as one with an excellent record at the box office. In terms of popular music, there are numerous artists, including Frank Sinatra, Bob Dylan, Otis Redding, and John Lennon, who are noteworthy for their personal styles, while in TV a similar argument could be made for some of the screenwriters of the Golden Age, like Rod Serling.

Thus, the contention—that the requirement that the mass art object address what is common in the audience is at odds with distinctive expressivity—does not seem to fit the facts. Perhaps this is because it rests on a confusion. When MacDonald is talking about individualized expressivity, he is referring to a property of the artist's production. But when he talks about what is common to the audience, he is talking about a property of the reception of the product. There is no reason to suppose that an uncommon production will not strike a common chord among diverse receivers.

Though 'uncommon' or 'distinctive' are logically contrary to 'common', *uncommon production* is not incompatible with *common reception*. That is, MacDonald's premiss seems to ride rhetorically on the supposition that, put crudely, what is common and what is distinctive don't mix. But this is hardly persuasive when we realize that, when stated non-elliptically, what we are talking about is what is common-to-receivers, and what is distinctive-of-senders. There is no reason to suppose that a distinctive expression will not be accessible to a large audience in virtue of their common interests and understandings. That a particular expression is original or unprecedented does not entail that it is inaccessible to the common understanding of a mass audience. And the counter-examples in the preceding paragraph illustrate that this is true not only in point of logic, but also in point of fact. That is, MacDonald's premiss about the necessity of the mass art object to address what is common in the audience appeals to the idea that the object must be broadly accessible. But as the examples of Chaplin, (early) Sinatra, and others show, a distinctively personal form of expression can be accessible to mass audiences. Fred Astaire's highly distinctive and expressive dance style was savoured by millions.

Likewise, MacDonald's seventh premiss is troubling. He contends that in order to seek the largest possible audience, the mass art product must gravitate toward the lowest common level of taste, sensitivity, and intelligence in the audience. This is a bit of armchair social science. It rests on some commonsensical assumptions. It is not an unreasonable, initial hypothesis, but it needs to be probed empirically. But when probed empirically, it does not appear to correspond to the facts. For by aiming at the very lowest levels of taste, intelligence, and sensitivity, the producer of mass art objects is standardly most likely to lose large segments of the audience.

Consider the case of hardcore violent pornography. Using MacDonald's reasoning, one might predict that the producers of mass art would gravitate toward it. However, in appealing to the low taste of some in the mass audience in this way, the producer risks alienating many consumers of average taste and sensibility. Often, appealing to the lowest side of the audience is counter-productive. That is why hardcore, violent pornography is generally avoided by makers of mass art who are concerned to secure the largest audiences. That is why hardcore pornography is produced cheaply for a specialized audience, and why it is not the common fare of the standard mass movie-market. And that is why Disney films are more marketable to mass audiences than overt bondage films. Indeed, throughout the history of mass art, one finds a marked tendency in pulp fictions to aim above the lowest common denominator of aesthetic taste and morality just because an appeal to higher values is itself an attractive calling card for the largest portion of the audience.[15]

MacDonald might respond to observations like these by claiming that these calling cards themselves are nothing but kitsch, yet then one wonders whether MacDonald's hypothesis about the downward vector of taste in the mass art market is really an empirical conjecture, or whether he intends to call anything that might garner attention in the mass art market an example of low taste, sensitivity, or intelligence. But in that case, premiss seven would turn out to be questionable inasmuch as it proposes what is nothing more than a stipulative definition as a substantive empirical generalization.

Premiss nine asserts that in order to compete with mass art, high art must gravitate toward lower levels of taste, sensitivity, and intelligence. But

[15] For example, Joseph McAleer notes the pronounced moral tone of Mills & Boon novels in his *Popular Reading and Publishing in Britain 1914–1950* (Oxford: Clarendon Press, 1992), especially ch. 4.

what is the force of 'must' here? Clearly, this is not the only avenue of serious art in the age of mass art. MacDonald himself admits that avant-garde art is another remaining option. Moreover, it is the option that many artists have taken in response to the rise of mass art. Indeed, as mass art becomes more pervasive, avant-garde art has grown apace both in terms of the amount of avant-garde art that has been produced and in terms of the scale of its audience (in both absolute and proportional terms).[16] That is, it is not evident that high art can only hold its own by degrading itself—by becoming middlebrow art—since, in fact, the historical record shows otherwise. So, it is not the case that in order to compete with mass art, high art *must* gravitate toward lower levels of taste, sensitivity, and intelligence. It is at best one temptation that some or maybe even many serious artists fail to resist.

Of course, MacDonald is right to assert that this tendency toward middlebrow art is rife in contemporary culture, as one can see in many of the offerings of public television. However, there is a question of how we are to interpret the existence of such a tendency versus the prospects for what MacDonald calls high art in the culture at large. For if high art today is avant-garde art, then it does not seem to me that the problem is so great, since avant-garde art, at present, is flourishing. It is certainly able to hold its own on the art market. That is, *pace* MacDonald, the competition with mass art has not driven high art from the scene, nor is there any reason, given the option of the avant-garde, to suppose that it necessarily will. Avant-garde artists may complain that the existence of mass art robs them of an audience that would otherwise be theirs. I am not so sure of that. But in any case, avant-garde art has probably never had it so good.

The model that MacDonald uses to characterize the relation of contemporary high art to mass art and middlebrow art is Gresham's law.[17] But it seems to me that a perhaps more compelling model may be found in the adage that when the level of water rises all boats are lifted. Thus when art production rises due to the demands of the mass art market, the avant-garde boats are lifted as well. It is when there is a great deal of artistic

---

[16] That is, throughout the twentieth century, as time marches on, there is more and more avant-garde art produced and a larger and larger avant-garde audience in absolute terms, and, I would conjecture, there is also a higher proportion of avant-garde artworks and avant-garde appreciators relative to mass art objects and appreciators today than there was fifty or so years ago. For example, there are more avant-garde films and avant-garde appreciators today than there were in 1945.

[17] Ernest van den Haag points out that MacDonald's use of the notion of Gresham's law really doesn't get him what he wants. According to Gresham's law, bad money drives good money out of the market-place because, inasmuch as people in such circumstances come to prize good money, they hoard it. If the art market were like this, then people would begin to prize the kind of art MacDonald endorses rather than mass art. But this is not what MacDonald thinks occurs. Therefore, he should not be alluding to Gresham's law. See Ernest van den Haag, 'Of Happiness and Despair We Have No Measure', *Mass Culture: The Popular Arts in America*, ed. Bernard Rosenberg and David Manning White (New York: Free Press, 1957), 524 n. 46.

activity that avant-garde artistic activity is most likely to take hold and flourish. Thus in contradistinction to premiss nine, the avant-garde or oppositional wing of high art thrives in the face of mass art without lowering its demanding standards of taste, sensitivity, and intelligence.

I have provided grounds for challenging the conclusions that MacDonald reaches in steps six, eight, and ten in the preceding argument. However, before taking leave of MacDonald, it is important to scrutinize one of the major underlying assumptions of his theory. Earlier I noted that MacDonald presumes an expression theory of art. Like Tolstoy, MacDonald appears to maintain implicitly that individualized expressivity is a necessary condition for art status. Mass art is not genuine art—neither high art nor folk art—because it precludes individualized expressivity. It is, MacDonald alleges, impersonal.

But it is hardly uncontroversial that individualized expressivity is a necessary condition for art status. On the one hand, some art may be art in virtue of its formal or aesthetic properties rather than its expressive qualities. This, of course, would leave open the possibility that some mass art, such as Busby Berkeley production numbers, are genuine art on formal grounds. Moreover, even if one is an expression theorist of art, one might not contend that the expressive properties that are relevant to art status need be individualized. In some artistic traditions, such as Chinese painting, the aim may be to approximate already existing expressive forms. Thus, if such cases count as counter-examples to the individualized expression theory of art, then that undercuts MacDonald's case against mass art that is expressive, albeit in a non-individualized way.

Of course, expression theories of art, including ones that rely on the notion of individualized expressivity, are open to so many objections that even if mass art failed to accord with them, that would not be decisive in showing that mass art is not genuine art. But even supposing for the purpose of argument that such theories were true, mass art, or, at least, some of it, would count as art inasmuch much of it is expressive and even—to address MacDonald's own position—distinctively expressive. The Marx Brothers refute MacDonald on his own terms. MacDonald has not shown, then, that some mass art is not genuine art.[18] He has not shown

In left margin, handwritten: No, but one might argue that it makes indiv. expression more difficult (pace Hitchcock etc.)

---

[18] In Ch. 3 of this book: I will defend the view that all mass art is art. However, at this point in the argument I only wish to show that MacDonald has failed to show that all mass art is not art. Moreover, I reject both broad-expression theories of art and the more narrow, individualized-expression theories of art. I only entertain them suppositionally above in order to show that even if these approaches were creditable, the case could be made that some mass art is art and thus represent legitimate concerns for aesthetic theory, MacDonald's view notwithstanding.

that all mass art is necessarily kitsch. Nor, for the same reason, has he shown that all mass art necessarily lowers standards of taste.

Because there are general problems with the sort of expression theory of art that MacDonald presumes, he is unable to prove that no mass art is art. Indeed, we may even grant him his favourite expression theory of art and still show that it must be conceded that some mass artworks are genuine art and, therefore, worthy of the attention of aesthetic theorists. But if this is so, then even MacDonald should admit that not all mass artworks participate in lowering standards of taste. Nor, as we have seen, is MacDonald's conjecture—that the very existence of mass art must cause the withering away of what he calls high art—convincing.[19] Therefore, none of the aesthetic charges that MacDonald levels at mass art are, in principle, theoretically compelling.

Of course, it may be charged that I have misconstrued MacDonald's argument entirely. Perhaps he does not intend to be drawing out the implications inherent in the nature of mass art. Maybe all he wants to say is that mass art, in fact, is conducive to a lowering of taste, sensitivity, and intelligence—that that is its leading tendency.

But then his claim is an empirical claim and not a philosophical one. And as an empirical claim, it is far from clear that it has much to recommend it. Has the general level of taste and intelligence—especially with reference to art—declined since the advent of mass art? Obviously, this would be a difficult question to answer without crafting precise definitions of taste, sensitivity, and intelligence. But, informally speaking, I see no reason to think that the taste, sensitivity, and intelligence of the audience hasn't been improving.

Michael Crichton, for example, is a better novelist in every way than Richard Howard. And movies like *Zombies of the Stratosphere* are certainly inferior in terms of taste, sensitivity, and intelligence to *St. Elsewhere* and even *Baywatch* and other sundry candidates. Yet such facts would appear to refute MacDonald's position reconstrued as a statistical summary about the downward-tending spiral of taste, sensitivity, and intelligence. In general, I conjecture that there is more reason empirically to suggest that the vector is pointed in the other direction.

---

[19] MacDonald's theory of mass art was influenced by Clement Greenberg, the subject of the next section of this chapter. Thus, like Greenberg, MacDonald's opposition to mass art is, to a significant degree, motivated by an attempt to protect modernism from the encroachment of mass art. That is why he is so concerned about the prospects of high art (modernism) in the age of mass art.

The passivity argument

The next argument against mass art comes from Clement Greenberg's seminal article 'Avant-Garde and Kitsch'.[20] Like MacDonald, Greenberg was not a philosopher. He was an art critic and theorist. Indeed, he was perhaps the most influential American art critic of the twentieth century. One might think of him as the theoretical architect of the notion of modernism that came to dominate American art and painting and the criticism thereof in the decades following World War II. Greenberg's legacy, in fact, is still with us, since it is Greenberg's theory of modernism that contemporary art critics and theorists most frequently attack when they attempt to draw the distinction between modernism and postmodernism in the realm of fine art. That Greenberg remains a viable target should come as no surprise, since his theory of modernism, with its accompanying arguments against what he calls kitsch, rests on a powerful philosophical conception of art.

At a number of points in 'Avant-Garde and Kitsch', Greenberg's argument recalls themes that we have already encountered in MacDonald's 'A Theory of Mass Culture'. The simple reason for this is that MacDonald's argument was influenced by Greenberg's, a fact MacDonald acknowledges by his footnotes. Yet, Greenberg develops certain aspects of that argument—such as the putative passivity of the mass art audience—in far more depth than MacDonald does.

One obvious point of tangency between the two articles is the notion of kitsch. However, as in the case of MacDonald, Greenberg also uses the concept in such a way that the extension to which it refers fluctuates. That is, Greenberg, like MacDonald, sometimes uses 'kitsch' to refer to what MacDonald thought of as middlebrow art, but also, again like MacDonald, Greenberg also uses it to refer to mass art. For example, Greenberg says: 'Kitsch is a product of the industrial revolution which urbanized the Masses of western Europe and America and established what is called universal literacy.'[21]

For Greenberg, kitsch is the art of the new mass society, comprised of the new urban masses who pressured society to provide them with a culture suited to their consumption. However, the art produced in this context is hardly genuine art from Greenberg's perspective. He writes:

[20] Clement Greenberg, 'Avant-garde and Kitsch', in *Clement Greenberg: The Collected Essays and Criticism*, vol. i, ed. John O'Brien (Chicago: University of Chicago Press, 1986), 5–22. This article was originally published in *Partisan Review* (Fall 1939).   [21] Ibid. 11.

Losing nevertheless their taste for the folk culture whose background was the countryside and discovering a new capacity for boredom at the same time, the new urban masses set up a pressure on society to provide them with a kind of culture fit for their own consumption. To fill this demand of the new market, a new commodity was devised: ersatz culture, kitsch, destined for those who, insensible to the values of genuine culture, are hungry nevertheless for the diversion that culture of some sort can provide.[22]

So, kitsch is not genuine culture, and the art objects that it proffers to the new urban audience are merely inauthentic substitutes for the real thing.

Why is it that mass artworks are merely ersatz substitutes for art proper? Because, Greenberg argues, in the present epoch, at least, authentic art or art proper is avant garde, since the avant garde preserves the values of past culture. One reason that the avant garde is capable of discharging this particular function is that it is putatively detached from the rest of contemporary culture which, according to Greenberg, in the industrialized epoch reduces all values to utilitarian value and which, in capitalist societies, reduces all values to market values. By means of its detachment from the rest of society, avant-garde art functions rather as a firebreak—protecting what remains of traditional values by becoming autonomous.

Greenberg writes:

Yet it is true that once the avant-garde has succeeded in 'detaching' itself from society, it proceeded to turn around and repudiate revolutionary as well as bourgeois politics. The revolution was left inside society, a part of that welter of ideological struggle which art and poetry find unpropitious as soon as it begins to involve those 'precious' axiomatic beliefs upon which culture thus far has had to rest. Hence it developed that the true and most important function of the avant-garde was not to 'experiment,' but to find a path along which it would be possible to keep culture *moving* in the midst of ideological confusion and violence. Retiring from [the] public altogether, the avant-garde poet or artist sought to maintain the high level of his art by both narrowing and raising it to the expression of an absolute in which all relativities and contradictions would be either resolved or beside the point. 'Art for art's sake' and 'pure poetry' appear, and subject matter or content becomes something to be avoided like the plague.[23]

Or, in other words, avant-garde art has detached itself from society by becoming autonomous—by becoming art for art's sake.

How has this process of detachment been achieved? With respect to painting and sculpture, art has secured this result by becoming abstract or non-objective. Indeed, the history of genuine modern art, as characterized by Greenberg, has been one of progressively more radical abstraction, as exemplified by the trajectory from Cubism to Abstract Expressionism.

---

[22] Ibid. 12.   [23] Ibid. 7–8.

By *abstraction*, Greenberg means that modern art has eschewed the representation of people, things, and events. Modern art does not offer us pictures of triumphant generals, but rather colour fields. Moreover, by opting for abstraction, Greenberg says, avant-garde art renounces 'the world of common, extroverted experience'.[24] The notion here appears to be that non-representational art divorces the artwork from the realm of ordinary experience, or, to put the matter in more technical philosophical jargon, avant-garde art—which in this context is genuine art—is disinterested in the sense that it is somehow disconnected from the world of practical affairs.[25] It is divorced from practical life; it is autonomous. It is art for its own sake. It is absolute art.

But given this line of argument, you might then very well wonder what it is that art of this sort is about. Greenberg's explicit answer is that it is about itself. Greenberg maintains:

The excitement of their art seems to lie most of all in its pure preoccupation with the invention and arrangement of spaces, surfaces, shapes, colors, etc. to the exclusion of what is not necessarily implicated in these factors.[26]

Or, in other words, at least with respect to painting and sculpture, art properly so-called is about its medium. It is reflexive.

If, historically, past art seemed much preoccupied with imitating the world, the art properly so-called of Greenberg's day is avant-garde or modernist, which means that it is about imitating imitation, or representing representation, or, to put it differently, it is about exploring its own nature as a pictorial medium. In this, its ultimate role is to provide a critique of its own conditions of possibility. And, as is well known, for Greenberg this became a matter of artists acknowledging the flatness of the picture plane as a way of asserting what they took to be the essential fact about the nature of painting.

It is against this understanding of avant-garde art, the genuine art of the contemporary world, that Greenberg articulates his understanding of mass art or kitsch. Avant-garde art is abstract, whereas mass art ostensibly favours representation. Avant-garde art is reflexive, whereas mass art is

---

[24] Greenberg, 'Avant-garde and Kitsch', 9.

[25] It should be evident to the reader that Greenberg's account of avant-garde art here represents a certain gerrymandering of the history of modern art, since this characterization only applies to selected specimens of twentieth-century avant-gardism. It does not apply to such movements as Dadaism, Surrealism, Futurism, or Soviet Contructivism, since these movements were involved in promoting social change. It does not apply to the theatre of Brecht. It is a rather formalist summation of the itinerary of the avant-garde which, of course, is why so many artists and critics are so hard on Greenberg nowadays.

[26] Greenberg, 'Avant-garde and Kitsch', 9.

generally imitative. Avant-garde art is introverted—it is about itself (it is about its medium). Kitsch is extroverted; it is about the world. Moreover, in being introverted, avant-garde art is detached from practical affairs and disinterested, whereas by representing the world, mass art is implicated in practical concerns.[27] Thus, avant-garde art is autonomous or pure art, whereas mass art is heteronomous or impure.

Furthermore, Greenberg draws another key distinction between avant-garde art and kitsch that is of crucial importance. Avant-garde art is committed to the general values of culture, something of which Greenberg maintains the masses are insensible. What are those general values? Greenberg makes this explicit in his discussion of the kitsch artist Repin in contrast to the avant-garde artist Picasso:

In Repin's picture the peasant recognizes and sees things in the way in which he recognizes and sees things outside of pictures—there is no discontinuity between art and life, no need to accept a convention and say to oneself, that icon represents Jesus because it intends to represent Jesus, even if it does not remind me very much of a man. That Repin can paint so realistically that identifications are self-evident immediately and without any effort on the part of the spectator—that is miraculous. The peasant is also pleased by the wealth of self-evident meanings which he finds in the picture: 'it tells a story.' Picasso and the icons are so austere and barren in comparison. What is more, Repin heightens reality and makes it dramatic; sunset, exploding shells, running and falling men. There is no longer any question of Picasso or icons. Repin is what the peasant wants, and nothing else but Repin. It is lucky, however, for Repin that the peasant is protected from the products of American capitalism, for he would not stand a chance next to a *Saturday Evening Post* cover by Norman Rockwell.

Ultimately, it can be said that the cultivated spectator derives the same values from Picasso that the peasant gets from Repin since what the latter enjoys in Repin is somehow art too, on however low a scale, and he is sent to look at pictures by the same instincts that send the cultivated spectator. But the ultimate values which the cultivated spectator derives from Picasso are derived at a second remove, as the result of reflection upon the immediate impression left by the plastic values. It is only then that the recognizable, the miraculous and the sympathetic enter. They are not immediately or externally present in Picasso's

[27] It should be pointed out here that Greenberg's analysis of the nature of avant-garde art and mass art is far more associative than one might wish. For example, he associates the absence of traditional representational content with detachment from practicality and disinterestedness. Perhaps he imagines that if a work does not represent features of the world it cannot address practical concerns. But this is clearly fallacious. An abstract design, like a swastika, can function politically, and, therefore, practically. Abstraction does not entail detachment or unworldliness. Similarly, that a work involves representational content, as much mass art does, does not indicate that it encourages what theoreticians call an interested response. Were that so, most of the painting of the past that we call art would be, on theories like Greenberg's, disqualified as genuine art. But that is a consequence that I conjecture even Greenberg would find unpalatable.

painting, but must be projected into it by the spectator sensitive enough to react sufficiently to plastic qualities. They belong to the 'reflected' effect. In Repin, on the other hand, the 'reflected' effect has already been included in the picture, ready for the spectator's unreflective enjoyment. Where Picasso paints *cause*, Repin paints *effect*. Repin predigests art for the spectator and spares him effort, provides him with a short cut to the pleasure of art that detours what is necessarily difficult in genuine art. Repin, or kitsch, is synthetic art.

The same point can be made with respect to kitsch literature; it provides vicarious experience for the insensitive with far greater immediacy than serious fiction can hope to do. And Eddie Guest and the *Indian Love Lyrics* are more poetic than T. S. Eliot and Shakespeare.[28]

Here it is quite clear that Greenberg identifies the value in genuine art with its capacity to elicit reflection or an active response from the spectator. In order to accomplish this, genuine art must be difficult, whereas Greenberg believes that kitsch or mass art can be enjoyed without effort. Moreover, this emphasis on the active response of the spectator in genuine art is what leads Greenberg to nominate avant-garde art as the genuine art of our times, since avant-garde art requires an active spectator to fill in its open structures. Thus, avant-garde art can be said to preserve the central value of art properly so-called. For art properly so-called has always, *ex hypothesi*, been dedicated to engendering active spectatorship. Indeed, commitment to this role, it would appear, is a necessary feature of art for Greenberg, as it is for many other modern theorists of art.[29]

On the other hand, Greenberg maintains that kitsch involves 'unreflective enjoyment'. It abets passive spectatorship—of the sort putatively evinced by 'couch potatoes'—whereas Greenberg, with the authority of a long tradition behind him, presumes that a necessary feature of genuine art involves a commitment to active spectatorship.[30]

Greenberg is certainly not idiosyncratic in the value he places on active spectatorship. Active spectatorship is a recurrent valorizing slogan of the avant-garde. It dominates the manifestos of avant-gardists from John Cage to recent interactive video artists like Ted Pope, and the group called Critical Art Ensemble.[31] Allan Kaprow was so obsessed with the notion of participation that by the mid-sixties he mandated that everyone who

[28]   Greenberg, 16–17.

[29]   For examples, see Jerome Stolnitz, *Aesthetics and the Philosophy of Criticism* (New York: Houghton Mifflin Co., 1960); and Monroe C. Beardsley, 'An Aesthetic Definition of Art', in *What is Art?* (New York: Haven Publication Inc., 1983), 15–29.

[30]   Similar arguments about the passivity of mass art continue into the present. See, for example, Hermann Lubbe, 'The Ethics of Media Use: Media Consumption as a Moral Challenge', in *Culture First: Promoting Standards in the New Media Age*, ed. Kenneth Dyson and Walter Homolka (London: Cassell, 1996), 57–65.

[31]   Critical Art Ensemble, *The Electronic Disturbance* (New York: Automedia, 1994).

attended one of his events be literally a participant, since he defined Happenings as 'an active art'.[32] Indeed, no one hails their own artistic breakthroughs by proclaiming that they encourage passive spectatorship. Moreover, critics and art theorists, as well, converge on their agreement in placing a premium on the importance of an active audience response. This is the reason that Roland Barthes commends the writerly text. Indeed, the excessive concern with interpretation as the paradigm of discourse about art in contemporary critical practice and theory appears to presume that an active response to artworks is the exemplary response. And philosophies of art as different as those of Arthur Danto and Monroe Beardsley likewise presuppose that artworks properly so-called have always been designed to elicit active responses from their prospective audiences.

Thus, Greenberg's assumption that genuine art requires that the audience add something to it—by way of reflection or interpretation—does not represent a radical departure from entrenched ways of thinking about art. Moreover, Greenberg's commitment to the essential importance of active spectatorship for genuine art is relevant to the case that he makes for modernist or avant-garde art as the genuine art of our epoch. Consider his emphasis on abstraction. In Greenberg's view, when a work is abstract, all things being equal, it calls for the 'spectator's reflection upon the immediate impression left by the plastic values'. That is, the spectator confronted by abstract art has to notice a pattern, or find the relevant details, or recognize the play of structure in the painting. One must, in other words, *work* in order to 'get' an abstract painting. In contrast to avant-garde art, mass art is generally representational and has content, often in terms of a narrative dimension. Undoubtedly, in certain respects, this makes mass art easy to consume.

But one suspects that it is this ease of consumption that Greenberg finds most offensive about mass art. For in Greenberg's view, genuine art must engender active spectatorship. And, in addition, Greenberg would appear to presume that in order to ensure such spectatorship the artwork must be difficult. Presumably the difficulty of the artwork abets the required state of active spectatorship by challenging the audience. That is, genuine art requires spectatorial activity; it requires work. And the natural way in which this working response is elicited is by creating artworks that are difficult.

Avant-garde art, of course, accords with this profile. In order to appreciate it, a certain sort of knowledge and background information will have to

---

[32] Allan Kaprow, *Essays on the Blurring of Art and Life*, ed. Jeff Kelley (Berkeley: University of California Press, 1992), 64.

come into play, if, for example, one is to identify the reflexive comment that an abstract array makes on the nature of painting. To interpret such a work one must be initiated into a certain discourse and, even after one assimilates the relevant art discourse, a great deal of cogitation will still be required in order to apply that discourse with understanding to the painting at hand. Such painting demands intellectual work from the spectator because of its hermetic structure, which serves as a difficult obstacle, or puzzle, or problem which the cognoscenti must solve.

Mass art, on the other hand, is easy to consume, and designedly so. It is made with the intention that it be assimilated with minimum effort. Ideally, it requires as little background information as is possible within the bounds of comprehension. It is made for fast pick-up. It is designed so that the audience can access it on 'first contact'. Indeed, one might say that it is the function of mass art to be accessible to maximum audiences, exercising minimum effort. But the very fact that mass art is designed to be accessible with minimum effort is what raises Greenberg's hackles, since he believes that genuine art is supposed to encourage discernible effort, whereas art, such as mass art, that attempts to minimize the effort the audience must invest in it, simultaneously invites passive spectatorship. And, for Greenberg, art that induces passive spectatorship is ersatz.

The central thrust of Greenberg's case against mass art or kitsch can be summarized by an argument, that for obvious reasons, I call the passivity argument. It goes like this:

1. If x is genuine art, then it abets active spectatorship.

By active spectatorship, Greenberg has in mind such audience responses as noticing details, recognizing patterns, making interpretations, filling in the work, etc. Abstract, avant-garde art functions this way. By being difficult, it challenges the audience in a way that is designed to activate participation with the artwork. Since Greenberg mentions no other way of eliciting active spectatorship in regard to a work, I suspect that he takes difficulty to be a *sine qua non* of genuine art.

2. If mass art is designed to be accessible (easy), then it abets passive spectatorship (i.e., non-active spectatorship).

3. Mass art is designed to be accessible.

4. Therefore, mass art abets passive spectatorship.

5. Therefore, mass art does not abet active spectatorship.

6. Therefore, mass art is not genuine art.

Though I have located this argument in Greenberg's 'Avant-Garde and Kitsch', it should also strike readers who are unacquainted with Greenberg's work as a familiar argument. It rehearses a recurrent jeremiad against mass art—one that has been heard throughout the twentieth century with respect to virtually every mass medium. It is, for example, the stuff of journalistic editorials against TV. The advantage of exploring this argument in the context of Greenberg's theory is that he makes apparent the serious philosophical concerns that underlie the passivity argument.

Greenberg situates the aesthetic problem with mass art in its failure to abet spectatorial activity. Genuine art elicits the contemplative activity of the audience. Mass art encourages passivity; therefore, mass art is not genuine art. Moreover, the cultural value of genuine art, in Greenberg's view (though he is hardly alone in this), is that genuine art exercises the audience's taste, their perceptual faculties, and intelligence. Mass art, in contrast, lets these human capacities lie fallow, so to say, or even more bleakly, it hastens their deterioration through disuse. This, of course, amounts to a significant loss of cultural value.

Thus, inasmuch as mass art threatens the eclipse of these talents, the passing of genuine art would deal a catastrophic blow to culture. What would be lost is an arena of human activity in which our powers can be exercised and expanded. If we substitute the sort of genuine art that Greenberg has in mind with ersatz art—i.e., mass art and / or kitsch—we will become passive spectators such that our human powers will diminish either by being left dormant or by deteriorating outright.

This cultural alarm, replete with predictions of the decline of civilization, is common coin among critics of the mass media. Where Greenberg differs from most others is not only in his theoretical sophistication, but in the use he makes of this diagnosis to advance the cause of the avant-garde. Written in 1939, Greenberg's article invokes then existing totalitarianism (which, of course, exploited mass art) to foretell the emergence of a new Dark Ages, with Fascist and Stalinist barbarians crowding at the gates. In this context, avant-garde art can be seen as a saving remnant. It will preserve the values of culture in a hostile environment. It will continue to encourage the perseverance of the sort of human powers that genuine art engenders through active spectatorship.

Let us begin dismantling Greenberg's argument by looking at his second premiss—If mass art is designed to be accessible, then it abets passive spectatorship. This does not seem to be true of mass art across the board. Consider some examples from film. Spike Lee's *Do the Right Thing* confronts the audience with a complex moral scenario that provokes the audience into reflecting upon the rights and wrongs of the case at hand, as well as the relevance of the philosophy of Martin Luther King versus that of Malcolm X to the situation. The film is accessible, but it has an 'in-your-face' way of presenting racial issues that demands an audience response. Likewise, *Citizen Kane* presents the audience with a contradiction—overtly claiming that a man's life cannot be explained by a single word, like 'Rosebud', while simultaneously suggesting such an explanation as Kane's sledge goes up in flames.[33] Again, the movie is accessible, but it leaves the audience with some provocative (contradictory) food for thought. Don't these examples indicate that there is no necessary connection between accessibility and a passive audience response?

Of course, the proponent of the passivity argument may balk at these counter-examples, maintaining that these films are not mass art, but something else—perhaps art cinema. I doubt that, but no matter, since one can argue for the proposition that accessibility is compatible with active spectatorship on the basis of more mundane cases as well. Mystery stories are a staple of mass art—of pulp fiction, movies, vintage radio, and TV. But consider the whodunit format where the audience does not learn the identity of the murderer until the detective wraps up the case with a bravura display of ratiocination. Such fictions are designed to engage the reader, listener, or viewer in a continuous process of interpretation and inference throughout our reception of the story. Like the fictional detective in the story, we attempt to figure out not only who committed the crime, but, often, how it was done. Mystery fictions like *Columbo* are surely mass art. But they are accessible *and* they presuppose active spectatorship. Moreover, this is not something new. Pulp fictions like Eric Bentley's *Trent's Last Case*, published in 1913, already exemplify this mode of address. Indeed, this novel even invites the reader to second guess the surmises of the detective figure. Similarly, this sort of audience ratiocination is not only presupposed in classically narrated detective fictions like Sue Grafton's *'I' Is For Innocent*, but for long sections of thrillers like Sidney Sheldon's *Morning Noon & Night*.

Nor is the invitation to fill in the story simply a feature of mystery fictions. There is also a long tradition in horror fiction that advocates that the best horror story is the one that leaves off graphic description or depiction, since, it is claimed, the audience will do a more effective job of imagining unseen monsters than the author ever could. This is not a recommendation that is always followed, but it is followed often enough for one to say that many mass horror fictions presuppose an active audience.

---

[33] See Noël Carroll, 'Interpreting *Citizen Kane*', in *Persistence of Vision*, 7 (1989), 51–62.

Likewise, radio fiction, as it is canonically described, encouraged its audience to perform feats of imagination.[34] The listener is said to have supplied the look of the Shadow. And stand-up comics on radio and TV require audiences who are prepared to interpret their punchlines in order for their jokes to succeed. That is, in order to 'get' a joke, the listener has to do something, namely figure out the implications of the incongruous concluding line of the joke, which often takes the form of a momentarily puzzling riddle that the audience must solve.[35] And cartoons with captions, like Gary Larsen's *The Far Side*, equally presuppose an interpretation by a reader piqued by the enigmatic juxtapositions of words and images,[36] while George Herriman's legendary comic strip *Krazy Kat* requires a reader prepared to track its multifarious details and juxtapositions, and to follow its surrealistic narratives. Even the music video by Meatloaf—'I'll Do Anything For Love But I Won't Do That'—invites the audience to answer the question of what 'that' might be. In these cases, accessibility does not preclude active spectatorship. In some cases, the very success of the mass artwork presupposes active spectatorship.

Nor are these examples exceptional. The presupposition of active spectatorship is a regularly recurring feature of mass artworks. Because this feature of mass artworks is so frequently overlooked, it is instructive to spend a few pages emphasizing it, even if I have already provided enough evidence to show that the second premiss of the passivity argument is questionable. The passivity argument is very strongly entrenched. So, rather than dismissing the second premiss of the argument with a few hasty counter-examples, let us look at the issue in more depth.

Perhaps the best place to start to establish the necessity of active spectatorship to much mass art is the case of mass fictions. I have already invoked mystery fiction. Here, I think that it is both obvious and non-controversial that the very structure of the classical whodunit (as opposed to the hardboiled detective story or thriller) is predicated upon drawing the audience into a continuous process of inference and interpretation. But it should also be noted that the kinds of spectatorial activity involved in response to mystery stories in terms of interpretation and inference are also available in every other genre of mass fiction. To illustrate this point, here are some more examples.

When reading Isaac Asimov's science fiction novel *Foundation*, the reader infers that the Empire has settled into a kind of medieval stagnation—where the capacity for original research and invention has been lost

---

[34] See, for example, Andrew Crisell, *Understanding Radio* (London: Methuen, 1986).
[35] See Noël Carroll, 'On Jokes', in *Midwest Studies in Philosophy: Philosophy and the Arts*, 16 (1991), 280–301. [36] Id., 'Words and Images', in *Persistence of Vision* (forthcoming).

and, in fact, is repressed in favour of reliance on the authority of the past—before this social malaise is explicitly diagnosed in the book. In much the same way, the reader has most likely surmised the identity of the Mule in Asimov's sequel, *Foundation and Empire*, way in advance of its explicit revelation in the text. Indeed, books like these are often designed in such a way that the reader is induced to make certain conjectures so that she will continue to read the book in order to see if they are fulfilled. This is one of the secrets to writing a successful 'page turner'. But this strategy, in turn, presupposes a cognitively active readership.

Moreover, this sort of activity can be engaged and promoted on a page-by-page basis. Toward the end of *The Rustlers of West Fork* by Louis L'Amour, the reader knows that Hopalong Cassidy is about to be ambushed on a wintery street by Johnny Rebb. Johnny Rebb is hiding out in a house that Hopalong has been told is empty. When Hopalong steps into the street, we learn that he is looking intently at something. L'Amour writes: 'No snow on the roof. He smiled. . . . ' This leads the reader to infer that Hopalong knows Johnny Rebb is in the house, because the house is obviously heated, and that inference, in turn, is confirmed on the next page. The confirmation of that inference is, of course, a minor readerly pleasure. But my point is that kind of pleasure would not be available if the reader were not active.

Likewise, in the pulp fantasy *The Shape-Changer's Wife* by Sharon Shinn, the reader speculates that Glyrendon's servants are really animals that have been transformed by his magic into humans long before the hero Aubrey comes to this conclusion. In effect, *The Shape-Changer's Wife* is a super-naturalized version of the *Island of Dr. Moreau*. It depends for its effect on encouraging the reader to fathom the identity of Glyrendon's household (including speculation on whence his servants and his wife came) and then rewards the reader by confirming her conjectures. From our perspective, what is, of course, noteworthy about this 'contract' with the audience, is that it presupposes an active, participant readership.

Harlequin Romances are often singled out as the very nadir of mass-market fiction. They are extremely formulaic. So many of these novels mobilize the same scenario: girl meets boy; girl misunderstands boy, or vice versa; the misunderstanding is cleared up; girl gets boy. However, what is generally neglected is that novels of this sort afford the reader an opportunity to expand his or her interpretive powers.

In *The Lake Effect* by Leigh Michaels, Alex Jacobi, a high-powered, woman lawyer, always dressed to the nines for success, has been told to lure her ex-colleague, Kane Forrestal, back to Pence Whitfield, the largest law firm in the Twin Cities. Kane says that he prefers beachcombing to big-time law. Alex assumes that this is a bargaining ploy and that her job is essentially to renegotiate Kane's contract. But the reader gradually hypothesizes that Kane is sincere in his distaste for Pence Whitfield, that he is attracted to Alex, and that she is attracted to him. Alex—one might say *of course*—is the last to know. She consistently misinterprets Kane's avowals and advances as negotiating gambits. Thus, the reader is constantly reinterpreting Alex's interpretations of what is going on.

Or, for a more compact example of the kind of interpretation that I have in mind, consider the Harlequin Romance *The Quiet Professor* by Betty Neels. Nurse Megan Rodner is convinced that Doctor Jake van Belfield is married. The reader realizes that despite his gruffness, he is attracted to Megan, and it also slowly dawns on us that we have no real evidence that van Belfield is married. In a conversation with Megan, he says that his house is too large, but that that can be remedied. She says, 'Oh, of course, when your wife and children live here.' We know that by this she means van Belfield's supposed present wife and children. He answers, 'As you say, when my wife and children live here,' which the reader understands is likely to mean van Belfield's future wife (whom Megan might become) and their children. Promoting this kind of interpretive activity in the reader is one of the central attractions of Harlequin Romances. But note that then it is the case that this highly accessible form of pulp fiction presupposes an active reader.[37]

So far I have advanced the case for active spectatorship with respect to mass fiction by citing genres. But the very act of comprehending a mass fiction of any genre will involve cognitive activity. For the reader, viewer, or listener of a mass fiction, like any other fiction, will be involved in following a story, and following a story is not simply a matter of passively absorbing the narrative. It involves a continual process of constructing a sense of where the story is headed. This may include predicting exactly what will happen next. But it need not.

Following a story requires audience activity. Generally, following a story engages us, at the very least, in envisioning or anticipating the *range* of things—will she get the job or not?—that are apt to happen next. In the movie *Sleepless in Seattle*, once the heroine finds the boy's backpack, the viewer tracks the action in terms of the question of whether our heroine and our heroes will meet up, or pass each other on the elevators. Earlier scenes in mass narratives, as in any narrative, are most frequently necessary causal conditions for later scenes. For this reason, earlier scenes

---

[37] For an even more ambitious defence of the interpretive activities of the audiences of mass art, see Alexander Nehamas, 'Plato and the Mass Media', *Monist*, 71 (1988), 214–35.

implicate or circumscribe a range of options concerning what will happen next, and a crucial aspect of what it is to follow a story is to evolve and to project a reasonable horizon or set of expectations about the direction of the events the story has put in motion. Indeed, it is only within the context of such a horizon of expectations that the reader or viewer can be said to know what is at stake in the action. Thus, in comprehending a mass narrative, the reader is not a passive sponge, but is engaged in filtering out possibilities from the incoming information.

Furthermore, following the story also requires filling in the pre-suppositions and implications of the fictional world of the narrative, an activity that can become challenging with cyberpunk fiction like William Gibson's *Virtual Light*. Undoubtedly, the implied background of much mass fiction is not as arcane as one often finds in cyberpunk. Nevertheless, there is never a narrative so simple and self-sufficient in terms of information that audiences need make no contribution in order to render the story intelligible. Thus, as of any fiction, mass-market fictions require active consumers.

Moreover, with many mass narratives, the audience is involved in the interpretation of what might be called narrative meaning.[38] For example, with the movie *The Searchers*, we are never told why Ethan does not kill the girl, as was his express intention. It is left up to the viewer to come up with an account of the significance of his behaviour and developing such an explanation requires audience activity. Many mass fictions are elliptical in a way that intentionally encourages the audience to speculate about lacunae in the text.

As well, many mass fictions take surprising plot turns, such as the revelation that Norman's mother is dead in *Psycho*. That these plot turns come as a surprise indicates not only that the audience has been actively constructing the narrative all along, but then calls for additional constructive activity in order to incorporate new information. And this is by no means a rare occurrence in response to mass fictions.

As Susan Feagin points out, appreciating a fiction 'requires adjusting oneself psychologically in ways one often can't anticipate. It requires shifting one's point of view and developing and utilizing various sensitivities.'[39] But changes in point of view, of course, involve audiences in actively reassessing what is going on in the fiction.

---

[38] For an account of narrative meaning, see George Wilson, 'On Film Narrative and Narrative Meaning', in *Philosophy and Film Theory*, ed. Richard Allen and Murray Smith (Oxford: Oxford University Press, forthcoming).

[39] Susan Feagin, *Reading with Feeling* (Ithaca, NY: Cornell University Press, 1996), 56. See also her ch. 3: 'Mental Shifts, Slides and Sensitivities'. My point in invoking Feagin here is to argue that there is no reason in principle to suppose that the mental shifts, slides, and sensitivities she describes do not frequently occur in mass fictions.

Thus far the audience activities I have been drawing attention to have been what might be called cognitive. But, of course, the consumers of mass fiction are not merely involved actively in a continuous process of cognition; they are also actively involved in response to mass fictions emotionally and morally. As Feagin puts it, responding to a mass fiction involves utilizing various sensitivities. For example, if in Ben Bova's novel *Mars*, the formation of our growing conviction—based on tracking various hints and clues dropped in the text—before it is stated that the expedition is deteriorating physically and psychologically is a cognitive judgement, then our classification of the newscaster Edith as an opportunist is a moral judgement, and our hatred of the Vice-President is emotional. Moreover, it should be eminently clear that virtually all mass-market fictions invite moral assessment and emotional responses as part of the glue that binds the audience to the text.[40] But why would one suppose that these responses are passive rather than active?[41]

Though I have been concentrating on mass fiction as evidence for active spectatorship in response to mass fiction, similar arguments can be made for other mass art modes. With respect to mass-market music, for example, it pays to note that the lyrics are often metaphorical and, therefore, invite exegesis. In Jackson Browne's 'For a Dancer' from his *Late for the Sky* album, we hear 'Just do the steps that you've been shown / By everyone you've ever known / Until the dance becomes your very own.' Yet, the listener does not take this at its literal, face-value, but rather interprets its symbolic portent, regarding dance as a figure for life and the stanza itself as a comment on the nature of the socialization process.[42] Likewise, in the popular song 'Memory', the careful listener interprets the transition from moonlight to daybreak as a metaphor of rebirth.[43]

One might object to these examples on the grounds that not every listener will make this interpretation, even if it is there to be made. But, by the same token, not every spectator, including appreciative spectators, performs the interpretive activity called for with respect to avant-garde

[40] Emotional and moral responses to mass art will be discussed respectively at greater length in Chs. 4 and 5 of this book.

[41] Some reasons for supposing this will be canvassed in the next section during our discussion of Collingwood where we will also provide some argumentation against this move.

[42] James F. Harris, *Philosophy at 33⅓ rpm: Themes of Classic Rock Music* (LaSalle, Ill.: Open Court Publishing Co., 1993), 68. This book provides a plethora of examples of the interpretive opportunities available in rock music.

[43] The interpretation of metaphors and symbols is also relevant to audience responses to mass fictions. For example, in the best-selling sword-and-sorcery novel *The Sword of Shannara* by Terry Brooks, the sword in the title of the novel is identified as an agency that causes the recognition of the truth in such a way that one of the metaphors that underpins the novel is that 'truth is a weapon'. Moreover, I would contend that this metaphor is in the novel so that the active reader is supposed to find it.

art. Nevertheless, we agree that avant-garde art generally abets active spectatorship in the sense that it not only makes the grounds for it available, but also that avant-garde art encourages it. Why should we regard the metaphors in mass market music differently?

MTV is frequently lambasted as a synonym for contemporary passivity. However, it is important to remember that some of its most popularly recurring strategies are predicated upon encouraging spectator activity. What I have in mind in particular is what we might call the recurrent rebus-like structure of many music videos. This involves matching the song in the music video with vague or fragmented episodes of action that might illustrate it, either as narratives or simply as images that somehow complement the words in the song. This structure invites the viewer to entertain different interpretations of the images in light of the song and vice versa.

For example, in Montell Jordan's 'This is How We Do it,' the song tells of a party. On the image track, among other things, we see images of a teenage party and a scene in an upscale restaurant. There are alternative ways of reading these narrative fragments. Perhaps these intercut semi-stories go from the singer's past to the present, showing him before and after he became a star. Or maybe the scenes in the expensive restaurant represent the young singer's wish-fulfilment fantasy. Or, yet again, maybe the imagery is merely an inventory of parties. The viewer can try out all of these alternatives, and others as well.

The rebus-like structure of music videos, like Montell Jordan's, is, to a limited extent, an open structure that affords the possibility of imaginative re-readings, both on first viewing and on subsequent ones. Undoubtedly, the cynic will charge that music videos are designed to allow for this minimal play of ambiguity because the viewer would go out of her mind with boredom otherwise. That may well be true. But even if the reason music videos encourage a limited range of imaginative play is a thoroughly venal one, that does not falsify my contention that music videos are frequently structured to encourage active spectatorship.[44]

This long excursus through pulp fiction, movies, and mass-market music, then, should make one thing clear: that mass art, despite its accessibility, may also abet active spectatorship. Thus, even if accessibility is a necessary condition or an essential feature of mass art, that does not entail that mass art, in virtue of its accessibility, abets passivity. For, given the preceding discussion, we have seen that much mass art—perhaps even

[44] Indeed, the ambiguity of many music videos involves the audience frequently in what I earlier referred to as the interpretation of narrative meaning. This is also true with respect to the suggestive use of photography in many advertisements.

most mass art—encourages some level of audience activity and, in many cases, mass artworks presuppose an active response on the part of viewers, listeners, and readers. Accessibility or ease of understanding is not incompatible with engendering active responses from audiences. Indeed, in some cases, it may be the opportunity to respond actively to the mass artwork that interests audiences in it in the first place.[45]

Of course, it may be said in reaction to my inventory of mass art that I have not really understood the passivity argument, in so far as most of my examples are of responses too rudimentary to be called active spectator responses. But I am not sure that this is my problem. It may be the problem of the passivity argument itself, inasmuch as its central terms— active and passive—are not sharply defined. For what could it mean to say that an audience is passive? Surely it cannot mean that there is no mental activity going on. That is implausible. After all, it is very difficult to conceive of a completely passive response to anything, especially a text, whether it is mass art or otherwise. Some cognitive processing must be going on. But, then, it falls to the proponent of the passivity argument to say, in some non-question-begging way, what kind of processing is passive and what kind of processing is active, as well as to show that, once the distinction is clearly drawn, mass art always turns out to be passive in principled contradistinction to other sorts of art, like avant-garde art.

Moreover, as long as we accept the distinction between active and passive responses to art, it seems to me that the things that I call active—such as inferring, interpreting, filling in presuppositions, tracking narrative events against a horizon of expectations, understanding metaphors, making moral assessments, responding emotionally, and so on—are the sorts of things that in ordinary language we are intuitively prone to call active. They are responses above and beyond rudimentary, automatic

---

[45] I have been emphasizing what might be called 'mentalistic' active responses on the part of the consumers of mass art. However, as Richard Shusterman points out, a great deal of mass-market music is designed for dancing, which is certainly an active response. On what grounds, Shusterman demands, is this kind of response ignored by the detractors of mass art when it comes to discussing the participatory dimension of popular music? See Richard Shusterman, *Pragmatist Aesthetics: Living Beauty, Rethinking Art* (Oxford: Blackwell, 1993), 184.

One genre of popular music that, by its nature, calls for active responses that are both interpretive and physical is the dance instruction song—such as Sam Cooke's 'Shake'—which encourages the listener to learn the dance from the words and rhythm of the song. This, of course, involves both interpretation (of the instructions in the song) and *action*. For a discussion of the dance instruction song, see Sally Banes and John F. Szwed, 'From "Messin' Around" to "Funky Western Civilization": The Rise and Fall of Dance Instruction Songs', in *New Formations*, 27 (1995–6), 59–79.

Furthermore, other genres that require an active physical response to mass artworks include not only interactive video games, but karaoke videos. Clearly, the prospects for such interactive technology have been only barely explored.

Also, for further arguments in defence of mass art, see Richard Shusterman, 'Don't Believe the Hype', *Poetics Today*, 14/1 (1993), 101–22.

cognitive-perceptual processing. Thus, if the proponent of the passivity argument wishes to discount this evidence, he or she must show why these examples are not evidence of active spectatorship.[46] Preferably, he should do this by crafting a clear distinction between active spectator responses and passive spectator responses such that the distinction does not also disqualify appropriate responses to whatever he believes counts as genuine art.[47]

Perhaps needless to say, I think that it will be very hard for a proponent of the passivity argument to do this. However, there is another option open to him. He might drop the distinction altogether (certainly a good idea from my point of view) and attempt to reframe the argument in other terms. Maybe he will attempt to rephrase it in terms of a distinction between ease of effort in comprehension versus difficulty of comprehension. This would surely be a reasonable move for someone like Greenberg to make, since, in fact, he talks in terms of effort rather than activity and passivity.

Recasting the argument in the vocabulary of effort, the first premiss would read 'If x is genuine art, then it requires effort on the part of the spectator in order to be comprehended and/or appreciated.' Stated more succinctly, this comes down to the idea that genuine art is difficult— difficult to comprehend, and, therefore, demanding in terms of effort. This way of stating the premiss has certain advantages over our previous formulation of it. For if my objections have hit their target, the original formulation was too loose—i.e., inasmuch as spectator activity is so vaguely defined, virtually anything might fall under its rubric. The first premiss in our initial formulation, though apparently true enough, ran the danger of being satisfied trivially by virtually anything. The reformulation in terms of difficulty is a little tighter and, therefore, more promising. However, on the debit side, it also gives every impression of being false.

For example, consider Picasso's *Bull's Head*, a construction comprised of the seat and handlebars of a bicycle that recalls the outline of a longhorn. This is, prima facie, avant-garde art, so it is presumably, by Greenberg's

[46] It has been charged by one reader of this manuscript that my criticism of Greenberg is unfair, since it is obvious that by passivity Greenberg never meant 'brain dead'. Two responses are in order. First: the responses that I have marshalled against Greenberg are way above the threshold of 'brain dead'. Second: what do Greenberg and others like him have in mind? It will not do to say they have some mysterious, undefined sophisticated distinction at their disposal that will save the day. That is simply evasive intellectually. At this point in the debate, the burden of proof belongs to Greenberg and his allies. To grumble that they are more sophisticated is a non-starter.

[47] The defender of the passivity argument might try to parse the active-versus-passive couplet in terms of conscious responses versus subconscious (or preconscious or tacit) responses. But that won't do, since the reflective response to so-called high art is often similarly subconscious (or preconscious or tacit).

lights, genuine art. But there is no difficulty in discerning the visual wit it evinces. The plain viewer can readily recognize the outline of the bull, while also appreciating the humour of building it out of a bicycle. Moreover, if we think about genuine art of the past—such as portraits by Velázquez of Charles V—it should be very apparent that difficulty is not a necessary prerequisite of genuine art. Thus, there is no impediment to regarding *The Gold Rush* as genuine art just because it is not difficult.

Perhaps Greenberg is tempted to speak of difficulty because he believes that difficulty is a necessary condition for an active spectator response. This might explain his apparent ambition to reconceive the appreciative response to art along the lines of the Protestant work ethic. However, as we have seen, it is false that an active spectator response requires that the work in question be difficult in terms of accessibility. Accessibility is not incompatible with active spectatorship. A work may require little effort in order to be assimilated and yet abet active spectatorship. The ease with which we comprehend and/or appreciate a work has no necessary connection with whether or not the work abets active spectatorship.

Moreover, if we disconnect the notion of the difficulty or effortfulness of a work from the prospect of active spectatorship, then it is hard to understand why Greenberg thinks that difficulty is important, let alone that it is a necessary condition for the status of genuine art. What's so great about difficulty in and of itself? If the answer is that it encourages work, then we are left to wonder what's so important about that? Work is valuable either for its external product or for purposes of self-realization. Work in response to art has no external product. And if it is not connected to the values of active spectatorship, then it is difficult to appreciate its contribution to self-realization. So, we may confront the Greenbergian with a dilemma. Either the requirement of difficulty is motivated for the sake of the kind of self-realization available through active spectatorship or it is motivated for its own sake, as if difficulty were an end in itself. The first horn of this dilemma is refuted by our long discussions of the compatibility of accessibility and effortless comprehension with active spectatorship. The second horn of the dilemma leaves the Greenbergian with a position that makes the value of genuine art virtually inexplicable— or, at least, as inexplicable as the notion that difficulty is valuable for its own sake, irrespective of what it brings about.

And, in any case, as we have seen, the first premiss of the argument— that genuine works of art demand effort—scarcely fits the facts. For there are many things that we can all agree are works of art—both traditional works and avant-garde works—that do not command an effortful response. Therefore, the passivity argument—cast in terms of either active spectatorship or difficulty is false—since its first premiss is either too slack to mark a distinction (on the active spectatorship reading) or it is false (on the difficulty reading); while the second premiss is outright false: neither is it the case that the accessibility of mass art precludes active spectatorship, nor that easy spectatorship differentiates mass art from genuine art of either a traditional or an avant-garde variety.

Greenberg's great worry about mass art or kitsch is that it threatens to undermine certain cultural values, namely those associated with active spectatorship. But as I hope that I have shown, mass artworks can be the source of what we can call transactional value, the value derived by audience members by exercising their powers of inference, interpretation, narrative understanding, metaphoric comprehension, and so on through their interaction with works that stimulate participatory spectatorship. In arguing thusly, I am obviously not claiming, as some might, that mass art has some unique standards of value of its own that are incommensurable with the standards of what Greenberg thinks of as genuine art. For the activities that make consuming mass art worthwhile are on a continuum with those available in genuine art.[48] Thus, Greenberg is wrong in supposing that the emergence of mass art threatens the total annihilation of the cultural values he prizes.

Of course, by saying that the transactional values available in mass art are on a continuum with those of Greenberg's brand of genuine art, I do not mean to claim that mass art is for its consumers an evolutionary way-station on a trajectory that culminates in modernism. In fact, I doubt that consuming mass art necessarily puts one on the pathway toward appreciating modernism. But this is compatible with maintaining that the values available in mass art are on a continuum with the values of modernism, even if consuming mass art does not lead one inexorably to cultivate more of the same transactional value by seeking out avant-garde art.

Just as a taste for beer does not inevitably lead to a taste for champagne, an appreciation of the transactional value of mass art does not lead typical consumers to a taste for modernist art. And even persons attuned to the transactional values of modernist art can savour the perhaps often lesser virtues of mass art in the same way that a connoisseur of champagne can appreciate beer. Indeed, even the wine taster may think that beer is what one should have some of the time, even though she thinks that, overall, champagne is finer. And, of course, it is also true that thinking that overall

---

[48] For further argumentation along these lines, see Noël Carroll, 'The Paradox of Junk Fiction', *Philosophy and Literature*, 18/2 (1994), 225–41.

champagne is superior to beer does not preclude the conviction that some beers can be superior to some champagnes.

Finally, it might be said that I have misunderstood Greenberg's case. He is not claiming, it might be said, that mass art is necessarily mindless, but only that some is, and, it might be added, who could deny that? Just look around; we are hemmed in at every side by mindless mass art. Thus, in my response to Greenberg, I have proven too much and I have tried to redeem all that mindless mass art.

Several points need to be made here. First, mindlessness is not simply a feature of mass art. There is a lot of mindless avant-garde art. I do not wish to deny that there is mindless mass art. I agree that there is a lot of it. I have only been at pains to show that mass art is not *necessarily* mindless: that there is some mass art that is mindful (that abets active spectatorship as we usually understand that concept); and that there is probably more mindful mass art around than the mandarins of modernism typically suppose.

As a last line of defence, the Greenbergian might challenge my method by noting that I have treated Greenberg's argument as one concerned with the essence of mass art. But perhaps Greenberg, and MacDonald before him, only meant to be talking about a pronounced tendency of mass art. Mass art tends to result in passive audiences. Even here, however, we must press the Greenbergian to clarify what is meant by 'active' and 'passive'. Thus, our argument against the passivity argument is the same, whether the argument is deduced from a notion of the nature of mass art or inferred as a statistical tendency. For how can we assess even an empirical claim until we have a precise idea of what is at stake in charges of passivity?

Moreover, 'passivity', in this debate, should not be confused with the allegation that people stay home and watch a lot of TV rather than going out and engaging in communal activities. For then we are no longer talking about the passivity induced by the structure of mass artworks, but the atomization of leisure time. Such audiences would be equally atomized if they stayed home and listened to Mozart rather than attending town meetings.

The formula argument

Perhaps the most philosophically fortified version of the formula argument against mass art is to be found in *The Principles of Art* by R. G. Collingwood.[49] Collingwood, unlike MacDonald, does not talk directly about

---

[49] R. G. Collingwood, *The Principles of Art* (Oxford: Oxford University Press, 1969). This book was first published by the Clarendon Press in 1938.

mass culture. Rather, the target of the formula argument is what Collingwood calls amusement art. However, it is very clear from Collingwood's
examples of amusement art that mass art is a major subspecies of amusement art and that, as such, mass art falls afoul of the formula argument.

For Collingwood, amusement art, of which mass art is a primary
example, comprises one of the categories of what Collingwood dubs
'pseudo art'. Pseudo art is something that is not art, but is mistaken for
art.[50] Pseudo art is a contrary of art proper. Pseudo art is false art. Thus,
like those of MacDonald and Greenberg, Collingwood's case against mass
art is primarily aesthetic, i.e., the formula argument is aimed at showing
that mass art is not really art properly so called.

In *The Principles of Art*, Collingwood is primarily concerned with producing a theory of art proper. His first order of business in this respect is to
eliminate what he regards to be certain competing theories of art which he
believes to be false. Two of these theories are the technical theory of art of
which a special instance is what we might call the representational theory
of art.[51] These theories are of special interest to us, since mass art could
pass as art proper on either of these theories. Thus, in order to appreciate
Collingwood's case against mass art, it is instructive to see why he rejects
the kinds of theories that would enfranchise mass art as art proper.

The technical theory of art is, roughly, the view that art is essentially a
matter of craft. It is a characteristically Greek idea. The Greeks discovered
the concept of craft. Notice how often the idea of a craft crops up in
Platonic dialogues. Analogies to medicine, shoemaking, farming, chariot-
making, and the crafts of war and government abound. One of the great
achievements of the Greeks was their grasp of the abstract logic of crafts.
So taken were they with the success of this idea that they attempted to
extrapolate it as an analysis of everything else, including the creation of the
universe. Among the activities that the Greeks attempted to assimilate
under the notion of craft was art. Collingwood, for reasons to be discussed
shortly, thought that this was a major error, since under the technical
theory of art all sorts of things that are not, by his lights, art, such as
amusement art and mass art, are categorized as art. The influence of the
technical theory of art, for Collingwood, is one of the reasons that we
mistakenly construe amusement art and mass art to be art proper.

The representational theory of art, according to Collingwood, is a
special instance of the view that all art is essentially a craft. Specifically,

---

[50] Collingwood, *The Principles of Art*, 33.
[51] The technical theory of art is discussed in ch. 2 of *Principles of Art*; the representational theory is
discussed in ch. 3.

the representational theory of art characterizes all art as the craft of arousing emotions in spectators. Indeed, even more specifically, the representational theory of art, according to Collingwood, maintains that art is the craft of evoking or arousing in spectators the self-same kinds of emotions that one would feel for the referent of a given representation. That is, the craft of representation aspires to get us to associate the same kinds of everyday emotions that we would be likely to bring to the sight of wounded soldiers to a movie image of the field of wounded soldiers such as the one that we see at the end of the first half of *Gone with the Wind*. According to the representational theory of art, the aim of the artist is to elicit everyday emotions by means of representation.

What Collingwood then goes on to call 'magical art' and 'amusement art' are both subcategories of representational art, because both types of art attempt to produce or to arouse everyday emotions by means of representations of referents that possess the power to provoke certain emotions, which will then be, so to speak, transferred to the representation itself.[52]

The technical theory of art maintains that all art is essentially craft; the representational theory of art specifies this assertion by claiming that all art is the craft of arousing emotions. Both theories, according to Collingwood, are false and need to be unhorsed in order to advance a theory of art proper. Both these theories impede the formulation of the theory of art properly so called, since, among other things, they regard as paradigmatic instances of 'art' candidates that are nothing more than instances of pseudo art. Thus, these theories muddy the waters with red herrings that are apt to draw attention away from examples of art properly so called and thus these theories confuse the data.

Collingwood attempts to refute the technical theory of art by enumerating six essential features of craft and then, in effect, arguing that not one of them is a necessary condition for art. By this manœuvre, he intends to show that art properly so called cannot be essentially a matter of craft, since it need not possess any of the necessary features of craft. The six necessary features of craft that Collingwood enumerates are: 1. craft always involves a distinction between means and ends; 2. craft always involves a distinction between planning and execution; 3. in craft, means are prior to ends in execution, but ends are prior in the process of planning; 4. in craft, there is a distinction between raw material and the finished product; 5. in craft, there is a distinction between form and matter; 6. in craft, there is a hierarchical relation between various crafts.

[52] Magical art is analysed in ch. 4 of *Principles of Art*; amusement art is analysed in ch. 5.

Putatively, these conditions obtain with respect to amusement art, but not to art proper.

Collingwood's basic line of attack here is to argue that none of the preceding necessary features of craft constitutes a necessary condition of art. For each criterion of craft, it is possible to imagine some artwork that lacks it, and it is also possible to imagine some artwork that fails to meet all six criteria. So none of these conditions is a condition for art proper nor is any nor are all of them necessary in combination.

In order to appreciate the way in which Collingwood conducts this argument, let us look at the first two conditions for craft status and at what Collingwood has to say about them. First, Collingwood argues that craft always involves a distinction between means and ends. Consider boot-making. When a craftsperson sets out to make a boot, she has an end in mind for which the boots in question serve as a means. The boot in question is designed to bring about some end—to serve some purpose. A riding boot is designed to serve a different purpose from a climbing boot. And both will be designed differently from a boot that is designed simply to look good. A climbing boot will be designed to take a lot of pressure, whereas that need not be of much concern in the design of a boot for the purposes of fashion—a boot that will be worn to cocktail parties and opera premières. The purpose for which the boot is designed governs the way in which the boot is constructed by the craftsperson. The boot is appreciated for what it does. It is not appreciated for its own sake, but for the way in which it serves some purpose.

That craft products are merely means to a predetermined end points to a second feature of crafts—that crafts involve distinctive stages: a planning stage and a stage of execution. First, the craftsperson thinks about the purpose of the product that she is supposed to make and then she figures out the means to facilitate that purpose. Having established that the boot that she has been commissioned to make is a climbing boot, the boot-maker plans out how to make a sturdy boot—she determines what materials are appropriate and assembles them so that they can take a beating. That is, she executes her plan. She knows exactly what she wants ahead of time and all of her activity is guided by a pre-ordained plan that itself is conceptually tied to the purpose of the product that she is constructing. Likewise, on Collingwood's view, a pornographer has a purpose—the sexual arousal of the audience—and he selects and arranges bodies to that end.

But this procedure is not, Collingwood argues, one that an artist properly so called must follow. Very often an artist does not start out knowing ahead of time exactly what the final product will be. For art, in contrast to craft, is exploratory. A writer might start out with some images, or some characters, or a situation, or just a phrase, and then experiment with them in order to see where it takes her. The writer may have no idea whether the outcome will be comic or tragic. If asked about this, she may say that she will just have to wait and see how it turns out.

Similarly, a composer may begin with a couple of notes and play around with them, trying out different combinations in order to see where they will go—to see where they will take her. Or, a painter may start with a few lines and test out different ways of developing them, just as a poet may start with just a phrase, waiting for the first phrase to call forth others.

Artmaking is a process, one in which very often the artist discovers where she is going only through the process of getting there. The artist often only learns what a piece is about in the process of creating it. The artist need not have an exact idea of where she is headed. This may be something that she negotiates or discovers along the way. This is not to say that an artist may not have a pre-ordained plan, but only that a pre-ordained plan, derived from a conception of the purpose or end of the work in question, is not a necessary or defining feature of all art properly so called.

But a pre-ordained plan, derived from a purpose that is distinct from the means at the artist's disposal, *must* be an element of all craft. No craftsperson could proceed in the way of the artists whom we have just envisioned. A shoemaker does not start working in leather without a clear idea of the outcome. Midway through working on a pair of shoes you do not hear shoemakers saying—'I'm not sure whether these will be bedroom slippers or riding boots, or whether they'll be penny loafers or half-Wellingtons.'

On the other hand, it might not sound strange for a playwright to say— 'I'm not sure whether this play is going to turn out to be a comedy or a tragedy; we'll just have to wait and see.' But, again, it would be absurd for a shoemaker to murmur: 'I'm not sure whether this will turn out to be a galosh or a toe shoe.' Who would ever hire such a shoemaker? When one orders a pair of boots, one expects boots, not slippers. When a shoemaker sets out to make something, she knows pretty much exactly what the endpoint of her activities and her product will be because she begins her activity apprised of a purpose that shapes her plan of attack.

Artists, however, frequently proceed differently; they often discover what they've made after they've made it. This is why it is not absurd to commission a choreographer to make a dance before you are told much about it. It may be that no conception of the prospective dance can be articulated until after the choreographer retreats to her studio and experiments with putting together different forms and figures in different patterns, incorporating some in her dance and rejecting others.

What considerations like this are meant to show is that there is a categorical distinction between art properly so called and craft. Craft necessarily involves exact plans that precede execution. But art need not necessarily involve planning. Artmaking can start without a specified plan and therefore the artist, as she works over her piece, is not implementing a preconceived blueprint.

Artists need not have exact plans because they need not set out to bring about pre-ordained purposes. Indeed, the artwork need have no pre-ordained purpose. It need not be designed to serve some pre-set purpose. Indeed, the artwork proper need not serve any ulterior purpose at all. The artwork may be valuable for its own sake. It is not a means to a preconceived end. Thus, the language of ends and means does not suit the artwork, whereas the idea of a craft for its own sake sounds like a contradiction in terms.

If you make a dance and someone asks you what it is for, you may, Collingwood might contend, say in a way that is perfectly intelligible that it is *not* for anything. It just is. And it is valuable for its own sake. Moreover, from this it follows that it is not the case that with regard to art proper that there is a necessary distinction between means and ends exactly because artworks properly so called may not have any specific purpose or end for which they have been produced, and, therefore, they will not possess any means to that end. This is not to say that some artworks, properly so called, may not have purposes. It is only to say that the possession of a purpose is not a necessary feature of art. Or, even if an artwork properly so called has some craft elements, it is not in virtue of its craft elements that it is an instance of art properly so called.

Art, then, can once again be seen to be essentially different from craft. For crafts always and essentially have purposes and ulterior ends in virtue of which means are selected and modified, and craft activity is dominated by pre-ordained plans that are conceptually tied to overriding purposes. But in so far as artworks need possess no ulterior purposes and may be processes of discovery without preconceived plans, artworks, properly so called, are categorically distinct from craftworks.

Or, what are essential features of craft—such as the distinctions between ends/means and plan/execution—are not necessary features of artworks. Thus, some artworks lack ulterior purposes and/or plans. So, artworks do not belong categorically to the class of craftworks. This is not to deny that some artworks may have craft features—like a plan or a technique. However, where artworks possess certain essential craft features, it will not be in virtue of those features (the ones they share with craftworks) that the artworks in question count as artworks. For example, artworks proper may possess certain representational properties—i.e., an artwork proper may picture something that arouses emotion—but the work in question will not be an instance of art proper in virtue of being representational.[53] It is another feature of the work, yet to be discussed, that accounts for its status as art, properly so called.

Space does not permit an examination of Collingwood's four other essential conditions of craft. Suffice it to say of those discussions that Collingwood offers similar arguments to the ones above with respect to the categorical distinction between craft and art proper. On the grounds of these arguments, he concludes that the technical theory of art is false, summarily claiming that the features of art that the technical theory of art as craft is prone to single out as essential features of art (since they are essential features of craft) are not essential features of art at all. If artworks proper possess these features, Collingwood argues, said features are only accidental to the art status of the work in question.

The refutation of the technical theory of art is important for Collingwood because it is the craft theory of art, on his view, that leads people to identify the wrong things—such as magical art and amusement art—as art proper, when, in fact, they are really pseudo art. Thus, if one is tempted to regard mass art as art proper, on Collingwood's account, this is probably due to one's allegiance to the technical theory of art, since mass art is at best a craft—the craft of arousing everyday emotions. In this sense, Collingwood's refutation of the technical theory of art is propaedeutic to his relegation of mass art to the status of pseudo-art.

In Collingwood's scheme of things, modern mass art probably falls into both the categories of magical art and amusement art. Both are species of representational art, i.e., craftworks whose express end is the 're-vocation of certain emotions'.[54] In the case of magical art, these emotions are aroused in order to be discharged into practical life. Religious art and propaganda are examples of magical art. The propagandist stirs up emotions—say, xenophobia—in order that audiences will vent that emotion in daily life by, the propagandist hopes, directing it at foreigners with whom the state is at war. Propaganda has a pre-ordained purpose, and the propagandist uses his craft to plan images and narratives that are likely

---

[53] This recalls Clive Bell's position that art proper can be representational, though not on account of its representational properties. Collingwood makes the same move, though for different reasons.

[54] Collingwood, *Principles of Art*, 57.

to engender hatred of the enemy. Inasmuch as propaganda takes the form of a craft, it is pseudo art—pseudo art of the magical variety.[55]

Amusement art, which is perhaps of more direct interest to us, likewise arouses emotions, not in order to bring about behaviour in everyday life, but for the sake of entertainment. Collingwood defines amusement art as a device for eliciting certain emotions in such a way that the venting or discharge of said emotions does not interfere with the concerns of ordinary practical life. Collingwood writes:

The artist as the purveyor of amusement makes it his business to please his audience by arousing certain emotions in them and providing them with a make-believe situation in which these emotions can be discharged.[56]

Basically, amusement art is theorized by Collingwood in a way that runs parallel to certain primitive theories of catharsis which maintain that the process of catharsis siphons off certain emotions, namely, the emotions that are aroused, but then dispelled, by a given spectacle.

Consider some examples of what Collingwood has in mind. Pornography aims at sexual arousal, which its imagery elicits, and then, in the ideal case, one supposes, which the pornographic work provides a felicitous opportunity for releasing. Detective *thrillers*—whose very name signals the emotional thrills the genre is designed to deliver—are also primary examples of amusement art, as are what Collingwood calls sob-stuff (which we are more likely to call tear-jerkers) which are aimed at bringing about a certain affect of sorrow (generally tinged by admiration).[57] That is, sob-stuff is designed to make us cry.

Moreover, similar points may be made about the other genres of amusement art that provide the staples of contemporary mass art. Horror, a very popular genre throughout the twentieth century, is predicated on raising definable feelings of fear and disgust in audiences.[58] The emotion of suspense is the aim of mass narrative fictions in many media, including pulp literature, comic books, films, TV programmes, radio shows, and the like, as is the affect of comic amusement. That is, pornography, detective

[55] Such art is 'magical' because it aims at being efficacious; it aims at bringing about changes in the real world of everyday life in contrast to amusement art which only aims at stirring up the imagination of the audience.

[56] Collingwood, *Principles of Art*, 81. NB: one wonders whether Collingwood's notion of 'make-believe' here doesn't anticipate Kendall Walton's.

[57] For an account of melodrama, see Flo Leibowitz, 'Apt Feelings: Why "Women's Films" Aren't Trivial', in *Post Theory: Reconstructing Film Studies*, ed. David Bordwell and Noël Carroll (Madison: University of Wisconsin Press, 1996), 219–29.

[58] For a theory of the horror genre, see Noël Carroll, *The Philosophy of Horror* (New York: Routledge, 1990), especially ch. 1.

thrillers, melodramas, horror fictions, suspense fictions, and comedies are all predicated upon raising a specifiable affect in the audience.

Furthermore, although our experience of the relevant affects with respect to the objects of mass art is not utilitarian—since our emotions, in these cases, are not carried over to practical affairs as in the case with magical art—nevertheless works of amusement art are designed within a strictly consequentialist framework, since the works in question are regarded by their producers (and their consumers) simply as a means to pre-given ends, namely the discharge of the emotions relevant to the kinds of works in question. That is, the discharge of certain emotions—horror, suspense, sorrow, and so on—is the purpose of these works; these works are not valuable for their own sake.

Like Greenberg and a great many others in the tradition of the philosophy of art, Collingwood maintains that art proper is intrinsically valuable. It is valuable for its own sake, and not for the sake of something else, like the relief of sexual tension. But *ex hypothesi* amusement art is produced for an ulterior motive or purpose. It is designed, planned, and executed for the purpose of discharging certain emotions. This, then, is one of the major reasons that Collingwood calls amusement art pseudo art. Mass art is not genuine art, properly so called, for it is not valuable for its own sake. Its purpose is to provide the audience with opportunities to vent certain emotions.

But Collingwood also has additional, related reasons for disparaging mass art. He argues that amusement art:

[I]s as skillfully constructed as a work of engineering, as skillfully compounded as a bottle of medicine, to produce a determinate and preconceived effect, the evocation of a certain kind of emotion in a certain kind of audience.[59]

This language, of course, given our earlier discussion of the technical theory of art, indicates that Collingwood regards the 'artist' who specializes in the production of amusement art as essentially a craftsperson. The producers of mass art, at best, exercise a skill, eliciting a preconceived reaction from audiences by means of a predetermined stimulus. That is, the artist who specializes in amusement art is really nothing more than a craftsperson, applying tried and true formulas, derived from traditional practice, in order to arouse pre-ordained or 'canned' emotional effects from audiences. People like Stephen King, Mary Higgins Clark, Steven Spielberg, Edgar Wallace, and Danielle Steel may be very good at doing this. But, in fact, they are merely recycling the well-worn plot techniques

---

[59] Collingwood, *Principles of Art*, 81.

of their respective genres, just as contemporary rock singers who arouse that satisfying feeling of defiance in teenage audiences are so often imitating strategies put in place by Mick Jagger decades earlier. In these cases, the mass artists function as craftspersons, selecting well-known devices as formulas to elicit an intended, pre-ordained response from audiences.

There can be little dispute that mass art is formulaic. Anne Rice's recent *Servant of the Bones* shamelessly recycles the narrative format of her *Interview with a Vampire*—once again presenting a supernatural being telling his story to a writer armed with tape recorders. Moreover, there are well-known strategies for achieving the purpose of many mass art genres. The successful whodunit involves hiding the culprit by means of routine strategies for distributing the suspicion of guilt to other suspects. Suspense can be predictably engendered by contriving a situation in which the characters that the narrative portrays as moral are threatened by dangers that threaten, in all probability, to overwhelm them.[60] The sentimental response in melodrama can be raised by placing admirable characters in pitiable circumstances. And so on.

Likewise, further evidence that mass art is formulaic can be found by considering the work of V. C. Andrews. After her death, her estate hired ghost writers (in this case, a very appropriate label) to continue writing novels under her signature. Moreover, the ghost writers are highly successful at counterfeiting the Andrews effect (mounting revulsion at the gradual revelation of incest) because they quickly identified Andrews' very recurrent formulas and recycled them. Indeed, when I was a graduate student, I received a form letter from a publisher inviting me to write a pornographic novel for money; included with the invitation were several pages of instructions on exactly how to write it. There was a copulation to page ratio, suggestions for motivating orgies (and a prohibition about bestiality–they were very leary of poultry, for some reason).

Not only are mass artworks formulaic. They are predicated, it is argued, on securing pre-ordained effects. On a given evening, one may feel in the mood for a melodrama, or a comedy, or a horror fiction. In such a case, being in the mood for x is a matter of wanting to undergo a certain emotional arousal. When one speaks of being in the mood for a comedy, one signals the generic affect one is interested in undergoing. It does not matter so much which comedy; one is simply interested in being comically amused, rather than being saddened by a melodrama, or horrified. Moreover, this way of speaking, which is very common, belies, Colling-

---

[60] See Noël Carroll, 'The Paradox of Suspense', in *Suspense: Conceptualizations, Theoretical Analyses and Empirical Explorations*, ed. Peter Vorderer, Hans J. Wulff, and Mike Friedrichsen (Matwah, NJ: Lawrence Erlbaum Associates, Publishers, 1996), 71–91.

wood might say, that the mass artworks in a given genre are pretty much replaceable. They are merely means to a certain desired emotional state, namely, the one that we make explicit by saying what the relevant mood is.

For example, when choosing a mass entertainment, someone may say 'I'd like a good cry tonight.' A melodrama might be the right choice in such a case. Or, Collingwood might add, a pill, if there was one, since a pill would be more reliable and faster than a movie or a novel. But, in any case, amusement art is strictly analogous to a pharmaceutical for Collingwood, inasmuch as it involves the application of craft skill to bring about a certain emotional effect that is pre-ordained—for example, the director, commissioned to produce a sitcom, aims at making us laugh.

The mass artist possesses craft knowledge about which formulas will bring about which emotional effects. Producing a mass artwork is very much like fitting someone for a pair of shoes or curing an allergy. Collingwood explicitly analogizes the creation of amusement art to engineering and medicine. Moreover, as we know from his arguments against the technical theory of art, the craft status of amusement art precludes the possibility that it is art properly so called. It is nothing more than the craft of arousing pre-ordained emotions of a highly generic nature—like suspense, pity, and horror—by means of reliable (tried and true) formulas with monotonously predictable results.

On the other hand, art proper, for Collingwood, is an end in itself, not a means to some other end. This is why Collingwood maintains that the means/ends distinction does not really correspond to art proper.[61] Moreover, Collingwood argues that in the case of genuine art, the artist need not start out with a plan for achieving some preconceived result. Indeed, paradigmatically, the genuine artist does not have a plan for where the artwork is headed. Rather, with art proper, the artist ideally begins with a vague feeling that she is trying to capture in the process of working on the feeling, working it up, so to speak, often, though not necessarily, through contact with her materials.[62]

That is, the artist starts with a vague feeling whose identity she gradually discovers in the process of creating the artwork. The work of creating the artwork proper is a matter of clarifying a vague feeling—a matter of making it definite or determinate, generally by working on it through a given medium. Art proper, like amusement art, is concerned with the

---

[61] Collingwood, *Principles of Art*, 20–1.

[62] The caveat 'not necessarily' here is meant to acknowledge Collingwood's view that an artwork, like a poem, could be completed 'in the head'. In fact, some commentators think that the artwork for Collingwood is essentially mental and use this as the basis of criticizing his position as Idealist.

emotions. But it does not aim at arousing emotions in spectators. Instead, it is a matter of expressing emotion, which involves a process of the artist clarifying a feeling for herself—a process of transforming an initial inchoate though suggestive feeling into an articulate emotion.

expression

Collingwood writes that:

the making of the poem begins in the poet's having an experience which demands expression in the form of a poem. But the description of the unwritten poem as the end to which his technique is means is false; it implies that before he has written his poem he knows and could state, the specification of it in the kind of way in which a joiner knows the specification of a table he is about to make. This is always true of a craftsman; it is therefore true of an artist in cases where the work of art is also a work of craft. But it is wholly untrue of the artist in those cases where the work of art is not a work of craft; the poet extemporizing his verses, the sculptor playing with his clay, and so forth. In these cases (which after all are cases of art, even though of art at a relatively humble level) the artist has no idea what the experience is which demands expression until he has expressed it. What he wants to say is not present to him as an end towards which means have to be devised; it becomes clear to him only as the poem takes shape in his mind, or the clay in his fingers.[63]

That is, in the case of art proper, the artist does not begin with a plan, but with a feeling that the artist wishes to express. That feeling is initially indistinct but compelling. It cries out, so to speak, to be expressed. There is some urgency about it. The composer tries out a couple of notes in order to capture it. This is a first approximation. But the first selection of notes is not quite right. So, the composer adds some more, subtracts some, and modifies others, until she believes that she has the feeling just right. Through this process of adjustment and modification, the composer is attempting to bring the initially vague feeling into sharp focus. Unlike amusement art, there is no preconceived plan, but rather a process of discovery, which can be called expressing emotion rather than arousing emotion. Moreover, this process of expression is, first and foremost, for the artist. She is getting clear for herself about the mood that she is feeling. If the phrase were not an article of psychobabble, we could say that she is 'getting in touch with her feelings' through the process of creating art.

Her energies are not directed at an audience. Whereas arousing emotions is audience-directed, expressing an emotion is a matter of self-clarification on the part of the artist. This is not to say that audiences cannot benefit from observing the artist's expression of a self-clarified

---

[63] Collingwood, *Principles of Art*, 28–9.

emotion, but only that the audience is secondary when it comes to art proper. However, on the other hand, amusement art would lose its *raison d'être* were the audience treated as merely secondary.

In the domain of art proper, when the painter surveys a landscape, some vague feeling about that *very* landscape is raised in her which she desires to express. Expressing that unique, though initially indistinct feeling, requires getting clear about it. Expression, according to Collingwood, is a process of clarification. Since the feeling in question is unique, it cannot be clarified by falling back on the rules, formulas, and laws for arousing *generic* emotions. Clarification can only be achieved in the process of working through or on that feeling (as a therapist might put it) most frequently in relation to some medium, experimenting with the form and the content of a sculpture or a poem or a painting until the artist is prepared to say 'That's it.' Once that 'eureka' experience is reached, the artwork is completed. When the artist presents it to the world, the audience may have the opportunity to 'relive' the artist's experience; however, presentation to an audience is not a necessary feature of art.

There are no antecedent rules for the artist to employ in order to 'get it right', because the emotion that the genuine artist is after is unique, according to Collingwood's definition of art proper.[64] Because the emotion that the artist finally clarifies is unique, there is no satisfactory paraphrase for it. The artwork is its own best expression of the emotion in question. Unlike the generic emotions in which amusement art traffics, our language does not have names for the relevant emotion in the case of art proper. Part of the point of art is to reveal the range of subtle emotional timbres for which language provides no names.[65]

So art proper is the pursuit of the expression of unique, initially heretofore unknown emotions through the process of clarification. Amusement art, on the other hand, involves the arousal of generic, fore-ordained emotions through the application of formulae. These features of amusement art render mass art a craft rather than art proper. In so far as mass

[64] Collingwood's theory of art proper may be summarized thus: if x is a work of art proper then x is 1. a process of 2. self 3. clarification of 4. an inner state (an emotion or feeling) 5. that the agent in question *actually* experienced 6. as an initially vague impulse 7. which becomes individualized (unique) as the agent works on it. The notion of self-clarification here stipulates that the process is one that the agent/artist carries out herself and which is undertaken for herself and not for some prospective audience. The requirement that the mood in question actually be experienced by the agent/artist amounts to the condition that the emotion in question be sincerely felt by the artist. This is a feature of expression theories of art that Collingwood shares with Tolstoy.

[65] Francis Sparshott, *The Theory of the Arts* (New York: Princeton University Press, 1982), 308–9. See also Curt L. Ducasse, *Art, The Critics and You* (Indianapolis: Bobbs-Merrill, 1955), 53.

art is amusement art, it is pseudo art. This argument, which I call the formula argument, may be summarized as follows:

1. If x is art proper, then x is essentially not formulaic in either its ends or its means.

2. Mass art objects are formulaic both in their ends (the specific, rather generic emotions, such as suspense, that they aim to bring about) and in their means (tried and true techniques, devices, and formulas that predictably elicit the relevant emotions).

3. Therefore, mass art objects are not instances of art proper. (They are pseudo art.)

Though I have introduced the formula argument through a consideration of Collingwood's philosophy of art, it should be obvious that it represents a common argument against mass art on the part of people who are unfamiliar with Collingwood's theory. However, before criticizing the argument as it might be advanced in common parlance, it is useful to confront it in terms of the sophisticated version propounded by Collingwood.

The first premiss of the argument—that art proper is not formulaic—although virtually a truism of post-Romantic culture, crucially depends upon what counts as formulaic. For, intuitively, it seems that many works that we might suspect are instances of art proper certainly have readily perceptible, recurring techniques. Think of impressionist artworks or Cubist artworks. Don't works in these styles evince recurrent structures that might, in all fairness, be thought of as formulaic? And if they are not formulaic, what is the relevant conception of formulaic? Collingwood can't beg the question by saying that it amounts to all and only the recurring techniques found in amusement art.[66]

Of course, Collingwood might concede this much, but then go on to say that even if such works are art, properly so called, and even if they have formulaic features, it is not in virtue of the formulaic features that they count as art proper. However, this response is at least questionable, in so far as many of the techniques (or formulas) that we find in artworks properly so called contribute in a constitutive way to the artistic identity

[66] As with the discussion of Greenberg, it is not acceptable for the defender of Collingwood to reject these arguments here out of hand on the grounds that Collingwood has something more complicated in mind than what is involved in my counter-examples. The burden of proof lies with Collingwood's allies to produce a conception of the formulaic which will evade my counter-examples and not invite others. To protest simply that Collingwood has a more sophisticated idea but to refrain from telling us what it is involves leaving off argumentation in favour of an altogether empty and heavy-handed appeal to authority.

of the works in question—even in terms of Collingwood's own conception of art. Consider the concluding couplet in an English sonnet. Surely it contributes to the clarification of the feeling expressed in such a poem, but it is a formulaic device. Moreover, if this is not an acceptable counter-example, the burden of proof falls to Collingwood and his allies to show why it is not. Thus, until that burden of proof is met, it would appear that the first premiss in the formula argument is wrong, and can be shown to be wrong even accepting Collingwood's view. That is, it is not the case that it is a necessary feature of art proper that it eschew formulas essentially.

Indeed, by excluding the formulaic from the domain of art proper, Collingwood is, in effect, denying that a great deal of past art that we heretofore regarded as art proper is art properly so called. In the art of different cultures and the art of our own culture in periods past, a premium has often been placed on attempting to abide by traditional paradigms assiduously. Such art has often demanded rigorous adherence to traditionally established rules of composition. Is it plausible to discount the history of art so radically? Can a conception of art that discounts most of the art of the past be convincing?

On the other hand, a defender of Collingwood might wave aside the preceding historical considerations by saying that Collingwood's theory of art is revisionist. Thus, we should expect that it will exclude from the domain of art proper many works that we antecedently regard as artworks proper—including English sonnets, impressionist and Cubist paintings, icons, Egyptian hieroglyphs, Chinese landscapes, and French academic art. But on what grounds should we accept such a radical revision of the conception of art? Collingwood himself seems to be committed to carving out a space for the modernist poetics of artists like Joyce and Stein. And, under the modernist dispensation, the ideal is that art eschew the formulaic and that each artwork invent a form unto itself. But even if the ideal of the artist as demiurge, creating a repertory of forms *ex nihilo*, captured the artistic imagination at one point in art history, why should the ideal of one moment in the history of art be elevated to the criterion of art proper? Surely this is an instance of revisionist overkill, even if it is motivated by the thoroughly respectable aim of providing a way in which to appreciate modernist masterpieces.

Collingwood's animus against the formulaic rests upon his admittedly sophisticated, positive conception of art proper—that art proper is a process of the self-clarification (by the artist) of an initially vague feeling which, once worked over, results in an individualized expression. Collingwood's conception undoubtedly sheds philosophical light on the often-neglected topic of artistic creation. However, Collingwood's theory of art, conceived as a comprehensive philosophy of art, raises questions at every turn, and, therefore, the proponent of the formula argument cannot rest his case on the unquestioned authority of Collingwood's philosophy of art.

Space does not permit a thoroughgoing refutation of Collingwood's theory of art. However, a few brief remarks about its inadequacies seem pertinent. First, the theory presupposes that emotion is the proper domain of art. But this ignores the possibility of emotively detached art. Can't art properly so called be rooted in the pleasing play of form with no attendant emotion? And what of a pure art of the play of ideas—such as conceptual art and the work of Duchamp, or the sort of modernist painting Greenberg has in mind, i.e., painting concerned to explore the conditions of painting. From a theoretically unprejudiced point of view, works of these sorts are respectable candidates for art status, though they may have nothing to do with the emotions as they are generally conceived—at least from a non-question-begging theoretical perspective. Thus, it would appear that Collingwood's philosophy of art is not universal.

Moreover, on Collingwood's philosophy of art, expression properly so called is a matter of clarifying a vague emotion. But this would appear to exclude art dedicated to presentation of vague emotions (like Symbolism) or unrevised emotion (like Surrealism) or raw emotion (like Beat poetry) from the domain of art. Again, Collingwood's theory of art seems to be too narrow from a theoretically unprejudiced point of view.

Collingwood places great emphasis on the artist's process of genuine self-clarification. This is one reason why he abhors formulas, since formulas substitute generic schemas in place of the authentic working out of unique expression. But doesn't this rather arbitrarily preclude the possibility that the feeling the artist wishes to express comes to her full-blown, as the opening lines of 'Kubla Khan' reportedly delivered themselves to Coleridge? And, in any case, doesn't Collingwood place too much emphasis on the process of creativity rather than its product? For example, in Collingwood's system, a work of art exists even if remains, so to speak, in the artist's head. If 'Kubla Khan' were just a dream that Coleridge never set down in print nor uttered to anyone, including himself, Collingwood would still count it as a work of art, though this, of course, would violate the intuition of many theoreticians, critics, and art lovers, that artworks must be at least artefacts with the capacity for public presentation.

Like many expression theorists of art, notably Tolstoy, Collingwood requires that the emotions expressed by a work of art proper actually originate in the artist, presumably as a vague feeling or some other sort of mental state. In other words, the mental state or feeling must originate in the experience of the artist. Call this the sincerity condition. However, this appears to raise the process/product confusion broached above. For if the product is the expression of a distinct emotion, why should we care if it was not arrived at though a process of an artist working over some vague intimation born in his own heart?[67]

What of commissioned art? Isn't it possible that an atheist or a confirmed sinner with no religious inclinations could produce a reverentially expressive portrait of a saint without consulting his own feelings? With art, we traditionally care about the results, it might be said. The process, including the question of whether the artist is sincerely working through her own experiences, may not always be germane to determining the art status of the product. Thus, Collingwood's emphasis on the putative process of genuine artmaking, irrespective of the art product, does not represent a necessary condition for art status.

Of course, mention of commissioned art once again brings us back to the revisionist character of Collingwood's theory. Much art of the past was commissioned—commissioned to express emotions that may or may not have coincided with the feelings of the artists in question. Moreover, from a theoretically unbiased standpoint, it is not clear why art must eschew the arousal of emotions altogether. Much of what we call art—including tragedy—does seem predicated on arousing emotion. Collingwood wants to rule such cases out of court. But his argument for this is inadequate. For all he has shown through his contrast with craft is that arousing emotions is not a necessary condition for *all* art. But that does not entail that some art is not dedicated to arousing emotions or that there is no art—such as tragedy—for which the arousal of emotion is an essential feature.

I concede that this hasty broadside against Collingwood's philosophy of art is rather scatter-shot. I realize that a friend of Collingwood's may have answers to many of the charges that I have laid at his doorstep. However, I think that even this brief rehearsal of the problems with Collingwood's philosophy of art reveals one thing, namely, that it is controversial enough that the proponent of the formula argument cannot appeal to it in order to settle the case against mass art. For even without addressing the problematic implications Collingwood's philosophy of art would encounter confronting troublesome cases of mass art—such as the highly expressive works of Chaplin, Keaton, and Hitchcock—Collingwood's philosophy of art appears to be flawed.

Turning from Collingwood's philosophy of art to the second premiss of the formula argument, further difficulties emerge. According to the for-

[67] Collingwood's theory also seems biased against aleatoric art, which art was undoubtedly designed to thwart expression theories of art of the sincerity variety, as well as the Romantic cult of the artistic personality.

mula argument, mass art is formulaic in both its ends—the emotions that it aims to engender—and its structures—the tried-and-true devices it elects in order to engender generic (or canned emotions). But I wonder whether either of these charges is genuinely intelligible, since both charges presuppose that a meaningful contrast is being drawn—between individualized versus generic emotions, on the one hand, and between the use of formulas versus the absence of formulas, on the other hand.

Concerning the distinction between generic and individualized emotions, it seems to me that all emotions have something generic about them. In the standard analysis of emotions, it is presumed that being in a given emotional state has necessary conditions; fear, for example, typically requires that the object of the state be taken by the agent in question to be harmful. But if each emotional state has a necessary condition, then, to that extent, every emotion is generic. The distinction between generic emotions and individualized emotions is not sharp. Even individualized emotions like a particular poet's joy in response to a sunset will have certain generic features. Moreover, even if one thinks that it would be better to talk about paradigm scenarios rather than necessary conditions with respect to the identity of emotional states, these scenarios will still be generic inasmuch as they are paradigmatic. Thus, in so far as emotions are in certain respects generic by their very nature, the principled distinction that Collingwood needs among different sorts of emotions may be unavailable to him.

The Collingwoodian may respond that he can draw the distinction between generic and individualized emotions in a way that eludes the previous objection . But then the burden of proof falls to him to show us how to do this in a way that will allow him to shore up the distinction he needs in a non-question-begging way. Needless to say, he should not attempt to shore up the distinction in such a way that it becomes the distinction between shallow and deep emotions, since it is not clear that deep emotions have not been expressed by some mass artworks, even if most of the emotions expressed in mass art have been shallow.

Of course, the case might be made as well that a great many of the emotions expressed in what we, and perhaps even Collingwood, would regard as high art have been shallow. Moreover, as this remark might indicate, if we make depth of emotional expression the criteria for art proper, then we risk turning the notion into a commendatory or evaluative criterion of art, rather than a classificatory notion. Only deep expression will count as art proper. But this brings with it the problem that there can be no bad art, since in order to qualify as art, the work must already be deeply expressive, and, therefore, *a fortiori*, good.

Needless to say, this problem may already be inherent in Collingwood's philosophy of art, since his theory requires that art must be expressive in his special sense, which would appear to entail that it necessarily possesses goodness (supposing that expressiveness is a necessarily good-making feature of a work of art). So, on Collingwood's theory, it may already be the case that all art is good. And this seems to me to be yet another reason to reject his overall philosophy of art.

At this point, the Collingwoodian may call for an end to all this palaver and say we all know the difference between generic and individualized emotions. But I'm not sure that we do, since I, at least, would count the expression of what is called Langian paranoia in mass-market films like *M* or *Scarlet Street* or *Woman in the Window* or *The Big Heat* as individualized. But then the second premiss of the formula argument would be false, since these would be mass artworks that achieve individualized emotional expression.

Likewise, the distinction between art that employs formulas versus art that eschews formulas is hardly clear-cut. Most art employs generic forms inherited from a tradition. To suppose that art can be produced without generic background traditions is simply Utopian or naïve. Moreover, these generic forms actually enable the kind of expressive achievements that Collingwood applauds so it would appear counter-productive for Collingwood to eschew formulas altogether for the sake of encouraging expressivity. It would be a classic case of throwing the baby out with the bath water. Or, to reverse metaphors, it would involve the use of a prophylactic (the prohibition against formulas) where one's aim is conception.

Of course, it is probably the case that Collingwood's notion of a formula is really evaluative and not descriptive. When he complains about formulas in amusement art, he, like many others, is really referring to boring formulas. But then the problem is not with formulas as such, but with their unimaginative use. However, if this diagnosis is correct, then there is no reason to suppose that the use of formulas or conventions in mass artworks need preclude their potential status as art properly so called, since mass artworks can use formulas and conventions inventively.

Consider the ways in which Agatha Christie uses the conventions of the classical detective story to 'hide' her murderers. In *The Murder of Roger Ackroyd*, she 'secretes' the murderer in the personage of the narrator;[68] in *Ten Little Indians*, the murderer is a 'dead man', while in *Murder on the Orient Express*, all the suspects did it. All of these examples involve imaginative play with mass genre formulas. Thus, if by 'formulaic', the

---

[68] As does the recent film *The Usual Suspects*.

proponent of the formula argument means that mass art necessarily employs formulas unimaginatively, then the premiss is dubious.[69]

Lastly, Collingwood correlates mass art with the attempt to arouse emotional states in audiences, whereas art proper expresses emotion. The pertinent contrast is arousal versus expression. However, it is not clear to me that Collingwood can sustain this distinction unequivocally, since he does think that typically audiences engage with art proper by reliving the process of clarification undergone by the artist. But isn't this process of 'reliving' a species of emotional arousal? It is true that Collingwood does not regard the audience's share as a necessary constituent of art proper. But inasmuch as it is a typically recurring, albeit contingent, feature of art proper, it seems to me that Collingwood overstates matters when he suggests that the arousal of emotion is foreign to the realm of art proper.

Perhaps enough has been said to undermine Collingwood's statement of the formula argument. But some readers may maintain that the argument can be advanced without allegiance to the idiosyncrasies of Collingwood's theory of art. Nevertheless, I think that many of the considerations brought against Collingwood are also sufficient to discount what we might call the 'plain formula argument' which contends: genuine art is not formulaic; mass art is formulaic; therefore mass art is not genuine art.

The first premiss is still Utopian. Most art, maybe all art, is formulaic to some degree. All artists use some conventions, formulas, rules of thumb, traditional forms, donnees, and so on. It is a Romantic myth (and perhaps a modernist ideal as well) that artists create *ex nihilo* and that some artists are altogether uniquely independent of traditional modes of composition. And even if it were true that the great artistic genius creates the rules of art for herself, it is surely too narrow a view of the nature of art to maintain that the extension of genuine art be restricted to the productions of all and only artistic geniuses. That is, even granting the possibility that the Romantic myth of the artist is a live option (something I am loathe to do myself), it still strikes me as inappropriate to take the romantic ideal as a comprehensive characterization of art properly so called. Surely one's conception of art should accommodate works of more modest ambition than those dreamt up in some Romantic fantasy.

Moreover, I suspect that the second premiss in the plain formula argument can be dispelled by means of a dilemma. On the one hand, if the second premiss is read literally, the claim that mass art is necessarily

---

[69] Furthermore, if this is what is meant by 'formulaic', then one would have to agree that much of what is thought of as 'high art' in the classificatory sense is also 'formulaic' in this evaluatory sense of the term.

formulaic is unexceptionable, but harmless, since most, if not all art is formulaic to some degree. On the other hand, if the second premiss is understood evaluatively—as the claim that all mass art is formulaic in the sense that it is boringly routine—then the second premiss is false, since it can be demonstrated that mass art can deploy its formulas imaginatively, and, thus, mass art is not necessarily numbingly routine. Perhaps much mass art is unimaginative. That may provide us with grounds for alleging that it is bad, as much mass art may be, but it does not provide us with grounds to suppose that mass art is not art; just as the fact that much 'high art' is formulaic in the sense of being predictably routine, and bad for that reason, does not provide us with grounds for cashiering it from the order of art.

Neither the Collingwoodian nor the plain version of the formula argument shows that mass art is not art properly so called. Ostensibly, the formula argument is different from the passivity argument, since as we saw in the last section, formulaic works can abet active spectatorship. However, there is probably a temptation to think of the two separate arguments as linked, since some people are likely to suppose that if a work is formulaic, then it encourages passive spectatorship. But that temptation should be resisted both for the logical reason that it is conceivable that some of the formulas in question may be designed to abet active spectatorship, and for the empirical reason that this logical possibility is in fact manifested, as we saw previously, in the devices of mass art.

According to the passivity argument, the response to mass art is passive. In dismissing that argument I rhetorically challenged the proponent of that argument to provide a principled way of distinguishing active from passive responses. Specifically, I demanded to know why we should think that the emotional responses to mass art were passive. Perhaps this discussion of Collingwood suggests an answer to my rhetorical question, namely, emotional responses are passive when they are elicited from audiences by routine formulas. But this seems wrong.

When I am angered because someone has gratuitously insulted me, that is an active response in common parlance. At the same time, it is true that the elicitation of anger requires that certain generic conditions be met. For example, I must believe that I or mine have been wronged in order to be in the state of anger. When we speak of formulas for eliciting anger in audiences, this generally involves portraying a fictional situation of the sort that draws the attention of the audience to features of the situation that meet the generic conditions for the emotional state of anger. Thus, we are shown characters for whom we are concerned being treated badly, thereby satisfying the generic condition of anger that it be directed at states of affairs where I or mine are wronged.[70] What is called the formulaic in this acount is the plot construction that instantiates the generic condition for the activation of the emotional state in the audience. However, since the existence of generic conditions for emotional responses in general does not preclude calling those responses active in ordinary parlance, I see no reason, *mutatis mutandis*, why we should speak differently about formulaically encouraged, emotional responses to mass art. Thus, a consideration of the formulaic in mass art gives us no reason to reopen the case for the passivity argument.

The freedom argument, the susceptibility argument, and the conditioning argument

The three arguments to be discussed in this section have been distilled from the writings of T. W. Adorno and Max Horkheimer.[71] These arguments emphasize a different direction in philosophy's case against mass art from the arguments we have been examining thus far. Whereas in our analyses of the arguments of MacDonald, Greenberg, and Collingwood, we have dwelt on what might be thought of as primarily aesthetic issues— i.e., the question of whether or not mass art is art properly so called—the discussion of Adorno and Horkheimer will involve more of the nature of social arguments against mass art—arguments that depict mass art as a social problem. Nevertheless, these arguments are still philosophical, since they attempt to show that the social problems that mass art precipitates are a function of the nature of mass art.

Of course, Collingwood, Greenberg, and MacDonald predicted unsavoury social consequences of what they called mass culture, kitsch, and amusement art respectively. And Adorno and Horkheimer discuss the aesthetic as well as the social problems of mass art, or, as they call it, the culture industry. However, the arguments of Adorno and Horkheimer to which I will be paying special attention are ones that are more directly political, although, of course, the distinction between the aesthetic and the

[70] See Ch. 4 of this book for a more detailed account of this relation between audience emotions and mass artworks.
[71] Especially T. W. Adorno and Max Horkheimer, 'The Culture Industry: Enlightenment as Mass Deception', in their book *Dialectic of Enlightenment* (New York: Continuum, 1990), 120–67; and T. W. Adorno, 'Culture Industry Reconsidered', *New German Critique*, 6 (1975), 12–19. Many of Adorno's writings on mass art have been anthologized in *The Culture Industry: Selected Essays on Mass Culture*, ed. J. M. Bernstein (London: Routledge, 1991). For an excellent overview of Adorno's philosophy of art— one from which I have benefited immensely—see Lambert Zuidervaart, *Adorno's Aesthetic Theory* (Cambridge: MIT Press, 1991).

political here is somewhat artificial, since, in ways, soon to be explored, Adorno and Horkheimer think that aesthetic shortcomings of a certain sort result in political problems.

As is well known, Adorno and Horkheimer are representatives of a form of marxism that is called Critical Theory that flourished in Germany before World War II. With the rise of Nazism, Adorno and Horkheimer emigrated to the United States, where their writings undoubtedly influenced intellectuals like MacDonald and perhaps Greenberg. Critical Theory, in the view of Adorno and Horkheimer, was a new form of sociology, one that was explicitly anti-positivist in that it was critical. That is, where positivist sociology might be construed as obsessed with what is—'just the facts, ma'am,' as Sgt Friday would say—Adorno and Horkheimer advocated that sociology be critical.

Positivism, on their account of it (which is also exemplified by certain tendencies in marxism) is also intimately connected to instrumental reason, i.e., reasoning devoted to deliberation over the means of bringing about effects. According to Adorno and Horkheimer, under the positivist dispensation, reason is thought to be solely a matter of the calculation of means. However, they regard this as a limited, and ultimately repressive, conception of reason, arguing that reason is not simply instrumental, since it is within the domain of reason to contemplate ends as well as means. Thus, hand in hand with Adorno's and Horkheimer's opposition to positivism is an opposition to instrumental reason as conceived to be the only sort of reason there is.

Antipathy to instrumental reason, in this sense, figures importantly in the background of Adorno's and Horkheimer's criticism of the culture industry (which is their name for what I am calling mass art). For in their view, the culture industry is yet another example of the positivist tendency to fetishize instrumental reason; since the culture industry is but another arena in which thought is dedicated to bringing about certain effects, specifically effects in the audience. That is, the culture industry is itself an exercise in instrumental reason because it treats the audience as a target—as a subject of calculation to be manipulated in certain specifiable ways.

In general, it is important to Critical Theorists like Adorno and Horkheimer to articulate the possibility of a space outside the realm of market or exchange value and the instrumental reason in which the market-place is implicated. For reason concerned with ends, such as critical reason, must be insulated from business as usual and instrumental reason as usual, if it is to develop a perspective on what is.

Adorno maintains genuine art provides such a space. Genuine art, with its claims to aesthetic autonomy, represents an attempted revolt against the clutches of exchange value and instrumental reason. Aesthetic autonomism is a gesture in the direction of affirming that there is the social possibility of living outside the nexus of exchange value and the preoccupation with instrumentality. Genuine art is an attempt to free itself from the social condition in which it finds itself. However, Adorno contends, though genuine art attempts to break away from society, as society is dominated by exchange value and instrumental reason, genuine art cannot really succeed in its aspiration inasmuch as it is impossible, as marxism presupposes, to transcend utterly the material conditions of social existence. Thus, genuine art inevitably fails to break free entirely from the conditions of bourgeois social existence. Nevertheless, in making the attempt to break away from the culture of exchange value and instrumental reason, the genuine work of art at least provides us with a picture of the central struggle within capitalist society—the struggle between the encroachment of exchange value and instrumental reason into every crack and crevice of social existence, and the resistance to that encroachment by the spirit of autonomy.

Genuine art is a monad of society, a microcosm that represents a truth about the social whole by exemplifying an awareness of the possibility of opposition to the imperialism of exchange value and instrumental reason. Genuine art functions as a kind of symbol, illuminating the nature of the social totality, particularly in terms of the struggle between exchange value and other sorts of value.

Here it is important to stress that the significance of genuine art for Adorno is not that it escapes from the bonds of capitalism, but that it reflects and, thereby, makes cognitively available the struggle between capitalist domination and autonomy. Thus, genuine art is not conceived to be autonomous for Adorno. What is important to him is that it *aspires* to autonomy, though this aspiration always inevitably fails to be realized completely.

This conception of genuine art makes the contrast between genuine art and mass art much more complicated than proponents of popular culture often realize. Too often they suppose that Adorno is claiming that genuine art is autonomous whereas mass culture is not, which then leads them to criticize Adorno by pointing out that he has failed to take into account that so-called genuine art is not really autonomous. But this is to refute a straw-Adorno. For in Adorno's view, it is not the case that the genuine work of art is autonomous and that the mass artwork is not. For Adorno, both types of work fail to escape from the grip of capitalist domination. However, *ex hypothesi*, the genuine work of art resists the domination of capitalism by attempting to secure what Kant would call a purposeful purposelessness—and, in doing so, the genuine artwork reflects a core feature of the modern social dialectic. On the other hand, mass art does not even attempt to resist the relevant forms of social domination, and, therefore, reveals nothing about the true nature of the social totality. Indeed, the mass art object is complicit with social domination, using its powers of instrumental reason to garner profit and to mask social domination.

The mass art object reinforces the instrumental ethos of society on Adorno's and Horkheimer's account, since, in ways that recall our discussion of Collingwood, they say that the mass art object doesn't aspire to purposelessness, but is, by its very nature, purposeful. It is a device for manipulating audiences in order to secure pre-planned results. The mass artwork treats the audience as an object for calculation to be shaped by the technicians of the culture industry. These technicians, like any other group of technocrats, specialize in the application of instrumental reason. As Collingwood might have it, they are just like engineers.

Undoubtedly the writings of Adorno and Horkheimer are somewhat rambling. They jump from extremely abstract discussions of the imagination to the fairly concrete discussions of advertising. However, the specific charges that they level at mass art are quite evident. Like Collingwood, they criticize mass art for being formulaic, especially for being repetitive. Like MacDonald, they criticize it for being a commodity as well as for being imposed on the people by technicians, and for being standardized. And, like Greenberg, they condemn mass art for failing to engage the imaginative (or contemplative) powers of the audience.

However, rather than reviewing the ways in which the criticisms of mass art by Adorno and Horkheimer overlap with previously rehearsed criticisms, it is more profitable here to look at the arguments they offer us that we have not already encountered in earlier sections. As I have already indicated, these arguments are particularly interesting because they move philosophy's case against mass art from the realm of aesthetics to the realm of politics, albeit to a politics that locates the pernicious effects of mass art in its aesthetic peculiarities.

To pinpoint at least one of the major problems that Adorno has with mass art, we can begin by taking note of a very telling sentence in Adorno's 'The Culture Industry Reconsidered'. There he writes that 'It [mass art] impedes the development of autonomous, independent individuals who judge and decide consciously for themselves. These, however, would be the precondition for a democratic society which needs adults who have come of age in order to sustain itself and develop.'[72] Mass art, in other words, obstructs human freedom and emancipation.

---

[72] Adorno, 'Culture Industry Reconsidered', 19.

Broadly speaking, it is clear that Adorno worries that mass art is an obstacle to freedom, where freedom is a matter of autonomy, which autonomy is itself comprised of individuality, where individuality, in turn, is a function of the exercise of reflection and the imagination. Thus, the question becomes: why is Adorno afraid that mass art is inimicable to the development of autonomous, free individuals?

In order to get to the bottom of this particular anxiety, it is initially convenient to divide Adorno's concerns into two parts. First, there is a formal part that pertains to the conditions necessary for the exercise of our powers of reflection and imagination.[73] And second, there is a content part that pertains to the beliefs that people are likely to derive from exposure to mass art.

By way of preview, let me say that with respect to their formal concerns, Adorno and Horkheimer are worried that mass art engenders a mental posture which is at odds with the exercise of our imaginative and reflective powers. Instead, they argue, mass art automatizes and stupefies our mental faculties. Mass art deadens our mental capacities. This is obviously related to the kind of position that one finds articulated in Greenberg, though Adorno is very explicit about what he believes to be the political consequences of passive spectatorship.[74]

According to Adorno's formal analysis of mass art, mass art stultifies, automatizes, and stupefies our mental capacities, thereby incapacitating their free and autonomous exercise with disastrous political effects. Moreover, it is not only the case that in some sense mass art interferes with the formal conditions of freedom by automatizing our mental faculties. It is also the case that the *content* of mass art impedes the development of autonomous individuals because it fills our mental stock with false and deceptive beliefs—deceptive beliefs that contribute to our domination by the social system and which enslave us.

For example, in 'The Culture Industry', Adorno and Horkheimer write: 'the deceived masses are today captivated by the myth of success even more than the successful are. Immovably they insist on the very ideology that enslaves them.'[75] That is, the audiences for mass art are enslaved by the belief that anyone can succeed, if they put their minds to it. This is generally false, given the structure of capitalist society, but the belief serves to encourage people to work hard and to conform. Mass art imparts false beliefs and ideas to people and thereby impedes the development of

---

[73] I call this part 'formal' because it pertains to the forms of mass art.

[74] It is worthwhile to note here that Adorno's conception of the spectator with regard to mass art is contrary to the commendatory notion of distracted spectatorship that we will encounter in our discussion of Walter Benjamin in the next chapter.

[75] Adorno and Horkheimer, 'The Culture Industry', 133–4.

authentically autonomous people by encumbering us with false, debilitating ideas that function to shackle us—that lead us into the social roles and conformist behaviours that society mandates.

Additionally, Adorno contends:

The concepts of order which it [the culture industry] hammers into human beings are always those of the status quo. They remain unquestioned, unanalyzed and undialectically presupposed, even if they no longer have any substance for those who accept them. In contrast to the Kantian, the categorical imperative of the culture industry no longer has anything in common with freedom. It proclaims: you shall conform, without instruction as to what; conform to that which exists anyway, and to that which everyone thinks is the reflex of its power and omnipresence. The power of the culture industry's ideology is such that conformity has replaced consciousness. The order that springs from it is never confronted with what it claims to be or with the real interests of human beings.[76]

What exactly is this deceptive concept of *order* that the culture industry promotes and that turns us into conformists? Adorno says:

While it [the culture industry] claims to lead the perplexed, it deludes them with false conflicts which they are to exchange for their own. It solves conflicts for them only in appearance, in a way that they can hardly be solved in their real lives. In the products of the culture industry human beings get into trouble only so that they can be rescued unharmed, usually by representatives of a benevolent collective; and then in empty harmony, they are reconciled with the general, whose demands they experienced at the outset as irreconcilable with their interests. For this purpose the culture industry has developed formulas which even reach into such non-conceptual areas as light musical entertainment. Here too one gets into a 'jam,' into rhythmic problems, which can be instantly disentangled by the triumph of the basic beat.[77]

That is, we take the formulas of the culture industry—for example, that when people get in trouble, they will be rescued—to heart as a reflection of reality. Thus, the culture industry deludes us with false conflicts that we transfer to our thinking about real-world conflicts, to our own detriment.

Furthermore, there is a way in which the stupefaction of our mental capacities—i.e., the stunting of our powers of imagination and reflection—by the devices of mass art further enhances our acceptance of the deceptive content that the mass-art industry relentlessly projects at us, thereby making us even more susceptible to the ideological blandishments that enslave us.

So, summarizing what we have said so far, there are at least three interrelated theses to the main line of argument that Adorno and Horkheimer

[76] Adorno, 'Culture Industry Reconsidered', 17.   [77] Ibid.

develop against mass art: first, the formal charge that maintains that the very form of address of mass art impedes the exercise of our faculties of imagination and reflection; second, the charge that the deceptive content of mass art enslaves us through false ideas; and third, the co-ordination or integration of the first two charges, which suggests (*a*) that the formal tendencies of mass art operate to make us susceptible to its deceptive content by, at the very least, blunting our imaginative and reflective powers, and (*b*) that the content of mass art—especially in terms of its relentless sameness—reciprocally undermines the free exercise of our imaginative and reflective capacities by automatizing them.

According to this view, our faculties of imagination and reflection are deadened by mass art, and this makes us more receptive to the ideational content of mass art than we might otherwise be, while, at the same time, the relentless repetition of the messages of mass art contributes, in part, to the deadening of our powers of imagination and reflection, and this atrophycation of our powers of imagination and reflection, in turn, has woeful consequences for our prospects for political and moral autonomy.

Part of this argument recalls Greenberg's worries about the way in which our mental capacities are, in effect, retired by mass art. Adorno and Horkheimer write:

The man with leisure has to accept what the culture industry manufacturers offer him. Kant's formalism still expected a contribution from the individual, who was thought to relate the varied experiences of the senses to fundamental concepts; but industry robs the individual of this function. Its prime service to the customer is to do his schematizing for him. Kant said that there was a secret mechanism in the soul which prepared direct intuition in such a way that they could be fitted into the system of pure reason. But today that secret has been deciphered. While the mechanism is to all appearances planned by those who serve up the data of experience, that is, by the culture industry, it is in fact forced upon the latter by the power of society, which remains irrational, however we may try to rationalize it; and this inescapable force is processed by commercial agencies so that they give an artificial impression of being in command. There is nothing left for the consumer to classify. Producers have done it for him. Art for the masses has destroyed the dream but still conforms to the tenets of that dreaming idealism which critical idealism balked at. Everything derives from consciousness: for Malebranche and Berkeley, from the consciousness of God; in mass art, from the consciousness of the producers.[78]

and

Real life is becoming indistinguishable from the movies. The sound film, far surpassing the theater of illusion, leaves no room for imagination or reflection on

[78] Adorno and Horkheimer, 'The Culture Industry', 124–5.

the part of the audience, who is unable to respond with the structure of the film, yet deviate from its precise detail without losing the thread of the story; hence the film forces its victims to equate it directly with reality. The stunting of the mass-media consumer's power of imagination and spontaneity does not have to be traced back to any psychological mechanisms; he must ascribe the loss of those attributes to the objective nature of the products themselves, especially to the most characteristic of them, the sound film. They are so designed that quickness, powers of observation and experience are undeniably needed to apprehend them at all; yet sustained thought is out of the question if the spectator is not to miss the relentless rush of facts. Even though the effort required for his response is semi-automatic, no scope is left for the imagination. Those who are so absorbed by the world of the movie—by its images, gestures and words—that they are unable to supply what really makes it a world, do not have to dwell on particular points of its mechanics during its screening. All the other films and products of the entertainment industry which they have seen have taught them what to expect; they react automatically [i.e., without reflection and imagination].[79]

The mass artwork precludes the contribution in terms of the play of imagination and reflection of the individual spectator to the artwork, thereby abetting the atrophy of the faculties in question. One way in which mass art contrives this result is a function of its pre-schematization, which effect is reinforced through its endless recycling of old formulas. This encourages the audience to put its mind on automatic pilot, rather than engaging in the free play of reflection and imagination. Adorno and Horkheimer note that: 'As soon as the film begins, it is quite clear how it will end, and who will be rewarded, punished and forgotten.'[80] The audience, in other words, has nothing to think about; everything is served up in an all-too-conveniently pre-digested form.

The unnerving sameness of content, along with other factors, such as the speed of delivery of information (in the movies) thrusts the consumer into the role of passive spectator. Moreover, this commerce in pre-ordained effects is antithetical to the autonomy of the individual spectator. It stultifies the possibility of a creative, individual response and substitutes for it a response that has been engineered from the outside by a production team working on behalf of the culture industry. Our faculties of imagination and reflection are not engaged in a process of spontaneous play, such as filling in the artwork. Rather, our faculties, operating at an

---

[79] Ibid. 126–7. In this quotation, Adorno and Horkheimer allege that the hurtling, forward movement of the narrative, sound film precludes the operation of the imagination. Presumably, the spectator has no time to think, as the narrative rushes forward. However, it has always struck me as logically incongruous that Adorno and Horkheimer refrain from making the same observation about music, since much music, including music Adorno would classify as genuine art, seems to me to have the same propulsive forward movement, delivered to the audience at comparably high velocities, that is here attributed to movies.   [80] Ibid. 125.

almost reflexive or automatic level, are dragooned into responding in the routine ways that have been described above.

Furthermore, for Adorno and Horkheimer, this is not simply an observation about cognitive processes. It is also of great political import. This may strike some readers as quite an astounding leap of logic. How does one get from the repression of the imaginative capacity in responses to artworks to any conclusions concerning political consequences?

Adorno and Horkheimer are not perhaps as forthcoming about this as they might be. However, I think that we can conjecture a hypothesis about what they might have in mind, if we recall the influential writings of Friedrich Schiller—particularly his *On the Aesthetic Education of Man*.[81] In Schiller's view, it is not only the case that our response to art involves free imaginative play. Schiller also thought that this capacity for play—first nurtured in our earliest aesthetic experiences—has important repercussions for morality and politics. For in exercising our capacity for imaginative play—by which we give form to nature—humans free themselves from nature in a way that sets them on the road to moral autonomy.

That is, our imagination enables us to recognize that humanity is not just a part of nature whose reality must be accepted as it is. Humans, through the exercise of their imagination, realize through their own case that they are free—that they in fact can impose form on reality. Thus, the freedom involved in aesthetic play is in fact a condition for moral autonomy, and, in consequence, for Schiller, aesthetic education through commerce with artworks is an ingredient in our development of our moral powers and political freedom. Aesthetic freedom is a first freedom. Indeed, it is a necessary pre-condition for any other sort of freedom. For the freedom from reality-as-it-is that is born of our experiences of art is a kind of original freedom—an experience of freedom that prepares us for the full acquisition of moral and political autonomy. In fact, without this original experience of freedom, the prospects for later development in the direction of further moral and political autonomy is at risk, if not impossible.

Now my proposal is that we interpret Adorno and Horkheimer as holding something *like* Schiller's view about the relation of aesthetic experience to moral and political education. This conjecture does not seem wayward, since Schiller's view's were well known to educated Germans of Adorno's and Horkheimer's generation. Perhaps this view was so well known to the audience Adorno and Horkheimer were addressing that

---

[81] Friedrich Schiller, *On the Aesthetic Education of Man: In a Series of Letters*, trans. Elizabeth M. Wilkenson and L. A. Willoughby (Oxford: Clarendon Press, 1967).

they felt little pressure to spell out their presumption of the broad contour of a view like Schiller's, according to which art and aesthetic education are conceived of as an integral part of moral and political education.

On Schiller's account, aesthetic education virtually plays the role of a developmental stage from the perspective of what we now call genetic epistemology. And if Adorno and Horkheimer share this view of the role of aesthetic education, it is easy to understand why they are so afraid of mass art. For they believe that mass art provides the wrong kind of aesthetic education. That is, they fear that mass art is not suitable for the development of autonomous citizens because in virtue of its automatizing sameness it stifles and even suppresses the play of the imagination and it standardizes taste. Mass art arrests the development of the cognitive play of the imagination and shackles our reflective powers, thus robbing us of a necessary condition for autonomy—not merely as aesthetic agents, but as political agents as well. Mass art suppresses our powers of imagination and reflection which undermines a 'precondition for democratic society' by literally interfering with the cognitive maturation processes of the prospective citizenry.[82]

Specifically, Adorno fears that the repression of the imagination through the exposure to mass art will have the consequence of inducing audiences to believe that situations—most notably social reality—cannot be other than the way they are. The imagination, that is, is a faculty that enables us to envision that reality can be otherwise. This is why Schiller thought that the development of the imagination was so crucial to morality and politics. For through the exercise of the imagination we can envision alternatives to what is, especially better alternatives to what is from a moral or a political point of view. Understood this way, the imagination is what makes change—changes in moral and political circumstances—possible. The imagination is what enables us to conceive of a better world and, therefore, is a pre-condition for changing it morally and politically.

Thus, Adorno fears that once our imaginations have been stultified by the operation of mass art, we shall be possessed by the conviction that situations—in particular and social reality as a whole—cannot be changed. This anxiety—that people will come to be hypnotized by the impression that social reality cannot be otherwise—is a recurring theme among radical theorists from Brecht to Barthes to contemporary, marxist semioticians, many of whom contend that a major function of ideology is to convince people that the form of social reality is given, inevitable, or 'natural', thereby undercutting a necessary condition for revolutionary

[82] Adorno, 'Culture Industry Reconsidered', 19.

activity, namely, faith in the possibility that things can be changed. In Adorno's case, the debilitation of our powers of imagination contributes to this ideological effect by arresting our cognitive capacity to project the possibility of things standing differently from the way they are.

Furthermore, Adorno and Horkheimer maintain that this process of shackling the imagination inclines us towards the acceptance of the representations of social reality proffered to us by mass art. Deadened to the possibility of alternatives, we putatively regard the picture of reality presented by mass art as reliable. It is our powers of imagination and reflection that afford us the space that we need to free ourselves from the grip of existing social reality by, for example, entertaining the possibility that reality could be otherwise.[83]

Critical Theorists often speak in the language of negation. One might say that they are believers in the positive power of negation. In this context, 'negation' applies to the negation of existing social reality. Social change, then, requires that people possess the capacity to negate what is, and that the imaginative capacity is a necessary condition for any substantial gesture of negation. However, inasmuch as our powers of imagination and reflection are not being exercised, and are even being allowed to atrophy through exposure to mass art, we are apt to accept the world as we find it as inevitable—including accepting as inevitable the world as it is represented in the products of the culture industry. Moreover, the reliance of mass art on repetition and stereotype reinforces this effect, the monotony of the formulas of mass art confirming the impression of the immutability of existing social circumstances. Thus, Adorno and Horkheimer write:

Anyone who doubts the power of monotony is a fool. The culture industry refutes the objection made against it just as well as that against the world which it impartially duplicates. The only choice is either to join in or to be left behind. . . . Continuing and continuing to join in are given as justification for the blind persistence of the system and even for its immutability. What repeats itself is healthy, like the natural or industrial cycle. The same babies grin eternally out of the magazines; the jazz machine will pound away forever. In spite of all the

---

[83] It is interesting to note that this worry about mass art appears to contradict another common complaint about mass art—namely, that it is escapist. The escapist argument contends that mass art departs from reality into fantasy and that the antidote to escapism is more realism. But the call for realism—for depicting things the way they are—seems to be the opposite prescription from what Adorno calls for.

For a discussion of escapism in general, see D. W .Harding, 'The Notion of Escape in Fiction and Entertainment', *Oxford Review*, 4 (1967), 23–32. In *The Origins of Totalitarianism* (New York: Harcourt Brace and World, Inc., 1966), Hannah Arendt discusses the escapist operation of totalitarian propaganda on pp. 352–4.

progress in reproduction techniques, in controls and the specialities, and in spite of all the restless industry, the bread which the culture industry offers man is the stone of the stereotype. In draws on the life cycle, on the well-founded amazement that mothers, in spite of everything, still go on bearing children and that the wheels still do not grind to a halt. This serves to confirm the immutability of circumstances.[84]

From this welter of charges against the culture industry, I believe that it is possible to abstract at least three arguments that I will call, respectively, the freedom argument, the susceptibility argument, and the conditioning argument. Let us examine them one at a time.

The freedom argument takes the following form:

1. If there is no aesthetic autonomy, there will be no moral and/or political autonomy. (There will be no freedom.)

2. If there is aesthetic autonomy, there is the play of the imagination and our powers of reflection.

3. With respect to mass art, there is no play of our imagination and our powers of reflection.

4. Therefore, in respect to mass art, there is no aesthetic autonomy.

5. Therefore, in respect to mass art, there will be no moral and/or political autonomy.

Moreover, in contemporary society, mass art is virtually the only available aesthetic staple for most people. Thus, most people in contemporary society will be deprived of the resources for developing moral and/or political autonomy. This would surely constitute a crisis of awesome proportions.

However, I am not persuaded that we need to take any of the premisses of the freedom argument very seriously. Considering the first premiss, I feel compelled to ask whether aesthetic autonomy is really necessary for moral and/or political autonomy. What Adorno and Horkheimer appear to regard as relevant to moral and political autonomy is the capacity to see or to imagine that things might be otherwise. This is reasonable. However, is it plausible to suppose that that capacity only correlates with aesthetic or artistic activities? Perhaps it is innate. But, in any case, it is certainly undeniable that the capacity to imagine that things could be otherwise is as intimately connected to practical activity as it is to aesthetic activity. After all, if I want to build a better chair, or if I want to get a different job, I will have to be able to envision alternatives to the way things are.

Practical activity, it seems to me, has at least as good a claim to be counted

[84] Adorno and Horkheimer, 'The Culture Industry', 148–9.

as the origin of our capacity to envision change in the world as does aesthetic activity, if not a better claim than aesthetic activity. But, be that as it may, I contend that we can readily conceive of people possessed of moral and political autonomy who have little or no intercourse with art, but who have a sturdy sense of the ways in which reality can be changed by practical activity. Therefore, if what is really at stake in this argument is the capacity to imagine the world differently, then it is not the case that aesthetic experience, in any non-question-begging sense of the term, is a necessary condition for moral and political freedom, since the relevant intimation of the alterability of reality can be derived from elsewhere. It could be derived from practical activity or it could even be an innate endowment.

The second premiss in the argument is somewhat harder to evaluate, since, to a certain extent, it looks as though it might be simply definitional. Whether the premiss is cogent will depend, in large measure, on how we understand the freedom that is putatively involved in the play of the imagination. Does it imply that the imagination must be altogether free of guidance by the object of our attention? If that is how we are to understand it, then we should reject the premiss, since under that conception of freedom, we would not be speaking of aesthetic autonomy, but of aesthetic fantasy. On the other hand, if by the freedom of the imagination, we have in mind the sort of active spectatorship discussed earlier in this chapter, then premiss two seems unobjectionable; but, at the same time, if our previous arguments were persuasive, then the notion of aesthetic autonomy would support no principled objection to mass art.

This issue is, of course, explicitly joined in the third premiss of the freedom argument, which contends that in the case of mass art there is no play of the imagination. But if we are to understand as examples of the play of the imagination such spectatorial activities as interpreting dramatic situations and metaphors, as well as inferring, mass art does afford the opportunity to exercise the imagination, not to mention some of the other active, imaginative audience responses that we canvassed in our discussion of Greenberg. Likewise, the viewer of a Busby Berkeley production number is involved in entertaining the play of pattern in exactly the way that Kant might have characterized a peasant rapt in the aesthetic appreciation of a landscape, which, for Kant, would be a matter of the free play of the imagination and the understanding.

Similarly many genre strategies are predicated on stimulating the imagination. Many of the creators of horror fiction have preferred to leave their monsters underdescribed or off-screen. They believe that it is better to proceed by suggestion, since they say that the audience can imagine things that are more horrible than they could ever depict. And sometimes this is true. But this strategy relies on the audience's use of its imagination. And at least some of the time, this technique works. Indeed, it is often employed in the contemporary TV series *The X Files*. Moreover, strategies that mandate the activation of the audience member's imagination can be cited in the case of other mass art genres. Thus, the worries of Adorno and Horkheimer with respect to the stultification of the bare powers of the imagination by mass art are empirically unfounded.

Adorno and Horkheimer regard the forward velocity of film (and, by extension, TV) editing as so hurried that there is no opportunity for the intervention of the imagination. Whether this is so is at least controversial. Certainly film theorists like V. I. Pudovkin have analysed what he calls montage in terms of the constructive activities of the spectator. It is not obvious that Pudovkin is wrong in the broad outlines of his theory, even if some of his specific hypotheses ring hollow. But, then, doesn't the construction of meaning by viewers of montage count as an example of the activity of our imaginative powers? And, if not, why not?

In short, it seems as though there is a great deal of audience activity involved in the response to mass art, or, at least, to a (substantial) number of mass artworks. For example, at the end of the movie *The Shawshank Redemption*, as all the details of the escape and its ramifications fall into place, the audience is involved in a pleasurable process of retrospection, recalling the ways in which the moral imbalances of certain earlier events are being redressed and fitted into a structure of justice (in the sense of just deserts). Likewise the ending of *The Usual Suspects* prompts the audience to reconfigure the earlier narrative. Certainly these examples involve the sort of cognitive engagement that Adorno and Horkheimer have in mind under the rubric of imagination and reflection. Therefore, the third premiss of the freedom argument seems false, as does the entire argument. Nor does it help to say that what Adorno and Horkheimer really mean is only that *some* mass art deadens the imagination, for inasmuch as it can be shown that some other mass art does not, they are no longer in a position to issue a blanket rebuke to mass art, or, as they call it, the culture industry.

A second argument against mass art that is discernible in the writings of Adorno and Horkheimer is what I call the susceptibility argument:

1. If we are unable to mobilize our imaginative and reflective capacities, then we are apt both to accept situations as unalterable and to accept representations of situations as showing the way in which things unalterably are.

2. In the case of mass art, we are unable to mobilize our imaginative and reflective capacities.

3. Therefore, with mass art we are apt to accept the representations of situations as showing the way in which things unalterably are.

Here, given a liberal understanding of what is involved in mobilizing our imaginative and reflective powers, it would appear that the first premiss is acceptable. However, the second premiss is troublesome, since, once again, everything hinges on whatever is meant by mobilizing our imaginative and reflective powers. Can those concepts be construed in such a way that it can be denied that mass art, or, at least, some of it, can be said to preclude the mobilization of the imagination and reflection, while, at the same time, those concepts, imagination and reflection, remain broad enough to command our assent to the first premiss? For if we construe these concepts broadly in the first premiss, but narrowly in the second premiss, the argument will be guilty of a fallacy of equivocation.

Obviously, it has been my contention throughout this chapter that on a broad, but unforced, conception of our mental powers, it must be conceded that mass artworks—not only perhaps special cases like *Citizen Kane*, but more mundane examples, like Harlequin Romances—can engage our imaginative and reflective powers. Consider all the moral reflection that so many mass artworks presuppose as a pre-condition for being simply intelligible to an audience. This may not strike Adorno and Horkheimer as a particularly strenuous exercise of our imaginative and reflective powers. But, then again, it would not appear to require a strenuous exercise of our imaginative and reflective powers to form the idea that things could be otherwise in general or in terms of social arrangements in particular.

On the other hand, if one wants to define our imaginative and reflective powers so that it is implausible that mass arts engage these faculties, then this must be done in such a way that it is consistent with the presiding definitions of those concepts in the first premiss of the argument. And this is what I think is so very hard to do.

If a narrow, or particularly demanding conception of our imaginative powers is introduced, then the first premiss starts to look false, even as the second premiss appears true. But if a broad conception of our imaginative and reflective powers prevails, the first premiss will turn out true, but the second premiss will turn out false, given the evidence that we have amassed throughout this chapter. Thus, the susceptibility argument faces a dilemma—whichever construal of our imaginative and reflective powers the Critical Theorist embraces, the argument must fail, since it will contain at least one false premiss.

The last of the arguments from the writings of Adorno and Horkheimer that I will discuss is the conditioning argument. It says that:

1. If certain stereotypes and stories are endlessly repeated, then they will project an image that circumstances (social realities) are immutable.

2. Mass art endlessly repeats its stereotypes and stories.

3. Therefore, mass art projects an image that circumstances (social reality) are immutable.

Whereas the susceptibility argument focuses upon the inanition of our faculties of imagination and reflection, the conditioning argument gives us some idea of one of the mechanisms that brings that inanition about, namely it is brought about by means of the monotonous repetition of stereotypes and stories.

Our imagination and our reflective powers are, one supposes, beaten down by the calculated repetition of routine representations so that these representations take full possession of our minds in such a way that we cannot conceive of anything, except in terms of these stories and stereotypes. Thus, these stories and stereotypes provide us with *the* way of seeing our world. Nothing outside the models provided by these stories and stereotypes appears comprehensible. They supply us with our limits of intelligibility, and they shape experience as implacably as Kantian forms of intuition, such as space and time.

These models structure our world and appear as immutable as laws of nature. Moreover, this is achieved by relentless conditioning—by the monotonous repetition of the same stories and stereotypes again and again. We are rather like the victims of an ideological indoctrination process—of the sort, once called brain-washing—where simple slogans are hammered into us repeatedly and without respite, until our minds are so taken over by them that we cannot but see the world under their aegis; we cannot see the world, especially social reality, differently from the way in which these stories and stereotypes command us to see it. And that way of seeing makes the world appear to us as immutable.

Though this argument makes a kind of abstract sense, it falls apart when one begins to consider its claims concretely. The first premiss maintains that if stereotypes and stories are monotonously recycled, the result will be the impression that social reality cannot be changed. Stereotypes become so ingrained that the status quo that they represent will appear immutable. However, if this seems persuasive, it is probably because it is being presupposed that the stories and stereotypes that are being repeated are ones that portray the status quo as unchangeable or natural or the way things must be. But what if the stories and stereotypes are about changing social reality? Why would that have the effect of leaving the impression that social reality is unchangeable?

For many of the stories and stereotypes of mass art are actually about the possibility of social change. Think how many episodes of *Star Trek* are about the possibility of cultural change. Of course, there is a federation directive that Captain Kirk, *et al.* refrain from intervening in the cultures of the planets where they find themselves. But then so many episodes are about circumventing this federation directive, or, albeit with heavy hearts, disregarding it. In *Star Trek*, episode after episode, it is shown again and again—monotonously, one might say—that the forces of oppression can be overcome by liberal democratic self-assertion. The series handles problems like racism and bigotry on a weekly basis, and it implies that they can be overcome by people of good will and gumption.[85]

Moreover, this is not an idiosyncratic feature of *Star Trek*, but something the TV programme inherited from the practice of science fiction in pulp literature, comic books, film, and the like. The possibility of social revolution is one of the major recurring themes of science fiction across the mass media. Remember Buck Rogers and Flash Gordon. It is also a theme of the *Planet of the Apes* series, not to mention *Star Wars*.

Nor is the possibility of social change restricted to the province of science fiction. Bible epics—like the *Ten Commandments*, *Ben Hur*, and *The Robe*—feature Jews and/or Christians waging ultimately successful revolts against various agencies of ancient tyranny, like Egypt and Rome. And so many westerns, in every media, feature the settlers staging successful resistance against tyrannical cattle barons and their hired mercenaries.

And there are also prison escape films, where venal and sadistic wardens representing an unjust social system are outsmarted by righteous convicts as is the case in *The Shawshank Redemption*. And even though Cool Hand Luke does not escape, his efforts are eulogized as heroic and are meant to symbolize an endorsement of the unquenchable human aspiration to freedom. Indeed, James Hilton's *Lost Horizon*—the first mass paperback ever published—provided a blueprint for social change, albeit an admittedly Utopian one.

Even TV sitcoms present scenarios of characters who undergo personal

---

[85] Here it might be said that Adorno and Horkheimer would never accept a *Star Trek* episode as being about *radical* social change. But what then would be an acceptable example of this sort of social change for Adorno and Horkheimer? Since they never say, their failure to address this problem raises a question about the empirical, cash value of their theory. On the other hand, if this issue is answered in such a way that none of the depictions of revolutionary self-assertion in mass art ever count as being about radical social change, then the suspicion is unavoidable that 'radical social change' is being implicitly defined in a way that begs the question.

changes, often overcoming socially oppressive biases; for example, in an episode of the programme *Roc*, the father is brought to accept his brother's homosexual marriage. And what about social message films—from *The Grapes of Wrath* to *Guess Who's Coming to Dinner* to *Philadelphia*? These films are underwritten by the sentiment that society ought to be changed, and they frequently hint that it can be changed.

So, it seems false to maintain that the repetition of stories and stereotypes *simpliciter* always imparts the impression that the status quo is immutable, since the stories and stereotypes that are being repeated may be ones that imply the mutability of social reality. Furthermore, many of the stories and stereotypes recycled by mass art are obviously of this sort. Thus, it would seem implausible to maintain that the repetition of stories of social mutability should result in the conviction of social immutability. And, if the proponent of the conditioning argument says that however implausible this sounds, this is nevertheless the case, then said proponent has a lot of explaining to do before we withdraw our suspicion concerning this hypothesis.

One gambit that the friend of the conditioning argument might try in this regard is to say of the preceding counter-examples that they make the possibility of social change appear too easy and that, in consequence, people become complacent about social change. They think, perhaps, that it will just come about with little or virtually no effort. But note that this concedes that it is not the mere repetition of stories and stereotypes that deters social change. Thus, the strongest version of the conditioning argument is false; it is not simply the repetitiveness of mass art that impedes social change. At best it is the content of what is repeated that makes a difference, if it does indeed make a difference, and, moreover, it is not the literal meaning of things like *Star Trek* that constitutes the problem, but only the impression that it leaves that progressive social change is not very difficult to achieve. A Vulcan can carry it off as easily as wiggling his ears.

But I am not sure that mass artworks always or necessarily insinuate that social change is easy. Surely, they frequently represent it as difficult and demanding; that is the manifest content, at least. And the problems with these fictions cannot be that they fail to represent social change as impossible. For the animating concern of the proponent of the conditioning argument is that society be recognized as mutable. It is true that the mass artworks in question portray social change as do-able. Perhaps they represent social change as easier to secure than it is. However, we are not compelled to explain this in terms of the purpose of engendering complacency. Rather, it might be explained as a rhetorical lever designed to encourage people to be optimistic enough to try to accomplish something. And surely this is not a motive that those who hope for social change should denigrate, especially since there is some evidence that the stories and stereotypes of actually existing mass art has, in fact, inspired some social change.[86]

But, in any case, the first premiss of the conditioning argument is an empirical conjecture. It relies on a constant correlation between the repetition of stories and stereotypes, on the one hand, and a kind of fatalism about the prospects for social change on the other. It is a hypothesis about the effects of repetition/conditioning, irrespective of the content of the independent variable. But this is a strange sort of conditioning, since it seems to allow that even if the repeated stimulus is of the sort that reinforces our convictions about the prospects for social change, the output will still be the belief that nothing can change.

Moreover, the second premiss of the conditioning argument appears hyperbolic. To a certain extent, all art involves the repetition of certain stereotypes and stories, and, in this respect, mass art is no different. But just as variation against a background of repetition is available in other forms of art, variation is also possible in mass art. Mass art does not merely repeat the same stories and stereotypes. Sometimes, it plays variations off its recurring strategies, as in the case of Alfred Hitchcock's *Psycho*, where audience expectations are subverted for expressive effect by killing off the putative heroine in the 'first act'.[87] Mass art is largely an affair of genres, but within the genre framework, mass artworks can evolve subtle variations that are often appreciated as such by plain viewers, readers, and listeners. Whether or not mass art is more reliant upon repetition than other forms of art, historically speaking, is a question that I am not sure I even know how to begin to answer. However, even if mass art is more formulaic, the formulas promote the possibility of variation against a generic background, and this possibility is one that has served as the basis of the reputations of many of the greatest masters of mass art, like Chaplin. Thus, the second premiss of the conditioning is too strong and cannot be endorsed without qualification, though, of course, the requisite qualifications will make it useless as a premiss in a philosophical argument about the essential nature of mass art.

So far we have seen that six of philosophy's major arguments against mass art—including the massification argument, the passivity argument, the formula argument, the freedom argument, the susceptibility argu-

---

[86] See Joshua Meyrowitz, *No Sense of Place* (New York: Oxford University Press, 1985).

[87] An effect that is often imitated, for example, as recently as in Wes Craven's *Scream*.

ment, and the conditioning argument—have all failed. But with so many arguments before us, it is natural to ask why philosophy bears such an obsessive antipathy toward mass art. Is it simply a peccadillo of the theorists that we have chosen to look at? Or are there deeper, conceptual grounds for philosophy's recurrent resistance to mass art?

Concluding remarks: a diagnosis of philosophy's resistance to mass art

There are a number of recurring themes that run through the preceding six arguments against mass art, including: that the mass artwork is formulaic, not unique; that it is a commodity, and, therefore, neither is it disconnected from society and practical concerns, nor is it disinterested; that mass art encourages neither an imaginative nor an active response from spectators; and that the responses it does elicit are 'canned' (i.e., generic) and not unique. Not all the different arguments that we have considered invoke every one of these themes; often they invoke only some of them. And, as well, each of the different arguments places different emphases on the factors from this group that they do employ. Nevertheless, these factors return, albeit often in different ways, with undeniable frequency in the thinking behind the arguments that we have just reviewed. Thus, one suspects that this particular package of concerns may tell us something about philosophy's resistance to mass art, or, at least about the type of philosophical resistance that we have encountered so far.

In order to get a handle on philosophy's resistance to mass art, our first question is whether one can identify the source of the package of concerns itemized above. I think that the answer to this question is pretty apparent. For these concerns and their systematic inter-relations derive from the aesthetic theory of Immanuel Kant, most particularly from Book I, 'The Analytic of the Beautiful', in his *Critique of Judgment*.[88] Indeed, it is to this text, or, to be more accurate, to misunderstandings of this text that I would trace one of the major, enduring sources of philosophy's resistance to mass art. What is the basis for this conjecture?

Needless to say, since there was no cable TV in Königsberg, Kant had no theory of mass art. In fact, he had no theory of art at all. Rather, the relevant sections of his third critique are not about art, but about judge-

---

[88] Immanuel Kant, *Critique of Judgment*, trans. Werner S. Pluhar (Indianapolis: Hackett Publishing Company, 1987).

ments of beauty and sublimity. However, in the course of the evolution of the philosophy of art throughout the nineteenth and twentieth centuries, parts of Kant's theory, especially his analysis of beauty, have been dragooned—inappropriately in my opinion—in various conceptions of the nature of art.[89] Often, Kant's theory of the aesthetic response has been turned into a theory of art—sometimes called the aesthetic theory of art[90]—by means of a functionalist pre-supposition, namely, that works of art are things that have been designed for the purpose of bringing about aesthetic responses of the sort characterized in Kant's theory of (free) beauty.[91] For example, one gripped by this way of thinking might hypothesize that a work of art, by definition, is the sort of thing that divorces us from practical concerns.

This kind of extrapolation of Kant's theory of beauty is a mistake, but it is a mistake that lies deep in the philosophical tradition, perhaps beginning with Schopenhauer. The upshot of this mistake for the theorization of mass art is that, in so far as philosophers attempt to understand mass art in terms of theories that they have misappropriated from Kant's theory of beauty, they are bound to misunderstand, to ignore, and/or to be hostile to mass art because they are employing a conceptual framework that is completely alien to the task. They are, perhaps unbeknown to themselves, trying to impose a framework for the analysis of free beauty on to the discussion of the nature of mass art. In what follows, I shall try to show how many of the fundamental premises in the arguments of Greenberg, Collingwood, MacDonald, and Adorno derive from Kant by way of some serious misunderstandings, while, at the same time, I will also indicate why these misunderstandings profoundly compromise any attempt to understand mass art philosophically from the get-go.

My central hypothesis is that a great deal of the philosophical resistance to mass art that we have discussed so far is the result of the misapplication of the terms of Kant's theory of free beauty to mass art. Equipped with such a conceptual framework, theorists often see no way to regard mass art as art proper, or, as is frequently the case, the theorist, like MacDonald, Greenberg, Collingwood, Adorno, or Horkheimer, sees mass art as essentially a deviant, perhaps degraded, but nevertheless ersatz form of art.

[89] For further substantiation of this point, see Noël Carroll, 'Beauty and the Genealogy of Art Theory', *Philosophical Forum*, 22/4 (1991).

[90] For an example of such a theory, see Monroe Beardsley, 'An Aesthetic Definition of Art', in *What is Art?* (New York: Haven Publications, Inc., 1983), 15–32.

[91] For Kant, the theory of free beauty is not a theory of art, however, it is my contention that many subsequent theorists, including those canvassed in this chapter, have attempted to turn it into one by presuming that an artwork's properly so-called function is to engender the experience of free beauty (or parts thereof) in audiences.

This central hypothesis, in turn, presupposes another hypothesis that I have defended at length elsewhere, namely that one of the major tendencies in the evolution of the modern philosophy of art has involved the mistaken transformation of Kant's theory of free beauty into a theory of art.[92] This development has distorted the development of the philosophy of art in many ways, including predisposing it toward formalism.

What I would like to do in the remainder of this chapter is to indicate the ways in which the misappropriation of at least fragments of Kant's theory of free beauty has also distorted various philosophical responses to mass art. In order to give substance to this allegation, I will once again consider some of the arguments of Greenberg, Collingwood, MacDonald, Adorno, and Horkheimer. But this time around, I will be less concerned with the truth of these arguments (having already called that into question in previous sections). Rather, I will focus instead on the way in which the central premisses of these theorists involve misappropriations of Kant's theory of free beauty. However, before discussing the latent Kantianism in these theories, it is useful to recall briefly the Kantian theory of beauty upon which these theories depend.

As already indicated, Kant's theory is not a theory of art, let alone mass art. The problem that concerned Kant in the 'Analytic of the Beautiful' is the analysis of judgements of free (rather than 'dependent') beauty, for example, judgements of things like sunsets (which judgements take the form 'This sunset is beautiful'). Kant wants to offer an account of the way in which such judgements can be universal and necessary even though they are based solely on our subjective feeling of pleasure when we see something like a stunning sunset. Put crudely, Kant wants to explain how, on the basis of my subjective experience alone, I can justifiably expect everyone else to assent to my judgement that 'this sunset is beautiful'.

To this end, Kant develops an elaborate theory of authentic judgements of taste. Stated very schematically, it goes like this: with respect to judgements of free beauty, 'x is beautiful' is an authentic judgement of taste (or, more simply, an aesthetic judgement) if and only if it is a 1. subjective, 2. disinterested, 3. universal, 4. necessary, 5. singular judgement concerning 6. the contemplative pleasure that everyone ought to derive from 7. the free play of the understanding and the imagination in relation to 8. forms of finality.

People, of course, spend lifetimes trying to unravel this theory precisely. So, clearly, I cannot offer an in-depth explication of it now. Rather, let me

---

[92] Noël Carroll, 'Beauty and the Genealogy of Art Theory', in *Philosophical Forum*, 22/4 (1991).

try to make a series of observations about it which will prove relevant to the discussion of mass art.

Aesthetic judgements can be universal—i.e., command the assent of all—on Kant's view because, though such judgements are based only on our subjective experience, they are made on the basis of what we have in common with everyone else, namely, on the basis of our cognitive and imaginative faculties in a disinterested state of mind. That our state of mind is disinterested—unconcerned with the practical consequences, advantages, disadvantages, and purport of the objects of attention—is thought to factor out all those interests in the object that might be suspected of making us judge the object differently from others. Thus the judgement is made on the basis of what everyone has in common—cognitive and perceptual faculties; the understanding and the imagination—without the interference of any idiosyncratic interests (such as practical or political utility, the prospect of personal gain, etc.) that might skew our judgement.

Moreover, the target of our attention—what it is directed at—is forms—like the patterns of a snowflake—rather than content. So the idea is that common faculties, such as cognition and perception, understanding and imagination, directed at forms, irrespective of content, while in a disinterested state of mind, will deliver to me the same sort of feeling that everyone else would also have were they to use their basic faculties unencumbered by the individuating particularities of interest and content. Absent interest and content, *ex hypothesi*, common human faculties should operate in the same way. Thus, if I can be sure that I am in a disinterested state, which is all the more likely if my response is to pure, unthematized form, then I am justified in thinking that anyone with the same basic faculties I possess should be stimulated as I am by the relevant input. If I am pleasured by it, then anyone just like me should be pleasured as well. This is why Kant thinks that I am justified in commanding the assent of all when I say 'This sunset is beautiful' where the judgement is disinterested and refers to the pleasure that arises from the free play of the understanding and imagination.

I will not comment at length on Kant's theory except to say that it is not altogether outlandish when what one is thinking about are things like our response to, say, foliage in autumn. However, as already noted, various elements of the theory have been extrapolated into theories of art. Many theorists, for example, think that the work of art is such that it puts us in a disinterested state of mind—that it frees us from concern with practical affairs and purposes; and, as well, some theorists have transformed the Kantian idea of disinterestedness into the idea that the work of art itself is autonomous, i.e., independent of ulterior cognitive and/or utilitarian purposes. And, of course, these two views can be connected by suggesting that it is the absence of utilitarian concerns in the object that is conducive to our disinterested response to it.

This interpretation may also seem to receive some correlative support from the emphasis that Kant's theory places on the nature of the object of aesthetic judgement, namely, what are called forms of finality (purposiveness without a purpose). That is, for Kant a sense of beauty is raised by a sense of the purposiveness of the object—i.e., its appearance of purpose—rather than by any actual purpose that the object might have been designed to discharge.

For example, when we appreciate the markings on a bird, we contemplate the configuration as if it were purposeful or designed, irrespective of the fact that it was not designed and that we may be unaware of any purpose it serves. This notion of purposiveness, in turn, has been transformed by theorists of art into the presupposition that art is without ulterior purpose, or, more jargonistically, that it is autonomous.

One feature of Kant's theory of beauty that I have not yet remarked upon, but which is central to many of the theories of art that have been constructed out of (or, in my view, imposed upon) Kant's speculations about beauty is that aesthetic judgement is singular. What Kant meant by this is that when we say 'x is beautiful' we are not applying a determinate concept to the object of our attention. There are no formulas or criteria for beauty. We can only tell whether something is beautiful by looking. If we look and, in consequence, feel disinterested pleasure, due to the play of our understanding and imagination, then it is beautiful. From this, it is conjectured that there are no general rules for what is beautiful. The proof of the pudding is in the tasting. If we say something is beautiful, this judgement rests on a unique, pleasurable experience; it is not deduced from a general rule.

Extrapolating from the theory of free beauty to a theory of art, this aspect of Kant's theory becomes the view that there are no rules or formulas in art. Each artwork, like each beautiful thing, is unique. It is not subsumable under a concept, just as it is not subsumable under a purpose. Following Kant's own theory of genius as exemplary originality,[93] the aesthetic theorist of art is tempted to maintain that anything that is properly called art must be unique and original, forging a law unto itself, rather than being tethered by determinate concepts or purposes or rules.

---

[93] Kant, *Critique of Judgment*, Bk. II, s. 49.

Perhaps needless to say, any theory like this—so biased toward original-ity—is not apt to be sympathetic to the formulaic strategies of mass art.

Lastly, for our purposes, in Kant's view, our response to the objects that give rise to aesthetic judgements is notably active and free. It is free in that it is not influenced by interests, nor is it constrained by determinate concepts and/or purposes. It is also free in that it is not driven by utilitarian desires. It is contemplative because it is open and playful. Indeed, Kant's notion of the free play of the faculties here is probably the origin of play theories of art from Schiller onwards. Moreover, it is cognitive and perceptual free play, involving the operation of the imagina-tion and the understanding in, so to speak, an exploratory mode. This entails the active exercise of our mental faculties. The judgement of beauty is not made passively; it is intellectually engaged and participatory.

Transforming this feature of aesthetic judgement into a capacity of the artwork involves theorizing that art objects properly so called are designed in such a way as to promote intellectually engaged, contemplative partici-pation. On the narrow formalist view, this might be construed as noticing the details and the inter-relations between parts of the work; but it might also be easily extended to the idea that artworks are designed to engage audiences actively in making meanings, inferences, and interpretations.

Again, Kant himself does not offer us a theory of art. He was involved in analysing aesthetic judgements, particularly with an eye to explaining how they could be universal and subjective at the same time. However, in attempting that explanation, he developed an account of the aesthetic which gradually became the source of various theories of art. The general way in which these theories came to be constructed involved reconceiving some feature or features of the Kantian aesthetic state, like disinterested-ness or active cognitive play, as the intended output of a capacity that art properly so called was designed to promote.

Outfitted with theories like this—which I tend to think of as distorted fragments of Kantian aesthetic theory—theorists of art who have attempted to negotiate the mass art of the twentieth century have con-cluded that mass art violates their conception of art, for mass art is not disinterested or autonomous in the ways they presuppose art ought to be, nor need it promote active contemplation, nor is it independent of desire, etc. Of course, Kant is not responsible for this misuse of his theory. Theorists like Greenberg, Collingwood, MacDonald, Adorno, and Hor-kheimer are.

Residues of Kantian aesthetic theory are very pronounced in Green-berg's theory of art. Its most striking presupposition—that the nature of art is reflexive; that art concerns the critique of the conditions that make artforms, like painting and sculpture, possible—is obviously a presumption that is Kantian in form, though not content. This presupposition, of course, seems to owe more to Kantian epistemology than it does to Kantian aesthetics. Nevertheless, Kantian aesthetic elements, in somewhat distorted variations, do make their appearance in subsidiary premisses of Greenberg's theory, notably in his discussion of mass art. Two notions that stand out particularly are the autonomy or disinterestedness of the genuine art object, on the one hand, and the active spectatorship of the audience, on the other.

In contrast to mass art or kitsch, Greenberg counterposes the avant-garde as the representative of genuine art. One reason why avant-garde art is capable of performing this role is that it is abstract, rather than representational. And this, in Greenberg's view, constitutes a renunciation of the 'world of common extroverted experience'. Moreover, this notion in Greenberg—which one finds echoed in other formalist opponents of mass art such as Ortega Y Gasset[94] and Clive Bell[95]—that non-representational art divorces work from ordinary experience seems to serve as a code for the conviction that genuine art is disinterested in—and therefore disconnected from—the world of practical affairs, and is, thereby, autonomous.

The reasoning here is hardly sound, but it is illustrative. Greenberg is trying to suggest that abstract, avant-garde art, in virtue of its non-representational explorations, is literally divorced from everyday reality, while implying that art—such as mass art typically is—that traffics in representation is mired in the everyday, which is almost synonymous rhetorically with practical concerns, interests, desires, and purposes. But representation hardly entails a concern with everyday or practical reality, just as the absence of representation does not entail disinterestedness. Greenberg invokes the authority of Kant by emphasizing the importance of disinterestedness, but then attempts to install that notion of disinterestedness in a barely plausible homology—disinterestedness/non-representation :: interestedness/representation. Moreover, this homology, apart from being an implausible generalization to begin with, is unKantian to boot, since Kant suggests no principled reason why a spectator could not, within the Kantian framework, have a disinterested, aesthetic response to a representation—to a watercolour of a landscape, for example.

Of course, by speaking of a disinterested *response*, another problem with Greenberg's use of the Kantian idiom is also sounded. For within the

[94] José Ortega Y Gasset, 'The Dehumanization of Art', in *The Dehumanization of Art and other Essays on Art, Culture and Literature* (Princeton: Princeton University Press, 1968).
[95] Clive Bell, *Art* (New York: Capricorn Books, 1958).

Kantian framework, that which is relevantly disinterested is our response to an object. It is not the object that is disinterested. Somewhere along the line historically, theorists—and Greenberg is not alone in this—transferred the notion of disinterestedness from the spectator to the art object.[96] Moreover, this distortion of Kantian aesthetic theory makes an important difference. For if we construe disinterestedness as a spectator's attention to an object for its own sake, then there is no reason to suspect that a spectator of mass art is not disinterested—that she is not attending to the mass art work for its own sake, rather than for personal gain, or for the purpose of advancing her moral, political, or financial agendas. That is, the interestedness of the object does not preclude that it is an occasion for disinterested attention, or that the pleasure that accrues is for any purpose other than the joy of attending to the object as an end in itself.

It is not my intention here to endorse the notion of disinterestedness as it is defined by Kant. In fact, in many ways, I am not a friend of the concept of disinterestedness. However, the point that I wish to make here is a logical point. If we grant the notion of disinterestedness for the sake of argument, and we note that the locus of this supposed state of disinterestedness is the audience, not the object that gives rise to the state, then I think it is clear that there is no reason to believe the spectator of a work of mass art cannot derive what is called disinterested pleasure from a work of mass art.

'Why', I might ask a fan of the *X-Files*, 'do you applaud the episode entitled "Ice?"' 'Because it was enjoyable,' she might answer. If I press on and ask 'Enjoyable to what end?' then there is no reason to deny that she can respond, in a perfectly intelligible manner—'To no end; watching it is pleasurable in and of itself.' Thus, if one allows that things can be valuable for their own sake (an admittedly controversial issue, one about which I frequently find myself on the side of the sceptics), then nevertheless there does not seem to be any reason, *pace* Greenberg and Adorno, to deny that that state can be an appropriate response to mass art. Thus, though Greenberg invokes the authority of the Kantian notion of disinterestedness in his argument against mass art, he has perverted Kant's idea in using it to promote the avant-garde and to demote mass art.

Of course, one might respond by charging that the fact that Greenberg has shifted the object of disinterestedness is not important, if what he says is true. But it does not seem that what Greenberg claims can be recuperated this way. For, on the one hand, the correlation that he draws between

---

[96] In our discussions, we have seen that Adorno also makes this move. Quite a few other theorists could be added to this list, including Schopenhauer in the nineteenth century and Peter Burger in the twentieth century.

disinterested avant-garde artworks versus interested mass artworks appears historically false when one considers the works of Soviet constructivism (surely politically interested avant-garde works). And, on the other hand, Greenberg has not noticed that even works that he considers interested can give rise to the sort of disinterested response he regards as the genuine value of culture, thereby undercutting the consequentialist considerations that he brings against mass art and kitsch.

Greenberg, like Adorno, uses what he thinks of as genuine art to tell an allegory about how genuine art, hypostasized as a historical agent, resists the encroachment of market value. Mass art, on the other hand, is complicit with market value. But I am suspicious of this sort of historical allegory for several reasons. First, it glosses over too many historical facts. Second, it is hard to imagine all art—all authentic art—as involved in a single, historical project of any sort, especially one as historically specific as resistance to utilitarian value. Indeed, it strikes me as rather sentimental—an attempt to turn all artworks into essentially good objects—to think of everything that we legitimately call art as being redemptive. Not all genuine art is dedicated to saving the world, and the correlation art/good :: commerce/bad smacks of a rationalization on the part of artists and theorists who fear that their social standing is threatened by other elements of the culture. And, finally, there are good reasons to think that history is not an allegory, but that such allegories—of the sort that are often called 'meta-narratives'—inform us more about the tellers of such stories than they do about actual historical processes.

In addition to the concept of disinterestedness, Greenberg appears to rely on the Kantian notion that active spectatorship is an essential ingredient in the genuine aesthetic response. To Kant's conception, however, Greenberg, like many other theorists, adds that it is only works of art that are designed to promote such responses which are art properly so called. Remember the contrast that he draws between Repin and Picasso. Here, I think that Greenberg reveals his revisionist version of Kant by identifying the value in genuine art with its capacity to elicit reflection from the spectator.

And, again departing from Kant, Greenberg correlates genuine art with difficult art, presumably on the grounds that what is difficult will incite the relevant sort of active spectatorship. Thus, since mass art or kitsch can be enjoyed without effort, or with very little effort, Greenberg is dubious about its status as art. He says it involves 'unreflective enjoyment'. Thus, he surmises that it abets passive reception, whereas the kind of reception that Greenberg, perhaps following his understanding of Kant, believes is normatively appropriate to genuine art is active.

Greenberg's stress upon the cultivated spectator's 'reflection upon the immediate impression left by the plastic values' of artworks, of course, calls to mind the Kantian emphasis on contemplation in the aesthetic response. Moreover, it is natural to suppose that the recognition Greenberg speaks of emerges from the play of the spectator's cognitive and perceptual faculties as she contemplates the surface of the painting. But to Greenberg, this sort of active, contemplative interaction is impossible, by definition, in the case of mass art and kitsch.

Yet if Kant believed that the active free play of the faculties is a constituent of the aesthetic response, as noted earlier, Greenberg has upped the ante in his analysis of genuine art. For genuine art by his accounting not only provokes active contemplation. Genuine art does this by being difficult. Genuine art is necessarily difficult; the participatory spectatorship it is designed to activate is demanding. This is a very energetic expansion of a Kantian theme, calling not merely for the active engagement of our mental faculties, but calling for them to be put to hard work.

Yet in Kant there is no suggestion that the active engagement of our faculties involves effort, nor that the object of aesthetic contemplation be difficult. In fact, quite the opposite would appear to be the case. The paradigm of an aesthetic response might be the appreciation of the starry sky at night. For Kant, being in an aesthetic state is as easy as rolling off a log, and, furthermore, it is available to everyone. There is no suggestion in Kant that the authentic aesthetic response requires effort, and certainly no implication that its object be difficult to assimilate. Greenberg has turned the response to aesthetic stimuli into work, thereby conflating a particular American obsession with aesthetic contemplation. But there are no theoretical grounds for this. The active spectatorship that Kant has in mind when he speaks of the play of the understanding and the imagination need not be arduous. Thus, it could not conceivably be a failing of mass art that, since it does not require effort, it does not, therefore, engage active spectatorship.

Greenberg's special variation on the theme of active spectatorship derives—unquestionably in a somewhat perverted form—from a strenuous, in a manner of speaking, misapplication of a central tenet of the *Critique of Judgment*. But in construing the active response of the spectator in terms of effort and difficulty, he loses sight of the degree to which Kant thought that aesthetic pleasure, rooted in the free play of the innate faculties, was available to all with little background and, standardly, without effort. Kant, that is, would not have denied that an artwork could afford aesthetic pleasure without effort. Nor should we, unless we feel compelled, as Greenberg surely did, to bring the Protestant work ethic into the gallery.

Of course, it is an empirical question whether all mass art fails to abet active spectatorship. As I have argued, there are many examples of mass art, such as *Citizen Kane*, that do elicit participatory rather than passive responses on any fair understanding of those concepts. But, at the same time, it is probably also true that a great deal of mass art—by which I mean popular art designed and produced for mass consumption and distributed by mass media—is assimilated without much effort by its consumers. Indeed, it is likely that the function of mass art is to be accessible to maximum audiences with minimum effort. But this is not incompatible with what Kant envisioned as the active aesthetic response. Thus, at the very least, Greenberg's extrapolation of Kant is problematic in so far as it offers no defence of its evident mismatching of a theory—which might pertain to some kinds of artistic activities, such as modernism, and their subtending aesthetic responses—to phenomena of a radically different sort, namely, mass artworks.

Indeed, one suspects that Greenberg's mistake here can be traced to his tailoring of the Kantian notion of active spectatorship to the purposes of avant-garde modernism. Avant-garde modernism may, in fact, mandate that the spectator's response be effortful and that her activity be of a demanding sort. But it is an exaggeration to suppose the kind of active spectatorship, suggested by Kant, be of this variety.

To sum up: Greenberg's argument against mass art seems to me to rest on a presumption, derived from Kant, of the centrality of active contemplation to aesthetic judgements. But there are at least three problems with Greenberg's use of his Kantian inheritance. First, it is not clear that Greenberg's version of active spectatorship corresponds to Kant's. Second, Greenberg, unlike Kant, appears to be talking about the kind of structure that is required to bring about an active response, but Kant is talking about the quality of the percipient's experience, not about the object that gives rise to it. Undoubtedly, Kant would have been loathe to make generalizations about the structure of such objects, since that would suggest the possibility of generalizations (and, thence, rules) about the stimulus that gives rise to the experience of free beauty. And lastly, even if Greenberg could, as he cannot, make out the case for some Kantian-derived theory of modernism, there is no reason to suppose that that theory is relevant when we turn to the very different realm of mass art.

Moreover, the only other available basis for defending Greenberg's view of genuine art, once the authority of Kant is cut out from under Greenberg, appears to be the presumption that art that requires effort is prima facie better than art that does not. But this is false. Art that is arduous may be no better for that; art that is easy can certainly be superior to art that is intentionally difficult. The assertion that art that you have to work for is the best art may, for some, have a morally uplifting ring to it, but I see little hope in establishing that the quality of art varies in proportion to its difficulty.

In this discussion of Greenberg, I think it is evident that he only relies upon extrapolating, perhaps unknowingly, fragments of Kant's aesthetic theory. He does not mobilize the whole architectonic, but only parts of it, parts, indeed, that he distorts. Similarly, Collingwood, MacDonald, Adorno, and Horkheimer also deploy only selected elements of what may be construed as Kantian theory in order to discount mass art.

Collingwood, of course, has a number of charges to lodge against mass art. On the one hand, he worries that mass art may draw away energies more appropriately expended on real life,[97] recalling perhaps the spirit, though not the letter, of Augustine's and Rousseau's criticisms of theatre.[98] And also, with explicit reference to cinema and the wireless, Collingwood fears that amusement art in times of unemployment will become the modern version of *panem et circenses*,[99] thereby recycling one of the most recurrent anxieties about mass culture available in the Western tradition.[100] However, Collingwood's central case against mass art appears to rely upon certain unacknowledged, Kantian-derived biases.

The element of Kant's theory of beauty that seems most relevant to Collingwood, and to MacDonald as well, is the notion that there are no rules for engendering aesthetic experience. For Collingwood (and MacDonald), this idea appears to turn into a conception of the artwork as singular, as not subsumable under a determinate concept, as creating its own aesthetic laws, rather than abiding by fixed laws or formulas. It is some such prejudice that guides Collingwood to hive off craft from art proper, and, in consequence, to disparage mass art as pseudo art. For amusement art, in so far as it is structured in terms of a predetermined plan—such as the formulas of mass art—is subsumable under a determinate concept (for example, the thriller), for a determinate purpose (for example 'tear-jerking'). Collingwood's distinction between art and craft is really a guise for expressing the Kantian-derived intuition that art works be unique. And, of course, once such an intuition is embraced, mass art,

---

[97]   Collingwood, *Principles of Art*, 99.
[98]   See St Augustine, *Confessions*, ed. W. H. D. Rouse (London: Loeb Classics, 1912), 101; and Jean-Jacques Rousseau, 'De inégalité', in *Œuvres complètes*, vol. iii, ed. Bernard Gagnebin and Marcel Raymond (Paris, 1964), 216.   [99]   Collingwood, *Principles of Art*, 102.
[100]   For a history of this recurring motif in our culture, see Patrick Brantlinger, *Bread and Circuses* (Ithaca, New York: Cornell University Press, 1983).

which gravitates toward the formulaic, can only seem to be deviant or pseudo art.

Here, nevertheless, it is important to indicate how alien this way of thinking is to its Kantian inspiration. I have stressed that Kant's theory concerns the experience of free beauty. Free beauty involves the apprehension of a stimulus—like a rolling pasture—without subsuming it under a concept. However, this is not the only kind of experience of beauty that Kant countenances. There is also dependent beauty. An experience of dependent beauty arises when we recognize that something fully realizes its concept. Pictures, for example, are designed to resemble their referents, and when we encounter a picture that shows its referent with striking verisimilitude, we may adjudge it beautiful—in the sense of dependent beauty—because it fulfils the concept of pictorial representation to an exceptional degree. Judgements of dependent beauty are made relative to concepts. Judgements that such and such is good of its kind are judgements of dependent beauty. So Kant does allow that concepts and rules have some relevance when making certain kinds of judgements of beauty.

Of course, Kant also argues that there are judgements of free beauty—judgements without concepts—in addition to judgements of dependent beauty. Judgements of natural beauty are often of this sort, since things like beautiful sunsets do not belong to a genre. In those cases, all we have to go on is our disinterested pleasure. However, Kant does not suppose that judgements of dependent beauty are flawed; they are just different from judgements of free beauty.

Moreover, it seems reasonable to say that Kant thought that many of the typical judgements that we make of artworks will involve judgements of dependent beauty—judgements geared to the kind or genre to which the relevant artwork belongs. Kant does not think that if we experience something in light of the dependent beauty it affords, the object in question is not art. In fact, Kant thinks that with artworks, we will, for the most part, experience them in terms of the genre to which they belong and in terms of the concepts appropriate to that genre. Kant does not hold to the slogan 'art yes; formula no.' Kant does not make the experience of free beauty the litmus test of art. He believes that in some of its aspects, an artwork may afford an experience of free beauty—for example, through the play of line and colour—but the same work is also assessable for Kant in terms of its genre and concept, that is, in terms of the notion of dependent beauty.

So, Collingwood's (and MacDonald's) appropriation of Kant's ideas involve several errors. First, they are applying the theory of free beauty as a criterion of art status. Kant has nothing to say explicitly about this one way or the other, but probably he would not be sympathetic to the idea, since he thinks that artworks in specified genres have concepts and that they can be appreciated in virtue of satisfying those concepts (i.e., in virtue of dependent beauty). Second, when Kant talks about free beauty, he is referring to the judgement of the percipient, not to the object. He says that in cases of free beauty, the percipient does not use a rule under which he may subsume his judgement. This says nothing about whether the object was constructed by means of a rule. And third, Kant agrees that there are artistic genres and formulas and, therefore, would not foreclose the potential art status of a work on the grounds that it belonged to a genre that possessed formulas and rules. Thus, Kant would not, on the basis of the theory that he bequeathed us, deny art status to mass artworks because they are formulaic. Collingwood and MacDonald do, but only by distorting their Kantian heritage.

Collingwood also implicitly invokes Kant by categorizing mass art as utilitarian, as MacDonald does by castigating it as a commodity. Here, it seems as though the Kantian notion of disinterestedness is being cited as the relevant authority. Apparently, if the artwork is utilitarian, then it possesses some extrinsic value, whereas the notion of disinterestedness is supposed to signal that we value the legitimate objects of aesthetic contemplation intrinsically or for their own sake. But, it is charged, the mass art object is not valued for its own sake, but for the sake of amusement or profit. Yet, as we have already seen, there is a *non sequitur* here, since there is no inconsistency involved in supposing that an object that is made for a utilitarian purpose cannot be engaged and appreciated for its own sake.

Collingwood also shares with Greenberg the anxiety that the products of mass art evoke passive rather than aesthetically active spectatorship. This is evident in his invocation of the stimulus/response model in describing our response to amusement art. He writes that 'the gramophone, the cinema and the wireless are perfectly serviceable as vehicles of amusement or of propaganda, for here the audience's function is *merely receptive* and not concreative.'[101] Thus, for Collingwood, not only should mass art be regarded as pseudo art because it is a formulaic craft predicated on utilitarian purposes, but also because it fails to engender the kind of creativity of the aesthetic response upon which the Kantian view putatively places such a premium. However it may be that Collingwood's estimate of what the relevant sort of creativity involves, like Greenberg's, vastly inflates Kant's views about creativity in these matters.

---

[101] Collingwood, *Principles of Art*, 323.

Moreover, and again like Greenberg, Collingwood's theory is ultimately in the service of a certain form of modernist, avant-garde art. His theory is designed to accommodate what is special about the poetics of Pound, Stein, and Joyce. Perhaps this supplies a motive lurking in the background for his expansion of the Kantian notion of free play into the conjecture that aesthetic appreciation involves a notably creative response to an artistic challenge (such as a modernist artwork). That is, Collingwood turns the Kantian aesthetic response into the preferred response for the modernist artwork as part and parcel of his implicit defence of avant-garde poetics.

Collingwood also belies his commitment to modernist aesthetics in his abhorrence of the formulaic, since the ideal of modernism is that the artwork be virtually a genre unto itself—that it be an unprecedented achievement in every respect. That is, the modernist artist aspires to make something utterly original. Thus, Collingwood's rejection of the formulaic is a variation on the modernist imperative to 'make it new'.

Like Collingwood, Adorno, another ardent defender of modernist art, is opposed to the formulaic, repetitive nature of mass art. Indeed, he meta-phorically characterizes the producers of mass art as the 'culture industry'. What for Collingwood was craft has undergone automation. Mass art objects are manufactured according to a plan.[102] And these objects are eternally the same.[103] This offends Adorno's underlying 'Kantian' prejudice on behalf of the unique and the singular. Adorno writes: 'Culture is the perennial pro-testation of the particular against the general.'[104] Moreover, Adorno's central arguments against mass art derive from the undeniably Kantian-inspired notion that genuine art is autonomous, or, at least, it aspires valiantly toward the goal of autonomy and freedom. Adorno's conception of the autonomy or freedom of art, it seems to me, includes two elements, both of them trace-able to Kant by way of intervening distortions.

There are two places where the notion of freedom enters into Kant's characterization of aesthetic judgement. Such judgements are supposed to be disinterested—to be free of practical and rational purposes. When Kant's theory is turned into a theory of art, this notion is transformed into the idea that the realm of art is divorced from other realms of human activity, including the practical, the social, the utilitarian, and the cognitive. The aesthetic realm, that is, is free from interests.

The second place where freedom enters Kant's picture of aesthetic appreciation is in his characterization of the free play of our faculties in response to beautiful stimuli. When Kant's theory is turned into an art

---

[102] Adorno, 'Culture Industry Reconsidered', 12.   [103] Ibid. 14.
[104] Adorno, 'Kultur und Verwaltung', in *Soziologische Schriften 1* (Frankfurt am Main, 1972), 128 as translated by Andreas Huyssen in *New German Critique*, 6 (1975), 6.

theory, this becomes the expectation that the artwork will excite such active free play.

Both these Kantian themes have a role in Adorno's characterization of autonomous art and his correlative dismissal of mass art. Art is autonomous, in the first instance, in so far as it 'dissociates itself from empirical reality and the functional complex that is society'.[105] Indeed, for Adorno, art is not only dissociated from society, but more specifically, it resists society.[106] Thus, in effect, Adorno politicizes the logical point that Kant tried to make about the putative distinction between the aesthetic realm and the practical.

Though Adorno criticizes Kant explicitly for details of the latter's concept of disinterestedness,[107] nevertheless Adorno's ideal of autonomous art remains heavily indebted to it. Moreover, it is specifically this notion of autonomous art that provides Adorno with his fundamental criticism of the culture industry. For the objects of mass art are embedded in the functional complex of society in a number of different, though interrelated ways: they are commodities; they manage the leisure time of consumers; they develop mass taste, including a taste for routinized rhythms that are synchronized to the rhythms of labour; and, most importantly, they render consumers conformists.

This last consequence of mass art, in effect, returns us to the second sense in which mass art is at odds with autonomy. On Kant's conception, aesthetic judgement involves the free play of the faculties which free play, as we have seen, Schiller parlayed into a pre-condition for moral autonomy. Mass art in its formulaic sameness blunts free play and standardizes taste. Presumably, if autonomous art has a role in the evolution of autonomous individuals, mass art, by subverting the free aesthetic response in favour of standardized mass taste, results in conformists rather than autonomous, free individuals.

However, as already observed, there is a problem with the invocation of the free play of the faculties here. Kant thinks that in judgements of free beauty, we respond with the free play of the faculties in the sense that we do not subsume the judgement of particulars under general concepts. However, these judgements are not the primary model of the aesthetic appreciation of artworks which typically, for Kant (and I think most of the rest of us) involves judging works as of a certain kind or genre, and which, therefore, also involves subsuming judgements of particulars under concepts. None of the opponents of mass art explains why judgements of free

---

[105] Adorno, *Aesthetic Theory*, ed. Gretel Adorno and Rolf Tiedemann (New York: Routledge, 1984), 358.   [106] Ibid. 320–2.

[107] Ibid. 14–15.

beauty rather than judgements of dependent beauty should serve as paradigmatic of the aesthetic response to artworks, including works of so-called high art, as well as mass artworks. Nor does Adorno explain why if the problem with mass art is that it encourages judgements of dependent beauty rather than free beauty, that the making of judgements of dependent beauty should be any impediment to the development of autonomous individuals.

Adorno, and theorists like him, may think that there is no call for explanations here because Kant has already established the centrality of the *free* play of the imagination and understanding to the aesthetic response to artworks. But that is simply a misinterpretation of the role that this sort of freedom plays in Kant's theory of taste, just as Adorno's personification of aesthetic disinterestedness into art's eternal resistance to society goes beyond Kant's epistemological point to create nothing less than a mythology of (modernist?) art.

Whether or not Adorno can respond to these criticisms of his appropriation of Kantian themes is not so important to the central point I want to make now, namely, that the interlocking senses of autonomy and freedom that are fundamental to Adorno's theory of genuine art and to his dismissal of mass art are fragments, albeit distorted fragments, of Kantian aesthetic theory. In this, Adorno exemplifies a tendency of other philosophical critics of mass art such as Greenberg, MacDonald, and Collingwood. Each, in turn, uses fragments of the Kantian theory of free beauty to presuppose a theory of art proper. Moreover, once this sort of theory, or parts of it, are enlisted as a framework for analysing mass art, mass art predictably is seen to be problematic in virtue of its very nature—its tendency toward the formulaic, its commitments to entertainment, to predetermined effects, and to easy and accessible consumption.

A major source, then, of philosophy's resistance to mass art is that it is the result of the tendency in Western aesthetics to misconstrue Kant's analysis of free beauty as a theory of art. Among other things, this putative theory identifies the experience of free beauty with the active response to phenomena for their own sake. For Kant, the aesthetic response is a free, spontaneous, cognitively engaged affair that eschews all rules and formulas and that appreciates the stimulus for its uniqueness and particularity, independently of morality and inclination.

Kant, of course, was writing about beauty—especially about our appreciation of natural beauty (comprising things like cherry blossoms and the plumage of peacocks). But what appears to have happened in European aesthetics after Kant is that Kant's account of free beauty—oddly enough, rather than his theory of dependent beauty—came to be regarded as proposing a theory of art and art appreciation. This is, of course, ironic, since, in fact, Kant's account of dependent beauty would appear to offer an account of art as we standardly conceive of it, whereas the account of free beauty does a much better job of tracking some of our typical responses to nature.

The form that this confusion over our Kantian heritage took was to regard artworks, properly so called, as objects and performances that are designed to cause aesthetic experiences in spectators, where aesthetic experiences, in turn, are characterized in the way that Kant characterizes experiences of free beauty. That is, artworks proper are characterized in terms of the capacity to engender in audiences active cognitive experiences of appreciation, marked by freedom, for objects that are not subsumable under formulas, rules, concepts, or purposes and that yield pleasure in the object for its own sake, independently of moral or practical factors.

I have not belaboured the ways in which this is an inadequate theory of art. The point that I wish to emphasize is that if philosophers of art harbour—if only subconsciously—something like this view of art proper, then they will have no way of coming to terms with mass art. They will observe, with some apparent justice, that mass art is formulaic; that, in certain pertinent respects, the response to mass art is easy; that mass art is not autonomous; that mass artworks are not often striking for their uniqueness and particularity; that mass art neither necessarily elicits the Kantian free play of the faculties (in the strictest, most technical sense of that concept), nor does it border on any other realm of freedom; and so on.

Furthermore and consequently, equipped with this misconstrual of Kant and the preceding observations, the philosopher of art is apt to conclude that mass art is not really art at all. Thus, mass art either falls outside the purview of the philosopher of art, or, if mass art becomes an object of theory, then it does so only in so far as the philosopher of art undertakes to explain why mass art is naught but pseudo art.

It is my historical conjecture that this misconstrual of Kant's theory of free beauty explains why so many philosophers of art—including Collingwood, Adorno, Horkheimer, Greenberg, Ortega Y Gasset, Bell, MacDonald, and others—have either ignored mass art or demoted it to the status of pseudo art. Of course, some of the theorists I have just mentioned would argue that they have explicitly departed from Kant in many of their writings. But in response, I claim that in their arguments with respect to mass art, they implicitly revert to the misappropriation of Kantian theory that I have been sketching. That philosophers and theorists from so many different traditions (from phenomenology to marxism) converge on the same mistake should, of course, come as no surprise, since Kant is probably the last philosopher whom the various diverse traditions of Western philosophy share in common.

If my diagnosis is correct, then a major source of the widespread failure of philosophical aesthetics with respect to mass art involves the frequent assumption of a framework—call it the ersatz Kantian theory of art—that is not only a controversial (indeed, I would say discredited) theory of art, but that—more importantly for our purposes—is categorically inhospitable to mass art. For the ersatz Kantian theory of art precludes from the outset the possibility that mass art is art and, therefore, a pressing object of attention for the philosophy of art. The ersatz Kantian theory of art is blind-sided or blinkered when it comes to mass art; it lacks the conceptual resources to characterize the nature of mass art as it is, because its subconscious philosophical conceptual framework was designed to track something else, namely the experience of free beauty.

Thus, my diagnosis of philosophy's resistance to mass art suggests at least one additional criticism of the philosophical tradition that we have been examining—namely, that it persists in using the wrong tool in analysing mass art. Kantian aesthetic theory was not a theory of art, either high or low. It is primarily a theory of free beauty and of the sublime, of our responses to flowers and cascades and the starry sky at night. Kantian aesthetic theory undoubtedly has a number of limited applications to some aspects of our intercourse with art. And as a theory of beauty and the sublime, it is perhaps not entirely implausible, although it is hotly disputed and probably false, though not wildly so.

But when the theory is extrapolated into a general theory of art, it becomes more and more implausible, even if it is nevertheless seductive to those who yearn for a way to distinguish art from everything else. Admittedly, the misappropriation of this theory, or, more accurately, fragments of this theory, has been influential in shaping various art movements that must be understood, in part, in terms of the influence of this theory on them. But the theory hardly suffices to characterize art in general, for the obvious reason that art as we know it is not divorced from the rest of society.

Moreover, there is also a sub-theme to this diagnosis of philosophy's resistance to mass art. For not only are the opponents of mass art reviewed in this chapter, perhaps subconsciously, wedded to fragments of Kantian aesthetic theory. They are also all proponents of various avant-garde or modernist movements. Indeed, they conflate modernist aesthetics with certain distorted fragments of Kantian aesthetic theory—by valorizing the notion of demanding participatory spectatorship. Thus, in effect, they have transformed modernist criteria of accomplishment into the paradigm of art properly so called. That is, theorists like Greenberg, Collingwood, and Adorno, collapse or confuse desiderata appropriate to modernist spectatorship with the less arduous notion of spectatorship suggested by Kant and widely accepted in the tradition. In this they adapt (or distort) Kant for modernist purposes, or, to put it differently, they have cobbled together, maybe subconsciously, a Kantian theory of the avant-garde which they, in turn, mistake for a theory of art properly so called. As a result, one can read their theoretical assault on mass art as a reflection of artworld politics where avant-garde and modernist artists experience the rise of mass art as a threat to their very existence. Theorists like Greenberg, MacDonald, Collingwood, Adorno, and Horkheimer attempt to make that threat disappear, so to speak, by banishing mass art from the artworld, properly so called. In order to do this, they weave together fragments of Kantian aesthetic theory into diverse versions of the aesthetic theory of art. Unfortunately, these theories of art fail as universal theories of art, perhaps because they are so concerned implicitly with valorizing the modernist avant-garde.

Furthermore, if Kantian-derived, aesthetic theories of art ill-suit the analysis of art in general, they are utterly insensitive to the fact of mass art in particular. Fundamental defining features of mass art—for example, that mass art objects be designed so that they are easily accessible—become disqualifying defects under the neo-Kantian (pro avant-garde) dispensation. But, then, let it be said, so much the worse for neo-Kantianism. That it fails to fit the aesthetic facts of mass art is no reason to rule mass art out of bounds.[108]

Progress in developing a theory of mass art will depend on evolving conceptual frameworks that are appropriate to the phenomena, not in denying the phenomena. Alien and/or obsolete frameworks, such as those derived from Kantian aesthetic theory (or Kantian aesthetic theory commingled with or melded into modernism), need to be superseded. In illuminating the grip that the Kantian tradition has exerted on philosophical thinking about mass art, I have intended to take a small step in preparing for that supersedure. In subsequent chapters, I shall try to

---

[108] Here, it might be said that my criticisms amount to the charge that the theorists canvassed in this chapter have advanced an evaluative theory of art as a classificatory theory of art. I think that this claim is uncontroversial, given the way in which the relevant theorists formulate their views. Additionally, one may say that my viewpoint presupposes that a classificatory theory of mass art is possible. That's right. Part of the reason for this presupposition on my part is that it seems to me that there is a great deal of agreement about the extension of the concept of mass art. And in Ch. 3 I will try to redeem my presupposition by showing that we can develop a convincing classificatory theory of mass art that accords with the prevailing consensus about the extension of the concept of mass art.

develop alternative frameworks for coming to terms with the aesthetics of mass art.[109]

[109] Throughout this chapter I have only concentrated on what might be called Kantian objections to mass art. I have done this, in part, because I think that the origin of philosophical resistance to mass art due to our Kantian heritage has been overlooked in discussions of mass art heretofore. However, I freely admit that there are other sources of philosophical resistance to mass art. For example, another notable source of philosophical arguments against mass art might be called Platonic. This involves recycling against mass art many of Plato's arguments against mimetic art, especially drama. These arguments charge that mass art appeals to the emotions, that it traffics in suspect psychological processes like identification, that it is necessarily sensational, that it is wedded to superficial appearances, that it indulges in mindless spectacles, and so on. Rather than summarizing these lines of argumentation here, however, I will take them up in the chapters on mass art and the emotions and on mass art and morality.

2 Philosophical Celebrations of Mass Art: The Minority Tradition

Introduction

Though most of the philosophical attention that has been directed to mass art has been negative, there is a minority tradition for whom mass art promises great things. Two of the leading figures in this tradition are Walter Benjamin and Marshall McLuhan, the subjects of this chapter. I call their responses to mass art *philosophical celebrations*. That these responses are celebratory is demonstrated by the extreme enthusiasm with which Benjamin and McLuhan, respectively, greet the emergence of the age of mechanical reproduction and the electronic future. Moreover, their defences of mass art are philosophical, since they are based upon conceptions of the nature of mass art.[1]

That is, unlike the proponent of such arts who defends mass art by showing that it is being produced by artists of the highest calibre, Benjamin and McLuhan defend mass art by attempting to show that the essential structures of the mass-art media are such that they have the capacity to produce effects of an order such that no one can gainsay their artistic status.

Someone like Gilbert Seldes, in contrast, attempts to show that mass art (or, for him, popular art) is defensible, since some of its practitioners–like Charlie Chaplin, Fanny Brice, Al Jolson, Ring Lardner, George Herriman,

---

[1] In this book, I treat positions on mass art—whether they are celebratory or resistant—as *philosophical*, if they are based on some conception of the nature or essence of mass art, since essences are the sorts of things in which philosophers trade. Of course, not all philosophers are essentialists. But a theoretical concern with essences is philosophical.

and others–are master artists.[2] The implicit assumption here is that where there are master artists, there is genuine art, perhaps even masterpieces. Seldes establishes the credentials of chosen artists by lovingly describing their accomplishments. His case for the genuine artistic status of what he calls the lively arts—his plea that said arts merit serious attention and respect—rests on establishing the existence of undeniable achievement in the entertainment practices in question.[3] He does not argue for the artistic status of the arts in question on conceptual grounds. His approach is, in a manner of speaking, empirical. He says, in effect, that these practices must be art, since they have already produced some artistic masters and masterpieces.

Philosophical defenders of mass art, however, proceed differently. They certify the artistic status of mass art by trying to show that various mass art-forms or media, by their very nature, have the capacity to elicit the kinds of responses—such as active spectatorship or critical reflection—that are thought to be the hallmarks of art. Whereas Seldes makes his argument on behalf of the lively arts on a case-by-case basis, the philosophical defender of mass art focuses on the media and the generic structures of mass art, arguing that they possess, naturally or essentially, the inherent potential to deliver the kind of effects that we associate with genuine art. Their defence of mass art is general or theoretical, where Seldes' defence is primarily dependent on examples.[4] Benjamin and McLuhan try to deduce the defence of mass art from the nature of mass art (or the nature of mass art media); in this, they are philosophical. Seldes, on the other hand, relies on specific case studies; in this, he is a critic rather than a philosopher.

There is much to be said for Seldes' approach. Indeed, I suspect that with respect to cultural debates about whether or not a practice is art, the issue is never really resolved until the practice in question produces either masterpieces or masters. With film, the appearance of works like Griffith's

---

[2] Gilbert Seldes, *The 7 Lively Arts* (New York: Sagamore Press, 1957). This book was originally published in 1924. See also Michael Kammen, *The Lively Arts: Gilbert Seldes and the Transformation of Cultural Criticism in the United States* (New York: Oxford University Press, 1996), especially ch. 3.

[3] For Seldes, achievement is a matter of producing a high degree of pleasure.

[4] I say 'primarily' here, since Seldes sometimes makes certain glancing claims that seem to be theoretical. At one point, for instance, he suggests that the lively arts may be defended on the grounds of a human need for art of the moment, as opposed to high or serious art, which is putatively for the ages. But Seldes never develops this supposed principle, nor is it notably coherent, given other things that he says. For example, he associates his lively arts with levity, and the high arts with seriousness. But this makes no sense when conjoined with what he says about the arts of the moment and art for the ages, since successful topical art can be serious, and enduring art (such as *A Midsummer's Night Dream*) can be marked by levity. Thus, since Seldes never really works out these 'theoretical' suggestions, and since these suggestions do not fit together nicely, I, in the spirit of interpretive charity, prefer to say that Seldes' primary defence of the art he loves is empirical and critical, rooted in cases. For examples of Seldes' 'theoretical suggestions', see the chapter entitled 'Before a Picture by Picasso' in *The 7 Lively Arts*, especially pp. 293–4.

Birth of a Nation and the films of Charlie Chaplin undermined the case against film as art. The empirical/critical approach works by arguing that a practice, like film, obviously can be art, if, in fact, it has produced some work that appears to be great art. However, the empirical/critical approach possesses a glaring limitation, since sceptics about a given practice may always deny that the examples adduced by a critic like Seldes are masterpieces, or even art, for that matter. The philosophical defender of mass art, on the other hand, does not descend into a debate over cases, but bases his argument on the nature, as such, of mass art.

The advantage of the philosophical defence of mass art is that it can bypass debates about particular cases. This advantage is especially important when, historically, one is interested in defending a mass art-form before it has produced any acknowledged masterpieces. For example, this was the only recourse that was available to Hugo Munsterberg, who desired to defend cinema before there were any cinematic masterpieces for him to allude to. And also, where a putative art-form abounds with substandard examples, the philosophical friend of mass art can wave them all aside and concentrate his argumentation on the possibilities of the practice. No number of egregious examples need deter him.

And even where a given medium or art-form has produced what are thought of as acknowledged masterpieces, the philosophical line of defence still has dialectical advantages over the critical approach, since sceptics can always dispute the status of any critical example. Benjamin and McLuhan rarely refer to specific cases of mass art and, instead, presume that a careful inspection of the structures of mass art show that they can produce effects that Benjamin and McLuhan imagine no one would deny are artistic.

A second similarity shared by Benjamin and McLuhan is that their defences of mass art are strongly Hegelian in stamp. If the most important philosophical sources of resistance to mass art appear to be Kantian (or ersatz Kantian), then the most sophisticated philosophical defences of mass art are Hegelian. This is very evident in the case of Benjamin because of his commitment to historical materialism (a derivative form of Hegelianism brought down to earth by Marx). But it is also the case for Marshall McLuhan, whose brief on behalf of the electronic mass media is that they expand consciousness by way of realizing the fullest potentials of the human sensorium.

For Hegel, different historical epochs, and their accompanying levels of consciousness, are emblematized by exemplary modes of art. The architecture of the pre-classic world of China and Egypt stands for the symbolic stage of the development of human consciousness. The sculpture of ancient Greece exemplifies the classic stage. And the poetry, painting, and music of Hegel's own time represented the romantic moment of consciousness. In the same vein, the arts of mechanical reproduction—such as film, photography, and radio—symbolize an emerging proletarian consiousness for Benjamin; while the electronic arts, exemplified most fully by TV signal for McLuhan, a stage of all-inclusive global consciousness whose potential reach is world-wide.

One obvious feature of the Hegelian approach to the philosophy of art is that it is historical. Certain art-forms exemplify certain stages in the development of consciousness for a time, and then things change. Consciousness changes, and the art that externalizes or embodies it changes in concert. Thus, art that is appropriate for one epoch is not necessarily appropriate to another. Art evolves over time. So, the criteria for art (and, presumably, even art status) that are fitting at one point in history, may not be appropriate at a later point in history.

Moreover, this feature of Hegelian aesthetics provides the celebrant of mass art with a strategic advantage in debates with many of the opponents of mass art. For many who criticize mass art do so from the perspective of more traditional art-forms and aesthetic theories. Mass art is not like previous art, and so the enemies of mass art argue that it is not art at all. However, a Hegelian art theorist does not presume that art is static. Art may change from epoch to epoch, and consequently, the Hegelian might contend, one should not assume that the criteria appropriate to earlier art-forms or the criteria developed by earlier theories of art are suitable for art of succeeding epochs. Furthermore, celebrants of mass art can exploit this Hegelian insight in order to argue that mass art is such a new form of art, an art-form for a new epoch, and, therefore, an art-form whose measure is not to be taken in the terms set out by previous artistic practice or by traditional artistic theories (such as ersatz Kantianism).

Because the Hegelian philosophical framework is historical in a way that allows that art may mutate over time, it is particularly attractive to the friends of mass art. It enables them to defend mass art on the grounds that it is the art (properly so called) of a new historical epoch—an art that emblematizes that epoch and its forms of consciousness—and, therefore, mass art is not to be foresworn simply because it does not accord with the criteria of art appropriate to previous practices and theories of art. Thus, it should come as no surprise that the most sophisticated philosophical attempts to defend mass art are Hegelian in their fundamental conception. But whether that fundamental conception is up to the task that Benjamin and McLuhan intend for it remains to be seen.

Walter Benjamin and the work of art in the age of mechanical reproduction

Mass art often suffers in the estimations of philosophers of art who approach it with theories calibrated to accommodate other forms of art. Thus, it is virtually predictable that mass art comes off badly when assessed by the lights of theories designed to illuminate other, often more traditional, types of art. Perhaps, then, it should be equally unsurprising that one way in which to defend mass art is to deny that the essence of art is fixed for all time, and to hold, instead, that art changes or evolves in such a way that art that is suitable for one epoch is not necessarily suitable for succeeding epochs. On this sort of (neo-Hegelian) approach, it may be argued that mass art is the art of a new historical era and that the fact that it does not abide by the standards and criteria of past art in nowise compromises its status as art.

For mass art represents a new form of art, one that is intimately related to the epoch in which it emerges as, for example, either a reflection of the times and/or as a causal ingredient in the distinctive spririt of age. 'The Work of Art in the Age of Its Technical Reproducibility'—or, as it is more frequently called, 'The Work of Art in the Age of Mechanical Reproduction'—by Walter Benjamin is probably the most sophisticated example that has ever been proposed of this type of defence of mass art—or, at least, of a defence of certain possibilities that are thought to be inherent in mass art.[5]

Benjamin's essay is notoriously difficult to understand. One reason for this is that, although Benjamin alludes to many of his central presuppositions, he often fails to spell them out explicitly. The most important of these unstated presuppositions, I think, is his philosophical commitment to a materialist conception of history. Since his case for the salutary prospects of mass art depends upon an argument about historical evolution, Benjamin needs a conception of the historical process in order to afford himself a framework for explicating the significance of and for assessing historical developments. And it is the materialist conception of history, I contend, that provides him with the requisite framework.[6]

[5] Walter Benjamin, 'The Work of Art in the Age of Mechanical Reproduction', trans. Harry Zorn, in *Illuminations*, ed. Hannah Arendt (New York: Schocken Books, 1969), 217–52.

[6] I am not the first person to associate Benjamin's essay with the materialist conception of history— Brecht called the essay a 'frightful' adaptation of this view. But, although I don't share Brecht's evaluation of the essay as frightful in any way, I think Brecht detected its philosophical leanings with x-ray accuracy. See Bertolt Brecht, *Arbeitsjournal*, vol. i, ed. Werner Hecht (Frankfurt: Surkamp, 1973), 16.

Consequently, given the importance of the materialist conception of history to Benjamin's argument, it is useful to begin the discussion of his argument in a way that Benjamin does not—that is, by sketching out the philosophy of history that is so material to Benjamin's defence of mass art.[7]

The materialist conception of history is a philosophical view of the basic laws of historical change. It was suggested by Marx and Engels[8] and refined by theorists like Plekhanov.[9] As is well known, it is Hegelian in origin, but instead of regarding the expansion of consciousness as the key to historical development, it regards the expansion of the forces of production as the fundamental agency of historical change. In this sense, it is a form of technological determinism, and, although it is most frequently associated with marxism, it is logically possible to assent to it without being a card-carrying communist.[10]

The materialist conception of history is an attempt to identify what might be called 'the motor' of history—that ensemble of forces that is causally responsible for mutations in every other dimension of the social fabric. According to the orthodox materialist conception of history—or, as it is sometimes called, 'historical materialism'—society is comprised of superstructural elements (ideology, art, religion, law, philosophy, and so on), production relations (the division of labour, the distribution of wealth and property rights, etc.), and productive forces (resources, both natural and human [physical and intellectual], raw materials, and technologies).[11]

[7] The philosophy of history that I will be associating with Benjamin's 'The Work of Art in the Age of Mechanical Reproduction' will be roughly the standard or orthodox account of historical materialism of the marxist variety rather than the theory of history that Benjamin suggests in his essay 'Theses on the Philosophy of History'. My reasons for proceeding in this manner are threefold: first, the 'Theses on the Philosophy of History' were written after 'The Work of Art in the Age of Mechanical Reproduction', *and* second, commentators such as Rolf Tiedemann and Gershom Scholem regard 'Theses on the Philosophy of History' as a departure from his earlier views as a result of the shock of the Hitler–Stalin pact, and third, the standard version of the materialist conception of history fits 'The Work of Art in the Age of Mechanical Reproduction' especially well, i.e., it meshes more neatly with the essay on mass art than does 'Theses on History'.

See Rolf Tiedemann, 'Historical Materialism or Political Messianism: An Interpretation of the Theses "On a Concept of History,"' in *Benjamin: Philosophy, Aesthetics, History*, ed. Gary Smith (Chicago: University of Chicago Press, 1983), 175–209.

[8] Karl Marx, *A Contribution to the Critique of Political Economy* (New York: International Publishers, 1970), 20–2; id. and Friedrich Engels, *The German Ideology* (New York: International Publishers, 1947), 6–43.

[9] Georgi Plekhanov, *The Materialist Conception of History* (New York: 1940). The most sophisticated recent presentation of this view may be found in G. A. Cohen, *Karl Marx's Theory of History: A Defence* (Princeton: Princeton University Press, 1978).

[10] Francis Fukuyama is a recent example of this possibility.

[11] Things, of course, are not as neat as this thumb-nail sketch suggests. There are important debates about which factors of society belong to which strata. Does the law, for example, count as a super-structural element, or should it be categorized along with the productive relations? However, for our purposes, I think that these debates can be ignored, since I am not aware of any theorist who would wish to propose that art is not a constituent of the superstructure of society.

Futhermore, the orthodox historical materialist claims to discern certain lawful relations between these features of society of which the most important law is that the influence of the productive forces is the predominant determining factor motivating social change.

That is, if we conceive of society as a three-tiered structure—with the superstructure on the top, the productive forces on the bottom, and the productive relations in the middle—then, according to orthodox historical materialism, the primary vector of social determination is from the bottom up. The superstructure and the relations of production take their shape in response to the developmental directions opened up by the productive forces. This is not to say that the superstructure and the organization of production relations never exert downward pressure on the productive forces, but only that the most significant line of historical causation goes from the bottom up. In any given society, the productive forces are, it is said, always the agents of social change in the last instance.

In order to get a concrete sense of this conception of history, consider the account it offers of medieval society. The productive base of medieval society was agricultural, with little technology. It was labour intensive. However, the fruits of this intensive labour could be expropriated or destroyed by alien invasion. As a result, a certain form of the division of labour—between a warrior class, on the one hand, and the peasantry, on the other—developed, which was predicated on the need for defence against alien incursions. The feudal system evolved, distributing proprietary rights and responsibilities with an eye toward supporting the central elements in this system of defence—mounted, heavily armoured horsemen (knights). Maintaining warriors of this sort was an expensive proposition, and the feudal system was a social instrument for fielding armoured cavalry. That is, feudal lords were allotted the services of serfs to provide them with the wherewithal to maintain themselves in a constant state of military preparedness.

Social relations, with knights (aristocrats) on the top and peasants on the bottom, were extremely hierarchical and rigorously enforced in the Middle Ages. At the level of the superstructure, religion reinforced this set of arrangements by preaching subservience, urging that everyone stay in their place in the social system. Thus, the peasants were encouraged to stay on the land, producing for the military in the name of both God and the sanctified order of his universe. And art, in this social context, served the purposes of religion—teaching the virtues that were conducive to the survival of the system, projecting a picture of the existing hierarchical order of social life on to a cosmic plane. Thus, at one point in the evolution of the feudal system, the ideology, religion, art, and laws of the system all conspired to make the system an ideally functioning whole.

Initially, this arrangement of the relation of the productive forces and the superstructure served to maximize the productive capacity of the economic base of society. The productive relations and the superstructure, so to speak, suited each other. They were, in general, synchronized. However, the historical materialist notes that the historical process is not static. As the productive powers of society are amplified under the pressure, for example, of constantly growing populations, new productive capacities emerge. With respect to feudalism, this involved the development of new industrial techniques, the discovery of new resources, and the emergence of new opportunities for trade.

These changes in the productive forces, in turn, called forth new forms of productive relations, including, most importantly, the nascent bourgeoisie, which spearheaded a new set of social relations called capitalism. But with the evolution of capitalism, superstructural elements of the feudal system—such as laws against usury, laws tying peasants to the lands, laws prohibiting the nobility from engaging in financial transactions, and so on—began to become obsolete, in the sense that they no longer abetted the smooth functioning of the newly available, emerging productive forces of society in the most efficient manner.

That is, as a marxist might put it, the ideology and the social arrangements in feudal society began to 'contradict' the economic base—began to stand in the way of (and, thereby, come into conflict with) the industrial potential of the productive base of society, which gravitated inexorably toward increased growth.

Notice that in this case, the higher tiers of society—the superstructure and productive relations—lagged behind the growth of the productive forces. Moreover, this lag exerted a downward pressure on the growth of the productive forces of society. In this respect, the superstructure and the arrangement of productive relations resist (or contradict) the expansion of the forces of production. Indeed, things like usury laws, inasmuch as they impede the development of banking, can be said to have shackled the development of the forces of production. The relations of production under feudalism, which valorized the artistocracy (the *ancien régime*), was out of step with the economic reality of capitalism, wherein the bourgeoisie is the dominant social class. According to the historical materialist, it finally took the French Revolution to redress this misalignment between the productive forces and social relations.

On the materialist conception of history, society naturally inclines in the long run toward the optimal synchronization of the forces of production, the relationships of production and the superstructure. However, this constellation of factors never remains stable because the productive forces are always changing. Specifically, they are always expanding, due to constant pressure of population increases. Moreover, the historical materialist maintains that the productive forces never return to lower levels of production because once humans experience more, they will never again be satisfied with less. Thus, there is a consistent pressure on the superstructure and productive relations to adapt eventually to the expansion of the productive forces. And where the superstructure and the productive relations of a given society resist adaptation—where they fetter the forces of production—they will inevitably be swept away and replaced by new social forms, ones more favourable to the expansion of productivity.

Typically, forms of social relations, the distribution of wealth, and the ideologies that were suitable to earlier developments of the productive capacities of society gradually come no longer to enhance economic growth, but eventually even come to impede it. Art, religion, law, and philosophy, which at one time served the function of facilitating the efficient running of the productive base of society, come to shackle or to contradict the means of production, as do archaic forms of social relations, such as the dominance of the bourgeoisie by the nobility prior to the French Revolution. And yet the growth of the productive powers of society is a constant that can never be stopped. It is inevitable. In time, it will overturn all resistance from other sectors of society, both at the level of the superstructure and at the level of social relations. The most dramatic way in which this occurs is through revolutions, like the French Revolution, in which aristocratic social relations broke apart due to the ascendency of the bourgeoisie in such a way that the engine of capitalism could be thrown into full throttle.

But, as is well known, the marxist historical materialist goes on to say that, though the triumph of bourgeois social relations and bourgeois ideology initially facilitated the development of the productive forces of society through capitalism, circumstances have reached a point where it is claimed that the bourgeoisie and the entire set of capitalist social relations and ideologies have come to fetter the productive forces of society. That is, capitalism with its abiding concept of the private ownership of the means of production is now thought to shackle the productive capacities of the economic base.[12]

Along with the development of new technologies—which enhance the productive powers of the economic base of society—a new industrial class,

---

[12] And this fettering of the forces of production, due to private ownership, will only be overcome, the marxist avers, by the socialization of ownership of the means of production.

the proletariat, has arisen, which class is best suited to facilitate the expansion of the productive forces of society, ultimately through the socialization of the means of production. The rise to power of the bourgeoisie becomes an impediment to the expansion of the industrial forces initially unleashed by capitalism, just as feudal productive relations were at odds with the relations most suitable to the capitalist exploitation of the productive base. Nevertheless, the vector of history is always, necessarily toward the expansion of the productive forces. So, the historical materialist predicts that capitalism and the proletariat are on a collision course—guaranteeing the revolution (peaceful or otherwise) of the proletariat—which revolution, in the long run, must redound to the favour of the proletariat just because it is on the side of the expansion of the productive forces, or, as it is sometimes said, 'on the side of history'.

The best way to understand Benjamin's essay 'The Work of Art in the Age of Mechanical Reproduction' is to see it as an attempt to situate the development of film and photography—along with printing and radio—as part and parcel of the process of historical process just sketched.

It would appear that Benjamin believes that art and the philosophies of art developed within the context of feudal and bourgeois social formations have lagged behind the productive capacities of the economic base of society. The expansion of the productive capacities of society brings about a new form of art, one that grows out of and that also facilitates the emerging economic base. This new type of art—including photography, film, and radio—is one with the emerging technologies of the productive forces in that this new art is itself technological. It is art that is reproducible on a mass scale. It is the art of the era of mass production which is itself mass produced.

Just as forms of private ownership will and must be replaced by social ownership, if the productive capabilities of modern industry are to expand unfettered, and just as the proletariat must supersede the bourgeoisie, so new forms of art—forms in greater concord with the new potentials of the productive forces than earlier art—must and will emerge. This new art, whose essential or defining characteristic, according to Benjamin, is mass reproducibility, has film and photography as paradigmatic examples. These art-forms are literally the product of new developments in the productive forces of society; they are literally new technologies.

Moreover, they are suited to the newly emerging social formation—mass society—for obviously they are mass reproducible. And, furthermore, because of their mass reproducibility and their internal technical structures, they can function in a way that both expresses and promotes the ethos of the new culture of the proletariat.

The mechanical arts realign art's function with respect to the relation of the superstructure to the expanding vector of development of the economic base and to the coincident evolution of proletarian productive relations. Art becomes transformed in a way that facilitates the proletarian reconception of productive social relations, which, in turn, facilitates the expansion of productive forces. (This transformation in art is heralded, to a certain extent, by developments in avant-garde art. The experiments of Dada, for example, are said to presage montage shock,[13] while Brechtian acting techniques anticipate the alienating, 'testable' character of film acting.[14] But such avant-garde effects await full realization in the arts of mechanical reproduction.)

Putatively, in Benjamin's view, the arts of mechanical reproduction possess certain features which enable them to implement the ethos of the proletariat. Purportedly, inherent to the nature of such art are certain features, including: 1. a specific kind of critical detachment; 2. an anti-traditional (indeed, a tradition-uprooting) bias; 3. a tendency to get close to and penetrate social reality (rather than to contemplate it); and 4. a tendency toward serving mass political ends—such as galvanizing concerted mass criticism on the part of a united audience—as a function of its mass reproducibility.

Mass reproducible art is radically different from the kind of art that has preceded it, as one would expect, given a materialist conception of history. For a historical materialist, like Benjamin, art is not thought of as something transhistorical. Mass reproducibility changes the structure of art. Each age evolves a different sort of art relative to its productive forces, since changes in the productive forces inevitably bring about changes in its historical relations to the ideological superstructure of society and to the existing social relations of the productive forces of the relevant epoch. Thus, in order to appreciate that which is new and significant about the art of mechanical reproduction, one must contrast it with the kind of art that preceded it, i.e., to the art that corresponded to earlier stages in the development of productive relations and productive forces.

According to Benjamin, one can describe the art that precedes mass art as auratic, contemplative, and cultic-traditional art. Mass art, in contradistinction, is putatively critical, penetrating, and anti-traditional. Whereas auratic art is marked by the presence of the original artwork to the percipient and by the attitude of aesthetic distance that the percipient takes toward the art object, in the case of mass art, the artwork (for

---

[13] Benjamin, 'The Work of Art in the Age of Mechanical Reproduction,' 237–8.
[14] Ibid. 246. n. 10.

example, in the case of a photographic reproduction of Rembrandt's *Night Watch*) is absent from the percipient; while Benjamin also contends that our characteristic posture to the artwork is to get closer to both it and what it represents, rather than to stand off, aesthetically distanced. Whereas auratic art is prized for its uniqueness, mass art, according to Benjamin, is by definition not unique, but mass produced (or reproduced). Such art is not fetishized in virtue of its uniqueness, just because it is mass reproducible.

Undoubtedly these contrasts are somewhat obscure. So let us work our way through the terms of Benjamin's analysis slowly. Benjamin maintains that before the era of technical reproduction, artworks had 'aura'. This aura is a function of several features. First, art was embedded in rituals, such as regional processions in honour of a local saint, and, therefore, was often situated in a definite geographical location. Moreover, as part of a specifically situated ritual with a definite location in space, the art object was unique. People travelled to see it. Being in the presence of the artwork—partaking of its aura was crucial—since the art object was a hierophany. Moreover, one stood back from the art object, perhaps in awe, and contemplated it from a distance.

Furthermore, if this describes features of the artwork in theocratic cultures, it is also the case that many of these attributes were carried over to secular art in the centuries during the Renaissance and after. If originally artworks were worshipped as hierophanies, secular high art becomes a virtual object of worship in itself—a 'religion' of art develops, the silence and serenity of the museum calling to mind that of the cathedral. Moreover, such high art continues to be prized for its uniqueness as a product of the hand of genius. People still travel to places like the Louvre and the Prado in order to be in the presence of the great artworks. And once there, they adopt the stance called aesthetic distance or contemplation.

But with the rise of mass industrialization, a new sort of art appears which no longer possesses an aura, since it is not religious in content, nor is it part of a ritual, nor is it aesthetically unique, since by its very nature it is involved with multiple, identical, reproducible copies of the same object. Industrially mass produced, the new art can be distributed everywhere. It is not bound to a unique spatial location. People no longer have to travel to see it. It can be delivered anywhere and everywhere. Art, in the age of mechanical reproduction, can be brought to the spectator, rather than vice versa, and by taking artworks out of unique ritual and cultic contexts, the aura of the artwork as such is further diminished.

This process especially undermines the impression of the auratic *presence* of the original artwork of previous periods, since copies of it, in the form of mass produced photographic reproductions, can circulate around the world, thereby enabling consumers to appreciate the object in its absence, sans auratic presence.

Likewise, where the auratic art object commands contemplative distance, the mass art object beckons us closer both to it and to whatever it represents (for example, the cinematic close-up). It does not attempt to absorb the percipient in the manner of religious or quasi-religious art or 'aesthetic' art, but encourages a critical stance at the same time that it invites us to take up a closer, penetrating point of view, ostensibly both to it and to whatever it represents.

Benjamin attempts to substantiate some of these claims about art in the age of mechanical reproduction by considering some of the devices of the emerging cinema, particularly as it was practised and theorized by Soviet film-makers. For example, comparing the painter with the film-maker, Benjamin claims that if 'the painter maintains in his work a natural distance from reality, the cameraman penetrates deeply into its web.'[15] Here Benjamin has in mind film-editing in general and the close-up in particular, which techniques, Benjamin, like the Russian film-maker and theoretician Dziga Vertov, associates with an epistemic stance that is inherent in the film medium—namely, a tendency to penetrate reality. This stance is also in evidence in other film devices, such as fast and slow motion, that enable us to see aspects of the world that are unavailable to the naked eye. Moreover, the epistemic attitude here is different from one taken toward auratic art, where one is distanced from the object of attention. In film, one is brought closer to the object putatively for the purpose of analysing it. The attitude inscribed in cinema is penetrative and analytic, not worshipfully distanced.

Benjamin believes that 'the mode of human sense perception changes with humanity's entire mode of existence'.[16] The introduction of new media participates in this transformation of human perception, not only by expressing or emblematizing it, but by encouraging its evolution. In this regard, artworks may serve as ideals symbolizing the direction that perception is taking while, at the same time, abetting the development of perception along unprecedented lines by providing opportunities for spectators to engender a foretaste of new or evolving forms of perception through trying on those forms in so far as said modes of perception are inscribed in emerging media. For example, perception in the modern age

---

[15] Benjamin, 'The Work of Art in the Age of Mechanical Reproduction', 233.
[16] Ibid. 222.

of psychoanalysis is putativley more attuned to pay attention to the small movements—the slips and gestures that make up the psychopathology of everyday life—and the cinema both expresses and celebrates this supposedly new awareness of the micro-mechanics of meaning, while also, so to speak, training the audience by means of close-ups to be attentive to the meaning of small, putatively 'unconscious' movements, like agitated fingers.[17] That is, for Benjamin, film is both an emblem of and an implementation of a new form of vision. It both symbolizes the transformation of perception and helps bring it about.

In fact, Benjamin believes that the film medium comes with a built-in critical stance. Part of his reason for this involves his interpretation of editing and other cinematic devices (such as the close-up and time-lapse photography) as essentially penetrative and analytic. But he also believes that the conditions of film-acting are such that the viewer is not drawn into the performance but stands ouside it critically.

Benjamin writes:

The artistic performance of a stage actor is definitely presented to the public by the actor in person; that of the screen actor, however, is presented by a camera, with twofold consequence. The camera that presents the performance of the film actor to the public need not respect the performance as an integral whole. Guided by the cameraman, the camera continually changes its position with respect to the performance. The sequence of positional views which the editor composes from the material supplied him constitutes the completed film. It comprises certain factors of movement which are in reality those of the camera, not to mention special camera angles, close-ups, etc. Hence, the performance of the actor is subjected to a series of optical tests. This is the first consequence of the fact that the actor's performance is presented by means of a camera. Also, the film actor lacks the opporunity of the stage actor to adjust to the audience during his performance, since he does not present his performance to the audience in person. This permits the audience to take the position of a critic, without experiencing any personal contact with the actor. The audience's identification with the actor is really an identification with the camera. Consequently the audience takes the position of the camera; its approach is that of testing. This is not the approach to which cult values may be exposed.[18]

Whether the camera engenders such a critical, virtually 'Brechtian' stance and whether the kind of criticism this might involve is unambiguously the sort of critical stance ideally relevant to working-class consciousness are controversial claims that I, at least, regard rather sceptically. Nevertheless, however strained Benjamin's analysis here appears, what is

---

[17] Benjamin explicitly analogizes 'filmic peception' with the Freudian analysis of parapraxes, ibid. 235.   [18] Ibid. 228–9.

clear is the theoretical work that Benjamin intends this notion of criticism to do in his account of mass art. Just as the penetrative and analytic techniques of film-editing both symbolize and are propaedeutic to the kind of perception that suits the emerging proletarian epoch, so film-acting engenders the kind of critical stance on the part of the spectator that emblematizes, and that will, in part, help to constitute a new way of seeing, one that is both reflective and productive of the formation of the new social order that historical materialism predicts.

In addition to the penetrative, analytical, and critical modes of perception expressed and engendered by arts of mechanical reproduction like film, Benjamin also commends the new media for their capacity to encourage distraction. Distraction, of course, contrasts with the characteristic mode of attention promoted by auratic art which involves modalities like concentration, worship, contemplation, and absorption.

Benjamin's concept of distraction is difficult to understand. It appears to involve at least two different things. On the one hand, it seems to refer to incidental attention.[19] For example, it is often said that people watch TV in a distracted manner. We do not gaze at the screen intently but glance at it, letting our attention wander, following TV programmes out of the corner of our eye, often while thinking about or doing other things. Of course, Benjamin was not writing about TV, but nevertheless he seems to have thought that our attention to film and perhaps radio also possessed the distractable quality that we now associate with TV.

Moreover, this distractability is noteworthy for him because it indicates that we are not in the thrall of mass-reproducible art as we are with auratic art, and, therefore, the room for critical disassociation with the mass art object is a greater possibility with mass art than with auratic art. That is, if the audience for mass art is absent-minded, rather than enveloped in contemplative rapture, it is in a better position to criticize the art object and whatever the art object represents. Thus, *contra* Adorno, Benjamin does not think that the audience is suborned by mass art, but rather that it enjoys a variety of critical detachment that is somehow built into mass media.[20]

On the other hand, Benjamin also thinks of distraction in terms of shock. Editing devices, such as montage, deal shocks to the audience.

---

[19] Benjamin, 'The Work of Art in the Age of Mechanical Reproduction', 240.

[20] The relevant sort of detachment here should not be confused with the disinterested attention often associated with auratic art. Disinterested attention is supposed to be focused on the object, albeit unconcerned with practical affairs. Distracted detachment, on the other hand, refers to a tendency to lose focus on the object intermittently. Disinterested attention is absorbed in the auratic art-work. But with distracted detachment, that sort of obsessive absorption is relaxed.

This, of course, is how Sergei Eisenstein once characterized the effects of montage. And, like Eisenstein, Benjamin also applauds this putative effect on the grounds that it possesses the capacity to focus the mind. Perhaps there is some notion of the subversion of expectations in the background here. But, in any case, editing, again *contra* Adorno, is thought to encourage active spectatorship—through shock, according to the Eisenstein/Benjamin line—and by galvanizing the mind, it opens the possibility of criticism. Benjamin says, reminding us of Brecht, that 'the film makes the cult value recede . . . by putting the public in the position of a critic. . . '.[21]

Though distraction in both the sense of incidental attention and shock cancels the contemplative response toward auratic art, these two senses of distraction appear to pull in opposite directions—one in which the mind is unfocused, or lazily focused, and the other in which it is concentrated. However, I think there may be no contradiction here inasmuch as Benjamin may be thinking of these different mental postures as occurring sequentially—i.e., as stages of the state of distraction he has in mind. With film, our attention is intermittent (distracted in the first sense), but one recurrent oscillation in this pattern is to be riveted by the shocks projected by cinematic structures like montage (distraction in the second sense). Moreover, both the detachment afforded by incidental attention and the mobilization of the mind in response to montage shocks encourage a critical stance, albeit in different modes and in different ways.

The forms of distraction manifested in mass-reproducible arts like the film both reflect the new industrial order and hasten its emergence by engendering new forms of perception. Aesthetic distraction reflects the environment of emerging industrial-*urban* society in that perception in the city is both distracted (the incidental, glancing attention of the *flâneur* being the apotheosis of this tendency) and constantly punctuated by shocks.[22] But in so far as this mandated mode of attention is also critical, it encourages the development of a mode of perception that is appropriate to the new, emerging industrial order. In addition to being distracted, this mode of perception is critical, penetrating, and analytic.

This mode of perception is an ideal that, according to historical materialism, modern consciousness—and most particularly proletarian consciousness as the most representative form of modern consciousness (i.e., the consciousness of a universal class)—aspires toward, and that aspiration is facilitated by new art forms, like film and photography, which have critical, penetrating, and analytic spectatorial responses built into

[21] Benjamin, 'The Work of Art in the Age of Mechanical Reproduction', 240.
[22] Ibid. 250.

their very nature. Thus, film and photography, among other arts of mass reproducibility, symbolize, while also helping to bring into existence, the kind of consciousness that is maximally consilient with expanding powers of the productive base of society. That is, film and photography are both emblems and agents of historical change.

Commenting on Benjamin, Joel Snyder writes:

> Benjamin wants to assert this: new methods of production engender new means of depiction because they bring about specifiable changes in the perception of the world. Art itself is intimately involved with the expression of perception. In a period of technical, industrial production in which the work of the hand is given over to the machine, the character of human perception—at least the perception of those who maintain and run the machines—the workers—changes in accord with the manner of production. Technical production brings about technically informed perception that, in turn, engenders technical depiction or reproduction. The standard for judging technically manufactured art cannot be the same standard used to judge manually produced art since the latter is derived from non-technically informed perception. This means that a film or a still photograph cannot be properly understood and evaluated by falling back onto the sense perception that characterized the pre-technical period. It demands a new standard and finds it in the revolutionary masses whose 'sense of reality' is in the process of being adjusted to the new means of technical production.[23]

Moreover, as we have seen, for Benjamin this new form of technical perception has an inherent critical dimension which, in turn, enables those possessed of it to realize better the potential of the new and still emerging technological order.

This view of mass art, articulated through the optic of historical materialism, provides Benjamin with two ways in which to defend mass art. The first way is fairly explicit in the text. Mass art is defensible because it is on the side of history. In participating in the transformation of perception—by both symbolizing it and facilitating it—mass art participates in the proletarian revolution and, thereby, ultimately participates in unleashing productive forces of society. Moreover, the capacity to participate in the transformation of perception, which is the relevant emancipatory potential of mass art for Benjamin, is immanent in mass art-forms like film with its inherent capacity for shock and for engendering critical consciousness. Thus, the arts of mechanical reproduction are defensible because they are *essentially* on the side of history.

Benjamin, of course, does not think that each and every artwork is

---

[23] Joel Snyder, 'Benjamin on Reproducibility and Aura: A Reading of "The Work of Art in the Age of its Technical Reproducibility"', in *Benjamin: Philosophy, Aesthetics, History*, ed. Gary Smith (Chicago: University of Chicago Press, 1989), 159–60.

emancipatory in this way. Individual works of mass art may be reactionary, and Benjamin points to the ways in which fascism can pervert the natural tendencies of mass art.[24] His position, rather, is that, on the whole, the mass arts of the age of mechanical reproduction are on the side of human emancipation—on the side of releasing the productive forces of society—both as emblems and facilitators of emancipation that herald a new mode of perception, one that is revolutionary—i.e., on the side of the proletariat in their role of liberators of the forces of production. It is the *telos* of mass media—in virtue of certain of its inherent features—that is emancipatory, rather than individual mass artworks.

But there is also another way of interpreting Benjamin's argument on behalf of mass art—a way that is perhaps only implicit in the text. In the last chapter, we noted that a great deal of philosophy's resistance to mass art can be attributed to a sort of residual Kantianism, which I called the ersatz Kantian theory of art. It is interesting to consider Benjamin's essay on art in the age of technical reproduction as a response to this species of philosophical resistance to mass art, since one might quite easily construe what Benjamin regards as auratic art as representing what under the influence of the ersatz Kantian theory (or fragments thereof) opponents of mass art regard as art properly so called. That art, ersatz-Kantian art, like auratic art, is marked by its uniqueness, its premium on the presence of the artwork to the percipient, and its call for contemplation. But, according to Benjamin, that is art whose time has past. It may be, as some commentators suggest, that Benjamin shows some nostalgia for auratic (or ersatz-Kantian) art, but he nevertheless acknowledges that history has passed it by.

Furthermore, Benjamin is arguing that art changes with the times and, presumably, that the theories of art based upon past conceptions of art are irrelevant to the new art. Thus, mass art is not to be assessed by defunct theories of art. That mass art cannot be comprehended by the theories appropriate to talking about auratic art does not show that mass art is not art. For it is art of a new sort, art that calls for new theories (theories, one supposes, like Benjamin's). So much, it seems to me, is implicit in Benjamin's extended contrast between auratic art and mass art, especially since the description of auratic art uses terminology that is strikingly Kantian with its emphases on distance, uniqueness, and so on.

So, then, Benjamin appears to defend mass art in at least two related ways. First, mass art contributes to historical progress both as an emblem

---

[24] Benjamin, 'The Work of Art in the Age of Mechanical Reproduction', 243–4. Samuel Weber points out that Benjamin holds that fascism offers the masses self-expression by allowing 'the mass to look itself in the face'. Samuel Weber, *Mass Mediauras* (Stanford, Calif.: Stanford University Press, 1996), 102.

and an exercise in the sort of technical (proletarian), emancipatory vision/consciousness that will release the productive forces—indeed, mass art is partially constitutive of the relevant evolving transformation of perception and consciousness. Second, since mass art is a new form of art, it cannot be measured by the standards of past artistic theories—such as the ersatz Kantian theory of art—but, rather, it calls for new forms of theorization. For historical reasons—since art mutates with the transformation of the productive base of society, all criticisms of mass art in terms of auratic or 'Kantian' categories (of the sort we encountered in the previous chapter) are conceptually inapposite, or even category errors.

Both these defences of mass art depend on the materialist conception of history, though with varying degrees of specificity. The first variation buys into a pretty substantial commitment concerning proletarian emancipation, whereas the second variation need only be committed to the view that features of the social superstructure, like art, change in response to seismic changes in the forces of material production.

These arguments may be called 'the progress argument' and the 'new art argument' respectively. They may be expressed, semi-formally, in the following ways. First, the progress argument:

1. If any art contributes to the expansion of the productive forces (call this progress), then it contributes to human emancipation. (This is a tenet of historical materialism of the marxian variety.)

2. If any art contributes to human emancipation, then it is eminently defensible.

3. If art symbolizes and encourages changes in perception that are suitable to the expansion of the productive forces, then it contributes to the expansion of the productive forces.

4. Mass art by its very nature symbolizes and encourages changes in perception that are suitable to the expansion of the productive forces. (It encourages the development of perceptual powers that are penetrating, scrutinizing [for example, close-up], analytical, critical, and distracted.)

5. Therefore, mass art is eminently defensible.

Moreover, the 'new art argument' may be stated thusly:

1. The nature of art changes with epochal or momentous changes in the forces and relations of the productive base of society. (This is a tenet of historical materialism.)

2. If the nature of art changes with epochal or momentous changes

in the forces and relations of the productive base of society, then it is a fundamental mistake to assess new art in terms of theories that are sensitive to the art of past epochs.

3. Mass art, the art of a new historical epoch, represents a change in the nature of art.

4. Detractors of mass art negatively assess the new art (mass art) in terms of theories that are at best sensitive to the art of past historical epochs (such as auratic art and/or ersatz-Kantian art).

5. Therefore, the detractors of mass art are fundamentally mistaken in their (negative) assessments of mass art.

Let us examine these arguments one at a time.

The progress argument begins with the historical materialist conviction that any art that contributes to the expansion of the forces of production contributes to human emancipation. This proposition, in turn, presupposes that the expansion of the forces of production contributes to human emancipation. But this proposition is at least controversial. Certainly environmentalists have a great deal of evidence that they believe shows that there are many cases where the expansion of productive forces creates more problems for human life than it solves. Perhaps environmentalists are not always correct in their assessments. But aren't they right at least some of the time? And, in any case, it is at least conceivable that there could be cases where the expansion of the productive forces might impede human emancipation.[25] The correlation between technological progress and human emancipation is far from straightforward.

Of course, the historical materialist might respond that he is talking about *genuine* expansions of the productive forces and that putative expansions of the productive forces that impede human emancipation are not genuine. But that transforms this tenet of historical materialism into a stipulative definition, whereas one would have thought that it was supposed to be an empirical, falsifiable law of historical development. Thus, the first premiss of the argument is at best on very shaky grounds.

The second premiss of the argument claims that any art that contributes to human emancipation is eminently defensible. This seems true enough. A contribution to human emancipation would appear to be at least a prima-facie good-making feature of any art, even if there are other good-making features of art. The premiss does not suggest that abetting human emancipation is the only grounds for defending art. That would

---

[25] Moreover, when it comes to the question of art, detractors of mass art are likely to analogize themselves to the environmentalists in the preceding argument.

certainly be problematic. However, claiming that, all things being equal, a contribution to human emancipation is a reason on behalf of certain art (though perhaps not in terms of art *qua* art) should raise no theoretical hackles.

The third premiss—'If art symbolizes and encourages changes in perception that are suitable for the expansion of the productive forces, then it contributes to the expansion of the productive forces'—appears to presume that it is possible 1. that art can function as a causal factor in changing perception; and 2. that symbolizing a form of perception can be a contribution to the expansion of the productive forces.

The plausibility of the first assumption depends upon whether art can cause a change in perception. This may be problematic in that perception is not something that is likely to change easily, let alone as the result of consuming artworks. The human perceptual system evolved over a long period of time, under the influence of natural selection. It is not particularly plastic. This is not to say that it could not change. Perhaps under the pressure of natural selection it will alter. However, for the forces of natural selection to take hold, a rather substantial period of time would be required. It is not plausible to think that the temporal scale—the industrial revolution—that a historical materialist like Benjamin has in mind is a substantial enough time slice to permit any interesting change in vision to occur. The life spans of an art movement, as we are familiar with them, seem incompatible with what would be required by natural selection to bring about a change in perception, whether or not that change were to be counted as abetting the expansion of the forces of production or not.[26]

Of course, everything depends on what one means by changing perception. Benjamin says that sense perception changes,[27] but perhaps that is not what he really means.[28] Since it is biologically unlikely that sense

---

[26] The issue of whether or not (*a*) sense perception changes; and (*b*) whether it changes as the result of the influence of media will be discussed at greater length in the next section of this chapter which concerns the work of Marshall McLuhan.

[27] Benjamin, 'The Work of Art in the Age of Mechanical Reproduction', 222.

[28] Benjamin is stingy when it comes to providing examples of the changes in sense perception that he has in mind. However, he does suggest that people see faster as a result of the arts of mechanical reproduction. But this raises a question about whether people confronted by urban life and cinematic montage have really developed a new perceptual ability to see faster, or whether the perceptual capacities that people already possessed were being stimulated to a greater extent than previously, but in such a way that the capacities already in place were able to process the increased stimulation.

I suspect that the modern age has not produced a new perceptual capacity, but that our already evolved perceptual capacities are being taxed by new levels of input. My reason for favouring this hypothesis has to do with my view that changes in sense perception via natural selection require much more time than Benjamin allows. Nevertheless, there is another problem with Benjamin's hypothesis, namely, how would we go about confirming it? What evidence is there for the notion that sense perception has changed in the direction of literally becoming faster. Certainly, the fact that movies deliver information faster than stained glass windows doesn't do the job, since this fact is compatible

perception is as plastic as Benjamin explicitly says it is, maybe a more charitable way to read him is to suppose that he does not believe that sense perception literally changes, but only that certain habits of perception change. For example, putatively under the influence of the close-up, people begin to *notice* small, expressive gestures more than they did in the past.

In so far as this is a matter of what people attend to and take note of, and not a matter of what they literally see, this conjecture does not run foul of the biological objections that I have just voiced. However, it does raise certain epistemological questions about how we could come to know that perceptual habits had changed over time. Inasmuch as this claim that perceptual habits change over time is an empirical, historical hypothesis, one would want to know how to go about confirming it. What would count as evidence?

Unfortunately, the kind of evidence Benjamin offers is inadequate. For he counts changes in art as evidence for changes in society's habits of perception. But this is circular, since Benjamin wants to maintain that changes in art mirror and/or cause changes in perceptual habits, and in order to do this, he needs independent grounds to establish that changes in art correspond to changes in perceptual habits. He cannot claim the existence of changes in perceptual habits on the grounds that art changes

with both the view that we have developed new perceptual capacities to assimilate movies, and my alternative hypothesis that the perceptual capacities we possessed prior to the advent of film already had the latent capacity to process montage.

Another possible example that Benjamin might have in mind as evidence that art changes perception is distraction. He claims that as a result of modern life and modern art perception is now distracted in the sense that it moves from one subject to the next rapidly. The Baudelairean flâneur is his epitome of this form of perception. However, this example is unconvincing for two reasons.

First, Benjamin seems confused about the facts of perception. The kind of perceptual movement that he discusses is not something that emerges in the late nineteenth century. It is a hard-wired feature of the perceptual apparatus that has been with us for millennia. It is a natural feature of the perceptual apparatus of humans, and of other animals, that we constantly shift our attention. The evolutionary grounds for this are obvious. Organisms are constantly on the look out for predators and prey, or other sources of nourishment. The natural disposition of our perceptual apparatus is to be constantly scanning the environment. The eye never stops moving; rapid eye movements and saccadic sweeps are hard-wired features of the apparatus. Neither the industrial urbanization nor the movies brought this about. The tendency constantly to shift attention is an enduring feature of the perceptual system. Moreover, this instinctual feature of the perceptual apparatus was already known to William James and H. Helmholtz. See David LaBerge, *Attentional Processing: The Brain's Art of Mindfulness* (Cambridge, Mass.: Harvard University Press, 1995), 35–8; and William James, *The Principles of Psychology* (New York: Dover Publications, Inc., 1950), vol. i, especially ch. 11.

A second problem with Benjamin's hypothesis that the arts, such as film, engender this mode of distraction is that it appears inconsistent with the data of film reception. Film viewers are typically glued to the screen. Their attention is not distracted. Indeed, film-makers have developed a very effective series of devices to block the percipient's natural perceptual tendency to shift attention. Film does not abet distraction. Cinema is a machine for keeping the audience's eyes riveted to the screen. For further argumentation along these lines, see: Noël Carrroll, 'Film, Attention and Communication', in *Great Ideas Today* (Chicago: Encyclopaedia Britannica Co., 1996).

in order to argue that changes in art correspond to changes in perceptual habits.[29]

What Benjamin needs is evidence that perceptual habits change which is independent of changes in art. Then he can go on to attempt to show that these changes correlate with changes in art. But Benjamin does not do this. He uses changes in art as evidence of changes in perceptual habits. And that is tantamount to presuming that his hypothesis has been established as a way of establishing his hypothesis. It is nothing short of begging the question.

Of course, this does not show that one might not be able to overcome this problem. Perhaps there is some evidence that would demonstrate in a non-circular way that perceptual habits have changed and that art has participated causally in that change. However, until that burden of proof is lifted, one may want to be sceptical about whether art has caused any change in perceptual habits, let alone changes in perceptual habits that might contribute to the expansion of the productive forces of society.[30] Thus, until some evidential justification can be provided for the presumption that art can change perceptual habits, we should approach the second premiss of the progress argument gingerly.

The second premiss of the argument also assumes that symbolizing a mode of perception that facilitates the expansion of the productive forces can contribute to the expansion of the productive forces. This presumes that there are special modes of perception that facilitate the expansion of the productive forces and that symbolizing them contributes to the expansion of the productive forces. Perhaps if we weaken what is meant by 'modes of perception' here, it is plausible to suppose that certain modes or, at least, habits of perception can contribute to the expansion of productive forces. Maybe becoming habituated to the use of computers—developing the hand/monitor co-ordination required by various video games—trains a work-force in the skills that are useful for fully exploiting the capacities requisite for consummate automation. But still, why does symbolizing these perceptual habits contribute to the expansion of the forces of production?

Two alternative ways of answering this question occur to me. On the one hand, symbolically reflecting new modes of perceptual habituation may serve to encourage people rhetorically to adopt them. And, on the other hand, symbolizing these putatively new habits of perception may, by

[29] Similar arguments can be found in David Bordwell's *On the History of Film Style* (Cambridge, Mass.: Harvard University Press, forthcoming), ch. 5.

[30] There is also the question of whether Benjamin believes that *acquired* perceptual habits are inherited by subsequent generations. If he does, he would be guilty of Lamarckianism.

externalizing them, so to speak, enable us to scrutinize them and, thereby, make oneself self-consciously aware of them, thus enabling one to understand them in ways that are conducive to making them one's own. These two explanations are not incompatible, and there may be other explanations that I have not thought of. Thus, I am at least willing to accept provisionally the proposition that symbolizing new habits of perception, if there are such habits, could be conducive to the expansion of the forces of production.

But if something can be said for the third premiss in the progress argument, the fourth premiss appears problematic in almost every way. The claim—that mass art symbolizes and encourages changes in perception that are suitable to the expansion of the forces of production—of course, runs into a difficulty that we have already encountered, namely, that it seems unlikely that any art, including mass art, literally changes perception. This objection is especially acute in the case of mass art, or mass-reproducible art, since the kinds of mass art Benjamin has in mind have hardly been in existence long enough to affect the relevant processes of natural selection, even if, in principle, it is imaginable that art could change human biology at the level of sense perception.

On the other hand, though Benjamin speaks of sense perception, the examples that he offers in terms of critical, analytical, penetrating, and distractive perception sound more like perceptual habits than like changes in our hard-wired, biological/perceptual apparatus. So, perhaps a charitable reading of Benjamin saves him from the criticism in the preceding paragraph. Nevertheless, the concrete claims that Benjamin makes about the changes in perceptual habits that mass-reproducible arts like film encourage are troublesome in at least two ways. First, there is the question of whether mass artworks, like film, engender the perceptual habits Benjamin has in mind. And second, there is what we might call the transfer problem—that is, why, even if film encourages the specific perceptual habits that Benjamin mentions, should these habits be taken as supporting the expansion of the forces of production?

Among the perceptual habits that Benjamin claims that the mass reproducible arts inculcate are a critical, analytical, penetrating stance toward mass artworks and what they represent, a tendency to look at things close up, and a tendency toward distraction, which also reinforces the critical habit. Supposing that film is the mass art-form that Benjamin is thinking about, I think that it is possible to challenge every one of his hypotheses about our perceptual habits.

Recall Benjamin's thesis about film-acting. Allegedly, the fact that a film performance is an assemblage of fragments makes the film audience more critically disposed toward it than they would be toward a stage performance. I doubt that this hypothesis would sustain empirical testing. But in the absence of testing, it still fails to be compelling, since, though the audience is aware of the way in which film performances are composed, this awareness does not seem to preclude their becoming wrapped up as intently in a film performance as they are in a stage performance. Indeed, the cutting in a film performance—with its changing points of view and scale—may engage their attention more than a stage play just because the perceptual array is more varied. That is, the visual activity on the screen, owing to the editing with its changing points of view on the action, may succeed in holding the audience's attention more effectively than a static stage performance.[31]

Benjamin thinks that the absence of the film-actor encourages a greater critical posture on the part of the film audience. Perhaps the idea here is that if the actor is not present, we will be more willing to criticize him. Benjamin himself says that a lack of an audience entails that the actor cannot adjust her performance to the audience. Thus, the film-actor is apt to appear awkward or out of synch with the audience. But surely if these factors come into play, they do so only on a case-by-case basis. It is not of the nature of the film performance to be necessarily awkward or out of synch with the audience, even considering the reasons that Benjamin offers. We know this because we know that as a matter of fact that many film performances have seduced audiences. Thus, the hypothesis about the heightened critical stance of the film viewer really claims to explain phenomena whose existence we have little reason to believe. Like phlogiston, the phenomenon Benjamin wants to explain doesn't seem to be there.

A critical attitude is not automatically delivered to the audience by viewing performances on film. Just think of all those fan clubs for galleries of film-actors. And, in any case, is it really evident that film audiences are more critical than theatre audiences? I cannot think that history will support this hypothesis in any convincing way.

Film is supposed to encourage an analytical, critical, penetrating frame of mind, as if the audience absorbed the stylistics of montage by osmosis while watching movies. Here, quite rightly, Benjamin stands in opposition to all those theorists encountered in the last chapter who maintained that mass art automatically precludes active spectatorship. But, though I agree with Benjamin that a film spectator is active, I doubt that

---

[31] See Noël Carroll, 'Film, Attention and Communication'.

that activity has carry-over value in terms of their ordinary cognitive and perceptual behaviour.

There are two reasons for this. First, there seems to be little evidence that watching films enhances analytical skills or makes movie viewers more penetrating in acquitting cognitive and perceptual tasks once they leave the movie theatre. And, alternatively, perhaps film techniques activate pre-existing skills, rather than instilling new ones. That is a more likely hypothesis than Benjamin's, given the rapid pick-up film viewers evince when exposed to new film techniques. But in any case, there is little reason to believe that film viewers derive new cognitive and perceptual skills, of the sort that might be manifested outside the screening room, from films.

One wonders whether the cognitive and perceptual habits that Benjamin attributes to film viewing—analysis, criticism, and penetration—are really parallel to any real-world cognitive and perceptual behaviours that we would refer to in terms of analysis, criticism and penetration. Certain kinds of editing patterns are called analytical and penetrating. These involve shots that break down the action and that close in on the action. But what does this necessarily have to do with people whom we call analytical and penetrating in their real-world activities? In film, these terms refer to the organization of cinematic space. But a real-world analytical or penetrating cast of mind is not necessarily spatial. The same words may be used to describe editing patterns and real-world cognitive styles, but it may be just an equivocation to suppose that these terms name cognate phenomena.

A critical person may say 'let's take a closer look at the problem.' But here 'closer' may be a metaphor. That films cut in for close-ups need have nothing to do with a critical mental posture. The metaphor in 'let's have a closer look' is not literally univocal with the spatial conception of 'close' in 'close-up'. To suppose that it is involves mistaking a pun for an analysis. Thus when Benjamin talks about the way in which film structures provoke analysis, criticism, and penetration of a sort that is on a continuum with analysis, criticism, and penetration in everyday life, he is not speaking about the actual phenomena of film viewing but conjuring the putative phenomena into existence by word magic. As in the case of his discussion of film-acting, the processes that he proposes to characterize seem non-existent, at least in the terms that he proposes to characterize them. The phlogiston problem once again!

Benjamin says that the film audience is distracted—both in the sense of being incidentally attentive and in the sense of being shocked. I do not believe that the notion that the film audience is typically distracted in the first sense is very plausible.[32] Standardly, the film audience is riveted to the screen, and when it isn't, that is due not to the nature of film, but probably to the film at hand, which may be boring, or to the mental state of the film viewer, which may be preoccupied because he is predisposed to be thinking about or doing something else. Nor do I think that distraction in this sense is a pre-condition for criticism. Anyone distracted from a film because she is thinking about something else is probably too busy with her own affairs to be concerned with criticism of either the film or what it represents.

It is true that the film viewer may be 'shocked' or galvanized by a stunning array of editing, but since this will generally involve the viewer in the process of trying to understand what the film-maker is trying to communicate, I do not see why Benjamin interprets this phenomenon as criticism. Indeed, advertisers use such effects all of the time to deflect critical scrutiny. Of course, I do not wish to recycle the old saw that montage is a way of bedazzling the spectator. Whether it bedazzles or promotes a critical stance is a matter of its use in a concrete situation. But just as there is no guarantee that montage editing necessarily short-circuits criticism, there is no guarantee that it encourages it either. Thus, I wonder whether Benjamin's characterization of the film viewer as a naturally inclined, distracted critic provides us with a reliable account of what actually goes on in film reception. Once again, it appears that Benjamin's description of the phenomenon, though it strains to show that film encourages analytical, penetrating, and critical cognitive and perceptual habits, falters because the characterizations of the nature of the cinematic phenomenon supposedly in question fail to be persuasive.

Benjamin claims that mass art encourages perceptual habits that are conducive to the expansion of the productive forces. This seems false at least in terms of the perceptual habits that he adduces because there are pressing questions about whether the perceptual habits that he describes really exist even with respect to film viewing. However, even if they do

---

[32] Also it should be noted that Benjamin's conception of modern perception as distracted is quite misleading. He talks about the flâneur who is always glancing elsewhere as a result of the diverse stimuli of the modern city. But hasn't Benjamin forgotten that saccadic eye movements are part of natural perception? The eye is always roving, on the lookout for predators and prey on the borders of perception. The tendency of the eye to be distractible is not modern. It is part of our hard-wired perceptual apparatus. Long before the advent of modern cities, people were keeping track of their peripheral vision and glancing elsewhere. This is assured by the operation of saccadic eye movement as well as by other evolutionary factors. Thus, the kind of distraction that Benjamin talks about is not modern, does not reflect the modern experience as such, nor does it require the emergence of film to cultivate it. Distractibility of the sort Benjamin has in mind has always been part of our perceptual make-up.

exist, there is still a question about whether they really have the transfer value that Benjamin thinks they have.

Presumably Benjamin thinks that something like what Snyder called technically informed perception serves the forces of production. The arts of technical reproduction putatively engender this technically informed mode of perception and that facilitates the expansion of the forces of production. But, once again, we must ask whether the specific perceptual habits that Benjamin describes, supposing they exist, would have much carry-over value in enhancing productivity. Certainly, being distracted in either of the senses that Benjamin uses this concept wouldn't. Incidentally attentive workers or shocked workers are unlikely to increase production.

Moreover, being analytical or penetrating in the manner of a film viewer would appear to be a somewhat modular expertise, hardly applicable to most of the tasks of industrial workers now or into the foreseeable future. Perhaps these skills would be suitable for the organization of work in some marxist Utopia; however, since no marxist has any idea of what work in that Utopia might entail, there seems to be little point in claiming that the skills involved in movie-viewing or radio-listening, even abstractly described, will be what is called for.

Of course, an obvious response to this criticism is that it misinterprets Benjamin. If he believes that the perceptual habits promoted by interaction with mass reproducible art figures in expanding the productive forces, it might be said that he does not believe that these perceptual habits are relevant at the level of industrial labour. Rather, he believes that the victory of the proletariat will release the forces of production and that the perceptual habits engendered by mass art will influence the development of a form of proletarian consciousness thereby bringing about the types of social change which, in turn, will facilitate the expansion of the productive forces. Thus, it is a mistake to suppose that the perceptual habits encouraged by mass art will carry over directly to skills that will improve productivity. Rather, the line of influence is indirect. Mass art contributes to working-class consciousness, and working-class consciousness will release the forces of production from the bondage of bourgeois-class consciousness.

Again, the relevant features of working-class consciousness involve a critical, analytical, penetrating attitude toward mass art and whatever it represents. It is not a matter of new perceptual habits with respect to the mechanisms of production, but a matter of a critical, analytical, and penetrating stance toward capitalist society. But this sounds almost as implausible as the notion that watching films supplies useful perceptual habits for the shop floor. Understanding editing or mastering montage thinking does not, in and of itself, promote penetrating social consciousness. One reason for this is that it typically involves following someone else's thought. I do not wish to suggest that this is not valuable. However, it is not an obvious method for engendering independent thinking of the sort the proletariat putatively needs to cultivate.

Furthermore, montage as such is not inherently critical socially. It is not of the nature of montage to encourage critical thinking, social or otherwise. This is not to say that a film-maker might not use montage, in concert with social or political content, to advance critical arguments and even to propose models for thinking critically about specific social issues. But, in such cases, we are not talking about some ontologically essential feature of montage, but about the uses to which montage can be put when it is deployed in connection with socially relevant content and a politically critical point of view. Thus, the assertion that there is something about mass art, due to its essential nature, that is conducive to the expansion of the forces of production—inasmuch as it promotes a critical, proletarian, class consciousness—seems mistaken.

Indeed, this objection is, I believe, the key to what is fatally flawed in Benjamin's approach to the defence of mass art. For behind the progress argument, there is the belief that a medium or a technology could have a mode of consciousness or a political stance inscribed in it. Specifically, Benjamin appears to believe that mass art has a proletarian viewpoint built into it, and, therefore, that it is inherently emancipatory (or, at least, that it *naturally* gravitates in that direction, all things being equal). This belies a faith in technological essentialism, a bias shared by other philosophical defenders of mass art, like Marshall McLuhan.[33]

But the question is whether it makes sense to suppose that a technology has an essence such that it entails a political commitment, especially a political commitment as specific as being on the side of proletarian emancipation. Such a view is strictly teleological. It presupposes that mass art has an ethical end toward which it gravitates naturally. In Benjamin's conception that end involves the emancipation of the working class and the liberation of the forces of production. It is as if mass art inherently possesses a moral-political destiny, or, at least, will, all things being equal, contribute to progress in human emancipation due to its very nature.

Yet this seems unlikely. Mass art may have a function—to address large numbers of people—but it does not appear to possess a *telos*, especially

---

[33] In fact, I call such defences *philosophical* just because they involve essentialism. That is, they are philosophical because they depend on premisses about the *nature* of mass art.

one as morally charged as that which Benjamin attributes to it. Whether or not mass art is conducive to moral and political progress depends on the ways in which it is used, not upon its nature *qua* mass art. Technologies, including mass art technologies, may be used in different ways for different purposes, just as drugs that can kill can also cure. Tractor treads can outfit tanks or combines. It is the human use of technologies to which moral evaluations accrue. Technologies, in and of themselves, are morally neutral, until they are put to use or enlisted in the service of human projects and purposes.

Technologies are not possessed of destinies. They may be invented for one thing, but used for another, as in the case of TV which was developed to be broadcast to public reception sites, but which was quickly adapted for home use. Moreover, it is even more implausible to imagine that such technologies have built-in moral/political agendas. Lenin and Limbaugh can use the radio for their own distinctive purposes. There is nothing about the technology of radio that determines what is broadcast, and so it does not appear that the technology has an ingrained moral/political commitment.

In response, it might be claimed that some technologies are designed in such a way that they can only be used for one purpose. For example, we often hear that a gun can only be used to ill effect. However, not only does this seem palpably false—for guns can be used to defeat fascism—but, even if there are some isolated cases where a technology can only be used to only one effect, mass art technologies do not appear to be of that sort. Over the last one hundred years, we have seen them deployed in the service of moral agendas of every stripe.

Of course, the way in which the reception of a technology is organized may be politically significant. But that brings us to a discussion of the distribution of mass art, and, therefore, to a discussion of the use of mass art. And that is a feature of mass art, as Adorno pointed out, that Benjamin ignores. For the most part, Benjamin examines what might be called intrinsic structural features of mass art, plumbing them in the hope of discerning their political significance, rather than concentrating on how mass art is used or distributed. But without attending to how mass art, or particular mass artworks, are used, I contend it is impossible to assess the moral or political significance of its structures. The structures are morally and politically neutral until they are used to some effect, where the effect or purpose in question determines their moral and/or political significance.

What it seems to me Benjamin wants to claim is that mass art, due to its nature, has certain built-in tendencies that favour human progress or emancipation, particularly in terms of enhancing working-class conscious-ness. This is problematic not only because his case for the specific features of consciousness he claims are inscribed in mass art is somewhat fanciful, but also because the suggestion that mass art is inherently disposed toward implementing his conception of progress presupposes the questionable notion that a technology, as opposed to those who use the technology, has any predetermined moral or political commitments. Hammers might enhance productive capacities or they might destroy them in the hands of a Luddite. Films might enhance socialist consciousness or they might impede it. It might go either way. There is no reason to suppose, as Benjamin seems to, that the medium predestines its use, where its use is, in fact, the locus of its moral and political significance.

To suppose that technologies have the sort of moral agenda that Benjamin ascribes to mass art built into them would appear to me to raise the metaphysical question of how this came about. Surely, the mass arts were not consciously designed to possess the revolutionary capacities they are said to have by Benjamin. So how would we go about explaining their possession of these capacities? Here perhaps the materialist concep-tion of history may be invoked, but I suspect that this will involve us in supposing that there is something like a supra-historical intelligence orchestrating the invention and development of the mass arts, and that is something that I, at least, find theoretically unappealing. Thus, I reject the progress argument,[34] though, of course, this is not to say that I believe that mass art (or, at least some of it) is not defensible, but only that this particular argument does not make the case.

If I have been rather hard on the progress argument, I am more sympathetic to the new art argument. Perhaps this should be expected, since, obviously, it is in some ways reminiscent of the diagnosis of philo-sophy's resistance to mass art that I offered at the end of the preceding chapter. However, though I welcome the conclusion of the new art argument, I suspect that its premises are far stronger than they need to

---

[34] Defenders of Benjamin might say that my objections to the progress argument on the grounds that technologies are morally and politically neutral is misdirected because Benjamin is not talking about technological features of mass art, but of stylistic features, like montage. I am not so convinced that Benjamin is aware of this distinction, since he writes as though he thinks that montage is an intrinsic feature of film. However, if he does make this distinction, I think that many of the arguments that I have made can be adjusted and remobilized in response in so far as stylistic features of montage, like the technology of the film camera, are also morally neutral and can be used for savoury and unsavoury purposes. That is, film styles, like montage, are not necessarily on the side of history. This is not to deny that people like Eisenstein, Vertov, and Pudovkin attempted to use montage—both in terms of style and content—to enhance their revolutionary projects. But capitalist advertisers can also use it—both in terms of style and content—in the service of an opposing agenda. And so could Leni Riefensthal.

be and that the argument can be made more plausibly with weaker premisses.

The first premiss of the argument maintains that the nature of art changes with epochal or momentous changes in the forces and relations of production. There are two claims here: first, that the nature of art changes over time, and, second, that the structuring cause of such changes are to be found in changes in the forces and relations of production. The latter claim, of course, derives from the materialist conception of history. However, both these claims are, to say the least, controversial.

If by 'the nature of art', we understand 'the essence of art', it is surely an open question whether or not it changes. Art-forms and genres, and their subtending purposes may emerge and disappear, but whether the essence of art can be said to change as a result of this sort of activity is problematic. For if the essence of art can be correctly characterized at a suitably abstract level, then changes in the styles, modes, genres, and purposes of art-forms may turn out to be merely different ways of instantiating the enduring essence of art. That art-forms, genres, styles, and their subtending purposes mutate, in other words, may not provide sufficient evidence that the essence of art, suitably construed, changes.

For example, the theories of the nature of art propounded by philosophers like George Dickie and Arthur Danto are putatively commodious enough conceptually to encompass most of what we call art.[35] They are certainly capable of counting both auratic art and mass-reproducible art as instances of art under their conceptions of the nature of art. Thus, unless such conceptions of art are decisively defeated, and no other comparably general theory of art can be developed, there is reason to doubt the proposition that the nature of art changes essentially. Indeed, even if no theory of art of this kind managed to discover the nature of art, it is still logically possible that art has an unchanging nature, though one of which we are unaware.

I am not hereby intending to endorse any essentialist theory of art. I am only pointing out that, as a matter of logic, the new art argument makes assumptions about the malleability of the nature of art that are far from settled. However, as we shall see, it is not clear that it is necessary to invoke the idea of changes in the nature of art in order to argue that the conceptual frameworks employed by the philosophical enemies of mass art are inappropriate. But more on that anon.

The new art argument presumes not only that the nature of art changes,

---

[35] George Dickie, *Art and the Aesthetic: An Institutional Analysis* (Ithaca, NY: Cornell University Press, 1974); Arthur C. Danto, *The Transfiguration of the Commonplace: A Philosophy of Art* (Cambridge, Mass.: Harvard University Press, 1981).

but that it does so under the influence of changes in the forces and relations of production. This is historical materialism. It is an empirical generalization—supposedly a law of history—but it has never been established uncontrovertibly. Perhaps this is because the dependent variable in this generalization has never been specified unambiguously. How are we to understand the notion of the nature of art?

If this amounts to the essence of art, then, of course, there is the issue of whether art does change. But maybe what is meant by the nature of art here applies to things like art-forms, styles, and genres. These surely change. But do they always change in response to changes in the forces and relations of production? In some cases, stylistic changes in art appear to change faster than changes in the forces and relations of production; the transition from abstract expressionism to minimalism to conceptual art occurred without corresponding changes in the nature of the forces and relations of production. Are these counter-examples to the theory?

And if they are not, why is it that these artistic changes are not the right sort of changes for us to be considering? Again, there is a lamentable laxness in the characterization of the dependent variable in the theory, inasmuch as it fails to specify the type of artistic changes to which we need to attend in order to evaluate the theory.

Moreover, it does not seem inconceivable that the forces and relations of production might change without corresponding changes in artistic practice. The forces and relations of production changed momentously in Russia during the reign of Stalin, but the stylistic structure of the Russian ballet remained virtually intact. Maybe the historical materialist will introduce some *ad hoc* hypothesis to handle this case, or, alternatively, he might claim that had the Soviet order persisted, the nature of the ballet would have changed under the influence of changes in the forces and relations of production. But, on the one hand, one fears that historical materialists will have to add so many *ad hoc* hypotheses to deal with cases such as that of the Russian ballet that the theory will be overloaded with epicycles, while, on the other hand, the prediction that, had the Soviet Union continued, given enough time the Russian ballet would have changed is hardly compelling, since given *enough* time, almost everything is likely to change in some way or other. At the very least, historical-materialist generalizations about artistic change appear too vague to be evaluated empirically, though they are advanced as empirical laws of the social system. Thus, it is epistemologically imprudent to grant the premiss that art changes in response to changes in the forces and relations of production.

Likewise, there may be some problems with the fourth premiss of the argument. As I have written it, it states that detractors of mass art negatively assess the relevant new art in terms of theories that are sensitive to the art of past historical epochs. This seems to accord with Benjamin's discussion of auratic art as the pertinent contrast to mass art. But it does not seem exactly right to regard the arguments of people like MacDonald, Greenberg, Collingwood, Adorno, and Horkheimer as rooted in a commitment to past art.[36] They seem to be contrasting mass art unfavourably to avant-garde and/or modernist art.

MacDonald, Greenberg, and Collingwood may have views of the enduring nature of art, which they believe applies to art of the past and the present. But at the same time, their theories are sensitive to the modernist art of their own times, and are not anachronistic. Adorno and Horkheimer, of course, at least appear more sympathetic to a historical-materialist conception of art, but they too are ostensibly in favour of the advanced art of their own times. So, the fourth premiss of the new art argument seems mistaken, at least if the detractors of mass art that we have in mind are people like MacDonald, Greenberg, Collingwood, Adorno, and Horkheimer.

But though the new art argument will not go through in the manner that I set it out previously, it can, I think, be rewritten in a more convincing form. We can jettison the commitments of the first premiss to the ontological mutability of the essence of art and to the historical-materialist conception of the origin of that change in the productive forces, and simply note that art is constantly undergoing change at the level of art-forms, genres, styles, and their subtending purposes. That is, all we need to claim is that art changes in many different ways. For if this is the case, then it is reasonable to suppose that it may be a mistake to assess new art—new art-forms, genres, styles, and their subtending purposes—by the lights of theories of art developed to be sensitive to features of other types of art. I say *other* types of art, rather than earlier forms of art, since some forms of new art may be misconstrued as a result of mobilizing theories developed to appreciate art that is contemporary to the relevant new forms of art—that is, to other new forms of art—as is the case when theorists attempt to come to terms with mass art armed with a conceptual framework appropriate to modernism.

Thus, rather than saying that 'if the nature of art changes with epochal or momentous changes in the forces and relation of production, then it is a fundamental mistake to assess new art in terms of theories that are sensitive to past art', we may make the weaker claim that 'If art changes in such a way that there are many different art-forms, genres, and styles

---

[36] I say 'people like' above, since Benjamin was not addressing MacDonald, Greenberg, or Collingwood, perhaps not even Adorno/Horkheimer.

with different subtending purposes, then it may be a mistake to mobilize theories appropriate to certain ensembles of art-forms, genres, styles, and purposes in order to understand and to assess other ensembles of art-forms, genres, styles, and purposes.'

Furthermore, rather than assert that detractors of mass art are wedded to conceptual frameworks that are appropriate to past, auratic art, one may charge that they are involved in importing criteria appropriate to one form of contemporary art, namely modernism, to a very different form of art, namely mass art.

Then, given that it is hard to deny that it is the case that art changes in such a way that there are many different art-forms, genres, styles, and often with subtending purposes, we can get to the conclusion that detractors of mass art may be involved in a mistake in their negative assessments of mass art in so far as they assess it in virtue of theories suitable for different kinds of art. Moreover, we can transform that *may be mistaken* to *are mistaken* by showing how many of the presuppositions of the practice of modernism, such as its commitment to singularity, are inapposite to the practice of mass art.[37] Thus, the new art argument can be given a new lease on life by weakening its premises in such a way that it becomes 'the different art argument'.

Some readers may feel that Benjamin has come in for an unfair drubbing in this discussion of the new art argument, since he never states the argument outright. Consequently, I may be charged with foisting a bad argument on him for the egotistical purpose of showing that I can do a better job of saying what he never tried to say. And I agree that the new art argument is at best implicit in 'The Work of Art in the Age of Mechanical Reproduction'. On behalf of my interpretive excavation of the new art argument, however, let me say that I think it makes sense to hypothesize Benjamin's commitment to it, given the distinction he is at pains to draw between auratic art and mechanically reproducible art, especially inas-

[37] Another diagnosis of the detractors of mass art is that they failed to see that mass art supports many of the same aims of modernist art, such as interpretive play, even if mass art supports these purposes to a lesser degree. Perhaps smitten by modernist paradigms, they were unable to recognize that many of the activities that are mandated by mass art are on a continuum with features that they prize in modernist art. That is, the difference between mass art and modernism is a difference of degree, not kind, even if critics like Greenberg and Collingwood failed to notice this.

I offered several variants of this approach in response to the massification, passivity, and formula arguments in the preceding chapter. This type of diagnosis differs from the one above in that the new art argument locates the problem in the importation of criteria from one kind of art—modernism—to another kind of art—mass art. However, rather than regarding these as competing accounts of what is wrong with the position of the enemies of mass art, I believe that they make both of these types of error, sometimes, as in the case of active spectatorship, by failing to see that much mass art, to at least some degree, meets their criteria, and, in other cases, such as their emphasis on uniqueness, by importing ideals appropriate to one sort of aesthetic practice into alien territory.

much as auratic art is characterized in the idiom of neo-Kantian aesthetics. Moreover, something like the new art argument seems not only compatible with historical materialism, but suggested by it, and 'The Work of Art in the Age of Mechanical Reproduction' does appear deeply committed to a materialist conception of history.

Indeed, I have tried to show throughout this section that many of the major problems with Benjamin's defence of mass art—in the context of both the progress argument and the new art argument—can be traced back to his commitment to the materialist conception of history. This disposes Benjamin to a belief that technology has a latent moral agenda— that technologies, both at the level of the economic base, and at the level of information technologies, are inherently biased in favour of emancipation. In contrast, I find such attributions of a morally charged *telos* to technologically reproducible art metaphysically perplexing, a matter of allegorically reading into mass art one's fondest wishes. Nevertheless, this tendency to project one's moral and political desires on to technology is the linchpin of the best-known philosophical celebrations of mass art—not only Benjamin's, but Marshall McLuhan's as well.

Marshall McLuhan and the electronic future

Like that of Walter Benjamin, Marshall McLuhan's defence of mass art rests upon an assessment of what he takes to be the inherent possibilities of the mass media.[38] He does not defend specific instances of mass art in the manner of someone like Gilbert Seldes. Rather, he defends mass art, or the mass media as such. It is the nature of the mass media—or, at least, of certain privileged instances of them, like TV—that, for McLuhan, commends them to us. This much is perhaps already evident in one of his favourite slogans—'the medium is the message'.[39] For what McLuhan has

---

[38] From the outset, it is important to acknowledge that McLuhan's own topic is larger than mass art. He is concerned with mass media, which include many things that are not usually considered to be art, such as newspapers, and, for him, clothing and clocks. However, I am presenting him as a defender of mass art, since in defending the mass media across the board, he is defending many things—such as movies, radio, comic books, and TV—that are examples of mass art. In other words, in so far as his arguments apply generally to mass media, they also apply specifically to mass art. Thus, I count him as at least a proponent of mass art, even though he might describe himself as engaged in a broader project.

Undoubtedly, McLuhan might also resist my characterization of him on the grounds that he is not a proponent of anything. He might say that he is merely describing, or, at most, explaining the way things are. However, I think that it is impossible to read his paeons to the electronic global village, along with his disparaging observations of linear print culture, without detecting the rhetoric of moral urgency.

[39] See Marshall McLuhan, *Understanding Media: The Extensions of Man* (Cambridge: The MIT Press, 1994), ch. 1, pp. 7–21. This book was originally published in 1964. All references to it in this chapter are to the MIT edition.

in mind by this mantra is that the content of mass media is less important than their structures, since it is at the level of structure, McLuhan contends, that the mass media engage and shape human consciousness in the profoundest of ways. Thus, when we come to evaluate TV, the content of its programmes is less important than its structure as a mode of communication, since it is its structure as a communication medium that influences the development of consciousness.

In principle, this is a very clever strategy for defending mass art. For in response to detractors of mass art who protest about this or that heinous example of mass art, McLuhan can flag the criticisms aside by claiming that it misses the point. For such criticism rests on the content (or the lack thereof) of specific examples, whereas the virtue of the mass arts, according to McLuhan, resides in their generic structures, not in their individualizing contents. That is, McLuhan can say to the enemy of mass art, exercised by a particular popular lyric, that she (Tipper Gore?) is missing the forest for the trees.

For McLuhan, technology is always an extension of our human powers. Technology is a prothesis. And when it comes to information technologies, the media are extensions of human mentalities. In this (recalling Benjamin again), the media symbolize consciousness at a certain level of its development, but also, inasmuch as the media are protheses, they also expand the range of the human sensorium and thereby raise consciousness to new levels. McLuhan does not hesitate to claim that media *create* new levels of human consciousness (for example, print is said to create individualism).[40] So the mass media, of which mass art is a subspecies, participate in the evolution of consciousness not only as a symbol of it, but as a causal ingredient.

Though McLuhan shares an inclination toward technological determinism with Benjamin,[41] he is not a historical materialist. For the historical materialist, the motor of history is the productive base of society. McLuhan, in contrast, locates the engine of history more narrowly. For McLuhan, *communication* technologies, rather than the entire ensemble of the forces of

---

[40] McLuhan, *Understanding Media*, 19.

[41] McLuhan might resist being called a technological determinist. In *The Global Village*, he denies that he is committed to the inevitability of the electronic age. But two things need to be said here: first, he certainly sounds like a technological determinist when he proposes *historical* hypotheses like the claim that printing created individualism. Specifically, he is a media (technology) determinist. Second, if he concedes that his prophecies about the future may not be inevitable, this merely shows that he is not a technological *fatalist*, not that he isn't a technological determinist. See Marshall McLuhan and Bruce R. Powers, *The Global Village: Transformations in World Life and Media in the 21st Century* (New York: Oxford University Press, 1989), 11–12.

production, represent the key to the historical process. Epochal historical transformations are brought about, that is, by changes in communication media. Thus, where the historical materialist locates the origin of the modern age in terms of the emergence of the capitalist exploitation of the means of production, McLuhan correlates it with the development of printing. And whereas the historical materialist predicts the shape of Utopia in terms of the socialization of the means of production, McLuhan prophesizes the approach of a global village as a result of the proliferation of electronic media.

Like the historical materialist, McLuhan's view of history is roughly Hegelian. It is divided into progressive stages. Indeed, in some respects, McLuhan's 'meta-narrative' is more akin to Hegel's than is that of the historical materialist, in so far as, like Hegel's, McLuhan's story focuses on the progressive evolution of consciousness *per se*. However, unlike in Hegel, that development is unpacked not in the idiom of spirit, but in terms of information-delivery technologies, or, less jargonistically, in terms of the structures of communication media. Thus, like Marx, McLuhan, so to speak, brings Hegel down to earth. And yet, McLuhan also evinces the sort of meliorism found in Hegel inasmuch as the story that McLuhan has to tell effectively rationalizes what is, reassuring one and all that the onset of the electronic media is the best of all possible futures. If Hegel's variation on theodicy was predicated on explaining the ways of history to 'man', McLuhan's is about explaining to (and, thereby, reconciling) us to the ways of the media.

McLuhan's argument on behalf of mass media—and of mass art as a subclass of mass media—is historical in the sense that, like Benjamin, he maintains that mass art is 'on the side of history'. That is, McLuhan surveys the historical process and discerns certain positive possibilities latent in it. These possibilities have to do with the enlargement of human consciousness in terms of achieving the fullest use of our sensory, cognitive, emotive, and social capacities. Implicitly, the story of humankind, for McLuhan, is (or should be) the story of our becoming whole (again).

The historical process is a matter of overcoming our alienation from our own powers. Anything that contributes to the actualization of our human potential—anything that contributes to making us whole—is salutary, or so McLuhan appears to presume. The post-print, electronic arts—such as radio, TV and perhaps computer art—can and are making teleologically significant contributions to the expansion and the fruition of human nature. Thus, contemporary mass art, given its virtually redemptive historical role, should not be condemned, but applauded. Why quibble about the paltry content of any number of the no-brainer TV programmes populating the so-called vast wasteland, when TV as such—the medium, not the message—will raise humanity to a higher plane of consciousness by engaging our human mental, sensory, and social capacities in a way that actualizes or fulfils the potentials of our very being?

In order to understand McLuhan's argument, it is helpful to review briefly his characterization of world history. According to McLuhan, history falls into three phases: the earliest stage extends from tribal times until roughly the Renaissance—call this the pre-Gutenberg epoch; next is the era of print culture, or the Gutenberg age—which extends into the present century, but which is giving way to a new age, the age of mass media, whose ultimate sign is electricity. This third age, the post-Gutenberg epoch, is already upon us, and its influence on our lives is being felt daily as computers play larger and larger roles in our lives.

When McLuhan popularized these ideas in the sixties in his book *Understanding Media*, TV, it seems to me, was his leading example. But much of what he had to say about electronic media in the sixties applies as well, if not better, to the possibilities opened up by the computer in the eighties and nineties. And McLuhan's rhetoric reminds one of contemporary talk about the information highway, the Internet, and the world wide web. Thus, McLuhan's assertions about electronic media are apt to strike many readers as uncannily prophetic (which is probably one of the reasons for the current renewed interest in McLuhan by figures like Baudrillard).[42]

McLuhan's first stage of historical development, the pre-Gutenberg epoch, is the longest, extending through three phases: a period of tribal, face-to-face oral communication, followed by an era of ideographic writing, followed by the age of alphabetic writing. The most primitive of these stages has something Edenic about it. Speech is said to free human consciousness from the domination by things,[43] and, at the same time, speech, as a primary means of communication, addresses the whole human person. That is, according to McLuhan, speech, as it is employed in face-to-face communication, does not appeal to one of our senses in isolation, but to all the senses.

McLuhan . . . holds this belief for two distinct reasons. . . . On the one hand he reminds us that although speech is designed to be heard, it is usually uttered in situations that call the other senses into play as well. That is to say, in order to make our spoken meaning clear we automatically use facial expressions and manual gestures; and we even use blows, grips and caresses to emphasize our

---

[42] Of course, one reason that contemporary talk about the Internet may recall McLuhan's rhetoric is simply that McLuhanism continues to exert a residual intellectual influence on present-day commentators.   [43] McLuhan, *Understanding Media*, 19.

meaning still further. For this reason, if for no other, the spoken word activates the entire human sensorium and thereby underwrites the accuracy with which the spoken message reproduces the mental state to which it supposedly corresponds.

McLuhan also claims that the channel of hearing itself is intrinsically richer, or, as he puts it, 'hotter' than that of sight, say. The result is that even if there were no other sensory clues coincident with those of speech, the listener would still be in receipt of a richer, hotter message than one coming at him through the eye alone.

For both these reasons McLuhan claims that spoken language exerts an irresistible power over the listener's imagination and that words have acquired the status of what the philosopher Hermann Usener has called 'momentary deities.' Primitive man, who relies almost entirely on oral exchanges, lives therefore in a condition of rich imaginative enchantment, his mentality galvanized throughout the length and breadth of its sensory repertoire.[44]

For McLuhan, human experience is multi-dimensional, appealing to the manifold of our senses in many ways. Sensory input comes to us in mosaic form—'sight, sound, taste and touch all at once.'[45] Optimally, McLuhan appears to assume, communication that preserves that complexity is best, inasmuch as communication is construed by him to be the communication of experience. In primitive societies, where oral exchanges predominate, McLuhan thinks that oral, face-to-face communication still roughly approximates and conveys the mosaic structure of experience. However, as communication media become more and more refined, the holistic, mosaic character of experience is diminished, because successive media come to specialize in engaging fewer and fewer of our sense modalities, until with the advent of print, communication is reduced to addressing one and only one sense, namely, sight.[46]

The rhythm of history for McLuhan is calibrated in terms of the degree to which dominant communication media conserve the variegated texture of the multi-channelled human sensorium. Speech does well on this grid, though ideographic writing and alphabetic writing represent diminutions, culminating in print culture—which is the nadir of communication history, in so far as it is said to reduce the operation of senses to the visual. However, all is not lost, since the advent of electronic media promises a restoration of the plurality of the human sensorium—an end to the alienation of the senses other than sight.

The progression from speech to ideographic and then alphabetic writing

---

[44] Jonathan Miller, *Marshall McLuhan* (New York: The Viking Press, 1971), 3–4.   [45] Ibid.

[46] Obviously a Derridean would have a field-day with the way in which McLuhan 'privileges' speech over (alphabetic) writing and printing. On the other hand, McLuhan's animus against the visual actually anticipates certain post-structuralist themes.

represents the first fall from grace in McLuhan's version of world history. He writes:

Pictographic and hieroglyphic writing as used in Babylonian, Mayan, and Chinese cultures represents an extension of the visual sense for storing and expediting access to human experience. All of these forms give pictorial expression to oral meanings. As such, they approximate the animated cartoon and are extremely unwieldy, requiring many signs for the infinity of data and operations of social action. In contrast, the phonetic alphabet, by a few letters only, was able to encompass all languages. Such an achievement, however, involved a *separation* of both signs and sounds from their semantic and dramatic meanings. No other system of writing had accomplished this feat.

The same *separation* of sight and sound and meaning that is peculiar to the phonetic alphabet also extends to its social and psychological effects. Literate man undergoes much *separation* of imaginative, emotional, and sense life.[47]

and

Civilization is built on literacy because literacy is a uniform processing of a culture by a visual sense extended in space and time by the alphabet. In tribal cultures, experience is arranged by a dominant auditory sense-life that represses visual values. The auditory sense, unlike the cool and neutral eye, is hyper-esthetic and delicate and *all-inclusive*. Oral cultures act and react at the same time. Phonetic culture endows men with the means of repressing their feelings and emotions when engaged in action. To act without reacting, without involvement, is the peculiar advantage of Western literate man.[48]

Moreover, crucial to the form of mentality that alphabetic writing introduces is a bias in favour of linear thinking. McLuhan says:

Consciousness is regarded as the mark of a rational being, yet there is nothing lineal or sequential about the total field of awareness that exists in any moment of consciousness. Consciousness is not a verbal process. Yet during all our centuries of phonetic literacy we have favored the chain of inference as the mark of logic and reason. Chinese writing, in contrast, invests each ideogram with a total intuition of being and reason that allows only a small role to visual sequence as a mark of mental effort and organization. In Western literate society it is still plausible and acceptable to say that something 'follows' from something, as if there were some cause at work that makes such a sequence. . . . [O]ur Western bias toward sequence as 'logic' [is hidden] in the all-pervasive technology of the alphabet. . . .

Only alphabetic cultures have ever mastered connected lineal sequences as pervasive forms of psychic and social organization. The breaking up of every kind of experience into uniform units in order to produce faster action and

---

[47] McLuhan, *Understanding Media*, 87–8 (emphasis added).   [48] Ibid. 86 (emphasis added).

change of form (applied knowledge) has been the secret of Western power over man and nature alike. That is the reason why our Western industrial programs have quite involuntarily been so militant and our military programs have been industrial. Both are shaped by the alphabet in their techniques of transformation and control by making all situations uniform and continuous. This procedure, manifest even in the Graeco-Roman phase, became more intense with the uniformity and repeatability of the Gutenberg development.[49]

With alphabetic writing, then, comes power, but at a price. On the one hand, writing comes to privilege the visual sense to the relative exclusion of the other senses, thereby subtracting from the richness of experience; the human sensorium is, in other words, running nearly on empty. But, as well, alphabetic writing also privileges linear modes of thought above other more imaginative, intuitive, perhaps juxtapositional ways of thinking. McLuhan claims:

Western history was shaped for some three thousand years by the introduction of the phonetic alephbet [*sic*], a medium that depends solely on the eye for comprehension. The alphabet is a construct of fragmented bits and parts which have no semantic meaning in themselves, and which must be strung together in a line, bead-like, and in a prescribed order. Its use fostered and encouraged the habit of perceiving all environment in visual and spatial terms—particularly in terms of a space and of a time that are uniform
    c,o,n,t,i,n,u,o,u,s
    and
    c-o-n-n-e-c-t-e-d.[50]

Thus, alphabetic culture fetters human consciousness by shackling it to the eye, repressing the other senses, while, at the same time, enforcing a regime of linear thinking, occluding, so to say, other, putatively non-linear modes of thought. Both these interconnected effects, of course, represent a diminution in the forms of consciousness available in tribal cultures, which cultures afforded a mosaic of experience both in the sense that a multiplicity of various sensory modes comprised experience, and in the sense that the presiding modes of thought were non-linear—metaphorical, mythic, juxtapositional, intuitively diverse, and imaginative. Moreover, the tendencies—toward the visualization and linearization of thought— already apparent in alphabetic writing were only intensified by the invention of printing, since printing is alphabetic writing plus mechanization/ standardization.

Of course, when McLuhan claims that a dominant communication

---

[49] Ibid. 85–6.
[50] Id. and Quentin Fiore, *The Medium is the Massage* (New York: Bantam Books, 1967), 44.

medium—like the alphabet—privileges one sense modality, like vision, over others, he does not mean that the other sense modalities disappear. We do not lose our auditory sensibility with the arrival of the alphabet. Nevertheless, in McLuhan's view, the balance between the relative importance of our senses—what McLuhan calls sense ratios—is altered by the hegemony of certain media. So, with the dominance of alphabetic writing as the primary communication medium, sight is valorized over the other senses, and this, in turn, has repercussions for thinking in general which, as we have seen, becomes for McLuhan linear and exclusive rather than non-linear and multi-dimensional (from the point of view of the number of senses that are engaged by the dominant form of thinking).

McLuhan claims:

The history of the Western world since the time of Aristotle has been a story of increasing linguistic specialism produced by the flat, uniform, homogeneous presentation of print. Orality wound down slowly. The scribal (or manuscript) culture of the Middle Ages was inherently oral/aural in character. Manuscripts were meant to be read aloud. Church chantry schools were set up to ensure oral fidelity. The Gutenberg technology siphoned off the aural-tactile quality of the Ancients, systemized language, and established heretofore unknown standards for pronunciation and meaning. Before typography there was no such thing as bad grammar.

After the public began to accept the book on a mass basis in the fourteenth and fifteenth century—and on a scale where literacy mattered—all knowledge that could not be so classified was tucked away into the new 'unconscious' of the folk tale and the myth.[51]

As this quotation makes evident, for McLuhan the invention of printing completes the alphabetic revolution by introducing regimentation and standardization. Of course, McLuhan does not see printing as all bad. Just as Marx regarded capitalism as a historically beneficial stage in human development, McLuhan concedes that print has made positive contributions to culture, including securement of the possibility of a certain form of historically important self-expression.[52] And again reminding us of Marx's conception of capitalism, print, according to McLuhan, changed every dimension of culture, bringing about, by his accounting, not only the dissociation of our senses, but also: specialization, detachment, indi-

---

[51] Marshall McLuhan and Bruce R. Powers, *The Global Village: Transformations in World Life and Media in the 21st Century* (New York: Oxford University Press, 1989), 46.

As this quotation may indicate, McLuhan's periodizations are not always consistent. One would have thought, for example, that medieval culture was alphabetic and, therefore, visual, but here we discover that it was auditory. McLuhan's periodizations, as well, are often so vague that he appears to play fast and loose with them; they seem to expand and contract in terms of what is convenient for making whatever point McLuhan wishes to at a given moment.   [52] McLuhan, *Understanding Media*, 176.

vidualism, privacy, linear perspective, mass production, nationalism, and even modern militarism.[53] That is, in so far as McLuhan regards communication media as the motor of history, the hegemony of printing changed the complexion of society in every way.

However, starting in the nineteenth century, with the emergence of the mass media—newspapers, photographs, comic strips, movies, the phonograph, radio, TV, and computers—the hegemony of print began to be contested. For in various ways these new media challenged the linear-visual mode of alphabetic/print consciousness, restoring to audiences those dimensions of experience that had been alienated by print culture. The newspaper, along with comics, for example, though printed, were laid out in a way that addressed the reader mosaically in so far as they were designed to be read (and viewed) juxtapositionally, rather than merely linearly.[54] Likewise, the photograph, according to McLuhan, recuperated gesture for the recording experience. He says:

If the phonetic alphabet was a technical means of severing the spoken word from its aspects of sound and gesture, the photograph and its development in the movie *restored* gesture to the human tendency of recording experience. In fact, the snapshot of arrested human postures by photography directed more attention to physical and psychic posture than ever before. The age of the photograph has become the age of gesture and mime and dance, as no other age has ever been.[55]

For McLuhan, what is important about the new mass media is that they restore dimensions of consciousness alienated by print culture. This includes the activation of more senses than only the visual and the encouragement of non-linear or mosaic thinking. TV is the medium that, for McLuhan, achieves this to the utmost, though had he lived to learn of CD-ROM he would undoubtedly have had much to say on its behalf as well.

TV, for McLuhan, addresses the whole human sensorium. However, perhaps the oddest claim he makes for it is that it is a tactile art. He writes:

The visual sense when extended by phonetic literacy fosters the analytic habit of perceiving the single facet in the life of forms. The visual power enables us to isolate the single incident in time and space, as in representational art. In visual representation of a person or an object, a single phase or moment or aspect is separated from the multitude of known and felt phases, moments and aspects of the person or object. By contrast, iconographic art uses the eye as we use our

---

[53] This list is derived from Anthony Quinton's extremely useful summary of McLuhan in his article 'McLuhan', in *Thoughts and Thinkers* (New York: Homes and Meier Publishers, Inc., 1982), 270. On the question of nationalism, see McLuhan, *Understanding Media*, 176–7.

[54] McLuhan, *Understanding Media*, 165.   [55] Ibid. 193.

hand in seeking to create an inclusive image, made up of many moments, phases, and aspects of the person or thing. Thus the iconic mode is not visual representation nor the specialization of visual stress as defined by viewing from a single position. The tactual mode of perceiving is sudden but not specialist. It is total, synesthetic, involving all the senses. Pervaded by the mosaic image of TV, the TV child encounters the world in a spirit antithetic to literacy.

The TV image that is to say, even more than the icon, is an extension of the sense of touch. Where it encounters literate culture, it necessarily thickens the sense-mix, transforming fragmented and specialist extensions into a seamless web of experience. . . .

The young people who have experienced a decade of TV have naturally imbibed an urge toward involvement in depth that makes all the remote visualized goals of usual culture seem not only unreal but irrelevant, and not only irrelevant but anemic. It is the total involvement in all-inclusive *nowness* that occurs in young lives via TV's mosaic image. This change of attitude has nothing to do with programming in any way, and would be the same if the programs consisted entirely of the highest cultural content. The change in attitude by means of relating themselves to the mosaic TV image would occur in any event.[56]

Clearly, McLuhan regards askance any media that separate (for example, the senses), and that exclude, whereas he commends media that include—both in terms of a number of the senses they activate, and in terms of encouraging involvement. Moreover, this contrast between the exclusive and the inclusive is related to his famous distinction between hot and cool media. Media that exclude are hot; those that include are cool.[57] Among the mass media of the twentieth century, photography, radio, and the movies are hot, while the cartoon, the telephone, and TV are cool. Hot media possess a high definition, are full of information, and, as a result, are comparatively self-sufficient. Cool media lack these properties and must be filled in or completed by audiences. They require the participation of the audience and, for McLuhan, it would appear, mass art forms that require participation are, all things being equal, superior to hot media. TV excels in this regard.

McLuhan claims:

Television completes the cycle of the human sensorium. With the omnipresent ear and the moving eye, we have abolished writing, the specialized acoustic-visual metaphor that established the dynamics of Western civilization.

In television there occurs an extension of the sense of active, exploratory touch which involves all the senses simultaneously, rather than that of sight alone. You have to be 'with' it. But in all electric phenomena, the visual is only one component in a complex interplay. Since, in the age of information, most transac-

---

[56] McLuhan, *Understanding Media*, 335.   [57] Ibid. 23.

tions are managed electrically, the electric technology has meant for Western man a considerable drop in the visual component, in his experience, and a corresponding increase in the activity of his other senses.

Television demands participation and involvement in depth of the whole being. It will not work as a background. It engages you. Perhaps this is why so many people feel their identity has been threatened. This charge of the light brigade has heightened our general awareness of the shape and meaning of lives and events to a level of extreme sensitivity.[58]

TV, that is, liberates us from the alienation of the senses and of the imagination that had been imposed upon us, and then enforced by the linear/visual regime of print culture. A mosaic medium (think of TV advertisements), promoting the imaginative (non-linear) participation of the mind and engaging all the senses, TV approximates a return to the unalienated form of consciousness enjoyed in tribal times. And, of course, in changing consciousness, the new, cool, participatory media will at the same time change social forms. Society will become a global village, decentralized, communitarian, and fraternal, with people involved in one another's concerns with scarcely a taint of individualism.

Central to McLuhan's conception of the positive value of the mass arts (like TV) is the notion of participation or 'involvement in depth'. The print medium is depicted as authoritarian; the text disciplines the reader. TV, on the other hand, encourages participation and in that sense is democratic. Print excludes non-linear responses; TV is more interactive. It invites the audience to respond, often by means of non-linear thinking.

Moreover, like Benjamin, McLuhan associates the structural potentials of the mass media (with respect to promoting participation) with certain avant-garde effects. Whereas Benjamin correlated Dada experiments with cinematic montage, and film-acting with certain of Brecht's alienation effects, McLuhan sees the so-called mosaic structures of the mass media as on a par with the open structures of the avant-garde. For McLuhan, the pastiche form of representation in TV correlates with the textual strategies of William Burroughs,[59] while the layout of a newspaper is Joycean. McLuhan claims:

Our ordinary newspaper page today is not only symbolist and surrealist in an *avant-garde way,* but it was the earlier *inspiration* of symbolism and surrealism in art and poetry, as anybody can discover by reading Flaubert or Rimbaud. Approached as newspaper form, any part of Joyce's *Ulysses* or any poem of T. S. Eliot's before the *Quartets* is more readily enjoyed.[60]

[58] McLuhan and Fiore, *The Medium is the Massage,* 125.
[59] McLuhan, *Understanding Media,* 230.   [60] Ibid. 216.

By aligning the structures of mass art with the aesthetics of the avant-garde, McLuhan is, in effect—at least rhetorically—outflanking many of the arguments of enemies of mass art such as Collingwood, Greenberg, Adorno, and Horkheimer, since these critics evolved their unfavourable assessments of mass art by contrasting it (if at times only implicitly) with the avant-garde. If Collingwood thought that his theory of art captured what was distinctive about the work of Joyce and T. S. Eliot, and that such a theory would, perforce, imply that mass art is ersatz, McLuhan responds, in effect, by attempting to level the contrast between the mass media and modernism, between mass art and the avant-garde, between TV and James Joyce. To charges that mass art induces passive spectatorship, McLuhan retorts that by its very nature mass art forms–like TV—with their mosaic structures, engender involvement in depth; they are, in short, the very epitome of interactivity (between art and audience), and they live on active, participatory spectatorship.

TV, for instance, requires an audience to fill it in—to respond imaginatively (and non-linearly) with all its senses and intuitive powers.[61] Thus, for McLuhan, TV achieves the condition of avant-garde art which, in parallel fashion, involves a restoration of something like the condition of tribal communication. TV re-tribalizes our culture by returning consciousness to a state where all of our senses and mental powers are given their due, after waning for centuries in a de-tribalized state, during the regime of print culture.[62] The new mass media, like TV, enable human consciousness to realize itself more fully than was possible during the hegemony of print media.

Of course, many of the enemies of mass media and mass art speak from the position of print culture and depend upon deploying its most prized criteria—visuality and linear thinking—against the mass arts. Thus, McLuhan's characterization of history provides him with an argument that more than defends mass media and mass art against the proponents of highest values (visuality and linearity) of print culture. Since this argument relies on the notion of the expansion of consciousness, I call it 'the consciousness argument'.

1. Communication media, at the level of structure, determine consciousness both in terms of sense ratios and in terms of dominant modes of thought processes.

2. Communication media that expand consciousness by enhancing

---

[61] One reason for this, McLuhan argues, is that the TV image (to date, it must be added) is very low in definition and that it requires the mental activity of the audience to fill it in.

[62] McLuhan, *Understanding Media*, 344.

the human sensorium (for example, that bring about a sense ratio in which each sense assumes something like its appropriate importance) and that make available more (rather than fewer) modes of thought are, all things being equal, superior to communication media that constrain consciousness by limiting the human sensorium and the availability of forms of thought.

3. Print media constrain consciousness by limiting it to the visual sense and linear modes of thought, whereas the new mass arts, as exemplified by TV, expand consciousness by restoring the richness of the human sensorium and non-linear thought.

4. Therefore, the new mass arts, as exemplified by TV, are superior to print media.

Thus, the new mass arts serve the prospects for the expansion of human consciousness better than previous art, or, at least, the art of the age of print culture. They represent a new level of artistic achievement, and presumably a superior level, indeed a level of accomplishment that continues and extends the work of the avant-garde by way of its inherent commitment to involvement in depth. Consequently, the new mass arts are not ersatz; they represent a new form of art properly so called; in fact, they represent a superior form of art.

This argument, moreover, can be further extended by claiming that in virtue of the changes in consciousness the new mass media facilitate, new and better forms of socialization will emerge, ones that involve global interactivity, decentralization, and communitarian (rather than individualistic) forms of life. That is, human life will become more participatory, not only at the level of consciousness, but politically and socially as well.

Fundamental to McLuhan's case is the premiss that communication media determine or change consciousness. Major support for this premiss derives from the notion that communication media shape our senses, at least in terms of sense ratios. But, as we have already seen in our discussion of Benjamin, the notion that communication media cause changes at the level of sense perception is highly dubious. Rather, it seems far more likely that communication media are designed to engage the sensory apparatus that humans already possess. How could a new communication medium engage audiences if it addressed us in terms of capacities that we do not yet possess? TV did not change our senses. It would not have succeeded if it required sensory dispositions that were not already in place. Instead of claiming that communication media structure our sensory apparatuses, a better hypothesis—and one that is incompatible with McLuhan's—is that our standing perceptual capacities influence the design of communication media, rather than vice versa. That is, our sensory capacities constrain the design of communication media, in so far as the success (the up-take) of any communication medium depends upon its addressing effectively our pre-existing sensory capacities.

Those pre-existing sensory capacities, of course, evolved biologically over millennia under the pressure of natural selection. As argued earlier, with respect to Benjamin, they are not particularly plastic. They are not likely to change as a result of, for example, fifty years of TV. Moreover, McLuhan's implication that the TV children of the sixties will bequeath their newly acquired perceptual habits to their progeny is embarrassingly Lamarckian. The human sensorium is a biological mechanism. But McLuhan's claims about its plasticity and malleability in response to the introduction of communication media is biologically unfathomable.

It might be thought that McLuhan's claims about changes in sense perception can appeal to the authority of Hegel. But Hegel's saga of the evolution of consciousness provides no support for the notion that our senses evolve over the course of history. Recall that in Hegel's view later stages in the history of consciousness involve not only the overcoming of aspects of previous stages of consciousness, but also involve the incorporation of aspects of ealier stages. Sense perception is an early stage of consciousness for Hegel, but it is taken up into later stages of consciousness intact. It remains a constituent of later stages of consciousness in an unrevised form. Consciousness changes historically for Hegel, but not at the level of sense perception. Thus, Hegel would not recognize as his own the claim of McLuhan (and other historicists of his ilk) that sense perception literally changes over the course of history. That is, McLuhan's hypothesis can find no succour in Jena.[63]

McLuhan's rhetoric is apt to resonate with the views of many contemporary relativists who believe that perception varies radically with culture. But this belief is generally based upon a confusion over two different senses of perception. On the one hand, we see x; on the other hand, we see x as a y, or we see that x is a y. That is, we see x as falling under some category; we see that x is a car. However, seeing that x is a car is different from seeing a material object in front of us on four wheels. Seeing that x is a car requires that we have the concept of a car, whereas seeing a car (a material object of a certain configuration) does not require having the concept car. Aborigines with no concept of a car, nevertheless see a car in front of them if their eyesight is sound.

Often those who think that perception changes confuse these two senses

---

[63] I owe this point to Ivan Soll.

of seeing. Seeing that x is a y is usually a matter of social training, in so far as we generally learn socially the categories to which things belong.[64] And, therefore, our capacities for seeing that x is a y may change as new categories are acquired culturally and/or historically. However, this is no evidence for the hypothesis that seeing in the sense of seeing x changes. For what we literally see is a matter of biology, not culture or history. A culture may only possess a few colour terms, but that does not imply that members of that culture do not see—in the sense of seeing x—thousands of different shades of colour. Thus, there is no argument from the fact that the seeing x as a y modality is open to historical variability to the hypothesis that literal sight, or any other sensory channel is historically variable. A case might be made that seeing x under a concept can be historically variable, but it gives no support to the kind of conjecture that McLuhan is advancing, namely, that literally seeing x is historically malleable.

McLuhan maintains that information technologies are an extension of our senses, including our nervous system. As a metaphor, this has some heuristic value. TV provides us with visual access to events from which we are remote. However, when taken literally, the slogan is implausible from a biological point of view, to say the least—especially if it is supposed to support the idea that communication media change our sensory apparatus, since there is no evidence that watching TV structurally alters our central nervous system.

Of course, at this point, the proponent of McLuhan is likely to say that I have got his argument all wrong, since his claim is not that communication media change our sensory apparatus, but that they change our 'sense ratios'. This does not, it might be said, involve changing the intrinsic structure of given sensory modalities, but only the relative importance that people place on the different organs of sense in their daily lives. What is changed is not the internal constitution of sensory apparatuses—which, indeed, requires the long-term operation of natural selection—but the emphasis that people in a given culture, dominated by certain communication media, place on various senses rather than others.

But this rejoinder is only as good as the concept of sense ratios upon which it depends. And that concept is very suspect, if not thoroughly meaningless, since, despite the scientific-sounding ring that talk of 'ratios' conjures up, McLuhan tells us nothing about the way in which we are to measure these ratios. If there are ratios here, then there should be some

---

[64] I say 'generally' because there are some categories—such as that of human being—that we may possess innately. Babies are said to recognize human faces without training, for example.

conception of sensory units in order for us to calculate different ratios. But McLuhan provides no inkling of the units of measurement which one might deploy in order to gauge the sense ratios determined by different communication media. Does it make sense to talk about ratios, if no metric is provided?[65] Moreover, it seems unlikely that such a metric could be provided, since our sensory faculties are triggered, *ex hypothesi*, in the same degree and in the same way whatever the dominant media. The crow of the rooster, one would retrodict, would have been as clarion during the pictographic era in Egypt as it is in the Gutenberg Age.

Printing supposedly valorizes sight—i.e., sight assumes a greater importance in alphabetic sense ratios than it possesses in the sense ratios of tribal cultures. And, presumably, other senses, like audition, are of lesser importance in the Gutenberg Age. But how plausible is this? Were European print people really less attentive to the sound of explosions in the eighteenth century than the tribal peoples they were shooting at? Or is it that print poeples experience such explosions less intensely than tribal peoples? But that seems unlikely, since the physiological structures of both print peoples and tribal peoples are the same. And if there is some measure of intensity that my argument is ignoring, the burden of proof falls to McLuhan and the McLuhanites to produce it.

Furthermore, McLuhan's hypothesis about differential sense ratios is difficult to operationalize experimentally not only because we have little or no way to understand the notion of sense ratios, but also because McLuhan never supplies us with a way in which to identify a dominant communication medium. How is it that print is the dominant communication medium before the advent of near-universal literacy (in the West), and why is it that when near-universal literacy does eventually arrive in the West, the dominant media are already electric? Indeed, in some sense, has speech ever lost its status as the dominant communication medium world-wide? Certainly during the era when alphabetic writing is said to dominate the scene, there was always more talking than there was reading and writing. So, how does one know when a given medium is dominant? Without knowing that, the hypothesis that sense ratios are determined by the dominant communication media is simply imponderable.

Furthermore, even if McLuhan could provide us with precise characterizations of 'sense ratios' and 'dominant media', there would still be devastating problems with his hypothesis. For what would be the evidence that either sense ratios or the intrinsic structure of the senses were changed under the influence of communication media? In his writing,

---

[65] For further development of this line of argument, see Jonathan Miller, *McLuhan*, 85–7.

the evidence that McLuhan seems to rely upon most is that there are changes in communication media. No concrete evidence is provided to establish changes in perception or sensory ratios from the reception side of things. Nothing is adduced concerning the effects of media on percipients. The putative effects are extrapolated from the alleged causes of those effects, i.e., the communication media. But that is circular. One does not show that something is the cause of x by merely hypothesizing that it is the cause of x. Thus, McLuhan's claims about the expansion of consciousness in response to communication media, in so far as it rests on claims about changes in our sensory faculties or sense ratios, is unfounded conceptually, epistemologically, and scientifically.

In the first premiss of the consciousness arugment, McLuhan contends that consciousness is altered by communication media not only in terms of changing the human sensorium, but in terms of changing modes of thought. Linear thinking, for example, is said to predominate in the Gutenberg Era, while other modes of thinking languish. But this conjecture is as slippery, for parallel reasons, as the conjecture about the human sensorium. What exactly is a mode of thinking and how does one tell when one predominates in a given culture? Whom should we be looking at when we wish to ascertain whether a certain mode of thinking is said to predominate? Should we be concerned with the population at large, or only subsegments? Presumably, with respect to print culture, we will get a very different picture of the dominant modes of thought if we look at peasants rather than intellectuals—indeed, if we concentrate on peasants, one imagines that one will get a very different and perhaps opposing idea of the dominant mode of thought than the one McLuhan proposes, supposing that some sense can be made of the very idea of modes of thought.

But this, in and of itself, is a large supposition. If modes of thought are characterized as loosely as linear versus non-linear thinking, then we will have a hard time classifying many thought processes, such as abduction. But if we cannot individuate thought processes adequately, then it will be impossible to discover whether or not changes in communication media correlate with changes in modes of thinking. For how will we know whether or not there has really been a change in the dominant thought process? McLuhan, as the reader has undoubtedly already surmised, paints with a very broad brush. But the brush is so broad that it paints over the details that one needs in order to assess the applicability of his grand hypotheses.

The hypothesis that communication media determine modes of thought also raises a 'chicken or egg' problem. That is, since communication media need to be invented and invention requires the operation of modes of thought, the case can be made that modes of thought determine the structure of communication media, rather than the other way around. If the correlative mode of thought for alphabetic culture is called linear thinking, doesn't alphabetic writing require the pre-existence of some linear thinkers who produce it? Or does alphabetic writing just pop into existence *ex nihilo*? Of course, if it is said that there is always both linear and non-linear thinking in any society and that it is really a matter of the ratio between them, then we are back to a problem analogous to the one we encountered with sense ratios—namely, how are these ratios to be measured?

Moreover, even if we could individuate thought processes, there is also the problem of how to tell which ones are dominant in a given culture. It sounds like a statistical nightmare, especially in historically remote cultures where even random sampling is out of the question. Here, the McLuhanite could agree but point out, in his own defence, that a social historian might be able to ascertain the *ideal* or most prized modes of thought in a given culture. And, though that might be possible, one still wants to say that a historical conjecture like McLuhan's can't rest on what people believe is the ideal mode of thought in their culture, but must locate what *is* the dominant mode of thought. After all, the relevant historical subjects might be wrong—they might idealize one mode of thinking when really another mode of thinking is the dominant one.

Given all these problems, I think that the first premiss of McLuhan's argument is too controversial to be embraced. Nor does the second premiss look very reliable. McLuhan presupposes that communication media that expand consciousness by enlarging the human sensorium and by amplifying the available modes of thought are better than ones that limit consciousness by diminishing the sensorium and the available repertory of modes of thought. This view, moreover, is a consequence of McLuhan's concept of communication.

For McLuhan, communication is the communication of experience. Since experience is sensorially multi-dimensional and non-linear, communication media that deliver multi-dimensional sensory information (i.e., information that appeals to many senses) and that are non-linear better approximate experience, and, therefore, are better *qua* communication (given that the putative function of communication is to do something like replicate experience). If I experience a fire, then that is an affair of sight, sound, touch, and smell. If I wish to communicate that experience to you in all its richness, then, McLuhan believes, it will be done most adequately by means of a medium that engages all these senses.

But surely it is a mistake to think that communication is essentially concerned with conveying the experience of the sender in all its richness. Perhaps communication sometimes has this goal. But most often, this is more information than we want. Because communication is connected to practical activity and/or to directing the attention of the receiver to this rather than to that, communication naturally tends toward being selective, abstract, and exclusive; too much inclusiveness is likely to thwart communication, rather than to realize its essence. Thus, McLuhan is plainly wrong in his conception of communication as aiming at the replication of the experience of the sender in all its richness.

Of course, a McLuhanite might claim that this argument is merely the dogma of an unreconstructed addict of print culture. But when we ask a sanitation engineer about the way in which a sewerage system operates, it is not clear to me that we also necessarily desire to experience exactly how it smells to him. Moreover, if the principle—that the purpose of communication is to convey experience in all its richness—is unacceptable, then it is not clear why communication media that convey experience richly are superior to media that communicate information more abstractly. That is, McLuhan supports the second premiss of the consciousness argument by means of the notion that communication media essentially aim at conserving sensory experience in the process of transmitting information. But that contention seems false, and without appeal to it, McLuhan has no other grounds for defending the second premiss of the consciousness argument.

According to McLuhan's third premiss, print media constrain consciousness by limiting the human sensorium to the visual and by enforcing linear thinking to the exclusion of other modes of thought; whereas the new mass arts, especially TV, restore the richness of the human sensorium and encourage non-linear thinking. Almost every one of these claims is problematic.

First, there is the question of whether printing as such is biased toward linear thinking rather than non-linear thinking. This seems unlikely. Printing as a technology is neutral to whatever is printed by means of it. Printing can produce logic textbooks, or poems, or the writings of mystics. Supposing that the latter two examples represent non-linear thinking, it must be emphasized that they are no more alien to the mechanical process of printing than are logical theorems. Printing presses do not break down when discourse marked by non-linear thought is typeset. Printing as such can convey any kind of thinking.

It does not seem defensible to say that printing as such is biased toward linear thinking. Printing is a physical procedure that is neutral with respect to its intellectual content. To suppose that a physical procedure like printing could influence the intellectual content—at the level of linear versus non-linear thinking—of what is printed is a category error.

McLuhan claims that TV involves all the senses. One must grant him that it involves sight and hearing. But all the senses? What about touch? We know that McLuhan thinks that TV is tactile, but the reason he offers for this is rather strained—that with TV our eye acts like our hand.[66] And movies are visceral too, since they emphasize gesture. But if we are as free as this in associating a given communication medium with this or that faculty of sense, why not say that the print medium also engages senses other than sight when, for example, dialogue is laid out on a page, or gestures are described in detail, or textures and smells are invoked?[67]

There is frequently something very arbitrary about the way in which McLuhan associates certain media with the senses—as when he discloses that TV is really tactile—such that one suspects one could, by aping McLuhan's 'method', associate any medium with any sense, or any combination of senses. But if that is the case, then we have little more reason to suppose that TV is tactile than we do to suppose that print—in some metaphorical sense—is also tactile. Of course, it might be argued that metaphorical correlations of a given communication medium with a given sense modality is illicit when calculating sense ratios, and that only literal correlations should count. But in that event, much of what McLuhan has to say about the putative enlargement of the human sensorium by the modern mass arts will go by the boards, since, for example, TV is not literally tactile. Yet, this concession would undermine the third premiss of the consciousness argument.

Therefore, in so far as each of the premisses of the consciousness argument is worrisome, the argument appears unsound.

Moreover, McLuhan's attempt to promote the new mass media in terms of the way in which they promise to bring into existence new, benevolent, social forms—such as the global village—is equally unpersuasive. Like Benjamin, McLuhan seems to believe that information technologies carry their own political and social agendas. Specifically, the electronic media, by McLuhan's lights, are inherently de-centralizing at the same time that they are global. However, as innumerable dystopian novelists, from Orwell onwards, have shown it is at least eminently conceivable that the electronic media might serve centralizing, totalitarian purposes. The electronic

---

[66] Indeed, reading typically would seem to have a better claim to being tactile than TV, since we use our hands to turn pages.

[67] Also, might not the print media be tactile for those who 'read' with their fingers, and aural for those who move their lips while whispering the words on the page?

media, indeed no media, have a pre-established moral destiny. They may be used for good or ill. There is no guarantee that the new mass media as such will deliver the kind of future that McLuhan finds morally attractive. Therefore, the putative moral attractiveness of the global village provides no grounds for defending the new mass media.

Throughout his writings, McLuhan puts too much faith in the power of the media to transform not only consciousness, but society. Of course, this is the central tenet of his philosophy of history—that communication media are the motor of the historical process. But this presuppostion is too strong. Undoubtedly, communication media make *some* contribution to the historical change,[68] but it is a mistaken, gross exaggeration to hold that they are the primary cause of change in every instance.

For example, McLuhan maintains that print is the cause of modern militarism, specifically in terms of the enlistment of large national armed forces. And certainly printing has something to do with the maintenance of massive armies, since printing makes possible the transmission of uniform commands across large bodies of troops, distributed over wide geographical expanses. But printing did not cause the emergence of large armies, even if it facilitates their existence, since the Gutenberg Era began several centuries before the kind of army that McLuhan has in mind made its appearance with the French Revolution. Printing may have been a necessary background condition for the possibility of fielding large armies, but it is not the triggering cause, as McLuhan is wont to imply.[69]

Indeed, McLuhan makes this error again and again. He repeatedly exaggerates the efficacy of communication media by claiming that communication media are the determining causes of all sorts of social phenomena for which they are at best necessary background causal conditions. In this respect, McLuhan's error resembles that of the historical materialist who rightfully notes that economic factors can be significant, though often overlooked, ingredients in social causation, but who then wrongly goes on to claim that they are always the determinant cause of social transformation in the last instance. Likewise, McLuhan is certainly correct in calling our attention to the role of communication media in history, but, equally, he is certainly wrong to maintain that it is always, or, even most often, that which finally determines social transformation. For in most cases where communication media figure in the causal matrix that

[68] Similarly, it may make sense to say that communication media make some difference to the way in which the people who use them think, i.e., to their *habits* of thought. However, such a trivial admission falls way short of McLuhan's assertions that communication media change the very structure of consciousness, the human sensorium and patterns of thought at the level of logical processing.   [69] Quinton, 'McLuhan', 273.

brings about historical change, they do so by way of functioning as necessary background conditions for initiatives, like mass conscription, that originate in other strata of the social fabric.

As noted, McLuhan also defends the new mass arts by aligning them with the avant-garde. Analogies between the new mass media and modernist art abound. For example, McLuhan says 'the viewer of the TV mosaic, with technical control of the image, unconsciously reconfigures the dots into an abstract work of art on the pattern of a Seurat or Rouault.'[70] And, as we have already seen, newspaper layouts are supposedly proto-Joycean. The crux of these analogies, for McLuhan, is the notion of participation. The avant-garde artwork is participatory because of its mosaic—often elliptical or juxtapositional—structure, which encourages the audience to fill it in or complete it. Likewise, McLuhan is at pains to show—again and again—that comparable mosaic forms are inherent in mass art media and, consequently, that mass art media also engender a form of audience participation that is strictly analogous to the modalities of participatory spectatorship called forth by the avant-garde.

This is at least a canny manœuvre on McLuhan's part given the history of the mass art debate, since the most sophisticated opponents of mass art have not only been friends of the avant-garde, but, more importantly, because their arguments against mass art are generally, if only implicitly, involved in demoting the status of mass art by contrasting it to the virtues of avant-garde or modernist art, especially in terms of the issue of participation. The mass arts are frequently condemned because they are passive rather than active. But passive in comparison with what? If one probes their arguments, the answer is almost always: in comparison with avant-garde or modernist art which is active and participatory, rather than passive, and non-participatory.

McLuhan meets this line of attack head-on—claiming that mass art media, in consequence of their nature, are not passive and non-participatory, but they promote active, participatory spectatorship of exactly the same sort provoked by the most ambitious work of the historical avant-garde. In this way, McLuhan directly confronts many of the arguments against mass art that we encountered in the last chapter.

But there are a number of problems with the way in which McLuhan stages this outflanking movement. First, even if one agrees, as I do, that the mass arts are more participatory than the philosophical opponents of mass art usually acknowledge, one cannot be too happy with the reasons— or, at least, the examples—that McLuhan generally advances in support of

---

[70] McLuhan, *Understanding Media*, 313.

this claim. The TV image, for instance, is said to possess a low definition, in terms of resolution, when compared to movie images. Thus, McLuhan surmises that the TV image must be filled in or completed by the spectator, and that this species of filling in is comparable to the participatory spectatorship required by the avant-garde audience. But there is a difficulty here. The sort of filling in or participation involved here is basically a matter of recognizing what the televised picture is a picture of. And this is an *automatic* process.

But one would suppose that the kinds of participation that the friends of the avant-garde have in mind are not automatic. I am not quibbling here over whether or not the audience is in some sense filling in the TV image, but only whether the psychological activity in question is of a piece with what modernist detractors of mass art have in mind when they disparage mass art. They talk in terms of mental activities like contemplation and reflection, which certainly sound like activities that obtain above the threshold of automatic perceptual responses. Thus, I suspect that they would challenge the kind of analogies, like the TV analogy, that McLuhan frequently deploys in order to hoist the modernists on their own petards.

That is, many of the analogies that McLuhan invokes are of the preceding sort—analogies that attempt to assimilate automatic perceptual responses to media technologies to avant-garde spectatorship. But these analogies, I suspect, can be rather easily deflected by philosophical modernists who are apt to argue that there are weighty and principled differences between automatic perceptual responses and aesthetic responses, properly so called.

Furthermore, I tend to side with the modernists in this dispute. Whatever is meant by participatory spectatorship in this debate, it does not refer to automatic perceptual responses. However, this does not entail that I agree with the modernist's argument against mass art on the grounds of participatory spectatorship, since I think that it can be shown (and that I have shown) that mass art can engage the active participation of the spectators at levels of intellective activity of a higher order than that of automatic perceptual responses. I only disagree with McLuhan's attempt to use the automatic responses engendered by mass art technologies as evidence that mass art promotes active spectatorship of a kind that is aesthetically relevant to the debate about audience participation.

A second problem with McLuhan's conflation of the mass arts and the avant-garde on the grounds of structure is that he ignores the commitment of the avant-garde to difficulty. The philosophical detractors of mass art are probably wrong (I think that they are certainly wrong) to take difficulty to be a necessary condition for the status of art proper. But I think that they are on much firmer ground, if their position is reconstrued as the proposition that difficulty is a necessary condition of avant-garde art. Moreover, if this is correct, then they, along with the rest of us, have the conceptual wherewithal to block McLuhan's attempt to level the difference between avant-garde or modernist art and mass art. For mass art, even though it abets certain levels of participation, does not do so in virtue of being difficult. So even if mass art and modernist art both engage participation, they are categorically different, since avant-garde art does it by means of difficulty—which, in turn, incurs an arduous, or, at least, recondite response in contrast to 'easy' responses elicited by mass art.

Thus, once again, there is a decisive disanalogy between avant-garde art and mass media art, such that the philosophical modernist can block McLuhan's attempted defence of mass art on the grounds that the (intentionally difficult) structures of avant-garde art and the challenging responses they are designed to engender are categorically different from the (intentionally easily accessible) structures of mass art and the undemanding response they are designed to promote in general audiences. That is, there is a distinction between mass art and avant-garde art, especially in terms of audience response, that calls into question McLuhan's attempt to assimilate mass-media art to the status of the avant-garde. Philosophical modernists were mistaken in presupposing that this distinction was enough to cashier mass art from the order of art proper, but they were not mistaken in discerning a distinction between mass art and the avant-garde, a distinction that undercuts McLuhan's attempt to defend mass-media art as nothing but the full-blooded successor of modernism.

Concluding remarks

Throughout this chapter, the philosophical defences of mass art proffered by Benjamin and McLuhan have been subjected to pretty intensive criticism. By my account, neither the progress argument nor the consciousness argument gets off the ground. However, it should be emphasized that it is not the case that, because these arguments fail, I think mass art is indefensible. The point of this chapter is that the arguments of Benjamin and McLuhan are flawed, but this is not a concession to the opponents of mass art encountered in the first chapter. Mass art is art for reasons yet to be discussed. But its art status is not to be secured by arguments of the sort advanced by Benjamin and McLuhan.

As already noted, Benjamin's and McLuhan's arguments on behalf of mass-art media are somewhat Hegelian. This is an attractive line of argument to take, since it provides the friend of mass art with the opportunity to claim that mass art is a *new* form of art (properly so called) and that, as such, it should not be assessed by criteria appropriate to the art or the art theory of a previous historical epoch. This affords the friend of mass art the wherewithal to make an end run around most of her critics, including most notably, the ersatz Kantians. Confronted by ersatz Kantians, a Hegelian-inspired Benjamin or McLuhan can respond: that was then; this is now. That mass art cannot be counted as art by the Kantian-derived lights of Greenberg, Collingwood, and Adorno does not show that mass art is not art properly so called, since it may be the art (properly so called) of a new era.

Under the inspiration of Hegel, both Benjamin and McLuhan suggest historical narratives, or perhaps 'metanarratives', that culminate with sanguine accounts of the flourishing of mass art. These Utopian narratives stand in stark contrast to the dystopian narratives told by Greenberg and Adorno, which end with prophecies of the collapse of civilization. On the one hand, the grand narratives of Benjamin and McLuhan are an antidote to the inveterate pessimism of folks like Greenberg and Adorno. But, on the other hand, one wonders whether or not there isn't something suspect about all these stories—the Utopian ones as well as the dystopian ones.

Adorno, Greenberg, Benjamin, and McLuhan all tell grand narratives that are virtually allegories and that project their hopes and dreams (including, sometimes, anxiety dreams) on to the historical process. None of these stories is a straightforward historical narrative, in so far as they all suppose knowledge of the future—for example, of the fall of civilization (Greenberg) or the advent of the global village (McLuhan)—that is far from certain. Unlike the ordinary historian, that is, Adorno, Greenberg, Benjamin, and McLuhan are presuming historical effects not known to obtain at the time they composed their grand historical panoramas. For this reason alone, we should suspect the status of their narratives as genuine history.[71]

But if they are not genuine histories, what are they? Again the notion of allegory comes to mind. But the historical process itself is not an allegory. And perhaps everyone would be better off if we just give up trying to treat it as such. This is more fruitful than trying to assess whether the dsytopian allegories of Greenberg and Adorno are more persuasive than the Utopian allegories of Benjamin and McLuhan. For the metaphysical presuppositions required to render the notion intelligible—that the historical process

[71] Arthur Danto makes this argument against all grand narratives of Hegelian vintage in 'Substantive and Analytical Philosophy of History', in his *Narration and Knowledge* (New York: Columbia University Press, 1985), 1–16.

is an allegory of some sort—are too speculative to warrant serious consideration. They invite the postulation of virtually magical agencies. Who, after all, writes these allegories in the flesh and blood of history?

Of course, Benjamin and McLuhan attempt to ground their stories materially. They discern the relevant futures as inscribed in various technologies. However, this too seems to me to indulge in a bit of magical thinking. For Benjamin and McLuhan descry a benevolent moral agenda, in the form of politically attractive modes of thought, to be inherent in the mass media. But neither moral nor political correctness is an intrinsic property of any information technology as such—indeed, they are not properties of any technology as such. The moral or political value of a technology, including a mass medium, is a property of the use of that technology in a concrete setting. Such media are morally and politically neutral *qua* technology. Thus, mass-art media cannot be defended on the basis of some putatively essential moral or political destiny that lies incarnate in their very nature. The presupposition that such an argument is legitimate is probably the deepest flaw in the most sophisticated celebrations of mass art. And both Benjamin and McLuhan, it seems to me, are guilty of it.

Another view that is shared by Benjamin and McLuhan is that there is a bond between the avant-garde arts and mass art. Benjamin regards Dada as an anticipation of cinematic (montage) shock, while he sees the alienating techniques of Brechtian acting as related to the distanciating (criticism-producing) effects of film-acting. McLuhan offers even more analogies between mass-art media and modernist poetics than these. As already noted, these analogies make a certain strategic sense, once one recalls that the leading arguments against mass art hail from theorists with a vested interest in championing avant-garde modernism. As argued in the last chapter, this includes transmogrifying elements of Kantian aesthetics into theories of art, biased in favour of modernism, that can then be used to bludgeon mass art.

Thus, by equating mass art with avant-garde art, Benjamin and McLuhan, like aikido masters, effectively attempt to appropriate the energy of their opponents for their own purposes. But these manœuvres, it seems to me, have more style than content. I find it difficult to agree that movie viewers are typically thrown into anything like the state of critical reflection that Brechtian alienation effects bring about, nor is watching TV programmes, no matter how many disjunctive commercials intervene, like reading *Finnegans Wake*. Nor does Hitchcock's editing standardly deliver the same kind of shocks that the aleatoric techniques of Dada provoke. Perhaps Benjamin and McLuhan can describe the effects that they

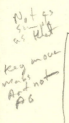

analogize vaguely enough to make it *sound* like there are real similarities here, but the experience of these techniques—avant-garde techniques, on the one hand, and mass art techniques, on the other—are so different that there is little point in equating them.

And yet there is something right about thinking of mass art and the avant-garde in tandem. So far, we have seen that all of our philosophical commentators on mass art—including Greenberg, Collingwood, MacDonald, Adorno, Horkheimer, Benjamin, and McLuhan—have, either implicitly or explicitly, linked their thinking about mass art with thinking about the avant-garde.[72] Of course, their theories also often diverge radically from each other in their assessments of the relative values of mass art and the avant-garde, and there are also significant differences of opinion here about the dissimilarities and the similarities that obtain between mass art and the avant-garde. But underneath this disagreement, there seems to be a consensus that talk about mass art naturally involves talk about the avant-garde.

Why does this couplet—mass art / avant-garde art—recur so frequently? Does it reveal something important about mass art? What makes it seem so natural to talk about mass art in tandem with the modernist avant-garde? Is the juxtaposition of mass art and the avant-garde right—i.e., is it theoretically apposite? I will attempt to answer these questions in the next chapter on the nature of mass art.

[72] I say implicitly here because MacDonald derives much of his theory from Greenberg where Greenberg's arguments presume that the avant-garde is the relevant, as well as the superior, foil to mass art. All the other commentators listed above make explicit reference to the avant-garde in the formulation of their theories of art.

3 The Nature of Mass Art

Introduction

The purpose of this chapter is to provide an analysis of the concept of mass art. That is, my aim is to produce a philosophical theory that isolates the common structural, functional, and ontological features that enable us to group assorted films, TV programmes, photographs, songs, pulp novels, fiction magazines, comics, broadcasts, and so on under the rubric of *mass art*.

Mass art has been with us, to a certain extent, since the invention of the printing press. But it has become increasingly omnipresent with the advent and expansion of the industrial revolution, due to the creation of new technologies for the mass production and distribution of pictures, stories, songs, and so on. Moreover, in the so-called information age, the electronic means for disseminating art have been further augmented to the point where it is conceivable that we will soon reach—if we have not already reached—a historical juncture where almost no human being on earth will be able to escape some exposure to mass art.

Nowadays it is commonplace to remark that we live in an environment dominated by mass art—dominated, that is, by TV, movies, popular music (both recorded and broadcast), best-selling blockbuster novels, photography, and the like. Undoubtedly this condition is most pronounced in the industrialized world, where mass art, or mass entertainment, is probably the most common form of aesthetic experience for the largest number of people. But mass art has also penetrated the non-industrial world as well, to such an extent that in many places something like a global mass culture is coming to exist—what Todd Gitlin has called a 'second culture'—alongside indigenous, traditional cultures. Indeed, in some cases, this second culture may have even begun to erode the first culture in certain third-world countries.[1] But in any case, as I have already conjectured, it is increasingly difficult to find people anywhere in the world today who have not had some experience of mass art as a result of the technologies of mass distribution.

Nor is any slackening of the grip of mass art likely. Even now, dreams of fibre-optic cable feeds running into every household keep media moguls panting, while Hollywood produces movies at a fevered pace, not simply to sell on the current market, but also in order to stockpile a larder sufficient to satisfy the gargantuan appetites of the home entertainment centres that, according to current predictions, will proliferate in the near future. Intellectual properties of all sorts are being produced and acquired at a delirious pitch in the expectation that the envisioned media technologies to come will require a simply colossal amount of product to transmit. Thus, if anything, we may anticipate the production and distribution of more mass art in the approaching future than ever before.

Mass art—at least in the statistical sense—is the most dominant art of our times. As such, it should command the attention of philosophers of art. My purpose here is to say something about the nature of this art, especially as it crystallized in the throes of the industrial revolution and as it continues to develop into the age of electronic reproduction. Though I think that my proposals do pertain, in many ways, to the forms of mass art that attended the rise of the printing press and other earlier forms of mass reproduction (such as popular Japanese woodcuts), my theory is particularly geared to mass art as it emerged in the industrial revolution and as it continues to evolve in the information age. Roughly stated, the extension of the items that I intend my theory to capture includes: popular commercial films, TV, commercial photography, pop music, broadcast radio, computer video games, comic strips, world wide web sites, and pulp literature.

Although, as I have just asserted, philosophers of art should be interested in mass art, as we saw in Chapter 1 they have not been. Throughout the period of the ascendency of mass art, most philosophers of art have either ignored mass art or have been outright hostile to it—demoting mass art to the rank of either kitsch or psuedo art. This philosophical resistance to mass art, I conjectured earlier, is in large measure the result of a

---

[1] For example, in the 1980s, the most popular TV programme in the People's Republic of China was a Disney compilation called *Mickey Mouse and Donald Duck*; it was so popular that it eclipsed folk heroes like Chi-Kung, the 'crazy Buddha'; and in some South American nations Disney characters are more familiar to children than the characters of their own native folklore. In Brazil, more villagers could identify Michael Jackson than their own presidential aspirants in 1984. See: James Lull, *Media, Communication, Culture: A Global Approach* (New York: Columbia University Press, 1995), 17; and A. Dorfman and A. Mattelart, *Para Leer al Pato Donald: Comunición de Masa y Colonialismo* (Mexico City: Siglo XXI, 1972).

mistaken attempt to fashion the Kantian theory of free beauty into theories of art proper that are particularly biased toward the modernist avant-garde.

Because of their misappropriation of Kantian aesthetic theory and their allegiance to modernism, theorists like Collingwood, Greenberg, Adorno, and Horkheimer tended to regard mass art as ersatz art. They observed, with some cause: that mass art is formulaic; that, in certain pertinent respects, the response to mass art was what they considered to be passive; that mass art is generally designed to induce certain predetermined effects; that mass artworks are not unique; and so on. Moreover, on the basis of such observations, they surmised that mass art was not art properly so called.

However, not only are the specific arguments advanced by MacDonald, Collingwood, Adorno, and Horkheimer beset with problems, but the Kantian-modernist framework that they employ to disqualify mass art from the order of art proper is conceptually ill-suited to theorize mass art. Kantian-modernist resistance to mass art lacks the conceptual resources to characterize the nature of mass art adequately, since its underlying philosophical framework was designed to track something almost entirely different.

Thus, at the risk of sounding presumptuous, my aim in this chapter is to begin to redress the failure of the philosophical tradition to come to terms with mass art. I intend to offer a theory of mass art as it is, rather than a polemic about what it should or should not be. But, of course, even this apparently simple statement of purpose is fraught with difficulties. One of those difficulties, some would contend, is the very way in which I have chosen to articulate my task.

I have called my object of study *mass art*. Others have adopted alternative labels, including popular art, kitsch, lowbrow art, the popular, and so on. Nor are these alternative labels merely matters of convenience. Many practitioners of what is coming to be called cultural studies, like Andrew Ross,[2] Patrick Brantlinger,[3] and John Fiske,[4] regard *mass art* as a suspect—if not altogether spurious–concept, preferring the notions of popular art and the popular as the most appropriate ones for surveying the field. Consequently, in the process of developing my theory of mass art, I will also need to provide arguments in favour of denominating the field of inquiry in the way I do.

This chapter is comprised of five more parts of substantive analysis and argumentation. The first part concerns an examination of a theory that I

---

[2] Andrew Ross, *No Respect* (New York: Routledge, 1989).

[3] Patrick Brantlinger, *Bread and Circuses* (Ithaca, NY: Cornell University Press, 1983).

[4] John Fiske, *Understanding the Popular* (London: Unwin Hyman, 1989); and id., *Reading the Popular* (London: Unwin Human, 1989).

call 'The Elimination Theory of Mass Art', or, alternatively, 'The Social Reduction Theory of Mass Art'. The Elimination Theory contends that there really is no such thing as popular or mass art, apart from the role that certain objects play in reinforcing pre-existing class distinctions and social identities. That is, there are no formal or structural features, nor are there any distinguishing affective consequences, that might serve to differentiate popular or mass art from any other sort of art. That some artworks are called 'mass artworks' is purely a sociological matter. It is an arbitrary convention that we group certain objects under the rubrics of popular art and mass art; the merely apparent aesthetic distinction here, in other words, can be reduced to and explained by social facts, such as the social need for signs or markers of certain class distinctions.

But, since my theory claims that mass art is a philosophically worthwhile distinction—one based on specific structural, functional, and ontological properties—The Elimination Theory is a rival to my view, one whose scepticism I need to undermine before I advance my own theory of the nature of mass art. For if mass art is purely a social construction, then my attempt to define mass art in terms of its structural and aesthetic properties is chimerical. Thus, refuting The Elimination Theory is my first order of business in this chapter.

In the next section of this chapter, I will develop my own theory of mass art by means of a formula, replete with necessary conditions that are jointly sufficient. I will also deal with some problems that the theory might be thought to incur, and, though my theoretical purpose here is first and foremost definitional, I will also make some conjectures about the value of my theory for empirical research.

In the third section of this chapter, I will discuss the ontological status of mass art. This section represents an extended clarification of the claim that mass art belongs to the broader category of multiple instance or type art.

The fourth section of the chapter reviews a rival theory of mass art that has recently been proposed by the philosopher David Novitz. Since Novitz advances his own theory by criticizing my theory of mass art, this section will involve both a refutation of Novitz's criticisms of my theory of mass art, and my criticisms of Novitz's theory of mass art.

Following the discussion of Novitz, I will go on in the next section of the chapter to entertain some objections to my approach that I anticipate might be advanced by proponents of cultural studies. This section is dialectically important, since, at present, cultural studies provides the major arena for the study of mass art in the contemporary academy. Specifically, I will address John Fiske's assertion that there is no such thing as mass culture. For, of course, if Fiske is right, then my project is doomed from the start. So, I must argue that Fiske's position is indefensible. Moreover, in the process of criticizing the shortcomings of Fiske's theory, I hope to advance further reasons for embracing my theory of mass art.

The Elimination Theory of mass art

According to the Elimination Theory of mass art, there are no formal features that distinguish popular art or mass art from other sorts of art, such as so-called high art. Nor are there any recurring affective features (such as certain types of emotional responses) that will do the job either. For the Eliminativist, the distinction between popular art (and mass art as the relevant subcategory of popular art), on the one hand, and high art, on the other hand, has no structural, functional, formal, or ontological basis. Rather, the distinction is really a class distinction. So-called high art is the art that is consumed by the members of the upper classes, and their consumption of high art is, in part, what signals their membership in that social stratum. Popular art and mass art are what everyone else consumes, and, likewise, their consumption of such art is a marker of their class affiliations. In short, the Eliminativist maintains that there is no such thing as popular art or mass art, apart from the role that certain objects play in marking and reinforcing certain class distinctions and class identities.[5]

[5] Originally, I thought that David Novitz's article 'Ways of Artmaking: The High and the Popular in Art' was a fair representative of the position that I am calling the Elimination Theory of Mass Art. Novitz, however, has charged that I have misconstrued his position. I am not completely convinced of this, and, as a result, Novitz and I have debated my interpretation of his position in print. Nevertheless, I think that even if I did misinterpret Novitz's intentions, Eliminativism is still an important position that needs to be addressed, since it is a powerful and coherent position. Thus, even if Novitz did not make the argument that I sketch above, it is philosophically necessary for me to deal with it, in so far as there is no point in my going on to construct my theory, if an argument like it is compelling. As well, the argument is worth scotching, since it represents a position that many theoreticians might be tempted to hold as a result of the influential writings of Pierre Bourdieu. Indeed, Eliminativism is a position naturally suggested by Bourdieu and his followers. Thus, eliminating Eliminativism has a certain heuristic value given the inclinations among contemporary art theorists.

However, since Novitz denies that he is an Eliminativist, rather than attacking him, I will direct my criticism at an anonymous theorist called the Eliminativist. Whether or not this position accurately reflects Novitz's view I will leave to the reader of the debate between Novitz and me.

The relevant contributions to that debate are: David Novitz, 'Ways of Artmaking: The High and the Popular in Art', *British Journal of Aesthetics*, 29/3 (1989), 213–29; Noël Carroll, 'The Nature of Mass Art', *Philosophic Exchange*, 23 (1992), 5–37; David Novitz, 'Noël Carroll's Theory of Mass Art', *Philosophic Exchange*, 23 (1992), 39–49; Noël Carroll, 'Mass Art, High Art and the Avant-Garde: A Response to David Novitz', *Philosophic Exchange*, 23 (1992), 51–62.

I also think that something like the Eliminativist's conclusion can be teased out of the writings of Pierre Bourdieu. See especially Pierre Bourdieu, 'The Production of Belief: Contribution to an Economy of Symbolic Goods', and id. 'The Aristocracy of Culture', in *Media, Culture and Society: A Reader*, ed. Richard Collins, James Curran, Nicholas Garnham, Paddy Scannell, Philip Schlesinger and Colin Sparks (Beverly Hills, Calif.: Sage Publications, 1986). See also Pierre Bourdieu, *Distinction: A Social Critique of the Judgment of Taste*, trans. Richard Nice (Cambridge, Mass.: Harvard University Press, 1984).

One may call this the Elimination Theory of Mass Art on the grounds that it maintains that there really is no such thing as popular art or mass art, apart from the social role they play.[6] However, in this context 'really' is meant to contrast with 'conventionally'. The Eliminativist does not want to deny that, as a matter of social fact, we do make a distinction between popular art and what is called high art. Rather, he contends that the distinction is nothing more than a convention. The distinction, in other words, reduces down to social facts about class differences. Thus, the Elimination Theory of Mass Art can also be called the 'Social Reduction Theory of Mass Art'.

But whether we call its proponent an Eliminativist or a Social Reductionist, his leading idea is that the distinction between what is called high art and popular (or mass) art rests not upon any formal, structural, or otherwise intrinsic properties of the works in question, but is merely a device through which society, notably industrialized Western society, elaborates pre-existing class distinctions in terms of putative differences in taste.

That is, just as class distinctions are said to be marked by one's choice of automobile, housing, and cuisine, so the art one consumes generally, according to the Eliminativist, signals one's class membership *and*, moreover, this social function is the real grounds for the distinction that we make between high art and popular art. A blue-collar worker drinks beer, reads the *New York Daily News*, and watches *Roseanne*; the upwardly mobile yuppie drinks Chablis, reads *The New York Times*, and attends ballet and the opera.

The Eliminativist's argument is debunking in nature. It proceeds by challenging an assortment of standard ways of attempting to negotiate the distinction between high art and popular art in accordance with some principle. After scouting various proposals, the Eliminativist concludes that there is no principled way of drawing the distinction. Nevertheless, the Eliminativist presumes that even if there is no theoretically principled way of drawing the distinction, there must still be some explanation of what we are trying to do by means of such a distinction. That is, even if the

---

[6] For most of this section, I set out the Eliminativist's argument primarily in terms of 'popular art', adding the notion of mass art either parenthetically or disjunctively (since it is the relevance of the argument to mass art that concerns us). My reason for proceeding in this fashion is that the Eliminativist's argument works better initially, if we are thinking in terms of popular art. That is, stating the argument with primary emphasis on the notion of popular art papers over some difficulties in the argument to which I will return in the concluding paragraphs of this section. Mass art, as we shall see, is a subcategory of popular art. But once we take the Eliminativist's argument to be aimed at mass art, it will be apparent that the Eliminativist has ignored certain important grounds for discriminating between it and the high art that evolves historically alongside mass art.

distinction is illusory from a philosophical point of view, we must still account for why we suffer the illusion.

Under the pressure of producing such an account, the Eliminativist proposes that the theoretically insubstantial distinction between so-called high art and popular art persists as part of an overall system of class distinctions; it serves to mark off an élite class from, presumably, everyone else. Moreover, this explanation debunks the distinction in question, in so far as it implies that the only way that someone could come to uphold it is through a commitment to some ideologically suspect social arrangement, such as class stratification.

In order to advance such an explanation, the first step for the Eliminativist is to show that there are no principled distinctions to be drawn between high art and popular art. This involves demonstrating that the bases upon which we are prone to draw distinctions between high art and popular art all collapse under the most meagre scrutiny.

What are some of the standard bases for distinguishing between what is called high art and popular art? Four putatively obvious ones are: 1. differences in form (for example, high art is complex, whereas popular art is simple); 2. differences in affect (for example, high art deals in or expresses profound, deep, and nuanced emotions, whereas popular art arouses routine, shallow, and commonplace emotions); 3. differences in origin (for example, high art is produced by individuals involved in adventures of self-discovery and exploration, whereas popular art is produced collectively or even corporately with no commitment to self-expression); and 4. differences in motivation (for example, high art, with its celebration of disinterestedness, is produced in opposition to capitalism's reduction of all value to market value, whereas popular art is a creature of the market-place).

Clearly none of these distinctions can, the Eliminativist notes, withstand the slightest historical pressure. Some high art is simple, described in terms like 'elegance', whereas, by many measures of complexity, popular or mass art can be complex: *The Hunt for Red October* and *Terminator 2* are technically complex, while *Twin Peaks* and its Danish cousin *The Kingdom* are structurally complex. Moreover, some fair examples of what is thought of as high art—like the religious art of the Middle Ages and the Renaissance—were predicated upon instilling the commonplace devotional attitudes of their times in their prospective audiences, whereas a TV drama like *Marty* explores some neglected emotions with subtlety. And there are many more examples where these came from. Thus, the Eliminativist takes it that a barrage of counter-examples like these readily establishes that there are no reasonable theoretical grounds for believing that popular art has any distinguishing formal or affective properties that hive it off from high art in a principled way.

Likewise, the thought that high art is to popular art as works of individual genius are to corporate productions can easily be dispelled. Drama, ballet, and opera—putatively high art—are often no less collaborative than commercial film-making or network TV, while some Hollywood productions—the works of Hitchcock and Keaton come to mind—bear the stamp of an individual artist. Nor can the relation between high art to the market-place drive a wedge between it and popular art. Are Julian Schnabel and David Salle less attuned to the siren call of money than Steven Spielberg and Madonna?[7]

In summary then, the Eliminativist's argument takes this form:

1. The distinction between high art and popular art is based upon either (a) a difference in formal structures; (b) a difference in affective properties; (c) a difference in origin (i.e., a difference of personal, individual creation versus anonymous corporate or collaborative creation); (d) a distinction in motive; or (e) a matter of class differentiation.

2. The distinction between high art and popular art cannot be based on (a), (b), (c), or (d). (This premiss is motivated by the preceding counter-examples).

3. Therefore, the distinction between high art and popular art is based on (e)—it is a matter of class differentiation.

Moreover, it seems that the way in which we are to interpret this conclusion is to regard so-called high art as the insignia of membership in the élite, whereas popular (or mass) art is the badge of the rest of us.

However, understanding the conclusion in this way already suggests that there is something wrong here. High art, at least in contemporary America, doesn't really seem to function as an emblem of membership in the dominant social classes. Not only does George Bush avow a love of country music and Bill Clinton a taste for rock, but popular (mass) art, statistically, is probably the art that most of our élite consume most frequently, while, at the same time, the largest portion of our élite are likely to be suspicious of contemporary high art.

Obviously, an interest in consuming or making contemporary high art (which is primarily avant-garde art) requires a degree of education, but

---

[7] For an account of the mendacious market mentality of the contemporary art scene, see Arthur Danto, 'Bad Aesthetic Times', in his *Encounters and Reflections: Art in the Historical Present* (New York: Farrar Strauss Giroux, 1990), 297–312.

that is readily available to anyone of any class who attends college, and, of course, the requisite background can also be acquired autodidactically without attending the university. Moreover, a roster of contemporary artists and critics quickly reveals that allegiance to the practices of high art (avant-garde art) does not depend on social background—though admittedly being in the upper middle class or the middle class may make such an allegiance more probable—while, at the same time, a taste for popular art and an aversion to high art seems to cut across class lines, at least in contemporary American society. The Eliminativist's account of the high art/popular art distinction can't be right, at least in the American context, because it is false that class distinctions map on to the high art/popular art distinction in the way that the Eliminativist's account requires, if it is to be indeed an explanation of the social persistence of the distinction.

In fact, from the viewpoint of social theory, there is something patently strained about dividing our society into two social classes—the élite and everyone else—and then mapping the high art/popular art distinction on to this division. Clearly, there are more social divisions than these two in the United States at least, and, though there are probably some important relations between some social affiliations and artistic consumption, it must be far more complex than the binary picture of society and art-making that our Eliminativist has proposed. The Eliminativist's account of the social function that the high art/popular art distinction plays simply cannot be correct, because our society cannot be plausibly taken to be structured or partitioned in the way he presumes, and, therefore, the distinction amongst the arts that concerns him cannot be regarded as mirroring a binary structure that does not exist.[8]

Our objections to the Eliminativist here are efficiently summarized by Russell A. Berman, who, writing in another context, notes:

It is not immediately obvious that the social and political elites constitute the primary recipients of 'high culture'—is it really the case that high income means high art, that Ted Kennedy and George Bush prefer Arnold Schoenberg to Wayne Newton? Nor is it self-evident that appreciation of high art is undeniable evidence of high social standing. While there is probably some connection between social status and aesthetic taste, it is simultaneously more flexible and complex than can

---

[8] At this point, it is open to the Eliminativist to offer a more complex picture of class stratification and its affiliated tastes, perhaps after the fashion of Bourdieu. But there will still be the problem that I will discuss shortly in the text, namely, that for artworks to perform the function for class differentiation that the Eliminativist alleges they do, they will have to possess some sort of internal features— such as formal features—that will enable social agents to choose the artworks that are appropriate to their social status.

be encompassed by a simplistic doubling of the vertical metaphor of high and low from society to art.[9]

Perhaps one way to attempt to reframe the distinction that the Eliminativist wants in such a way that it deflects the Teddy Kennedy/George Bush type of example might be to say that the élite, as a result of their class status, are able to appreciate *both* high art and popular art, whereas the non-élite only have access to popular art. But this seems false. Membership in the real, social élite need not correlate with an appreciation of high art—does Jesse Helms secretly admire Surrealism?—while many (most?) of the connoisseurs of contemporary high art are socially marginal. Of course, the latter may think of themselves as '*élite*', but that would be a matter of equivocating on the relevant meaning of the term. And, in any case, the Eliminativist cannot simply stipulate that the consumers of high art are the élite without begging the question. That is, the Elininativist cannot definitionally defend the proposition that high art always correlates with élite consumption at the same time that he (the Eliminativist) claims to be drawing an informative, empirical social distinction concerning the world as we know it.

In terms of the Elininativist's argument, then, I want to, in effect, deny that (*e*) is a live option. Given the preceding considerations, the distinction between high art and popular (mass) art must rest on something other than matters of class distinction. This suggests two ways in which the Elininativist's argument may have gone wrong: first, certain of the options that the argument rejects may have been dismissed too hastily; second, there may be other grounds for the distinction that the Eliminativist has overlooked. In fact, I think that the Eliminativist's argument errs in both of these directions.

It seems obvious that the Eliminativist's dismissal of the possibility of some formal differentiae between high art and popular art is too quick. For the Eliminativist, as we have represented him, considers only one possible formal distinction—simplicity—and then he rejects the prospects for any formal distinction in short order. But surely it is a mistake to jump from the notion that simplicity won't do the job to concluding that there are no formal features that are characteristic of popular art.

Indeed, if there were no formal difference between high art and popular art, it would be at least difficult to see how the distinction could serve the social role that the Eliminativist attributes to it. How would the élite be able to identify which objects were the 'right' ones with which to affiliate or disaffiliate? Moreover, if it were perfectly arbitrary—if so-called high art

[9] Russell A. Berman, 'Popular Culture and Populist Culture', *Telos*, 87 (1991), 61–2.

were whatever some suitably defined group consumes—then we would expect to find that the class of high art objects would be just as likely to contain Garbage Pail Kids trading-cards and Care Bears paraphernalia as it does works by Anselm Kiefer. But the set of works of high art is not such a hodgepodge.

In fact, how could it be, if it is to serve as a stable means for differentiating classes? That is, if people, at least in part, emblematize their social identity through their exercises in taste, they would have to have some way of determining whether or not they were attending to the right sort of things. And formal differences seem a very likely candidate here for determining whether something is a matter of high or popular art.[10]

For example, in Chapter 1 we saw that Greenberg identified what we might call contemporary high art in terms of difficulty. This would give someone at least a rough guide for ascertaining whether an artwork belonged to the species of contemporary high art. But difficulty is arguably a formal characteristic of an artwork. And it is hard to imagine how, without reference to some such formal characteristics, the élite would be able to identify the artworks that are suitable to their social station. And even if formal differentiae do not play this role, the Eliminativist must still explain how members of different social classes go about choosing the objects that are appropriate to their class standing.[11] Thus, the Eliminativist must concede that at the very least social differentiation is not the sole basis upon which the distinction between high art and popular art rests.

However, this qualification allows that the distinction may, in part, have something to do with formal differentiae, since other candidates, like content, appear unlikely.[12] Thus, given his own theory, the Eliminativist seems to have ruled formal differentiae off the court too abruptly. For the Eliminativist himself will probably have to incorporate something like formal criteria as a measure of the difference between high art and popular art in order for his own hypothesis about social differentiation to be feasible.

Moreover, against the Eliminativist's putative dismissal of the relevance

[10] A radical Eliminativist might counter that the élite have no such implicit means for segregating high art from other sorts. High art is just whatever they choose, and there's an end to it. However, this seems implausible since the corpus of high art has much more unity than this view would predict and the Eliminativist cannot ignore this. In so far as he is offering an account of social reality, he is obliged to explain it.

[11] It seems obvious that the élite should have such means at their disposal—that they do not simply christen works as high art—since there is often disagreement about what counts as high art in the magazines and discourses that the Elininativist regards as élite.

[12] And the same point might be made about affective properties, since, in terms of both affective properties and content, works of so-called high art and popular art frequently converge. Think of revenge plots.

of formal criteria, I will, in the next section of this chapter, explore the possibility of crafting a formal distinction between (contemporary) high art and mass art in the process of defining the nature of mass art. And if the arguments on behalf of that distinction are successful, then the second premiss of the Eliminativist's argument, as stated above, is false.

However, before developing that line of argumentation, let me call attention to another problem with the Eliminativist's argument. The Eliminativist's case takes the form of a disjunctive syllogism—an argument by elimination of all the rival alternatives. An argument of this sort depends upon successfully setting forth all the competing alternatives. Thus, if the Eliminativist has failed to consider all the alternatives, then his argument is inconclusive. Furthermore, I think that it is the case that the Eliminativist has failed to countenance all the relevant alternatives for considering the distinction that concerns him.

In order to see the alternative that the Eliminativist has overlooked, it is useful to recall that throughout this section I have articulated the Eliminativist's position primarily in terms of 'popular art', adding 'mass art' either parenthetically or disjunctively. But in our contemporary context, the idiom of 'popular art' masks a possible way of drawing the distinction between high art and popular art, of which mass art is the primary example. Why? Because 'popular art' can be a very ahistorical concept. Arguably, in some sense the high art/popular art distinction can be marshalled to apply to many different cultures and historical eras. On the other hand, the central question in the contemporary debates in which the Eliminativist argument figures is not about some eternal contrast between popular art and high art, but about the putative nature of popular art in what Walter Benjamin called the age of mechanical reproduction (which nowadays is becoming the age of electronic reproduction). That is, the concerns that motivate contemporary theoretical discussions about the popular arts occur in a historical context where we understand that the label 'popular art' refers discursively to the arts of mechanical and electronic reproduction.

When pundits decry the plight of culture in industrial and so-called post-industrial society, they are not referring to the probable pernicious effects of medieval miracle plays. They are talking about the art that is disseminated by mass technologies. Similarly, when the Eliminativist speaks of popular art, he should be taken to be speaking about what I call mass art—art that is produced and distributed on a mass scale. But once we see that this is the pertinent, historically specific referent of 'popular art' in the Eliminativist's argument, then it seems likely that the Eliminativist may have neglected a crucial alternative for discriminating popular—that is to say mass—art from contemporary high art. For what is it that makes such art *mass* art? That is, there may indeed be certain structural differences between mass art—*art produced by mass technologies for mass distribution*—and other sorts of art that contribute in part to the disctinction the Eliminativist aspires to reject. In order to make good on this possibility, let me turn directly to the project of defining mass art.

Defining mass art

I have promised to propose a theory of the nature of mass art. By claiming that this theory pertains to the *nature* of mass art, I maintain that my theory is concerned with classifying mass art, rather than with either condemning or commending it. This is meant to distinguish my approach from previous philosophical theories of mass art, which seem preoccupied, at least implicitly, with evaluating mass art either morally, politically, or aesthetically. Dwight MacDonald, Collingwood, Adorno, Horkheimer, Greenberg, and, more recently, Guy Debord[13] and Jean Baudrillard,[14] all appear to me to provide characterizations of mass art primarily in order to condemn it, while Walter Benjamin and Marshall McLuhan present theories meant to valorize it. I, on the other hand, hope merely to say what it is—to classify mass art rather than to judge it morally, politically, or aesthetically.

By identifying my project as classificatory, I mean, among other things, that I intend neither to excoriate nor to defend mass art. This is not because I feel that mass art is indefensible. One can defend it by pointing to mass artworks—such as *Citizen Kane*—that are valuable from both an artistic and a moral perspective. That is, it makes no sense to condemn mass art, as such, if it has produced works of value, including some masterpieces.

But, the task of either condemning or praising mass art in virtue of its very nature seems to me to be quixotic. Like most human practices, mass art involves worthy and unworthy examples (morally, politically, and aesthetically), and it is at the level of particular cases that praise or blame seems appropriate. I suppose that one could say in broad defence of mass art that it is valuable because it brings aesthetic experience to a great many people. But I think that the real defence of it is that it has produced some works of the highest achievement. And yet, establishing that in detail is a

[13] Guy Debord, *Society of the Spectacle* (Detroit: Black and Red, 1977).
[14] Jean Baudrillard, *Selected Writings*, ed. Mark Poster (Stanford: Stanford University Press, 1988).

critical task, not a philosophical one.[15] What philosophy can contribute to that project, at the present juncture is to say what mass art is in a classificatory sense, since we need a way, logically speaking, in which to identify mass artworks before we commend them as the relevant sorts of achievement.

Furthermore, unlike the Eliminativist, I maintain that we can say something substantive about the nature of mass art, i.e., about its essential (as opposed to its socially adventitious) properties. We need not reduce mass art to something else—for example, a marker of class relations. Mass art, on my understanding, has certain features—internal features—that lead us to classify it as mass art. That is, something is not mass art simply in virtue of external features, such as the social class that consumes it.

Part of the key to characterizing mass art is to realize the importance that the word 'mass' plays in naming it. For, as noted previously, there are other candidates for naming the phenomenon in question. But I contend that many of them are misleading. Perhaps the most misleading way to label the phenomenon is to call it *popular* art.

For, as I noted in my criticisms of the Eliminativist, calling the phenomenon 'popular art' fails to signal that the type of production that concerns us has a certain historical specificity. 'Popular art' is an ahistorical term. Popular art, in some sense, might be said to have existed throughout the centuries. It is not historically specific. If by popular art one means the art of the common people, then there has always been what is called folk art. Moreover, if popular art just means art that is liked by lots of people, then it seems fair to say that every society has had some popular art.

But, on the other hand, what is called 'mass art' has not existed everywhere throughout human history. The kind of art—of which movies, photography, and rock-and-roll recordings provide ready examples—that surfeits contemporary culture has a certain historical specificity. It is the art of a particular type of culture. It has arisen in the context of modern industrial mass society and it is expressly designed for use by that society, employing, as it does, the characteristic productive forces of that society—namely, mass technologies of production and distribution—in order to deliver art to enormous consuming populations—populations that are 'mass' in the sense that they cross national, class, religious, political, ethnic, racial, and gender boundaries.[16]

In addition, the theories of popular art with which we are familiar

---

[15] Moreover, I think that it is a critical task that has been accomplished any number of times in the twentieth century.

[16] John B. Thompson captures this sense of mass by speaking of mass art as being aimed at 'an indefinite range of potential recipients'. John B. Thompson, *The Media and Modernity: A Social Theory of the Media* (Stanford: Stanford University Press, 1995), 84.

regard the phenomenon in question—whatever it's called—as representing some kind of historical break. Thus, if what I've just said about the universalist connotations of 'popular art' is accurate, then that notion doesn't highlight the historical specificity of the phenomenon. Mass art, unlike popular art *simpliciter*, is not the sort of art that might be found in any society. It emerges in a historical context, namely mass society. And it is art that is designed to serve mass society by using the means of that society—mass technologies—as a way of performing this service.

Precisely dating the emergence of this social formation (mass society) and of dating the correlative emergence of mass art would be difficult. But we can speak about it in a general way. Mass society began to emerge in tandem with capitalism, urbanization, and industrialization. Mass art undoubtedly made some sort of significant initial appearance with the first mass-information technology—the printing press—which produced some of the first potentially mass-art forms, such as the novel. But then later forms of mass art began to command a more and more dominating position, especially in industrialized societies in the nineteenth and twentieth centuries, as more and more mass information technologies developed—such as photography, sound recording, motion pictures, radio, TV, and so on. Though we might not be able to specify the date when the age of mass art dawned, we can certainly say by now that we are in the thick of it.

As noted earlier, a number of cultural theorists, like Andrew Ross and Patrick Brantlinger, shun the label *mass art*. Instead they prefer to continue to call the phenomenon popular art. Their motivation, if I understand it correclty, is that the label *mass* has unsavoury political connotations. For when people like Dwight MacDonald called the phenomenon mass art, the term reeked with disdain—notably the disdain of an élitist, undemocratic sort, a disdain that regards those who do not belong to some mandarin company of intellectuals and modernist aesthetes as part of some *shapeless blob*.

This shapeless blob—the masses— is, according to theorists like MacDonald, easily given shape and manipulated by the technocrats of popular culture. Moreover, this supposedly shapeless blob is comprised, first and foremost, of the working classes and/or the underclass. Thus, scholars in what is now called cultural studies worry that in speaking of *mass* art, *mass* culture, or *mass* anything, one is buying into an élitist view of society, and perhaps even conspiring with it.

Undoubtedly, it is true that the term 'mass culture' may have once been given a contemptuous spin by theorists like MacDonald. However, that need not be its intended connotation. When I use the term *mass art*, I do not intend any derogation of its consumers. I simply mean that it is art that is made on a mass scale, i.e., art that is, first of all, made by and distributed by means of a mass technology. It is made for mass consumption. But here *mass* is used in a strictly *numerical* sense. It is not used in the pejorative— 'shapeless blob'—sense. Nor are the numerical masses that I have in mind reducible to the *masses* in the class sense of the term—to the proletariat, to the working class, to blue-collar workers, to the lumpen-proletariat, or to the underclass. Mass art is designed to seek out a mass audience, irrespective of class. Moreover, mass art succeeds in great measure in this endeavour. People of different classes and income brackets—indeed, of altogether different cultures—consume it, as evinced by the distribution of TV sets across class and ethnic lines in much of the industrial West, and beyond.

My sense of mass art is simply numerical, not evaluative and certainly not pejorative. Mass art is art that is designed to be consumed by lots and lots of people. That is why it is produced on such a large scale and distributed by mass technologies. Thus I am willing to run the risk of calling the phenomenon 'mass art', despite the potentially, politically incorrect sound of the label because: first, it points to *the* significant feature of the phenomenon—that it is essentially involved in production and distribution on a mass scale; and, second, because the alternative way of naming it—calling it 'popular art'—fails to acknowledge the way in which scale is utterly relevant to its nature, and, in consequence, fails to acknowledge its historical specificity as a product of industrial urban mass society.

Mass art is *for* mass consumption. The first and most obvious way in which it is for mass consumption is that it is produced and distributed by the mass media—radio, TV, photography, cinema, sound recording, etc. As Walter Benjamin pointed out, it is art that can be mass reproduced and transported in bulk; or, in some cases, it is beamed across great distances so that it can engage indefinitely large numbers of consumers in different places, often simultaneously.

Vaudeville, as practised in late nineteenth- and early twentieth-century theatres, was a popular art, but not yet a mass art, because the vaudeville performer could only play before one audience of limited size, in one playhouse at a time. On the other hand, when vaudeville and music hall performers, like Charlie Chaplin, Buster Keaton, Harry Langdon, and W. C. Fields, incorporated their stage routines into their films, their performances became mass art, in so far as their performances became available to mass audiences all over the world, at the same time.

As these examples should indicate, in refusing to label this phenomenon popular art, I do not mean to deny that there is frequently a historical connection between popular art, broadly so-called, and mass art. Quite often, mass art evolves out of already existing popular art. Ballads first disseminated through live performance and preserved in memory, in turn, give way to ballad sheets and sheet music, and, ultimately, evolve into records, audio cassettes, and compact disks. Carnival freak shows perhaps become one source of horror movies, while nineteenth-century melodramas provide a repertory of stories and techniques to be mined by early films, just as story-telling, stylized joking and badinage, and finally the stand-up comedy routine remain the provenance of much late-night TV, not to mention sitcoms.

But of course, not all traditional forms of popular entertainments, broadly construed, have been transformed into mass art forms. Cock-fighting, for example, has not found its way into mass art, nor have bear-baiting or medicine shows. Moreover, mass art has developed forms with no debt at all to the traditional popular arts. Music television, for instance, owes its heritage to pre-existing mass art forms, such as film. In short, though all mass art may belong to the broader, ahistorical class of popular art, not all popular art is mass art.

Ex hypothesi, what marks mass art from the broader class of ahistorical popular art is, as the label 'mass art' signals, that it is produced and disseminated by means of mass industrial technologies, technologies capable of delivering multiple instances or tokens of mass artworks to widely disparate reception points.[17] Like the mass manufacture of automobiles, mass art is a form of mass production and distribution, designed to deliver a multiplicity of tokens of a particular artwork to frequently geographically remote mass consuming audiences. Mass art is the art of mass society, predicated on addressing mass audiences by means of the opportunities afforded by mass technologies. Mass art is produced and delivered by mass media. These media are called *mass* because they make products available to relatively large audiences simultaneously.

Here it is important to stress that these media are called 'mass' because they make their products technologically available to large audiences, even if they do not actually command large audiences. TV, that is, was a mass medium in this sense before large numbers of people possessed TV sets. The products of mass art are, in principle, produced for a plurality of recipients, and mass technology contributes to the realization of this aim by, as John B. Thompson puts it, extending 'the availability of symbolic

---

[17] I am generally in agreement with John B. Thompson's statement that 'what is unique about receptive activity [with respect to mass media] is that a) the spatial-temporal context of reception does not overlap with that of production and b) there are multiple reception contexts that do not overlap with each other.' Thompson, *The Media and Modernity*, 109.

forms in space and time'.[18] Walter Benjamin intended to make the same point when he emphasized the capacity for reproducibility and global transportability of the arts of the mechanical age.

But that something is produced and distributed by a mass technology is not enough to guarantee that a candidate is an example of mass art. For an artwork may be produced and distributed by a mass technology at the same time that it is not designed for mass consumption. That is, though production and delivery by mass media technologies represents a necessary condition for mass art, it is not a sufficient condition for identifying a candidate as a mass artwork. Why not?

Because, for example, avant-garde art, that has not been designed for mass consumption, can be produced and distributed by a mass medium. That is, avant-garde art that is expressly designed to frustrate mass consumption—for instance, to outrage the bourgeoisie—has been produced in and distributed by mass media. Consider Cocteau's *Blood of a Poet* or Buñuel's *Age of Gold*. These films were produced and distributed by the same mass technologies that produced and distributed Frank Capra's films. But neither Cocteau's nor Buñuel's films are mass art, since they were not designed for mass consumption.

Similar cases can be multiplied with respect to avant-garde music. Works by Meredith Monk and Robert Ashley are produced and distributed by means of the same technologies of sound recording that are employed in producing and distributing the work of Whitney Houston and Billy Joel. Indeed, every mass medium has supported some avant-garde experimentation. TV has Nam June Paik, and avant-garde broadcast radio has the German poet Schuldt and the American Richard Kostelanetz. Likewise film-makers like Michael Snow and Jean-Luc Godard deploy the same cinematic apparatus that David O. Selznick and Victor Fleming did in their production of *Gone with the Wind*.

Yet clearly avant-garde artworks, when produced by means of mass media, are not mass artworks proper. For they are not designed for easy consumption by mass, indefinitely large, undifferentiated audiences. Quite frequently they are designed to confound mass audiences. And even when they are not directly intended to do this, they invariably do so nevertheless, since it is a necessary condition of being avant-garde that the works in question subvert, or, at least, go beyond conventional expectations and understandings.

Avant-garde artworks are not designed to be immediately accessible to

[18] John B. Thompson, *Ideology and Modern Culture: Critical Social Theory in the Era of Mass Communication* (Stanford: Stanford University Press, 1990), 221.

mass audiences. They are meant to challenge or to transgress the common cognitive and emotive stock that the mass consuming audience brings to the relevant art-form. This is not to say that an avant-garde work cannot be a bestseller. Salman Rushdie's *Satanic Verses* was. However, the explanation in this case has more to do with the fact that people in places like Iowa defiantly refused to allow an Iranian dictator to tell them what they might read and less to do with their appreciation of Rushdie's disjunctive narrative strategies.

Indeed, I conjecture that Rushdie's book, though widely purchased, was not widely read. For in order to be read with understanding and appreciation, *Satanic Verses* requires a background of literary history, literary theory, and the related discourses of the divided or multiple subject, which discourse is not at the fingertips of most of the Anglophone reading public. *Satanic Verses* was a *succès de scandale*, and, furthermore, I suspect that generally when avant-garde artworks turn into bestsellers, it is the aura of scandal that explains this phenomenon. That a work is a bestseller, in other words, does not necessarily show that it is a mass artwork. People may purchase it simply for its notoriety.

On the other hand, *Bridges of Madison County* (to stay in Iowa) is a mass artwork, while *Satanic Verses* is not. What is the difference? That the former is designed to be accessible to the mass reading public and the latter is not. All things being equal, any literate consumer should be able to understand the *Bridges of Madison County* without any specialized background, save the ability to read and a rudimentary mastery of the practice of fiction.[19] *Satanic Verses*, on the other hand, requires a special background in order to be understood, though of course that background can be acquired autodidactically.

Avant-garde artworks can be produced and delivered by mass technologies, but they are not mass artworks. For though produced and delivered by mass technologies, such avant-garde artworks are not structured for ready assimilation and reception by mass audiences. Indeed, they are designed to thwart ready assimilation. In the most benign cases, avant-garde artworks are intended to stretch common sensibilities, while in the more standard cases, they are designed to disrupt them, often for the sake of disturbing what are perceived to be aesthetic and/or moral laxities. Indeed, throughout the epoch of mass art, it has been the defenders of the avant-garde, modernist aesthetic (for example, Collingwood, Adorno, and Greenberg) who have been the harshest critics of mass art. For them, the

---

[19] This, of course, is not to deny that some people, especially Fundamentalist zealots, might not be offended by it, since it appears to condone adultery.

avant-garde has been both the historical and the conceptual antithesis of mass art.

Something can be produced and delivered by a mass technology, then, but not be designed for mass consumption—such as avant-garde films, music recordings, video, novels, broadcasts, and the like. The pertinent reason that such works are not examples of mass art, however, does not have to do with technology, but rather with the ways in which the works in question are designed in terms of structures (formal and otherwise), styles, and ease of comprehension.

Avant-garde artworks are not designed to be consumed by mass audiences. They are enigmatic or mysterious—indeed, designedly so—for the average consumer, unless he or she has a certain background, comprising some art-historical knowledge about the context in which the work of art is made along with some operational understanding of the kinds of associations, modes of interpretation, and reasoning that are appropriate to bring to bear on the work. Avant-garde works are challenging, or, as a Greenbergian might put it, 'difficult'; in order to meet their challenge, one typically needs some knowledge of the relevant background frameworks— which even when known may be difficult to apply.

Thus, avant-garde artworks are not standardly accessible to wide numbers of people. Moreover, since the requisite background frameworks are not always straightforward in terms of their applicability to a given case, avant-garde artworks are often not readily accessible in the sense that they are not easily deciphered even for one who has access to relevant background frameworks.

In the world as we know it (as opposed to a world in which everyone is steeped in the dialectics of the avant-garde), avant-garde art, even if it is produced and delivered by a mass technology, cannot be said to be *designed* for mass consumption, since it is not accessible to large numbers of people without training and since it is not easy to assimilate. The fact that the avant-garde is not easy to assimilate is perhaps signalled by its very name—it is *in advance* of the main body; it is the leading edge, leaving many of the rest of us behind.

But if the avant-garde art produced by a mass medium is not designed for mass consumption, it may nevertheless provide valuable clues about what is involved in eliciting mass consumption. That is, inasmuch as the avant-garde is the antithesis of mass art, it affords, in a Hegelian fashion, insight into the 'thesis'—mass art—against which it draws its programme and its purpose. Avant-garde art is designed to be difficult, to be intellectually, aesthetically, and often morally challenging, and it is inaccessible to those without certain background of knowledge and acquired sensibilities.

Mass art, in contrast, is designed to be easy, to be readily accessible, with minimum effort, to the largest number of people possible.

Avant-garde art is esoteric; mass art is exoteric. Mass art is meant to command a mass audience. That is its function. Thus it is designed to be user friendly. Ideally, it is structured in such a way that large numbers of people will be able to understand and appreciate it, virtually without effort. It is made in order to capture and to hold the attention of large audiences, while avant-garde art is made to be effortful and to rebuff easy assimilation by large audiences. In so far as mass art is meant to capture large markets, it gravitates toward the choice of devices that will make it accessible to mass untutored audiences.

Obviously, mass consumption involves accessibility. As the case of the avant-garde indicates in a negative way, accessibility is partly a function of background knowledge. In order for mass art to be accessible in this sense, it must be designed for fast pickup by what I have called *untutored* audiences. That is, mass art has to be comprehensible for untrained audiences, virtually on the first go-around. So the modes of communication and the conventions of mass art have to meet certain *design considerations*, namely, they have to be such that they can be grasped and understood almost on first contact. They must, as already noted, be very, very user friendly.

For example, comic books, commercial movies, and TV tell stories by means of pictorial representation. Furthermore, there is a large body of psychological argumentation to the effect that pictorial recognition is, in large measure, an innate capacity,[20] acquired in the process of learning to recognize objects. That is, pictorial recognition arises in tandem with object recognition. A child, for instance, is able to recognize the subject of any typical picture where antecedently the child is already able to recognize the real-world referent of said picture. Pictorial recognition does not involve a process of learning over and above object recognition. It does not involve training in a code, a language, or any special procedure of inference. Anyone with normal perceptual capacities can recognize the referent of a standard motion-picture image (whether on film, TV, or CD-ROM) simply by looking, without the intervention of a subtending process of reading or inferring.[21] Thus, in so far as movies and TV images rely heavily upon pictorial symbols, they are virtually immediately accessible to untutored audiences world-wide.

Story-telling by pictures, that is, expeditiously satisfies one of the major

---

[20] Or one which unfolds naturally given the proper (minimal) environmental circumstances.
[21] For further defence of this hypothesis, see Noël Carroll, *Mystifying Movies* (New York: Columbia University Press, 1988), 137–46.

desiderata of mass art design, since it guarantees virtually immediate pickup by audiences, without those audiences requiring an education in specialized codes of reading or inferential procedures. Since pictorial representation is accessible to anyone, the mass arts that are based upon them have, in principle, unlimited audiences.

Of course, this is not to say that the mass arts don't educate audiences in the way in which to receive them. Often this education proceeds, as critics of mass art have observed (but misunderstood) by repetition and formula. That is, what critics condemn as a failing of mass art—formulaic repetition—is actually a design feature that ensures that people will be able to understand mass art by becoming familiar with its conventions and formulas. Moreover, the formulas towards which mass art gravitates are not ones that must be learned by prior exposure, but ones that almost always can be picked up on first exposure. Further exposure to such formulas and conventions by repetition serves, then, to make the productions of mass art more and more intelligible to audiences.[22]

Whereas avant-garde art is frequently—and perhaps ideally *most frequently*—a matter of subverting people's expectations (often through the so-called deconstruction of formulas and conventions), mass art proper is the opposite—a matter of building and reinforcing audience expectations by means of repetition and formula. Moreover, where it makes sense to call the audience 'trained' with respect to mass culture, the training, in the main, has proceeded through the repetition of already fairly accessible formulas.[23] That is, it is training by example.[24]

Mass art is designed to be accessible in the sense that it is, ideally, as

[22] Thomas J. Roberts writes 'There are traditions that we learn in school and others we learn informally, by word of mouth, by example.' It is my hypothesis that access to the avant-garde tradition is *primarily* of the former variety, while access to mass art is primarily of the latter variety, especially in terms of examples. See Thomas Roberts, *An Aesthetics of Junk Fiction* (Athens: University of Georgia Press, 1990), 36.

[23] This is not to deny that there may be other devices for 'training' the audience of mass art. For example, there are publicity campaigns that encourage preview articles and interviews in newspapers and magazines, and there are also TV and radio interviews through which the producers of albums, TV programmes, and so on prepare the audiences for their latest productions. This provides a certain degree of 'word-of-mouth' training, though I think that the primary means for educating the mass audience, to the limited extent to which it is plausible to call the process 'education', is by means of repetition and formula.

[24] For instance, in response to Christopher Pike's science fiction novel *The Season of Passage*, the reader infers that the Russian astronaut Ivan has been possessed by an alien force before the protagonists in the novel realize this. Part of the grounds for their inference is the way in which Ivan is depicted; he is, for example, affectless. Having encountered this clue in other works of science fiction, like *Invasion of the Body Snatchers*, the description of Ivan prompts the audience to regard him with suspicion. But in this case the audience has picked up this inference ticket through experience with comparable mass fictions where it is formulaically repeated. This, then, is a case where it may be argued that the audience has been, in part, tutored by previous mass artworks. (I say 'in part', since even without prior experience of this device, the reader would notice that Ivan is behaving extremely strangely; the formula itself, that is, is already very accessible even upon first encounter.)

close as possible to being legible to the average untutored audience member, virtually on contact. This, at least, is the ideal toward which mass art gravitates. This implies that the mass artwork is designed for easy consumption. Moreover, not only is mass art designed for ease of comprehension and consumption in the first instance. It is easy to follow and to understand in every instance thereafter.

This ease of comprehension has its origins in the design features of mass art. For example, the narrative structures deployed in the mass market novels of Stephen King and Mary Higgins Clark proceed by encouraging audiences to entertain certain questions that the novels in question then go on to answer. This question/answer format—which I call erotetic narration—has a kind of natural logic that is easy to follow, in contrast to the narrative structure of a modernist work like *Last Year at Marienbad*, which presents a barrage of questions that are never decisively answered. Because of design features, like erotetic narration, the products of mass art are easy to follow, whereas examples of modernist art are not.[25]

Indeed, the search for what is massively accessible even tends to influence the choice of content in mass art entertainments. Action/adventure scenarios are so serviceable for the purposes of mass art, because physical competition between starkly defined forces of good and evil are easier for almost anyone to track than are complex psychological dramas, which may, for example, require background cultural information that the common audience member is apt to lack. That is, it is easier for the randomly selected plain viewer to understand *Mortal Kombat* than *Blow-up*.

Clearly, the accessibility of mass art is also connected with its reliance on the formulaic and on repetition. For when I pick up a work of mass art, if it involves a narrative, then, most often, I will have a pretty reliable horizon of expectations about the course or trajectory that the events in the story are likely to take. As critics of mass art, such as Adorno, have noted, with mass narratives we know which characters are the ones we'll be hearing about for the rest of the story, and we know, pretty reliably, which characters are likely to be alive by the end of the story, which ones are likely to be married, and so on. Moreover, we have reliable knowledge of these things, because mass narratives are formulaic.

In so far as mass artworks are formulaic, they are easy to follow, i.e., they accord with our expectations. And inasmuch as mass artworks are easy to follow, they are also apt to appeal to more and more people as suitable or appropriate objects with which to occupy one's leisure time. Of course, in order to command large audiences, mass artworks must be

---

[25] For a discussion of erotetic narration, see Noël Carroll, *Mystifying Movies*, 170–81.

more than merely easy to consume. They must also invite or excite our interest. But a precondition, here, of exciting interest, is nevertheless that they be easily comprehended. That is, before mass artworks can be widely enjoyable, they must be widely accessible, at least in terms of comprehensibility.

So once again, in certain respects, critics of mass art, like Clement Greenberg, were right. Mass art *is* easy, especially when compared to the difficulty—perhaps the self-imposed difficulty–of avant-garde art. However, the ease with which mass art is consumed is not a flaw, but rather a design element, which is predicated on the function of mass art as an instrument for addressing mass audiences.

Whether this ease of comprehension implies that the consumer of mass art is passive is, as we have seen, another question. Its answer depends upon how one defines 'passive'. Is the reader of a mystery story who is informed about the formulas of fiction *passive* when she tries to infer the identity of the criminal? That is, it is not exactly clear whether the contrast between easy comprehension versus difficult comprehension maps neatly on to the dichotomy between passive reception versus active reception. Nevertheless, it is the case that we can say from a factual point of view—without drawing any evaluative conclusions—that, all things being equal, a work of mass art will be designed for easy comprehension, i.e., intended for access by large numbers of untutored consumers expending a minimum amount of effort in order to understand the mass artwork.

Moreover, *pace* the excoriations of the critics of mass art, this feature of mass art is not a source of shame. It is a condition for the possibility of mass art in the world as we know it. For if mass art were not expressly designed for easy access—i.e., for intelligibility on the part of a maximum number of people with little effort—it would not be able to command mass audiences.

What earlier critics of mass art saw as a reason to condemn mass art— its easy accessibility (which in some ways derives from its tendencies toward the formulaic)—is in fact a central design feature of mass art, properly so called. For without this ease of accessibility for untutored audiences, mass art could not function to secure or elicit mass consumption. Furthermore, unless we can provide some reason why eliciting mass consumption in the world as we know it is always, in principle, condemnable, then the fact that mass art is designed for mass consumption should not present us with any conspicuous problem.

It is the point or function of mass art to address mass audiences. This may be driven by the profit motive in capitalist countries or by ideological purposes in totalitarian regimes. But that, in turn, dictates certain desiderata concerning the internal structures of mass artworks, namely, that mass artworks will gravitate towards structures, like pictorial representation and erotetic narration, and even content, that will be accessible virtually on contact, without specialized background training and/or effort by vast numbers of people. Mass artworks tend toward a certain kind of homogeneity exactly because they aim at engaging what is common among huge populations.

Frequently it is this tendency toward homogenization that critics, generally avant-garde critics, single out for loathing when it comes to discussions of mass art. Recall MacDonald. However, the search for common denominators in mass art (which need not involve a search for the 'lowest' common denominator), at the level of both style and content, is not a failing, but rather a design consideration, given the function of mass art. For it is the point of mass art to engage mass audiences, and that mandates an inclination toward structures that will be readily accessible—virtually on contact and with little effort—to audiences with widely differing backgrounds.

Gathering together and amplifying some of these observations, then, we may attempt to define the mass artwork in the following way:

> X is a mass artwork if and only if 1. x is a multiple instance or type artwork, 2. produced and distributed by a mass technology, 3. which artwork is intentionally designed to gravitate in its structural choices (for example, its narrative forms, symbolism, intended affect, and even its content) toward those choices that promise accessibility with minimum effort, virtually on first contact, for the largest number of untutored (or relatively untutored) audiences.

Here, the parenthetical qualification concerning 'relatively untutored audiences' is meant to accommodate the fact that, to a certain extent, audiences may be tutored by the repetition and formulas of mass art itself.[26]

I have arrived at the first condition by stipulating that my domain of concern is mass *art*, not mass culture, which would represent a broader category. That is, my concern is with those items of mass culture that are more narrowly identifiable as art—such as dramas, stories, and songs—

---

[26] Of course, by calling the audiences of mass art untutored, I don't mean that people cannot learn things from mass art. Many immigrants in America learnt English and American folkways by listening to the radio. In this way, radio functioned to consolidate the nation in a way that is analogous to the function of national literatures for nation building. For a discussion of this aspect of radio, see: Michele Hilmes, *The Nation's Voice: Radio Broadcasting and the Shaping of American Culture, 1922–1952* (Oxford: Oxford University Press, forthcoming).

rather than news programmes, cooking shows, sporting events, or talk shows. Since mass artworks are not avant-garde, there should be little problem classifying items in terms of whether or not they fall into already entrenched art-forms—such as drama or song—or in terms of whether they discharge traditionally recognized artistic purposes like representation or expression. Thus, if questioned as to why I suppose that the mass artwork is art, my first impulse is to respond by asking, 'What else could it be?'[27]

Of course, some readers may not be happy with this. They are apt to challenge the first condition of my definition on the grounds that it is a contested issue as to whether or not what I call mass art is art properly so called. They will object that you just can't stipulate that it is such. In response, I argue that inasmuch as mass art-forms are descended from traditional art-forms, they have a prima-facie claim to art status. That is, inasmuch as many of the genres and forms of mass art are extensions of genres and art-forms that are already regarded as art proper, there seems to be no principled reason to deny that mass art is art.

Furthermore, the creators of mass art are typically engaged in the sorts of activities that artists in traditional artistic practices engage in—not only drawing, writing, and acting, but, more abstractly, representing, expressing, and discovering suitable forms in which to convey content. For example, the directors of *All in the Family* and *M*A*S*H* had to determine which of alternative shooting styles best expressively realized their goals—choosing, in the former case, a frontal, distanced, closed, 'proscenium' approach to underscore a universe that revolved around a central patriarchal figure (Archie Bunker), while in the latter case choosing a penetrative, moving-camera style to highlight the ensemble and more egalitarian world of *M*A*S*H*.[28] That the people who create mass art are involved in discovering appropriate forms of content and that they, in consequence, create works that may be contemplated in terms of the expressive relation of form to content is another reason to think that what I call mass art is an instance of art proper.

In addition, I think that there is no question that mass art would count as art in terms of the leading *classificatory* approaches to identifying art. Here I have in mind institutional theories of art, the open-concept approach, aesthetic theories of art, historical theories, and my own

[27] That mass artworks are what I have called 'multiple instance or type artworks' is a feature of these works that, if not already apparent, will be explicated in the next section of this chapter, concerning the ontology of mass art.

[28] David Barker, 'Television Production Techniques as Communication', in *Television: The Critical View*, 5th edn., ed. Horace Newcomb (New York: Oxford University Press, 1994), 87–100.

approach to identifying art, which I call narrativism.[29] A major source of difficulty for identifying works of art is the avant-garde, since avant-garde art, generally by design, seeks to stretch our conception of art in unprecedented ways. However, mass art does not raise that problem, since it typically is involved in mining traditional art-forms and genres. Thus, it is likely to fall squarely in the domain of art on any reasonable, classificatory approach to identifying art.

Doesn't question [handwritten margin note]

For readers who worry about how we are able to determine whether a given candidate is art, then, I would, of course, first recommend that they use my own notion of identifying narration, but, if one does not like that approach, then let her use any of the other classificatory approaches to identifying art. I predict that they will all count mass art—or, at least, the majority of mass art objects—as art proper.[30]

This prediction may sound overly adventurous, since in Chapter 1 we encountered a number of commentators bent on denying that mass art is art proper, on the basis of the theories of art to which they were aligned. How, then, can I say that mass art will count as art on any approach to identifying art? Here two comments seem pertinent. First, in some cases, the theorists in question withheld the status of art from mass art because their conception of it was ill-conceived. For instance, Greenberg thought that mass art induced passivity, but he was wrong. Second, and perhaps more importantly, I have claimed that mass art will turn out to be art proper on any *classificatory* approach to the problem of identifying art. But many of the theories of art that we encountered in the first chapter were not classificatory in nature, but evaluative. For example, when Greenberg supposes that art proper engenders high-calibre states of reflection, he is perhaps identifying a good-making feature of art (or, at least, some art), but not a generic feature. Thus, his approach to identifying art is not classificatory, but ultimately evaluative, and, therefore, it is not a counter-example to my conjecture.

The second condition of this definition—that the mass artwork is produced and distributed by a mass-delivery technology—is putatively derived from the insight that what everyone is always talking about in the debates that have raged in our culture since the late nineteenth and early twentieth centuries under various guises—such as the debate

---

[29] See Noël Carroll, 'Identifying Art', in *Institutions of Art: Reconsiderations of George Dickie's Philosophy*, ed. Robert J. Yanal (University Park: Pennsylvania State University Press, 1994), 3–38.

[30] The requirement that the mass artwork be art may play a role in dealing with certain types of counter-examples. For instance, the contention that things like Roman tiles and manufactured textiles should not count as mass art may be grounded in the observation that they are not art in the classificatory sense, though, of course, this will depend on one's method for identifying artworks.

between high art and low art, or serious art versus popular art—has really been concerned with mass art, the art that began to appear and that increasingly appears in the age of mass industrial society via the agency of mass technologies. Mass art is art that is produced and distributed by a mass delivery system, the first major one of which to emerge in the West was printing, which was later followed in rapid succession by photography, sound recording, film, radio, and TV, and which undoubtedly will be augmented by laser technology, holography, HDTV, computer technology, and who knows what.

Mass art emerged historically; it has not always been with us. It arrived on the scene only when technologies capable of mass production and distribution did. Mass art is not popular art *simpliciter*. It requires a mass production and delivery technology, where such a technology is defined as one that is capable of simultaneously delivering multiple (at least two) tokens of a mass artwork-type to more than one reception site. The concept of mass art, that is, is derived by drawing a contrast within popular art broadly construed.

By identifying mass art in terms of mass delivery systems, a difference is marked between mass art and the more generic notion of popular art. Mass art is popular art, but a noteworthy subspecies, distinguished by its reliance upon mass delivery systems capable of reaching non-overlapping reception sites simultaneously.

But what exactly is a mass delivery system? Walter Benjamin suggests that it is a technology for the mass reproduction of images and stories. But this is not exactly right. It does a nice job for things like certain photographs, but it does not capture the possibility of such things as one-time, live radio dramas broadcast to multiple reception sites. But such broadcasts should count as examples of mass art, even though they may never be 'reproduced' in Benjamin's sense. So, in contrast to Benjamin's notion of mass reproducibility, I propose to define a mass delivery system as a technology with the capacity to deliver the same performance or the same object to more than one reception site simultaneously.

The frescos on the ceilings of Renaissance cathedrals, though they might be viewed simultaneously by large numbers of people, are not cases of mass art, for such frescos cannot be in two or more places at the same time. On the other hand, the self-same radio performance or live-TV performance has the capacity to be transmitted to many disparate, non-overlapping reception sites; while films and photos are objects that can be reproduced multiply and transported to many different places, thereby affording the possibility that effectively exact tokens of the film-type or the photo-type in question can be consumed simultaneously.

Of course, the notion of a discrete reception site here is a bit tricky. It cannot be specified in terms of precise, measurable distances between reception sites. An average-sized household with two TV sets standardly has at least two discrete, non-overlapping reception sites, whereas Mt Rushmore constitutes one reception site, though it can be viewed by many people from many different standpoints, which encompass an area greater than that of the average household.[31] What counts as a discrete reception site depends upon what is the normatively correct focus of audience attention within a given practice. Mt Rushmore is a single, spatially continuous reception point covering an indeterminately large expanse, whereas two TV sets are, in standard conditions, two reception sites. Discriminating reception sites, it seems to me, must proceed on a case by case basis, often by attending to the criteria already in ordinary language, which, in turn, identify the normatively correct focus of audience attention. And attending to ordinary language usage in this way, I think, confirms the intuition that Mt Rushmore is one reception site (with continuously overlapping viewing-points), whereas standardly each TV set is its own reception site. Likewise, each theatre stage is a discrete reception site, though unlike in TV, in theatre it is impossible to deliver the same token performance of a play to two different non-overlapping reception sites simultaneously, whereas this capability is a *sine qua non* of mass-technology art.

Another reason for not wishing to count Mt Rushmore as an example of mass art is that it is not the product of a mass delivery system. If one were to admit Mt Rushmore into the class of mass artworks, then cathedrals, palaces, and tourist attractions would be mass art, but it seems wrong to me to count the Washington Monument as mass art. Thus, conceiving Mt Rushmore as mass art puts us on a slippery, indeed, treacherous slope.[32]

Ontologically, as we shall see at greater length in the next section of this

---

[31] The caveat 'standardly' is included here in order to block counter-examples such as two or more televisions being set side by side and tuned to the same channel. We often see such arrangements in futuristic fictions about the living rooms to come. Also the qualification 'standardly' is meant to pre-empt cases such as those where different TV monitors convey parts of a single image after the fashion of a mosaic (as in some of the work of Nam June Paik).

[32] One possible counter-example to my conservatism in these matters might be Disneyland. My initial response to a case like this is to reject it on the same grounds that I rejected Mt Rushmore. If Disneyland is mass art, then won't St Peter's and Notre-Dame de Paris be mass art as well?

However, some may feel that there is a worthwhile difference to be noticed here. For there may be a sense in which there is more than one Disneyland, whereas there is not more than one St Peter's. Disneylands can crop up in more than one place—not only in California, but in Orlando, Florida and outside Paris. Moreover, these Disneylands or Disneyworlds may be cut from the same mould. And with the proliferation of Disneylands, it may be possible for different audiences to experience the same Disneyworld rides in different sites at the same time.

Nevertheless, several things are worth noting here. In general, fairgrounds like Disneyland do not—perhaps for economic reasons—replicate exactly the same rides in different locales. Moreover, mass technology need not be essential to the production of such rides. For example, carpeted, wooden water

chapter, the mass artwork is a type whose numerically distinct tokens are identical in the sense that two dimes of the same minting are identical. Moreover, a mass artwork, such as film, differs from a play, which, in certain respects, is also a type, in so far as different tokens of a play—i.e., different productions—are not identical, inasmuch as they will enlist non-identical casts, sets, and so on. And this, of course, is one reason why plays are not automatically cases of mass art. For identical productions of them (if they are not filmed or taped) cannot be delivered to two or more disparate, non-overlapping reception sites simultaneously.[33]

Previously I claimed that the Eliminativist's argument—that mass art has no intrinsic, distinguishing attributes—ignored certain alternative options for characterizing a distinguishing feature of mass art. The notion that mass art is produced and distributed by a mass delivery system is such an alternative. Call it a necessary structural feature of mass art. Moreover, this feature commands our attention once we try to differentiate the kind of art people are attempting to characterize in debates about contemporary art. For the connection with mass delivery systems is what differentiates the relevant popular art of our times from popular art construed ahistorically.

However, though production and distribution of the relevant artworks by mass industrial technologies is an essential feature of mass artworks, it is not sufficient alone to identify a candidate as a mass artwork, since, as we have seen, it seems counter-intuitive to count avant-garde artworks, such as films by Stan Brakhage, as mass artworks. Such artworks may be produced and delivered through the agency of a mass medium, but they cannot reasonably be expected to enlist mass untutored audiences. They are not readily accessible, cognitively and emotively, to plain viewers. That is why Brakhage introduces his films with lectures; he is trying to tutor his

---

slides—sometimes called flumes—may be constructed in accordance with a preset design, but it does not seem appropriate to call them mass art.

Of course, in principle, it may be the case that fairground rides could be completely prefabricated and mass produced. Were this the case, I would be more willing to consider them as examples of mass art. There are perhaps already architectural cases like this, such as the golden arches of McDonald's Hamburger outlets. Here, we might have to begin to countenance the idea of mass architecture, which, in turn, might count as mass art.

[33] Some commentators have worried that, given a performance of a play before an audience which is simultaneously broadcast around the nation, we will have to say that we have two artworks—the play enacted before the audience and the broadcasted play—such that one is a mass artwork and the other is not. On the one hand, we can dissolve this apparent incongruity in a great many cases like this by drawing a distinction between one artwork and a mere recording thereof. On the other hand, if what is broadcast involves editing and changes in camera positions such that we do not feel that the broadcasted play should be delegated to the status of a *mere* recording, then I see no problem with admitting that there are two artworks here—the live play and the broadcast play—only one of which is mass art. For editing and changes in camera position and framing do constitute a layer of artistic interpretation and creativity not standardly available in the enacted performance.

audiences in the way in which to view, to understand and to appreciate his films. But mass art is designed to elicit mass consumption and, though being produced by a mass medium makes this possible in one sense, it is not, in and of itself, enough to discharge the function of engaging mass audiences. For avant-garde art can be produced and distributed by a mass medium, but avant-garde art is typically designed to frustrate or problematize mass consumption, whereas mass artworks proper are ones whose design choices are made with an eye to guaranteeing their accessibility to viewers who, with no specialized background, can understand and appreciate them virtually on contact, while expending little effort.

Identifying mass art with art produced in a mass medium does not yield a full account of mass art proper. A full account of the nature of mass art proper is a matter of saying in virtue of what features mass art fulfils the function of engaging mass audiences. So, a full account of the nature of mass art must provide some indication of how art produced in a mass medium is designed to command the attention of mass audiences. And it is the third condition in my theory that is supposed to supply an indication of the design considerations that ideally enable mass art to fulfil its function.

Mass art is differentiated from the more amorphous category of popular art in terms of mass-delivery technologies. Furthermore, mass art is differentiated from other forms of art that exploit mass delivery systems in virtue of the functional tendency of mass art to gravitate toward choices of devices, structures, affects, and even contents that promise easy accessibility with minimum effort for the largest number of untutored audiences.

Rock and Roll music, for example, in addition to its harmonic simplicity, employs a readily detectable backbeat that helps organize the rest of the sound.[34] This beat is a pronounced or foregrounded frame of reference, whose repetitiveness grants easy entry into the rhythmic structure that converges on it. As the old Beatles' song 'Rock and Roll Music' has it: 'It's got a backbeat, you can't lose it.' Most people can pick it up quickly and move to it, at least in terms of toe- and finger-tapping and rhythmic nodding. It is this internal structural feature, among others, that makes rock and roll music accessible globally.

One might think that, in so far as most rock is song-in-a-natural-language, it would not travel well. However, sociologists have discovered that listeners do not primarily attend to the lyrics in rock, but rather to the

---

[34] See Theodore Gracyk, *Rhythm and Noise: An Aesthetics of Rock* (Durham, NC: Duke University Press, 1996), ch. 5.

broad emotive contour of a piece.[35] Thus, teenagers in Moscow can savour the same tones of euphoria or defiance that their opposite number in Liverpool does.

In so far as my definition of mass art emphasizes its search for structures that can command mass audiences, the formula suggests a rich empirical research programme for studying mass art, namely, that, with mass art-works, an always useful question to ask concerns what it is about the relevant works that enables them to command the attention of large audiences. That the cutting rates in MTV videos average 19.94 shots per minute helps explain why music videos rivet viewers to the screen, since such a pattern provides little opportunity for attention to flag.[36] Indeed, given the way in which our perceptual system operates, i.e., given the involuntary tendency of our attention to reawaken (for sound adaptive reasons) upon the onset of new stimuli, MTV might be said to be exploiting our hard-wiring in such a way that most viewers find themselves irresistibly drawn to its imagery.[37]

Since mass art depends for its success upon being accessible, an instructive research question to ask about particular mass art-forms is what features of the works in question contribute to this effect and why. For example, one might analyse the ways in which certain devices of mass-movie narration and TV narration—such as point-of-view editing—are keyed to innate dispositions of primate perception.[38] For, obviously, where the devices of mass art mobilize innate responses, their accessibility to mass audiences is virtually guaranteed.[39]

Of course, I do not mean to suggest that all or even most of the central

---

[35] Roger Jon Desmond, 'Adolescents and Music Lyrics: Implications of a Cognitive Perspective', *Communications Quarterly*, 35 (1987), 278; Simon Frith, *Music for Pleasure* (New York: Routledge, 1988), 154; and Quentin Schultze, *et al.*, *Dancing in the Dark: Youth, Popular Culture and the Electronic Media* (Grand Rapids: William B. Eerdmans Publishing Company, 1991), 160–3.

[36] Donald L. Fry and Virginia H. Fry, 'Some Structural Characteristics of Music Television Video', a paper presented at the meetings of the Speech Communication Association in Chicago in November of 1984, cited in *Dancing in the Dark*, 206.

[37] Perhaps what is called channel surfing is a related phenomenon. As our attention sags, we try (often subconsciously) to reactivate it by changing the channel, thereby introducing a burst of new stimulation. What we do to ourselves by way of channel surfing is roughly what MTV editing does for us automatically and at a much faster pace.

For further discussion of these sorts of effects on audience attention, see Noël Carroll, 'Film, Attention and Communication', *Great Ideas Today 1996* (Chicago: Encyclopaedia Britannica Corp., 1996).

[38] Noël Carroll, 'Toward a Theory of Point-of-View Editing: Communication, Emotion and the Movies', *Theorizing the Moving Image* (New York: Cambridge, 1996).

[39] For further examples of this see Noël Carroll, 'Film, Attention and Communication'; and Joseph D. Anderson, *The Reality of Illusion: An Ecological Approach to Cognitive Film Theory* (Carbondale: Southern Illinois University Press, 1996). In ch. 6, 'Continuity', Anderson is especially adept at showing how cinematic and televisual space is constructed, especially in terms of Hollywood 'conventions', in such a way as to mesh with our innate capacities for spatial understanding.

structures of mass art are connected to hard-wired features of the human organism. Some may be, and in those cases, it is theoretically valuable to take note of them. In other cases, however, the analysis of the accessibility of the central devices of the various mass arts may require amplification in terms of historical and cultural considerations that explain how audiences pick up these conventions almost on contact.[40]

For example, the convention of the 'fade-out' and its virtually immediate recognition by audiences would not be explained in terms of innate perceptual dispositions of the human organism, but in terms of the way in which this convention expanded upon techniques—such as dimming the lighting and dropping the curtain—that were already known to audiences familiar with these theatrical markers for scene endings. That is, the intelligibility and accessibility of the 'fade-out' would be explained in virtue of its historical transposition of pre-existing cultural practices rather than in terms of exclusively hard-wired perceptual capacities.[41] Nevertheless, whether the explanations depend on biological, psychological, social, or historical factors, or upon a mix thereof, an unavoidable avenue of empirical research into the phenomenon of mass art is the isolation and characterization of the structures that secure widespread accessibility.

Moreover, as I suggest parenthetically in the third condition of my definition, mass art gravitates not only toward certain formal features for the sake of accessibility; mass art may also gravitate toward the

[40] For further discussion, see David Bordwell, 'Convention, Construction and Cinematic Vision', in *Post-Theory*, 87–107.

[41] Furthermore, much of the reasoning that we mobilize in order to follow films, TV programmes and comic strips is continuous with ordinary, everyday reasoning. Editing generally accords with our stored schemas and scripts for recognizing and organizing situations in everyday life, and films, TV programmes, and comic strips can generally be followed by using ordinary practical reasoning, including folk psychological understandings of human motivation. Thus, to a great extent, analysing the structures of such mass artworks and explaining their accessibility will involve determining the way in which they activate cognitive skills that the audience already possesses. Therefore, explaining why such mass artworks are accessible will involve identifying the psychological and social factors that account for the audience's possession of the cognitive stock that enables them to follow the relevant works, along with an account of the ways in which the pertinent mass art structures activate the mobilization of those cognitive capacities.

That much of what you need to know in order to follow such mass artworks is of the nature of what people already know in terms of cognitive skills, moreover, is a decided advantage for the purposes of mass communication. Understanding film and TV does not require special cinematic or televisual literacy; it relies in large measure upon engaging the inferential and interpretational skills that people already deploy in everyday life. Explaining the accessibility of film and TV then, to a large extent, involves noting how specific cinematic and televisual configurations link up with everyday cognitive skills.

For a useful summary of research in this area as well as an insightful discussion of its significance, see Paul Messaris, *Visual Literacy: Image, Mind & Reality* (Boulder, Colo.: Westview Press, 1994), especially ch. 3.

For further discussion of the notion of schema, notably what is called the person schema, see Ch. 5 of this book.

exploration of certain generic affects— such as teenage love, as enshrined in countless popular songs—because they are commonly recognized. And, as I mentioned earlier, certain types of content, like action/adventure stories, may be natural for mass art, since it is easier for the average movie-goer to comprehend how a kick-boxer fights his way out of an ambush than it is to comprehend the intricate and crafty financial man-œuvrings of leveraged corporate take-overs or the behaviour of people with infinitely subtle sexual preferences.

One objection to the emphasis that I place on accessibility in the definition of mass art is that certain forms of mass art may in fact be inaccessible to large groups of people. My students, for example, tell me that heavy metal music is inaccessible to their parents. Indeed, they add, it may even be part of the attraction of heavy metal that it is somehow inaccessible to the older set.

However, I wonder if heavy metal music is really inaccessible, rather than simply distasteful to my students' parents. These oldsters could certainly comprehend it without putting very much mental energy into it, even if they didn't like it. In fact, many of these parents may really comprehend it, and that may be the very reason that they dislike it. But, in any case, the question of whether the Lawrence Welk generation or the folk-song generation can literally understand Guns N'Roses is different from the question of whether they enjoy them, even if old-timers tend to couch their dislike misleadingly in phrases like 'I just can't understand x'. They really mean 'I can't stand x', or 'I can't understand why you (their teenage child) like x.'[42]

My emphasis on accessibility may also seem to be at odds with the fact that certain mass art is targeted at specialized audiences. For example, on cable TV, there is now at least one comedy channel and a science fiction channel. In my view, mass art aims at securing the largest audience possible. But how can we square this hypothesis with the fact that some mass art is customized for limited audiences—audiences, for example, with a taste for science fiction, on the one hand, and for comedy, on the other hand?

[42] Similar comments might be relevant to comic books, especially violent ones. Moreover, it may be parental dislike of certain comic books that, in part, makes them attractive to young readers. Martin Barker's findings with respect to *Action* is very suggestive here. Many of the committed readers he interviewed identified the comics as for young or even rebellious readers or for modern teenagers who enjoy new freedom, while many casual readers thought the comics were ones that parents wouldn't want one to read or that their parents wouldn't like and that reading them was 'naughty'. One might speculate that the anti-authority connotations of such comics was part of the reasons that young readers, involved in the adolescent project of differentiating themselves from their parents, were drawn to them. See Martin Barker, *Comics: Ideology, Power and the Critics* (Manchester: Manchester University Press, 1989), 58–9.

However, granting that mass art may be moulded to serve special audience interests should not obscure the equally important fact that in terms of basic stylistic choices—of modes of representation and narrative structures—there is not that great a difference between what would be shown on a comedy channel and what would be shown on a science fiction channel. *Seinfeld* and *Green Acres* are not really that different from *Babylon 5* and *Lost in Space* in terms of features like these. They all tell different stories, but their narrative and visual structures are similar. Their point-of-view editing structures are not different, for example. That is, the structures that secure the possibility for mass accessibility are common to mass art comedy and science fiction. So even if certain mass art products are, in virtue of their content, tailored to spectators with special interests and tastes, nevertheless, such works still gravitate toward securing the largest possible audience in terms of their fundamental structural choices. Mass art comedies are constructed in such a way that they are accessible to science fiction afficionados along with virtually everyone else. That a work appeals to certain tastes should not be confused with its generic accessibility.[43]

In my previous criticism of the Elimination Theory, I asked whether the denial of the relevance of formal and affective properties for the purpose of identifying mass art wasn't too hasty. Now, perhaps, the basis for my suspicion is evident. The third condition of my theory implies that formal and affective factors do have a role to play in identifying mass art. Mass art is, in part, a functional concept. The intended function of mass art is to elicit mass engagement. Thus, mass art will gravitate to formal and affective choices that facilitate the function of mass art. We may not be able to draw up a list of the formal features of mass art. However, this does not mean that formal features are irrelevant to identifying mass art. For, given an artwork produced and distributed by a mass delivery system, we will count it as an instance of mass art only if its formal features, whatever they might be, are conducive to mass accessibility.

Proleptically, let me point out that in my view mass art is such that it is *designed* to promote mass accessibility. This concedes that something may

---

[43] A similar point can be made with respect to what is called 'quality television'. The early eighties saw the emergence of programming targeted at an an upscale audience. Some examples include *Hillstreet Blues*, *St Elsewhere*, *L.A. Law*, *Northern Exposure*, *Moonlighting*, *China Beach*, *Picket Fences*, *thirtysomething*, *NYPD Blue*, and *Chicago Hope*. However, these series, despite their play for college educated yuppies, did not employ techniques that were different in kind from other forms of TV. Often their narrative structures were derived from soap opera narration, while their visual devices were never really different in kind from those found in *SeaQuest DSV*. For a discussion of 'quality television', see Robert J. Thompson, *Television's Second Golden Age* (New York: Continuum Publishing Company, 1996).

be an instance of mass art even if it fails to promote mass accessibility. A production may be a work of mass art even if it is a bungled attempt—that is, as the result of ineptitude, something that is inaccessible. But on my theory, as long as it can be established that the work in question was intentionally designed to be generally accessible, even if it is not, it still counts as a work of mass art.

Also, I claim that works of mass art *gravitate* toward formal choices that enhance accessibility. This language allows that accessibility is a degree concept, and that establishing whether a given formal choice is to be assessed as accessible or inaccessible will depend upon judgement calls based upon reflecting on comparisons and contrasts between a candidate strategy and alternative strategies of construction that are available within the same historical context.

Throughout my discussion of the formal/functional differentiae that demarcate mass art, I have repeatedly used avant-garde art—specifically avant-garde art produced by a mass medium—as the pertinent *logical* contrast to mass art proper. By mobilizing this contrast—i.e., by asking what is the difference between art produced in a mass medium (such as avant-garde art) and mass art proper—I put myself argumentatively in the position to hypothesize the third condition of my theory.

However, it pays to note that avant-garde art, as we saw in preceding chapters, is not only a conceptual foil to mass art proper. It is also, I believe, the relevant *historical* form of art that contrasts with mass art. Throughout the various debates that have been staged about mass art in this century, critics of mass art have consistently disparaged mass art because of its failure to measure up to the standard of avant-garde art. Critics of mass art—like Greenberg, Collingwood, Adorno, and Horkheimer—have all been proponents of avant-garde art, and the features of mass art that lead them to consign it to the realm of pseudo art are really features that derive from the brutal fact that mass art is not avant-garde art, where the notion of avant-garde art itself is generally bound up with some misunderstanding of Kantian aesthetics. Moreover, since avant-garde art has the best claim to being the high art of our epoch, it is easy to see why many commentators mis-describe the contrast between avant-garde art and mass art in terms of a distinction between high art and popular art.

I hypothesize that mass art and avant-garde art, in our times, have developed in contrast to each other, and, historically, the most important boundaries in the contemporary conception of the arts have to do with the way in which they carve up much of the genus of art into two highly visible, contrary species. This is not to say that there are not other sorts of arts existing at present, including folk art (such as break-dancing before it was commercialized) and what is sometimes called middlebrow art (as defined by MacDonald as the contemporary recycling of the structures of previous art-forms, both canonical and avant-garde). None the less, the highly structured distinction between mass art and avant-garde art marks the most significant theoretical boundary between the arts in contemporary Western culture.[44] And that is why all the theorists we have encountered feel as though they must treat mass art and the avant-garde in tandem.

Of course, by stressing the distinction between the avant-garde and mass art, I do not intend to deny the historical fact that these two distinct forms of art frequently borrow from each other. Avant-gardists—from Eisenstein with his interests in the circus, through the Surrealists with their interests in film, to the quotations of mass art by Pop artists and postmodernists—have perennially treated mass art as a source of themes and techniques; while mass artists often look to the avant-garde for inspiration—Hollywood moguls bought *Bolero* before they even knew what it was.

However, even though there is this movement between mass art and the avant-garde, the borrowings in both directions tend to change the purport of the themes and devices that cross the boundary between mass art and the avant-garde. For when the avant-garde adopts a theme or device from mass art, that theme or device acquires a kind of reflexive dimension that it lacks in its native land. For example, that the theme or device comes from the domain of mass art becomes part of its meaning or significance once it is incorporated in an avant-garde work, as in the case of Eisenstein's appropriation of circus devices as a celebration of the energy of the people. Of course, the case is even more pronounced in the postmodernist appropriation of vernacular imagery where said imagery is held up for semiotic dissection.

Likewise, when mass art incorporates elements of the avant-garde, it may be in order to appropriate the prestige of the high art of our times, or

---

[44] Though I am primarily concerned with mass art of a modern vintage—most notably mass art in the industrial age—I am also willing to admit that there may be examples, such as popular Japanese woodcuts, that meet my criteria of mass art but which pre-date industrialization. Today, it may be the case that we especially value such woodcuts because they are rare, that we display them in our museums of fine art, and that we treat them as what is called high art. But all this seems to me compatible with the fact that they are early (perhaps in some sense even 'technologically primitive') examples of mass art. That we treat such specimens as so-called high art due to their scarcity and/or their beauty does not preclude their status as early mass art. Maybe some of our contemporary fashion photography will be treated with the same esteem in the twenty-fourth century. And, in any case, where I invoke the notion of 'high art' in the sense of contemporary high art, I mean it to be understood primarily in terms of the avant-garde. So even if we honorifically treat some popular, preindustrial, Japanese woodcuts as high art today (in the somewhat dubious, honorific sense of 'high art'), we certainly do not mean to imply that they are avant-garde art.

to exploit the sensational aura or shock value that often surrounds this or that avant-garde 'scandal'. But in any case, when mass art borrows from the avant-garde it always adapts the relevant devices and themes to its own purposes by making them more accessible.[45] In film and TV, one example of this is to motivate disjunctive avant-garde cutting patterns psychologically, or to render dream sequences—like Dali's sets for *Spellbound*—fully explicable.

Thus, the fact that the traffic between the avant-garde and mass art is sometimes heavy does not refute my contention that these two domains are contrary. For each domain transforms whatever it borrows from the other in profound respects. When the avant-garde takes over a technique or a theme from mass art, that technique or theme acquires a new hermetic significance, such as the postmodernist's ironization of mass art iconography. This, of course, turns the mass art item into something that demands deciphering—something that is difficult for the ordinary viewer to understand and interpret without instruction. In contrast, when mass art incorporates avant-garde material, it attempts to render it accessible to the plain viewer, reader, or listener. That is, when avant-garde art appropriates mass art material, it attempts to transform it into an avant-garde challenge, whereas when mass art borrows an avant-garde theme or device it attempts to transform it into mass art by making it accessible. Therefore, for all the theft that goes on between mass art and the avant-garde, the two realms remain categorically distinct.

Inasmuch as mass art is to be understood functionally, according to my theory, a question arises about evaluation. Should a mass artwork be deemed good just in case it is accessible to large numbers of people? Here I would want to argue that being accessible is a good-making feature of a work *qua* mass artwork—since this realizes a design intention of mass artworks—but that this does not entail that the mass artwork is good, all things considered. There are several reasons for this.

The first is that the mass artwork does not only belong to the category of mass art. Typically, it also falls into some genre. Thus, its evaluation hinges not only on its success as an example of the mass art kind, but also on its success according to the evaluative criteria of the genre to which it belongs—suspense, romance, science fiction, melodrama, horror, and so on. As well, the mass artwork is also an artwork, so its comparative evaluation also involves considering its goodness as an example of one genre *vis-à-vis* the goodness available in other genres. An all-things-

---

[45] Raymond Williams appears to find this sort of appropriation of modernism somewhat alarming. See Raymond Williams, 'Culture and Technology', in his book *Towards 2000* (London: Hogarth Press/Chatto & Windus, 1983), 142.

considered evaluation of a particular instance of mass art involves an assessment of its virtues or blemishes not only *qua* mass art and *qua* the genre it belongs to, but also in terms of its standing as a work of art.

Moreover, though accessibility is a good-making feature of such a work *qua* mass art, it does not even entail that a candidate is good in any unqualified way as a mass artwork. For accessibility is only a precondition for mass art status. A mass artwork can be accessible but lack-lustre. Simply being accessible does not guarantee that it is enjoyable, appealing, interesting, or possessed of any other quality that might recommend it to a mass audience, or to any audience for that matter. Being accessible is simply *a* good-making feature of a mass artwork, for the reasons already given. However, it does not provide grounds for judging a work to be good overall, nor even good as a mass artwork. For a work that has a good-making feature can still be aesthetically weak. Perhaps in securing accessibility, a given mass artwork can be said to be not altogether bad. It has achieved something. But accessibility does not indicate goodness in any robust sense.

A mass artwork may be adjudged bad, if it fails to be accessible—i.e., if it fails to secure what it set out to achieve. But accessibility, though it counts for something, doesn't count for very much in terms of evaluation. It may be a *sine qua non* of other dimensions of aesthetic accomplishment in a mass artwork. But from the point of view of evaluation, it is to be regarded as a minimal achievement.

Another query that my theory may raise concerns its domain. I have developed a view of mass artworks. But, it might be observed, I might have initially oriented my project differently. I might have attempted to identify something called *mass cultural productions*. By opting for an analysis of mass artworks, rather than mass cultural productions, I have excluded from my purview such things as network news programmes and game shows. But, it might be charged, isn't this unconscionably arbitrary?

Perhaps there is some arbitrariness involved. But at the same time, the realm of mass cultural productions represents a larger class of things than I am, at present, prepared to theorize. I expect that much of what I say about mass artworks will pertain to mass cultural productions in general. This is especially apt to be the case with respect to accessibility. But, for the present, my target is narrower. I am concerned to identify only those mass cultural productions that are connected to recognizable art-forms, such as sculpture, music, drama, dance, literature, and, to a certain extent, architecture. I see no problem in principle, in attempting to characterize this subset of mass cultural production, even if some of my findings may apply to other sorts of mass cultural productions.

My analysis of mass art will not collapse into a characterization of mass cultural productions in general, of course, because not all mass cultural productions will be categorizable as art. Where there is overlap between my theory of mass art and a theory of mass cultural productions, it will concern my technology and accessibility conditions. However, I do not believe that it is a disadvantage of my theory of mass art that it suggests how we might begin to go on to characterize mass cultural productions in general.

The ontology of mass art

Having defined the nature of the mass artwork, I would now like to turn to the question of its ontological status—to the question of the mode of existence of the mass artwork. In my definition of the mass artwork, I have already partially answered this question by claiming that the mass artwork is a multiple instance or type artwork. In this section, I would like to clarify further precisely what I mean by this claim and to defend it. The strategy that I will adopt is first to attempt to characterize the ontological status of film, in order then to go on to see whether that characterization can be generalized, with suitable adjustments, to other mass art-forms such as photography, sound recording, broadcast radio, and telecommunications.

A useful way to get at the ontology of film is to focus on the difference between theatrical performances and film performances.[46] Say that there is a performance of *The Master Builder* tonight at the local repertory theatre and a performance of *Waterworld* at the same time in the neighbourhood multiplex cinema. One might go to either. In both cases, we are likely to be seated in an auditorium, and each performance might begin as a curtain rises. But despite surface similarities, there are ontologically profound differences between the two performances.

Undoubtedly, this assertion will seem odd to some philosophers. For if one distinguishes between two kinds of art—those that are singular and those that are multiple—then film performances and theatre performances appear to be on a par ontologically. That is, both the theatre performance

---

[46] This account of the ontology of film builds on earlier attempts of mine, including Noël Carroll, 'Towards an Ontology of the Moving Image', in *Philosophy and Film*, ed. Cynthia Freeland and Thomas Wartenberg (New York: Routledge, 1995); and Noël Carroll, 'Defining the Moving Image', in my *Theorizing the Moving Image* (New York: Cambridge University Press, 1996).

and the film performance will count as tokens of a type. In each case, the performance is a token of an art type—*The Master Builder*, on the one hand, and *Waterworld*, on the other—in the sense that any token of the type in question may undergo destruction—say, by fire—while the type continues to exist.[47]

Clearly, the type/token distinction, though helpful in locating the ontological distinction between certain paintings and sculptures, on the one hand, and things like plays, films, novels, and symphonies, on the other hand, is not fine-grained enough to distinguish between film performances and theatre performances. In order to secure a handle on this distinction, it is instructive to consider the different route by which we get from a play-type to a dramatic performance token versus the route from a film-type to a performance (i.e., a showing or a screening) of a film.

To get from a film-type to a token performance, we require a *template*; to get from a play-type to a token performance, we require an *interpretation*.[48] Moreover, the different routes from type to token performance in theatre, versus film, explains why we regard different theatrical performances of the same play as artworks in their own right, while, at the same time, we do not regard film performances (i.e., film showings) as individual artworks.

The film performance is generated from a template—standardly a film print, but it might also be a videotape, a laser disk, or a computer program, coded in a physical medium. Such templates are themselves tokens; each one of them can be destroyed without the film-type being destroyed, and each of these token-templates can be assigned a spatial location, though the film-type—say, *Waterworld*—cannot. Nor is the negative of the work the film-type. It is but one token among many. The original negative of F. W. Murnau's *Nosferatu* was destroyed in accordance with a court order, but the film still exists.

Each film showing is a token of the film-type; each token showing gives us access to the film-type. But in order to present a token performance of a film, we require a template—a film print or a video cassette or a laser disk—which template itself is a token of the film-type. The token film performance is generated from the template mechanically (or electroni-

---

[47] The application of the type/token distinction to art derives from Richard Wollheim, *Art and its Objects* (Cambridge: Cambridge University Press, 1980), especially ss. 35–8. The distinction in general appears to have been first proposed by C. S. Peirce, *Collected Papers*, vol. iv (Cambridge: Harvard University Press), 537.

[48] Here, I mean interpretation in the sense of the filling in of a recipe. The play is a recipe to be filled in by the performers of a play. The text is a set of instructions, but the instructions need to be filled in imaginatively by actors, directors, lighting designers, and so on. That process of filling in the recipe is what I mean by an interpretation in this context.

cally), in accordance with routine technical procedures. Thus, the token film performance—the film-showing—is not an artistic performance and does not warrant aesthetic appreciation.

Of course, one may complain if the film is shown out of focus, or if it burns up in the projector, but these complaints are not aesthetic. They are complaints about the mechanical expertise of the projectionist. The expertise of the projectionist, undoubtedly, is a precondition for access to the artwork *qua* film-type. But it is not an object of aesthetic commendation.

But the story is very different when it comes to plays. The difference is partly a function of the fact that plays may be considered either as literary works or as performance works.. When a play, like the dramatic text of *Strange Interlude*, is considered as a literary work, then my copy of *Strange Interlude* is a token of the art-type *Strange Interlude* in the same way that my copy of *The Warden* is a token of Trollope's novel. But when regarded from the perspective of theatrical performance, a token of *Strange Interlude* is a particular performance, which occurs at a specifiable time and place.

Whereas a film performance is generated from a template, and not an interpretation, a theatrical performance of *Strange Interlude* is generated by an interpretation and not a template. When used in the context of performance, the play-type *Strange Interlude* by Eugene O'Neill functions as a recipe which is to be filled out by other artists—by directors, actors, set designers, and the like. O'Neill composed the play—which is a type—but the play must be brought to life by an interpretation, or a conjunction of interpretations (by directors, actors, etc.), and, furthermore, this interpretation governs the performance tokens of the play as it is offered to the public on a nightly basis.

Moreover, this interpretation is a type; the same interpretation of a play can be revived after a substantial temporal hiatus and can be tokened in different theatres with numerically different but qualitatively identical sets. So, the performance token of a play-type is generated through an interpretation, which is itself a type. Consequently, theatrical interpretations are types within a type.[49] We get from a play-type to a performance through an interpretation which is itself a type. This contrasts with the route from a film-type to a token film-showing, which is mediated through a template which is itself a token.

Earlier I noted that a film performance—that is to say a film-showing at your local multiplex—is not itself an artwork, while matters stand differently with theatre. Theatrical performances are artworks in their own right. It takes artistry and imagination to embody an interpretation,

---

[49] See R. A. Sharpe, 'Type, Token, Interpretation, Performance', *Mind* (1979), 437–40.

whereas film performances require nothing more than technical compe-tence. In theatre as we know it, the interpretation and the performance are each candidates for aesthetic appreciation.

In the best case, the play, its interpretation, and its performance are integrated, though we recognize that these are discriminable layers of artistry, even if one person writes the play, directs it, and acts in it as well. For there are many cases where a bad play finds a commendable interpretation, embodied in superb performances, while, at other times, a good play is poorly interpreted but performed well, and so on. That we make these distinctions so easily indicates that there are different ontolo-gical strata of artistry when it comes to the stage—strata of artistry that do not obtain in film in the same way.

For if with theatre, the play-type is a recipe that directors and other artists interpret, yielding different (though related) artworks, with film, the recipe (for example, the shooting script) and the artistic interpretations of the director, actors, etc. are non-detachable constituents of the same artwork. We do not evaluate shooting scripts independently of the film production,[50] and we do not evaluate film-showings *aesthetically* at all.

It is fairly standard to regard works of film art as types. But if the preceding comparison with theatre is persuasive, then we can characterize films in a more fine-grained way, namely: a film is a type whose token performances are generated by templates that are themselves tokens. Our next question, then, is whether this pattern of analysis can be generalized to other forms of mass art, including photography, radio, telecommunica-tions, music recordings, and best-selling pulp fiction.

Best-selling pulp fiction, like literature in general, is a type art-form. My copy of *The Gift* is a token of Danielle Steel's novel in the same way that my copy of *The Magic Mountain* is a token of Thomas Mann's novel. In either case, the destruction of my copy would not standardly occasion the destruction of Steel's or Mann's novel. Indeed, every graphic token of Steel's novel might be burnt up and yet the novel might continue to exist if, à la *Fahrenheit 451*, one person remembered the text.

Of course, it strains English usage to call my token copy of *The Gift* a performance. So, it is perhaps better to speak of token instances, or of token reception-instances, here, rather than of token performances, as we expand our characterization of the pattern of analysis that we have already developed with respect to cinema to other mass art-forms. Moreover, as in the case of film, we have access to works of pulp literature through token

---

[50] For example, when scripts are published, that is typically because the films in question are thought to be aesthetically important. We do not generally read scripts as literature in their own right.

reception-instances that are themselves generated from templates, including hard-typography and, perhaps at the limit, memory traces.

Turning from pulp fiction to photography, the first thing to be noted is that it may not be the case that photography is uniformly a multiple art-form from an ontological point of view. There may be, due to their method of production, photographic artworks that are one of a kind, such as Polaroids and daguerreotypes.[51] Such photographs have an onto-logical status that is characteristic of the status of paintings.

If a daguerreotype by Niépce is destroyed, we have lost the daguerreo-type, even if photographic reproductions of it remain, in the same way that if the *Mona Lisa* in the Louvre were shredded, we would lose da Vinci's masterpiece, despite the continued existence of all those museum postcards. With such single-instance photographs, the so-called reproduc-tions thereof are not tokens of the work in question, but documentations of it. Thus, I do not wish to call single-instance photographs mass art proper, for the same reason that the *Mona Lisa* is not an example of mass art, despite the fact that it has been photographically documented end-lessly in art history texts and travel books.

On the other hand, in addition to single-instance photographs, there are many photographs that fall squarely into the category of mass art. And, predictably enough, given the photographic basis of film in general, the pattern developed to analyse cinema suits such photographs quite nicely. For token reception-instances of such photographs are generated from templates, like negatives, which are themselves tokens, and the works in question continue to exist even if the negatives and most of the other tokens of the relevant photograph are lost or destroyed.

Considering radio and TV, the first point to make is that, in a great many cases, programmes in these media are recorded on such things as audio magnetic tape, kinescopes, videotapes, or digital programs for subsequent broadcasting. This practice became fairly standard in radio by the late nineteen-forties. In cases like this, the pattern of analysis matches the one introduced for film, since the token instances of tape serve as the requisite templates that make token reception-instances pos-sible. But what of one-time broadcasts that are not taped or artistically modified (by things like mixing) at the message source?

Clearly, one-time broadcasts in radio and TV should count as examples of mass art, since they can simultaneously afford a multiplicity of token reception-instances of the same work—a song or a drama—in non-over-

---

[51] Patrick Maynard has pointed out to me that some modern photography collectors count individual daguerreotype prints as one of a kind.

lapping reception sites that are geographically remote from each other. But what is the template in these cases?

My suggestion is that the template is the transmission signal that has been derived from the message source by coding and modulating devices for the purpose of transmission, and which is received by demodulation and decoding devices such as household radios and TVs. Each token reception-instance is derived from the template by a mechanical/electrical (as opposed to an artistic) process. Just as projecting a film is neither artistic nor interpretive, neither is turning on or tuning a radio or a TV. The token reception-instances of the programmes in question are physical processes. The broadcast signal is a physical structure and certain token reception-instances of these programmes can be destroyed—by jamming, for example—while the radio mass artwork and the TV mass artwork continue to exist. Of course, where the programme signal derives from a magnetic template, we find a relay of templates, including the transmission signal, as well as the tape, mediating between the mass art type and its token reception-instances.

One complication should be mentioned here. Suppose a TV programme is being shot before a live audience. In such cases, we might want to talk about two artworks. There is the work of theatre, which is performed in front of the specific studio audience, and there is something else. In one case, where what is broadcast is being edited and structured (for example, in terms of long-shots, close-ups, etc.), there is another artwork, which, if it meets the accessibility condition, is a mass artwork, one that differs in important respects from what the studio audience sees. And in another case, where there may be no additional structuration (a prospect that some, on compelling grounds, might deny is a live one), the something else is a documentation of the theatrical artwork, something on a par with a museum postcard of the *Mona Lisa*. Similar distinctions can be drawn with respect to live radio broadcasts, which will comprise a live performance artwork for the immediate studio audience, and either a straight documentation or recording of it (if one concedes that there are such things), *or*, more standardly, a mass artwork which has been modulated, mixed, and enhanced electronically for the radio audience.

Some commentators worry that, given a performance of a play before an audience that is simultaneously broadcast around the nation, we will have to say that we have two artworks—the play enacted before an audience and the broadcast play—such that one is a mass artwork and the other is not. On the one hand, we can dissolve the apparent incongruity in a great many cases like this by drawing a distinction between an artwork and a mere recording thereof. On the other hand, if what is broadcast involves editing and changes in camera positions such that we do not feel that the broadcasted play should be delegated to the status of *mere* recording, then I see no problem with admitting that there are two artworks here—the live play and the broadcast play—only one of which is mass art. For editing and changes in camera position and framing do constitute the addition of a layer of artistic interpretation and creativity not available in the enacted performance before the studio audience.

Of course, where a one-time broadcast involves a script, in the case of a drama—or a score, in the case of music—we have no problem thinking that we are dealing with a type, that, in principle, can be tokened more than once. However, a problem may appear to arise when one thinks of broadcasts that involve improvisation (and no taping, or editing or mixing), since one may worry that in such cases one will be unable to specify the type of which the reception-instances are tokens. Here I think that our anxieties rest on the intuition that improvisations are one-of-a-kind events.

I believe that there are two ways to handle this problem. The first is to concede that improvisations are singular artworks and to argue that, as in the case of single-instance photographs, reception-instances of improvisations are documentations rather than tokens of the works in question. However, the second solution, and the one I prefer, is to deny that improvisations are, in principle, single-instance artworks. For improvisations can be memorized and played again and again by the original artists or by someone else;[52] they can be notated (as they were in the classical tradition), and played again; and in the age of mass art, they can be taped and/or memorized by listeners who, in turn, can notate them and/or reproduce them. An improvisation continues to exist as long as token performances of it can be executed. A painting ceases to exist when the 'original' is destroyed. But, in this sense, there are not strictly speaking originals in the case of improvised musical or dramatic productions. It is conceptually possible to replicate an improvisation, but it is not possible to replicate paintings under the standard concept of a painting.

Improvisations are not, in principle, singular artworks. Thus, the pattern developed to characterize film artworks can be applied to broadcast improvisations. That is, we see and/or hear token reception-instances of the improvisation type through the mediation of a token transmission template.

[52] For example, Robert B. Ray notes: 'To avoid paying royalties, groups like King Oliver's Creole Jazz Band and Armstrong's Hot Five replaced published songs with on-the-spot improvisations whose recording granted them a permanence they would otherwise never have had.' See Robert B. Ray, 'Tracking', *The South Atlantic Quarterly*, 90/4 (1991), 784.

The story to be told about popular sound recordings resembles the account of typical broadcasting, for the straightforward reason that most typical broadcasting of popular music already involves sound recording. In sound recording, a microphone transforms aural vibrations into electrical pulses which are amplified and converted by a recording head, an electro-magnet that produces patterns on the coating of the recording tape. This process, in turn, is reversed in playback when the magnetic patterns are converted back into vibrations, amplified by some type of loudspeaker or headphone. Once again, the musical work, which is a type, generates a token reception-instance in my living room, via a token template, which in this case is a magnetic pattern or a relay token thereof.

However, as with some of the media we have already examined, with sound recording, we may wish to distinguish between two kinds of cases: pieces created in the studio by mixing, dubbing, etc., which we might regard as constructed mass art types,[53] and pieces of music that are virtually unvarnished documentations of independently existing musical performances.[54] Though the former probably have the best claim concep-tually—and probably statistically—to be considered mass art proper, the latter have played an undeniable role historically in the evolution of mass culture, even if the future seems to belong to studio constructed mass art.[55]

Provisionally, then, the pattern of analysis developed to isolate the ontological status of cinema appears to work across the board for mass artworks in general. Mass artworks are multiple instance or type artworks. Specifically, they are types whose token reception-instances are generated by templates, or by relays of templates that are themselves tokens. This serves to distinguish the works in question from singular artworks, on the one hand, and from type artworks whose token are generated by inter-pretations, on the other hand. Of course, this does not separate the works in question from certain non-artworks—like TV news programmes—that

[53] Perhaps Glenn Gould was one of the first people to recognize the analogy between the ontology of sound recording and the ontology of film. He wrote that 'one should be free to "shoot" a Beethoven sonata or a Bach fugue in or out of sequence, intercut almost without restriction, apply postproduction techniques as required, and the composer, the performer and above all the listener will be better served thereby.' Glenn Gould, *The Glenn Gould Reader*, ed. Tim Page (New York, 1984), 359.

[54] Many might wish to deny the possibility of what I call unvarnished recordings, and, therefore, regard all musical sound recording in terms of the category of constructed mass art types. For an extended, though controversial, discussion of the significance of sound recording for rock music, see Theodore Gracyk, *Rhythm and Noise: The Aesthetics of Rock Music* (Durham, NC: Duke University Press, 1996).

[55] It perhaps pays to remark here that rock music played by garage bands, bar bands, and the like is not mass art proper by my construal. It may count as popular art, but it is not mass art because it is not, in the basic case, delivered to multiple reception sites simultaneously.

are also produced and delivered by the relevant mass technologies. TV news programmes and sitcoms share the same mode of existence, inasmuch as they are the same kind of types. Where they differ is in their respective claims to art status.

Before concluding this discussion of the ontological status of mass artworks, it is important to consider a serious objection that might be raised against it. In my attempt to isolate the ontological status of mass artworks I have, in part, relied upon a distinction between singular and multiple arts. However, this distinction has been challenged by Gregory Currie in his important monograph *An Ontology of Art*.[56] In this book, Currie advances the Instance Multiplicity Hypothesis, according to which all art is multiple.[57] There are no singular arts in Currie's view, our intuitions about paradigmatic cases of fine art, such as painting and sculpture, notwithstanding. Thus, to the extent that my theory of the ontology of mass art depends on a distinction between singular arts and multiple arts, it appears to rely upon a distinction where there is none. Therefore, in order to defend my theory, I need to show that the contrast between multiple arts and singular arts is a distinction with a difference.

Currie introduces his defence of the Instance Multiplicity Hypothesis by claiming that there is a presumption in favour of any ontological theory of art that offers a unified perspective on the field—that says that all art is singular or that all art is multiple. Moreover, it is fairly obvious that it cannot be the case that every art-form is singular. Consider literature. So, the hypothesis that all the arts are multiple has a better chance of providing a unified theory of the field. Or, in other words, Currie thinks that there is a presumption in favour of the view that artworks are multiple across the board. Thus, if there are no considerations that threaten to defeat it, the Instance Multiplicity Hypothesis is the ontological theory that we should endorse.

Currie argues that it is logically possible to produce molecule-for-molecule versions of any work of fine art. Imagine a super-xerox machine that can replicate any painting, sculpture, and so on. Since it is identical, molecule for molecule, to the original, it has the same perceptible structure as the original. And since the replicas are counterfactually dependent on the originals in the sense that every feature in the replica is causally dependent on a corresponding feature in the original, then the presence of features in the replica are explained by the same historical and intentional

---

[56] Gregory Currie, *An Ontology of Art* (New York: St Martin's Press, 1989).
[57] See Ibid., ch. 4.

factors that explain the presence of those features in the original.[58] Thus, these super-xeroxes are alleged to deliver the same aesthetic stimulation as the original and putatively grant access to the historical significance of the original. Therefore, they are perfectly satisfactory targets for artistic (i.e., aesthetic plus historical) attention—from the viewpoint of appreciating the accomplishment of the work in question. That is, they are on a par with the originals. Indeed, Currie writes as though all fine art is, via his super-xeroxing machine, mass-producible art (at least in principle).

Currie's argumentative strategy, in effect, is to challenge opponents to find something wrong with his conjecture. Thus, most of Currie's energy is spent showing what is misguided about possible objections to his theory. However, I think that there are some pretty decisive considerations that he never addresses and that indicate that the Instance Multiplicity Hypothesis does not offer a general theory of all the arts. For example, Currie never discusses site-specific works of art—that is, sculptures and architectural artworks that take their character from the environments in which they are constructed, and that are altered over time by the conditions of the surrounding environment in ways that are intended to constitute part of what viewers are to take as their object of appreciation. That is, works of sculpture and architecture may be such that they are designed to interact with the specific sites upon which or in which they are constructed, and that interactive process can itself be intended to be part of what is significant about the piece.

Robert Smithson's *Spiral Jetty* was constructed on a site notable for its unique possession of a certain strain of algae that guaranteed the reddish hue that he was after, and the shape of the jetty was a response to the formation of the surrounding site. Moreover, part of what was to be appreciated in the work was the differing appearances of the jetty as the water levels altered. Similarly, Walter De Maria's *Lightning Field* was situated as it was because of the high intensity of electrical activity in the environment and because of the way in which the surrounding mountains framed that activity. And, of course, part of the piece involved the

---

[58] I am not completely convinced by Currie's assertion here. I would have thought that the relevant historical and intentional factors to consider in terms of one of his super-xeroxes would be those that are pertinent to the operation of the super-xeroxing machine—for example, the intentions of the operator of the machine as he or she sets the dials on the super-xeroxing apparatus. Using Currie's own terminology from earlier chapters in his monograph, I think that the relevant heuristic pathway of the super-xeroxed replica should be the historical considerations and intentions of the operator of the super-xerox apparatus, and not the heuristic pathway of the original artwork. That heuristic pathway may be available in the replica, but it should not be the relevant focus of our attention when we come to consider the nature of the accomplishment that the super-xeroxed replica represents. Nevertheless, for purposes of argument, I will grant Currie his assertion in the following discussion above.

way in which the piece engaged actual, specific, recurrent lightning storms.[59]

These pieces are representatives of an important genre in contemporary art, sometimes called 'earthworks'. Their relevance to the discussion of singular versus multiple arts is, of course, that the very vicissitudes these works undergo as they interact with their actual environments are part of what these works are about. These works are involved with processes, not merely with products. It is hard to imagine that, in the known physical universe, one could regularly replicate the exact processes undergone by the original site-specific works by means of Currie's super-xerox machine.

Let us grant, for the sake of argument, that Currie's super-xeroxing machine can replicate a site-specific structure and its surrounding environment at time T1. Yet, it is virtually unimaginable that, physically, all of the events that the original undergoes from time T2 through Tn will occur in the putative replica. And if it happened once, that would be a fluke event, hardly replicable with any degree of reliability on all subsequent occasions of super-xeroxing.

But if the future histories of the supposed replica do not regularly suffer the same events as the original, then the putative artworks in question are not identical. It is highly unlikely, given the structure of the physical universe, that Currie's super-xeroxes of site-specific works will standardly weather in exactly the same way that the originals do. But since the weathering process can be an element of artistic attention in site-specific works, site-specific works are singular artworks—works that are not, in principle, regularly multipliable in the known physical universe. For in the known physical universe, the probability that the original site-specific work and all the super-xeroxes thereof might undergo the same physical transformations is wildly freakish.

Nor can these considerations be turned aside on the grounds that the works cited are of contestable artistic status. For the same case can be made on the basis of acknowledged architectural masterpieces such as Frank Lloyd Wright's *Taliesin* and *Falling Waters*. Furthermore, site specificity is arguably a central feature of Greek temple architecture.[60] At one point Currie briefly considers architecture, and surmises that the surrounding environment is irrelevant to the identity of the work—perhaps because he senses that if his super-xeroxes must replicate entire, indeterminately

[59] Descriptions and photographs of the pieces by Smithson and De Maria can be found in John Beardsley, *Earthworks and Beyond: Contemporary Art in the Landscape* (New York: Abbeville Press Publishers, 1989).
[60] See, for example, Vincent Scully's *The Earth, The Temple and The Gods: Greek Sacred Architecture* (New York: Praeger Publishers, 1969).

bounded environments and their vicissitudes, the possibility of super-xeroxed replicas, produced on a regular basis, will seem immensely implausible, even in principle. But he is just wrong if he thinks that a unique environment and its vicissitudes cannot be part of a site-specific work. And that error spells the defeat of the Instance Multiplicity Hypothesis, for the reasons I have already rehearsed.[61]

Currie says that there is a presumption in favour of a unified theory of the ontology of art and that the view that all art is multiple is the most credible unified theory. I see no reason to believe that there is such a presumption, and, in any case, if the facts are otherwise, all claims about such a presumption must be retired. Furthermore, I think that the fact of site-specific artworks of the sort to which I have alluded shows the so-called presumption to be extravagant. There are at least these singular artworks, and that is enough to sustain the distinction between singular and multiple artworks that I have invoked in developing my theory of the ontology of mass art. Even if super-xeroxing were possible in some cases, there would still be a contrast class of singular artworks. Not all art is, in principle, super-xeroxable. There is still a distinction with a difference worth marking here. Moreover, even if it were the case that all art is multiple in the way that Currie speculates, my theory of the ontology of mass art would still be informative, since I draw a contrast between multiple art whose token instances are generated by interpretations, and mass art whose tokens are necessarily generated by templates that are themselves tokens and/or relays of tokens.[62]

David Novitz's theory of mass art

Since the first publication of my proposal for a theory of mass art, at least one competing theory has emerged.[63] Advanced by David Novitz, this theory maintains that:

[61] For further objections to Currie's theory, see Christopher Shields, Critical Notice of Currie's *Ontology of Art*, *Australasian Journal of Philosophy*, 73/2 (1995), 293–300.

[62] One reader, inspired by Currie, advanced as a counter-example a work of high art produced by Currie's super-xerox machine. I am not convinced that this work would be of equal artistic standing with the original, because what Currie calls the heuristic pathway of the original would differ from the heuristic pathway of the copy (since that would involve a story about using the super-xerox machine). However, for the sake of argument, let us assume that the super-xerox is an artwork. Is it a mass artwork? It is not, on my account, if it is not accessible. A super-xerox of a Braque is not mass art. But would it have the same mode of existence as mass art? Yes, it would, even though it is not an example of mass art. I have already admitted that avant-garde artworks can be produced and distributed by mass technologies. But what if it were an instance of more traditional high art. Then it might be an example of what in the next section I call technologically distributed, traditional esoteric art.

[63] David Novitz, 'Noël Carroll's Theory of Mass Art', *Philosophic Exchange*, 23 (1992), 39–50.

A mass work of art is 1. a work of art 2. whose production or delivery involves the use of mass technology 3. with the intention thereby of delivering the work to as many people as possible.[64]

Novitz introduces his own theory by criticizing my theory at length and then offering his own, not unrelated view, as an improvement over mine. For our purposes, it is useful to consider both Novitz's criticisms and his alternative theory, since doing so will enable me to clarify my own theory further, to introduce some further distinctions, and to show the advantages of my theory over competitors like Novitz's.

One of Novitz's objections to my theory is that it will count nineteenth-century novels—such as those of Jane Austen's[65]—as mass art. I don't really see the problem here. Though my theory is offered primarily as an analysis of mass art in the contemporary world, I explicitly admit that the novel is one important potential source of mass art which pre-dates our current age of mass culture. Thus, I don't understand why Novitz thinks that the possible inclusion of certain nineteenth-century novels under the category of mass art in my theory should be a counter-example to my view. Indeed, I would count most eighteenth-century novels of the gothic variety as mass art. And, of course, I will count pulp novels of any vintage as mass art. Thus, why Novitz thinks that the inclusion of some novels in the category of mass art is a problem remains a mystery to me.

Of course, I would question whether novels like James Joyce's *Ulysses* or Virginia Woolf's *To the Lighthouse* are instances of mass art. But these are avant-garde novels. I am committed to the view that avant-garde novels are not mass art. But none of Novitz's counter-examples are avant-garde. Whether Jane Austen's novels are mass art depends, for me, upon whether or not they are designed to be accessible for mass audiences. But, unfortunately, Novitz does not tell us whether he thinks this to be so or not. But *if* it turns out that they were so designed, then I have no problem with counting Jane Austen's novels as mass art. In my view, we need more literary-historical knowledge than Novitz supplies in order to adjudicate his counter-example.

Novitz places a great deal of emphasis on the fact that my theory may classify works from earlier centuries as mass art. I certainly concede this, and with certain cases, I am more than willing to bite the bullet and agree that they are mass art—for example, as noted earlier, I admit the possibility of classifying certain popular Japanese woodcuts as mass art. Novitz seems to think that this is a problem, but I don't. Rather, it is to be

---

[64] Ibid. 48.   [65] Ibid. 47.

expected when one is analysing the concept of a historical phenomenon that emerges over time.

When Marx analyses the concept of the commodity which was and remains central to capitalist exchange, he admits that the account may apply to some pre-capitalist objects as well. Indeed, this is what we would anticipate of a form that evolved over a historical process. But his account is not compromised by this. His analysis is no less instructive. Similarly, when I analyse the notion of the mass art objects that are central to contemporary mass culture, the fact that my analysis picks out historical forebears and precursors should not problematize my project.

Speaking broadly, the biggest worry that Novitz has about my theory is that he believes that it precludes the possibility of what he calls high art being mass art. But here I believe that he has simply misread me. I never claim that high art as such cannot be mass art. I don't even deploy the notion of high art in an unqualified way in my theory. Rather, I maintain that avant-garde art—which, I assert, has the best claim to being the high art of our time—cannot be mass art. Though I may be wrong in regarding avant-garde art as what should count as the high art of our times, from a logical point of view, I have not precluded the possibility that some of what people call high art is mass art. If *Oliver Twist* or *Silas Marner* are what people call high art, then they may very well be mass art as well.

My theory of mass art states three conditions that are individually necessary and jointly sufficient for something to count as mass art. To iterate: x is a mass artwork if and only if 1. x is a type artwork 2. produced and distributed by a mass delivery technology 3. which is intentionally designed to gravitate toward those choices which promise accessibility for the largest number of untutored (or relatively untutored) audiences. Novitz leaves the first condition unquestioned, lavishing his attention on the second and third conditions.

Novitz's attack on the second condition—the mass technology condition—is strange in several respects. On the one hand, he introduces certain counter-examples, like trinkets, against this condition—as if this condition alone were both necessary and sufficient for counting something as mass art. But, of course, since this condition is only a necessary condition, it should come as no surprise that non-mass art objects might share this feature with mass art objects and yet not count as mass art, since they are precluded by other conditions in the theory. For example, trinkets may not count as mass art because they fail to meet my first condition—i.e., they may not be art. (I say 'may' here because in some instances certain so-called trinkets may be art; what would be needed to make this discussion fruitful would be a concrete, historical case of the sort that Novitz fails to provide.)

On the other hand, a second jarring feature of Novitz's attack on the mass-technology condition is that, despite his objections to it, he appears to take it up unrevised when he comes to advancing his own theory of mass art. One must wonder why, if the mass-technology condition is so flimsy when I state it, Novitz later embraces it.

One of Novitz's counter-examples to my theory is a recording of a piece by Mozart. This example is ambiguous. It blurs the distinction between the artwork as composition and the artwork as performance. Surely, Mozart's original composition is not mass art. So we must be talking about some performance, where the performance in question is an electronically constructed one, rather than a mere recording. Is this a counter-example to my theory of mass art?

I think not. For I do not preclude that a work of so-called high art can be a work of mass art. I only deny that a work of avant-garde art can be mass art. And Mozart's music is not avant-garde. So a Mozart recording *may* be a work of mass art, depending upon whether it meets my other criteria—notably the third condition, which we may call the accessibility condition. My hunch is that such a performance will not meet the accessibility condition, but I could be wrong here. And if I am wrong, I am nevertheless willing to live with the consequence that part of the contemporary recording industry's production of what is called classical music may belong to mass culture.

Again, I doubt that I will be driven to this conclusion in any way that I should find embarrassing, once we attend to particular cases. For I predict that most of the relevant classical music will fail to meet the accessibility condition. Of course, there is what might be labelled the 'Boston Pops/Hollywood Bowl phenomenon'—classical music that has been doctored or edited or taken out of context in order to make it accessible. Recordings of this sort might plausibly count as mass art, or, perhaps more accurately, as middlebrow art. But the existence of such recordings does not compromise the distinction that I am out to draw between contemporary mass art and avant-garde art that is produced and delivered by mass technology.

Undoubtedly, Novitz would attempt to block the move I attempted to make two paragraphs ago when I denied that Mozart's compositions were mass art. For Novitz has a very expansive view of mass technology. For him, very few works of art do not involve mass-delivery technology. Among these mass technologies he includes paper and pencil, inked quills and vellum, fountain pens and sketch books. So if Mozart had access to a pen and a piece of paper, then he had access to a mass-delivery technology.

However, I think that it violates our ordinary sense of English to regard a pen and a piece of paper as a mass-delivery technology. Indeed, I think that in ordinary English it is bizarre to call pen and ink a 'mass technology'. Doesn't the relevant sense of 'mass technology' have connotations of industrial production? 'Technology' suggests power machinery to my ear. And a pen is not an example of power machinery.

I stipulated that a mass-delivery technology was a technology with the capacity to deliver the same performance or object to more than one reception site simultaneously. And I not only question whether Mozart could write fast enough to do this; I also wonder whether pencil and paper constitutes a *mass technology* in any natural understanding of that phrase.

Novitz also claims that the belly of a violin is a mass technology according to my stipulation, since it can deliver a sound to more than one reception site at the same time. However, here he overlooks my observation that in discriminating discrete reception sites, we will need to seek guidance from ordinary language where, of course, it is not customary to regard the front and the back of a concert hall as discrete reception sites. Moreover, the front and the back of a concert hall are not typically non-overlapping reception sites.

In disputing the mass technology condition of my theory of mass art, Novitz raises the case of Steven Spielberg's thinking up the plot of his next movie. This is supposed to count against the requirement that mass art-works be produced and distributed by a mass technology. I don't see why. If Steven Spielberg fails to make that plot into a film by means of the mass technology of the movies, his musings hardly comprise a mass artwork or even part of one. Any Hollywood contract lawyer will support me on this one. Of course, I never maintained that a mass technology is the only ingredient in the production of a mass artwork, but that it was simply a necessary ingredient. On the other hand, doesn't Novitz's Spielberg example begin to insinuate a commitment to a rather suspicious tenet of Idealism (namely, that artworks proper are mental)?

In my view, the most interesting condition in my theory is the third condition—the accessibility condition. This condition distinguishes mass art from avant-garde art—the art with the best credentials to being what might be thought of as the high art of our time—and, therefore, the accessibility condition distinguishes mass art from avant-garde art that is produced and delivered by a mass-delivery technology. However, it is the accessibility condition that Novitz appears to regard as the least-palatable element in my theory. Indeed, it is by dropping the accessibility condition from the theory of mass art that Novitz paves the way for the proposal of his own theory.

According to the accessibility condition, what we refer to as mass art in our culture must be such that it is designed to gravitate in its structural and stylistic choices (and perhaps even in its content) toward articulations that are easily accessible to mass untutored audiences. Mass art must be designed in a way that is accessible to mass audiences. This, in turn, broadly determines or constrains the structures, styles, and even subjects that mass art tends to deploy. Specifically, mass art gravitates to those structural and stylistic choices that best realize its function, namely, to engage mass audiences by means of choices that are easily accessible, virtually on first exposure, to mass untutored audiences.

Novitz questions the notion of untutored audiences that I invoke in the accessibility condition. He thinks that if a specimen of mass art involves the use of a natural language, then the audiences must at least be tutored in the language in question. In order to understand an English-language film, one needs to understand English. And the acquisition of English requires tutoring.

First, it is not clear that following an English-language film like *Mad Max* or *Twister* always does require facility in English (and my account of mass art helps explain why this should be so). Many English-language films, especially action films, minimize the use of dialogue, perhaps in order to enhance international accessibility—and there is some indication that the popularity of mass-market films varies inversely with the amount of language in it.[66] And it is for this reason—a reason connected with accessibility—that many mass-market movies minimize dependence on language.

But even granting that much mass art may require facility in a relevant natural language, this does not cut against my claims about untutored audiences. For in my sense of 'tutored', the tutoring at issue involves training in *specialized* background knowledge, including training in deciphering erudite codes, cues, implications, and allusions. But one does not need specialized training in order to understand mass artworks in one's own language; one already knows one's own language. No special tutoring is required. After all, when I spoke of 'untutored audiences', I did not mean to refer to wolf children.

Moreover, the English speaker who watches a Hong Kong film does not

[66] That is, more language often translates into less popularity, and, apprized of this, Hollywood producers aim at using less language and more action. See Terry Ilot, 'Look at Who's Talking Too Much', *Variety* (9 Sept. 1991), 110. Moreover, it should be added that mass-market American films and TV programmes derive a special advantage inasmuch as English is becoming the *de facto* international language—world-wide, one person in seven speaks it. See Susanna McBee, 'English: Out to Conquer the World', *U.S. News and World Report* (18 Sept. 1985).

require special tutorials to follow the mass-art structures deployed in a Jackie Chan movie. And in order to deal with whatever language difficulties these films may present, mass film distributors most frequently resort to dubbing such films into the languages the relevant audiences already speak, or, less frequently, they resort to subtitles in languages the relevant audiences already read. Indeed, the preference for dubbing over subtitles confirms the tendency in the mass arts to gravitate toward choices that presuppose the least amount of uncommon knowledge across the targeted mass audiences (since dubbing does not presuppose literacy).[67]

Novitz finds my claims about untutored audiences unconvincing because he thinks that audiences need background knowledge about the law, about mental illness, parody, human foibles, and so on in order to follow *L.A. Law* and *Twin Peaks*. Now I'm not sure you need to know anything about actual mental illness in order to follow *Twin Peaks*. The background information relevant here would be better found in horror films than in medical journals, while most of the required legal 'knowledge' required by *L.A. Law* that is not supplied directly (and accessibly) by the narration itself probably comes to the viewer from having been exposed to previous law shows. That is, if these TV programmes require any background training, it comes from the province of mass art itself which, as my theory contends, tutors its audience to a limited extent through formulaic repetition. Thus, neither *L.A. Law* nor *Twin Peaks* confounds what I say about untutored audiences.

Novitz fears that the notion of accessibility that I employ is dubious. For what is accessible to one person may not be accessible to another. Some people may find Mozart and Shakespeare more accessible than rap. Granted. But this misses the issue. The question is about what *masses* of untutored people find easily accessible. It does not seem plausible to suppose that *masses* of untutored people find *The Tempest* more accessible than 'Fight the Power'. Novitz may respond that masses of people could be trained so that they find *The Tempest* accessible. But then they would not be untutored. Nor would their new-found access to *The Tempest* diminish their grasp of 'Fight the Power'.

Novitz notes that accessibility may change over time. I wouldn't want to dispute this. But that does not challenge my theory. My theory maintains that mass art has a function that predisposes it to search out easily accessible structures. At time T5, mass art gravitates toward the most easily accessible structures at time T5. At time T15, a mass artwork of that

[67] For further discussion of the issue of natural languages and movies, see: Noël Carroll, 'Film, Attention and Communication'.

vintage will seek out the most easily accessible structure available at T15. Needless to say, the most easily accessible structure at T15 may differ from those at T5. Iris shots, for example, may be later replaced by close-ups.

Thus, that degrees of accessibility may change with history does not challenge the claim that mass art gravitates toward what is most accessible, where accessibility is time-indexed. Mass art tends in the direction of accessibility, specifically in terms of what is accessible in the context of its production, even though what counts as accessible at one point in time may undergo mutation later.

My third condition—the accessibility condition—is a functional/structural requirement for mass art. That the function in question might be realized by different structures at different times does not contravene the requirement in question. Marx claimed that the forces of production gravitate toward maximizing productivity. This generalization, though perhaps false, is not undermined by noting that at one point the forces of production are steam-driven while, at another point in time, they are electrically powered. Likewise, mass art, given its function, gravitates toward accessible structures—i.e., accessible in context. This is a structural requirement even if, given historical circumstances, the specific structures in question may vary.

Nor is this concession to history on my part something that should astound the reader. I have advertised more than once that I am dealing with historical phenomena. I have only denied that exclusively historical (and/or social) considerations can provide an account of mass art. I have never contended that history (including social history) should have no role to play in our understanding of mass art.

Novitz's leading counter-example to the accessibility condition is *Sense and Sensibility*. Presumably it is art; I won't quibble with that. And it is certainly distributed by means of a mass-delivery technology, the printing press. Is it mass art? In my view, that depends upon whether it meets the accessibility condition. Whether it does so requires a careful inspection of the novel in question. But Novitz is not very forthcoming about how we are to understand this example. So I am unsure about both how we should categorize it and how Novitz thinks that it should be categorized.

Nevertheless, if, once scrutinized, the novel is categorized as mass art, my theory is not threatened, since I countenance some (indeed, a great many) widely marketed novels—including not only pulps but well-written ones as well—as mass artworks. On the other hand, if, upon close examination, *Sense and Sensibility* turns out not to be mass art because it is not easily accessible to mass audiences (and was not intended to be), then that's okay too, since I agree that some novels are not mass art. In any case, *Sense and Sensibility* will not present a clear-cut counter-example to my theory until Novitz tells us more about it, or, at least, more about what he thinks about it.

Actually I have to confess that I'm not really sure what Novitz intends to prove by means of *Sense and Sensibility*. Is it that he thinks that it is mass art, but my theory unjustifiably excludes it? Or, is it that he thinks that it is not mass art, but that my theory includes it as he, Novitz, thinks that my theory should not? Novitz's article unpromisingly suggests each of these problems in different places. At one point, Novitz says that Austen did design her works to be accessible, which suggests the former objection, but later he says that her works were not so designed, which suggests the latter objection. But these objections cancel each other out. Novitz can't have it both ways.

I think that a charitable interpretation of Novitz's understanding of *Sense and Sensibility* is that his considered judgement is that Austen intended her novels to be accessible to her readership, but not to be accessible to mass untutored audiences where 'her readership' and 'mass untutored audiences' are not co-extensive. But, of course, whether Austen designed *Sense and Sensibility* to be accessible to her readership is irrelevant to whether it is mass art in my sense of the category; Stockhausen undoubtedly designed his works to be accessible to his (rather specialized) audience. Thus, if Novitz in his role as literary historian is right—and, of course, I am not agreeing that he is—*and* Austen did not design *Sense and Sensibility* for easy accessibility by mass untutored audiences, then, on my theory, it would not count as mass art.

Yet in his conclusion Novitz maintains that he has shown that on my theory Jane Austen's novels are mass art. Of course, this conclusion will not upset my applecart for reasons I've already rehearsed. However, I cannot refrain from remarking that this surmise on Novitz's part contradicts what seems to be his earlier assessment of the significance of *Sense and Sensibility* to the debate.

Many of Novitz's objections, it seems to me, ride on a misconstrual about what I am trying to do with the concept of mass art. I am not trying to map all art into the couplet mass art/not mass art. I think that there are more distinctions than this. I am primarily interested in the distinction between mass art and avant-garde art, since I think that this is the most important division in the contemporary art world, and that it has been since some point in the nineteenth century. But there are other distinctions that can be made between the various artworks available to us, and it may be that certain of Novitz's counter-examples, such as *Sense and Sensibility*, are better categorized under these labels.

For example, avant-garde art is not the only sort of esoteric art. There is what might be called traditional or canonical esoteric art. This is art designed for a highly educated audience that is equipped with the skills necessary to comprehend it.[68] Most of the canonical works of English literature probably fall into this category, and, moreover, there are still people working in this tradition. A. S. Byatt's novella *The Conjugial Angel* might be an example here, since it requires a reader with the learned hermeneutical skills to decipher the significance of all the poetical quotations for the ongoing plot. Similarly, Gabriel García Márquez's *Of Love and Other Demons* would also appear to fall into this category because of the hermeneutical expertise required of an appreciative reader to track his thematic comparisons between religion and science.[69]

Where works of traditional esoteric art are wedded to a mass production/distribution technology, we may refer to them as technologically distributed traditional esoteric art. And it is into such a category that I suspect that Novitz thinks *Sense and Sensibility* probably falls.

Traditional esoteric art, whether produced by a historical figure or a contemporary artist, contrasts with avant-garde art, since avant-garde art repudiates traditional art as well as repudiating popular art. Both traditional art and avant-garde art are esoteric, but they are esoteric in different ways. And, of course, both traditional esoteric art and avant-garde art can be produced and distributed by means of a mass technology. Nevertheless, both can be distinguished from mass art along the axis of accessibility. Novitz's dissatisfaction with my theory of mass art, it seems to me, may stem from his belief that I intend to sort all art by means of the mass art/avant-garde couplet. This leaves us with a great deal of art that one doesn't know how to classify. But rather than incorporating works like *Sense and Sensibility* and, perhaps, *The Conjugial Angel* into the category of mass art, as Novitz seems wont to do, I suggest that we locate it in the alternative category of technologically distributed traditional esoteric art.

The category of technologically distributed traditional esoteric art is the one that is most likely to appear to problematize the boundary that I am attempting to draw around mass art proper, especially because some canonical art of this sort that was once inaccessible is accessible now, as

---

[68] The distinction between esoteric and exoteric art can already be located in the Middle Ages. See Peter Burke, *Popular Culture in Early Modern Europe* (New York: Harper, 1978), 28. And, of course, most of the canonical classical art in the West was designed for educated citizens, not for slaves, peasants, and the urban masses of ancient Greece and Rome.

[69] In contrast to *The Conjugial Angel* and *Of Love and Other Demons*, Kathy Acker's *Pussy King of the Pirates*, Don DeLillo's *Mao II* and Milan Kundera's *Kindness* fall into the category of avant-garde art— the former because of its radically disjunctive grammatical deviations and all three due to their disjunctive narrative strategies.

a result of mass education. Two things need to be said about such cases. First, since accessibility is time-indexed, we will determine the accessibility of a work of Austen or Mozart in terms of the context of its production, not in terms of the context of its contemporary reception. And, second, in certain cases, the technological reproductions of certain artworks, such as Caruso singing an aria, are not themselves artworks, but only recordings thereof. Thus, the *recordings qua* recordings of traditional esoteric art for wide-scale distribution are not artworks, let alone mass artworks.

In contrast to simple recordings of canonical artworks, an example of a full-blooded case of technologically produced and distributed traditional esoteric art would be a classical piece of music (of historical or contemporary origin) performed by a contemporary orchestra that was mixed and modulated via sound recording, and which was inaccessible to mass audiences originally, and which continues to be inaccessible to such audiences. For my money, most of the productions of the classical music industry would appear to fall into this category, rather than the category of mass art, where I suspect Novitz thinks they should go.

Of course, traditional esoteric art should not be confused with middlebrow art. Middlebrow art, following Dwight MacDonald, is art that imitates the structures of past avant-garde art or traditional esoteric art in the way, say, of *Masterpiece Theatre*. Such art is more accessible than contemporary avant-garde art, but less accessible than mass art. Whereas avant-garde art repudiates the approach of traditional esoteric art, and whereas contemporary artists in the arena of traditional esoteric art seek to continue it, changing it perhaps only incrementally, middlebrow art *imitates* past esoteric traditions, either of the avant-garde variety or of what I call the traditional esoteric variety. Nevertheless, middlebrow art still belongs on the esoteric side of the ledger when contrasted to mass art, since it requires a specialized background in order to be appreciated, even if it is not the same kind or degree of specialization required by avant-garde art or traditional esoteric art.

When middlebrow art like various BBC productions are wedded to a mass delivery system, Novitz, I think, is prone to categorize them as mass art, whereas I would prefer to categorize them as *technologically distributed middlebrow art*, since they are designed to appeal to people of a certain educational background and are not fully comprehensible to people without that background.

To summarize, then, the strategy I would employ to handle most of Novitz's counter-examples to my theory would be to argue that there are more suitable categories—such as technologically distributed esoteric art, recordings of such art (and, indeed, recordings of folk art and even popular art), as well as technologically distributed middlebrow art—that accommodate them more perspicuously than does the category of mass art. That is, rather than collapsing all these distinctions into the category of mass art—just because they may be technologically distributed—as Novitz tends to do, I would prefer to generate more categories, capable of marking fine-grained distinctions of greater accuracy.[70]

Novitz concludes his criticisms of my theory of mass art by proposing a theory of his own. As already noted, for Novitz, a mass work of art is 1. a work of art 2. whose production or delivery involves the use of mass technology 3. with the intention thereby of delivering the work to as many people as possible. The major difference between my theory and Novitz's is that his theory is not committed to the view that mass artworks are always designed to be understood by large numbers of viewers. They need only be capable of being delivered to lots of people.

According to Novitz there are two senses of mass art. The first sense of mass art pertains to items produced and delivered by a technology capable of reaching two or more reception sites simultaneously. The second sense of mass art pertains to items designed to be understood by large numbers of untutored people. Novitz says that I run these two senses together. I wouldn't have thought that I conflated these two senses. I constructed an account of mass art where each of these discriminable senses plays a role as a necessary condition of mass art. Is that a matter of running the two senses together? Or, is it a matter of constructing a third, more adequate, sense of the term?

Novitz also contends that I have given no argument for my 'running together' of these conditions. Specifically, Novitz is leery of my invocation of the accessibility condition. But despite Novitz's accusation, I thought that I offered a number of arguments in favour of this move. The first was that it did a better job than rival accounts of tracking the notion of mass art as that term has been used in our common discourse throughout this century. When someone like Dwight MacDonald heaps scorn on mass culture and its products, what he is talking about are putative artworks that are not only mass-produced but that are designed for easy consumption by mass audiences.

Novitz points out that his theory only emphasizes the first sense of mass art. But his first sense of mass art is not enough. In ordinary discourse, most of us would hesitate to call the videos of Bill Viola mass art, though they are produced and distributed by a mass technology. My theory of

---

[70] Obviously more could be said about these distinctions. But, inasmuch as my primary concern is with conceptualizing mass art, to do so now would be digressive. Thus, working out this map of different types of art will, for the time being, remain a topic for future research.

mass art is sensitive to that hesitancy. My theory tracks usage here better than a view of mass art that relies primarily on Novitz's first sense of the term. And that is a dialectical argument in favour of the way that I build my theory.

Second, I maintain that my theory of mass art has useful explanatory consequences. For one can derive an instructive explanatory hypothesis from the accessibility condition of my theory. Indeed, my third condition might be read as informing a broad research programme, namely, if one wishes to isolate the key features of what in our culture we refer to as mass art, look for those structures, stylistic choices, and even narrative themes that enhance the accessibility of the objects in question for mass untutored audiences. That is, investigate the structures of the items that we pre-theoretically think of as mass art in terms of their capacity to engage mass untutored audiences. Therein lies an important part of an account of their emergence, their popularity, and their continued existence. I have already given some examples of the way in which such investigations might proceed, and I noted even more research in this direction in my footnotes. That my theory of mass art promises explanatory bonuses for empirical research represents yet another consideration in favour of the way in which I construct my theory.

On the other hand, Novitz says that his theory emphasizes the first sense of mass art noted above—the technology sense. I am not sure why Novitz is so relaxed about this, given the pummelling to which he subjected my technology condition in his article. Perhaps by his conclusion he felt that he had learned to live with my technology condition. But I think that it is obvious that one cannot hope to proffer a theory of what we call mass art that places primary emphasis on the technology sense of mass art. That simply ignores too much avant-garde art of the sort that is produced and delivered by means of mass technology.

According to Novitz's theory, something is a mass artwork when it is a work of art involving the use of a mass distribution system with the intention to deliver the work to as many people as possible. Thus, if a group of avant-gardists commandeered a network TV frequency in order to present a highly hermetic drama for the express purpose of not only outraging the bourgeoisie but of confusing just about everyone else that would count as a work of mass art in Novitz's view. That is, our avant-gardists intend to deliver their production to as many people as possible, while at the same time they intend to dumbfound the audience in a gesture of artistic contempt. But is this the sort of phenomenon that people have in mind when they talk about mass art?

Novitz thinks that an advantage of his theory over mine is that he can count a BBC production as mass art, whereas I do not. But I am not so sure that the issue is so clear-cut. If the BBC production is designed to be accessible to mass untutored audiences—layered with explanatory inter-ludes, parsed by a barrage of cinematic techniques, and edited for TV—such a production might be mass art in my view. On the other hand, if the performance is intentionally designed in a way that renders it still inacces-sible to a mass audience—as are certain productions of Britain's Channel Four—then I see no problem in treating it on a par with avant-garde art that is produced and delivered by means of a mass technology. Surely it cannot count as a virtue of Novitz's theory that it can regard esoteric art as mass art. Of course, many of the BBC productions of the sort that concern us may be examples of neither avant-garde art nor mass art. They may be recordings of canonical art (or folk art, or popular art, or avant-garde art, etc.), or technologically distributed traditional esoteric art, or, even more likely, technologically distributed middlebrow art. But such middlebrow art is not mass art proper, since middlebrow art is designed to be acces-sible for a target audience, one that shares what might be broadly called a liberal, higher education.[71]

Clearly, the major bone of contention between Novitz and myself is that I see our reigning concept of mass art as bound up in large part with a contrast between it and esoteric avant-garde art. Though these two art practices do not exhaust the full range of the art of our time, they are the most conspicuous and the most dominant art practices in our culture—practices that define themselves in large measure in opposition to each other. That my theory tracks this central distinction—which is reflected in our continuing common discourse about mass art—and what Novitz's theory erases this opposition counts in favour of my theory and against Novitz's. That my theory, in addition, suggests a plausible empirical research programme with informative results, also, I submit, makes my theory more attractive than Novitz's. Of course, in a certain sense, Novitz is free to stipulate any sense of mass art that he wishes. However, the advisability of Novitz's stipulation must be weighed against the advantages of a rival theory like mine which (a) does a better job tracking ordinary usage; (b) sharply marks the central conceptual and historic contrast between mass art and the avant-garde; and (c) abets a robust empirical research programme.

---

[71] Here I am not reverting to the social reduction theory of art, since, in my view, possession of higher education in the liberal arts is not necessarily a matter of class or income status.

John Fiske's rejection of the concept of mass art

I have already noted that many practitioners of what is called cultural studies, such as Brantlinger and Ross, find the notion of mass art distasteful. But if it is simply a matter of distastefulness, then I think that my comments about the numerical sense of mass art should allay their worries. However, there is one theorist of cultural studies who appears to believe that the notion of mass art is not only distasteful, but that the very concept of mass art is metaphysically impossible. And, of course, if such a view is convincing, then my theory of mass art must be wrong. For one should be willing to abandon any theory of something that doesn't exist. Whereas Novitz thinks that my account of mass art is inaccurate, the view that mass art is non-existent is an even deeper challenge, one that I associate with the influential writings of John Fiske.

In his *Understanding Popular Culture*, John Fiske writes:

What popular culture is not, however, is mass culture. *Mass culture* is a term used by those who believe that the cultural commodities produced and distributed by the industries can be imposed upon the people in a way that irons out social differences and produces a unified culture for a passive, alienated mass audience. Such a process, if it existed and it does not, would be anticultural and antipopular; it would be the antithesis of culture understood as the production and circulation of meanings and pleasures, and of the popular as an intransigent, oppositional, scandalous set of forces. There is no mass culture. . . .[72]

Fiske comes to this conclusion about mass culture, and, presumably, about mass art as a subcategory thereof, because he has a very special theory of popular culture. Ordinarily, we think that popular culture is comprised of objects, like books and toys, and mass-produced events, like TV miniseries. That is, ordinarily, we think of popular culture and popular arts from the production/distribution side of things. And this leads us to think of popular art as a collection of certain types of products, namely those designed for popular consumption.

But Fiske thinks of popular culture differently—not from the producer's side of things, but from the audience's side. Popular culture is something that the people, so-called, *do*, and not something that the culture industry produces. Indeed, popular culture is something that people do with the commodities that the so-called culture industry produces. Popular culture comprises the ways in which people use these products for their own purposes—which uses are at variance with the uses intended by the

[72] John Fiske, *Understanding Popular Culture*, 176–7.

dominant ideology and are, therefore, at least in this sense, oppositional and even progressive politically (though not radical politically).

For Fiske, popular culture is, by definition, a site of resistance. Certain urban aborigines in Australia, for example, may use TV westerns for their own purposes; they cheer at the slaughter of white settlers as their wagon trains are surrounded by Indians.[73] This, of course, is at variance with the intentions of the producers of the westerns in question, who undoubtedly anticipated that audiences would be horrified by the massacre of the white settlers. But the aborigine audience has, so to speak, recoded such scenes as occasions for celebrating set-backs to white imperialism. Fiske calls this type of cultural resistance to the intended point of such westerns *producerly* (alluding to, while also freely adapting, Roland Barthes' distinction between the readerly and the writerly[74]). That is, the aborigines use the relevant commodity in a way in which it was not intended to be used; they produce an alternative 'meaning' for the scene that is important for the aborigine community and its interests.

People not only resist the commodities of the culture industry by producing alternative significations for said commodities. They may also purportedly use the commodities of the culture industries to evade the disciplinary regimes of the dominant ideology. Fiske cites TV wrestling programmes as an example of the evasion of the dictates of the dominant ideology.[75] For the audience of wrestling programmes supposedly celebrates grotesque body types that are putatively in violation of the norms of the dominant ideology—i.e., André the Giant is no one's idea of the ideal model for Armani tailoring. Likewise, adolescents who loiter in shopping malls, buying nothing, are said to evade, subvert, and ostensibly resist the imperatives of consumer society by eschewing its norms of conduct.[76]

Whether or not these examples are persuasive, they nevertheless give us a sense of how John Fiske conceives of popular culture. Popular culture is a particular kind of use that a certain group—called the people (as in 'the people united will never be defeated')—make of industrially produced

---

[73]   Ibid. 25.
[74]   See Roland Barthes, *The Pleasure of the Text* (New York: Hill and Wang, 1976).
In terms of earlier chapters in this book, it is interesting that Fiske has appropriated Barthes' concept for the response to avant-garde art for his own characterization of popular responses to art. Like McLuhan, Fiske is, in effect, attempting to align responses to popular and mass art with the response to avant-garde art by underscoring the active nature of the response to what I refer to as mass art. The people, according to Fiske, are not the docile recipients of mass culture; they respond to it creatively, as do the ideal audiences for avant-garde art according to people like Greenberg. Thus, in a roundabout and perhaps distorted way, Fiske confirms that it is the issue of participation that is at the crux of modern debates in this arena. Even though Fiske might be averse to speaking of art proper, he, perhaps like those urban aborigines, has appropriated a central historical view of art proper—namely, that it should be participatory—for his own purposes.
[75]   Fiske, *Understanding Popular Culture*, 82–102.   [76]   Id., *Reading the Popular*, 14–18.

commodities and their venues of distribution. The relevant kind of use in this regard is resistant or oppositional. That is, popular culture is the use of commodities by the people in ways, either producerly or evasive, that vary from those intended by the culture industry's technocrats and which alternative uses, in turn, serve the purposes of the people.

Stated schematically, Fiske's theory of popular culture is:

> X is an instance of popular culture if and only if 1. x is a *use* of a commodity by and for the people 2. that is producerly and/or 3. evasive and 4. that is relevant to the everyday lives (and struggles) of the people.

Speaking diagnostically, it is evident how Fiske came to this view. Reacting to the Althusserian approach in cultural studies, which seemed to entail that resistance to the ideology communicated by the products of the popular culture industry is impossible, Fiske set out in exactly the opposite theoretical direction.[77] If Althusserians appeared to provide no theoretical accommodation for the fact that people were not always invariably positioned by pop culture (conceived of as what Althusserians called an 'ideological state apparatus') Fiske responds by reconstruing popular culture as nothing but a site of resistance to the dominant ideology.

Surely, as I myself have argued, the Althusserian viewpoint is flawed, in so far as it entails that people are utterly incapable of rejecting the ideology communicated through popular culture. But this flaw is an empirical flaw; it simply doesn't square with the facts. Yet it is not clear that moving, as Fiske does, to a position that is the polar opposite of Althusserianism has much to recommend it, empirically either. Certainly, the empirical point to make against an Althusserian approach to popular culture is that sometimes people resist the ideological address implicit in popular art. But Fiske opposes Althusserianism by maintaining that people are almost always resisting the ideological address of the products of the culture industry. And the view that people are always resisting the products of the culture industry seems hardly more plausible empirically than the view that they are never resisting.

Of course, when one looks closely at Fiske's theory of popular culture, it becomes apparent almost immediately that Fiske's theory is not an empirical theory. For him, popular culture is always a site of resistance—of either the producerly or the evasive variety—as a matter of definition, rather than as a matter of fact.

---

[77] For an account of the Althusserian approach, see Noël Carroll, *Mystifying Movies*.

Furthermore, popular culture and popular art cannot be reconceived as mass culture or mass art in the ways I propose, because of the manner in which Fiske defines the popular. For the popular, according to Fiske, is a matter of resistant usages to which commodities are adapted, whereas mass art, in my sense, refers to products with certain properties and structures. Moreover, since my conception of mass art presupposes that the products of mass art are often successfully designed to elicit convergent responses from large numbers of people, there is no place for my version of mass art in the universe as stipulated by Fiske's definition, since in that universe, when it comes to popular culture, all is difference—different uses and meanings that people find to answer to their purposes and needs in their situated struggles with the hegemonic ideology.

But if the issue is really a matter of definition, let us ask whether Fiske's definition is a good one. I cannot see that it is. Whether or not you agree with my contention that popular art is better conceived in terms of mass art, and, for that matter, that popular culture is nowadays better understood as mass culture, we nevertheless probably pretty much agree upon what falls into the categories of popular culture and popular art respectively. Will Fiske's definition of popular culture coincide with our pre-theoretical intuitions about the extension of the concept of popular culture? I doubt it.

Presumably, we all agree that Anton von Webern's atonal music is not an example of popular culture. Any theory of popular culture that incorporates a piece by Webern into the category of popular culture surely has something wrong with it. But why can't a piece of Webern's atonal music become a piece of popular culture for Fiske, if it is used by the people for purposes of resistance?

Suppose a rap group plays a recorded selection of Webern at a concert for the purpose of deriding Eurocentric culture. That is, the rap group uses Webern much in the way that the aborigines used the dying settlers in TV westerns.

Thus, a piece by Webern, say his *Funf Satz* for string quartet, Op. 5 (1909), enters the corpus of popular culture. But certainly any theory of popular culture that, for any reason, counts this piece as an example of popular art or culture is way off the mark. Moreover, if Fiske's definition of popular culture is false, and if his rejection of the existence of mass art depends solely upon this easily contested definition, then Fiske's definition poses no threat to my theory of mass art.

Of course, we should have anticipated that Fiske's definition of popular culture would bear little resemblance to the ordinary concept of popular culture. For our ordinary concept of popular culture is geared to thinking of popular culture as a collection of products, whereas, for Fiske, popular culture is comprised of uses or processes, namely, *processes* of resistance.[78] Thus, if we assess Fiske's theory as a reconstruction of our ordinary concept of popular culture, it is bound to fail.

But perhaps it will be argued that one misconstrues Fiske's theory as a reconstruction of our ordinary concept of popular culture. Maybe it is a revisionist, stipulative redefinition, one, which like certain scientific stipulations, should be assessed not in terms of its capacity to track our ordinary concepts of things like gold, but in terms of the way in which it abets empirical discoveries about the nature of things, rather than our concepts of things. Fiske's theory may be at variance with received notions of popular culture. But, it might be suggested, we should accept his radical revision of these notions because of the discoveries, notably the empirical discoveries, that his revision makes possible.

Yet, even if we are to regard Fiske's definition as a stipulative definition of this sort, I think we still have good empirical reasons to reject it. For the research programme that Fiske's stipulative definition suggests unavoidably distorts the nature of popular culture, rather than revealing it in a new light. Fiske's theory is not empirically enabling; instead, it obscures an empirical understanding of popular culture.

Put succinctly: the problem with Fiske's theory is that it is overly and unrealistically obsessed with difference. Fiske's theory identifies culture with responses to the commodities of the culture industry that are at variance with the intended or anticipated or designed responses to things like movies and TV shows, to popular songs and advertisements. It skews empirical research in the direction of always seeking out the differential, putatively resistant, responses of the people to the products of what, if we are not Fiskeans, we would call 'popular culture'. For under Fiske's dispensation, it is just the differential responses that comprise popular culture.

But this is clearly misguided. People may have differential responses to the commodities of the culture industry. But at the same time, they often have convergent responses too. For example, many of the responses of Fiske's urban aborigines must coincide perfectly with the responses that the makers of the westerns in question intentionally designed their movies to elicit. The aborigines, for instance, recognize certain of the characters in the programmes under discussion as *white settlers*, rather than as tree stumps or dung beetles or rocks or planets or even Indians. The aborigines

---

[78] Interestingly, Fiske is ensnared in the notorious process/product ambiguity—which beset earlier philosophers of art—in a new way. This problem may have a bearing on the work of other proponents of cultural studies beyond Fiske as well.

could not have mobilized their differential, adversarial response, if they did not already, antecedently embrace the intended meaning of the sequences in question—namely, that these sequences represented white settlers being massacred.

A theory of differential responses of the sort Fiske endorses, then, makes no sense if one denies that there is a substratum of convergent meanings, and recognitions thereof, on the part of even resistant audiences. In so far as Fiske's theory seems to countenance only differential responses—summarily precluding from the purview of theory the relevance of convergent responses to what we pre-theoretically call popular culture—Fiske's theory is bound to distort the phenomenon rather than to illuminate it empirically.

Fiske's definition of popular culture neither adequately reconstructs our ordinary concept of popular culture, nor is it an empirically fruitful, stipulative redefinition of popular culture. In so far as Fiske's rejection of the existence of mass culture, and by extension mass art depends on his definition of popular culture, my commitment to the notion of mass art is not threatened by Fiske. For there seems to be nothing backing Fiske's definition other than his wish that popular culture be an altogether good object (as a Kleinian psychoanalyst might put it).

Furthermore, if I am correct in maintaining that any empirically satisfactory account of popular culture needs to attend to convergent responses—indeed, needs to explain convergent responses, in general, before differential responses are explained—then my hypotheses about mass art have much to recommend them. For I start by thinking of popular art, construed as mass art, in terms of its capacities to elicit convergent responses and understandings amongst vast audiences. That is what my emphasis on accessibility is all about.

This, of course, is not the whole story. There are undoubtedly some examples of resistance to and recodings of mass art of the sort that intrigues John Fiske. And these are certainly worthy of investigation. My point is simply that it does not seem plausible to believe that there is as much resistance and recoding as Fiske insinuates.[79] And there is—more importantly—a great deal of convergent response of a sort that Fiske ignores and that is, in addition, often presupposed as a necessary condition for the kind of differential responses that Fiske prefers to talk about. My theory of mass art, of course, tracks this convergence with a passion. And though this might not be the whole story, it may be a very good beginning.

---

[79] For a more politicized set of objections than mine to the kind of active audience approach Fiske endorses, see William R. Seaman, 'Active Audience Theory: Pointless Populism', in *Media, Culture and Society*, vol. xiv (1992), 301–11.

242 The Nature of Mass Art

Concluding remarks

In this chapter I have attempted to develop and to defend a theory of mass
art. I have argued that the category of mass art is not exclusively reducible
to the role it plays in a system of pre-existing class distinctions, but that it
primarily tracks certain intrinsic structural features of the artworks that
we classify as mass artworks. Those structural features include the use of
mass technologies of production and distribution as well as the use of
formal and/or stylistic devices that promote easy accessibility for mass
untutored audiences. Mass art, by my account, can be contrasted with the
broader category of popular art *simpliciter* in virtue of its reliance on mass-
media modes of production and distribution; while mass art, inasmuch as
it is exoteric, is to be distinguished from technologically distributed esoteric art—such as avant-garde art, what I call traditional esoteric art, and
middlebrow art—along the dimension of accessibility. For mass art is
designed to be comprehensible to untutored audiences, whereas the
various forms of esoteric art presuppose audiences equipped with specialized knowledge of various kinds and degrees.

Of the various forms of esoteric art, the one that contrasts most starkly
with mass art is avant-garde art, especially avant-garde art that is produced
and distributed by means of mass media technologies. For although such
avant-garde art may have the technological capacity to be delivered to
mass audiences, it is not designed for mass consumption. Indeed, it is
expressly designed to thwart mass consumption, particularly where a
hallmark of mass consumption is a matter of the ease of accessibility for
untutored audiences. Avant-garde art, more than any other form of esoteric art, is intentionally designed to problematize easy consumption and
comprehension, often for the purpose of assaulting what it conceives to be
the aesthetic, intellectual, and moral complacency of the general run of
humanity. The rallying cry of much avant-garde art, for example, is to
outrage the bourgeoisie. Avant-garde art, that is, stakes its identity explicitly
on its inaccessibility, whereas mass art, operating on the opposite pole of
aesthetic address, aims at accessibility of the most generic sort. Thus, avant-
garde art, particularly technologically produced and distributed avant-
garde art, is the most pronounced conceptual foil to mass art available.

Moreover, the antithesis between mass art and avant-garde art is not
merely logical. It is also historical. The age of mass art is also the age of
avant-garde art. The history of art in the twentieth century—in terms of its
major developments—is largely a chronicle of the history of avant-garde
art, on the one side, and of mass art on the other. Indeed, it is common-

place to chart the history of twentieth-century art by citing the successive appearance of movements like cubism, surrealism, abstract expressionism, pop art, and other developments within the evolution of modernism and postmodernism, while, at the same time, also calling film the premier art-form of the twentieth century. The Museum of Modern Art, for example, does this all the time.

That is, when we think of the history of art of the past one hundred or so years, it seems natural to think of it in terms of emergence and development of avant-garde art-forms, on the one hand, and mass art, on the other hand. Nor is this way of thinking happenstance. For if my theory is right, mass art and avant-garde art are intimately related conceptually, in so far as avant-garde art takes mass art as one of its animating points of departure. Avant-garde art is, among other things, expressly designed to be the antithesis of mass art. It is exactly the accessibility that mass art affords that avant-garde art is intended to disturb. And, contrariwise, it is the inaccessibility of avant-garde art that mass art strives to avoid. Just ask any producer of mass art as he or she contemplates the bottom line.

The conclusion of the preceding chapter ended with a question, namely, why does theoretical thinking about mass art appear to come in tandem so frequently with either explicit or implicit considerations of avant-garde art?[80] By now, my answer to that question should be apparent. Mass art and avant-garde art are conceptually antithetical in such a way that the identity of the one depends upon its contrast to the other. Mention of one, thus, calls for mention of the other in the way that mention of the individual calls forth mention of the collective, or that mention of mind depends on the concept of matter, or that talk of masters requires talk of slaves, or, at least, servants.

In other words, one half of the mass art/avant-garde couplet, especially from the avant-garde side of things, depends dialectically on the other half of the dichotomy—mass art—for contrast. Moreover, this logical contrast acquires a particular sense of historical urgency—again, especially from the avant-garde side of things—in so far as these conceptually contrasting modes of art are conceived to be in competition for both audiences and prestige. Thus theorists of mass art in the past have consistently returned to the relation between mass art and avant-garde art because the two art-

---

[80] The MacDonald essay that we discussed in Ch. 1 did not discuss the avant-garde. However, inasmuch as MacDonald's essay derives from Greenberg's theory, it is implicitly alluding to the avant-garde, for Greenberg's arguments presume that the avant-garde is the relevant, as well as the superior, foil to mass art. On the other hand, Collingwood and Adorno make explicit reference to the avant-garde.

making practices are intimately linked both logically and historically. That is, conceptually and historically, the two forms of art-making are tied inescapably.

In defining mass art—particularly in terms of the contrast between mass art and avant-garde art—I have emphasized the relation that mass art aspires to secure with its audience. And clearly the history of the discussion of mass art has always revolved around its putative effects on audiences. So far, I have considered the relation of mass art to its audience in terms of accessibility, which I have parsed primarily as a matter of comprehensibility. And comprehensibility, as I have treated it so far, has been, first and foremost, a matter of cognition, narrowly construed. However, the relation of mass art to its audience has traditionally, for good reason, been an object of concern beyond issues of cognition, narrowly construed. The relation of mass art to the emotional, moral, and political life of its audiences has certainly been of equal importance. Thus, in the ensuing chapters of this book, I will discuss, respectively, the relation of mass art to the emotions, to morality, and to ideology. In these discussions, the importance of accessibility will not disappear. Rather, its significance for the ways in which the emotional, moral, and political address of mass art impacts on audiences will be developed in greater depth.

4 Mass Art and the Emotions

Introduction

In Chapter 1, I reviewed a series of arguments against mass art that I attempted to trace back to Kantian aesthetics, or, rather, to a misunderstanding thereof. However, these arguments are not the only claims made against mass art. There is also a long-standing tendency to associate mass art with the provocation of untoward emotional states. This line of attack is popular among pundits of all sorts, including philosophers. Abraham Kaplan, for example, maintains that:

Popular art wallows in emotion while art transcends it, giving us understanding and thereby mastery of our feelings. For popular art, feelings themselves are the ultimate subject matter; they are not present as a quality of the experience of something objectified, but are only stimulated by the object. The addiction to such stimuli is like the frenzied and forever frustrated pursuit of happiness by those lost souls who have never learned that happiness accrues only when the object of pursuit has its own substance. Popular art ministers to this misery, panders to it, we may say. . . . Popular art . . . deals in nothing else. That is why it is so commonly judged by its impact.[1]

Kaplan goes on to add that:

The popular audience may be chronically bored, but this is not to say that it is without feeling. On the contrary, it is feeling above all that the audience

---

[1] Abraham Kaplan, 'The Aesthetics of Popular Arts', *Modern Culture and the Arts*, 2nd edn., ed. James B. Hall and Barry Ulanov (New York: McGraw Hill, 1972), 71–2. Kaplan's notion of 'a quality of experience of something objectified' shows the influence of expression theorists of art such as R. G. Collingwood and S. K. Langer.

contributes to the aesthetic situation and that the popular artist then exploits. Popular art does not supply a missing ingredient in our lives, but cooks up a savory mess from the ingredients at hand. In a word, feelings are usually lacking in depth, whatever their intensity. Popular art is correspondingly shallow.[2]

In a similar vein, Daniel Bell associates the emphasis on visuality in many of the contemporary mass arts with the stimulation of the emotions. He claims that it 'is the nature of the contemporary temper, with its hunger for action (as against contemplation), its search for novelty, and its lust for *sensation* [that causes us to want to see things]. And it is this visual element in the arts that best appeases these compulsions.'[3] F. R. Leavis chides the motion pictures by alleging that they fundamentally appeal to cheap emotions,[4] while Allan Bloom chastises rock music for encouraging the passions.[5] John Fuller goes so far as to claim that rock music hypercharges the emotions of young listeners in ways that will seriously damage their will to live,[6] while Herbert Blumer and Philip Hauser state that motion pictures can induce a state which they call 'emotional possession', which they allege can lead to delinquency. Explaining their hypothesis they say:

The chief characteristics of emotional possession may be mentioned here: the inciting of impulses, the arousing of a given emotion, a relaxing of ordinary control, and so an increased readiness to yield to the impulses aroused. These states of mind and feelings come, usually, as a result of the individual 'losing himself' in the picture, or becoming deeply preoccupied with its drama or movement. Thus in witnessing a mystery picture, a child may become frightened; in viewing a sad picture, a young man or young woman may experience a strong impulse to love relations. In the case of delinquents or of criminals, or of those marginal to these types, pictures of excitement, adventure and daring seem most

---

[2] Kaplan, 'The Aesthetics of Popular Arts', 72.

[3] Daniel Bell, *The Cultural Contradictions of Capitalism* (New York: Basic Books, 1976), 106 (emphasis added).

[4] F. R. Leavis, *Mass Civilisation and Minority Culture* (Cambridge: Gordon Frazer at St John's College, 1930), 8–10. Here Leavis may be getting at the idea that mass art's arousal of emotions may attach said emotions to things that are not fit to be their proper object. This raises the issue of sentimentality which I address in the concluding remarks of this chapter.

[5] Allan Bloom, *The Closing of the American Mind* (New York: Simon and Schuster, 1987), 60. Though Bloom makes this passing reference to the emotions, he is most concerned to denounce what he believes to be the unhealthy arousal of the sexual drives by rock music. Theodore Gracyk thoroughly undermines Bloom's attacks in *Rhythm and Noise*, 124–47.

[6] John G. Fuller, *Are the Kids All Right? The Rock Generation and its Hidden Death Wish* (New York: Times Books, 1981), 240–56.

likely to induce emotional possession, and, in doing so, to give impetus to delinquent tendencies.[7]

Quotations like these can be multiplied endlessly. They may be stated in such abbreviated form that they may appear to be little more than *ad hominem* canards. They hardly seem philosophical. Rather, they may appear just plain cranky. And yet, at the same time, they have an undeniable resonance. There is an obvious reason for this—namely, that these jeremiads rest upon the philosophical arguments developed at length in Books II, III, and X of Plato's *Republic*. That is, many of the most persistent, recurring arguments against mass art are actually quite ancient in origin. The arguments that Plato advanced against Greek drama and painting supply an arsenal of rebuke from which twentieth-century commentators frequently recycle their deprecations of mass art. Thus, if a great deal of philosophy's resistance to mass art can be labelled Kantian, much of the remaining resistance can be instructively regarded as Platonic.

The Platonic influence is quite apparent in our quotations from Kaplan, since Kaplan's resistance to mass art rides on a contrast between emotion and understanding. His talk of pandering to the emotions is, of course, unmistakably an allusion to Plato, reminding one, perhaps, of the *Gorgias*. Likewise, Leavis and Bloom do not even seem to have to bother to spell out what is wrong with the correlation of mass art with the passions, so deep is their Platonic heritage.

Plato's suspicion of representations, moreover, is paralleled by Bell's suspicion of visual media, while the notion of emotional possession is basically a return, in social-scientific lingo, to Plato's fear that audiences are likely to take on the emotions of the characters portrayed in drama. Fuller, in turn, identifies the emotions putatively induced by rock music with the height of irrationality, claiming that they embody a death wish.

Since the presuppositions of the Platonic form of the philosophical resistance to mass art often remain implicit in the arguments of twentieth-century commentators, perhaps the best way to approach this source of philosophical resistance to mass art is to return to the source—Plato's dialogue. For though Plato had no intimation of the emergence of mass art, his arguments, scarcely updated, provide one of the richest sources of philosophical resistance to mass art. Thus, in what follows, I will begin by critically reviewing Plato's arguments, eventually using them dialectically in order to develop an alternative framework for thinking about the

---

[7] Herbert Blumer and Philip M. Hauser, *Movies, Delinquency and Crime* (New York: Macmillan Co., 1933), 47.

relation of the emotions to mass art. This alternative framework will depend in large measure on exploiting what, in the recent philosophical and psychological literature, is often called the cognitive theory of the emotions.[8]

Clearly, there is an important, though perhaps not unique, relation between mass art and the emotions, especially the garden-variety emotions—that is, those that are marked in ordinary speech—such as fear, awe, pity, admiration, and the like. For mass artworks are unquestionably designed to elicit these garden-variety emotional responses from readers, listeners, and viewers. In large measure, what commands and shapes the audience's attention to the mass artwork, what enables the audience to follow and to comprehend it, and what energizes our commitment to seeing the artwork through to its conclusion is the emotional address of the mass artwork. Speaking metaphorically, we might say that, to a large extent, emotions are the cement that keeps audiences connected to the mass artworks that they consume—especially those mass artworks of a narrative variety, which include not only TV programmes, movies, pulp fictions, and comic strips, but also popular songs whose lyrics often tell a story outright, or presuppose one underlying their dramatic (often romantic) monologues.[9]

Moreover, the emotions in question here are generally what I have called 'garden-variety' ones—such as fear, anger, horror, reverence, suspense, pity, admiration, indignation, awe, repugnance, grief, compassion, infatuation, comic amusement, and so on. Mass fictions, including songs, rely heavily on the activation of specific garden-variety emotions. So many melodramas, for example, depend upon the audience's concern for the protagonists, whom we not only pity for their misfortunes, but whom we also admire for their character, especially as it is manifested in their self-sacrificing behaviour, such as Stella Dallas's self-willed separation from her beloved daughter.[10] Horror fictions, of course, require not only that we be

---

[8] A useful survey of cognitive theories of emotion in the philosophical literature is John Deigh's 'Cognitivism in the Theory of the Emotions', in *Ethics*, 104 (1994). For a discussion of a wide range of research in psychology of this sort, see Keith Oatley, *Best Laid Schemes: The Psychology of the Emotions* (Cambridge: Cambridge University Press, 1994).

[9] In this chapter, I will focus on the relation of the emotions to mass artworks of a narrative variety. This covers quite a lot of territory, since it includes songs with stories and dramatic monologues, such as 'Yesterday' (which elicits nostalgic yearning for a past love affair) or 'Smoke Gets In Your Eyes' (which tries to capture the illusive emotive timbre of love). Statistically, songs probably comprise the largest segment of the mass output of the music industry. The theory advanced in this chapter, however, does not apply to orchestral music. That is, as they say, a project for future research.

[10] For an account of the emotional response to melodrama, see Flo Leibowitz, 'Apt Feelings, or Why "Women's Pictures" Aren't Trivial', in *Post-Theory: Reconstructing Film Studies*, ed. David Bordwell and Noël Carroll (Madison: University of Wisconsin Press, 1996). Nor is this sort of melodramatic address merely an artefact of yesteryear. Danielle Steel's recent bestseller *Lightning* revolves around instilling admiration in the reader for Alexandra Parker's courageous confrontation of personal disasters, including cancer and marital separation.

thrown into a state of fear and repulsion toward the monsters that threaten the human race, but that we feel mounting anxiety as the protagonist ventures into the hidden recesses of the old dark house.[11]

Indeed, with much mass art, especially narrative fictions (including song lyrics[12]), eliciting the appropriate emotional response from the audience is generally a condition of our comprehending and following the story successfully as it unfolds. For example, if we do not hate certain characters, then the trajectory of a narrative bent upon punishing them may not only be unsatisfying, but even unintelligible.[13] What, we may ask ourselves, is the author's point in detailing their come-uppance at such length? Why is so much time and elaboration being spent on showing us how this vicious character gets his just deserts? It will generally not compute, unless we are attending to the story in the emotionally appropriate way.

But the emotions engaged by the plot of a mass artwork are typically not only a standard condition of the intelligibility of the successful story. They are most often what keeps us glued, so to say, to the narrative. In both life and in art, the emotions have the function of focusing attention (as well as of mobilizing responses). And with mass fictions, the emotions keep us focused on the plot on a moment-to-moment basis. They organize our attention in terms of what is going on in a scene, and they also prime our attention to the kinds of things to expect in future scenes.

To be more specific: our emotional responses to earlier scenes will generally contribute to organizing the way in which we attend to later scenes. If we are indignant about a character's behaviour when we first encounter her, then, when she next appears, we will be on the look-out for more evidence of nastiness on her part. Emotions organize perception. Emotions shape the way in which we follow character behaviour, just as in everyday life they enable us to track the actions of others.

Moreover, although most of my examples so far have relied on our emotional involvement with characters, clearly what I have said can also apply to situations and events. The horror that we feel about the initial

[11] For an account of the emotional response to horror fictions, see Noël Carroll, *The Philosophy of Horror, or Paradoxes of the Heart* (New York: Routledge, 1990).

[12] Broadly speaking, I think that the analysis of the expression of emotions in songs involving lyrics can be accommodated by the theory of 'modifying music' that I develop in Noël Carroll, 'Notes on Movie Music', in *Theorizing the Moving Image* (Cambridge: Cambridge University Press, 1996).

[13] Some readers have argued that it may be possible to understand a successful narrative dispassionately. That is, one may not feel the relevant emotion, but recognize that others feel it or are supposed to feel it, and then they go on to understand the narrative through this indirect route. I would not wish to deny that this sort of *meta-understanding* is possible. Nevertheless, with respect to the successful narrative, such meta-understanding still depends, albeit obliquely, on the work's capacity to elicit the appropriate response from the general audience.

outbreak of vampirism in *Salem's Lot* emotionally colours the way in which we attend to subsequent scenes. Our emotional involvement alerts us to the potential dangers in situations which we might otherwise ignore. Indeed, such emotions quite frequently alert us to dangers in situations that the characters overlook. Small animal-bites on the neck might mean little to them, but they loom large emotionally in our attention.

So, we must concede that the Platonic critics are right to point to the importance of the emotions to mass art. And, as a result, any account of mass art owes us a framework for understanding the relation of mass art to the emotions. But, at the same time, these critics are wrong in their Platonic assumptions (as well as in the assumption that they are saying something distinctive about all and only mass art). Thus, in what follows, I will attempt to show what is wrong with the Platonic approach with the aim of evolving a better framework for analysing the relationship of mass art to the emotions.

Plato versus the cognitive theory of the emotions

In his *Republic*, Plato developed a battery of arguments against drama and painting. Many of the arguments that one finds against mass art in the twentieth century are merely transparent adaptations of Plato's arguments. Perhaps one of the reasons that contemporary commentators are so brief in their statement of these arguments is that they are resting on the authority of Plato. Moreover, Plato's arguments were introduced in order to state the case for banishing the arts from the good city. Likewise, many latter-day Platonists are in favour of censoring mass art.

Plato's arguments against the arts are premised on the way in which he thought that drama and painting address the emotions of spectators. Plato's central argument hinged on his conviction that the emotions are irrational in the sense that they undermine the rule of reason, both in the individual and, in consequence, in society. Certain emotions, like pity and the fear of death, were of particular concern for Plato, since he believed that they would undermine the citizen-soldier's capacity to wage war. That is, Plato thought that these emotions were maladaptive. One did not want troops disposed to pity themselves or the enemy, or troops who at the sound of battle trembled with the fear of death.

Plato believed that by using dramatic texts as the Greeks did, reading them aloud in the process of education, people would acquire these untoward emotional dispositions by playing certain roles—that is, by identifying with the characters who vented these emotions. Latter-day

Platonists, vexed by mass art, are less worried about the audience's acquisition of dispositions toward pity and fear, and more worried about the acquisition of emotional dispositions such as aggressiveness. Moreover, identification or notions like 'emotional possession' are still regarded by them as the primary mechanism by which such emotional dispositions are inculcated.[14]

But Plato was not simply concerned that certain particular unsavoury emotions might be disseminated through the influence of and identification with art. He distrusted the emotional address of poetry and painting irrespective of the specific emotions they elicited just because he believed that the excitation of the emotions in general is problematic. For the emotions, in his view, oppose reason, and, for Plato, any threat to reason constitutes a threat to the community at large. Furthermore, the displacement of reason by the emotions in the life of the individual was, according to Plato, psychically unhealthy. The life ruled by the passions rather than by reason is not balanced and cannot be a happy one. Kaplan, speaking of the emotions versus understanding, lays similar charges at the door of mass art, charging that it yields ersatz happiness and psychic incompleteness. This prejudice is so ingrained in our culture that writers like Leavis and Bloom hardly even need to spell it out.

Moreover, Plato thought that drama, his primary target, was inexorably bound to promote emotion over reason, because artists would have to pander to the emotions of untutored audiences if they were to have audiences at all. That is, Plato argued, the general audience, knowing little, would have to be addressed in terms of their emotions rather than their understanding. That is why, a contemporary Platonist might say, shows like *L. A. Law* are preoccupied with the drama of office romance rather than the drama of legal research. The latter requires a background of legal education in order to be comprehended; the former needs only gut reactions. Thus, Plato, in effect, proposed the first economic theory of art, explaining why consumption dictated the unavoidably emotional address of drama. Clearly such a functional perspective on the influence of demand on artistic production has influenced contemporary critics of mass art like Dwight MacDonald, as we have seen; while Plato himself could only approve of Bell's correlation of the visual with sensation, spectacle, and emotion in his disparagement of contemporary mass art.

---

[14] Interestingly, Plato's fears that mimesis enjoins a morally suspect process of identification is echoed in the analyses of contemporary Althusserian-Lacanian cultural critics of mass art. But where Plato worried that identification threatened to destabilize the psyche, these contemporary Platonists charge that identification unifies the subject for ideological effect. This influential brand of contemporary Platonism will be discussed at length in Ch. 6 of this book.

Of these Platonic arguments, the most general and deepest is that art—
and, for our purposes, mass art—essentially addresses the emotions and,
thereby, undermines reason. If contemporary critics of mass art do not
always lay out the presumed linkage between the emotions and the
irrational, it is because they rely on a well-established philosophical tradition, beginning at least with Plato, to secure this correlation. According to
this tradition, reason and the emotions are in some sense at odds. Reason—or, for Kaplan, the understanding—must dominate the emotions.
Left to their own devices, so to speak, the emotions will gravitate toward
the irrational. In Plato's conception of human psychology, and in that of
contemporary Platonists, reason and emotion appear to occupy different
regions of the psyche. There is no expectation from the Platonic point of
view that they will converge, and there are even more grounds to anticipate that they will pull in opposite directions.

The Platonic tendency is to think that the emotions are irrational or
opposed to reason. Thus if art—drama or mass art—addresses the emotions, it will address the irrational in us and, in consequence, undermine
reason's control. But the obvious question to ask about this argument is
whether in fact the distinction between reason and the emotions is as
sharp and antagonistic as the Platonist maintains. Are the emotions necessarily irrational forces in the way that Plato and the critics of mass art
presume?

The tendency in contemporary psychology and in analytic philosophy is
to reject the Platonic presupposition that the emotions are irrational.
Instead, it is more common to propose that reason and the emotions
are not opposed, inasmuch as reason is an ineliminable constituent of the
emotions. Thus, in order to undercut Platonic arguments and to set the
stage for our own positive account of the relation of the emotions to mass
art, it is profitable to look at the picture of the emotions—often called the
cognitive theory of the emotions[15]—that has been developed by contemporary researchers and that challenges the prejudice that the emotions are
by their very nature irrational.

In order to determine whether or not the emotions are irrational, we
need some conception of what an emotion is. Perhaps the first answer that
might naturally tempt us in order to answer this question is that an

---

[15] For different versions of this view, see, for example, William Lyons, *Emotion* (Cambridge: Cam-
bridge University Press, 1980); George Rey, 'Functionalism and the Emotions', *Explaining Emotions*, ed.
Amelie Oksenberg Rorty (Berkeley: University of California Press, 1980), 163–96; Robert C. Solomon,
The Passions (Garden City: Anchor/Doubleday, 1976); Irving Thalberg Jr., 'Emotion and Thought',
American Philosophical Quarterly, 1 (1964), 45–55; and Thalberg, 'Avoiding the Emotion–Thought
Conundrum', *Philosophy*, 55 (1980), 396–402.

emotion is a feeling. When we're in an emotional state, our body changes. Our heart-rate might alter; we might feel our chest expanding or contracting. Physical changes occur as we move into an emotional state—the adrenal glands produce corticosteroids, and there are phychological or phenomenological changes as well. When we are angry, we may feel 'hot under the collar'. But are these physical and phenomenological changes in the body the whole story? Supporting this view, we might notice that in English we often do refer to the emotions as 'feelings'.

But there are reasons to deny that emotions are simply feelings—neither merely physical alterations, nor phenomenological flutters, nor a combination thereof. Why not? Because it is easy to imagine chemically inducing the sorts of bodily feeling states that are typically associated with emotions where there is no question of our being in an emotional state. Suppose we chemically induce the feeling states in you that you exhibited the last time you were angry. Here you are now alone in a room in exactly the same physical state you were in when your boss said something sarcastic to you during a business meeting last month. Are you angry? Not if there is no one or no thing with whom or with which you are angry. Remember that you are only in the same bodily state that you were in last month. But you are not in the same mental state. *Ex hypothesi*, you are not thinking about your boss nor about anyone else. The chemicals only induce certain changes in your body.

Admittedly, you may be in an unpleasant physical state. But you cannot be said to be in an emotional state of anger, unless there is someone or something that you think has done wrong to you or yours. For emotional states are directed—you are afraid *of* war, or you are in love *with* Clara, or you are angry *at* the boss. Bodily feelings, however, are not directed at anything. They are physical states. They are internal events without external reference.

But what is it that links our internal feeling states to external objects and events? What's the bridge, so to speak? Cognitive theorists of the emotions say that it is our cognitive states (that's why they're called cognitive theorists). For example, it may be our states of belief that connect our internal feelings to external situations. Suppose that I believe that Michael stole my money and that, in doing so, he has wronged me. This is, all things being equal, apt to give rise to anger. That is, taken by this belief—which is directed at Michael—my sympathetic nervous system is activated, and I begin to feel tension throughout my body. I feel myself tightening up. The reason that I am in this physical state is my belief that Michael has stolen my money. That is why my blood boils and my temples throb whenever I see him. In short, my belief that Michael has stolen my money *causes* my blood to boil and my temples to throb.

So as an initial approximation, let us say provisionally that an emotion is made up of at least two components: a cognitive component such as a belief or a thought about some person, place, or thing, real or imagined; and a feeling component (a bodily change and/or a phenomenological experience), where, additionally, the feeling state has been caused by the relevant cognitive state, such as a belief or a belief-like state.[16] Furthermore, a conception of the emotions like this is bad news for the Platonists, since it incorporates cognition and understanding into the emotions, thereby denying that reason is totally opposed to the emotions. For if reason/cognition is a constituent of an emotion, then emotion cannot be the antithesis of reason/cognition. But in order to make the problem for the Platonist even more explicit, let's look a bit more closely at the cognitive component of an emotion.

I am angry at Michael because I believe that he has stolen my money. But theft is not the only grounds that I might have for being angry. I could be angry at Michael for cutting ahead of me in line, or for throttling my little brother. Theft, queue-breaking, throttling, and so on are instances of a broader class of things, any of which might warrant anger. What is the relevant broader class of things—i.e., what must I believe about someone if I am to be angry with him? I must believe that he has done wrong to me or mine. I think that Michael has stolen my money, and that falls into this larger class of things. So, in order to be angry with someone, I must believe that the object of my anger has done some wrong to me or mine.

Similarly, other emotions are directed at objects that belong to a specifiable or delimited class of things. In order to be afraid of x, I must think that x is dangerous—that it belongs to the class of harmful things. X might not really be dangerous. But to fear x, I must perceive it to be harmful, even if it is not. In order to pity x, I must think that x has suffered misfortune. I cannot pity someone whom I think is on top of the world in every way. In order to envy x, I need to think that x has something that I lack. I cannot envy Quasimodo's good looks, if I believe that Quasimodo is grotesque. And so on. In short, what emotional state I am in is determined

[16] The caveat 'at least' here is meant to acknowledge that desires may also be constituents of many everyday emotions. Some theorists even argue that desires are constituents of all emotions, though I am not sure that we need to be committed to such a strong hypothesis. For theorists who maintain that desires are constituents of all emotions, see Jenefer Robinson, 'Emotion, Judgment and Desire', in *Journal of Philosophy*, 80/11 (1983), 731–41; and O. H. Green, *The Emotions: A Philosophical Theory* (Dordrecht: Kluwer Academic Publishers, 1992).

by my cognitive state—by, for example, beliefs or thoughts about the objects of the emotional state in question.

If I believe that I've been wronged and this causes a feeling of agitation in me, then, all things being equal, the state is anger. But if I believe that I'm in danger, and this causes my blood to freeze, then the emotional state I am in is fear. That is, as these examples should indicate, emotional states are governed by *criteria*. But what exactly does this mean?

In order to be angry with x, in the standard case, I must believe that certain criteria have been met, for example, I must believe that x has wronged me or mine.[17] To fear x, I must believe that x is harmful; to pity x, I must believe that x has suffered misfortune; to envy x, I must believe that x has something I have not got. To be in these emotional states, I must be in the relevant cognitive states. These cognitive states are constitutive of the very identity of the emotional states in which I am. Having the relevant cognitive states is a necessary condition for being in these emotional states.[18] These cognitive appraisals of the situations in question are criterial for being in just these emotional states. Indeed, the relevant cognitive appraisals are the *reasons* that I am in these states.

If you ask me why I am angry, my reason is that I think that I or mine have been wronged. If you ask me why I'm afraid, my reason is that I believe I've been threatened. Perhaps I believe that you are about to shoot me. Why do I pity Oedipus? Because he's suffered grievous misfortune. Why do I envy Donald Trump? Because he's got lots and lots of money, and I don't.

Now if what I've said so far is persuasive, then it looks as though the emotions are necessarily governed by reason. Indeed, to say that I am in one of these emotional states, sans the requisite cognitive appraisals, would be virtually self-contradictory, the very height of irrationality. To say that I am afraid of potatoes at the same time that I genuinely believe in my heart of hearts that they are not harmful is sheer nonsense, a logical absurdity—what Gilbert Ryle called a category error. Indeed, if I made such a claim, you would probably either attempt to find some hidden,

---

[17] By speaking of the 'standard case', here, I am excluding the case of fiction where entertaining thoughts, rather than believing, is the pertinent mental modality. But more on that later.

[18] This is not to say that we always recognize the emotional state that we are in by reference to the necessary criteria for being in that state, nor that everyone can explicitly articulate the necessary criteria for being in a given emotional state. Often we identify the state that we are in by means of what Ronald de Sousa has called paradigm scenarios—narrative prototypes that we use to match emotions to certain types of situations. For a discussion of paradigm scenarios, see Ronald de Sousa, *The Rationality of the Emotions* (Cambridge, Mass.: MIT Press, 1987). For an initial attempt to explore the relevance of paradigm scenarios for aesthetic research, see Noël Carroll, 'The Image of Women in Film: A Defense of a Paradigm', in *Theorizing the Moving Image* (New York: Cambridge University Press, 1996).

unacknowledged reason why I think that potatoes are dangerous or suspect that I did not understand the meaning of my own words. These explanations might account for the utter irrationality of my assertion. But the very search for these kinds of explanations shows that, in the standard case, we think that, *contra* the Platonists, the emotions naturally possess a kind of rationality.

Perhaps further evidence for the view that emotions possess some sort of rationality—that they are governed by reasons—is that our emotions can be modified or altered by changing our beliefs or reasons. Our emotions are educable. If reasons can be given to show that the object of our fear is not harmful, then the emotion of fear typically evaporates. We try to convince the child not to be afraid of the ogre in the closet by proving to him that there is no such ogre.

Furthermore, if I can be shown that an action that I thought was cowardly is courageous, then my emotion standardly will shift from contempt to admiration. Why does this happen? Because inasmuch as emotions are determined by cognitive states, like belief, a change in the relevant cognitive state will change the emotional state, either by transforming it into another emotional state or by sublating it entirely. The relation of emotions to cognitive states, like beliefs, is, of course, the basis for the psychoanalytic talking cure which, in effect, modifies dysfunctional or inappropriate emotional behaviours by disentangling our sedimented, mistaken, or erroneously associated beliefs and patterns of attention. Thus, though certain emotional episodes may be irrational in the sense that they are based on defective beliefs or confused patterns of attention, the emotions themselves are rationally tractable.

Moreover, if emotions are susceptible to being changed by reasons and to being modified by cognitive states, such as belief states, then we must conclude that, *contra* the Platonists, the emotions respond to knowledge. They respond to knowledge naturally, since knowledge-like cognitive states, such as beliefs, are components of all emotional states. The consequences of these observations for the Platonic view should be straightforward. The emotions are not necessarily irrational. They have rational criteria of appropriateness that are open to logical assessment. They are naturally responsive to reason and to knowledge. Thus, addressing the emotions in the manner that mass art does need not necessarily be thought to undermine reason.

Indeed, the emotions may serve reason in general by effectively guiding our attention to important information. Therefore, there are no grounds for worrying that the emotions—such as the emotions elicited by mass art—will necessarily subvert reason, since, among other things, reason or cognition is an ineliminable constituent, in fact a determining force, of the emotions. Thus, it is not the case that all mass art representations threaten reason; only those that encourage defective cognitive states, like false beliefs or inaccurate patterns of attention, are affronts to reason—and not because they are emotional states, but only because they are epistemically defective. Or, in short, the Platonist's most general argument about the relation between mass art and the emotions must be rejected.

In addition to his general argument about art and the emotions, Plato himself also claims that the specific emotions—like pity and fear—that are engendered by dramatic poetry are maladaptive, while contemporary Platonists often complain about the supposed dysfunctional tendency of mass art to engender aggressiveness. Encouraging these emotions, the Platonists believe, imperils the good of society. This is perhaps another reason why the Platonists think that certain specific emotions are irrational. Of course, whether the specific emotions in question pose the social problems the Platonists allege raises at least two kinds of questions that are not of direct interest to us in this chapter: whether, in fact, these emotions really have the consequences that the Platonist attributes to them, and whether, in specific cultural contexts, these emotions are dysfunctional.[19] However, if the Platonist is trying to suggest that the emotions are maladaptive in general, then he is surely wrong.

For emotions are part of our biological makeup. This is not to deny that they are culturally modified. To be angered, we must believe that we have been wronged, but, of course, what counts as a wrong is in a great many cases a matter of cultural determination. Yet, along with the influence of culture, the emotions are also rooted in biology. And as biological phenomena, their persistence can be explained according to principles of natural selection. That is, in opposition to the suspicion that the emotions are maladaptive, we may argue that we have the emotions because they contribute to the fitness of the organism. In other words, we have the emotions because they enhance our prospects for survival. Undoubtedly, this is connected to the fact that they respond to knowledge and reason. But, in any case, the emotions are hardly impediments to adaptation; rather, they are biologically rooted devices in the service of adaptation.

Moreover, we need not base this claim on the abstract supposition that any biological component as entrenched as the emotions must provide some adaptive advantage. I think that we can begin to specify with some precision the evolutionary service that the emotions perform for the human organism. Of course, the most obvious service that the emotions

---

[19] These questions, especially the first one, will be addressed in the next chapter.

perform for the organism is that they motivate behaviour, since emotions are typically made up of desires, as well as cognitive states. But the emotions also contribute to perception. That is, emotional states cognitively organize our perceptions of situations in light of our desires and values, and thereby prepare the organism to act in its perceived interests. Anger and fear, for example, prime the organism to fight or to flee respectively.

The bodily changes that the emotions induce ready the organism to carry out certain activities effectively. But connected to their role in the preparation of the organism for action, the emotions also shape our perception of situations.[20] And this, of course, rather than their action-motivating potentials, is what should be most interesting for aestheticians.

Perception and the emotions are interrelated in a number of ways. First, it is our attention to certain aspects of a situation—say, the harmful ones—that moves us into certain emotional states in the first instance. But then the emotions provide feedback to our processes of attention. Once alerted to the harmful aspects of a situation, our fear will impel us to search the situation—to scan the scene—for further evidence of harmfulness. The emotions focus our attention. They make certain features of situations salient, and they cast those features in a special phenomenological light. The emotions 'gestalt' situations, we might say. They organize them. They make certain elements of the situation stand out. They are sensitive to certain aspects of various recurring situations, like danger, and they size up and organize certain situations rapidly. And then they hold our attention on the relevant features of the situation, often compelling us to pick out further aspects of the situation under the relevant criteria that defines the emotional state that we are in. As Jenefer Robinson puts it: 'If I respond emotionally . . . then my body alerts me to my conception of the situation and registers it as personally significant to me.'[21] For example, we might first detect the large wave coming at us and then our fear further apprises us of or draws our attention to its lethal velocity.

Clearly, the attention-guiding function of the emotions is connected to the role the emotions play in determining action. The emotions focus attention on those elements of situations that are relevant for action, given our desires, interests, and values. The emotions are evolutionary mechanisms for identifying the significance—generally the significance for effec-

---

[20] S. Tomkins, 'Script Theory: Differential Magnification of Affect', in *Nebraska Symposium on Motivation*, 26 (1979), 201–40; Kent Bach, 'Emotional Disorder and Attention', in *Philosophical Pathology*, ed. George Graham and G. Lynn Stephens (Cambridge, Mass.: MIT Press, 1994), 51–72; and Jenefer Robinson, 'Startle', *Journal of Philosophy*, 92/2 (1995), 53–74.   [21] Robinson, 'Startle', 65.

tive action—of the situations in which we find ourselves. And they are very economical devices in this respect, especially when contrasted to other, slower mental processes, like deliberation. The emotions are good things to have when the organism has to scope out a situation immediately. Thus, in terms of both their action-guiding potential and their service to attention, the emotions are optimal adaptive mechanisms. This is not to say that particular emotional episodes are not frequently out of place or inappropriate, just as certain logical deductions may be unsound. Nevertheless, the emotions as a general feature of human nature are adaptive.

Thus, the Platonist is wrong, should he suspect that the emotions are maladaptive. Nor do I think that he can make the case that particular emotions—like pity and fear—are always maladaptive. For example, fear of death may sometimes be maladaptive for a soldier in battle, but it is not for someone like a philosopher king, stepping out of the way of an oncoming chariot. Similarly neo-Platonic critics who charge that mass art engenders aggressiveness, supposing that they could support this charge empirically, forget not only that aggressiveness is not only often useful, but also that the aggressiveness portrayed in mass art is generally appropriate, inasmuch as it is most frequently tied to questions of injustice and other forms of wrongdoing. That is, when aggression is portrayed positively, it is represented as a morally correct alternative, quite often in contexts where no other morally correct alternative is available. And in cases where aggression is wanton, it is typically represented in mass art as morally repugnant. Therefore, if aggression is encouraged by mass art, this occurs within a moral framework that one supposes, all things being equal, is socially adaptive.

As you will recall, Plato also has a theory of the way in which the emotions are engaged by drama. His theory is probably the first theory of identification in Western civilization. It is so influential that contemporary Platonic critics of mass art typically take it over whole. According to Plato, when people read plays aloud, a practice that was quite common in Athenian culture (perhaps akin to family TV viewing), they would take on the emotions of the characters whose parts they were reading. And this was problematic, Plato thought, because in doing so they would not only risk contamination by unsavoury emotions, but also in giving vent to the emotions through play-acting, they would send reason on a holiday. Neo-Platonic critics of mass art, of course, extend this analysis of play-reading to the silent consumption of representations of mass art, claiming that by representing the emotions of characters, mass artworks encourage audiences to take on particular anti-social emotions while, in general, wallowing in irrationality to the detriment of understanding. We have already seen why these worries about irrationality are misplaced. But it also pays to note that the Platonic theory of how the emotions are communicated by way of identification is also mistaken.

In the standard case, when we are emotionally engaged by fictions, we do not identify emotionally with characters by, so to say, taking on their emotions. When we are happy at the end of the TV programme because the lovers have finally got together, that is not a function of the fact that we are in love with the characters. Which one of the characters would it be, anyway? Both? But if we are in love with both of the characters, then we are in an emotional state that neither of the characters is in, since each one of them is only in love with one person. And actually, we are in love with neither of them. We are happy that they have got together, but we are happy in a way similar to onlookers or observers, not participants.[22] Our emotions do not duplicate theirs, although our recognition of what their emotions are and that the lovers' desires have been satisfied are ingredients in our rather different (not identical) emotional states.

Similarly, when we are angered by the behaviour of both Antigone and Creon, our anger is based on our assessment that both of them are unyieldingly stubborn, an assessment that neither one of them shares with us. And when Creon's son and then his wife commit suicide, we pity him, whereas his emotional state is one of self-recrimination.

Likewise, when consuming a melodrama, readers, viewers, and listeners are not only often saddened by the protagonist's misfortune, but also, often that sadness is conjoined with a feeling of admiration for the character in question. We admire, for example, her fortitude or her willingness to sacrifice for others. However, this emotional state on the part of the audience is not one of identifying with the character's emotion. She is not admiring herself. Probably, if the character did admire herself, many of us would cease to admire her, since vanity is something that generally turns us off. Thus, our psychological state differs from that of the character in cases of 'melodramatic emotion', perhaps necessarily so.

In short, in the standard case, there is an asymmetrical relation between the emotional states that characters undergo and those of the audience, whereas identification of the sort advanced by Platonists requires identity

---

[22] Though I do not agree with all of his conclusions, I think that it is important to note that Nico Frijda also stresses that our stance toward fictions is that of an observer, not a participant. See Nico A. Frijda, 'Aesthetic Emotions and Reality', *American Psychologist* (December 1989), 1546.

(of emotions), which is a symmetrical relation.[23] Therefore, the notion of identification cannot provide us, *contra* Plato and his contemporary avatars, with a general theory of our emotional involvement with dramas in particular or mass art in general.[24]

For heuristic purposes, I have spent a great deal of time elaborating the problems with the Platonic conception of our emotional involvement with various forms of art. For in laying out what is wrong with the Platonic position, I have been able to introduce enough information about the nature of the emotions so as to construct a positive account of the way in which the emotions are engaged by mass art. In my criticisms of the Platonists, I have rejected the possibility that emotional identification characterizes the general mechanism or structure that elicits the audience's emotional response. In its place, let me offer an alternative account.

Criterial prefocusing: An alternative to identification

As we have already seen, the emotions are intimately related to attention. It is this feature of the emotions that should be important to art theorists, rather than the action-mobilizing feature of the emotions, since artworks, in the typical case, command attention, not action. I have suggested, furthermore, that the emotions are related to our attention-focusing mechanisms. They direct our attention to certain details in an array, rather than to others. The emotions enable us to organize those details into significant wholes or gestalts, so that, for example, our attention selects out or battens upon the concatenations of details in the situation that are, for instance, relevant to harm or to misfortune. The emotions operate like

[23] On pp. 99–100 of *Reading with Feeling*, Susan Feagin challenges my arguments against identification. She claims that my position is based on noting only one structural asymmetry between the characters and the audience, namely, that the character is in a belief state, whereas the audience is only entertaining certain thoughts. Moreover, she contends that the difference between thoughts and beliefs is not so different as to preclude the notion of identification. However, even if Prof. Feagin is right about this, it does not compromise my argument. Because, as I have shown above, there are typically many other asymmetries between the mental state of the audience and that of the character. For example, with many melodramas, it is generally the case that my sadness for a character is compounded with admiration, whereas this is not something that the character feels. Similar asymmetries can be found across the board for our emotional responses to characters. Therefore, the notion of identification cannot supply us with a general account of our emotional response to fictions. We do not identify with characters. We are in the position of observers; we do not 'become' the agents in stories. The objects of our emotional states standardly differ from the objects of the emotional states of characters in stories. For generally the characters in said stories are the objects of our emotional states in a way that these characters are not objects of their own emotional states. We pity characters beset by misfortune, though these characters are not generally self-pitying. See Susan Feagin, *Reading With Feeling: The Aesthetics of Appreciation* (Ithaca, NY: Cornell University Press, 1996), 99–100.

[24] The question of identification will be discussed further in the next chapter.

a searchlight, foregrounding those details in a special phenomenological glow. And, as well, once we are in the midst of an emotional state, we not only hold to those details, often obsessively, but we are also prompted to search out more details with similar relevance to our presiding emotional assessment of the situation. The emotions manage our attention when we are in their grip. And that management undergoes changes in the sense that it first alerts our attention to certain gestalts and holds our attention on them and then encourages further elaboration of our attention, inclining us to search for further elements of the relevant gestalt in the stimulus, and leading us to form expectations about the kinds of things we should be on the lookout for as the situation evolves.

Now if this picture of the way in which our emotions and attention mesh is accurate, then it should provide us with a useful way in which to think about how our emotions are involved with respect to mass artworks, particularly those of a narrative variety—including movies, 'junk' fictions, TV and radio dramas and comedies, comic strips and comic books, popular songs, and so on.

In life, as opposed to fiction, our emotions have to pick up on the relevant details of a situation for us out of a welter of unstructured details. We are sitting in a room talking distractedly to some friends; we notice a faint smell of something burning. Our emotions alert us to danger. Our attention is riveted on the odour. We begin to look and to sniff about for further evidence of fire, readying ourselves to confront it or to flee.

But in fictions, of course, including those of mass art, the situation has already been prestructured for our attention. The author has already done much of the work of focusing our attention through the way in which she has foregrounded what features of the event are salient. After all, the author has not only chosen—indeed invented—the situations we encounter; but she has also decided what features of those fictional events are worthy of direct comment or implication. Thus, again and again in *Uncle Tom's Cabin*, Harriet Beecher Stowe confronts us with scenes of families being separated, and, in case after case, she emphasizes the innocence and decency of the slaves whose family ties are being sundered, and the cruelty and callousness with which it is being done. These perhaps none-too-subtle promptings lead us to perceive the scenes under the category of injustice which, in turn, elicits the affect of indignation from us. And this indignation, in consequence, bonds us to the details of the text as well as preparing us to anticipate and to be on the look-out for further evidences of injustice—which, of course, Stowe's text delivers in abundance.

Or consider the character Fledgeby in Dickens's novel *Our Mutual Friend*. As Fledgeby taunts his factotum Riah, Dickens keeps in the foreground of our attention Fledgeby's viciousness, underscoring his abusiveness and his unflinching anti-semitism, which he, Fledgeby, attempts to pass off as humour. Through Dickens's descriptions, Riah is shown to be Fledgeby's moral and human superior in every way. All Fledgeby has is a little money which he uses to subordinate everyone else, including Riah. Dickens does not have to come right out and say that Fledgeby is contemptible. Rather, the way in which he has described the situation engenders in us hatred of and contempt for Fledgeby, which primes the way in which we attend to Fledgeby's appearance in other scenes, and which encourages us to hope for his downfall.

Or think about how suspense is engendered in fictions and how it keeps us riveted to the action.[25] Suspense is an emotion, one that in fictions generally involves an event where some outcome which we regard to be morally righteous is improbable. For example, in the recent motion picture *Speed*, it is likely that the bus will explode; in *True Lies*, that the nuclear device will detonate; and in *Outbreak*, that the antidote will be blown away along with the rest of the town when the army drops its firebomb. In each of these cases, the outcome that I've mentioned has been depicted as immoral in the relevant fictions, but, at the same time, it is the one that is most likely, given the world of the fiction as it has been presented to us. Or, to put it alternatively, the moral outcome is presented as if it were improbable. When confronted with such prospects, we attend to the events onscreen with suspense; it rivets us to the screen, and it shapes our attention in such a way that our mind is preoccupied with tracking the features of the event that are relevant to the emotional state in which we find ourselves. And with suspense, that means keeping track of the shifting probabilities for the forces of good versus the forces of evil.[26]

Whether verbal, visual, or aural, the text will be prefocused. Certain features of situations and characters will be made salient through description or depiction. These features will be such that they will be subsumable

[25] For further elaboration of the view of suspense suggested in this paragraph, see Noël Carroll, 'The Paradox of Suspense', in *Suspense: Conceptualizations, Theoretical Analyses and Empirical Explorations*, ed. Peter Vorderer, Hans J. Wulff, and Mike Friedrichsen (Mahwah, NJ: Lawrence Erlbaum Associates, Publishers, 1996), 71–92.

[26] I have chosen examples where the emotions involved are somewhat intense and where their elicitation has a forceful, one might say, an 'in-your-face' character. I have opted for such examples not only because, for reasons to be discussed later, this is typical of mass fictions, but also because I think that intense examples show the dynamics of our emotional response to fictions in general in bold relief. However, there is no reason to think that the elicitation of emotions by fictions is always as aggressive as it is in these examples. The emotional cues in a text may be more recessive or subtle, they may be initially obscured by irony or ambiguity, and it may take them longer to hit the audience than the examples that I have mentioned. This may be especially the case as we ascend from routine examples of mass art to the more 'difficult' products of so-called high art. And yet, even in these cases, I think that we will discern the same regularities in operation.

under the categories or concepts that, as I argued earlier, govern or determine the identity of the emotional states we are in. Let us refer to this attribute of texts by saying that the texts are *criterially prefocused*.[27]

For example, horror is an emotion that involves fear and revulsion.[28] The criterion of fear is the harmful; the criterion of revulsion is the impure. Events are horrific when they are subsumable under the categories of the harmful and the impure, i.e., when they satisfy the criteria for horror by being harmful and impure. Thus, when authors of horror describe or depict events which they intend to elicit horror from us, they describe or depict events, situations, and characters that are harmful and impure—for example, slavering, fetid mounds of cankerous flesh with razor sharp claws and cosmic antipathy to all things human. That is, the author will describe or depict the putative objects of our emotional state so that the *salient* features of that object are apt, for the normal audience member, to be slotted under the categories of the harmful and the impure. This categorization need not be a conscious operation, any more than my recognition that the oncoming car is potentially harmful need be accompanied by my saying it, even subvocally.

So the first step in the elicitation of an emotional response from the audience is a criterially prefocused text—a text structured in such a way that the description or the depiction of the object of our attention is such that it will activate our subsumption of the situation or event under the categories that are criterially relevant to certain emotional states. Once we recognize the object under those categories, the relevant emotion is apt, and, in certain conditions to be discussed below, likely to be raised in us. We will be likely to undergo some physical changes—with horror fictions, our flesh may begin, as they say, to crawl; with suspense, we may feel our muscles tense; with melodrama, we may shed a tear; with comedy, we may laugh. And, in addition, our attention becomes emotively charged: the object of the emotion rivets our attention, while our emotionally governed perception casts its object in a special phenomenological light.

The emotion glues our attention to those features of the object of the emotion that are apposite to the emotional state we are in; it encourages us to survey the event for further features that may support or sustain the prevailing emotional state in which we find ourselves; and protentively, our emotively charged state shapes our anticipation of what is to come by priming us to be on the lookout for the emergence or appearance of

---

[27] I think that it is the fact of criterial prefocusing that Jenefer Robinson leaves out in her essay on the emotions in fiction in 'Experiencing Art', *Proceedings of the 11th International Congress of Aesthetics*, ed. Richard Woodfield (Nottingham: Nottingham Polytechnic Press, 1988), 156–60.

[28] This conception of horror is defended in Noël Carroll, *The Philosophy of Horror*.

further details subsumable under the categories of the reigning emotion. Or, in short, the criterially prefocused text gives rise, in the right circumstances, to *emotive focus* in the audience, where by 'emotive focus' I am referring both to the way in which the emotional state of the reader, listener, or viewer fixes but also shapes her attention.

The Platonic story of our emotional involvement to the text posits characters, venting certain emotions, with whom we identify in such a way that their emotions are transferred to the audience. In contrast, I maintain that the structure involves a criterially prefocused text that elicits an emotively focused response. This is, a criterially prefocused text brings our attention to certain details, alerting an emotional response which quickens our attentiveness and which binds us to the text so that we are ready to assimilate it in the relevant way. Relevant to what? Relevant to the presiding emotional state which, in the standard case, is the one which the author designed the text to engender in us.

The emotional states of characters may be pertinent to the emotional state we are in; that we perceive a character to be in anguish may be material to our pity for him. His anguish is part of his misfortune, after all. But it is the way in which the text is criterially prefocused and not some putative process of character identification that is crucially determinant to the audience's emotive response. Rather than character identification, it is our own pre-existing emotional constitution, with its standing dispositions, that the text activates. This, in large measure, is what accounts for our emotional involvement with narrative fictions in general and mass fictions in particular.

Of course, simply presenting a reader, viewer, or listener with a criterially prefocused text does not guarantee that the reader, viewer, or listener will respond emotionally. For a criterially prefocused text can be read dispassionately. Something more is required to elicit successfully a passionate response. And what that 'something more' is amounts to a concern or a pro-attitude on the part of the reader, viewer, or listener of the fiction regarding the way in which the situation depicted in the fiction is or is not going. These concerns function like the desires in many everyday emotions, and when added to the mental content or conception derived from the criterially prefocused text, the combination, all things being equal, should elicit an emotional response in the normal audience member in accordance with the criterial features of the situation that the text has made pertinent for attention.

The structure of our emotional involvement with a fiction comprises at least a criterially prefocused text plus certain concerns or pro-attitudes, and together these are apt to elicit broadly predictable responses in standard audiences. The criterially prefocused text embodies a conception of a situation. But a conception of a situation alone is not sufficient to motivate an emotional response, as is evident from the reactions of certain sociopaths. To prompt such a response requires that audiences be invested with concerns—certain pro and con attitudes—about what is going on in the story.[29]

This suggestion makes the assumption that narrative structures can enlist audiences in preferences about the ways in which a story might go. This is not to say that all stories do this—narrative instructions about how to fix a broken water pipe may not. Nevertheless, I think that it is equally non-controversial to suppose that many narratives do induce readers, listeners, and viewers to form preferences about how a story should evolve. For example, in Grant Allen's *The Woman Who Did*—called 'the bestseller that scandalized Victorian Great Britain'—the implied reader is concerned for Herminia Barton (the woman who believed in the moral legitimacy of sexual relations outside of marriage). Said readers respect her sincerity and prefer that Herminia be spared from harm. Thus, at the end of the story, when Herminia feels compelled to commit suicide, the reader is moved to sadness, not simply because the story has portrayed her plight melodramatically, but because the story has elicited a pro attitude toward Herminia from the reader as well.

Typically, narratives develop in such a way that readers, viewers, and listeners have a structured horizon of expectations about what might and what might not happen. And in addition to a sense of the possible outcomes of the ongoing courses of events, one also, generally under the guidance of the author, has convictions about what outcomes she would, in a certain sense, prefer to obtain versus those she would prefer not to obtain. In some cases, the preferred course of events correlates with the express goals and plans of the protagonists in the story; what they want—say, averting nuclear disaster—is what the audience also wants to happen. However, in a great many other cases, the story may proffer preferred outcomes independently of the express goals and plans of any of the characters. That is, the story may have its own agenda, as in the case of all those fictional lovers who find themselves amorously involved in ways they never planned and even might have abhorred antecedently.

But, however motivated, audiences develop concerns regarding the situations in stories, and when those concerns are threatened, we tend to react with dysphoric (or discomforting) emotions, whereas when the

---

[29] As I understand these pro-attitudes, they are not themselves emotions, but rather like the desires that comprise many everyday emotions.

concern in question is abetted by narrative developments, our emotions tend to be euphoric.[30] Which particular dysphoric or euphoric emotion is engaged, of course, depends upon the way in which the text is criterially prefocused. For example, considering some dysphoric emotions, if I have a pro attitude toward a character and he is morally wronged in a way that the text makes criterially salient, then, all things being equal, I will feel anger toward those characters who have wronged him; whereas if presented with the gross misfortune of a group—say the passengers entrapped in a doomed jumbo jet—that has elicited my concern in a criterially prefocused way, then I am to feel pity for them. And even if some callous audience member does not feel pity in this case, pity is the normatively correct or warranted response to the text as well as the necessarily typical response.

Furthermore, euphoric emotions of different sorts are also likely to evolve in accordance with the way in which the text is criterially prefocused (where our concerns and desires about the direction of courses and events are also satisfied). When a character toward whom we bear a pro attitude overcomes obstacles, we are likely to respond with joy and admiration, whereas the manifestation of virtually limitless power by an agency of which we approve—for instance, nature or a god—will tend to evoke awe or reverence, or, at least, reverence, will be the normatively correct or necessarily typical response.

Authors of narratives, including mass fictions, are able, fairly reliably, to induce the emotions they set out to evoke—especially basic emotions (like anger, fear, hatred, and so on)—because of the fact that they share a common background (cultural, but biological as well) with their audiences, both in terms of the criteria relevant to the experience of certain emotions as well as in terms of what it standardly takes to elicit concern for given characters and their goals, and for the alternative directions that situations may take. Inasmuch as authors generally share a common background, cultural and otherwise, with their audiences, they may use themselves as detectors to gauge how audiences are likely to respond to their texts. They can use their own reactions to predict the direction of the standard audience members' concern as well as the specific emotional states which the criterial prefocusing will encourage.

Of course, authors are not infallible in this regard. In his book *American Psycho*, Brett Easton Ellis expected audiences to respond with hilarity—

---

[30] Here I am extrapolating from what is sometimes called the conflict theory of the emotions. Representatives include: F. Paulhan, *The Laws of Feeling*, trans. C. K. Ogden (New York: Harcourt, Brace and Company, 1930); G. Mandler, *Mind and Body: Psychology of Emotions and Stress* (New York: Norton, 1984); and Keith Oatley, *Best Laid Schemes*, especially pp. 107–9 and 174–7.

since he intended a postmodern send-up of the Reaganite rapacity of the eighties—whereas they greeted the book with disgust. Nevertheless, with most narrative fiction, such wild mismatches of intended affect with actual affect are the exception rather than the rule. Most narratives are relatively successful in raising the *kind* of emotion they aim at, though not always successful in the degree to which they aspire (frequently erring in the direction of eliciting too much or too little of the intended affect).

The reason for what accuracy there is in this matter is that, generally, authors, in sharing a background (an ethos, a moral and emotive repertoire, a cognitive stock, and so on) with audiences, are able to conjecture creatively what their confreres' reaction should be in terms of which emotional responses are appropriate to situations depicted in certain ways. Within the boundaries of certain cultures, there are certain criteria concerning what emotionally responses are normatively correct—i.e., what emotions certain situations are supposed to elicit. Authors, as members of that culture, possessed in common with audiences, use their knowledge of what is normatively correct in terms of emotional responses and compose narrative situations accordingly. Moreover, some emotions and their situational antecedents may be universal, a fact, as we shall see, of especial importance for mass art. Thus, in those cases, authors can use their own generic emotional responses to guide the elicitation of emotional responses from audiences.

Authors, then, can broadly predict how readers, listeners, and viewers will respond to the events they construct because said authors know the way in which members of their own culture, such as themselves, and, in some cases, members of all cultures, are supposed to respond to situations of various sorts. Where most story-tellers fail (when they fail), it seems to me, is usually not in evoking the emotions they intend to evoke, but in evoking them at the wrong level of intensity. And this, I speculate, is very frequently a matter of the failure to elicit the appropriate amount or type of concern for the characters and situations depicted.

But, be that as it may, emotional involvement with narratives in general and mass fictions in particular depends upon a combination of a criterially prefocused text with pro and/or con attitudes about the ways the narrative situation can develop—that is to say, a combination of a conception of the situation along with some relevant concerns, preferences, and desires. Together, these provide necessary and sufficient conditions for an emotional response to the text to take hold in such a way that the reader, viewer, or listener becomes emotionally focused, i.e., in such a way that the abiding emotional state fixes and shapes her attention in a manner warranted by the text.

In so far as audience concern often takes its cue from the goals of characters, it may be tempting to reintroduce the Platonic notion of identification at this point, claiming that audiences take on the goals of characters in fictional narratives by identifying with the characters and deriving their (the audience's) concerns by means of this process. But this brand of identification cannot provide us with a general theory of how concerns are engendered by narratives, since the direction of our concern in many stories runs in different directions from those of the protagonists. So it cannot, across the board, be the case that, in order to form our concerns, we must be identifying with characters and their express goals. Often we form our concerns about how the story should go in a paternalistic rather than an identificatory fashion. Frequently, we do not think that the characters should get what they want. For example, we may not think that the hero should marry the woman he wishes to marry, but that he should prefer the heroine (for example, the movie *Bringing Up Baby*). Thus, identification once again fails as a general account of how we are emotionally engaged by narrative fictions.

Contra the Platonists, the relevant mechanism is not a matter of identification. We do not become the character or acquire her goals. The character's emotion does not transmigrate into us. Rather, our pre-existing dispositions to certain values and preferences are mobilized by the text's providing an affective cement that fixes our attention on the text and shapes our attention to ongoing situations.

Furthermore, as the reader will remember, Plato and latter-day Platonists have tried to explain the function of the emotions with respect to drama and mass art respectively in terms of purely economic necessity. The audience understands little, Plato and his followers contend, so that the only way in which to engage it is through the emotions, understood as irrational forces. I, of course, reject this account in so far as I think that the emotions are connected to cognition. Indeed, addressing the emotions may in fact in some (even many) cases provide an opportunity for understanding. Thus the elicitation of emotional responses from audiences is not an alternative to cognition and understanding.

Rather, the real function of the emotions for narrative fictions and mass art, on my account, is, first and foremost, the management of the audience's attention. Of course, successful management of the audience's attention may be economically beneficial. But this may be regarded as a secondary effect and not the primary reason that emotions are indispensable to fictions, including the narrative fictions of mass art. Attention management is the central function of the emotions with respect to fiction.

Ramifications for research

If my account of the emotional involvement of the audience with regard to narrative fictions is acceptable, it suggests a certain direction of research. In order to analyse how a text elicits an emotional response, it is of crucial importance to isolate the way in which the text is criterially prefocused. Using oneself as a detector, the critic begins with a global sense of the emotions that the text has elicited in her. Then, using the criterion of the emotion in question as a hypothesis, one may review the way in which the text is articulated in order to isolate the relevant descriptions or depictions in the text that instantiate the concept of the emotion in question. In following this procedure, one can generally pith the emotive structure of the text.

What 'pithing the emotive structure of the text' amounts to here is finding the aspects of the depictions or descriptions of the object of the emotion that satisfy the necessary conditions for being in whatever emotional state the audience is in. This is what explaining the emotional state of the audience generally comes to (along with identifying the concerns or preferences with which the narrative invests the audience).

For example, I cite the descriptions of the putatively rancid odour of the monster in a mass horror fiction because it contributes to the satisfaction of one of the necessary conditions of being horrified (namely, that the object of the emotion be perceived as impure) and thus my citation contributes to explaining why the audience both is and is warranted in being horrified by the novel. Of course, it is impossible to predict exhaustively every way in which authors will satisfy the necessary conditions of the emotional states that concern them. After all, artists can be original. However, there is room for limited generalization in this area where theorists are able to identify recurring formulae—both in terms of constructing emotive salience and enlisting audience preferences—that are routinely used to secure certain affects in various mass art genres.

Admittedly, this order of research may not always be practicable. For example, one may not always be able to articulate with precision one's emotional response to a text. In that case, one might be better advised to tackle the descriptions and depictions with an eye to seeing what they make salient and then compare those saliencies with the criteria for the better-known emotional states. This may lead to a clarification of the emotional address in question. Needless to say, I would not wish to claim that the emotional address of a text is always unambiguous, nor would I deny that some texts may introduce novel emotional timbres.[31] Nevertheless, in these cases the procedure that I have recommended is still valuable, since it will enable us to identify the general contours of the emotional ambiguities and novel emotional timbres in the text.[32]

My emphasis on the emotional address of texts may trouble some researchers who might worry that it makes textual analysis sound too much like sociology. It may sound as though I am advocating that we must go out into the field and find out how audiences actually respond to texts. We could do that, and I see no reason to expect that the results of such research might not be interesting and informative. However, I am not here proposing that sort of empirical sociology. For I am concerned now with the normatively correct address of the text—the emotive effect that the text is supposed to have or is designed to have on the normal audience, that is, the emotive response that is warranted by the text or that is typically necessary with regard to the text.

Some people may find decapitation humorous. But that is not the emotional response that the film *Braveheart* is designed to promote with respect to the demise of its central protagonist. Throughout this chapter, I have been concerned with the normatively correct emotional response to texts and with the general structure that encourages that response. Identifying the operation of that structure in a given work is a matter of textual analysis, albeit against the cultural and biological background in which the text is produced. It is not a matter of sociological polling. This, of course, is not said to deny that the results of sociological polling can be instructive. But in many cases, perhaps most, I suspect that it is redundant, since, to a surprising extent, it seems to me, texts tend to elicit actual emotional responses that are normatively appropriate to them, as a result of what is generally shared—culturally and biologically—by the producers and consumers of the relevant texts.

---

[31] One should also mention the case of mixed emotions. A mass fiction may, for example, be referred to as 'bittersweet'. In such a case, the audience will be in a state that mixes sadness with some positive emotion. Here, our analyses will proceed by examining the text in terms of the criteria relevant to each of the component emotions.

[32] Of course, in many cases, especially where ordinary readers are dealing with texts, including mass artworks, that are somewhat remote from us in time and/or place, we will not be able to depend on our own emotional responses to the text because we do not have the appropriate cultural background. This is exactly where literary history, film history, dance history, and the like have an indispensable role to play. For historians can supply us with the background necessary to make the emotive address of texts from other cultures and other periods in the history of our own culture emotionally accessible to us.

Fiction and the emotions

So far I have been developing a framework for understanding our emotional engagement with fictions, including mass-art narratives. In doing so, I have presumed that such engagement is logically possible. But there are certain theoretical considerations that suggest that the relations I have attempted to unravel simply can't obtain. Thus I need to address these worries in order to allay them.

I have embraced a cognitive theory of the emotions in order to characterize our emotional involvement with fictions. Cognitive theories of the emotions maintain that a central component of the emotions is a cognitive state, such as a belief. But if the requisite cognitive state that is partly constitutive of an emotion must be a belief, then, as some cognitive theorists contend, it is difficult to understand how readers, viewers, and listeners can be emotionally moved by narrative fictions, because such audiences know the narratives in question are fictions, and therefore, on one standard account of knowledge, they do not believe them. To fear x, under one widely accepted analysis of fear, is, among other things, to believe that x is harmful. But then how can I be in the state of fear with regard to a vampire movie, since I know that the movie is a fiction, that vampires do not exist, and, consequently, that the vampires depicted in the movie cannot really be harmful? Similarly, in so far as other emotions involve other sorts of beliefs, which, like fear, putatively cannot be sustained for persons, objects, and events we know and, therefore, believe do not exist, how is any emotional response to fiction possible at all? Perhaps, it might be argued, emotional responses to fiction are just logically impossible, and our indulgence in them is irrational (thereby raising Platonic anxieties once again).

My answer to this challenge relies on my rejection of the supposition that emotions require beliefs in all cases.[33] The cognitive theory of the emotions requires a cognitive component, but, I would argue, the form that that component may take is diverse, including not only beliefs, but thoughts and perhaps even patterns of attention.[34] And, furthermore, the form of the cognitive component that is most relevant to understanding our emotional responses to fictional narratives is thought, not belief.

But what do I mean by 'thought' in this context? In order to answer that question, let me contrast what I am calling thoughts to beliefs. A belief, for

[33] This view is defended at greater length in Noël Carroll, *The Philosophy of Horror*, especially ch. 2.
[34] Concerning the relevant patterns of attention, see Amelie Rorty, 'Explaining Emotion', in *Explaining Emotion*, 103–26.

my purposes, can be conceived as a proposition held in the mind as asserted. To believe that there is a table in front of me is to be committed to the truth of the assertion of the proposition 'that there is a table in front of me'. A thought, on the other hand, is a matter of entertaining a proposition in the mind unasserted, as one does when I ask you to suppose 'that Albania has conquered the United States' or to imagine 'that Manhattan is made of pizza'. To imagine is to remain neutral about whether we know or believe whatever it is that we imagine.[35] It is to entertain a thought-content, to entertain a proposition as unasserted, to understand the meaning of the proposition (to grasp its propositional content or sense), but to refrain from taking it as an assertion, and therefore, to be neutral about its truth value.

Moreover, it seems to be indisputable that emotions can be engendered in the process of holding propositions before the mind unasserted. While cutting vegetables, imagine putting the very sharp knife in your hand into your eye. You suddenly feel a shudder. You need not *believe* that the knife is in your eye, nor even that you are really going to put it into your eye. Indeed, you know that you are not going to do this. Yet merely entertaining the thought, or the propositional content of the thought (that I am putting this knife into my eye) can be sufficient for playing a role in causing a tremor of terror. For emotions may rest on thoughts and not merely upon beliefs.

We can evoke bodily changes in ourselves by means of thoughts. We, or at least many of us, do this all the time when we stimulate ourselves sexually in the process of imagining compliant beauties (of any gender, depending on one's own sexual preference) beckoning us to embrace them (or whatever else we enjoy). Arachnophobes can send a chill of fear down their spine by imagining that a tarantula is in their underwear, and most of us can make ourselves gag with disgust, if we imagine the food in our mouth is someone else's vomit. Thoughts, that is, can play a role in generating emotional states.

Furthermore, this aspect of the emotions is particularly pertinent to our commerce with fictions. For fictions are stories that authors intend readers, listeners, and viewers to imagine.[36] Fictions are comprised of sentences and other sense-bearing vehicles (like televisual images) that communicate propositions to audiences, which propositions the author of the fiction

---

[35] Kerry S. Walters also stresses the role of the imagination in emotional responses to fiction in his 'The Law of Apparent Reality and Aesthetic Emotions', *American Psychologist* (December 1989), 1545–6.
[36] This view of fiction is advanced in Gregory Currie, *The Nature of Fiction* (Cambridge: Cambridge University Press, 1990); and in Peter Lamarque and Stein Haugom Olsen, *Truth, Fiction and Literature: A Philosophical Perspective* (Oxford: Clarendon Press, 1994).

intends the audience to imagine or to entertain in the mind unasserted as a result of the audience's recognition of the author's intention that that is what they are meant to do. In making a fiction, an author is creating an assemblage of propositions for prospective readers, viewers, and listeners which the author intends them to entertain in thought. The author presenting a fiction in effect says to the audience: 'hold these propositions before your mind unasserted'—i.e., 'suppose p' or 'imagine p' or 'entertain p unasserted'.

Thus, if thoughts, as distinct from beliefs, can also support emotional responses, then we may have emotional responses to fictions concerning situations, persons, objects, and things that do not exist. For we can imagine or suppose that they exist, and entertaining unasserted the propositional content of the relevant thoughts can figure in the aetiology of the emotional state. Fictions, construed as propositions to be imagined, supply us with the relevant unasserted propositional content, and in entertaining that content as the author mandates, we can be emotionally moved by fictions.

It is not impossible to be moved emotionally by fictions. It is quite natural as we can see by putting together two theses: 1. the thesis that fictions are propositions that authors proffer to us with the express intention that they be imagined or entertained as unasserted, and 2. the thesis that thoughts, construed as propositions held in the mind as unasserted, can play the role of the cognitive constituent in the activation of an emotional state.

On my account of our emotional involvement with fictional narratives (including pulp literature, movies, TV programmes, comics, songs, radio soaps, and the like), authors present readers, listeners, and viewers with propositions to be imagined that depict or describe situations that have been criterially prefocused and that arouse our concern so that we become emotionally focused on the text—i.e., attention 1. becomes riveted to the objects of our emotional state (said objects are lit, in a manner of speaking, in a special phenomenological glow); 2. our attention is virtually inexorably drawn to those features of the object of the emotion that are apposite to the emotional state we are in; 3. we are encouraged to search the situation for more features of the sort that will support and sustain the prevailing emotional state; and 4. we are prompted to anticipate further details of the evolving story that are subsumable under the categories relevant to the presiding emotion.[37]

---

[37] As points 3 and 4 above indicate, emotional engagement is sustained, in part, by feedback mechanisms.

Emotions are a central device that authors have for managing the attention of readers, listeners, and viewers. Not only do authors use our already existing emotional constitution to direct our attention and to fill in the story in a way that makes it intelligible. Through our emotions, they keep us locked on the text on a moment-to-moment basis. Nor is there anything irrational about this. For it is not irrational to respond to the situations depicted in texts in accordance with the cognitively appropriate criteria. Nor is it irrational to respond emotionally to fictions, since thoughts, of the sort communicated by fictions, which are held before the mind as unasserted propositions, are a perfectly reasonable source of emotional excitement.[38]

But What About Mass Art?

A possible criticism of what has been said about the emotions thus far might be that it is too general. For the account that I have offered would appear to apply to the relationship of the emotions to narrative fictions across the board. Nothing has been said about what might be the unique relationship of the emotions to mass art. The structures that I have isolated would appear to be as relevant to so-called high art as they are to mass art. That is true. The emotional mechanisms that are operative with respect to art in general are also operative with respect to mass art. That is to be expected, since mass artworks are very often intimately related to histor-ical forms and genres of art in general. Mass art is not completely different in kind from art in general; apart from its reliance on mass technologies, it primarily differs in degree, along certain dimensions (such as accessibility) from other sorts of art, like esoteric art. Thus, the emotional address and the structures of emotional engagement that we find in mass art are not categorically different in kind from what we find operative in cases of narrative and representational art in general.[39]

But does this mean that there is altogether nothing specific to say about

[38] An alternative view of the relation of fiction to the emotions is developed in Kendall Walton, *Mimesis as Make-Believe: On the Foundations of the Representational Arts* (Cambridge: Harvard University Press, 1990). I have criticized this view in Noël Carroll, 'On Kendall Walton's Mimesis as Make-Believe', *Philosophy and Phenomenological Research*, 51/2 (1991); Noël Carroll, 'A Critical Study of *Mimesis as Make-Believe*', *Philosophical Quarterly*, 45/178 (1995); and Noël Carroll, 'The Paradox of Suspense', *Suspense: Conceptualizations, Theoretical Analyses and Empirical Explorations*, ed. Peter Vor-derer, Hans Wulff, and Mike Friedrichsen (Mahwah, NJ: Lawrence Erlbaum Associates, 1996). I also criticized an earlier version of Walton's approach in my book *The Philosophy of Horror*.

[39] Though in this chapter I focus on emotion and mass art narratives, the theoretical apparatus I develop can also be deployed to analyse mass art representations that tell no explicit story—such as those posters of children with large, dark eyes. Some of the material that I discuss at the end of this section with reference to emotional recognitional capacities would be relevant to explicating the emotional address of such posters.

the relationship between mass art and the emotions? Perhaps we can say this much: in so far as mass art gravitates toward mass accessibility, mass art will tend toward engaging emotional responses that are relatively generic. This much is suggested by our theory of mass art. For if—as was argued in the previous chapter—mass art tends toward those structures and effects that address mass audiences, then when it comes to eliciting emotional responses, mass art will gravitate (ideally) toward appealing to the emotional dispositions that are distributed amongst the largest numbers of people.

For example, there is evidence that there are some emotional states that are nearly universal across the human race.[40] This is perhaps predictable, not only in virtue of our shared biological endowment, but also because many of the situations in which humans find themselves—and found themselves in prehistoric times—recur. This is not to deny that there are cultural variations in the emotions, but only that there is also some evidence of some nearly universal emotions as well. By saying that an emotion is nearly universal, here, I mean that certain antecedent situations have the probable propensity to elicit cognate emotional responses cross-culturally. Moreover, if our theory of mass art is right, then we would predict at least a marked tendency in mass artworks toward the attempted elicitation of nearly universal emotions.

Some candidates for emotions of this sort include anger, disgust, fear, happiness, sadness, and surprise.[41] And clearly quite certain mass-art genres are expressly devoted to the elicitation of just such emotional states in audiences as their primary aim or purpose. Anger, of course, is not simply one emotion, but a syndrome or family of emotions, including subcategories like revenge and indignation.[42] And revenge supplies the motor of innumerable action fictions, including many westerns, such as *The Bravados*. The exploitation of this emotion is so recurrent that we, in

---

[40] See, for example, J. D. Boucher, 'Antecedents to Emotions across Cultures', in *Human Assessment and Cultural Factors*, ed. S. H. Irvine and J. W. Berry (New York: Plenum, 1983), 407–20; J. D. Boucher and M. E. Brant, 'Judgment of Emotion: American and Malay Antecedents', *Journal of Cross-Cultural Psychology*, 12 (1981), 272–83; K. R. Scherer, H. G. Wallbott, and W. B. Summerfield (eds.), *Experiencing Emotion: A Cross-Cultural Study* (Cambridge: Cambridge University Press, 1986); Nancy L. Stein and Keith Oatley, 'Basic Emotions: Theory and Measurement', in *Cognition and Emotion*, 6 (1992), 161–8; Paul Ekman, 'An Argument for Basic Emotions', ibid. 169–200; P. N. Johnson-Laird and Keith Oatley, 'Basic Emotion, Rationality, and Folk Theory', ibid. 201–23; Paul Ekman 'Antecedent Events and Emotion Metaphors', in *The Nature of Emotion: Fundamental Questions* (New York: Oxford University Press, 1994), 146–9; Phoebe Ellsworth, 'Some Reasons to Expect Universal Antecedents of Emotion', ibid. 150–4; Nico Fridja, 'Universal Antecedents Exist, and Are Interesting', ibid. 155–62; Richard Lazarus, 'Universal Antecedents of Emotions', ibid. 163–171; K. R. Scherer, 'Evidence for Both Universality and Cultural Specificity of Emotion Elicitation', ibid. 172–4; Keith Oatley and Jennifer M. Jenkins, *Understanding Emotions* (Oxford: Blackwell Publishers, 1996), 49–59.

[41] Oatley and Jenkins, *Understanding Emotions*, 51.

[42] On the notion of emotional syndromes, see James R. Averill, 'It's a Small World, But a Large Stage', in *The Nature of Emotion*, 143–5.

fact, often refer to 'revenge narratives'. Even some songs, such as 'My Boyfriend's Back', would appear to fall into this category.

Likewise, indignation is a key emotion in mass art, frequently figuring in political dramas. Quite often in such fictions, authors are careful to include scenes of the villains slaughtering children, women, and old people in order to stoke the audience's hatred of tyranny. Even Bruce Lee uses racial discrimination ('No dogs or Chinese') in order to motivate the anger of his audiences, while so many war stories are based on indignation directed against the injustices of the enemy. Most prison-camp narratives involve cruel and unusual torture scenes for this purpose. And *Seven Samurai* is sustained in part by our sense of outrage directed toward the brigands who oppress the villagers.

Fear is the metier of many action and detection genres from suspense to thrillers, from disaster scenarios to sci-fi sagas of alien invasion. Suspense accrues when we fear that the forces of right are virtually assured to be overwhelmed by the forces of evil,[43] and suspense is an emotional state that almost no action story forgoes, while disaster scenarios (on the large screen and TV, and in pulp novels) prey on anxieties not only about the reliability of everyday technologies, but also on basic fears concerning earth, air, fire, and water—fears of being drowned, burnt, smothered beneath an avalanche, and suffocation. And fear of nuclear destruction has been the staple of innumerable mass fictions, including the song 'Eve of Destruction'.

Fear coupled with disgust is the basis of all horror fictions.[44] For the monsters who serve to demarcate this genre conceptually are not only fearsome, but impure. In the *Outer Limits* (the new series) episode entitled 'Sandkings', the proverbial mad scientist breeds hordes of insects that are not only lethally dangerous, but which elicit our repulsion toward crawling things. When armies of these creatures swarm over human bodies, one's tendency is not only to be frightened, but to gag. This is the quintessential moment in horror fiction, and literally thousands of stories, movies, TV programmes, and even rock videos have been dedicated to provoking it. The horror genre, in short, is systematically predicated on eliciting the nearly universal emotional states of fear and disgust.

Surprise figures in many mass-art genres, especially in action stories where unexpected explosions, gunshots, screams, ambushes, unholy apparitions, last-minute rescues, and the like are the order of the day. However, surprise need not only occur in violent situations. It may involve melodramatic revelations and disclosures that take the audience off-guard. Such revelations often supply the 'cliff hanger' at the end of an instalment in

---

[43] See Noël Carroll, 'The Paradox of Suspense'.
[44] This hypothesis is defended in Noël Carroll, *The Philosophy of Horror*.

soap-operas. Whole genres that are devoted to special effects also seem energized by the commitment to surprise the audience. When the mother ship finally appears at the end of *Close Encounters of the Third Kind*, the audience is surprised by its heretofore unsuspected scale, and that surprise holds the audience in rapt attention.

Many popular songs, like 'Under the Boardwalk' and the 'Good Old Summertime'—specialize in the celebration of well-being, exhilaration, and enthusiasm—a kind of overflowing happiness or exuberance, while others address a generic sense of loss, as does 'September Song' and all those songs about teenagers dying, including 'Tell Laura I Love Her' or 'Teen Angel'.

What leads researchers to say that certain emotions are nearly universal is that there are grounds for believing that they can be evoked by similar types of antecedent conditions or situations cross-culturally. Sadness, for example, is generally elicited by antecedent situations involving irrevocable loss,[45] generally of a significant other, perhaps most frequently of a family relation. Sadness of this sort, of course, is a staple of melodramas and tear-jerkers where characters are continually losing or being separated from their loved ones, including spouses, children, parents, siblings, mates, and even pets. Researchers, for example, have found that people of different cultures are able not only to recognize the sadness of the mother deer's death in *Bambi*, but to be moved by it.[46] Mukul Anand's international blockbuster *God Is My Witness* relies on wringing the maximum amount of pity through a story of separation.

In cases like these, the audience is prone to commiserate with those suffering the pangs of loss. Indeed, not only loss, but any threat to family unity can elicit pity from a mass audience. In general, misfortune, appropriately dramatized, can readily serve to elicit sorrow from randomly selected viewers, listeners, and readers.

Summarizing the immensely successful 1990s Chinese TV serial *Yearning*, Jianying Zha says of its major character Huifang: 'She has the worst luck in the world. By the end of the show, she is divorced from her ungrateful husband, hit by a car, paralyzed and bedridden, and has to give back the adopted daughter so dear to her.'[47] The scenario for *Yearning*, in turn, was based on the theme of the lost child which Zha maintains

[45] See Lazarus, 'Universals in Antecedents of Emotion', 164, and id., *Emotion and Adaptation* (New York: Oxford University Press, 1991), 249–51.

[46] James Gross and Robert Levenson, 'Emotion Elicitation Using Films', *Cognition and Emotion*, 9 (1995), 87–108.

[47] Jianying Zha, *China Pop: How Soap Operas, Tabloids and Bestsellers are Transforming a Culture* (New York: New Press, 1995), 26.

was often an important ingredient in the Taiwanese soap-operas that had already enthralled audiences on mainland China.[48] And stateside, TV tear-jerkers, like the series *Highway to Heaven*, serve up family calamities portending separations of various sorts almost on a weekly basis.

Of course, many melodramas not only involve sadness, but also elicit a species of joy or happiness (understood as an emotional episode) as well. The relevant antecedent situation for joy is the realization of a goal or, at least, progress in that direction. Thus, in one instalment of *Little House on the Prairie*—called 'The Lord Is My Shepherd'—Charles's family not only loses its first boy-child to the grim reaper, but one of his daughters, Laura, runs away from home. This latter sorrow, however, is eventually reversed when Laura is restored to the family. A similar rhythm of sorrow and joy marks the episode of *Highway to Heaven* entitled 'Thoroughbreds'. Lizzie is stricken with cancer, but her ex-husband Garth realizes that he has mis-understood her and plans to remarry her, against his wealthy father's wishes. However, at the promptings of the angelic interloper (played by Michael Landon, whose exploits the programme recounts), the father eventually relents, and the family is heartfully reunited during the wed-ding of Lizzie and Garth, thereby realizing the true goals of everyone concerned. In a slow-motion epilogue, we also learn that Lizzie has survived cancer and bears a child, recuperating past losses in a mist of joyful tears.

In melodramas, the budget of sadness and joy need not be distributed over different moments in the story. Often the self-same event can be the occasion of both sorrow and happiness. This is due to the fact that frequently an instance of loss or separation in a melodrama is also an occasion for the protagonist to exhibit a trait of character, like fortitude or self-sacrifice, that gladdens the audience as a result of its nobility. Thus, when *Stella Dallas* relinquishes her hold on her daughter, so that the daughter may flourish with all the benefits high society has to offer her, the audience is saddened, but also happy that Stella Dallas has achieved her goal and, in the process, evinced the highest degree of motherly love. Similarly, it seems to me, the most tearful moments of the movie *Backstreet* and of the novel *The Bridges of Madison County* occur when the sadnesses of the major women characters are recounted at the same time that their successful commitment to protecting others is also pronounced.

The novel *Max* by Howard Fast distributes sadness and joy in a different way. Max is a fictionalized pioneer of the movie industry. When each of his experiments—such as the introduction of the feature-length motion

---

[48] Ibid. 38.

picture—succeeds, the audience feels joy or gladness. We 'cheer him on', and when the character achieves his goal—a nearly universal antecedent for the feeling of joy or happiness—a feeling of good cheer overcomes us. But then at the end of the narrative, when through various betrayals Max irrevocably loses his studio, sadness predominates. The narrative is one of the rise and fall of Max's fortunes, and these plot turns are accompanied by alternating feelings of gladness and sorrow. Of course, some business sagas—like the tales of Horatio Alger—involve only ever mounting successes. In them, all the protagonist's aims appear to come to fruition. These genres are dedicated to provoking gladness in the audience. That is why they are referred to as 'feel-good' stories.

Thus far, I have been stressing the correlation between nearly universal emotions and specific mass-art genres. I think it is hardly surprising that the correlation is impressive, since mass art is designed for a mass audience, and since, all things being equal, nearly universal emotions can command larger audiences than more esoteric ones. Sartre's novel *Nausea*, for instance, revolves around the distinctive emotional state of existential anxiety. It takes as its object things that the major character Roquentin regards as meaningless. The perceived meaningless of the universe is the cause of a kind of visceral loathing in him. But in so far as the emotion in question is a rather specialized one, *Nausea* is an unlikely subject for a mass artwork. The emotions associated with filial affection, as in *Bambi*, on the other hand, are, since filial affection is widely distributed in a way that a background in the dialectics of being is not. Thus, melodrama, rather than existentialist philosophy, is the sort of thing we find dominating pulp fiction, TV, movies, and popular songs. *Angst*, of the Sartrean variety, is too esoteric an emotion for uptake on a large scale.

By associating specific mass-art genres with nearly universal emotions, I do not mean to suggest that the elicitation of emotions, like fear or cheer, figures all and only in response to certain specifiable genres. By focusing on the way in which many genres are predicated on evoking specifiable emotions—like horror and revenge—I mean only to point to some graphic evidence of the correlation of mass art to nearly universal emotions. But, at the same time, it is also true that individual works in each genre of mass art may elicit a gamut of nearly universal emotions in the course of their narration. Anger, hatred, fear, disgust, surprise, joy, and sadness can alternate in every sort of mass artwork. Though specific genres may place primary emphasis on eliciting certain emotions above all—in the way that horror stresses the fear/disgust complex—each genre may exploit the resources of many nearly universal emotions in order to keep the audience glued to the story on a moment-to-moment basis.

Anger, for example, appears across mass-art genres and is remarkably pervasive. Danielle Steel's bestseller *Malice*, though ultimately a melodrama with a happy ending, crucially depends upon enlisting the reader's indignation at the characters who victimize Grace, beginning with her father who sexually abuses her and continuing through a host of other exploitative male figures. The novel rides on engendering feelings of injustice in us on behalf of Grace. So many recent potboilers—like Mary Higgins Clark's *Where Are the Children?* and *Gerald's Game* and *Dolores Claiborne* by Stephen King—are organized around the issue of child abuse because it is virtually guaranteed to mobilize the audience's anger and indignation in ways that accelerate the intensity of the overarching feelings of suspense that grips the reader.

Moreover, perhaps needless to say, anger can appear as an ingredient in any mass-art genre. Heroes and heroines generally stand in opposition to nemeses who thwart their projects. These can range from obdurate parents to alien emperors. These are characters whom we love to hate, such as Jennifer Malone in Michael Crichton's *Airframe* and Daphne in Danielle Steel's *Lightning*. The degree to which anger supplies a major bond to mass narrative fictions is quite arresting. Hatred, one is tempted to say, is a major calling-card of mass art. Furthermore, the anger that we bring to bear on antagonists—because of the wrongs they inflict on the protagonists—also encourages a taste for revenge in us, inviting us to stay with the story in the hope that the villains will be dealt their well-deserved punishment.[49]

Likewise, the kind of joy or happiness or gladness or good cheer that accompanies the realization of a goal or project is in evidence across mass-art genres whenever the protagonists secure their ends, whether those ends be marriage, some sort of martial victory, success in business, the discovery of a lost child, the elimination of a monster, and so on.[50] In these cases, the audience feels happy not because of some accomplishment of its own, but because someone for whom the audience possesses a pro-attitude, such as care or concern, has secured his/her/their ends. And this can occur at virtually any point in virtually any mass-art genre.

Nearly universal emotions are elicited by mass artworks because such works recurrently address such widespread human interests as love, sex, violence, mystery, heroism, and wealth.[51] But by emphasizing

---

[49] The song 'These Boots Were Made For Walking' is perhaps a musical example of a mass artwork predicated on revenge.

[50] Joy, of course, need not only be a response to a character's realization of a goal. The TV series *Cheers* specialized in another kind of happiness—a pervasive sense of belonging.

[51] Samuel P. Huntington, *The Clash of Civilizations and the Remaking of World Order* (New York: Simon and Schuster, 1996), 58.

the correlation between mass art and nearly universal emotions, I do not mean to gainsay that mass artworks may not also address more culturally specific emotions. Many American mass artworks, for example, make a special fetish out of Christmas, presumably in the expectation that Yuletide imagery will stir up a wealth of warm emotional associations in viewers, listeners, and readers. Obviously, the accessibility of these emotions has a certain cultural specificity. They may not be available to all peoples, everywhere. Nevertheless, it should also be clear that when not nearly universal emotions, such as what we might call Christmas cheer (or nostalgia), are the subject of a mass artwork, the emotions in question still have to be fairly pervasive.

Christmas cheer is not a nearly universal emotion and it is culturally specific, but, at the same time, it is very widespread across its target audiences. Indeed, it is probably the case that even those who have no antecedent associations with Christmas can develop some appropriate emotional responses to the relevant imagery, since it usually betokens belonging, especially familial belonging (a theme of nearly universal resonance). But, be that as it may, it is still the case that where a mass artwork traffics in culturally specific emotions, it will ideally gravitate to those culturally specific emotions that are widely accessible to its culturally specific target audience.

Christmas cheer is not universal, but it is widely available in Christian audiences, especially American ones. That is, the emotional address of works of this sort—like 'White Christmas'—will still aim at engaging mass audiences and, thus, at enlisting the emotional resources that vast numbers of people possess. Undoubtedly, Mary Higgins Clark's *Silent Night* gains added poignancy by situating the kidnapping of the seven-year-old Brian on Christmas Eve, thereby correlating the reunion of the Dornan family with Christendom's celebration of its first family.

Critical to an audience's capacity to be moved by a mass fiction is its ability to recognize the emotional states that the relevant characters exhibit. Our pity for a character who has been separated from her husband depends, in large measure, on our recognition that she has been saddened by this event. For if she is glad to be rid of him, then, all things being equal, there will be little cause for us to pity her. We must recognize that she is miserable, and that her misery is part of her misfortune.

This is not to say that our sorrow for such a character is identical to hers. We are not sad because we have lost our own spouse. Her sorrow has her husband as its object, whereas our sadness has as its object her sorrow. Her sadness and pain contribute to our sadness for her (it is part of her misfortune), but it is not the same as her sadness, since we are sorry that she is feeling the disturbing pangs of her sadness, while she, presumably, is not focusing reflexively on the discomfiture of her psychological state.

A great many of the emotions that are directed at mass artworks are of this sort. The emotional states that characters undergo are material to our own emotional responses to the characters in question. We feel anger on behalf of a character in part because he feels insulted. We do not feel insulted, but we are angry that the object of our pro attitude has been insulted. Thus, in order to be moved by mass artworks of this sort, the fictions must be such that readers, viewers, and listeners are able to recognize the emotional states of the characters in such stories. That is, the capacity to recognize what emotional states a character is in is often a condition for responding with emotional appropriateness to a mass artwork.

And in this respect, the relevance of nearly universal emotions surfaces once again. For not only are certain emotional states shared cross-culturally, but so is the human capacity to recognize certain emotions. One reason that familial loss is such a recurrent theme in mass fictions undoubtedly has to do with the fact that most audiences can readily identify the emotions that the victims of such misfortunes, like Bambi, are suffering. Thus, mass artworks, again given their preoccupation with wide-scale accessibility, tend to portray states of affairs and events whose emotional effects on characters will be readily recognized by mass audiences either because the emotional states of the characters in question are of a nearly universal sort, or otherwise widely pervasive culturally.

For the purpose of demonstrating the importance of nearly universal emotions and the recognition thereof for mass art, it is instructive to conclude this section by looking in depth at the way in which one of the most frequently deployed structures of communication in mass art depends on these phenomena in order to function effectively. The structure that I have in mind is point-of-view editing. It is a staple device in film and TV, and something very much like it is often used in comic-book illustration.

Point-of-view editing is a widely used technique.[52] One commentator claims that it amounts to as many as 97% of the cuts in contemporary television.[53] This is undoubtedly a much higher rate of incidence than one would find in the majority of theatrically released films. However, few mass-distribution films forgo the use of this device entirely, and most

[52] According to David Bordwell, the technique I am about to discuss is more technically called eyeline matching. I'm not completely convinced of this. However, be that as it may, I will continue to call it point-of-view editing, since I think that this is how most non-specialist readers use the term.
[53] Paul Messaris, *Visual Literacy: Image, Mind and Reality* (Boulder: Westview Press, 1994), 85.

films resort to it many times in the course of a narrative. The introduction and popularization of this device in the early decades of this century is always listed among the major stylistic breakthroughs in film style. By anyone's account, it is a central structure of the international mode of communication known as motion pictures (under which rubric I mean to include TV). What is less frequently appreciated, however, is that this device depends generally upon the recognitional capacities of mass audiences to identify nearly universal emotions.

The point-of-view schema is minimally comprised of two images—the point/glance shot and the point/object shot.[54] The point/glance shot involves a character in the act of looking, generally off-screen (or, in comics, off-panel). The point/object shot then follows, putatively showing us what the person in the point/glance shot sees. The elements in this structure can be iterated. Often in early cinema, the structure as a whole was repeated several times, but nowadays it is customary to exhibit the pattern only once.

Moreover, the point/glance shot may precede the point/object shot, or the order may be reversed, giving rise to what Edward Branigan calls respectively the prospective and the retrospective structures of point-of-view editing. Through the point-of-view schema, the author can narrate by showing us what a character is looking at and, thereby, indicate what is on her mind, as well as conveying with some precision what the character feels about whatever it is that she is seeing. Given the pervasiveness of this structure, the question naturally arises as to how mass audiences are able to understand such editing patterns so effortlessly.

An important clue to answering this question is recent psychological research that supports the hypothesis that for certain *basic* ranges of emotional expression cross-culturally humans are able to recognize and identify emotional states on the basis of facial expression alone.[55] It is well known that humans have an innate capacity to recognize the faces of other humans as human. But it also appears to be the case that affect manifested by the face, to a certain extent, can also be readily identified by means of our natural recognitional capacities.

That is, when members of divergent cultural groups, including peoples unfamiliar with mass-media representations, are shown pictures of facial

---

[54] Edward Branigan, *Point of View in the Cinema* (Amsterdam: Mouton Publishers, 1984), 103.

[55] See Paul Ekman, 'Expression and the Nature of Emotion', in *Approaches to Emotion*, ed. Klaus Scherer and Paul Ekman (Hillsdale, NJ: Lawrence Erlbaum, 1984), 319–43; id., 'Cross-Cultural Studies of Facial Expression', in *Darwin and Facial Expression*, ed. Paul Ekman (New York: Academic Press, 1973), 169–222; id. and Wallace Friesen, *Unmasking the Face* (Cambridge: Cambridge University Press, 1972); eid. and Phoebe Ellsworth, *Emotion in the Human Face* (Englewood Cliffs, NJ: Prentice-Hall, 1975); Carroll Izard, *The Face of Emotion* (New York: Appleton-Crofts, 1971).

expressions of emotion, they converge in their categorization of the emotions in the pictures they are exposed to, at rates that preclude the possibility that the coincidence is random. People, indeed people from different cultures, are able to identify certain rudimentary ranges of affect—including enjoyment/joy; surprise/startle; distress/anguish; disgust/contempt; anger/rage; shame/humiliation; and fear/terror—on the basis of facial expression.[56]

Moreover, it seems reasonable on the grounds of such empirical evidence to suppose that the existence of this recognitional capacity is important to the way in which point-of-view editing secures uptake.[57] That is, the point/glance shot in the point-of-view figure is able to convey information to mass audiences about the emotional states of characters. An obvious hypothesis here is that it is likely that the point-of-view structure is able to do this by activating the spectator's innate capacities to recognize the gross category into which a character's facial expression falls. In short, the point/glance shot is a device that is predicated upon engaging natural recognitional capacities in such a way that mass audiences are able to identify the global emotional state of the relevant character in the point/glance shot.

This is not to deny that audiences may also determine the emotional state of the character in virtue of the narrative context of a motion picture or illustrated comic. Rather, my point is simply that in addition to the narrative context, the facial expression of the character in the point/glance shot provides further information about the character's emotional state. And, of course, the point/glance shot can also supply that information about the character's emotional state by itself, where the narrative context has not prepared us for it.

However, I do not want to overestimate the importance of the point/glance shot for the point-of-view figure. Both the point/glance and the point/object shot contribute to the expression of character emotion via point-of-view editing. The point/glance shot activates our recognition of the global emotional state of the character. But then the point/object further refines our understanding of the character's emotional state.

[56] Indeed, another sort of evidence for the hypothesis for the cross-cultural correlation of certain facial expressions with certain basic emotions is that blind children exhibit the same facial expressions for the relevant emotions that sighted people do. But how is that possible, unless certain aspects of emotional expression are innate? Moreover, there is a ready evolutionary explanation for this inasmuch as emotional display is a crucial factor in communication between conspecifics. That is, it is an adaptive advantage, for all sorts of reasons, that humans are able to recognize—almost automatically—many of the emotional states that fellow members of their species are in.

[57] Though I am here discussing the relevance of this recognitional capacity to point-of-view editing, this phenomenon is also relevant to other shooting formats, such as the deep-focus, long shot wherein we may see the face of one character responding emotionally to something else on screen.

The emotions expressed by motion pictures are often fine-grained. The fear on the character's face is not fear *simpliciter*, but vertigo in the film of the same name. How do we get from recognition of the global emotion of fear, signalled by the point/glance shot, to the more specific realization that the fear in question is vertigo? It is here that the contribution of the point/object shot becomes especially relevant. For the point/object shot presents the audience with the object of the character's emotional state.

As we have already seen, emotions are marked by intentionality. That is, they are directed. One is jealous *of* someone. One is not characteristically just afraid. One is afraid *of* something or someone. Emotions have objects—objects toward which they are directed: the person of whom I am jealous, or the thing of which I am afraid. In some cases, the object of my emotional state may also be its cause.[58] Moreover, the way in which I perceive the object of my emotional state serves to identify the nature of the emotional state in which I find myself. If the object of my state is something that I regard to be harmful, then the emotional state I am in is fear; if the object of my state is someone who I think has wronged me or mine, then the state is anger. Thus, in supplying us with the object of the character's emotional state, the point/object shot in the point-of-view schema helps to define the emotional state of the character.

Though the human face can give us very broad, generally reliable information about the basic emotional states of others, that information can still be somewhat ambiguous. It may be hard for us to differentiate closely related emotions like fear and surprise, or to specify the emotion in a fine-grained way. Is this the face of a lover, a religious worshipper, or a patriot? In order to arrive at more fine-grained discriminations, we generally depend upon knowing the object and/or cause of the emotional state. And when it comes to point-of-view editing, the point/object shot generally supplies us with this information.

That is, the function of the point/object shot is to supply the audience with the cause and/or object of the character's emotional state in order to define the emotional state of the character in a fine-grained way. In *Vertigo*, the character who is terrified of heights attempts to overcome his phobia by climbing up a short kitchen ladder. Suddenly, his face, shown to us in a point/glance shot, manifests terror. Then the point/object shot shows us the object of his emotion. He is looking, not at the floor, but out the window and down at the street several storeys below him. Once apprised

[58] Helen Nissenbaum, *Emotion and Focus* (Stanford, Calif.: Stanford University Center for the Study of Language and Information, 1985), 15–21.

of the object of his emotion, we are able to specify it. It is not merely fear; more precisely, it is fear of heights. It is vertigo.

The relation of the point/glance shot to the point/object shot, where point-of-view editing is being used to portray character emotion, has a reciprocal structure. The point/glance shot sets forth a global range of emotions that we recognize as broadly characterizing the neighbourhood of affective states that the character could be in. Then, the point/object shot shows us the object and/or cause of the emotion, thereby enabling us to focus upon the particular emotion—within the affective range set by the point/glance shot—that pertains to the character in question. The point/object shot focuses or selects the particular emotion being portrayed, out of the wider spectrum of emotional timbres afforded by the point/glance shot.

In other words, the point/glance shot functions as a *range finder*, whereas the point/object shot functions as a *focuser*, specifying the relevant affect of the character as a particular emotional state within the range set out by the point/glance shot. Thus, both the point/glance shot and the point/object shot are key in the articulation of character emotion by means of editing.

Moreover, in addition to the preceding reciprocal relation between the point/glance and the point/object shot, there are further functional relationships within the point-of-view structure. For example, broadly speaking, the point/glance shot provides the viewer with a rough guide to what is emotionally salient about the point/object shot. The reason for this has to do with the fact, as we have seen, that emotional states of a given sort are typically elicited by objects that share certain general characteristics or that meet certain criteria. The emotion of disgust, for instance, is elicited by objects that the emoter regards as noxious or impure. Thus, when a point/glance shot represents a character evincing the global state of disgust, that primes the viewer to expect that whatever is eliciting this state will meet the criterion of impurity. In a manner of speaking, the point/glance shot criterially prefocuses the point/object shot. Consequently, when the point/object shot arrives on the screen, the viewer will survey it in terms of those features that correspond to impurity—to the zombie's festering sores rather than to his Gucci loafers.

The point/glance shot provides a rough anticipation of what, emotionally speaking, should be salient in the point/object shot. So, if the point/glance shot presents us with a character transfixed by fear, then that indicates that we should attend to the lethal axe being wielded in the ensuing point/object shot and not to the flowers in the background.

In this way, the point/glance shot in the point-of-view structure functions as a means for managing the audience's attention.

In mass-art spectacles, the point-of-view structure functions because of the way in which the point/glance shot engages our constitutional make-up in terms of activating our cross-culturally endowed capacity to recognize at least certain gross categories of emotions. But the assimilation of the point/object shot in mass artworks also depends on the audience's generic emotional capacities, since, in order to be comprehended, the situations depicted in the point/object shots are generally either situations that are nearly universal antecedents for basic emotional states or, if they are not universal antecedents, they need to be widely pervasive ones, particularly where they are targeted at culturally specific audiences. Thus, the existence of generic emotions, especially of the nearly universal variety, is key to the operation of the point-of-view schema which, in turn, is one of the central narrative devices for communication in the visual repertory of mass art. That is, it is the existence of nearly universal emotions and of recognitional capacities that can track them that makes point-of-view editing, as a particularly viable structure of mass art, possible. Such editing would be inaccessible for mass audiences if it did not exploit generic features of the emotional make-up of vast numbers of spectators.

Not only entire mass-art genres, but also its small-scale communicative structures, like point-of-view editing, are connected to the activation of the generic emotional capacities of its audiences. Mass art has no special purchase on the emotions. All sorts of artworks engage the emotions. But mass art does, for what we called in the previous chapter design considerations, take a special, though not unique, interest in the basic or nearly universal emotional capacities that viewers, listeners, and readers possess, so to speak, as part of their standard operating equipment. Mass art presupposes the existence of such emotional equipment for success (uptake) not only at the level of specific scenes and overarching narrative structures, but also at the level of small-scale structuration, such as point-of-view editing. Mass art does not engage the emotions differently from other artistic practices. But it does have a noteworthy affinity for basic emotions (and otherwise widely distributed emotions).

Concluding remarks

Having associated mass art with basic or nearly universal or even just widely pervasive (though culturally specific) emotions, I may appear to have conceded to one of the arguments against mass art that was presented by Collingwood in the first chapter of this book. Collingwood, it will be recalled, dismissed mass art on the grounds that it was involved exclusively in the arousal of canned emotions. Haven't I just granted him his point by contending that, given the nature of mass art, it has a tendency to gravitate toward the elicitation of basic or nearly universal emotions?

Not really. For Collingwood, the expression of originally experienced emotions in contrast to the arousal of what he thinks of as canned emotions marks the boundary between authentic art and amusement art. I, on the other hand, not only question whether it is appropriate to think of basic or nearly universal emotions as necessarily 'canned', but, on the other hand, I also deny that his putative distinction can actually distinguish, in a classificatory sense, between art properly so called and pseudo-art. On any fair view of the history of art, I think it is undeniable that major works in the canon are dedicated to arousing basic or nearly universal emotions. Such works are typically appreciated because of their power to evoke basic or nearly universal emotions. Thus, that mass art, among other sorts of art, stimulates basic emotional responses should not disqualify it from the order of art, inasmuch as commerce with basic emotions is frequently what reasonable art appreciators admire about the achievements of so-called high art. Mass art may have a functional affinity for the basic emotions that is not necessarily shared by every other sort of art. But that feature notwithstanding, in so far as addressing basic emotions is a legitimate feature of canonical art, it cannot be held against mass art.

Earlier, we quoted Abraham Kaplan who maintains that mass art is shallow because it 'wallows' in superficial emotions. But, in response, I would argue not only that the emotions as such are not necessarily superficial, but also that it is a mistake to suppose that the emotions engaged by mass art are inevitably shallow. I agree that for design reasons mass art is apt to gravitate toward nearly universal or, at least, widely pervasive emotions. But it is surely an error to conflate generically distributed emotions with shallow emotions. Nearly universal emotions can certainly be deep. Sadness over the loss of a loved one is not shallow just because it is experienced by nearly everyone. Kaplan's contention here may rest upon supposing that something that is *widely* distributed must be shallow, but, then again, a river that is broad can also be very deep.

Of course, in defending mass art against Collingwood and Kaplan, I do not want to leave the impression that I think that there is no room to criticize the emotional address of mass art. However, I think that such criticism should be done on a case-by-case basis. I believe that summary dismissals of mass art *tout court* on the basis of the way in which it excites audiences emotionally is ill-advised. But this is not to deny that particular mass artworks may be chastised for the inappropriateness of their emotional address.

As Aristotle noted, appropriateness with respect to an emotion is a matter of bringing the right emotion to bear on the right object with the right level of intensity for the right reason. This suggests that there are several grounds from which to criticize the emotional address of a mass artwork. A mass artwork can be judged to be emotionally inappropriate, for example, if it mismatches the emotion it propones with an unsuitable object, as it might if it encourages race hatred (for example, Nazi propaganda fictions that portray Jewish people as insects or vermin for the purpose of eliciting disgust).

Or, a work may be open to criticism, if the level of emotional intensity that it engenders is out of proportion with its object. Many mass artworks that are called sentimental (in the sense that the emotions they invite are excessive) may offend in this direction; too much angst over the death of a dog might be an example here (though not one apt to persuade dog-lovers). And, undoubtedly, many pop love songs may lavish too much fervour over slight infatuations. Lastly, in addition, emotional episodes in mass art can also be criticized on the grounds that they elicit certain emotions for the wrong reasons—by, for example, intercutting images of Stalin with battle scenes so as to suggest that the grounds for cheering the defeat of fascism is simply that it makes Papa Joe happy.

Emotions, then, can be criticized or, as we shall see in the next chapter, commended on the basis of their objects, their intensity, and their motivating reasons. This is true not only of 'real life' emotions, but also of the emotions elicited by mass art. The Platonists are wrong to reject the emotional address of mass art across the board. But it would be equally wrong to suggest that there is never anything problematic about the emotions elicited by certain mass artworks. However, where problems arise with respect to the emotional address of mass art, it is at the level of particular works and not at the level of mass art as such. Quite frequently, these problems will arise because of the way in which the emotions are connected to morality. Thus, to complete this discussion of the relation of mass art to the emotions, we must turn to a discussion of the relation of mass art to morality.

5 Mass Art and Morality

Introduction

Perhaps the greatest anxieties about mass art concern morality. During the 1996 presidential campaign in the United States, Democrats and Republicans vied with each other to see who could raise the greater alarm about the moral dangers of mass art. While at the same time pocketing enormous campaign contributions from leaders in the entertainment industry, Bill Clinton, taking his cue from Bob Dole, used the presidency as a 'bully pulpit', urging Hollywood, TV, and the music industry to clean up their act.[1] In America, politicians and other pundits are fond of citing statistics about the number of hours children spend before the TV set, contrasting it with the number of hours they spend in school. Emboldened by these figures, they are wont to declare that TV has become the major educator of Americans, and, when it comes to moral education, the mass media are generally found to be wanting on every side. Thus, special computer chips—V-chips—are being installed in every newly manufactured TV set in order to assure that our children will not be corrupted.

Of course, such criticisms of the mass media in Western Culture harken back to Plato. For Plato's suspicion of the relationship of art to the emotions was ultimately motivated by ethical concerns, since the emotions are connected to action. Plato's fear was that by roiling the emotions, art was apt to give rise to ethically unpalatable behaviours, encouraging not only specific, morally obnoxious emotional dispositions like cowardice,

---

[1] After denouncing the entertainment industry for their indulgence of violence, both Clinton and Dole went on record—this time Dole imitating Clinton—praising *Independence Day*, a film in which probably more human beings are wantonly murdered than in any other in recent memory.

but also promoting a general tendency to relax the vigilance of reason over behaviour, thereby giving vent to irrational impulses that would finally manifest themselves in anti-social activities.

Present-day Platonists likewise fear that mass art will produce similar effects in contemporary audiences. They worry that mass art provides bad role models with whom spectators are bound to identify, resulting, in all manner of wickedness, especially in terms of rampant violence and sexual promiscuity. They also predict that the audiences of mass art will derive morally false beliefs from their TV and movie screens which, in turn, will motivate immoral behaviour. With respect to sexually graphic mass art, for example, feminists frequently charge that pornography is the theory and rape is the practice. The underlying thought here is that mass art disseminates morally flawed views and sentiments that will then erupt into everyday life with disastrous repercussions morally.

This general cultural preoccupation with the moral threat posed by mass art is also reflected in academia. For as mass art becomes increasingly central as an object of university study in humanities departments, it is treated primarily as a phenomenon that requires intense moral scrutiny. Academic paper after academic paper interrogates selected mass artworks for their contributions to racism, sexism, homophobia, classism, and so on. And though admittedly often excessive, and sometimes even paranoid, this academic obsession with the moral significance of mass art is certainly humane and has a point, since I think that most of us would agree that mass art has *something* to do with morality. The question is how to be more explicit about what that 'something' comes to.

Obviously, the moral considerations that energize contemporary academic concern with the morals of mass art are often very different from the issues that irritate politicians, especially conservative ones. Nevertheless, there is an apparent consensus among contemporary public spokespersons—including academics, religious leaders, and politicos—that responsible talk about mass art should address its moral credentials.

Of course, there also is an important difference worth noting between Plato and contemporary critics of the morals of mass art. Plato was convinced that art *as such* was necessarily morally corrupting. His was a blanket criticism of art. Contemporary critics, on the other hand, are somewhat more judicious. They do not believe (rightly, I think) that all mass art is necessarily damnable. Even if much of it is, for them, the situation is remediable, since mass art can serve the forces of light as well as those of darkness. For contemporary critics, the cure for what is wrong with mass art is more mass art, but mass art committed to morally enlightened perspectives.

Nevertheless, contemporary critics of mass art do agree with Plato in the belief that art needs to be discussed and assessed morally, although, unlike Plato they allow that these assessments can be variable. Not all art nor even all mass art is irredeemably evil, as Plato would have thought. Even if much of it is wicked, that does not preclude the possibility that mass art might also be a force for positive moral education. Plato thought that if poetry was the educator of the Greeks, it should be replaced by philosophy. Contemporary critics think that if predominantly bad mass art is the educator of modern audiences, then it should be replaced by morally enlightened mass art. The common assumption here is that mass art is connected to moral education and that it can be assessed ethically in light of its contribution to moral education.

I do not wish to challenge this view.[2] I take it that this is virtually self-evident. However, these assumptions do raise certain theoretical questions about the specific ways in which art, including mass art, intersects with moral education, and about how the relation of mass art to moral education provides grounds for evaluating mass art morally. Thus, in this chapter my central concern will be with developing a theory of a general relation of mass art to morality, especially with an eye to showing how my conception of that relation can provide a basis for evaluating the moral status of particular mass artworks. Unlike Plato, I do not think that we can render a summary judgement on (mass) art—claiming that it is all (morally) bad. Rather, we must proceed on a case-by-case basis. But having said that much, I owe it to the reader to provide some general guidance about how we might handle the particular cases.

As I have already mentioned, a great deal of contemporary criticism of mass art presupposes that it can be discussed and evaluated morally. However, little effort has been devoted to working out the theoretical foundations of the moral criticism of mass art by contemporary commentators of mass art, especially those in the humanities who identify themselves with cultural studies and who make such criticism their bread and butter. In general, they presume the possibility of the moral criticism of mass art without demonstrating its foundations. Thus, in this chapter I will attempt to suggest a foundation for the discussion and evaluation of mass art (or, at least, much mass art) from a moral point of view. Of course, in pointing out that there has been little sustained work on this topic in the

---

[2] Possible challenges to the view that art, including (presumably) mass art, has nothing to do with moral education are frequently advanced by those whom I have elsewhere called autonomists. For arguments against autonomism, see Noël Carroll, 'Moderate Moralism', *British Journal of Aesthetics*, 36/3 (July 1996), 223–38; and id., 'Art, Narrative and Moral Understanding', in *Aesthetics and Ethics*, ed. Jerrold Levinson (Cambridge: Cambridge University Press, forthcoming).

humanities, I do not mean to suggest that there are no existing views available. So, in order to motivate my own position, I will begin by looking at some influential existing perspectives, examining their shortcomings in the hope of preparing the ground dialectically for my own proposals.

Consequentialism, propositionalism, and identificationism

Though contemporary academic criticism of mass art, especially of the cultural studies variety, is notorious for its frequently abstruse jargon, many of the fundamental ideas that it presupposes as a basis for criticizing mass art morally are not very different from ideas found in the broader culture and employed not only in journalism, but also in everyday conversation about mass art. Three such ideas are what may be called *consequentialism, propositionalism*, and *identificationism*, respectively. By introducing these terms as labels for *three* different ideas, I do not mean to suggest that they are mutually exclusive. They can be connected in various ways, and I conjecture that many people, even most people, including both academics and plain speakers, often hold all three. Nevertheless, they are discriminable.

By *consequentialism*, I mean to refer to the belief that mass artworks have causal consequences, of a predictable sort, for the moral behaviour of viewers, listeners, and readers. Exposure to mass art influences or shapes behaviour. This part of the consequentialist hypothesis is advanced as commonsensical. Especially given the amount of exposure to which the average audience member submits himself/herself, mass art would, it is said, have to have *some* effect, So much, it would seem, stands to reason.

However, the consequentialist also believes that one can say fairly accurately what those behavioural consequences are likely to be. Violent mass art will promote violent behaviour; lascivious mass art will cause sexual promiscuity of a morally undesirable sort. Moreover, the consequentialist is able to ground the moral evaluation of particular mass artworks on the basis of its predicted behavioural effects. Violent mass art can be condemned as morally evil because it ostensibly results in aggressive activity; lascivious mass art is bad because it is said to cause sexual exploitation.

On the other hand, consequentialism also has the wherewithal to render variable moral assessments of mass art. Mass art that represents and/or recommends tolerance will count, all things being equal, as good, in so far as it promotes tolerant behaviour in whatever way lascivious mass art provokes sexually exploitative behaviour.[3] For the consequentialist, it is the presumed moral status of the putatively predictable consequences of consuming certain types of mass art that determines the moral status of the pertinent mass art. Consequentialism, then, provides a clear-cut way to evaluate mass art morally.

Of course, a commitment to consequentialism need not coincide with a willingness to evaluate art variably. Plato was a consequentialist, and, as a result of his predictions about art, he declared it all condemnable. But contemporary critics seem to agree that mass art might be morally good or bad. It all depends upon what these critics presume about the moral status of the consequences that they predict concerning the works in question.

Moreover, I submit, if push comes to shove, and one demands to know the grounds for their moral assessments of the relevant artworks, most critics nowadays will—sooner or later—advert to the consequences they believe that the work wil bring about in the pertinent audiences. That is, even if this is not the initial charge they make, in the background they will harbour a conviction about the behavioural consequences of particular artworks, and they will transfer their moral assessments of those presumed behavioural consequences to the artwork itself.

If consequentialism supplies the leading candidate for grounding the moral assessment of mass artworks, there still remains a question about the way in which the mass artwork manages to bring about the relevant behavioural consequences. What is the mechanism or the set of mechanisms that impel the predicted behaviour whose moral status enables the consequentialist to assess the mass artwork. Here, there are at least two popular candidates for identifying the operative mechanism. One is propositionalism, while the other might be called identificationism. Again a critic might believe that the mechanisms isolated by these positions are *both* relevant to producing the behavioural effects in question and even that they work in tandem. But since the mechanisms are discriminable in principle, let us discuss them one at a time.

According to the *propositionalist*,[4] the artwork may contain certain

---

[3] Undoubtedly, one 'way' such works might be said to promote the behaviour in question is by making it appear attractive. How exactly authors make such behaviours attractive, in turn, would then need to be investigated by means of textual analysis, perhaps in conjunction with psychological experimentation.

[4] See Morris Weitz, 'Truth in Literature', *Revue internationale de philosophie*, 9 (1955), 116–29; John Hospers, 'Implied Truths in Literature', *Journal of Aesthetics and Art Criticism*, 19 (1960–1), 37–47; Peter McCormick, 'Moral Knowledge and Fiction', in his book *Fictions, Philosophies and the Problems of Poetics* (Ithaca, NY: Cornell University Press, 1988), 106–30; Gerald Graff, *Literature Against Itself: Literary Ideas in Modern Society* (Chicago: University of Chicago Press, 1979); Peter Lamarque and Stein Haugom Olsen, 'The Propositional Theory of Literary Truth', in their book *Truth, Fiction and Literature: A Philosophical Perspective* (Oxford: Clarendon Press, 1994), 289–321.

propositions, either explicitly or implicitly.[5] These propositions may also be moral in nature.[6] Often they take the form of general moral (or immoral) maxims.[7] For example, some feminists believe that pornography generically implies—even if it does not state outright—that women are merely objects whose sole purpose is to pleasure males.[8] Pornography, on

[5] A work may state certain propositions outright. Think of a silent film with an intertitle that says 'All people should love one another'. Or, the proposition may be put in the mouth of a protagonist whose authority is not only unchallenged, but endorsed by the work in question. Imagine a reverential video fiction of Christ delivering the Sermon on the Mount. Or, the proposition in question can be implied, entailed, or presupposed by the work. It might never be explicitly presented, but nevertheless the work may appear committed to it. Since most propositional critical interpretation is of this sort, my examples will generally be of propositions that are putatively implicit in artworks. Perhaps critics are most frequently drawn to these sorts of propositions because they often require an interpretation to unearth them, and most critics are in the business of interpreting. In a moment I will talk about how such propositions might be said to be implied by mass artworks. But, in any event, the reader should not take my emphasis on implicit propositions as I signal that I think that propositionalism is not also a doctrine concerning explicit propositions.

[6] The propositions may also concern non-moral affairs. Propositionalism is not only a doctrine about the acquisition of moral knowledge and/or beliefs. It can be a doctrine about the acquisition of any kind of knowledge and/or belief from artworks. For example, one might say a given novel is about the theme that everyone is mortal, or that love is fleeting, or that Napoleon was a genius. However, since this chapter is concerned with moral education, I will restrict my attention to propositionalism as it pertains to morality.

[7] Propositionalism need not be restricted to general propositions. A given work may—explicitly or implicitly—convey propositions about particulars. Here, the work may be a source of knowledge and/ or beliefs—moral or otherwise—about individuals. For example, a movie might convey the proposition that Rasputin was mad, that New York is disgusting, or that Henry VIII was evil. Nevertheless, it does seem that academic critics usually prefer to look for general propositions or themes when they interpret artworks. For example, in *Structuralist Poetics*, Jonathan Culler, perhaps following Aristotle, suggests that there is a convention of reading literature that tells us to read for highly general significance. I am not sure what Culler thinks justifies this convention, but I do think that Culler's citation of this supposed convention at least tracks the standard operating procedure of most exegetes (who are usually propositionalists) in the contemporary literary establishment.

The question of why there should be a preference for finding general rather than particular propositions in literary interpretation is an intriguing theoretical issue, but not one to be explored at this time. However, since I think that most propositionalists nowadays act as though there is a bias in favour of general propositions, my examples will be of that sort, though I readily admit that a propositionalist could be a particularist, even in terms of moral content. One would still be a propositionalist if one maintained that a story implied (or stated outright) that King John was a thug.

For Culler on general significance, see Jonathan Culler, *Structuralist Poetics: Structuralism, Linguistics and the Study of Literature* (Ithaca, NY: Cornell University Press, 1975), 115.

[8] Some feminists, like Catherine McKinnon and Andrea Dworkin, take this to be the definition of pornography. Many, including other feminists, have pointed out that this is not an empirically convincing generalization about pornography under any pretheoretical understanding of the concept of pornography. That is, examples can be produced of what we pretheoretically think of as pornography where women are not represented as merely the tools of male pleasure, but are fully co-participants in the erotic fun and games. And there is also male, homosexual pornography that has no women in it. So, it might be argued that the correlation of pornography with female subjection is purely stipulative—a definition masquerading as an empirical generalization. However, a propositionalist who is also a feminist need not be deterred by these objections so long as she/he only claims that some pornography is of the sort that implies that all women are the morally appropriate object of male sexual domination, or even that some women—say those who wear short skirts—should be regarded as sex toys for men.

For MacKinnon's and Dworkin's characterization of pornography, see Indianapolis and Marion County, Ind. Ordinance 35, sec. 2 #16–3 (15 June 1984).

this account, contravenes the Kantian moral principle that all persons should be treated not merely as means, but as ends. Pornography reduces female persons to the status of objects, often called 'sexual objects'. Indeed, pornography is said to entail and to endorse an alternative principle to that which recognizes persons as ends in themselves, namely, the principle that women are nothing but a means to male pleasure, or even that women should be regarded as nothing but instruments of male sexual desire. At the very least, if such an account of all or even some pornography is accurate, the propositionalist could condemn the pornographic works in question for their expression of immoral ideas.

Moreover, it is easy to see how one might go about connecting propositionalism to consequentialism. The propositionalist may argue that a work of art may not only express a moral belief;[9] it may also promote it—that is to say, encourage its adoption, perhaps by making it seem attractive. A pornographic video or novel may give people moral, or, according to feminists, immoral ideas. Pornography is said, by certain feminists, to function as a potential *source* of immoral beliefs.

Furthermore, if these moral beliefs become incorporated in the viewer's, listener's, or reader's cognitive stock, they can provide a motive for action—a pretext for men to treat women in morally demeaning ways. And if the feminist critic presumes that this is likely to happen on a regular, predictable, and wide-scale basis, then she becomes a consequentialist as described above. She condemns pornography on the grounds of its predictable propensity to play a causal role in the aetiology of immoral behaviour—the treatment of women as merely means by men. The extreme form of this behaviour is rape. Thus, the dictum that pornography is the theory and rape is the practice is really a combination of propositionalism (pornography is the theory) and consequentialism (rape is the practice).[10]

Of course, the propositionalist need not only assess mass art negatively. One may also find with certain works that the propositions implied are morally correct, and, then, if one is, in addition, a consequentialist, one may commend the work in question on the supposition that it will encourage morally admirable behaviour. Thus, some feminists might

[9] Propositionalists may differ here over whether they regard artworks as a source of belief or of knowledge. Since, for reasons to be discussed, the notion that artworks are a source of beliefs rather than of knowledge is the weaker (and more plausible) view, I will, for the sake of charity, represent the standard propositionalist as committed to the view that artworks, notably fictions, are a source of beliefs rather than of knowledge.

[10] This position is a theme of a number of articles in *Take Back the Night: Women on Pornography*, ed. Laura Lederer (New York: William Morrow and Company, 1980).

endorse what they call erotic art,[11] as distinct from what they stipulate to be pornographic art, on the grounds that by graphically portraying sexual relations as loving—that is, in part, as equally respectful of the claims to sexual pleasure of all the participants concerned—the relevant work implies that no one should be the mere instrument of another's desire, which idea, if it becomes rooted in belief (as the favourably disposed critic almost always implicitly predicts it will), produces humane sexual behaviour. The work in question then can be evaluated positively from the moral point of view on the grounds of its propensity to promote morally correct behaviour.

On the propositionalist view, especially where the propositions in question are general, art functions as a source of education pretty much in the way that science does. It invests us with general ideas. These ideas are non-trivial—they are interesting and informative. Art serves as the source for new beliefs, which when justified by commerce with the world, yield new knowledge. Moral education through art operates like scientific education.[12] Art provides us with moral principles which we can test by observation and experience. Art can initiate moral discoveries. But, like science, when art dispenses false propositions and serves as the source of defective beliefs, it is bad. And where those false propositions concern allegedly moral truths, they are morally bad.

Moreover, if the false moral beliefs disseminated and encouraged by an artwork are likely to result in morally disreputable behaviour, then the artwork can also be criticized in light of its consequences. If art serves as a source of the ideas and beliefs that cause immorality, then the artworks in question deserve condemnation in light of their non-accidental, putatively regularly recurring, behavioural consequences.

Of course, behaviour may not be motivated solely on the basis of beliefs—even general moral beliefs—where moral beliefs are understood on the model of scientific generalizations. Actions are also motivated by emotions. So the consequentialist may also be interested in isolating a

[11] Gloria Steinem, 'Erotica and Pornography: A Clear and Present Difference', in *Pornography: Private Right or Public Menace*, ed. Robert Baird and Stuart Rosenbaum (Buffalo: Prometheus Books, 1991), 51–5.

[12] Indeed, propositionalism is perhaps the reflection of the anxiety that those in the humanities often feel in the shadows of science. Propositionalism is a way of defending the value of art, especially literature, in the face of the fear that science has greater authority and greater claims to the academic and/or cultural pie. The propositionalist responds to the lustre of science by asserting that literature and other art forms are just like the sciences, since they too have interesting and informative propositions to advance. That is, as a matter of sociological conjecture, I submit that whatever attractiveness propositionalism has it possesses as a blocker to science in academic and cultural debates. That is perhaps why it claims for the arts a capacity to communicate general, interesting propositions on the model of scientific education.

mechanism by which action-motivating emotions are instilled in readers, viewers, and spectators. And here, as we saw in the last chapter, one of the most enduring theories of the way in which this comes about is the theory of identification. On the *identificationist* view, readers, viewers, and listeners take on the emotions of fictional characters.[13] Where those emotions are morally suspect, the consequentialist predicts that they will result in immoral behaviour and the identificationist-cum-consequentialist will criticize the work in question on the grounds that it is highly likely to produce immoral actions.[14]

Violent comic books have often been attacked in this way. Whereas identification with morally upright characters, exhibiting the ethically proper emotions, is applauded because such characters provide good emotional role models, Barney the Dinosaur, ever considerate and even tempered, is to be preferred morally to overly aggressive, hot-headed, and truculent cartoon super-heroes like Wolverine.

Perhaps needless to say, there is no reason to restrict the operation of the mechanism (or process) of identification to the emotions. One may argue that readers, viewers, and listeners identify not only with the emotions of characters, but with their ideas as well. In this way, one may segue from identificationism into propositionalism. Thus, to return to the example of pornography, one might suggest that the way in which the proposition that women are merely a means to male sexual gratification is conveyed is by the reader's, viewer's, or listener's identifying with some character or characters in the relevant fictions who believe and/or endorse this immoral precept. In this case, identification would explain how the propositions implied by the pornographic work get lodged in the audience member (no pun intended). And, once so lodged, the consequentialist + propositionalist + identificationist predicts that it is likely to produce the sort of immoral behaviour that warrants censure. Moreover, works that one can reliably predict will serve as causal agencies in the production of such censurable behaviour themselves warrant censorship. Producing such works is like giving a drunk a loaded gun and encouraging him to discharge it in a crowded pub.

---

[13] One variation here might be to say that the reader, listener, or viewer identifies with the emotional perspective of the implied narrator. For the sake of brevity, I will forgo working through this variation at this time.

[14] A similar story can be told about desires. For the identificationist, the reader, viewer, or listener will take on the desires of characters and/or implied narrators in much the same way that they take on the emotions of said entities. Because the theory of identification for desire parallels the way the theory handles emotions (perhaps since desires are very often constituents of emotions), I will not develop this variation at this point. However, there will be a discussion of desire with respect to mass art in the last chapter in this book.

Now, I suspect that most critics of mass art buy into all three of these views. That is, even if they are unaware of it, most are a combination of the consequentialist, the propositionalist, and the identificationist (in terms of emotions [desires] and beliefs). But each of these views might be held in isolation from the others. One can be a propositionalist without being a consequentialist—supposing, for example, that what is wrong with artworks that express evil maxims is that holding or asserting false moral principles is bad in itself. And, similarly, one could maintain that inducing others to take on immoral emotions and/or beliefs is morally contemptible, even if it does not result in the production of evil behaviour. One could be a consequentialist without specifying the mechanisms by which immoral (or moral) behaviour issues from artworks (including mass artworks). Thus, in what follows, I will criticize consequentialism, propositionalism, and identificationism consecutively. However, it should be borne in mind that if most commentators, if only tacitly, buy into the combined package of these three views, then the package itself is undermined if each element in it is discredited.

Consequentialism is one of the oldest views about how we might go about discussing and evaluating art morally. It can claim a lineage all the way back to Plato. In our own times, it remains a furiously debated hypothesis by politicians and social scientists alike. Because it often comes in the company of discussions of censorship, it is of especial importance in liberal societies where the harm principle supplies virtually the only uncontroversially recognized warrant for state interference. For if consequentialism could be shown to be true, then the harm principle could be mobilized to sanction artworks with demonstrably harmful consequences. That is why, I hypothesize, many feminists find strength in the allegation that pornography causes rape. It is just the sort of accusation which, if substantiated, would provide grounds for invoking the harm principle and removing pornography from circulation.

But, of course, it is just this kind of causal nexus that has proven illusive. Thus, the prospects for state censorship of art, including mass art, have remained a perennially contested issue. And it will probably remain that way, unless and until the proponents of consequentialism are able to meet some fairly steep standards of proof.

But putting the question of state sanctions and government coercion to one side, the question might still be raised about whether consequentialism supplies us with a way of morally evaluating mass art where, for example, a negative evaluation would not be grounds for mobilizing state power against the relevant miscreants. We might think that adultery is morally wrong but also want to refrain from having adulterers incarcerated or put in stocks. Something can be morally wrong and not warrant coercive enforcement by the state. I take it that most of us want to be in a position to criticize mass art from a moral point of view, even if at this time, given the relevant research, we are not yet prepared to endorse thoroughgoing censorship.

Might not consequentialism be serviceable in this regard? Might not moral condemnation (or commendation) in this arena require lower epistemic standards than would the mobilization of state power in the form of coercive censorship? Isn't consequentialism just plausible enough that it can provide the basis for justifying the typical moral evaluations of artworks and mass entertainments that all of us, or most of us, make all of the time?

Yet here, I think, that we must admit that we know virtually nothing about the consequences of consuming art, including mass art. For example, we have no precise, reliable account about why violence is high in Detroit but low in Toronto, where the respective populations are exposed to the same violent entertainment media; nor do we have anything but exceedingly general ideas about why there is less violent crime in Japan than in the United States, despite the fact that Japanese programming is far more violent than ours. At this point, the notion of a *difference in culture* is apt to be bruited about, but that is not an explanation. It is what needs to be explained, if we are to determine the relevant differential behavioural responses to mass art. Thus, it may be argued that since we don't know how to calculate the behavioural consequences of mass art for morality, we should refrain from bluffing about our knowledge of the supposed behavioural consequences of mass art and stop trying to invoke knowledge we do not have to justify our moral evaluations of it.

Critics of consequentialism, in short, greet the best-known consequentialist attempts to assess art in terms of its behavioural repercussions by emphasizing that we really don't know enough about the ways in which mass art might influence behaviour to make such a standard persuasive. Any group that claims to be able to predict the behavioural consequences of, for example, pornography, it might be said, is simply trying to advance its own sensitivities and moral preferences under the guise of a 'theory'.

Of course, anyone but the most vociferous sceptic has to admit that there is some evidence in favour of consequentialism. However, much of the evidence vastly underdetermines the kind of ambitious generalizations that consequentialists might hope to draw from it. For example, if there is evidence that children exposed to violent cartoons are more likely to hit punching dolls than children who have not been so exposed, that hardly indicates that the cartoons are likely to promote violent interpersonal behaviour in everyday social life, since, after all, the children are attacking dolls, dolls that are okay to hit. The children are not attacking people. There is nothing morally wrong about striking inflated clowns and the like, and, in any case, there are lots of reasons to be cautious in extrapolating from the way a child handles a doll to the way in which he handles (or manhandles) other people.

Undoubtedly, it may be said that morality prohibits structuring experimental designs where real harm to people is a genuine option. But that just means that consequentialism remains poorly confirmed. Similarly, what adolescent males are willing to write down on a questionnaire after seeing a film full of rough sex may not be a reliable predictor of their future behaviour in real sexual situations.

In addition, often it seems that consequentialist hypotheses about the behavioural consequences of mass art are so qualified and hedged that they appear irrelevant for purposes of general moral evaluation where that is to be tied to prediction. If we are told that certain violent stimuli may dispose certain people with pre-existing violent tendencies toward immoral acts of agression under certain either very vague or very limited conditions, we will want to be sure that the people in question have not been so defined as to make the consequentialist hypothesis either unfalsifiably vague or trivial.

Nor is anecdotal evidence very compelling. Ted Bundy probably told jailers that pornography made him do it because that was what he thought they wanted to hear, or because he thought that by hearing it, the powers that be might grant him leniency, whereas Jeffrey Dahmer's confession that he was influenced by *Exorcist III* hardly suggests the basis of a general standard of evaluation. How could anyone predict on the basis of looking at *Exorcist III* that anyone would behave as Dahmer did? How can one extrapolate from the case of Dahmer to that of normal people? And anyway, there is no other reported case of serial cannibalism as a result of watching *Exorcist III*.

Furthermore, there is also another problem with trying to predict immoral behaviour on the basis of audience exposure to standard cases of mass art. Namely, the behaviour exhibited in mass art usually comes morally marked. When the Mighty Morphin Power Rangers adopt what some call their violent solutions to their problems, there is generally no other moral alternative open to them. As earth is threatened by powers of inhuman origin, calling 911 may just not be an option. The police can't stand up against the alien invaders' array of lethal force. Thus, the Rangers' response is morally justified in the world described in the fiction.

Similarly, morally unjustified violence is typically framed as repugnant in mass fictions. So, we might ask, why does the consequentialist predict that exposure to morally appropriate violence will result in immoral violence? If the spectator is cast in the role of a copycat, then shouldn't one predict that he will be instructed in the ways of morally appropriate violence and repulsed by morally unjustified violence? And if not, why not?

If morally inappropriate violence is systematically presented as unattractive by the media, why does the consequentialist fear that it will appeal to the audience? Violence researchers tabulate an amazing amount of violence on our TV screens. Granted. But since that violence is usually marked in the morally appropriate ways, why do they suppose that audiences are being tutored in immoral behaviour rather than in the conditions under which aggression may be morally acceptable versus the conditions when it is unacceptable?

And, of course, viewers realize that the violence on TV is fictional. So why are researchers so convinced that there will be a slippage effect on real world behaviour. That Superman can fly to the moon doesn't encourage viewers to try to do likewise with any appreciable frequency. Thus, since mass fictions present activities—including, for example, aggressive activities—internally contextualized in morally motivated ways and externally contextualized as fictional, one would suspect that there are enough brakes on what is represented to prevent the eruption into everyday life of copycat behaviour from the direction of normal viewers, listeners, and readers.[15] And, if this is not the case, then consequentialists owe us not only behavioural evidence to the contrary, but also some explanation of why these brakes don't work. Otherwise consequentialism seems nothing short of a rather large promissory note instead of a viable standard for evaluating mass art morally.

Of course, none of the objections to consequentialism so far is insurmountable. They are requests for more evidence, for more precision, and for more theory. And there is no reason to suppose that consequentialism might not be able to rise to the occasion. However, I think it is fair to say that, at present, consequentialism has not met anything like the burden of proof that would be required to turn it into a justifiable standard for evaluating mass art morally. But, interestingly, the very fact that, after over two millennia, consequentialism is still inconclusive as an evaluative standard for assessing art morally may supply us with a different kind of argument against consequentialism.

---

[15] Moreover, if we are not talking about normal audiences, might we not wonder why it should not be the case that all bets are off on predictions of the sort that are relevant to making moral evaluation? Wouldn't those predictions have to be keyed to standard or average responses?

For at least two-and-a-half millennia, we have been evaluating art morally. This form of evaluation is deeply embedded in our practices. *Ex hypothesi*, this form of evaluation is legitimate. It works, even if we do not know how it works. We know how to carry it off intelligibly and rationally. But if, despite the beliefs of many theorists since Plato, this form of evaluation cannot, for the reasons given, be dependent on consequentialism, then it must rest on something else. Whatever that 'something else' is, supposing that it can be be specified, renders consequentialism beside the point. Maybe the super social sciences of the future will discover and confirm consequentialist theories of unimagined power. Perhaps these theories will be so compelling that we will even feel confident about using coercive state power to censor the mass artworks about which it can be demonstrated that they are very likely to cause morally deplorable, serious harm to others. Given sufficient proof, I, for one, would not necessarily be opposed to censorship in the right circumstances. But if (and that's a very big *if*) such a day ever arrives, that will be then; this is now.

And now we do not have such a theory, and there is no use pretending that we do. However, and this is the good news, we don't need such a theory now nor have we needed such a theory up until now. Or, we don't need such a super scientific theory now because we haven't needed one up until now. We have been able to get along morally evaluating art, including (for the last century or so) mass art, without a complete, scientifically impeccable consequentialist theory. Moreover, if we can say how the moral evaluation of art has been and presently is possible without a viable theory of the behavioural impact of art, then consequentialism is to a certain extent extraneous. It might be nice to have such a theory. Indeed, our sense of social responsibility suggests that research into the influence of art, especially mass art, should continue. But for the purposes of evaluating mass art morally in the manner that is common to our practices, such a super-scientific theory may be ultimately unnecessary.

Of course, there is a promissory note in what I have just said too. It is not enough for me to advertise that we can get along without consequentialism and simply leave it at that. I ought to be able to say positively how it is that we can get and have got along evaluating art morally without consequentialism. And that will be the burden of proof of the next section of this chapter. However, before advancing my own theory of the foundations of the moral criticism of mass art, I have yet to look at the claims of propositionalism and identificationism.

Propositionalism claims that art, including mass art, can be a source of information about the world. On one version of propositionalism, art is said to be a source of knowledge; on a weaker version it is said to be a source of beliefs. Moreover, propositionalists usually think of this information as general in nature.

Of course, in one sense, this position is unobjectionable. Many works of art state certain generalizations outright. One character may say to another, 'Everyone needs love.' But propositionalism would not be very interesting, if this is all it meant to claim. It would be obvious. But typically, propositionalists do not merely contend that artworks often contain explicit statements of putative fact. They also maintain that artworks suggest, imply, entail, or presuppose other general propositions. This too, in a way, is unexceptionable. Probably most novels suggest that people live in groups. But the propositionalist does not want to emphasize that artworks suggest general truths of a trivial nature. The propositionalist maintains that works like novels often implicitly suggest, imply, entail, or presuppose interesting and informative generalizations, and that, as a result, they can be educative.

Thus, artists can educate audiences in the same way natural scientists do—by providing us with informative generalizations. Where the artist differs from the natural scientist is that the artist's generalizations pertain to human affairs and not to subatomic particles or galaxies. Art operates at the level of persons, not synaptic pathways. Consequently, often the relevant generalizations suggested, implied and/or presupposed by artworks are moral.[16]

Art educates by providing information. Where the generalizations in question pertain to ethics, that education is moral. Art—especially narrative, representational, and dramatic art—suggests, implies, or presupposes, among other things, informative, non-trivial moral information. Audiences derive this moral information by picking up on these suggestions, implications and/or presuppositions. Where the information is counterfeit, the work is

[16] One reason that propositionalists typically make their claims in terms of general propositions might be their desire to connect art with knowledge about the world. For if a propositionalist is a particularist—claiming that art either states and/or implies propositions about particulars—then it would be questionable whether, for example, a fiction could yield knowledge about the world. For if a novel stated or implied that its major character was good that would not count as knowledge about the world because the character is made up. It would not amount to knowledge about the world or even a hypothesis that might be tested against the world, since the character is a fiction. Consequently, the propositionalist is likely to argue that the knowledge available in fictions is abstracted from the story in the form of a generalization, where the generalization in question can be true of the world. That is, where the propositionalist wants to claim that fiction yields knowledge, he/she will be inclined to claim that the prospective knowledge is general rather than particular, because it is hard, otherwise, to see how the propositions could yield knowledge. Knowledge with reference to fictional particulars seems unlikely, since the relevant particulars do not exist in the real world. So the propositionalist is apt to claim that it is the general claims, abstractable by interpretation from fictional particulars that concern him.

morally bad; where morally enlightening, the work is good. Thus, propositionalism appears to provide the means to evaluate artworks morally.

Propositionalism is a view that has not only been advanced by philosophers; it also appears to represent the implicit or underlying theory behind much of the moral criticism of texts that we encounter in academic, journalistic, and informal talk about texts. TV reviewers as well as literature and cinema professors proceed by identifying a moral thesis with which they maintain the text under consideration is associated, and they go on to evaluate the text by praising or excoriating its moral viewpoint. The text is said to imply a racist prejudice, which the critic then goes on to castigate.

The propositionalist thinks that narratives can be a source of moral knowledge, or at least moral beliefs, in terms of general moral propositions—either explicitly stated in texts, or, more importantly, implied by them.[17] Narratives especially but also representations of human affairs, in general are thought of as instruments of moral learning. They contain implicit moral propositions which audiences acquire in the course of consuming texts. Like scientific texts, these texts are cognitively valuable because of the information they convey, though artistic texts are distinguishable from scientific ones, in part because much of the information that they specialize in is moral. Nevertheless, such texts are still thought to provide us with propositions we may apply to situations in the world.

This conception of the relation of artworks to morality provides a ready standard with which to evaluate narratives and other forms of representation morally. Narratives and representations that make moral discoveries or that impart informative or true or reasonable beliefs are, *ceteris paribus*, good, whereas those that advance false or otherwise defective moral propositions are flawed. The feminists, mentioned earlier, who criticize pornography do so in part by dint of propositionalism, maintaining that pornography purveys bad moral theory in its suggestion that women are not genuine moral agents, but only ever sexual objects. Here the defectiveness of the moral maxim that pornography presupposes, suggests and/or implies is grounds enough for regarding pornography as morally despicable.

Propositionalists may argue, alternatively, either that artworks are sources of knowledge—of informative moral truths—or that artworks

---

[17] The implied propositions are of more interest to professional critics (academic and otherwise), since implications are literally non-obvious and therefore require interpretation. And, in our present culture, professional critics are primarily interpreters. That is how they see themselves. That is why they have a vested interest in the widespread existence of interesting, implied propositions in their objects of criticism.

are only the source of interesting moral propositions. The former view is the more ambitious one. It suggests that works of art not only communicate moral propositions, but that they provide justification for them as well. But this claim is subject to the well-known objection that, since most of the artworks that provide the best evidence for propositionalism are fictions, it is hard to see how a fiction, by itself, could supply a warrant for whatever general moral claims it advances. Since a fiction concerns particulars, it is not clear how one could find in it an adequate evidential basis for a generalization. Indeed, since fictions are made up, it does not seem that they provide any real evidence for the generalizations that they suggest. And finally, since authors make up the particular cases they narrate often in order to advance the moral generalizations in question, whatever 'evidence' they proffer would appear to be question-begging, if not tainted. So, it is better to understand propositionalism as the doctrine that certain artworks—including narratives and representations—suggest, imply, entail, and/or presuppose moral beliefs, rather than knowledge. These beliefs may then be regarded as hypotheses to check against the world. But it is the world and not the work that warrants or justifies the beliefs found in art. The artworks do not provide knowledge in and of themselves.

However, even if propositionalism is taken as a theory about belief, rather than knowledge, it is still susceptible to objections from another direction. For even though propositionalism is a mainstay of criticism as we know it, sceptics worry especially about the notion that texts contain implicit moral reflections of a general nature. How are these reflections conveyed? Propositionalists say by suggestion and implication. But the idea that texts imply or entail general propositions is thought to be too strong. The entailment seems to be nothing like logical entailment. Yet to say that the general propositions are merely suggested by texts seems far too weak. What a text suggests to some people, as we all know, frequently has nothing to do with what the text is about.[18]

However, this problem may not be as daunting as it first appears. Clearly, the propositionalist is not talking about deduction when she speaks of texts implying propositions. But there are other alternatives. Peter McCormick has likened the derivation of propositions from texts to abduction, by which, if I understand him correctly, he means something like inference to the best explanation.[19] Narratives present us with events that ask us to think about why they transpire as they do. Watching

---

[18] For criticism of the viability of the notion that texts imply propositions, see Mary Sirridge, 'Truth from Fiction?' *Philosophy and Phenomenological Research*, 35 (1974–5), 453–71.

[19] McCormick, 'Moral Knowledge and Fiction'.

Antigone, for example, we may ask ourselves why Creon loses his family. Likely answers include: because he's too resolute; because he doesn't know when to look the other way; because he is too implacably wedded to his own proclamation (he's the ultimate bureaucrat). If these hypotheses are superior to others—if they explain what happens in the text's presentation of events better than other explanations—then we infer that they are what Sophocles intends us to take away from his play.[20]

Furthermore, it is possible to abstract from these explanations to some broader principles, for example, that: in general, refusing to bend the rules sometimes courts disaster; or, one should judge particular situations, and sometimes bend the rules. This is a moral generalization of sorts (even if it is not Kantian). It can be derived from the text by a combination of inference to the best explanation, or what McCormick (following Pierce) calls abduction, plus abstraction. The way we infer this proposition— which might also be referred to as the theme or the thesis of the play— is not as rigorous as a deduction from general premises, but it is not free association either. It seems like a respectable species of induction (not enumerative induction, but inference to the best explanation), or, if you prefer, abduction. Moreover, it enables us to parse what is meant by the notion that texts imply propositions, namely, they arrange conditions in such a way that readers, listeners, and viewers make textually constrained, warranted inferences about the underlying general themes or theses of the text. Thus, the sceptic's charge that the propositionalist can give no respectable account of what he means by implication is excessive.

Of course, McCormick may be wrong if he is suggesting that the audience always derives the general propositions in a text by way of abduction. However, maybe the propositionalist does not need a universal theory of the logic of textual implication here. Perhaps there is no special form of textual implication. But we do have some reliable practices of interpretation, and, in light of those practices, perhaps we can say that what a text is thought to imply is just what a reliable interpretation of the text would identify as the theme or thesis of the text in question.[21] And though it might be difficult for us to propose a theory of reliable interpretation, all the propositionalist really requires is that there be some reliable interpretive strategies for texts in order to claim that sometimes texts 'imply' general moral propositions. Thus, the propositionalist does not even need a conjecture as ambitious as McCormick's in

---

[20] I have used this example rather than McCormick's. McCormick's example is the inference that, in reference to *Anna Karenina*, Vronsky's and Anna's adultery is wrong. I don't see why McCormick uses this example, however, since it doesn't get you to a general proposition.

[21] Lamarque and Olsen, *Truth, Fiction and Literature*, 327–8.

order to counter the sceptic and to motivate the notion that texts carry implications.[22]

If we have been able to defend propositionalism thus far, there is nevertheless one further objection that I think it cannot evade. According to the propositionalist, in the standard case, we derive interesting, informative, general propositions—very often moral principles and maxims—from artworks, notably from narratives and representations of human affairs. But this seems wrong. For in the standard case, the propositions implied, presupposed, or suggested by artworks are generally truisms. They are not interesting and informative. In some sense, *Macbeth* may show the wrongness of unbridled ambition, but it can hardly be said to reveal it. No one with the capacity to understand *Macbeth* is likely to learn the abstract proposition—that unbridled ambition is wrong—from it, because such audiences are apt to command this knowledge already.[23] Indeed, it may even be a condition of comprehending *Macbeth* that the ideally informed, implied viewer already have this proposition at her disposal. But in any case, it makes little sense to say that the narrative is important for the way in which it provides the audience with informative moral ideas or new moral beliefs.

We may infer that this abstract proposition is the theme of *Macbeth*, but not as the result of some subtle maieutic process whereby knowledge hidden in the recesses of the mind is suddenly brought to the fore and recognized, the scales falling from our eyes. The relevant abstract proposition is a piece of common moral wisdom. Very often, the propositions that we are apt to attach to certain narrative artworks, including very distinguished ones, approach the status of truisms. That hypocrisy is repugnant may be the moral of *Tartuffe*, but this cannot be thought of as something that Molière discovered. Rather, audiences knew it before encountering the play, and, in fact, could only understand the play in virtue of their antecedent moral convictions.

Too often the propositions purportedly disclosed by narrative artworks and representations are such commonplaces that the propositionalist's hypothesis that we learn from such texts seems disingenuous and strained, since most of the moral beliefs that we might be said to acquire from art are things we already know and which, in fact, we must bring to the text in

---

[22] Though McCormick may not be correct in thinking of abduction as the only reliable procedure for textual interpretation, he certainly is not wrong in thinking that is one procedure—indeed, a very pervasive one.

[23] It might be said that this dismissal of propositionalism rides on misidentifying the knowledge that *Macbeth* affords. It is not that unbridled ambition is wrong, but that any wrongdoer, including oneself, is likely to suffer in the way that Macbeth does. But this strikes me as being almost as much of a cliché as the notion that unbridled ambition is wrong.

order to understand it. Moreover, if what we have said about mass art in previous chapters holds, this will be especially true in regard to it. For the moral address of mass art will have to be accessible and that will predispose it toward the mobilization of widely known moral precepts.

Propositionalism suggests that art can be a means of moral education. But if the notion of education implies the learning of informative propositions, the notion of education—especially moral education—seems ill-suited to our standard commerce with art. For usually the general moral propositions associated with texts, or implied by texts, or, at least, found in texts by reliable interpretations are truisms of such striking banality that we must hesitate to say that typical audiences learn them from narratives. Admittedly, there are exceptions to my generalization. Perhaps from *Native Son*, readers may learn that racism literally brings its own worst nightmares into existence. But such cases are rare, indicating that, at best, the propositionalist has identified *a* possible relation of morality to art, but a far from comprehensive one—indeed, perhaps an unusual one. Propositionalism cannot supply us with a general framework for assessing the moral status of artworks, because there are so few interesting and informative moral propositions to be derived from art. Since most are truisms, there isn't enough of a data base for propositionalism to get out of the gate as a general theory of the relation of art to morality.

One might think that propositionalism could evade this objection by dropping its commitment to informative propositions. But there are several problems with this gambit. First, propositionalism is clearly a premiss in a larger argument about the value of art, especially literature. Part of that value is supposed to be that it is on a par with science in its production of new, interesting, and informative propositions. The doctrine of propositionalism is thus useless for this project if it gives up the commitment to informative, non-trivial ideas. If the propositionalist is attempting to put literature on a par with science, the parallel is lost, unless the propositionalist can show that literature and the arts in general have comparably informative ideas and discoveries to offer audiences.

Moreover, if the propositionalist is not talking about informative ideas, then he is left with a lot of explaining to do. For example, the propositionalist has no way of accounting for why art trades in truisms. And further, why might it be a good-making feature of art that it implies moral commonplaces? Why does art create elaborate fabrics of truisms that might be as easily derived from sermons, catechisms, pamphlets, and the like? Propositionalism has no answer to these questions.

Furthermore, if propositionalism concedes that the general propositions available from art are truisms, the link with moral education seems broken. For if art typically presupposes that we already know—and believe that we know—the general propositions it seeks to draw out from us, how can it make sense to say it teaches them to us? And anyway, what moral virtue is there in repeating moral truisms to audiences who already know them? That seems to be the definition of a bore, not of a paragon.

Since the theory of identification was broached in the last chapter, I will be brief in my criticism of the simple version of it here. Later, after I have proposed my own account of the relation of mass art to morality, I will return to a discussion of recent, more-sophisticated theories of identification. Nevertheless, a quick review of the shortcomings of the simple version of the identification theory will be useful at this time in order to prepare for the alternative theory of the relation of mass art to morality that I intend to defend.

The simple theory of identification is not only an article of common speech—where plain speakers constantly talk of identifying with the characters they like[24]—it also has a long and continuing theoretical heritage.[25] Perhaps first articulated by Plato, it has remained a persistent model for talking about narrative and representational art throughout the history of western aesthetics. Of course, the case that Plato had in mind was one in which people read plays aloud to each other. His fear was that in speaking the lines of various characters, readers would take on the values of those characters by identifying with them. In modern times, given that we do not often read plays aloud to each other anymore, this would seem to be primarily a problem for actors.

But it is very easy to adjust Plato's theory of identification to modern conditions of reception. One need only postulate two stages of identification. First, the actor identifies with a character in order to read the character's lines effectively, and then the spectator identifies with the actor playing the character. In this way, the actor's primary identification with the character is, so to speak, relayed to the audience. Such theories of 'relayed' identification are evident throughout the tradition of Western theatrical aesthetics from the seventeenth-century French cleric Jacques Benigne Bossuet to the contemporary phenomenologist Bruce Wilshire.[26]

---

[24] See, for example, Leo Handel, *Hollywood Looks at its Audience: A Report of Film Audience Research* (Urbana: University of Illinois Press, 1950).

[25] For an example from contemporary psychology, see W. F. Brewer and P. E. Jose, 'Development of Story Liking: Character, Identification, Suspense and Outcome Resolution', *Developmental Psychology*, 20/5 (1984), 911–24. K. Oatley also espouses identificationism in his book *The Best Laid Schemes*.

[26] Jacques Benigne Bossuet, *Maximes et réflexions sur la comédie* (1694), in *L'Église et le théâtre*, ed. C. Urbain et E. Levesque (Paris, 1930), 212; Bruce Wilshire, *Role Playing and Identity: The Limits of Theatre as Metaphor* (Bloomington, Ind.: Indiana Press, 1982). See also Jonas Barish, *The Antitheatrical Prejudice* (Berkeley: University of California Press, 1981).

Moreover, it is the fear of this putative propensity of dramatic representation that, in part, motivated Brecht to design his alienation effects, an innovation that has exerted immense influence on recent academic discussions of mass art largely through the midwifery of Roland Barthes.

According to the simple version of the theory of identification, in the course of consuming narratives, the spectator somehow becomes one with fictional characters, taking on their values and their emotions (including their morally relevant emotions) and vicariously experiencing their circumstances. We put ourselves in their shoes, so to speak. However, putting on those shoes involves taking on their values, their emotions, their desires, and so on. And, I suppose, the worry of many moralists is that once we put those shoes on, we might not take them off, or that we might be predisposed to put them on again, sometimes in the course of everyday life.

As Bossuet puts it, one takes over the 'spirit and nature' of the character.[27] Via identification, the values and morally relevant emotions of the characters penetrate us, as if by a process of osmosis. Thus, the proponent of the simple theory of identification explains the relation of art to morality as a matter of moral education—a process by which artworks invest spectators with moral ideas, outlooks, and emotions by inducing them to identify with actors playing characters who hold the relevant moral ideas and outlooks and who exhibit the emotional states in question.

This is a neat theory of the means by which art—especially representational, narrative, and dramatic art—performs the function of moral education. However, in almost all its details, it seems wrong. Audiences do not appear to undergo the same experiences as the fictional characters that are the objects of their attention. If they did, it would be hard to account for their behaviour. If citizens of Washington DC identified in this way with the human characters onscreen in *Independence Day*, they would not stay to the end of the film. They would evacuate. Thus, it cannot be the case that the audience has identified with the characters; the audience must not be taking certain of the characters' ideas with the same degree of seriousness that the characters do. And this is one reason to suspect the notion of identification—understood as the mind-melding of the character and the audience—is altogether unlikely, or, at least, insufficiently precise.[28]

---

[27] Bossuet as translated in Barish, *The Antitheatrical Prejudice*, 194.

[28] In the preceding case, I have taken identification to be a matter of imagining oneself to be the character, where this is thought to involve taking on the emotions, beliefs, etc. of the character. However, sometimes identification is described as a matter of projecting oneself into the character's situation or imagining what it would be like if the character were me. In this case, somewhat like

Moreover, with respect to the moral values of fictional characters, identification seems to be an infelicitous explanation of the responses of readers, viewers, and listeners to them. Almost all fictions present audiences with a range of moral values and ideas, including—very often, if not typically—ones that are conflicting and even contradictory. The audience endorses only some of them for this very reason. That is, the audience doesn't align itself with all of the moral values of all of the characters—how could it, since they are often patently contradictory (in a way made salient in the narrative)? But how does the theory of identification explain this differential endorsement? It cannot say that the audience endorses only the values of characters with whom it identifies, since identification is supposed to explain how it is that the audience comes to take on the values it does. Rather, the audience's pre-existing values seem to explain the audience's response to the characters, however we describe that response (though I would prefer not to call it identification), instead of the character's manifestation of certain values somehow taking over the audience.

This is not to deny that the audience may share certain values with characters, or even that our sharing of these values shapes our response to the relevant characters. Perhaps, most often, we tend to develop care and concern for characters with whom we share certain values, including, most notably, moral values. But sharing the same values need not be explained by a process as arcane as identification. I share moral values with the other subscribers to *Dissent*, but I identify with neither any nor all of the other subscribers, nor with the writers and the editorial staff of the magazine.

Sharing moral values can be explained in everyday life without adverting to identification, and I see no reason to invoke it in order to explain how it is we come to endorse the values of some fictional characters over others. That is, if the tendency to endorse the projects of like-minded people can be explained in many cases without the concept of identification—as it can in the case of my subscription to *Dissent*—then why not, on the grounds of theoretical economy, proceed on the hypothesis that it can

---

Walter Mitty, I imagine that I am in the character's situation. I ask myself what I would do if I found myself in a position like his. I do not take on his emotional make-up, but rather I project my own emotional make-up into the character and think about how I would behave.

But I do not think that this projection model of identification provides a very plausible picture of audience response. In fact, it appears to me that, if it ever happens, it involves a failure to pay attention to the fiction. It is more like daydreaming than attending to the fiction. Perhaps after a movie is over, people ask themselves questions about how they would have responded to the circumstances in the fiction. But I hardly think that they can be doing much or any of this sort of speculation during the fiction and be paying attention to the fiction at the same time. And, in any case, the response that the author intends the audience to have toward the fiction can't involve our thinking about the character in our own terms, since the author knows nothing about us.

be explained in all cases by means of the same considerations that enable us to explain it where the operation of identification is, prima facie, out of the question.[29]

In everyday talk, the notion of identification is often used to say that a viewer likes certain characters. But clearly the notion of identification has no explanatory payload here. For we do not like all of the characters in most narratives. Our response is differential. We like some characters and dislike others. And we dislike some more than others. Moreover, this kind of differential response is a condition of possibility for most dramas as we know them. It is the basis of what is called dramatic conflict. But one cannot use the notion of identification to say why we like some characters rather than others, since 'identification', in this usage, is synonymous with 'liking'. Thus, using this notion of identification to explain why we like a character would be tantamount to saying that we identify with the character because we identify with the character.

Of course, it is not necessary for us to share the entire value structure of a character—as the simple theory of identification (the view that we become the character) would suggest—in order to be favourably disposed to a character. In mass fictions about the ancient world, I may be sympathetic to the ambitions of a certain Roman consul without taking on board all of the values of that character, such as his tolerance (as represented in the fiction) of slavery. Obviously we will have to explain this sort of favourable response to a character—that is, our endorsement of the moral claims of such a character on us—without reference to identification. And if we are able to explain cases like this (as I will try to do later in this chapter) without recourse to identification, why suppose that such an explanation will not work across the board? Perhaps the notion of 'partial identification' will be introduced here. But *partial* identification doesn't sound to me like identification at all!

Our moral endorsement of characters is selective—selective in that we do not endorse every character paraded before us, and selective in the sense that we may not endorse all of any given character's attributes. The

---

[29] Of course, this principle can be challenged by the identificationist, if she can show that there is something about the data with respect to certain cases that warrants the extra explanatory apparatus of identification. But note that the burden of proof here lies with the identificationist. And, to my knowledge, no identificationist so far has met this burden of proof. Moreover, it will not do to claim that identification is necessary to account for the intensity of the emotional responses observable in some cases. For emotional responses of the highest levels of intensity can be observed in cases where there is no question of identification. I was outraged by the assassination of Israeli Prime Minister Yitzhak Rabin, but I did not identify with him. That is, intense emotional response can be explained in cases where there is no question of identification. Therefore, why suppose that other cases cannot be explained in the same way without postulating the extra added explanatory machinery involved in the alleged process of identification?

simple theory of identification has no way to explain either of these forms of selectivity. The notion of identification that is suggested by Plato and Bossuet makes it sound as though we will identify (and thereby come to endorse) any character presented to us; perhaps latter-day Platonists who fear that audiences will imitate the violence of villains subscribe to a similar view. But such views of the sheer infectious power of mere character portrayal do not square with the data. For there are too many characters who do not win our moral endorsement, and therefore (presumably) with whom we cannot be said to identify. But how will the identificationist explain this selectivity? Note that if the answer is that we will identify only with the characters whom we morally endorse, then identification makes no explanatory contribution to the phenomenon of moral endorsement, but rather vice versa.

On the other hand, the simple theory of identification also lacks the means to say how it is that we may morally endorse only certain of a character's moral attributes and outlooks, but not all of them. Yet, if we did tend to identify ourselves with a character, wouldn't we take on all of their moral attributes? Isn't that what *identity* means?[30]

Undoubtedly, when we morally endorse a certain character and her projects, that is typically done on the basis of our recognition that we share certain moral allegiance with the character in question. But similarity is not identity, and recognition is not identification. We can recognize that x has a property, even a property we share and/or admire, without becoming x, even imaginatively.

Identification is a mechanism that is supposed to explain the intensity of our response to the plights of characters. We respond to those plights by becoming the character, if only vicariously. But this does not correspond to the facts. For example, very often the cognitive stock of the spectator contains information that the character lacks; we know that the character is being stalked, but she doesn't. And, as well, our emotional state is different from that of the character, on the basis of this

---

[30] Here it is important not to confuse identification with what is called empathy. According to Mark Barnett, empathy is 'the vicarious experiencing of an emotion that is congruent with, but not necessarily identical to, the emotion of another individual'. Empathy is a matter of a disposition toward a character on the basis of a similarity with my own emotional state, a similarity that may be as broad as a correspondence of positive or negative emotional valence—the character feels sorrow, whereas I feel pity toward her. Thus, the fact that we empathize with characters is not evidence that we identify with them. If anything, identification is a strong theory of empathy. But it is needlessly strong.

For Mark Barnett's definition of empathy, see Mark Barnett, 'Empathy and Related Responses in Children', in *Empathy and its Development*, ed. N. Eisenberg and J. Strayer (Cambridge: Cambridge University Press, 1987).

knowledge.[31] We are not identical with the character with respect to either cognition or emotion, and yet our response is intense.[32] Thus, if we can explain cases like these without invoking the notion of identification, why talk about it in cases where the cognitive and emotive states of the audience and the characters are more similar (though never precisely identical[33]) than I have stipulated in the case just imagined? Isn't identification just excess theoretical baggage? An epicycle whose explanatory irrelevance suggests its non-existence?

As we saw in the last chapter, quite often the emotional state of characters, as well as their cognitive states, are very different from the states of an audience member.[34] The hero in a ninja film may be cool as a cucumber, while the audience, caught up in the thrall of suspense, is anxiously biting its fingernails. Some may be disposed to explain this in terms of identification. But can that be right, given the striking difference between the emotional states of the audience and the character? And if we have the conceptual resources—such as those sketched in the previous chapter—to explain emotional engagement in response to situations that seem oddly suited to identification, why suspect that those resources, sans identification, can't do the job in cases where the audience's emotional state is closer to that of the protagonist—for example, where our karate hero is nervous about a confrontation. In both situations, it is our recognition of the potential danger of the situation in the world of the fiction that *primarily* exercises us, not the protagonist's

---

[31] This is also quite common in melodramas, where we often know the problems a character will confront before she does. We are, so to speak, waiting for her to learn that she has been betrayed or that her loved ones are endangered. In such circumstances, which are quite standard, there is no sense to the notion of identification, since our cognitive and related emotive states differ widely from those of the character.

[32] Moreover, if holding a moral belief is a cognitive state (as I think it is), then it is also the case that we may be intensely moved by a character whose moral beliefs are different from and even counter to our own. We may cringe when an unprincipled businessman is about to be crushed in a towering inferno though our cognitive stock, in terms of moral beliefs, is quite different from his.

[33] Since we are always aware that the situation is fictional and the character is not. One exception here might appear to be cases of reflexive comedies, such as cartoons, where a character makes an aside about its fictional status to the audience, perhaps in a suspended moment in a chase scene. However, that is a momentary ascesis, after which the character leaves the meta-fictional frame of his comment and steps back into the fictional world where once again he, unlike the viewer, no longer takes his situation to be fictional.

[34] Murray Smith has offered a counter-example to this claim. With respect to the film *Deception* he argues that the state of the audience and the state of the character Christine are identical. They may both be described as curiosity. But our mental state is not the same as Christine's. Yes, we may both be curious about the transaction between Hollenius and Gribble, but we are *also* curious about whether Christine will figure it out, and I think that it is reasonable to suppose that this added layer of curiosity is not part of Christine's mental state.

See Murray Smith, *Engaging Characters*, 181.

attitude toward it.[35] Thus, the simple theory of identification has dubious explanatory power.

Undoubtedly, it is sometimes the case that the audience shares a similar state with a character; perhaps the audience even shares the same *kind* of state with the character. With respect to a movie, the characters are horrified by a monster; so is the audience. But there is no reason to explain this correlation in terms of identification. Rather, the audience and the characters are both horrified by the image of the monster, which is fearsome and disgusting. We need not route the audience's horror through the character. The audience would be horrified by it on its own, even if there were no character shown reacting to the monster, as is often the case in horror films.

Typically, the fictional situation grounds the audience's parallel response to the monster. There is no compelling theoretical reason to add that the audience has psychologically fused with a character. If we are startled by the loudness of the roar of a monster in a film, the loudness accounts for our response as it does for the character's parallel response. The character jumps; we jump. The cause of our response and the separate but converging response of the character are the same. We have no theoretical motivation for adding an additional causal step like identification. We need not postulate that we have merged with the character. Rather, our responses are convergent because the stimulus is the same. Thus, we can do without the concept of identification.

On the simple theory of identification, representational, narrative, and dramatic artworks concerned with human affairs are a source of moral education—for good or ill—because by means of identification audiences are thought to be inculcated with the moral views and ideas of characters, as well as with their morally relevant emotional and conative dispositions. The audience is said to adopt these by being presented with characters who display these qualities, including vices and virtues. The audience adopts these qualities by identifying with the characters, and, by becoming them, taking on their vices, virtues, principles, and purposes.

But if with respect to morality, the sign of identification is moral endorsement of the character, then identification cannot be what causes moral endorsement. For, as we have already argued, the audience does not endorse just any character. If anything, the audience endorses those characters who evince moral properties and principled commitments

---

[35] This is not to say that the protagonist's attitude may not make a difference. If he is very nervous, we may become more fearful for his prospects, but not because we identify with him, but because we realize that his nervousness may make him less effective in the confrontation at hand.

that the audience already shares with the character. Therefore, the identificationist has, in fact, reversed the order of explanation here.[36]

That is, given the data (our differential moral responses to characters),
even if there were a process of character identification (a view about which
I am obviously extremely sceptical), one would have to rely on the
audience's pre-existing moral dispositions (including moral beliefs and
emotions) in order to get the process of identification off the ground to
begin with. Identification would not explain the audience's acquisition of
moral beliefs and emotions. Rather, the audience's possession of antecedent moral beliefs and emotions would have to be invoked in order to
explain the operation of identification.

Though (as I hope I have shown) we have ample reason to believe that
there is, strictly speaking, no such thing as character identification, even if
there were such a process it would be of no use for explaining how art—
including mass art—functions to promote moral education, if we suppose
that education involves the acquisition of new moral beliefs and emotions.
For if there were something to the idea of identification, it would seem to
require the antecedent moral beliefs and emotions of spectator in order to
gain a foothold in the audience's inclinations. Rather than a source of
moral education, identification—supposing there is such a thing—would
have to be parasitical on the audience's antecedent moral education. Thus,
interestingly enough, identificationism would appear to confront a problem similar to that of propositionalism.

Both propositionalism and identificationism are advanced as accounts of
how artworks imbue audiences with new moral beliefs and/or emotions.
But the beliefs and emotions that artworks typically have to propose are
ones that the audience already possesses. So in what sense can art really be
said to educate its audiences morally on either of these accounts? And if art
does not educate its audiences morally, how can it be evaluated? Ultimately, neither propositionalism nor identificationism seems to have
answers to these questions.

If the preceding argumentation is compelling, consequentialism, propositionalism, and identificationism, though widely held views of the relation
of art, including mass art, to morality, all appear to fail. Propositionalism
and identificationism are especially problematic as putative models of
moral education. However, the process of working through these posi-

---

[36] For further arguments against identificationism, see D. Zillman, 'Anatomy of Suspense', *The
Entertainment Functions of Television*, ed. P. H. Tannenbaum (Hillsdale, NJ: Lawrence Erlbaum Associates, 1980); D. W. Harding, 'Psychological Process in the Reading of Fiction', *Aesthetics in the Modern
World*, ed. H. Osborne (New York: Weybright and Talley, 1968), 300–17; D. W. Harding, 'The Role of
the Onlooker', *Scrutiny* 6/3 (December 1937); Noël Carroll, *The Philosophy of Horror*, ch. 2.

tions in such critical detail has not been wasted. It has at least indicated certain mistakes that any theory of the relation of art to morality—particularly one which exploits the notion of moral education—should avoid. Thus, in developing my own theory of the relation of art to morality, I need to heed the lessons derived from criticizing consequentialism, propositionalism, and identificationism. Those lessons include: 1. refraining from assuming that one can predict the behavioural consequences of artworks and from tying the moral evaluation of artworks to those supposed predictions; 2. acknowledging that artworks operate on moral beliefs and emotions already at the audience's disposal and avoiding the presumption that artworks typically function as original sources of moral beliefs and emotions. Those are the constraints which my account must respect. Here is the theory.

Clarificationism

In this section, I would like to develop a theoretical account—by which I mean a general account—of *one* of the most important and comprehensive relations of art, especially mass art, to morality. I do not mean to suggest that the relation that I have in mind is the only possible one between mass art and morality. It is *a* relation. However, I do think that it is the most pertinent relation between art and morality in the sense that it is the one that obtains in the largest number of cases. Moreover, I conjecture that it is on the basis of this relation that the moral evaluation of art is usually grounded.

As in the previous chapter, the theory developed here will pertain first and foremost to mass narratives—including pulp fiction, movies, TV, cartoons, comics, pictorial representations, programme music, and songs (that either tell stories outright, for example, 'A Boy Named Sue', or that involve lyric narrators, for example, 'Mr Piano Man').[37] With reference to mass art, this covers quite a lot of ground, though it does exclude pure instrumental music like 'Wipeout' and 'Classical Gas', as well as abstract visual art, like psychedelic posters.[38] Those remain topics of further study.

Much mass art is narrative. Perhaps mass art gravitates toward narrative so frequently because narrative is a means of generally securing accessibility. That is not to say that all narratives are accessible. Certainly Robbe-

[37] Moreover, many songs contain explicit moral content, such as 'Respect'.
[38] However, it should be also noted that programme music—such as movie soundtracks—often has a role to play in narrating. For a theory of the way in which this occurs, see Noël Carroll, 'Notes on Movie Music' in *Theorizing the Moving Image*.

Grillet's novels are not. But, at the same time, narrative is a practice common in everyday discourse cross-culturally. It represents a mode of widely distributed thinking and, in that sense, it possesses a prima facie, though hardly guaranteed, promise of accessibility. This may be one reason why avant-gardists often eschew or seek to subvert narrative, and even adopt the stance of anti-narrativism. But much—possibly most—mass art is narrative, concerned with stories and implied stories of human affairs, including anthropomorphized ones like *The Wind in the Willows*, *Charlotte's Web*, *Raptor Red*, Disney and Warner Brothers cartoons, and so on. Moreover, I maintain that the nature of such narratives make our discussion and evaluation of them in moral terms apposite.[39] Thus, in order to advance my theory of the pertinent relation of mass art to morality, it is necessary to begin by discussing the nature of narrative.

As is well known, narratives (and representations with narrative implications) make all sorts of presuppositions, and it is the task of the reader, viewer, or listener to fill these in. It is of the nature of narrative to be essentially incomplete. Every narrative makes an indeterminate number of presuppositions that the audience must bring, in a manner of speaking, to the text. Authors always write in the expectation that the audience will correctly fill in what has been left unsaid. Zane Gray presumes that the audience will not suppose that his cowboys' innards are made of sawdust, and popular writers in general assume that their audiences will suppose that their characters possess the same structure of beliefs, desires, and emotions that they do and that the characters are not alien changelings with unheard-of psychologies.

That is, authors presuppose that the audience has a pre-established schema for what constitutes a human person and that, unless informed otherwise, the audience will use that schema to fill-out the human and otherwise person-like (for example, Klingon) characters in the story.[40] The author does not have to specify everything about a character, or even that much, because she relies upon the audience's mobilization of its person

---

[39] For further argumentation for this claim, see Noël Carroll, 'Moderate Moralism'; and 'Art, Narrative and Moral Understanding'.

[40] For a discussion of the relevance of person schemas to fiction, see Murray Smith, *Engaging Characters: Fiction, Emotion, and Cinema* (Oxford: Clarendon Press, 1995), especially ch. 1. Smith's notion of the person schema is preceded by David Bordwell's, where it is presented as a way of explaining critical interpretations. See David Bordwell, *Making Meaning* (Cambridge, Mass.: Harvard University Press, 1989), 151–68; and id., 'Cognition and Comprehension: Viewing and Forgetting in *Mildred Pierce*', *Journal of Dramatic Theory and Criticism*, 6/2 (1992), 183–98.

Interestingly, given the fact that narratives require the mobilization of our everyday person schemas in order to be understood, the doctrine of formalists, like Boris Tomashevsky, that art (including literature) and life are separate must be false. Most narratives are unintelligible unless the audience accesses everyday person schemas in the process of consuming artworks concerned with human affairs. The penetration of life into art is a necessary condition of narrative literature.

schema to do the work for her. Conan Doyle does not go out of his way to say that Sherlock Holmes has only one heart, since he reliably predicts that most readers will assume so, unless told otherwise. Likewise, the author does not have to spell out that the characters possess the standard complement of beliefs, desires, and emotions except, where there are deviations from the norm of our person schemas such as Mr Spock, who reputedly lacks emotions.

The ordinary person schema of the audience is the default value. Authors presuppose that audiences will access it in order to follow the story. This is not to say that the audience may not have to revise the schema under the guidance of the text. In science fictions like *The Midwich Cuckoos*, the audience is informed that one mind possesses the many bodies of the children of the village of the damned. But, unless told otherwise by the author, the audience will fill in the characters according to their standing-person schemas. And, moreover, as a condition of narrating, authors assume that they will do so. No artist can say or depict everything there is to say or to depict about the fictional events she is narrating. She depends upon the audience to fill in a great deal and that filling-in is an indispensable part of what it is to follow and to comprehend a narrative. When the author of a novel about the eighteenth century notes that the characters travelled from one province to another, she expects that, unless she wrote otherwise, the audience will not imagine that the characters were teleported, but that they travelled by carriage, horse, or on foot.[41]

The kinds of details that authors rely on audiences to supply come in all different shapes and sizes, ranging from facts about human biology to facts about geography, history, politics, religion, and so on. In many cases, the author relies upon what we know or believe about human psychology in order for her narrative to be intelligible. For example, in *Eugénie Grandet*, Balzac presumes that the readership has enough understanding of the ways of the human heart to see how it is that Eugénie's betrayal at the hands of her cousin can precipitate the irreparable bitterness that turns her into the very image of her father. That is, he presumes that the audience grasps how becoming her father is a kind of psychological armour or protective shielding against future emotional damage. Authors presume that audiences bring a working folk psychology to the text—one shared by the author—as a condition of narrative intelligibility, and, in that sense, the audience's mobilization of that folk psychology for the purpose of filling in

---

[41] See Christopher Butler, *Interpretation, Deconstruction, and Ideology* (Oxford: Clarendon Press, 1984), 7, 53.

the story is a condition of the very possibility of the text as a form of narrative communication.

Moreover, the audience's activity of filling in the narrative does not simply have to do with recognizing what the text suggests, implies, or presupposes about the contours of its fictional world and about the nature and psychology of the human characters that inhabit that world. To understand a text successfully also involves mobilizing the emotions requisite for the text. One does not understand *Trilby* unless one finds Svengali repugnant, whereas anyone left unmoved by the experiences of the members of the Joy Luck Club would find the point of the novel incomprehensible.

A narrative by its very nature is selective and therefore incomplete in certain specifiable senses. It is for this reason that the author requires an audience to be able to bring to the text, among other things, what is not explicit in it. This further dictates that, to a large extent, the author and the audience need to share a common background of beliefs about the world and about human nature, as well as a relatively common emotional stock. The author designs her work with an implicit working hypothesis about the knowledge that her anticipated reader will bring to the text, along with knowledge of how the reader will feel toward the characters. For unless the readers feel toward the characters in certain ways, the readers will be unlikely to comprehend the narrative.[42]

Of course, the cognitive stock that the audience needs to possess in order to understand a narrative fiction successfully includes not only knowledge of geography and human nature, but moral knowledge as well. For example, in an episode of the TV series *Family Ties*, one can only understand the jokes at the expense of the character Alex if one realizes his failure to recognize that women are not objects available, as he puts it, from a 'girl tree'.[43] The vignette revolves around the principle that women are persons and should not be treated like things. There should not be, as Alex opines, 'a girl store'. Alex's failure to woo Sharon is attributable to his failure to treat her as an end in herself, as a person in her own right. Instead, Alex tries unsuccessfully to mould Sharon into the image of his former girlfriend, Ellen. His failure to do so supplies the narrative with its *raison d'être*.

The audience is able to follow the logic of this story just because it is able to supply the unstated moral premiss the narrative presumes, namely, that women should be treated as persons. Admittedly, this example may

---

[42] One qualification here is what I call meta-understanding. See Ch. 4 n. 13.
[43] This episode of *Family Ties* aired on ABC on 2 Oct. 1986; it has no title.

seem trivial, but it is hardly unrepresentative. Most narratives rely on the activation of moral beliefs on the part of the audience, and the relevance of what goes on in the story to those moral beliefs is indispensable to the audience for grasping the point of the narrative.

Of course, audience emotions are equally important in following a narrative, and those emotions are quite frequently moral both in the sense that many emotions are shot through with moral concepts—in the way that anger is (since 'being wronged' is conceptually criterial for feeling it)—and in the sense that the relevant emotions are themselves very often moral emotions, such as the contempt for wanton brutality and the indignation that pervade every instalment of the TV miniseries *Roots*.[44]

In the last chapter, we saw how often anger serves to glue the audience to the text. In Stephen King's *The Green Mile*, hatred of Percy Wetmore and Brad Dolan is part of what it is to follow the text successfully, while in Lorenzo Carcaterra's *Sleepers*, outrage at Sean Nokes is indispensable for the revenge plot to be effective. Anger is so central to Hong Kong film-making that one book on it is entitled *Kung Fu! Cinema of Vengeance*.[45] Of course, the anger induced by mass fictions is moral in nature, inasmuch as it is frequently connected with papable injustice—for example, the attempted rape of his sister in Bruce Lee's film *Enter the Dragon* or the domestic abuse in Stephen King's *Rose Madder*. But in David Morrell's *The Totem*, our moral contempt for Mayor Parsons rests on our recognition of his attempt to pull off a cover-up, as is the case with a similar figure in the TV movie *The Beast* and with the Secretary of Defense in the novelization of *Independence Day*. In all these cases, the fictioneers depend on the audience's filling in the text with moral judgement and moral emotion. Without the audience's contributions, the fictions would typically remain inert.

Nor is the anger family the only relevant emotional syndrome here. One cannot, for example, admire Schindler in the way the film *Schindler's List* encourages, if one does not feel that the Nazis are morally loathsome. And even melodramas, like *Backstreet*, as we have seen, typically evoke an emotional response that is a mixture of moral admiration for the protagonists—often as a result of their self-sacrificing behaviour—compounded with sorrow over their adversity. There is no 'melodramatic response', just as according to Aristotle there is no tragic response, where the audience misconstrues the moral standing of the relevant characters. Nor is it likely that there can be a successful narrative of any substance that would not

[44] See Boris Tomashevsky, 'Thematics', in *Russian Formalist Criticism*, ed. Lee T. Lemon and Marion J. Reis (Lincoln: University of Nebraska Press, 1965), 65.

[45] Verina Glaessner, *Kung Fu! Cinema of Vengeance* (New York: Bounty Books, Crown Publishers, 1974).

rely upon activating the moral powers of the audience—their moral emotions and judgements—against a background of moral beliefs. Part of what it is standardly to follow a narrative is to bring our moral beliefs, judgements, and emotions to bear on it in a way that completes the narrative. Moreover, in the general case, authors can rely upon the audience to fill in the narrative with the right beliefs, judgements, and emotions, because the audience and the author share a roughly common background.

In his *Letter to M. D'Alembert on the Theater*,[46] Jean-Jacques Rousseau argues that theatre cannot transform a community morally or reform it. Rousseau believes this because he points out that in order to succeed an author has to write within the moral framework of his times. Rousseau notes, 'An author who would brave the general taste would soon write for himself alone.'[47] That is, there are 'market pressures', so to speak, that incline authors to design their works in such a way that they rely upon a fit between their narratives and a roughly common cognitive, emotive, and moral stock that is shared by the readers, viewers, and listeners who make up the expected audience of the work. If there were no such common background, there would be no successful communication, since there would be no uptake.[48]

A successful narrative is built so that its anticipated audience can understand it, and in order to understand a narrative successfully, an audience will have to mobilize its knowledge and its emotions, moral and otherwise, in the process of filling in a story. This means that in order to understand a narrative successfully, we must use many of the same beliefs and emotions, generally rooted in our common culture and our common biological endowment, that we use to navigate everyday human events for the purpose of filling in and getting the point of stories. In this sense, it is not the case, *pace* propositionalism and identificationism, that the narrative teaches us something brand new, but rather it activates the knowledge and emotions, moral and otherwise, that we already possess.

That is, the narrative becomes the occasion for exercising knowledge, concepts, and emotions that we have already, in one sense, learnt. Filling in the narrative is a matter of mobilizing or accessing the cognitive, emotive, and moral repertoire that, for the most part, we already have

[46] Jean-Jacques Rousseau, 'Letter to M. D'Alembert on the Theater', in *Politics and the Arts*, ed. Allan Bloom (Ithaca, NY: Cornell University Press, 1973).   [47] Ibid. 19.

[48] This sort of argument looks back to Plato's about the necessity of emotional address in theatre, while also looking forward, at least in its structure, to MacDonald's lowest common denominator argument. That is, Plato, Rousseau, and MacDonald all look to what we might broadly call market circumstances to explain the necessity of certain structural features of the artworks that concern them.

at our disposal. Narratives, in other words, provide us with opportunities to, among other things, exercise our moral powers, because the very process of understanding a narrative is itself, to a significant degree, an exercise of our moral powers.

Because narratives are so inextricably bound up with the exercise of our moral powers, it is quite natural for ethical concerns to recur frequently when we discuss stories. In so far as narratives necessarily depend upon activating our moral beliefs, concepts, and feelings, it comes as no surprise that we should want to discuss them and to share and compare (with other audience members) our moral reactions to the characters, situations, and overall texts that authors present to us with the clear intention of eliciting—among other things—moral responses. That is, it is natural for us to think about and discuss narratives in terms of ethics, because narratives, due to the kinds of things they are, awaken, stir up, and engage our moral powers of recognition and judgement.

But if this account is correct, and if we suppose additionally that learning is a matter of the acquisition of interesting, non-trivial propositions, heretofore unknown, and/or of freshly minted moral emotions, then (as we saw earlier) we may be sceptical about whether there is such a thing as moral education when it comes to mass narratives, since, in the standard case, there is no moral learning of this sort. For in the vast majority of narrative artworks, and especially in the case of mass artworks, such narratives depend—as a condition of their very intelligibility—upon our antecedent possession of knowledge of various moral precepts, and of concepts of vice and virtue, and so on. Nor do such narratives invest us with, and thereby teach, new emotions; rather, typically they exercise the emotions that we already possess.

And yet, it does seem that the operative sense of learning in the preceding sceptical argument is too restrictive. For there is another sense of learning—both moral and otherwise—that is being ignored and that applies to the kinds of activities that narrative artworks abet. It is this: that in mobilizing what we already know and what we can already feel, the narrative artwork can become an occasion for us to deepen our understanding of what we know and feel. Notably, for our purposes, a narrative can become an opportunity for us to deepen our grasp of the moral knowledge and emotions already at our command.

This conception of the relation of art, especially narrative art, to morality might be called transactionalism (because of its emphasis on the transaction between the narrative artwork and moral understanding), or it might be called, as I prefer to call it, *clarificationism*, in honour of the most prized transaction that might transpire between the narrative artwork and the moral understanding. Clarificationism does not claim that, in the typical case, we acquire new propositional knowledge from artworks, but rather that the artworks in question can deepen our moral understanding by, among other things, encouraging us to apply our moral knowledge and emotions to specific cases. For in being prompted to apply and engage our antecedent moral powers, we may come to augment them.

In the course of engaging a given narrative, we may need to reorganize the hierarchical orderings of our moral categories and premises, or to reinterpret those categories and premises in the light of new paradigm instances and hard cases, or to reclassify barely acknowledged moral phenomena afresh—something that we might be provoked to do by a feminist author who is able to show us injustice where before all we saw was culture as usual. Or, a mass fiction, like the television series *Cagney and Lacey*, may, for example, prompt us to revise our morally charged cultural schemas by presenting women as serious candidates for police officers.

A movie such as *A Raisin in the Sun* addresses white audiences in such a way as to incite vividly their recognition that African Americans are persons, like any others, and, therefore, should be accorded the kind of equal treatment for persons that such audiences already verbally endorse as a matter of moral principle. The film does this by showing that the dreams and the family bonds of the protagonists are no different from those of others—that is to say of persons of other races, notably the white race—and, thereby, the film prompts the audience to subsume African-Americans under a moral precept concerning equal treatment that the audience already believes. The film shows that the life of the characters is no different from the lives of other Americans, and that the life of such characters calls for the same moral protection that every other life requires. The film makes our precepts about equality hit home with particular force. And this, in turn, encourages the white audience to form the moral judgement that the way in which the potential neighbours of the black family respond to their purchasing their new house is wrong.

In this case, as in many others, it seems accurate to describe what goes on in white audiences as a discovery about something about what they already knew—i.e., they put together previously disconnected belief fragments in a new gestalt in a way that changes their moral perception. Ideally, they 'get' something about equality that they haven't 'got' before. Here it is not primarily the case that the white audience acquires a new piece of moral knowledge—an interesting, new general proposition; rather, they seem to be prompted to make connections between the moral beliefs they already possess in a way that illuminates their grasp of the case at hand, as well as possibly spotlighting a heretofore unrecognized application of their precepts about equality. The film, that is, may provoke a 'gestalt switch'.

The characters and the situations presented in the movie afford an occasion to reorganize or to reshuffle the moral beliefs that the white audience already has at its disposal. Its system of beliefs undergoes clarification. Its grasp and understanding of what it already knows is deepened in a way that counts, I contend, as learning, though it may not primarily be a matter of learning a new proposition, since in some sense, the white audience already knows that African Americans are persons and that all persons deserve equal treatment. What the movie succeeds in doing is in bringing together those two pieces of knowledge in a forceful way. It creates a situation that encourages the audience to forge a salient connection between heretofore perhaps isolated beliefs. Here, we are given the opportunity to deepen our grasp and our understanding of what we already know in a way that also counts as learning, though not necessarily as a matter of learning, as propositionalism would have it, new, non-trivial and interesting propositions. Rather, it is more a matter of grasping the connection between pieces of antecedently possessed knowledge.[49]

Similarly, a mass fiction like Erich Maria Remarque's *All Quiet on the Western Front* presents the reader with the opportunity to reflect on what he really values. The reader may already agree that in some sense war is an evil. But reading Remarque's book can become an occasion for coming to appreciate the value of dry socks, a warm meal, a sunny day and camaraderie over the claims of national honour. The book presents us with situations that cause us to reflect upon and perhaps reorder our heretofore complacent hierarchy of values, making us vividly aware of what we value

---

[49] I would not wish to deny that there is a sense in which one might describe what the audience has learnt by means of a general proposition. Perhaps, one might describe the reaction to *A Raisin in the Sun* in terms of the audience's possession of a new proposition—that African Americans deserve equal treatment. But I don't think that the audience has simply deduced this from other general propositions that it holds antecedently. That is something that they could have done by rote. Rather, they come to see that this perhaps already known fact is deeply embedded in their structure of moral beliefs. That is, they come to appreciate this belief in the sense in which one appreciates a chess move. They not only acknowledge it, but they see its interrelation to other beliefs in a way that also makes those other beliefs more vivid and compelling, inasmuch as their relevance is brought home by a particular case.

Phenomenologically, it is not like simply acquiring a new proposition like the sum of 47,832 and 91,247 is 139,079. Rather, it is a matter of an abstract proposition falling into place and resounding in a larger system of beliefs. Simply describing what happens as the acquisition of a new proposition, even if it is in some sense formally true, misses this dimension of the transaction.

Of course, I would not wish to deny that *some* narrative artworks convey novel general moral propositions to audiences. My contention is that this is not the standard case. In the standard case, the narrative artwork functions more as an occasion to promote (or, as we shall see, to degrade) moral understanding by activating moral propositions already at our disposal.

or what we ought to value.[50] In other words, the fiction functions as a suitable occasion for getting clearer about our values.

Here I intend to draw a contrast between knowledge and *understanding* such that understanding is meant to mark our capacity to manipulate what we know and to apply it with a sense of intelligibility—not simply to have access to abstract propositions and concepts, but to be able to employ them intelligibly and appropriately. Understanding is a capacity to see and to be responsive to connections between our beliefs. A person with understanding has the ability to find her way around in the mental geography of her own cognitive stock.[51] Understanding is the ability to make connections between what we already know. With understanding we acquire increasing familiarity with concepts and principles whose generality may at first be bewildering. Understanding is the activity of refining what we already know, of recognizing connections between parts of our knowledge stock, and of bringing what we already know to clarity through a process of practice and use.

We may possess abstract principles—such as 'all persons should be given their due'—and abstract concepts—such as 'virtue is what promotes human flourishing'—without being able to connect these abstractions to concrete situations. For that requires not only knowing these abstractions, but understanding them. Moreover, this is the kind of understanding—particularly with respect to moral understanding—to which engaging with narrative artworks may contribute.

Inasmuch as understanding is often a function of correctly classifying things, fictional narratives frequently present us with opportunities to deliberate about how to categorize behaviours and character traits, and, thereby, they can enhance our capacity for classifying the human environment—by encouraging us to link abstract concepts to percepts in ways that can make us more sensitive and adept at applying them to real-world cases. As I have already suggested, it seems to me that the work of many feminist artists has been to get people to reclassify a great many everyday practices under the category of injustice. They have got many—men and women alike—to see certain behaviours as exploitative. I see no reason to refrain from calling this process one of moral education, even if the audience already possesses the idea that exploitation is morally bad. What audiences learn from these feminists is not that exploitation is bad—they already knew that. Rather they learn to see and to appreciate

[50] Robert Stecker, *Artworks: Definition, Meaning, Value* (University Park: Pennsylvania University Press), 284–5.
[51] See Neil Cooper, 'Understanding', *Aristotelian Society*, Supplementary Volume, lxviii, 1–26.

that certain customary folkways are, in fact, exploitative. And that, I submit, constitutes moral education.

Moreover, in so far as the emotions involve a conceptual component—in terms of formal criteria for what can serve as the appropriate object of an emotional state—it is coherent to talk about deepening our emotional understanding, which involves treating the narrative as an occasion for clarifying our emotions, i.e., in Aristotle's terms, of learning to apply the right emotion to the appropriate object with suitable intensity. This, of course, presupposes that the emotions are educable. But inasmuch as we showed grounds for this in the last chapter, I see no reason for denying that narratives might not be the occasion for educating the emotions morally—not by investing us with new moral emotions, but by correctly exercising the ones we already possess.

As is probably apparent, for the clarificationist, engaging with or coming to understand a narrative artwork can itself simultaneously be a process of deepening one's own moral understanding. A classic example of this is the reader's recognition that there is something deeply wrong morally with Emma's 'guidance' of Harriet in Jane Austen's novel. That is, recognizing that Emma is treating Harriet as a means to satisfy her own vanity is not only requisite for understanding the novel successfully, but it also deepens our moral understanding by providing the reader with a portrait of the sort of interpersonal manipulation that is rife in everyday life, which, though well-intentioned, is ultimately self-deceptive as well as wicked. Moreover, the fact that we must resist the allure of Emma's otherwise attractive personality before we reach this insight about the wrongness of her interference with Harriet's life makes the novel *Emma* all the more serviceable as an occasion where we have the opportunity for expanding our moral understanding, though not our knowledge (in so far as we already knew the abstract maxim that treating people merely as a means is immoral).[52]

It might be argued that this case does not come from the province of mass art. But, of course, it is easy to find parallel cases in the corpus of mass art. In *Mr. Deeds Goes to Town*, I suspect that the audience begins to recognize the wrongness of the subterfuge that the newspaperwoman, Babe, plays on Longfellow Deeds before she does. She is presented as an attractive character—savvy, ambitious, energetic, and smart. The audience is favourably disposed toward her. She is your basic spunky thirties heroine. And yet, the audience, I think, realizes that she has made a terrible, morally serious mistake before she does.

[52] See Gilbert Ryle, 'Jane Austen and the Moralists', *Oxford Review*, 1 (1966).

Likewise, in the best-selling novel, *Gentleman's Agreement*, by Laura Z. Hobson, though one is almost always on the side of Phil Green, the crusading journalist who pretends he is Jewish in order to unmask anti-semitism, one also hesitates at points over what he is doing, since one wonders whether he has really thought through the consequences of what he is doing for some of the people closest to him. He never thinks to warn his young son about what might befall him, or even to explain to the child what he is doing, until after the boy becomes the victim of discrimination. Should Green be drawing a child into his project, even if the child ultimately (perhaps for the wrong reason) consents? Is Green, blinded by his own self-righteousness, sometimes morally reckless in this and some other instances? Is he using his son as a means, albeit a means to a just cause (confronting anti-semitism), but a just cause that will also win Green money and prestige?

The novel may not answer these questions, but raises them in a way that invites the reader to deliberate about them and to try to come to an all-things-considered judgement about them. The case is a hard one, because one must weigh the undeniable overall good of what Green is doing against certain possibly wrong aspects of it. But that it is not an absolutely clear-cut case makes it a productive opportunity for the audience to expand its moral powers.

In the early scenes of the film *A Face in the Crowd*, the character Lonesome Roads, toward whom the audience is encouraged to be favourably disposed, incites his TV audience to demonstrate against his commercial advertiser, a mattress company. The president of the company is portrayed as a stuffy arrogant snob, and the film audience is likely to be gladdened when his mattresses are burned in the street by unhappy customers agitating against the cancellation of Lonesome's contract. However, as the story goes on and Lonesome is revealed to be a cruel demagogue, the audience is apt to revise its evaluation of this scene retrospectively. Moreover, that the film prompts retrospective revision contributes to the sophistication of our powers of moral judgement.[53]

Many of Alfred Hitchcock's films prod the audience to wrestle with moral ambiguities. For example, in *Shadow of Doubt*, when, during a

---

[53] For a recent film example that encourages the audience to revise its moral judgements consider the character of Archibald Cunningham, played by Tim Roth, in *Rob Roy*. At one point, we are invited to extend some sympathy for him, when he narrates his unfortunate upbringing. However, we come to resist any temptations along these lines as his villainy continues. He is just too vicious for his childhood experiences to excuse him. Nevertheless, the film is interesting for the way in which it prompts us to revise our moral judgement of the character at least twice—first by encouraging us to ameliorate our initial unfavourable assessment of him and then by prompting us to revise our moral judgement of the relevance of the extenuating circumstances.

cocktail party, Young Charley signals to her uncle that she knows that he is a serial killer, she seems satisfied that it is enough that he leave town. This will save her family, especially her mother, great embarrassment and pain, to say the least, but Young Charley's behaviour still allows a dangerous killer to remain free to prey upon 'merry widows' elsewhere. Here, Hitchcock invites the audience to consider whether Young Charley's apparent moral victory isn't somehow morally irresponsible.[54]

On the clarificationist view, learning from a narrative artwork through the enlargement or expansion of one's moral understanding is not well described as a *consequence* of engaging the story. Understanding the work, enlarging one's moral understanding, and learning from the narrative are all part and parcel of the same process, which might be called comprehending or following the narrative. When reading a novel or watching a film, our moral understanding is engaged already. Reading a novel, for example, is itself generally a moral activity in so far as reading narrative literature—from Thackeray to Patricia Cornwell—typically involves us in a *continuous process of moral judgement*, which continuous exercise of moral judgement itself can contribute to the expansion of our moral understanding. When reading a novel or watching a TV drama, we are engaged in a moral activity already, inasmuch as our powers of moral judgement and understanding have been drawn into play, and, as we shall see later, our moral assessment of a narrative artwork may rest upon the quality of that moral activity or experience, rather than, *pace* the consequentialist, upon speculations about the probable behavioural consequences of reading, hearing, or viewing that fiction.

In order to avoid obscurity, it will be useful for me to provide some examples of the way in which narrative artworks can enhance the understanding. As Sir Philip Sidney[55] and Immanuel Kant[56] point out, we are often possessed of general propositions that are very abstract and that we may not be able to connect to particular situations. That is, they are so abstract that they leave us at a loss about how to apply them. But narrative artworks can supply us with vivid examples that enable us to see how to apply abstractions to particulars. For example, *King Lear* gives us an arresting example with which to understand the general proposition that 'a

---

[54] This interpretation is derived from George Wilson's, 'The Importance of Being Enigmatic', a talk delivered at the Honolulu Arts Academy Theater, 22 Aug. 1996.

[55] Sir Philip Sidney, 'An Apology for Poetry', in *Criticism: The Major Texts*, ed. Walter Jackson Bates (New York: Harcourt, Brace, Jovanovich, Inc., 1970), 82–106.

[56] Immanuel Kant, 'Methodology of Pure Practical Reason', in *Critique of Practical Reason* (Indianapolis: Bobbs-Merrill, 1956), 155–65. See also what Kant says about judgement in 'On the Common Saying: "This May be True in Theory, but it does not Apply in Practice"', in Immanuel Kant, *Political Writings*, ed. Hans Reiss (Cambridge: Cambridge University Press, 1995), 61.

house divided shall not stand'; while the early twentieth-century film serial *Judex* dramatizes the moral adage 'Judge not, lest ye be judged'.

This recognition of the importance of examples for moral understanding, of course, was also acknowledged by medieval theologians in their recommendation of the use of the *exemplum*, a recommendation that can be traced back to Aristotle's discussion of illustrations in his *Rhetoric*. Much modern moral theory has placed a great deal of emphasis on rules in its conception of moral deliberation. However, this overlooks the problem that often our moral rules and concepts are too thin to determine the particular situations that fall under them.[57] That requires moral judgement, which in turn requires examples in order to develop, and the capacity for moral judgement is exactly what is ideally exercised and refined through our encounters with narrative artworks. Thus, George Eliot and D. H. Lawrence recommend literature as a means of augmenting our powers of moral judgement in terms of our capacity to interpret the content of abstract, general rules in response to particular situations.[58]

Here, it is not my intention to disparage the role of rules for moral deliberation, but merely to point out that rules need to be negotiated by the capacity for judgement. In order to know how to apply moral rules, the moral imagination requires examples for reflection. Examples call into play the operation of moral judgement to adjudicate the application of rules and roles with reference to particular cases. And it is this capacity for moral judgement that can be enhanced by traffic with narrative artworks just because narrative artworks, as a feature of their essential nature, require moral judgements in order to be intelligible.

For example, Mary Shelley's *Frankenstein* exemplifies the point that evil proceeds from nurture, not nature—from the environment and social conditioning, or the lack thereof—and, hence, that blame needs to be apportioned with respect to this principle. Victor Frankenstein, that is, must bear a large measure of guilt for the mayhem he has unleashed through being 'a bad father'. Moreover, as this example should indicate, the way in which moral understanding is enhanced by narrative artworks need not be thought of as a matter of the fiction supplying audiences with precise templates that they then go on to match with real cases. For obviously there can be no real case anywhere like the one portrayed in *Frankenstein*.

Instead, the moral understanding can be refined and deepened in the

---

[57] See Charles Larmore, *Patterns of Moral Complexity* (Cambridge: Cambridge University Press, 1987), ch. 1.

[58] Ibid. 21; and George Eliot, 'The Natural History of German Life', in her *Selected Essays, Poems and Other Writings* (London: Penguin Books, 1990), 110.

process of coming to terms with this story and its characters, especially the monster and his claims to justice. We are not in a position to measure real-life on a one-to-one basis against the story of *Frankenstein*—since nothing like the story could occur—but after reading the novel our moral under-standing may be more sophisticated in such a way that we can identify cases of injustice quite unlike that portrayed in *Frankenstein*. Thus, we see why authors need not—and often do not—trade in typical cases, but favour rather extraordinary ones in order to provoke an expansion of our moral powers.

Mass fictions are very frequently involved in exemplifying moral prin-ciples. In the episode of the TV series *The Waltons* entitled 'The Pursuit', the importance of honesty in marital relations is stressed. Set during World War II, Jim-Bob has lied in the heat of passion about his military exploits to a young woman named Cathy. He has never been overseas. But he thought that he was about to be shipped off to the European theatre of operations, and the suggestion is that he feared that this might be his last chance to shed his virginity. However, he is not shipped off. Cathy, mean-while, believes that she is in love with him. When he resists her aggressive advances, she tells him, falsely, that she is pregnant. Marriage preparations begin, but in a defeated spirit of tangible resignation on Jim-Bob's part which, in turn, causes Cathy anxiety. The situation is one of ill-ease.

Jim-Bob's father (called 'Daddy') talks to the couple about his own marriage and about the importance of truthfulness to a relationship. Gradually, the lesson sinks in, and the youngsters talk through their predicament honestly, thereby averting what the fiction suggests would be a disaster. Here, the truism that honesty is the best policy is given weight by having its content interpreted by an example that illustrates a not infrequent moral predicament in everyday life. Moreover, though this case may be aesthetically unremarkable, it represents the moral structure of many mass fictions, including not only TV dramas, but many situation comedies as well.

In addition, just as narrative artworks may enable us to clarify our moral comprehension of abstract moral principles, so too do they enlarge our powers of recognition with respect to abstract virtues and vices. As is well known, in *Pride and Prejudice*, Jane Austen presents the reader with an array of different kinds and degrees of pride in order to coax the reader into recognizing which type of pride, as Gilbert Ryle puts it, goes best with right thinking and right acting.[59] Similar strategies of comparing and contrasting character traits along a single dimension regularly recur in

---

[59] Ryle, 'Jane Austen and the Moralists', 8.

mass art. In martial arts films, such as *The Karate Kid*, both the characters of the karate masters and their students are presented to the audience for us to recognize the morally correct attitude, as well as the appropriate conduct, of an athlete. Likewise, so many western novels and movies, like *Shane*, are about the virtue of restraint—about its proper scope and limits as exemplified by a case study.

And many mass fictions are about vice, as the titles of movies like Erich von Stroheim's *Greed*, *Foolish Wives*, and *Blind Husbands* indicate. *Ace in the Hole* provides a concrete portrait of ruthless ambition. In *Barchester Towers* by Trollope, Mr Slope exemplifies a paradigm of manipulativeness, whereas in Dickens *Bleak House*, the reader gradually comes to see Mr Skimpole's charm and frivolity as a form of callous egoism, thereby receiving a lesson in what, *avant la lettre*, we might call the passive-aggressive personality. Again, the fact that we must revise our moral assessment of Skimpole as the narrative goes on provides an opportunity for us to exercise our powers of moral perception and judgement. Moreover, that *Barchester Towers* and *Bleak House* were originally released in serial form, of course, encouraged readers to compare their moral judgements of evolving characters and situations with each other, much in the way that contemporary soap-operas provide communities of viewers with a common source of gossip, where gossip itself has the salutary function of enabling discussants to clarify their understanding of abstract moral principles and concepts, as well as their application through feelings, by means of conversation and comparison with others.[60]

Narratives involve audiences in processes of moral reasoning and deliberation. As the father in *Meet Me in St. Louis* considers moving to New York, the viewer also weighs the claims of the emotional cost such a move will exact from his family against the abstract claims of the future and progress. And, of course, some narratives, including mass narratives, present audiences with moral problems that appear to have no satisfactorily resolvable solution. Think of the plight of the officer-aristocrats in Renoir's *The Grand Illusion*. This too seems to enrich the moral understanding by stretching its reflective resources.

As Martha Nussbaum argues, narratives may not only serve as models of moral reflection and deliberation, they may be occasions for moral understanding. Nussbaum, of course, believes that there is little legitimate room for moral principles and abstract moral concepts in literary-cum-moral understanding, emphasizing, as she does, perception as the model

---

[60] This view of soap-operas is defended in Noël Carroll, 'As the Dial Turns: Notes on Soap Operas', in my *Theorizing the Moving Image*.

for moral reflection.[61] However, though I do not want to preclude that there may be cases of the kind of moral perception that Nussbaum valorizes, I do not feel any pressure to deny that there are also cases where the moral understanding comes to appreciate abstractions via concrete narratives. Why not have it both ways—so long as we acknowledge that the process of reflection involved in understanding narrative artworks is at the same time a process of moral understanding, often, at least in the most felicitous cases, involving the reorganization and clarification of our moral beliefs and emotions.

Rousseau, it will be recalled, claimed that drama could not reform its audience, since a public artform must, in order to persist, root itself in the beliefs and moral predispositions that its audiences already embrace, lest the work appear unintelligible to them only to be rejected out of hand in consequence. Now surely Rousseau is right that in the standard case, living artworks must share a background of belief and feeling with their audience, but Rousseau oversteps himself when he infers from this that art cannot contribute to moral reform, at least incrementally. For moral reform is often connected to reorganizing, or refocalizing, or 're-gestalting' what people already believe and feel. That is, moral progress frequently relies upon operating on moral beliefs and moral sentiments that people already possess.

For example, by calling attention to and emphasizing the fact that gays and lesbians are fully human persons, one can often convince heterosexuals that gays and lesbians are fully deserving of the rights that those heterosexuals in question already believe should be accorded to all persons. And, of course, this type of gestalt switch, which often contributes to the refinement of moral understanding, is easily within the grasp of narratives, as topical novels and films such as *Philadelphia* attest. By showing its protagonist home for the holidays, amidst a loving and admiring family, *Philadelphia* is capable of prompting the viewer to recognize that gay people are members of the kinds of human communities characteristic of persons, worthy of full civil rights and equal respect.[62]

Undoubtedly, some reformist fictions, like *To Kill a Mockingbird*, are

[61] See, for example, Martha Nussbaum, 'Perceptive Equilibrium: Literary Theory and Ethical Theory', in her book *Love's Knowledge: Essays on Philosophy and Literature* (New York: Oxford University Press, 1990), 168–94.

[62] The use of families in this sort of narrative would appear to be very important, since there is psychological evidence that viewers will tend to be more favourably disposed to characters who are similar to themselves and one widely distributed dimension of similarity is the family and familial bonds of affection.

On the bias of empathy for similarity, see Martin Hoffman, 'The contribution of empathy to justice', in *Empathy and its Development*.

frequently criticized for trafficking in victims who are too pure, too saintly, too unrealistically good, and, in that sense, somewhat misleading in the long run. But I think that, in the short run, these choices are certainly tactically justified in order to get the job done, where the job in question is to coax the reconfiguration of popular thinking about oppressed groups, including blacks, gays, Jews, women, and so on. And to the extent that people can be incrementally enlightened by narratives that operate on the audience's antecedent ethical beliefs and emotions, Rousseau is wrong. For narratives can contribute to moral reform by deepening our moral understanding by means of engaging that which we already believe and feel with reference to particular cases.

By focusing on the nature of narrative and by taking note of the way in which narratives require audiences to fill in stories by means of their own beliefs and emotions, including, unavoidably, moral ones, I think that I have shown why it is natural for us to discuss narrative artworks in terms of ethical considerations. For, simply put, much of our activity as readers, listeners, and viewers with respect to narratives engages our moral understanding. *Pace* formalists who regard the moral discussion of art as either a failure of intelligence or taste or both, we may argue that it is neither, given the kind of artefacts narratives are. For given the nature of narrative, the activity of reading, viewing, or listening to one is, in large measure, a matter of exercising our moral understanding. It is appropriate to think and to talk about narrative artworks in light of morality because of the nature of narrative artworks and the responses—such as moral judgements—that they are meant to elicit as a condition for being intelligible, given the kinds of things they are. Indeed, it would be a failure of intelligence and taste if one did not respond to narratives morally.

Moreover, if what I have argued so far is compelling, then perhaps the clarificationist picture of the relation of morality to narrative art can also suggest certain grounds for the moral assessments that we make of characters and of complete narratives as well. Obviously, the moral judgements and understandings achieved in response to a narrative artwork differ in at least one way from those essayed in everyday life, since the moral experience that we have in response to a narrative is guided by the author of the story. There is a level of moral experience available from the narrative that depends on the guidance with which the author intends to provide us. I contend that our moral assessments of the narrative, then, can be grounded in the quality of the moral experiences that the author's guidance is designed to invite and abet.

Some narratives may stretch and deepen our moral understanding quite a lot. And these, all things being equal, will raise our moral estimate of the work, which may, in turn, even contribute to our artistic evaluation of the work, in so far as a narrative artwork which engages our moral understanding will be all the more absorbing, for that very reason.[63] *Do the Right Thing* may be a recent example of a mass artwork of this sort.

On the other hand, narratives that mislead or confuse moral understanding deserve criticism—as does Michael Crichton's recent, morally frivolous novel *Disclosure*, which pretends to explore the issue of sexual harassment through a case that really has more to do with thriller-type cover-ups than it has to do with sexual politics. The particular instance of alleged sexual harassment is actually a gambit in a corporate take-over. It is hardly a productive case for thinking about sexual harassment. In other words, it focuses attention on the wrong kind of particular. Here, the problem with the novel is that it is essentially digressive, and, in that respect, it misdirects our moral understanding on the issue of sexual harassment. Likewise, narratives that pervert and confuse moral understanding by connecting moral principles, concepts, and emotions to dubious particulars—as often happens in political propaganda—also fare badly on the clarificationist model, since they obfuscate rather than clarify.

The recent film *Natural Born Killers*, for instance, advertises itself as a meditation on violence, but it neither affords a consistent emotional stance on serial killing, nor does it deliver its promised insight on the relation of serial killing to the media, if only because it neglects to show how the media might have affected the relevant characters. Indeed, its very title— *Natural Born Killers*—would seem at odds with the hypothesis of media-made murder. The media references in the film appear to divert our attention away from the moral issues at hand, and in confusing or even perverting our moral grasp of the issue, they are, along with the film as a whole, candidates for moral rebuke.

Throughout this chapter and the previous one, I have emphasized the importance in narratives of enlisting the audience's emotional response to the situations that narratives present. Because of this, narratives can be morally assessed in terms of whether they contribute to emotional understanding—where that pertains to morality—or whether they obfuscate it. For example, in many fictions about psychotic killers, like the film (as opposed to the novel) *Silence of the Lambs*, the murderers are presented as gay. Gayness is advanced as part of their monstrosity, and the audience is encouraged to regard these killers with horror. Gayness is thus represented as literally unnatural. Gayness and monstrosity are superimposed on each other in such a way that gayness is turned into a

---

[63] For further argumentation of this point, see Noël Carroll, 'Moderate Moralism'.

suitable object of the emotion of horror. That is, gayness is conflated with horrific monstrosity.

But this is to mismatch gayness with a morally inappropriate emotion. It is to confuse homosexuals with the kinds of creatures—like alien beings—that warrant emotional responses of fear and disgust. To engender this kind of loathing for homosexuality by enlisting a response to homosexuals that is emotionally suitable for horrific monsters is morally obnoxious as a result of the way in which it misdirects our feelings. It confuses matters morally by inviting us to forge an emotive link between gayness and the horrific. It tendentiously promotes the wrong kind of object for the emotional state in question.

The ways in which the quality of our moral experience of a narrative artwork can vary—either positively or negatively—are quite diverse. Many different things can go right or wrong in terms of how our moral understanding is engaged, or perverted or frustrated by a narrative artwork. Thus, it is unlikely that there is a single dimension along which the qualities of all our moral experiences of narratives can be plotted or ranked. And since we possess no algorithm, we will have to make our moral assessments on a case-by-case basis, aided, at most, by some very crude rules of thumb, like those operative in the preceding examples.

For instance, in the movie version of *Schindler's List* in the scene where Schindler leaves the factory, director Steven Spielberg strong-arms our emotions by trying to force us to accord Schindler a level of moral admiration that the character has already won from us. As Schindler whines about his Nazi lapel-pin, we are coerced into virtually subvocalizing 'It's okay Oskar. You're a hero and the pin probably helped you fool the SS officers anyway.' Here, our moral emotions are engaged, I think, excessively. Spielberg asks for too much, too late. But, of course, this flaw is rather different and nowhere as problematic as the case of the gay serial killers. In that case, the emotions get attached to morally unsuitable objects for the wrong reasons. At least Schindler appears to be the right kind of object for the emotion in question.

On the clarificationist model, moral asessments of narrative artworks can be grounded in the quality of our moral engagement with and experience of the narrative object. This engagement can be positive, where our moral understanding and/or emotions are deepened and clarified, or it can be negative, where the moral understanding is misled, confused, perverted, muddied, and so on. Moreover, there are many ways in which moral understanding and feeling can be facilitated. For example, a novel—even a bestseller—may subvert complacent views, prompting a reorganization that expands our moral understanding, where such an expansion may count as a good-making feature of the work. And, of course, many narrative artworks, undoubtedly most, engage our moral understanding and emotions without challenging, stretching, or degrading them. Such narrative artworks probably deserve to be assessed positively from the moral point of view, since they do exercise our moral understanding and emotions, but maybe it is best to think of them as *morally good but without distinction.*

One advantage of grounding our moral assessments of narrative artworks in the quality of our moral engagement with said artworks—in contrast to attempts to base our moral assessments on the predicted behavioural consequences of reading, hearing, and listening to such narratives—is that, as we have seen, we have little or no idea about how to determine with any reliability the behavioural consequences of such activities for real-world contexts. And if we can't predict the consequences with precision, there seems to be no acceptable method here.

But, on the other hand, using ourselves as detectors, we can make reasonable conjectures about how those who share the same cultural and genetic backgrounds as we do are apt to understand and be moved by given characters and situations. That is, it is difficult to imagine participants in Western culture who could mistake Darth Vadar as generous.

Clarificationism, then, is not subject to the same criticisms that were levelled at consequentialism. For the clarificationist can deal with those who are suspicious of moral assessments of art on the grounds that such assessments appear to rest upon unwarranted presumptions about the behavioural consequences of consuming artworks. Instead, the clarificationist contends that the relevant moral assessment is keyed to the very process itself of consuming the narrative artwork and not to the supposed behavioural consequences of that process. This is not to deny that the way in which narrative artworks might interact with our moral understanding may have repercussions for behaviour. Nor would I reject the possibility that certain narrative artworks might be censored, if someone could finally prove that they cause actual harmful behaviour systematically. Rather, the clarificationist merely maintains that the moral assessment of narratives, including mass fictions, continues to be possible, as it always has been, in the absence of any well-confirmed theory about the impact of consuming narratives on behaviour.

Not only can the clarificationist meet the possible objection that we cannot assess art morally because we lack the theoretical wherewithal to gauge the behavioural consequences of art. The clarificationist can also explain how art might have something to teach, even though the maxims and concepts it deals with are so often routinely known. For, in the most typical case, narrative art can educate the moral understanding and the emotions by using what we already believe and feel—mobilizing it, exercising it, sometimes reorienting it, and sometimes enlarging it—rather than primarily by introducing us to interesting new propositions and concepts.[64]

On the propositionalist view of the morally educative powers of narrative, it is supposed that audiences derive general, novel, interesting moral propositions from texts and then they apply them to the world. I have argued that this is not an accurate, comprehensive account because most of the propositions derivable from narratives are truisms. But this is not the picture of the educative powers of narrative that the clarificationist advances. The clarificationist acknowledges that narratives generally play off the moral beliefs and emotions that we already possess. However, in *exercising* these pre-existing moral powers in response to texts, the texts may become opportunities for enhancing our already existing moral understanding. Thus, the direction of moral education with respect to narratives is not *from the text to the world* by way of newly acquired and interesting moral propositions, as the propositionalist suggests. Rather, antecedent moral beliefs about the world may be augmented in the understanding by commerce with texts. That is, the pertinent direction of moral education for the clarificationist is, so to speak, *from the world to the text.*[65]

Since I have attempted to ground moral assessments of narrative artworks in what might be broadly construed as a learning model, it may appear that I have walked into the cross-hairs of a well-known, long-standing argument by formalists that contends that artworks cannot be the instruments of moral education, nor is it their function to promote moral education. Rather, art is valuable for its own sake; it is not supposed to serve ulterior ends, such as moral education.

---

[64] The caveat 'primarily' in the preceding sentence is meant to allow for the possibility that, in exceptional cases, the kind of reorienting, reorganizing, and regestalting that I have been talking about may yield an interesting, new proposition or concept. This is not, I contend, the general course of events, but I do not wish to argue that it could never happen. But it is rare enough that it cannot provide the basis of a general theory of the relation of fictional narratives to the moral understanding. Moreover, it needs to be stressed that even where there is the acquisition of a new proposition or concept, the fictional narrative itself provides no probative force for the acquired 'knowledge', since the fiction is made up. If the proposition is to be justified, it must find warrant in the real world. The concession that interesting new propositions may be acquired in the process of deepening our moral understanding of fictional narratives is a response to a comment by Jerrold Levinson. However, I remain sceptical about his suggestion that the fictional narrative can serve as part of the database for newly acquired principles and concepts.

[65] In stressing the world-to-text direction between moral understanding and narratives, rather than the text-to-world direction, my position converges on the one defended by Peter Lamarque and Stein Haugom Olsen in *Truth, Fiction and Literature: A Philosophical Perspective.*

However, though I think I have shown how moral learning can issue from commerce with narrative artworks, I have not proposed the reduction of narrative art to an instrumentality of moral education. For the learning that may take place here, though it emerges because of the kind of work a narrative artwork is, need not be the aim of the narrative artwork, but rather a concomitant, one of which the author may take no self-conscious notice. For if it is the purpose of the narrative artwork to absorb the audience in it, to draw the audience into the story, to capture our interest and to stimulate our imagination, then it is also apparent that by engaging moral judgement and the moral emotions, the story may thereby discharge its primary aim or purpose by secondarily stimulating and sometimes deepening the moral understanding of the audience.

It is not the function of narrative artworks to provide moral education. Typically, the purpose of a narrative artwork is to absorb the reader, viewer, or listener. Nevertheless, frequently the narrative may bequeath moral learning to the audience while in pursuit of its goal of riveting audience attention and making the audience care about what happens next by means of enlisting our moral understanding, judgement, and emotions. That is, what the author explicitly seeks is to engage the audience. And engaging the audience's moral understanding may be and very often is a means to this end.

The formalist is correct in denying that narrative art necessarily serves such ulterior purposes as moral education. But, none the less, that does not preclude that there is moral learning with respect to narrative art-works. For in those cases, which I believe are quite frequent, moral learning issues—in a non-accidental way, but rather like fallout or a regularly recurring side reaction—as the author seeks to absorb readers in narratives of human affairs by addressing, exercising, and sometimes deepening our moral understanding and emotions. This need not be what the author has in the forefront of her intention, but it happens very often in narratives of human affairs, where it is our moral interest in a work and our moral activity in response to the work that keeps us interested in the object for its own sake.

I have tried to show why we are naturally inclined to advert to morality when we discuss narrative artworks, and I have also attempted to ground the variable moral assessments we make concerning narratives in our experiences of them.[66] I have focused on one very important relation

---

[66] Some formalists may say that, though this may be how moral assessments of narrative artworks are grounded, this sort of moral assessment is *never* relevant to the aesthetic assessment of the work. I have tried to deal with this objection in Noël Carroll, 'Moderate Moralism'.

between morality and the narrative artwork, specifically upon the way in which the narrative artwork unavoidably engages, exercises, and sometimes clarifies and deepens moral understanding and the moral emotions. Indeed, it is my contention that this is the most comprehensive or most general relation that we can find between narrative art—including mass fictions—and morality.

By saying this, I certainly acknowledge that there may be other relations between narrative and morality. Certain didactic genres may operate a bit differently from what the preceding picture suggests. Some tales, like the story of the Roman General Regulus, are explicitly designed to make virtues, such as honesty, more and more attractive, while others, like 'The Pied Piper of Hamlin', are intended to make vices, like dishonesty, seem profoundly ill-advised. However, such overt moral didacticism is not the mark of most narratives, but only of a limited segment, often dedicated to the young and disseminated by the mass media in the form of children's books and cartoons.

Likewise, some narratives are devoted to extending moral sympathies by inducing some of us to see things from foreign or alien points of view, for example, *Native Son* and *Bicycle Thieves*. But though this is an undeniable way in which a narrative might address its audience, it is not a phenomenon that we find operative in all or even most narratives of human affairs, since not all such narratives typically possess viewpoints that differ in any appreciable degree from their audiences.

Consequently, clarificationism attempts to stress the most comprehensive relation between narrative artworks and morality. It is as comprehensive as it is because it focuses on the way in which narrative artworks, given their nature, unavoidably bring moral understanding into contact with the artwork as virtually a condition for comprehending the artwork. I have pursued this line of approach because it seems to me to isolate the most general stratum of the relation of morality to narrative art, though, of course, I would be the first to agree that other strata also welcome further excavation. My claim is only that clarificationism picks out the deepest layer of the engagement of art and morality, and not that there may not be other layers.

Simulation, or back to identification?

Recently, a new theory of the way in which narrative fictions are pertinent to morality has come to the fore. Advanced by Gregory Currie and others, it attempts to exploit a theory developed in the context of the philosophy of mind in order to characterize our engagement with fictions.[67] This view may be called simulation theory. Stated roughly, simulation theory in the philosophy of mind is the hypothesis that we predict, understand, and interpret others by putting ourselves in their place, that is to say, by adopting their point of view.[68] Philosophers of art like Currie suggest that the apparatus of simulation is what we use when we read, view, or listen to narratives. The grain of truth in identification theory is, *ex hypothesi*, the process of simulation. Currie writes: 'What is so often called audience identification with a character is best described as mental simulation of the character's situation by the audience who are then better able to imagine the character's experience'.[69]

By simulating the mental states of fictional characters, we come to experience what it would be like to be in situations such as those in which the characters find themselves. This is relevant to morality, inasmuch as we learn, by acquaintance, what it would feel like to undertake certain courses of action—what it would be like to murder someone, for example. Furthermore, knowing what it would be like to murder someone or to steal is relevant information when it comes to moral deliberation, since before we undertake a certain line of action, it is important to have a sense of how we will feel about it, once we act.[70] Thus, engaging fictions by simulation is a source of knowledge that is relevant to moral deliberation and, therefore, to morality. For in deliberating about whether one will commit adultery, it is pertinent to ask oneself what it will feel like once one has done it. Will one feel unbearable pangs of conscience and

[67] See Gregory Currie, 'The Moral Psychology of Fiction', *Australasian Journal of Philosophy*, 73/2 (June 1995), 250–9; and Gregory Currie, 'Imagination and Simulation: Aesthetics Meets Cognitive Science', *Mental Simulations*, ed. Martin Davies and Tony Stone (Oxford: Blackwell, 1995), 151–69. Susan Feagin also endorses the notion of simulation in her book *Reading With Feeling*, as does Murray Smith in *Engaging Characters*.

[68] See, especially, Robert Gordon, 'Folk Psychology as Simulation', in *Folk Psychology*, ed. Martin Davies and Tony Stone (Oxford: Blackwell, 1995), 60–73; Robert Gordon, 'Simulation Without Introspection or Inference from Me to You', *Mental Simulations*, 53–67; Alvin Goldman, 'Empathy, Mind and Morals', ibid. 185–208. These books contain a wealth of information about simulation theory, including arguments for and against. Robert Gordon also discusses simulation in his book *The Structure of Emotions: Investigations in Cognitive Psychology* (Cambridge: Cambridge University Press, 1987), 149–55. [69] Currie, 'The Moral Psychology of Fiction', 257.

[70] Such a theory of the relevance of literature to moral learning, sans the apparatus of simulation, can also be found in Dorothy Walsh, *Literature and Knowledge* (Middletown, Conn.: Wesleyan University Press, 1969); Catherine Wilson, 'Literature and Knowledge', *Philosophy*, 58 (1983), 226; Frank Palmer, *Literature and Moral Understanding: A Philosophical Essay on Ethics, Aesthetics, Education, and Culture* (Oxford: Clarendon Press, 1992); and Roger Scruton, *Art and Imagination: A Study in the Philosophy of Mind* (London: Routledge, 1974). In contrast to propositionalism—which emphasizes *knowing-that*—these authors stress a form of knowledge by acquaintance—i.e., *knowing-what-it-would-be-like*. What contemporary simulation theorists do—it seems to me—is to supply the psychological mechanism that makes this possible.

remorse? One way to find this out is by simulating the experience of fictional adulterers.

The notion of simulation has arisen in a context of debate in the philosophy of mind over the best way in which to explain how we predict the behaviour of other people in everyday life. One view of how we do this can be called the Theory Theory. On this view, as we mature, we learn a lot about how people behave. We learn that in certain situations, people will react in certain predictable ways. For example, if you aggressively accuse someone of something, they are likely to deny it. Gradually, our knowledge of other people grows. We acquire a great deal of folk-psychological knowledge about human behaviour. Moreover, this folk-psychological knowledge of other people's behaviour, it is said, has the structure of something like a theory—a very powerful theory, indeed, when you think about how often we are right in our predictions about the behaviour of others.

This view is called the Theory Theory because it is the *theory* that we predict and understand the behaviour of others on the basis of our possession of an implicit folk-psychological *theory* of human behaviour, a folk-psychological theory whose level of accuracy should be the envy of any social scientist. In other words, it is the theory that folk psychology is a theory. According to the Theory Theory, when we observe another person, we apply our implicit folk-psychological theory of human behaviour to predict and to understand what they will do. We mobilize, so the story goes, the generalizations of our folk-psychological theory, much in the manner of a scientist.

There are some obvious questions, however, that the Theory Theory raises. Is it plausible to think that people really possess such a theory subconsciously—a theory whose predictive power is beyond anything available at present to conscious social scientists? Such a theory would be more complex than our most complicated physical theories. Isn't it quite a stretch to think that we are all in possession of such a powerful theory subconsciously, especially given how weak our explicit, formal psychological theories are in terms of their predictive power? How is it that we are so smart in constructing our theories subconsciously, but so bad at replicating them consciously? In addition, the computations that the Theory Theory imputes to us are quite complex and would appear to require a great deal of real time to work through. However, our predictions of how others will behave often transpires in an instant.

Simulation theory is proposed as an alternative to the Theory Theory— an alternative that overcomes its shortcomings. It denies that we possess a complex theory of human behaviour. Rather, it argues that when we want to predict or understand the behaviour of others, we put ourselves in their shoes. We use our own complement of background beliefs, desires, and emotions in order to see how we would respond were we in the situation of the person in question, and then we predict that that person would act as we would. If we want to know how someone else would feel in a certain situation, we put ourselves in their situation, taking on their beliefs about the situation and their values concerning it, and then we observe how we would feel. We use ourselves, in other words, as simulators.

Your belief-desire *system* and mine are pretty much the same. So, if you want to learn about how I am feeling, put yourself in my position—entertain the specific beliefs and desires that are pertinent for me in the situation at hand—and the emotion that I am feeling is apt to arise in you. This is likely to happen because the networks of believing, desiring, and emoting that you and I possess are roughly congruent. So input my beliefs and desires into your cognitive / conative system, and the output is likely to be the same.

Similarly, if one wants to predict what someone else will do, input that person's beliefs, desires, and emotions into your own cognitive / conative system and observe what you yourself are disposed to do. This is how Sherlock Holmes proceeds in the 'Musgrave Ritual' when he tells Watson: 'You know my methods in such cases, Watson. I put myself in the man's place, and, having first gauged his intelligence, I try to imagine how I should myself have proceeded under the same circumstances.' Thus, Sherlock Holmes is able to discover Brunton's behaviour by simulating it—by asking what he himself would have done in Brunton's place—by running Brunton's program, so to speak, on his own system of beliefs, desires, and emotions. Or, as Kant says: 'It is obvious that, if I wish to represent to myself a thinking being, I put myself in his place, and thus substitute, as it were, my own subject for the object I am seeking to consider (which does not occur in any other kind of investigation).'[71]

Of course, simulation theory does not suppose that our mental state is exactly the same as that of our target. For when we simulate another, we de-couple, so to speak, our mental system from our action system. Or, as simulation theorists like to say, we go off-line. Our cogitations do not issue in actions; they stop short of that. Simulation is a mode of imagination. According to the simulation theorist, this is how we predict the behaviour of others in everyday life. Folk psychology is not a theory; folk psychology is simulation. That is, simulation provides, in large measure, the means by

[71] Immanuel Kant, *Critique of Pure Reason*, 1st edn., trans. Norman Kemp Smith (London: Macmillan, 1953), 336.

which we predict the behaviour of others; we use ourselves as detectors of their intentions.

Moreover, we do not just simulate the behavioural intentions of others. When we deliberate about practical decisions, we simulate our own prospective activities. We imagine different lines of action and run them off-line on our own cognitive/conative system in order to gain a sense of how we would react in different circumstances as well as how we would feel about undertaking different lines of action. Thus, simulation is a crucial ingredient in practical deliberation about our own actions.

In the case of simulating others, we input their relevant beliefs and desires into the black box of our own off-line cognitive/conative system and then consider the output as a predictor of their behaviour. With respect to our own prospective actions, we input our own beliefs about some possible future state into our off-line or disengaged cognitive/conative system and contemplate our reactions to alternative states of affairs. Obviously, from an evolutionary point of view the capacity to run these off-line simulations is an advantage. It is an economical way to figure out what others (including other people and perhaps sometimes animals) will do. But we do not just simulate the behavioural dispositions of others. We simulate our own prospective, future selves. This enables us to test out alternative strategies in thought.

From the viewpoint of evolutionary theory, the explanation for why we have the faculty of imagination/simulation is that it affords the capacity for strategy testing.[72] By entertaining thoughts about future states, we are able to get a handle on how we will feel and act in alternative situations, and, as well, are able to work up informed hypotheses about how others are likely to respond to us (which is useful in testing out our own prospective strategies). Simulation is a means for constructing cost-free test-runs of future actions that can provide us with knowledge about ourselves and others.

Clearly, the theory that folk psychology is simulation rather than a complex psychological theory avoids some of the problems of the Theory Theory. According to the simulation theory, there is no reason to hypothesize our dubious possession of an immensely elaborate, subconscious psychological theory. Moreover, the mobilization of such an elaborate theory with respect to particular cases would seem to require a large amount of computing time, whereas running a simulation is a much faster

---

[72] Ruth Millikan, *Language, Thought and Other Biological Categories* (Cambridge, Mass.: MIT Press, 1984).

process—one whose speed is much more in keeping with our actual, real-time predictions of the behaviour of others.

Moving from the realm of predicting actual behaviour to the realm of aesthetics, the application of simulation theory to the consumption of fiction is very straightforward. When we read, view, or listen to a fiction, we are running our cognitive/conative system off-line already; that is, we are imagining the story. Moreover, simulation is a special case of imagining. It is one of the primary resources of the imagination that we employ when following texts.

With respect to fictional texts, Gregory Currie distinguishes between two types of imagining. Primary imagining is a matter of what in the previous chapter I called entertaining a proposition as unasserted. It is imagining, under the guidance of the author, that such and such is the case in the world of the fiction. But there is another kind of imagining that Currie believes comes into play in response to the fiction. It involves imagining—that is, simulating—the experience of a character.

Currie writes:

Secondary imagining occurs when we imagine various things so as to imagine what is fictional. Sometimes, secondary imaginings are not required for primary imagining to take place: the story has it that a certain character walked down a dark street, and we simply imagine that. Then we have primary imagining without secondary imagining. Primary imagining most notably requires the support of secondary imagining in cases where what we are primarily to imagine is the experience of a character. If the dark street hides something threatening, the character who walks may have thoughts, anxieties, visual and auditory experiences and bodily sensations about which it would be important for readers to imagine something. The author may indicate to greater or lesser degree of specificity, what the character's experience is. But it is notoriously difficult, and in some cases perhaps impossible, for us to describe people's mental states precisely. Authors who adopt stream of consciousness and other subjective styles have failed to do it, and so have film makers like Hitchcock who try to recreate the character's visual experiences on screen. Anyway, the attempt at full specificity and precision in this regard would usually be regarded as a stylistic vice, leaving, as we significantly say, 'nothing to the imagination.' What the author explicitly says and what can be inferred therefrom, will constrain our understanding of the character's mental state. It will set signposts and boundaries. But if these are all we have to go on in a fiction, it will seem dull and lifeless. It is when we are able, in imagination [through simulation], to feel as the character feels that fictions of character take hold of us. It is this process of empathetic re-enactment which I call secondary imagination.[73]

---

[73] Currie, 'The Moral Psychology of Fiction', 256.

Simulation or secondary imagining, moreover, can be relevant to moral deliberation.

We imagine ourselves in a certain situation which the fiction describes, imagining ourselves to have the same relevant beliefs, desires and values as the character whose situation it is. If our imagining goes well, it will tell us something about how we would respond to the situation, and what it would be like to experience it: a response and a phenomenology we can then transfer to the character. That way we learn something about the character. More importantly, from the point of view of moral knowledge, we learn something about ourselves and about the things, we regard or might regard as putative values.[74]

Fictions, by way of simulation, then, supply us with the kind of knowledge that would be relevant to making a moral decision about a course of action—knowledge of what it would be like (for instance, what it would feel like) to be a liar, a cheat, or a philanthropist. If we killed someone, could we live with ourselves? Simulation can provide some information toward answering such questions.

Moreover, this conception of the relation of fiction to morality provides a means for evaluating narratives from an ethical point of view. For example, 'fictions that encourage secondary imaginings, while providing signposts for those imaginings which systematically distort their outcomes, may do moral damage by persuading us to value that which is not valuable.'[75] And, presumably, fictions that encourage us to value what is morally valuable are, *ceteris paribus*, to be assessed positively from the moral point of view.

There is, of course, a debate in the philosophy of mind about whether simulation is the correct conception of folk psychology.[76] This is not a debate about whether there is such a thing as simulation, but whether folk psychology is basically a matter of simulation. But those arguments, interesting as they may be, are not what we need to consider now. Rather, ours is the question of whether the notion of simulation—whether or not it best models folk psychology—is really relevant to aesthetics, specifically to our typical intercourse with fictions and the moral evaluation thereof.

For Currie, simulation is not the whole story of our engagement with fiction. Nor does he claim that simulation is the only relation of narrative fiction to morality. It is *a* relation, though one does have the impression that Currie thinks that it is a rather central and comprehensive one. Thus,

---

[74] Currie, 'The Moral Psychology of Fiction', 257.   [75] Ibid. 258.

[76] See, for example, Stephen Stich and Shaun Nichols, 'Folk Psychology: Simulation or Tacit Theory', in *Folk Psychology*, 123–58; and eid. 'Second Thoughts on Simulation', *Mental Simulation*, 87–108. Both these volumes also contain answers to Stich and Nichols, as well as further rebuttals and defences of simulation theory.

the issue arises about whether it is a compelling rival to the theory propounded in the preceding section of this chapter.

Simulation or secondary imagining, as Currie describes it, is not the same thing as identification. For unlike identification, simulation does not presuppose that all of our cognitive and/or emotional states are identical to those of the character whom we are simulating. As in everyday life, simulation only requires rough similarity, not mental fusion. There is psychological evidence that audiences do represent the emotional states of characters mentally.[77] One issue is whether that representation takes the form of simulation. At least one psychologist has suggested that something like simulation might play a role in understanding the emotions of fictional characters; but this has not yet been substantiated empirically.[78] However, supposing simulation sometimes comes into play, the question is how often does this happen? How useful is simulation theory as a comprehensive model of our commerce with fictions, especially with reference to morality? Is it a more attractive model than the clarificationist model?

Obviously, the two theories are not incompatible. They could work in tandem. For example, simulation could be the means by which clarification is secured. Or, one might think that simulation and clarification are both equally important means for comprehending narratives from the moral point of view. However, there are some important differences between Currie's version of simulation and my account of clarification— differences that may be relevant to determining whether or not one has better claims to being more comprehensive than the other.

In order to contemplate the differences between the two approaches, it is useful to recall a distinction made by Richard Wollheim. With reference to the imagination, Wollheim distinguishes between central imagining and acentral imagining.[79] Acentral imagining is a matter of my imagining *that* such and such; central imagining is a matter of my imagining x. Acentral imagination is exemplified by the case where I imagine that Kubla Khan built Xanadu; central imagining is exemplified by the case where I imagine building Xanadu. Acentral imagining is from the outside, so to speak; central imagining is from the inside. Given this rough distinction, Currie's notion of simulation (or secondary imagining) is a case of central imagining, whereas the clarificationist view, as propounded by me, is involved

---

[77] Morton Ann Gernsbacher, H. Hill Goldsmith, and Rachel R. W. Robertson, 'Do Readers Mentally Represent Characters' Emotional States?' *Cognition and Emotion*, 6 (1992), 89–111.

[78] D. S. Miall, 'Beyond the Schema Given: Affective Comprehension of Literary Narratives', *Cognition and Emotion*, 3 (1989), 55–78. Miall is discussed in Gernsbacher, *et al.*, 'Do Readers Mentally Represent Characters' Emotional States?' 109.

[79] Richard Wollheim, *On Art and the Mind* (Cambridge, Mass.: Harvard University Press, 1974), 59.

with acentral imagining. We respond to fictional situations as outside observers, *assimilating* our conception of the character's mental state into our overall response as a sort of onlooker with respect to the situation in which the character finds himself; whereas for Currie, when we are involved in simulation or secondary imagining, we are centrally imagining that we are the characters. Which, if either, of these approaches is more comprehensive? Which models our response to fictional narratives better?

I think that quite clearly as consumers of fictions we are typically in the position of outside observers, or, as Richard Gerrig and Deborah Prentice call it, side-participants.[80] Of course, the simulationist can respond that outside observers can employ simulation. However, I wonder how often we do. After all, with most narratives, especially mass narratives, omniscient narrators tell us what is going on in the minds of the characters. Simulation theory putatively informs us about how we go about predicting the behaviour of others and understanding their affective states. But most narratives, it seems to me, give us ready access to the mental states—the intentions, desires, and emotions—of characters. So what need do we have for simulation? We have the information already in most cases. Furthermore, this often happens in visual narratives as well; with respect to *Casablanca*, we do not have to simulate Rick's feelings about Ilsa; Rick tells us all we need to know in order to feel sorry for him.

Nor does this entail that the 'direct access' to character's inner states renders narrative representations affectively lifeless. For we use that information, along with the information about the situation the character is in, in order to generate *our own* emotional reaction to the character and his/her circumstances. There is no need to suppose that our affective state has to be channelled through a simulation of a character's putative state. We can generate our own emotional reaction directly (that is to say, without an intervening stage of simulation) by using the information that the narrator supplies us about the character about whom we are concerned—including explicitly given information about her intentions, desires, emotions, plans, and so on.

There are two parts to this objection. The first is that with the typical narrative there is little role for simulation with respect to fictions—especially written fictions—because the determination of what is going on in the mind of characters is generally supplied by omniscient narrators. Such narrators may describe events from the outside and then go

---

[80] Richard Gerrig and Deborah Prentice, 'Notes on Audience Response', in *Post-Theory: Reconstructing Film Studies*, ed. David Bordwell and Noël Carroll (Madison: University of Wisconsin Press, 1996), 388–403.

inside the mind of the character to tell us their reactions. Thus, the pressure for philosophers of art to use simulation to explain our grasp of a character's state of mind does not match up with the pressure for simulation theorists in the philosophy of mind to explain our real-life predictions and understandings.

Second, as with the objections offered previously to the notion of identification, simulation theory seems to overestimate the degree to which responding emotionally to a fiction requires centrally imagining the states of characters. Most often, I would contend that the emotionally appropriate object of our attention is the situation in which a character finds herself and not the situation as the character experiences it. The character feels grief, but we feel pity for her, in part, because she is feeling grief. The object of her emotion is, say, her child. The object of our emotion is her situation—a situation in which she is feeling sorrow. We do not simulate her situation; rather, we respond emotionally with our own feeling of pity to a situation in which someone, namely the relevant character, is feeling sorrow.

Putting these two objections together, then, we can argue that typically we do not need to postulate the operation of simulation because our emotional response is finally that of an observer (not a direct participant, as simulation might suggest), and the relevant information needed to form the appropriate emotional response from an observer's point of view is generally supplied by omniscient narrators. Thus, there is no reason to postulate the operation of simulation in the typical case of responding to fiction.

Of course, this argument, if it is persuasive, might be thought to apply primarily to written and perhaps spoken narratives. It might be said that it is less compelling when it comes to visual narratives like movies and TV programmes. For with visual narratives, it is far less customary to have the sort of omniscient narration where we are given direct access to the minds of the characters. Running voice-over commentary on the characters' internal states—in either the first person or the third person—is, for example, rare. So, it might be argued that in general when it comes to visual narration, simulation usually has a role to play of a sort that I have denied it plays with standard cases of written narration. In visual narration, we are given the character's overt behaviour and have to go on from there. Might it not be the case that we go on by way of simulation?

My inclination is to resist this suggestion. First of all, as the example of *Casablanca* indicates, characters often tell us about their mental states—their intentions and their feelings—outright. But, in addition, once again there is the asymmetry problem discussed earlier. Typically our emotional responses to characters are different from their emotional responses. We are paralysed by fear when the heroine is trapped on the edge of a parapet, but she, undaunted and fearless, plunges into the moat several hundred feet below.[81] We feel sorrow for characters wracked with guilt. And so on. Simulation just doesn't seem to be the right model for these audience responses.

But how, it might be asked, do we know the characters are wracked with guilt, since without knowing that, we may not respond with pity? Don't we need simulation to explain this? I think not, and not only because characters often verbalize their internal states. Rather, we can recognize the states of others without simulation.[82] This is not a reversion to the Theory Theory. Rather, we need only suppose that people have the power to recognize certain patterns. This does not require having a full-blown theory, but only a repertory of sometimes related, sometimes unrelated schemas or prototypes for assessing situations. For example, in order to interpret the emotions underlying a convicted criminal's effort to shield his face from a TV camera, I need not simulate his mental state in order to recognize that it is connected to his sense of shame. Likewise, tracking the emotional states of characters in films and TV programmes rarely requires simulation. It is easy to recognize their states without simulating them.[83]

In the last chapter, we discussed point-of-view editing. Surely, it might be suggested that that is a form of visual narration that must involve simulation. The character looks off-screen, and in the succeeding shot we see molten lava streaming toward the camera. Don't we feel fear because we are simulating the character's response? I don't think so. We know that molten lava is dangerous without imagining ourselves to be in the character's position. If we are concerned about the character, the knowledge

[81] Moreover, in such a case, is it likely that if we used ourselves as simulators, we would predict that she would take the plunge? Wouldn't we predict that she would surrender? Wouldn't we?

[82] Recall, for example, that in the last chapter we cited research to the effect that the recognition of certain basic emotions on the basis of facial expressions may be an innate capacity. It is not at all clear that when I recognize a picture of a face etched in the characteristic contours of fear that I am simulating. For if I am just shown the picture of a face, I really don't have enough of the character's situation at my disposal to know which of his beliefs, desires, and so on to run off-line. And yet I am able to identify his mental state accurately.

[83] Here it might be suggested that recognition just is simulation. But I suspect that this begs the question. Moreover, I think that we need to postulate some capacity of recognition that is independent of simulation. It can't be simulation all the way down. For simulation would appear to require powers of recognition in order to get off the ground. For example, suppose I wanted to simulate the state of someone who is embarrassed by being in the presence of someone else who is suffering an intense state of humiliation. Wouldn't I have to take on board the first person's recognition that the second person is humiliated? Simulators require the beliefs of the simulatee, and some of those beliefs must often be of the nature of recognitions. The possibility that everything is a matter of simulations nested in simulations is too baroque for my sensibilities, unless some compelling reason can be found to force us to postulate it.

that molten lava is heading her way is enough to engender fear for the character in us. The added step of imagining that we are in the character's shoes is unnecessary.[84]

Moreover, we can confirm that this is enough to explain our response by noting that our fear for the character may be no different whether we suppose the character knows she is about to be engulfed in lava or not. Presumably, the simulation theory would predict different responses, since we would be simulating different mental states. But I suspect that we can vary the mental states of the characters without provoking a difference in our emotional response to the alternative stagings.

Similarly, when a fast movement toward the camera in a point-of-view schema startles us, it startles *us* directly without our simulating the character's being startled. Our cognitive/conative system may be off-line, but we need not be running the character's program in order to be startled. Nor do we need to simulate the character's mental state in order to recognize that he's been startled. And a similar explanation can be given for our response of disgust when a putrid monster lurches from a dark corridor. We have direct access to our own response; we need not imagine ourselves to be the character. For once again, the character might just be unaware of the putrid monster.

Currie says that when we watch a character walking down a dark street, perhaps in a detective thriller, we enliven the situation by simulating the character's mental state. But I think that this is not usually the case. Rather, we are onlookers. We are more likely to subvocalize our concern in terms of thinking almost aloud: 'Get out of there', or 'Watch out!' We are not necessarily replicating the mental state of the character. For again, remember that this could be a situation in which the character feels no sense of danger. Will it make a difference or not? Perhaps we need some experiments here, though my prediction about their outcome should be evident.

According to the simulationist, we use simulation in order to predict and understand characters. On the other hand, I claim that simulation

---

[84] That we are able to recognize emotions on the basis of facial displays indicates that it cannot be the case that it is always simulation all the way down. For the photos that psychologists like Ekman have used to elicit these responses are simply photos of faces. They are not photos of bodies nor of the situations in which characters find themselves. Thus the percipient does not have enough information to simulate what the person in the photo is believing and feeling. The percipient's response, then, is based on recognition without simulation. Thus, with facial expression, it cannot be simulation all the way down. There is a bedrock of recognition. Simulation is not then a fully comprehensive account of folk psychology. Nor does it appear to handle every case of emotional detection in mass art. It does not fully account for the phenomena of point-of-view editing. Of course, there is still a question of how pervasive simulation really is with respect to fiction in general and mass fiction in particular. My suggestion is that it is at best very rare.

doesn't play much of a role in the typical case. Is there any way to motivate my claim? Perhaps our response to villains is relevant here. Often villains are the characters whom it is most difficult to understand—in mass narratives, they are often evil incarnate. Thus, one would predict that they would be especial targets of simulation. But, I suspect that even simulation theorists will admit that we rarely try to put ourselves in the place of villains, though *ex hypothesi*, these characters would seem to be the ones who cry out most for simulation.

Also, I question how useful simulation is for following narratives. Simulation is supposed to be a device for predicting behaviour. But very often, the cognitive stock of characters is beyond what the average audience member can simulate. Who could have simulated the incredible catch that Buster Keaton executes when his girlfriend goes over the falls in *Our Hospitality*? Characters often surprise us just because their imagination is beyond simulation by average viewers, listeners, and readers. Had one been simulating Rick's state in *Casablanca*, it would have been more likely to predict that he would fly off with Ilsa. But he surprises us. Perhaps, most often when we consume fictions our posture is that of expecting the characters to surprise us rather than that of simulating them.[85]

But, in any event, I think that we do have reason to believe that our relation to characters is less often a matter of simulation than of what I have called elsewhere assimilation.[86] That is, rather than centrally imagining that we are the character, we adopt the stance of an observer or an onlooker and form an overall emotional response of the situation in which the character finds herself. This may involve an assessment of the character's emotional state. His anger may be relevant to our indignation. But our access to his anger need not, and I claim, most often does not, require simulation in order to be detected; and, in any case, our emotional

[85] Also, there is a question about how much prediction actually goes on in following a narrative? When a character is surrounded by the villains, are we predicting what he will do, or waiting to see what he will do?

Also, it seems to me that when we follow a narrative, we more often than not are keeping track of possible future lines of action—for example, will she be captured or not—rather than making exact predictions about the outcomes of earlier events, since the later events in the narrative are generally so underdetermined by the previous events in the story that precise predictions are out of place. And, of course, sometimes we know what will happen next, because either the narrator or the characters tell us, thereby obviating the need for our own predictions.

Prediction, that is, may not be a general model of what we usually do when following narratives. Thus, if prediction is what makes simulation theory attractive to philosophers of mind, it may be of little applicability in aesthetics, since following narratives to a large extent does not call for prediction.

For further argumentation about the unimportance of prediction for narratives, see Noël Carroll, 'The Narrative Connection' *Narrative: Emotion and Cognition*, ed. Seymour Chatman and Will van Peer (forthcoming).

[86] Noël Carroll, *The Philosophy of Horror*, 95–6.

response is different from his, since our emotional response has as part of its object a man who has been angered.

I am not prepared to claim that simulation never happens. Perhaps sometimes it even happens as a sub-routine in the process of assimilating the situation of the character. But I do think that it happens much less frequently than theorists like Currie appear to think it does. They leave the impression that it is very pervasive. But I think that, supposing it does occur, it is very rare. Like the identification theorist, the simulation theorist, in my view, overestimates the importance of central imagining for our response to fiction. Indeed, sometimes the emphasis on central imagining, where simulation is supposed to tell us something about ourselves (about how we would act or feel) seems to me to be an inappropriate response to fiction, since the author generally does not intend that we *imagine* how we, as readers, feel. That may be to leave off paying attention to the story and instead to wander off into some fantasy.

But, in any case, it is my contention that, in the main, central imaginings, such as simulations, have little to do with our typical response to fictions. That is more a matter of acentral imagining where, on the basis of acentrally imagining the situation of the character (i.e., entertaining it in thought) from the perspective of an onlooker, we go on to formulate our own emotional response to it, often assimilating the character's emotional state as part of the object of our more encompassing emotional state.

Thus far I have been focusing on the story the simulation theorist tells about our emotional response to fiction. I have not addressed the link that the simulation theorist alleges obtains between simulation and moral deliberation. This linkage, of course, is what the simulation theorist regards as one of the most important relations, if not the most important relation between narrative fiction and morality. Needless to say, if simulation occurs as rarely as I assert, then this relation to morality cannot be very comprehensive. It is not, for example, as comprehensive as the relation isolated by clarificationism. However, it also pays to ask how significant this putative link between simulating fictions and morality really is.

According to Currie, fiction serves moral deliberation by providing information about what it would be like to do certain things. Watching *Sunrise* and simulating the mental state of the husband, I putatively learn what it would feel like to intend to kill my wife. This sort of information is relevant to moral reasoning, since knowing what it would feel like to nurture this intention is something one should consider before acting on it.[87] For example, if as a result of such an exercise of the imagination one thinks that doing x would bring about insufferable discomfiture (in the form of pangs of conscience), that should count as a reason against doing x.

But I am very sceptical about this picture of the relation of morality to fiction, not only because I think that our perspective on characters is, in the vast majority of cases, that of an onlooker rather than a simulator, but also because I doubt whether the simulation of characters plays much of a role in moral deliberation, since we know that the situations that characters find themselves in are contrived; we know that they have been made up by the author.

I would not deny that simulation may play a role in moral deliberation. However, I think that when it does play a role, we are simulating ourselves undertaking alternative courses of action tailored to our own situations. Since the situations of characters are known to be made up, I doubt that moral agents frequently use simulations of the states of fictional characters to assess alternative lines of action. Thus, if this kind of simulation occurs rarely in moral deliberation, Currie's account of the relation of fiction to morality is not a very comprehensive one. Rather, clarificationism is the better candidate for isolating a more comprehensive account of the most frequently occurring relation between morality and narrative fiction.

Concluding remarks

In the last chapter, I noted that many readers might worry that my theory of the relation of mass fiction to the emotions was too general. If it modelled anything at all, it was a comprehensive relation of narrative and perhaps all representational art to the emotions. In other words, I did not say enough about the specific relations of mass art to the emotions. A similar question may arise with respect to this chapter. Though I have used many examples from mass art in order to motivate clarificationism, it might be charged that this theory does not say anything about a unique relation between mass fictions and morality. The theory, if it applies at all, would appear to be a comprehensive theory of the relation of morality to any sort of narrative, whether it be an instance of mass art or esoteric art.

---

[87] There is, of course, the question of whether this sort of information is usually derived from simulation with respect to fictions. In one of the most famous examples of this kind, *Crime and Punishment*, I do not think that we need to simulate the phenomenology of Raskolnikov because Dostoevsky does such a graphic job describing it. Similarly, I do not believe that we need to simulate the husband's torment with regard to *Sunrise*; we are shown it.

That's right, but, once again, as in the previous chapter, I think that we can say this much about the relation of mass art to morality: in general, mass art will gravitate toward the activation of the moral maxims, concepts, presuppositions, and emotions that are distributed most widely amongst its potential audiences. As with the emotions, there is evidence that there are nearly universal, or at least very widely distributed moral presuppositions globally—that is, values and prohibitions that are at least recognized (though not always acted upon) cross-culturally. These include the recognition of positive duties of mutual support, loyalty, and reciprocity. The acknowledgement of something like the Golden Rule as well as of family responsibilities, such as the care of children and the sick, are nearly universal. Likewise admiration of generosity, especially as a virtue in leaders, is nearly universal.[88] Thus, mass narratives that rely on the recognition of such values and their power to address audiences can travel transculturally. They need not be inaccessible. And there are also nearly universal prohibitions against violence, rape, and deceit. It is perceived almost everywhere, from childhood up, that it is unfair to punish one person for another's wrongdoing. Such prohibitions, of course, supply the engine that powers a great deal of mass art, engendering the anger, indignation, and allegiance that so many mass artworks require for intelligibility.

This is not to say that specific cultures do not elaborate moral codes in their own ways, ways that are sometimes non-converging. However, these codes most often appear to contain overlapping, core elements.[89] And so it should not be surprising that mass art tends toward activating moral responses by addressing such widely distributed and even nearly universal moral dispositions.

Though most cultures seek to restrict the operation of vengeance by means of alternative forms of redress, most understand the moral basis of retaliation for wrongs. That is why they seek alternatives to violent revenge. But, in any case, the motive for revenge and a comprehension of its rough justice, especially in cases where judicial redress is foreclosed, is recognizable cross-culturally. Thus, the immense number of mass artworks dedicated to revenge should, in principle, be accessible nearly everywhere.

Many mass artworks concern love, and the rights and wrongs of it. Where this pertains to familial affections, it has obvious global purchase.

[88] Donald E. Brown, *Human Universals* (Philadelphia: Temple University Press, 1991), 138. This disposition to admire generosity in leaders is especially significant for mass narratives where heroes—the pertinent leader figures—are regularly marked by their generosity to others.

[89] Sissela Bok, *Common Values* (Columbia: University of Missouri Press, 1995).

But it is also the case that romantic love can be recognized, appreciated, and morally assessed cross-culturally. There is anthropological evidence that the practice of romantic love is widely distributed internationally, and that it is perhaps nearly universal.[90] Moreover, there are reasonable evolutionary grounds for believing that love is nearly universal because it afforded an adaptive advantage to humans by providing the glue that kept early hominid parents together, thereby enhancing the survival prospects of offspring.[91] But, however we came by it, the ability to recognize and assess romantic love relations is widely distributed—which is why Mizoguchi's major films can move audiences morally whether they are Japanese or French.

Different cultures evolve their own elaborate moral codes which prescribe behaviours that guide agents along the paths of righteousness appropriate to the culture they inhabit.[92] Michael Walzer calls these cultural elaborations 'thick'.[93] But these 'thick' moralities correspond to each other along certain 'thin' dimensions, i.e., reiterated features found across the thick moralities. For example, minimal moral concepts of truth and justice are found across thick moralities and are indispensable to them, and 'the minimal demands that we make on one another are, when denied, repeated with passionate insistence.'[94] Similarly, this minimal or thin morality is comprised of various negative injunctions such as rules against murder, deceit, torture, oppression, and tyranny.[95]

Ex hypothesi, this minimal or thin morality derives from common features of the recurring situations humans perennially find themselves in, and such experience accounts for 'universal dispositions . . . found in all cultures.'[96] Furthermore, given the nature of mass art, it should come as no surprise that mass art tends to traffic predominantly in what Walzer calls thin morality as its fundamental line of address. Its villains typically violate minimal standards of morality and its protagonists, contrastively, fight for justice, truth, and loyalty, especially in terms of the bonds of family, love, and friendship.[97]

[90] See William Jankowski and Edward Fischer, 'A Cross-Cultural Perspective on Romantic Love', *Ethnology*, 31/2 (1992), 149–55; and William Jankowski, 'Introduction', *Romantic Love: A Universal Experience?* (New York: Columbia University Press, 1995), 1–19.

[91] See Helen Fisher, *The Anatomy of Love* (New York: Norton, 1992); and ead., 'The Nature and Evolution of Romantic Love', in Jankowski, *Romantic Love*, 23–41.

[92] Huntington, *The Clash of Civilizations*, 318.

[93] Michael Walzer, *Thick and Thin: Moral Argument at Home and Abroad* (Notre Dame: University of Notre Dame Press, 1994), 1–11.   [94] Ibid. 6.

[95] Ibid. 10.   [96] James Q. Wilson, *The Moral Sense* (New York: Free Press, 1993), 225.

[97] My stress on the correlation of mass art to nearly universal emotions is, of course, connected to the capacity of mass art to travel globally. For, as Samuel Huntington says in another context, 'a global phenomenon demands a global explanation'. Huntington, *The Clash of Civilizations*, 97.

As with our claims about the emotions, there is no reason now to claim that all the moral sensibilities addressed by mass art are nearly universal in nature. It is enough to suggest that mass artworks typically aim at activating widely distributed moral presuppositions, judgements, and emotions. Mass artworks, in this regard, are standardly designed to foreground the 'thin' moral dimensions of situations rather than elaborating their thick implications. I hope that there is little dispute about that.

However, agreeing on this much, the critic of mass art may be tempted to charge that the moral judgements and responses elicited by mass art are paltry. They may often be morally good, but they are good, as I put it earlier, without distinction. Thus, they contribute little to anyone's genuine moral education.

But, as in the previous chapter, there are two responses to be made here. It is not clear that most art—whether mass art or otherwise— generally achieves much more than the moral status of being good, but with no special distinction.[98] *And*, furthermore, there is no reason to assert that mass art cannot engage our moral powers in subtle and enlarging ways even in respect to 'thin' morality. Surely, we have examples of this ready to hand. Renoir's *Grand Illusion* is a case in point. It engages our moral understanding of phenomena like class, ethnicity (anti-semitism), war, and nationalism in compelling ways—ways that depend upon activating the application of 'thin' moral concepts. Thus, there are no grounds, in principle, to suppose that mass art can only be wicked or good but without distinction. It can be morally enlarging. And clarificationism can account for this.

---

[98] Nor should we disparage the moral value of artworks that, in my language, are good but without distinction. They are still valuable from an ethical point of view for the way in which they exercise our moral powers. This is not an inconsequential service when one thinks about how infrequently we are called upon to make moral judgements. In this way, artworks, even ones that are good without distinction, may help keep our moral talents from rusting.

6 Mass Art and Ideology

Introduction

There is perhaps no aspect of mass art that concerns scholars in the humanities today more than its relation to ideology.[1] Randomly perusing academic journals of film, literature, and so on, one finds article after article devoted to revealing the classist, racist, sexist, homophobic, and/or militarist tendencies in this or that product of mass art. And most books in what is called cultural studies, I would dare to guess, concern the ideological operation of mass art, regarding mass art as either complicit with the interests of the hegemonic forces of society, or, at least, as a site of ideological struggle. At this time, one has the feeling that the study of mass art in the humanities nowadays is almost virtually co-extensive with the study of ideology. Thus, it would be remiss in a treatise of this sort not to address the topic of the ideological criticism of mass art directly. Moreover, the topic of ideology also follows quite naturally from the preceding chapter, since ideology raises moral issues.[2] Therefore, a discussion of ideology seems a fitting way in which to conclude the line of inquiry that we have been pursuing so far.

Undoubtedly the reason that contemporary critics in the humanities are

---

[1] I speak of 'scholars in the humanities' here because the researchers concerned with mass art in the social sciences appear less obsessed with the topic of ideology than their peers in arts and letters.

[2] Perhaps some old-time marxists might deny this, since they believe that marxism has nothing to do with morality. I think that this is false, but I will not argue the case now, since I believe that most contemporary critics in the humanities will have little problem with my claiming that the disclosure of ideology is concerned with morality. They might prefer to use the term 'politics' where I say 'morality', but perhaps we can all agree on the formulation that the concerns are ethical-political, since they would appear to presume background notions of justice.

so preoccupied with the topic of ideology with respect to mass art rests on their conviction that the propagation of ideology by mass art is a major lever by which oppression is sustained in the modern world. The presiding idea here is that by means of ideology, systems of social domination seize control of the consciousness of citizens in such a way that they find domination acceptable. Ideology may function either to invest people with false desires that come to enslave them and/or function to counterfeit the legitimatization of unjust social practices. Mass art, in turn, is eminently serviceable for the purposes of ideology because it disseminates its tenets so pervasively. Herbert Marcuse, for example, claims that 'The power of corporate capitalism has stifled the emergence of . . . [emancipatory] consciousness and its imagination; its mass media have adjusted the rational and emotional faculties to its market and its policies and steered them to a defence of its domination.'[3]

Inasmuch as the concern of contemporary critics of the ideological operation of mass art is motivated by a commitment to social justice, their project seems impeccable. However, such critics do often seem to overestimate the importance of ideology for maintaining systems of social domination. In their view, ideology, especially in capitalist states, is the primary lever of social domination. But, as I have argued elsewhere,[4] along with others,[5] the structure of economic arrangements may be of far greater importance for explaining the persistence of systems of social domination than ideology is. That is, the criticism of ideology, or, as it is sometimes called, *ideology critique*, may not be as centrally significant to the struggle against domination as scholars in the humanities today suppose it to be.[6]

But, having voiced that qualification, I must hasten to add that, though ideological criticism may not be of central importance, I still agree that it is of some importance. There is such a thing as ideology, and it seems reasonable to presume that it plays some role in sustaining regimes of domination. And, in addition, in so far as ideology involves dissembling, it is the responsibility of scholars to unmask it. That alone is enough to make

---

[3] Herbert Marcuse, *An Essay on Liberation* (Harmondsworth: Penguin, 1969), 24.

[4] Noël Carroll, *Mystifying Movies* (New York: Columbia University Press, 1988), 84–8.

[5] Nicholas Abercrombie, Stephen Hill, and Bryan S. Turner, *The Dominant Ideology Thesis* (London: George Allen & Unwin, 1980).

[6] Hereafter I will refer to what these scholars do as ideological criticism, since it is less cumbersome than the more grammatically accurate 'criticism of ideology'. I do not want to use the term *ideology critique* because I do not think that what is involved is generally of the nature of a critique. It is not usually an investigation into the conditions of possibility of the objects of study at hand in the way that a critique of pure reason or of political economy is. It is criticism—most frequently negative criticism—and not critique, properly so called. To call it ideological critique is a self-aggrandizing euphemism after the fashion of rubbish collectors calling themselves sanitation engineers.

the criticism of ideology a worthwhile subject of inquiry. Moreover, mass art is one of the major means through which ideology is communicated. Thus, contemporary ideological critics, even if they overestimate the overall efficacy of the ideology promoted in mass artworks, are not mistaken in drawing our attention to it.

Consequently, in this chapter I would like to contribute to the theory of the ideology with respect to mass art. This contribution has two parts. First, I want to develop a concept of ideology that I think suits the purposes of contemporary critical practice better than any existing alternative view. And second, I would like to speculate about the operation of some of the devices that are frequently employed by mass art in order to transmit ideology.

The devices that I have in mind are what I call, broadly speaking, rhetorical in nature. But since I do not think that rhetoric is inherently ideological, it is not my contention that the deployment of the devices in question is automatically ideological. What determines whether the use of these devices is ideological depends on the content that the relevant devices are used to communicate. Thus, I need a concept of ideology in order to determine whether or not the rhetoric of a particular instance of mass art is to count as ideological. In this regard, the two contributions that I hope to make to the theory of ideology in this chapter are integrally linked.

As in my discussions of the emotions of morality, the notion of ideology that I associate herein with mass art, as well as the rhetorical devices that it uses to disseminate ideology, are not unique to mass art. They are in evidence in other sorts of art. This, as I have already argued with reference to the moral and emotional address of mass art, is to be expected, since mass art evolves out of other sorts of art. Consequently, I should say proleptically that I do not regard it as a compelling criticism of my findings that the rhetorical devices I isolate can be found outside of mass art.

To suppose that there are rhetorical devices for the promulgation of ideology that are necessarily unique to mass art belies an essentialist bias that I find implausible. Historically, it is unlikely that there could be such devices. Where would they have come from? And, in any event, since much mass art evolved out of previous artistic practices, it is reasonable to suppose that they took previously existing ideological devices on board as part of the process of their historical development.

Moreover, even if there were some rhetorical device that were unique to mass art, that could only be a contingent matter, since, as we know, different artistic formations imitate each other all of the time. Thus, if there were some rhetorical device that as a matter of fact were only to be found in mass art, there would be no reason to believe that it could not be imitated in some other artistic practice. That is, if it were a fact that some device were *historically* unique to mass art, it would not be *necessarily* unique to it.

Furthermore, I see no point in looking for some unique devices for disseminating ideology that pertain to all and only mass artworks, since my intention is to develop a theory that suits contemporary ideological criticism as it is practised in the humanities today. That project is dedicated to examining the dissemination of ideology in mass art in general, not to the putative discovery of merely that quotient of ideology that is delivered to its audiences by the purportedly unique means of mass art.

Suppose, for the sake of argument, that there are some necessarily unique mass-art mechanisms for the transmission of ideology. It is also the case that many of the devices for transmitting ideology in mass art are not unique in this way. The contemporary humanistic critic of mass art is concerned with all the kinds of ideology disseminated by mass art. So whether or not the devices I characterize are unique to mass art or not is irrelevant. If I manage to find some fairly pervasive conduits of ideology that frequently recur in mass art, that will be of use to the contemporary critic. It will not disturb such critics if it turns out that these vehicles are not peculiar to all and only mass art.

Moreover, since I think that even if we grant the essentialist the unlikely possibility that there are some unique mechanisms for disseminating ideology by means of mass art, even he must concede that such pure mass art devices are few and far between. Thus, if one wishes to make a contribution to the foundations of the contemporary practice of the criticism of ideology in mass art, then it is much more to the point to focus our attention on relatively generic devices for the dissemination of ideology in mass art, rather than on the (however few) necessarily unique ones there might be.[7]

What follows is divided into two parts: a discussion of the concept of ideology and a more empirical examination of some of the most frequently recurring strategies that operate to transmit ideology in mass art. This review of the rhetorical devices employed in mass art to advance ideology is not exhaustive, nor do I contend that the devices that I enumerate are mutually exclusive. In this respect, my speculations are exploratory and provisional, though I hope they may be helpful or at least

---

[7] Of course, I think that there are no such necessarily unique mass art devices. I have made the assumption that there might be only for the sake of argument.

suggestive to practical critics concerned to pinpoint the operation of ideology in mass art.

Since the devices in question are what I call rhetorical and since rhetoric is not necessarily always in the service of ideology, in my view we can only call a specimen ideological in virtue of the content that the rhetorical device in question advances. Thus, in order to isolate instances of ideology in mass art, we need a conception of ideological content, or what we might less pedantically call a theory of ideology.

Thus, the next section of this chapter is preoccupied with developing a theory of ideology. But the theory has a purpose which, in turn, constrains the way in which I build it. I want to craft a concept of ideology that I think suits the practices of sound contemporary ideological criticism in the humanities. Consequently, I will reject conceptions of ideology that do not appear to mesh with those purposes. The concept of ideology that I finally advance may not be the one that every practical critic would offer if asked. But I hope that it is *a* concept of ideology that expeditiously serves the purposes of valid ideological criticism better than rival formulations and that contemporary critics can recognize it as such.

A theory of ideology

The notion of ideology is very confusing. There are many conceptions of ideology abroad and in use. Moreover, many of them are incompatible. Some commentators regard adherence to ideology as irrational,[8] whereas others argue that an ideology can be embraced rationally.[9] Sometimes ideology is referred to as a system of beliefs—for example, Nazi Ideology—whereas we also often speak of isolated beliefs as ideological, even if they are not part of a larger system or world view. For example, it is at least conceivable that someone accepts the ideological explanation that the poor are unemployed solely because they are lazy without buying into some larger framework of beliefs.

On some accounts, the concept of ideology is very broad. It amounts to

---

[8] Jon Elster, 'Belief, Bias and Ideology', in *Rationality and Relativism*, ed. Martin Hollis and Steven Lukes (Cambridge, Mass.: MIT Press, 1982), 123–48; Edward Shils, 'The Concept and Function of Ideology', *International Encyclopedia of the Social Sciences*, vii. 66–76; Louis Althusser, 'Ideology and Ideological State Apparatuses (Notes towards an Investigation)', in *Lenin and Philosophy and other Essays* (New York: Monthly Review Press, 1971), 189–220; David Weberman, 'Towards a Genetic Conception of Ideology' (unpub. MS).

[9] Raymond Boudon, *The Analysis of Ideology* (Chicago: University of Chicago Press, 1989). Boudon also counts Karl Mannheim in this persuasion, since Mannheim thinks of ideology as the belief in norms that have been adapted to a historical situation. See Karl Mannheim, *Ideology and Utopia* (London: Routledge and Kegan Paul, 1954).

'the process of production of meanings, signs and values in social life.'[10] For example, Clifford Geertz equates ideology with symbolic action.[11] Such conceptions of ideology make it virtually co-extensive with what is ordinarily called culture. Similarly, some theorists, emboldened by the promise of semiotics, identify ideology with discursive closure.[12] This makes ideology at least as wide as all linguistic culture.

Still broad, but less broad than the notion of ideology-as-culture, are the conceptions of ideology that define it as a body of ideas expressive or characteristic of a particular social group or class,[13] or as action-oriented sets of political beliefs.[14] These notions of ideology distinguish ideology from culture as a whole by correlating it to the beliefs of certain groups or classes, on the one hand, and with politics, on the other hand.

However, what unites the notions of ideology cited in the preceding two paragraphs is that they are not necessarily pejorative. There is no reason to be suspicious of every cultural belief. Is there anything wrong in thinking that one should drive on the right side of the road in Texas? Nor are the beliefs that are expressive or characteristic of a certain group or class necessarily disreputable. There was nothing wrong with Martin Luther King's convictions about the equality of the races, though it would count as ideology, if it were expressive or characteristic of African-American thinking on the matter. Likewise, for the same reasons, if we define ideology as action-oriented political beliefs, there appears to be no a priori reason to distrust all ideology, since in this view, the beliefs of emancipatory political movements will be ideological.

So, there are non-pejorative usages of the concept of ideology. But, in addition, there are, at the same time, other usages—quite common in ordinary speech as well as in academic discourse—where to call something ideological is to upbraid it. For example, when I dismiss the vituperations of *The Weekly Standard* as ideological, I do not mean to say that they merely are an example of culture, semiosis, symbolic activity, or the characteristic expression of neo-conservatives and their political aspirations. I mean to say that there is something wrong with them—that they are biased and distorted in a way that serves some dubious social agenda. This informal usage is suggested by John Thompson when he says

[10] This usage is cited, but not endorsed, by Terry Eagleton in *Ideology: An Introduction* (London: Verso, 1991), 1.
[11] C. Geertz, 'Ideology as a Cultural System', in *Ideology and Discontent*, ed. D. Apter (Glencoe, Ill.: Free Press, 1964), 25–49. [12] See Eagleton, *Ideology*, 2.
[13] Ibid. 1. [14] Martin Seliger, *Ideology and Politics* (London: Allen and Unwin, 1976).

ideology comprises 'the ways in which meaning (or signification) serves to sustain relations of domination.'[15]

Examples of both the broad, non-pejorative sense of ideology and the more narrow pejorative sense are not hard to find, either in technical writing or ordinary speech. However, these usages are not usually consistent with each other. If one is employing the notion of ideology as culture, one should not assume that it carries a pejorative spin, unless one is explicitly committed to the extreme and rather unpromising hypothesis that every cultural expression of every conceivable culture—past, present, and future—is suspect, including one's own conception of ideology, inasmuch as it is an instance of symbolic activity. Moreover, this sort of tension is apt to arise when contemporary critics, armed with a broad conception of ideology, such as ideology as semiosis, attempt to use it to unmask oppression, since presumably their own critical work is an example of semiosis. This does not entail that broad conceptions of ideology are without bona fide precedents, but only that pejorative senses of ideology and broad senses of ideology may be at odds with each other, and that the failure to recognize this may lead to talking at cross purposes.

Unquestionably, the confusion that persists over this notion is rooted in the history of the short-lived concept of ideology. Introduced by Destutt de Tracy at the end of the eighteenth century, ideology was supposed to be the study of the origin of ideas—notably ideas derived from sensation. Understood this way, ideology is of the nature of what we would think of as psychology today. It was Napoleon who gave the term political associations—indeed, pejorative ones—when he criticized Destutt de Tracy and Volney for being *ideologues*, i.e., people concerned with abstractions, rather than real-world politics.[16] This sense of ideology is echoed, at least to a certain extent, by Hegel in his *Philosophy of History* when he contrasts ideologues, construed as persons of principle, to statesmen.[17]

These usages of the notion of ideology, if they exist at all today, are rare. Undoubtedly, the most influential early conception of ideology is that of Marx and Engels, especially as it is employed in their *German Ideology*. In their view, ideology is thought—often systematic thought (such as philosophy or economics)—that expresses and facilitates the interests of the dominant class, notably the bourgeoisie under capitalism and the aristocracy under feudalism. This conception of ideology is pejorative. According to it, ideology represents social reality upside down, as if, Marx says, in a

---

[15] John B. Thompson, *Studies in the Theory of Ideology* (Cambridge: Polity Press, 1984), 4.

[16] Boudon, *Analysis of Ideology*, 25.

[17] See Z. Pelczynski, 'The Roots of Ideology in Hegel's Political Philosophy', in *Ideology and Politics*, ed. M. Cranston and P. Mair (The Hague: Sijthoff and Noordhoff, 1981), 65–74.

camera obscura. Moreover, this mystification has a social function. It expresses and advances the interests of the dominant social class. This notion underwrites the later marxist notion of false consciousness according to which dominated classes, as a result of ideology, come to mistake their own real interests for those of the ruling class.

Historically, the marxist tradition has exerted a great deal of influence on contemporary critics of ideology. For example, though feminists may wish to part company with Marx's emphasis on class, they nevertheless continue to look back to the marxist tradition for rough models for discussing oppression; for some feminists, sexism, as endorsed by women, is akin to false consciousness.

Unfortunately, however, the marxist tradition itself does not use the concept of ideology univocally. In *What Is To Be Done?*, Lenin correlates ideology with the systems of beliefs of the major players in the class struggle. Thus, there is socialist ideology as well as bourgeois ideology. But if Lenin and his followers are willing to speak of socialist ideology, then they cannot be using the term pejoratively in the way that Marx did, since obviously they do not intend to demean socialism.

With so many conflicting notions of ideology on offer, it is natural to wonder which, if any, of these conceptions contemporary ideological critics should endorse. Each of these usages has precedent in current linguistic usage, and each is intelligible when used and duly flagged in the appropriate context. None is obviously inadmissable on a priori grounds. But, at the same time, one cannot endorse all of them without the threat of inconsistency looming. Thus, a choice needs to be made between them. But which one is best for the purposes of sound ideological criticism?

I think that we can make some headway here if we begin by sorting these candidates into two large categories. Let us say that there are broad, non-pejorative conceptions of ideology and narrow pejorative ones. Next, let me add that I think it is fairly obvious that contemporary critics should favour a pejorative conception of ideology over non-pejorative conceptions.

This seems obvious to me in so far as contemporary ideological critics are, by their own account, first and foremost social *critics*—that is, they are in the business of advancing negative judgements of that which they identify as ideology. They justify their pedagogical practice, for example, on the grounds that they are advancing the cause of justice by revealing the ideology that enslaves people, including their students, who, as unwitting dupes of ideology (in the form of racism, sexism, homophobia, classism, and so on) are complicit not only in the oppression of others, but in their own domination as well. That is, they may be victims of false consciousness. Professors teach students to decode ideology, putatively to disabuse students of their acceptance of ideological beliefs and in order to equip them to resist the blandishments of ideology for the rest of their lives.

Academic critics of the ideology disseminated by mass art are committed to autonomy—to the autonomy of oppressed peoples, including their students. They engage in the criticism of ideology for the sake of justice. But if they employ a broad, non-pejorative conception of ideology, then they will lose their moral edge. For if ideology is simply symbolic activity, then their lectures and articles are ideology too. Why should a student trade in her traditional ideology for a new one, if both are equally ideological? Moreover, if ideology is equated as anything cultural, why should anyone even attempt to divest themselves of ideology, since human life is inextricably bound up with culture? What point is there in urging students to shed ideology, if it is impossible? Thus, I surmise, if contemporary scholars of mass art intend to use the notion of ideology *critically*, then they ought to prefer a pejorative conception of it. For what *critical* means in this context is virtually equivalent to *pejorative*.

And yet, even if it seems as though contemporary critics should opt for a pejorative conception of ideology, they often tend explicitly to endorse broader, non-pejorative notions of ideology. This is the case with Althusserians, for example, whose mentor alleges 'ideology is therefore an organic part, as such, of every social totality. . . . Human societies secrete ideology as the very element and atmosphere indispensable to their historical respiration and life. . . . Historical materialism cannot conceive that even a communism society could ever do without ideology.'[18] Moreover, where Althusserianism is wedded to semiotics, as it often is, all symbolic activity becomes ideological, by necessity. Thus, where critics believe that

[18] Louis Althusser, *For Marx* (London: New Left Books, 1977), 232.

It should be noted that Althusser himself does have various ways to recuperate the pejorative dimension of the notion of ideology. For example, in 'Teoría, Práctica teórica y formación teórica. Ideología y lucha ideológica' (Theory, Theoretical Practice, and Theoretical Formation. Ideology and Ideological Struggle), *Casa de las Americas*, 34 (1996), a journal published in Havana, Cuba, he offers a distinction between ideology in class-dominated societies versus classless societies. Presumably, the notion of a class-dominated ideology is a pejorative one. However, here I think Althusser is introducing two concepts of ideology where most of us think one would suffice, namely the pejorative notion of ideology. After all, we already have the notion of culture—or even of symbolic culture—in order to characterize the meanings, signs, and values of putatively classless societies.

Althusser also sometimes draws a distinction between ideology and science. This might enable him to mobilize a pejorative sense of ideology, but it will be of little use to his adherents in the Anglophone world, since they regard this as 'privileging' science and feel compelled to deconstruct any purported contrasts between ideology and science.

Althusser's 'Teoría, Práctica teórica y formación teórica' is discussed by Jorge Larrain in *The Concept of Ideology* (Brookfield, Vt.: Gregg Revivals, 1982), 154–7.

there is nothing outside ideology, including their own symbolic activity, the critical dimension of the notion of ideology is undermined.

But if such an approach is as logically self-defeating as I have argued, one must ask why contemporary critics of ideology are so eager to embrace it? I think that contemporary critics are often disposed toward broad conceptions of ideology because they can use it as a universal premiss to justify the employment of ideological criticism anywhere they wish with virtually no need for argument. If all culture is ideological, it follows that one may scrutinize any aspect of culture from the point of view of ideological criticism. There is no apparent need to argue for ideological analysis in a special case. Every case is automatically ripe for ideological analysis.

This can appear quite liberating, especially in the short run. It seems to supply critics with the philosophical wherewithal to go searching for ideology in places where no one heretofore believed that ideology existed. Fashion photography, diet regimes, and exercise manuals—not to mention movies, TV, and popular songs—are all automatically ideological under this dispensation. Thus, broad conceptions of ideology give enterprising social critics the conceptual means to outflank more conservatively minded critics in the short run. To colleagues who say that movie projectors are beyond or beneath critical appreciation, the contemporary critic deftly demurs, responding that *everything* is ideological.

But, I would argue, these short-run advantages come at a price that should be too steep for the ideological critic to be willing to pay. For in buying into the broad concept of ideology, the scholar sells off his birthright as a social critic. For, as I have already suggested, in labelling everything ideological, one tars one's own analyses and political agendas with the same brush one is using against the forces of reactionary oppression. However intellectually liberating broad conceptions of ideology may appear to be, they are self-defeating in the long run, and, for that reason, contemporary critics of ideology with respect to the mass arts should assiduously steer clear of them.

Yet, even if we agree that what contemporary criticism needs is a pejorative conception of ideology, we are still not out of the woods. For there are quite a few pejorative conceptions of ideology from which to choose. How, then, are we to proceed? My suggestion is that we begin with one of Marx's versions of ideology and consider its shortcomings in the hope that by dialectically correcting it, we may eventually arrive at a serviceable conception of ideology.

Marx, of course, presents us several different alternative formulations. For our purposes, let us simplify matters and say that for Marx, ideology involves thought, often systematic thought (such as philosophy or economics), that gives the appearance of being objectively true, but that in fact is biased in favour of the interests of the dominant social class, generally expressing and/or advancing those interests. Ideology is a matter of ideas and concepts, often organized systematically. But these ideas and concepts are mystificatory. They dissimulate. They, in effect, lie. They are false.

But they are not merely false. Their falsity has a function. It masks the interests of the dominant class, thereby encouraging everyone, including members of the dominant class, to mistake the ruling class's perspective as the unvarnished truth. For example, if economists maintain that wages cannot be higher without risking massive unemployment, then that may be ideological if the predictions are false, and, at the same time, they serve the interests of the owners of factories in making larger profits. And, in turn, workers who accept these prognostications would be victims of false consciousness.

This conception of ideology has two components—what we can call the epistemic component and the domination component. The first component requires that the ideas, concepts, beliefs, etc. in question be flawed epistemically in some way: that they be false, mystifying, and so on;[19] the second component refers to social oppression. On the marxist version, ideology expresses and advances the interests of the dominant social class, often by disguising those interests. But at the same time it is important to note that ideology need not be conspiratorial. Ideologues may sincerely believe what they say. Thus, intentions notwithstanding, what they say is ideological only if it serves to express and/or advance the interests of the dominant class. Let us begin by looking at the domination component of the theory first.

The domination component of the marxist notion of ideology is too narrow for the purposes of contemporary ideological criticism. It is tied too closely to the notion of class. Thus, it can only be applied to societies that have social classes and, indeed, to societies that have dominant social classes. Moreover, it is explicitly linked to class domination. But, arguably, phenomena like sexism and racism are ideological, yet they may not be reducible to class relationships. Thus, one way in which contemporary critics need to adjust the marxist conception of ideology is to refrain from keying it exclusively to class domination.

Domination or oppression is important to the conception of ideology

---

[19] For example, according to Michele Barrett, 'the consensual definition of ideology [is] . . . mystification that serves class interests.' Barrett, *The Politics of Truth* (Stanford, Calif.: Stanford University Press, 1991), 14.

that is relevant for contemporary criticism. But it should not be restricted to notions of ruling-class domination. Hitler's *Mein Kampf* was, for example, ideological *before* he assumed political power in 1933 when the Nazis came to constitute the ruling class in Germany. And similarly, the doctrines of the Ku Klux Klan and those of the various unofficial militias that are to be found throughout the USA today are ideological, even if they do not serve the interests of the ruling class. In fact, one suspects that the dominant classes in America not only would prefer to do without such social formations, but would be better off without them.[20]

Thus, it seems mistaken to tie the notion of ideology so closely to the interests of the dominant class for two reasons: ideology may not have to do with class relationships at all (for example, homophobia), and even where it has to do with class relationships, ideology need not be in the service of a *dominant* class (for example, the sexism of various socially marginal religious groups). The domination component of the concept of ideology, in other words, needs to be weakened. My suggestion is to drop talk about dominant or ruling classes and to associate ideology with any form of domination or social oppression, whether it is an expression or implementation of an interest of a *ruling class* or not.[21]

That is, I recommend dropping the supposition that ideology must be connected exclusively to *class* phenomena.[22] On such an approach, the sexism of marginal social groups, such as ethnic or religious subcultures, could also count as ideology, as long as the epistemic component of the concept of ideology is also satisfied. This concept of ideology, I think, suits to purposes of sound social criticism better than approaches that depend exclusively on class analysis. So, on my provisional construal, something would be ideology if it were both false and in the service of some form of social domination.

Here domination need not be associated with the dominant social class, or, indeed, with any class. Homophobic remarks by anyone, of any social class, would be ideological where they posed as objective truths (for example, 'gay men are all child molesters') that, in turn, were linked to

[20] That is, the doctrines of the Ku Klux Klan are probably not in either the perceived or the real interests of the dominant social classes in America.

[21] In order to be viable, this approach assumes that we have some reliable way of identifying forms of social domination. This would probably require something like a theory of justice and obviously this is not the place to attempt to develop one. Thus, if there are sceptical readers who are convinced that there can be no theory of justice, they might want to stop reading right now. On the other hand, I suspect that most contemporary critics think that a conception of justice is within their reach, so they at least have grounds for believing that we can identify the relevant forms of social domination.

[22] I also suggest that we drop talk about interests, because a tenet may be ideological whether or not it is in either the perceived interests of a group (a group's ideology may call for mass suicide as a result of what they conceive to be a disinterested philosophical imperative) or its real interests.

forms of social domination (for example, discrimination against homosexual school teachers). Nor need we suppose that homophobia is in the real interests of any class, including the dominant class. Homophobia is ideological in so far as it advances false views complicit with some form of social domination.

Such forms of social domination are often thought of as systems, such as capitalism or patriarchy. However, I see no compelling reason to require that ideology be linked with social practices that are exclusively of the nature of systems. Isolated social practices might be ideological without being part of an overarching, systematic ensemble of practices of social oppression. Refusing to sell Irish people liquor on the grounds that they are all drunkards would be ideological, even if there is no systematic persecution of the Irish in the offing. Thus, rather than associating ideology narrowly with *systems* of domination, I think that it is wiser to work with a more modest claim and to say that x is ideological only if x is complicit with *practices* of social domination.

This, of course, does not exclude the possibility that ideology is also complicit with systems of social domination, since systems of social domination are comprised of practices. But speaking more broadly of practices of domination also allows us to deal with cases of ideology that may not appear to be part of a fully articulated system of oppression. Moreover, when I say that something is a practice of social domination, I do not mean that it is actually an effective practice; something can be ideological if it recommends a practice of domination that is not yet in place. Something may be ideological if it is only a blueprint for a prospective practice of domination. Thus, the hate literature of many marginal groups may satisfy the domination condition of the concept of ideology in this way.

So far I have been working on the domination component of the concept of ideology. Let us put that to one side for the moment and turn to the epistemic component. One very standard way to flesh out this condition is to say that something is ideological only if it is false. When ideology is associated with illusion, the idea of falsity seems to be what one has in mind. Moreover, this formulation, though broader than the case of false consciousness, also handles it, since the notion of false consciousness presupposes that agents have *mistaken* beliefs about their interests. Likewise, those who regard ideology as necessarily involved in contradictions should be attracted to this conception, since contradictions are necessarily false.

Undoubtedly this is a very typical way of characterizing ideology because it is very clear-cut. If ideology is epistemically flawed thought, the most straightforward way in which something can be epistemically flawed is for it to be false. The view that the poor are just lazy is ideological, in part, because it is empirically false.

Often ideology is associated with systems of beliefs, such as philosophical systems, religious world views, and economic theories. However, I, at least, find no compulsion to restrict ideological thought to systems of belief. It seems plausible to suppose that one might be committed to the isolated proposition that the poor are simply lazy without endorsing an entire *system* of beliefs. Such a view might be part of a commonplace *collection* of beliefs, but it often seems exaggerated to me to speak of such collections as systems—as if they were on a par with an organized, reflectively constructed body of thought.

Thus, it may be more advisable to start by speaking of propositions, rather than of systems, as the relevant basic unit of ideological thought. This, of course, does not preclude that in particular instances ideology is systematic. But since systems of thought will be composed of propositions, it seems more economical as well as more accurate to think at ground level of ideology in terms of propositions, rather than only in terms of systems of thought.

So, as a first approximation of the epistemic component of one of the most typical views of ideology, we might suggest that a proposition x is ideological only if x is false.[23] This coincides with the views of theorists who regard ideology as unscientific.[24] But this is only a necessary condition for ideology. In order to be ideological, a proposition will not only have to be false; it will also have to be linked to some practice of social domination. My belief that I have the longest fingers in Wisconsin, though false, is not ideological, since it is not connected to any practice of social domination. The epistemic condition and the domination condition are each necessary conditions for ideology; together they are jointly sufficient.

This is a neat theory of ideology. Unfortunately, it is inadequate. One of the reasons that it is inadequate is that the epistemic condition is too narrow. It is too narrow in a number of respects. First, the notion of falsity is too restrictive; sometimes true propositions are used to advance ideology. Terry Eagleton offers the example of a management spokesperson during a hospital strike who says to the ambulance drivers that unless they

---

[23] For example, though Raymond Aron does not think of ideology as directly deriving from the criterion of truth or falsity, he does think of it as deriving indirectly from it. See Raymond Aron, *The Opium of the Intellectuals* (London: Greenwood, 1977).

[24] Talcott Parsons, 'An Approach to the Sociology of Knowledge', in *Transactions of the Fourth Congress of Sociology* (Milan, 1959), 25–49.

go back to work people will die in the streets.[25] This might very well be true, but it is also, in context, misleading. For it carries the implication that it is the fault of the strikers that people will die in the streets, whereas it may very well be the refusal of management to negotiate that should be held accountable. In this case, management uses a true statement to confuse the issue.

Similarly, in Wisconsin, conservatives advanced the cause of what they called welfare 'reform' by citing cases of welfare embezzlers who, though they lived in Chicago, registered in Milwaukee, where the benefits were more generous. Time after time, critics of welfare alluded to well-documented cases of people arriving from Illinois to cheat the Wisconsin system. The cases were true enough. But they were used in a discursive context where it was implied that they were paradigmatic cases, rather than exceptional ones. Needless to say, this use of tendentious paradigms disposed many angry voters against welfare.

Here, then, was a case where true propositions were deployed ideologically. Moreover, parallel examples of tendentious paradigms are quite frequent in national discussions of welfare, where some substantiated cases of several generations of women who have made Aid to Dependent Children into a way of life are cited with the misleading, pragmatic implication that they represent the typical circumstances of women on the welfare rolls. The anecdotes may be true, but what they insinuate, in context, is misleading.

True propositions, in short, can be used to advance ideology. Test scores, accurately compiled, may be complicit in the operation of ideology when they are cited to suggest that whole groups of people are inferior with respect to quantitative skills. The reports in question may be true, but in the relevant discursive context they may be cited in a way that is both misleading and that is connected to some practice of social domination. Obviously, truths can be marshalled in recommendations for unjust social policies that involve avoidable social oppression. Thus, it will not do to articulate the epistemic condition of our theory of ideology solely in terms of falsity. We must cast our nets more broadly and say that a proposition x is ideological only if x is false or otherwise epistemically defective (as is the case where, in context, x is very apt to be misleading, or is ambiguous, or is connected to other beliefs in a way that is unwarranted).[26]

---

[25] Eagleton, *Ideology*, 16.

[26] As noted, a true proposition may be embedded in an otherwise ideological discourse in such a way that its import, overall, is misleading owing to its discursive contextualization. The ideologue may use a true proposition in a context where other relevant propositions are omitted. Or, he may surround the proposition with evasions and *non sequiturs* in what has come to be called 'spin-doctoring'.

Since the ways in which a proposition can be epistemically defective or misleading are various, it is perhaps best to leave this condition somewhat unspecified, relying on the ideological critic to spell out exactly what is epistemically wrong with the relevant propositions on a case-by-case basis. Sometimes it may involve eliciting misleading implications or presuppositions. Sometimes it may involve tendentious paradigms. But since ideologues can be very inventive at discovering new ways of 'twisting' the facts, one should be wary of attempting to specify in advance all the ways in which ideology can be epistemically defective, other than being just false.

Restricting the epistemic condition of the concept of ideology to falsity is one way in which the standard conception may be too narrow. Another way is by speaking only of propositions. For ideology may not only be comprised of propositions. It may also be comprised of concepts and categorical frameworks, i.e., ways of carving up phenomena. For example, if a society tends to represent women as either madonna-types or whores, then that grid distorts the way in which someone who employs this optic forms assessments and expectations about the behaviour of women. This framework, moreover, may readily perform a service in continuing social oppression, since women failing to evince the salient characteristics of madonna-hood are more likely than not to be treated like prostitutes, which treatment, of course, in our society, is standardly not particularly respectful or deferential.

Conceptual categories and conceptual schemas can distort social phenomena in a way that is complicit with social domination. They can do this either by being too gross and unrefined, thereby failing to pick out pertinent grades of difference and distinction as do portrayals of African-American males as either saints (*To Sir With Love*) or criminals. Or, categorical frameworks can be too rarefied—defining phenomena out of existence (the death of a thousand conceptual cuts).

That concepts and categorical schemas are relevant to ideology shows that the correlation of ideology with false propositions is too restrictive in two senses, since: first, ideology may involve concepts and categorical frameworks, rather than only propositions; and, second, because concepts and categorical frameworks are not epistemically assessed in terms of truth, but in terms of notions such as fitness to the phenomena. Where categories and conceptual frameworks fail to fit the phenomena by demarcating it inaccurately, they may obscure the phenomena and distort it, for example, by over-simplifying the relevant forces in play. Or categories can draw distinctions where they should not be drawn. (Perhaps the notion of the deserving poor is a pertinent example here.) Moreover, such distortion can be relevant to practices of social domination. Thus, in order to speak of the epistemic dimension of ideology, we need to speak not only of propositions, but of concepts and categorical frameworks. Nor is this an obstacle to those who wish to talk about ideological systems of belief, since such systems will be composed of propositions, concepts, and categorical frameworks which, in salient respects, are epistemically flawed as well as being complicit in practices of social domination.

Summarizing our results so far, then, we may say: that a proposition x is ideological only if x is false or otherwise epistemically defective; and that a concept, category, or categorical framework y is ideological only if y fails to fit the phenomena (is inaccurate, distorting, obscuring, or otherwise epistemically defective).[27]

Here epistemic defectiveness, of whatever sort, is only a necessary condition for ideology.[28] It must be linked to some practice of social domination before we can call a candidate a full-blooded instance of ideology. But what is the nature of that linkage? How must epistemically defective propositions and concepts be connected to practices of social domination in order to count as cases of ideology?

The most popular way to characterize that linkage is to say that the epistemically defective content of ideological thought performs some *function* for practices of domination. For example, John Plamenatz characterizes ideology as 'a whole set of beliefs that serves to hold a group together or to justify its activities or to promote its interest.'[29] Here the ideological thought in question performs such functions as facilitating group cohesion and promoting interests. But there is a general problem with making the attribution of functions criterial to the identification of ideology, and it is a problem that we are familiar with from the preceding chapter. Namely, it presumes that we are in a position reliably to predict the consequences of broadcasting thoughts. But as we suggested in our discussion of consequentialism—to which genus this species of function-

[27] Though I think that epistemic defectiveness is a necessary condition for ideology, this does not commit me to the view that ideology is either necessarily rational or necessarily irrational. I suspect that an ideological conviction can be acquired in either way. Whether adherence to an ideological belief is rational or irrational is to be determined by the particularities of the case at hand.

Though I only discuss propositions and categorical schemas in the epistemic half of my formula here, other plausible candidates are discussed in my 'Film, Rhetoric and Ideology', *Theorizing the Moving Image* (New York: Cambridge University Press, 1996), 287 n. 15.

[28] There is perhaps a use of the term ideology that considers it to be any politically biased proposition. One might say that a proposal is biased because it is simply Democratic Party boilerplate. This, in effect, is to regard epistemic defectiveness—political bias of any sort—as sufficient for calling something ideological. I do not deny that this usage may be out there. However, I think that this conception of ideology is not what contemporary critics are after, since it regards any sort of political bias as ideological whether or not it contributes to practices of social domination. And, it seems to me, that some political bromides, though biased, may be benign.

[29] John Plamenatz, *Ideology* (London: Macmillan, 1970), 31.

alism belongs—the claim to be able to make such predictions reliably is vastly exaggerated.

Thus, if in order to call something ideology, we must be in a position to forecast accurately the actual consequences of airing epistemically defective thoughts for practices of social domination, then we would rarely, if ever, be in a position to do so. Here, it might be suggested that we only need to be able to say that the thought in question has the capacity to promote some practice of domination. But this is rather lame, since probably any intellectual content in certain circumstances has the capacity to promote practices of domination. In order to make capacity-talk persuasive, its proponent will have to say that the cognitive content of the thought in question has a *predictable* propensity to elicit support for practices of social domination in standard contexts. But then we are back to making implicit predictions once again.[30]

Is there a way around this problem? Gordon Graham, with reference to ideologies like Fascism, has said: 'By "ideologies" I mean those sets of beliefs which have or are meant to have wide implications for the conduct of political life and even, in some cases, for its complete refashioning.'[31] Here Graham's concerns are broader than mine, since he has in mind systems of explicit political belief. Nevertheless, his suggestion that the relation of ideas in such systems to conduct is one of *implication* is useful.

The problem with functionalist constructions of the domination component of the concept of ideology is that they may presuppose a degree of causal knowledge that we have not got about the consequences of disseminating thought, including epistemically defective thought. But we are on far better footing to say what the implications of saying something in a given cultural-political context are without committing ourselves to sociological predictions. As competent language users, for example, we are very good at picking up the pragmatic implications of assertions. So, perhaps we can say that an epistemically defective proposition, concept or combination thereof is ideological just in case it has favourable (often contextually motivated) implications for some practice of social domination.

Practices, of course, are not simply behaviours. They are underwritten by, among other things, presuppositions, categories, and concepts. Thus, one relation that propositions, concepts, categorical frameworks, or combinations thereof can have to a practice is that they serve as tenets or premises of the practice. Moreover, in other cases, propositions, concepts, and so on may have favourable implications for practices. The discovery

---

[30] For further criticism of the implicit functionalism in ideological attributions, see Ian Adams, *The Logic of Political Belief: A Philosophical Analysis of Ideology* (Savage, Md.: Barnes and Nobles, 1989).

[31] Gordon Graham, *Politics in Place: A Study of Six Ideologies* (Oxford: Clarendon Press, 1986), 48.

that a certain metal is highly durable may have favourable implications for the practice of mining that metal. Similarly, a thought introduced in false or misleading ways in a given social-political context can have 'favourable' implications for a practice of domination. Advancing tendentious paradigms of welfare cheats has favourable implications in so far as it serves as a premiss in policy recommendations that portend social domination.

Therefore, let us say that a proposition x is ideological if and only if 1. x is false (or otherwise epistemically defective) and 2. x is a tenet of or has contextually grounded implications favourable to some practice of social domination. Likewise, a concept or categorical framework y is ideological if and only if 1. y fails to fit the phenomenon (or is otherwise epistemically defective) and 2. y serves as a tenet of or has contextually grounded implications favourable to some practice of social domination.

These formulas appear to work nicely for famous cases of ideology. Consider the Noble Lie in Plato's *Republic*. Socrates is asked why people would accept the hierarchical arrangements he proposes for the ideal state. Let us assume—the gyrations of Plato exegesis aside—that most of us think that the republic in question involves practices of domination (merchants, for example, subservient to philosophers). Socrates suggests that the dominated might be persuaded to accept their own subjugation by means of a myth.

According to this myth, all the citizens are born of the same earth—the state is a Mother Land, if you will. Some are people of gold, some of silver, and some of base metal. However, though they are of different metals, they are still blood relatives. All are brothers and sisters. All issue from the same mother. The gold people are the rulers or guardians, the silver people are the military and the police, and the rest of us are base metals. Why should we obey the people of gold?

Here the family analogy comes into play. In a family we are willing to accept certain lines of authority because of our understanding of kinship relations. Perhaps the oldest brother or sister is automatically first in command in the event of the death of the parents. Authority exerts itself in a family in a way that does not obtain in relations between strangers. But by means of the Noble Lie, Socrates is suggesting that the willingness to accept authority within family relations be transferred to political relationships.

Purportedly, we are all consanguineously linked in Plato's republic. The guardians are effectively our older brothers and sisters. We should accept their authority as we do that of our older siblings. This is clearly ideological on my account. The Noble Lie is comprised of false propositions—Socrates admits as much. We are not born of the earth; we do not all share the same parent. Moreover, the categorical framework—people of various metals—fails to fit the phenomena. At the same time, the myth has favourable implications for the relevant practices of domination—obey the guardians, as you would an older brother or sister. Whether or not anyone would be taken in by the Noble Lie, we can still call it ideological, because it involves epistemically defective thought that provides tenets of and has implications favourable for a practice of political domination.

Though I hope that I have improved upon it and made it somewhat more precise, the characterization of ideology that I have presented so far is rather standard in its broad contours. And inasmuch as it is somewhat conventional, it is also the target of some pretty standard objections. Thus, in order to defend my theory of ideology, I need to show how it can address standard objections to theories like it.

Two leading objections to theories like mine are: 1. if this is what ideology is, then we do not need a special science (in the European sense) of ideology critique;[32] and 2. this theory, with its emphasis on epistemic considerations, makes ideology largely an affair of cognition, ignoring the fact that ideology is equally, if not more, concerned with affects, such as emotion and desire.[33] Let me address these objections one at a time.

The first objection is that there is no such thing as a science of ideology critique, if ideology is as I parse it. My account of ideology is componential, and each of the components can be addressed by existing practices of inquiry. The propositions and concepts that I speak of can be assessed for epistemic defectiveness by existing disciplines. If the relevant proposition concerns developmental psychology, let psychologists examine it; if it is a matter of financial statistics, send it to the economists. Likewise, the domination component would appear to fall squarely into the domain of political scientists. That is, we already have the methods and disciplines for investigating ideology at hand, if ideology is as I depict it. We do not need new methods of inquiry nor do we need a new, specially trained cadre of scholars to deal with ideology on my construal.

The presupposition of this argument seems to be that ideology should constitute a unique object of study, one that calls for new methodologies. And it is true that on my account it looks like we are already in a position to examine ideology, since ideology is built up from already familiar

---

[32] This seems to me to be a theme of Raymond Geuss's *The Idea of A Critical Theory: Habermas and the Frankfurt School* (Cambridge: Cambridge University Press, 1981). The charge has been explicitly voiced by David Weberman in his 'Towards A Genetic Conception of Ideology', a paper presented to the Philosophy Colloquium at the University of Wisconsin.

[33] Terry Eagleton attributes such a criticism to Althusser in his book *Ideology* (p. 19). David Weberman also advanced this objection in his lecture 'Towards A Genetic Conception of Ideology'.

components. But, as you might predict, I reject the presupposition of this argument. It is not clear to me why we should believe that a constraint on any theory of ideology must be that it makes of ideology a unique object of study. One may be moved, as I am, to study ideology because it exists and because it is important. That it need not require its own unique methodology is hardly a compelling reason not to study it. Who cares whether or not it constitutes a unique object of study? To demand that ideology be construed in such a way that it calls for a unique theoretical approach seems to be nothing more than the tail wagging the dog.

The second objection to my account of ideology seems more troubling. Ideology addresses the affective life of people. Althusser says that ideology 'expresses a will, a hope, a nostalgia rather than describing reality'.[34] I would hesitate to say that ideology has nothing to do with describing reality. But reading Althusser charitably, we can agree that it may involve more than describing reality. It also involves engaging emotion and desire. Advertisements provide constant examples of this: they employ all manner of devices in order to encourage our admiration of large corporations—portrayed as bastions of strength or friendly systems of hospitality (reach out and touch someone)—and to encourage us to desire their products. If any theory of ideology excluded the affective dimension of such things as advertising, it would surely be a bad theory. The question is whether my theory is flawed in this way.

I think that it is not. To show why it is not, let us see how the theory can accommodate the affective dimension of ideology. Let's start with the emotions, since we have already discussed them at length in relation to mass art. The objection seems to presuppose that if a theory stresses epistemic defectiveness in terms of propositions and concepts, then it is linked to cognition in a way that excludes a consideration of the emotions. But this is to presume a poor theory of the emotions. For, as we saw in Chapter 4, the emotions have cognitive ingredients. The emotions involve entertaining propositions and subsuming objects under concepts and categories.

There is a long-standing prejudice that the emotions have no cognitive content. In *A Treatise on Human Nature*, Hume famously separated reason and passion, declaring reason to be the slave of the passions and adding that the passions do not contain 'any representative quality which renders it a copy of any other existence or modification.'[35] But, as I have argued previously, the notion that emotions lack any representational content is dubious. If I believe that someone has insulted me, that, all things being

---

[34] Althusser, *For Marx*, 234.
[35] David Hume, *A Treatise on Human Nature*, ed. Selby Bigge (Oxford: Oxford University Press, 1960), Bk. II, s. iii. 415.

equal, is likely to cause me to be angry. Anger does not arise without thought contents nor is it indifferent to thought contents. In standard conditions, people are not angered by learning the velocity of a meteor landing on Jupiter. But they are typically angered by being told that they are racially inferior. Emotions have propositional content or, although Hume denied it, they have representational content.

In addition, emotions involve concepts that serve as criteria of appropriateness for being in an emotional state. In order to be angry, I must subsume the object of my state under the concept of a wrong done to me or mine. An emotion is appropriate where its object is of the criterially correct sort. But if emotions have propositions and concepts as intrinsic ingredients, and these representational constituents are epistemically assessable—in terms of truth and falsity, or appropriateness or inappropriateness, or epistemic clarity or confusion—then a theory of ideology like mine need not be regarded as inapplicable to the emotions. If it is said that my theory is primarily concerned with cognition, that does not imply that it has nothing to say about the emotions, since cognition is an essential ingredient in the emotions. And, inasmuch as cognition is an ingredient in the emotions, emotions are epistemically assessable. An emotion can be epistemically defective if it is false, inappropriate, confused, and so on. Similarly, a message can be ideological if it addresses our emotions by means of epistemically defective cognitive content that is appropriate to emotional states that, in turn, serve as tenets or have favourable implications for some practice of social domination.

The Noble Lie is a case in point. It encourages its target audience to regard their rulers as older siblings by asking them to entertain the belief that they all derive from a common parent—the Mother Land. This is designed to promote filial affection for the authorities and a sense of unity (family-unity) with other citizens. The lie also suggests that the nation itself be conceptualized as a parent, thereby inviting listeners to transfer their love for their mother to the state. In all these instances, the myth presents incongruous objects under the figure of the family in order to bring the emotions appropriate to family relations to alien and inappropriate objects. In this respect, the emotional address of the myth is epistemically defective. Moreover, inasmuch as that epistemic defectiveness has favourable implications for practices of social domination, the myth is a vehicle of ideology. In this case, it is an instance of ideology working on the emotions.

Obviously, the Noble Lie is not an isolated case. Similar invocations of the Mother Land (or the Father Land) as well as claims on the loyalty of people in the name of shared kinship (racial purity) and blood lines are still unfortunately widespread in the twentieth century. These are cases where ideology addresses the emotions. Any theory of ideology should be able to deal with them. And mine can.

For example, in the nineteenth century, journalists frequently published caricatures of the Irish that represented them as simian.[36] The features of an ape or a monkey were superimposed on a stereotypical Irish figure. The effect of such cartoons was to equate Irishmen with apes and monkeys, thereby implying that they are less than human. A similar form of pictorial rhetoric has also been employed against African-Americans. These caricatures address the emotions. Depending on the specifics of the case, they represent the Irish, on the one hand, and blacks, on the other hand, as at least incongruous but also hybrid, impure, probably subhuman beings. Thus, again depending on the illustration at hand, they represent the Irish and African-Americans either as the appropriate objects of comic amusement or as the appropriate object of disgust and possibly horror.

These caricatures disseminate ideology by means of their emotional address. They are obviously epistemically defective. Neither the Irish nor Africans (nor the descendants of Africans) are either monkeys or apes or admixtures thereof. The cartoons are epistemically flawed representations. And they are also emotionally inappropriate, since they present their images of the Irish and the African (and the African-American) under the wrong categories. Moreover, that epistemic defectiveness has implications that are favourable to practices of ethnic and racial discrimination that are socially oppressive. To lay out images in a way that appears to make it emotionally appropriate to regard persons of other ethnic groups and races as subhuman objects of humour or horror advances a tenet of social domination—for example, those people should not be accorded equal treatment; they are so disgusting.

If I have shown that my theory of ideology can accommodate the emotional address of ideology, it remains to be shown that it can also handle the relation of ideology to desires. Clearly, the strategy that I will employ here is parallel to the one that I have used to deal with the question of the emotions. As with the emotions, there is also a long-standing philosophical conviction that desires are not connected to cognition. Thus, it is supposed that a theory of ideology that emphasizes epistemic defectiveness and that is cognitively oriented cannot model the relation of ideology to desire.

Our previous quotation from Hume on the passions is often taken to

[36] L. Perry Curtis, *Apes and Angels* (Washington, DC: Smithsonian Press, 1971).

apply to desire; that is, the passions are taken to be a matter of both the emotions and desire. Thus, on the Humean view, desire has no representational content. It is akin to pure energy—the pure energy that moves us to action.[37] Desire is the fuel. Reason is the slave of desire; it figures out how to get what desire wants. But desire itself has no representational or cognitive content.

But this view of desire seems mistaken. It pictures desire as a pure push with no steering mechanism of its own.[38] But desires have intentional content. Desires are directed. Desires have objects. How would reason be able to implement desires if they had no intentional content?

The object of a desire—what I want—is the thing the possession of which would satisfy my desire.[39] Or, more broadly, desire aims at some state of affairs which, should it obtain, would satisfy my desire. If I want a car, then I desire that I should have one. The representational content of my desire is a state of affairs that, by my lights, should obtain.

Whereas the representational content of a belief in the typical case concerns a state of affairs thought to obtain, the representational content of a desire often is of a state of affairs that does not yet obtain, but that I think should obtain. Bringing about that state of affairs motivates my action. Metaphorically speaking, a belief ideally presents a picture of the way the world is, whereas a desire presents a picture of how I think the world should be. The direction of fit between a belief and the world is from world to mind; the direction of fit with respect to desire is from mind to world. The representational content of a desire guides action dedicated to changing the world in its image.

However, a desire is not merely a disposition to act. It is also a reason to act. That I have a desire for lunch is a reason for me to go across the street and buy some food. But how does a desire function as a reason? By representing a situation—like having lunch—as something that should obtain, as a state of affairs that it would be good, if it did obtain.

That is, desire provides a reason to act. What could that reason be? That it would be good to have the state of affairs that is the object of the desire obtain. I desire lunch. This is a reason to have lunch. Why is this desire reasonable or appropriate? Because it represents lunch to me as a good

[37] Perhaps a modern psychological example of this view is to be found in C. L. Hull, *Principles of Behavior* (New York: Appleton-Crofts, 1943).

[38] See Andrew Woodfield, 'Desire, Intentional Content and Teleological Explanation', *Proceedings of the Aristotelian Society*, NS lxxxii (1982), 67–87.

[39] My account of desire follows that of Dennis Stampe's, especially his article 'Desire', in *Companion to the Philosophy of Mind*, ed. S. Guttenplan (Oxford: Blackwell Publishers, 1995), 243–9. See also id., 'The Authority of Desire', *Philosophical Review*, 96/3 (1987), 335–81; and id., 'Reasons and Desires', in *Philosophy and Phenomenological Research*, xiv.

thing to have. As Dennis Stampe puts it: 'we may say that the object of a desire (whether it exists or not) is therein represented as something the possession of which would be good. In the desire that P, it is represented as being the case that it would be good were it the case that P.'[40] Thus, a plausible case can be made for the claim that desires have representational content,[41] and, of course, if desires have representational content, then they are not necessarily recalcitrant to a theory of ideology like mine.

Desires represent their objects as good things to have. If I have a desire for x then x is represented as a good state of affairs, one that should obtain. But, then, desires can be epistemically defective. And desires that are epistemically defective and that have favourable implications for some practice of domination can be called ideological desires.

For example, an advertisement might be misleading; it might represent a sports-car as a good thing to have, but by way of obfuscating associations (it suggests that such cars come equipped with beautiful playmates or that they guarantee popularity). Or, an ad might falsely represent something as something good to have. A real estate prospectus might show us some pictures, putatively of a majestic natural scene, but that really denote land that is four feet underwater. Should we take these representations on as our own, our desires would be epistemically defective. Moreover, if possessed of epistemically defective desires that are either tenets of or that have favourable implications for some practice of social domination, they would be ideological. The desire to rape women—the representation that raping women would be good—is ideological in this way, since, as feminists have shown, rape is in large measure about power.

Thus, if a film-maker employs the sense-bearing signs of his medium to suggest that raping women is good, he or she (for example, Lina Wertmuller) at least provides the grounds for the formation of an ideological desire, even if viewers do not act on it. The message in this respect can be regarded as ideological because of the way in which it addresses the desires of the audience. In this case, the film can, in terms of the framework of the last chapter, be said to be morally flawed, in so far as it seeds confusion

[40] Stampe, 'Desire', 246. Here it is being claimed that a desire for x represents x as a good thing to have. This contrasts with the more radical hypothesis advanced in Platonic dialogues that a desire represents its object as the *best* thing to have. See Plato, *Gorgias*, 467c–468e; and Plato, *Lysis*, 279d–282a.

[41] It should be noted that theories of desire of this sort are not uncontroversial. There has been a resurgence of neo-Humean arguments of late, including Michael Smith, 'The Humean Theory of Motivation', *Mind* (1987), 36–61; David Lewis, 'Desire as Belief', *Mind* (1988), 323–32; John Collins, 'Belief, Desire and Revision', ibid. 333–42. Engaging these articles here would take us too far afield into the details of decision theory. For interested readers, Huw Price attempts to deal with these articles in his 'Defending Desire-as-Belief', *Mind* (1989), 119–27.

over the proper objects of desire. But the flaw is also ideological, since the moral infraction here involves a practice of social domination.

So far I have attempted to show that my theory is not blind to the affective dimension of ideology. The stress it lays on epistemic defectiveness does not render it ineffective in addressing issues of emotion and desire. Furthermore, on behalf of my concept of ideology, I should also point out that it meshes nicely with many of the models of ideology popular in the humanities today. For example, it is often said that ideology operates by naturalizing its object—by portraying certain social phenomena, such as greed, as natural, i.e., as a feature of human nature (and, therefore, unavoidable).

Now in my view, calling something natural is not necessarily ideological. I don't see why saying that humans are naturally disposed to be language users is ideological. So, I do not agree that claims about human nature are necessarily ideological, nor do I agree that naturalization is the only way in which ideology operates. However, where naturalization is ideological, my theory can say why. Suppose greed is advanced as a piece of human nature in a context where a certain form of aggressive capitalist behaviour represents a practice of social domination. My theory says that this is ideological because the claim that greed is natural is false and that its presumed truth is a tenet that has implications favourable to a certain practice of social domination.[42] That is, where the notion of naturalization picks out the operation of ideology, my concept of ideology explains how it is able to do so.

Similarly, contemporary critics align ideology with the tendencies to universalize and to de-historicize. As in the case of naturalization, these tendencies are said to represent socially contingent, oppressive phenomena as unavoidable—as the way all people for all time always have and always will behave. Don't whine about the avariciousness of our robber barons, it might be said; such behaviour is an eternal, universal human constant. There's nothing to be done about it; learn to live with it.

Whether or not there are human universals of any sort is an open question. I suspect that there may be some universal, or nearly universal features of human nature and I, unlike many contemporary humanists, think that said universals and their invocation may be ideologically benign. But I also do agree that the rhetoric of human universals can be ideological, and that contemporary critics have pointed to some compelling cases of this. Moreover, I think that those critics should like my proposed

---

[42] For example, it may imply that there is no sense in trying to rein in the behaviour by means of social prohibitions, since the behaviour is inevitable.

concept of ideology, since it can clarify why charges of universalization and de-historicizing are ideological in those cases where the allegations make sense. Claims for universal, eternal human verities will be ideological where they are false or otherwise epistemically defective and when they provide either tenets or favourable implications for some practice of social domination. Unlike many contemporary critics, I do not reduce ideology to naturalization, universalization, eternalization, or a combination thereof, since I think that there are more ways to ideology than just these. However, my conception of ideology nevertheless suits the purposes of these critics, since it will track all the cases where strategies such as these are used in the service of ideology.

As I have conceded, my view, for all the twists and turns, derives from a fairly standard take on the nature of ideology. However, there is one very frequent component of some typical views of ideology that my position has left out—what might be called the genetic component. That is, certain theorists maintain that ideas and concepts are not simply ideological because they are epistemically defective and oppressive, but also because of the way in which they are acquired. For this position, a view is ideological only if it has been acquired in the wrong way, notably, if it has been acquired or formed in a situation where believers come to embrace it as a result of coercion or deception. An ideological belief, that is, is tainted in its very origin. And that is one of the reasons that it is ideological. The question before us now is, should I build a genetic component into the conception of ideology that I propose?

Genetic taintedness is not a sufficient condition for counting a belief as ideological. Were it so, then many worthy beliefs that serve just social practices, which we acquired as a result of parental coercion or guile, would be ideological. Suppose that I came to believe that women should be treated fairly as a result of my father's threat that if I did not share my toys with my sister and her girlfriends, then I would have to stay in my room. Or, maybe he used deception, conjuring up visions of hellfire and eternal perdition, if I failed to treat my sister and her friends appropriately. Why should that matter now in assessing my belief? For the conviction itself is not epistemically defective, and it is a tenet of just social practices. Surely we initially acquire many worthy beliefs as the result of parental practices that fall short of the ideal of open and uncoerced discussion between equals. Are all those beliefs ideological? This seems counter-intuitive. It seems to commit what is generally called a genetic fallacy and it is so unlikely that we should not even consider it a necessary condition for ideology.

Of course, this objection rides on considering the genetic component in terms of actual belief formation. It asks whether, in fact, a given belief has a tainted origin. And given the way in which children are educated (and may have to be educated) coercion (within reasonable bounds) and guile may play an inevitable role here.

However, at this point in the dialectic, a proponent of the genetic conception may say that the test is not whether coercion or deception actually played some part in the acquisition of the belief, but whether the belief could only have been acquired in the context of coercion and/or guile. That is, the proponent of the genetic condition goes counter-factual.

On a view like this, suggested by the work of Jurgen Habermas,[43] the ideal situation for acquiring the relevant sort of belief is one in which I come to embrace it as the result of free and open, uncoerced discussion, with access to full information, between equals. If a belief could only be acquired in a situation that falls short of this—if it could only happen in a speech situation where coercion and deception prevail—then it is tainted. My beliefs about the treatment of women, though secured by parental force and guile, are not ideological on this view, since I could have been brought to a recognition of their rectitude—perhaps when I grew up—in the pertinent sort of ideal speech situation. This formulation circumvents the charge of committing a genetic fallacy. Perhaps we should incorporate it into our conception of ideology.

But I am inclined not to. My reason is that I see little need for the addition of this notion of counter-factual taintedness to our theory. For what will discussants deliberate about in such ideal speech situations? Presumably they will be primarily concerned with the epistemic credentials of certain propositions. They will consider whether the propositions in question are true, whether the concepts are fit, and whether both are used in a way that is not misleading or unwarranted. For if the content of their discussion meets these criteria, it is unlikely that their implications in terms of a given social practice are avoidable.[44]

Yet if this is what deliberation in an ideal speech situation involves, then talk about the genesis of the ideas is just excess theoretical baggage. For we already implicitly have some such notion of the ideal speech situation built into the epistemic defectiveness condition of our theory. So to say additionally that beliefs must be genetically untainted in the relevant respects is not necessary.[45]

[43] Jurgen Habermas, *Legimationsprobleme im Spatkapitalismus* (Frankfurt: Suhrkamp, 1971), 125, 148.

[44] And if they are not avoidable, on the supposition that 'if' implies 'can', then they are not unjust.

[45] Further arguments against the genetic conception of ideology can be found in Raymond Geuss, *The Idea of A Critical Theory: Habermas and the Frankfurt School* (Cambridge: Cambridge University Press, 1981).

The ideal speech situation, that is, is nothing but the ideal situation for assessing the epistemic probity of propositions and concepts. That, ideally, discussion be open, uncoerced, and non-deceptive and that ideally it avail itself of full information represents nothing but the conditions that should obtain for carrying out any epistemic evaluation effectively. Thus, something like the ideal speech condition is already presupposed in our epistemic defectiveness condition. Consequently, there is no reason to add a condition about counter-factual genesis to our theory as it stands. The theory as it stands is already equipped to deal with the problem of necessary counter-factual taintedness.

So much then for the formulation of the concept of ideology; now let us apply it.

Ideology and rhetoric

During the nineteen seventies and eighties, an approach to the study of ideology coalesced in the humanities that associates ideology with discourse (where discourse itself is understood not only narrowly in terms of language, but as any ensemble of sense-bearing signs).[46] We can call this the ideology-as-discourse view. According to this still influential approach, all discourse serves the purposes of ideology by positioning subjects. By *positioning subjects*, theorists have in mind that discourse—any coherent discourse, at least—addresses readers, listeners, and viewers so that they come to think of themselves in a particular way. All discourse has an implied audience position, and audiences take or *misrecognize* this position to be an accurate reflection of their nature as agents.

Specifically, audiences take themselves to be what are called (misleadingly, I think) Cartesian subjects. That is, discourse imposes a certain conception of the subject on its readers, viewers, and listeners; it causes us to misrecognize the kind of beings we are. This is not the only function of ideology, but it is perhaps the most central one or fundamental one, since, on this account, it is believed that discourse puts in place a self-conception that serves as the support—sometimes called the subject support—for the acquisition of further ideological roles and values.

---

[46] This approach is represented by Rosalind Coward and John Ellis, *Language and Materialism* (London: Routledge and Kegan Paul, 1977); Catherine Belsey, *Critical Practice* (London: Methuen, 1980); and Kaja Silverman, *The Subject of Semiotics* (New York: Oxford University Press, 1983). Since I have criticized this approach at length elsewhere, I will not dwell on its detailed shortcomings here. Instead, see Noël Carroll, 'Belsey, Language and Realism', in *Philosophy and Literature* (April, 1987); and id., *Mystifying Movies*.

What is the nature of this Cartesian subject and why do theorists think that it secures a necessary condition for ideology? A Cartesian subject is one that takes itself to be a unified and autonomous subject. This is a result of coherent discourse transferring, so to speak, its appearance of unity to the audience member, who, in turn, reprojects his or her sense of unity back on to the discourse. This impression of unity on the part of the audience member is, according to theorists of the ideology-as-discourse persuasion, inaccurate from a theoretical point of view, so the process is called *misrecognition*. Moreover, this process of misrecognition serves an ideological function. For by encouraging the impression that the subject is free (unified and autonomous), it abets the belief that our choices are free choices.

In any culture, individuals are shaped by existing social structures. Their choices of roles and values, so the story goes, are socially mandated. By reinforcing the impression that we are free agents in this matter, discourse has a function for the status quo. It creates the impression that the choices dictated by the culture at large are free choices, thereby confirming the individual in the conviction that the roles, choices, and beliefs imposed upon her are really her own. Thus, the individual becomes a participant in her own domination.

The dominant social system functions smoothly, that is, by instilling the conviction in its subjects that their decisions are freely made, whereas, according to the ideology-as-discourse view, they are in reality completely constructed by the social system in the interests of the dominant order. Discourse provides compliant subject supports eagerly awaiting further elaboration in terms of the roles, values, choices, and beliefs of the prevailing order. Subject supports are a necessary condition for ideology; co-operative subject supports (ones that misrecognize themselves as free agents) make the operation of social domination frictionless. Thus, the view that discourse as such constructs subject supports appears to be the royal road for studying the effective operation of ideology.

On such a conception of ideology, the critic of mass art has a ready-made research agenda. Pith all those structures that make discourse appear coherent and one will at the same time identify the fundamental instruments in the construction of ideological subject supports. This project has been immensely influential in film studies, where such elements of discursive address as point-of-view editing, the perspectival image, the projection apparatus, and so on have been interrogated as mechanisms of ideological subject-positioning. The putative success of this programme in film studies has encouraged its adoption in cultural studies across the mass arts, and, even where certain of its tenets are criticized, much of its conceptual machinery—such as the language of subject-positioning—continues.[47] For example, the suspicion that narrative closure—in any discursive practice (mass art or otherwise)—constructs subjects who misrecognize themselves as unified and autonomous agents is still widely abroad.

Two presuppositions of the ideology-as-discourse view are that 1. all discourse is ideological, including 2. what one might think of as all the 'formal' elements of discourse—grammatical personhood, tense, perspective, narrative closure, and so on. Indeed, these presuppositions reinforce each other. The first presupposition, given its universality, entails that *everything* is ideological, including all formal or structural elements, whereas the second presupposition invites a research programme that is bent on showing how these apparently 'innocent' elements of discourse in fact function ideologically.

Nevertheless, both these presuppositions seem extravagant. The notion that all discourse is ideological—especially given the extremely expansive notion of discourse popularized by semiotics—turns the ideology-as-discourse view virtually into a variant of the ideology-as-culture view and, therefore, is susceptible to the criticisms offered in the preceding section of broad conceptions of ideology. Furthermore, the supposition that every formal or structural device found in mass art is ideological seems counterintuitive. One reason for this, among others, is that it seems that mass artworks that are, on balance, progressive, like Gorky's novel *Mother* and Pudovkin's film adaptation of it, employ the same sorts of formal and structural devices that reactionary ones do. But if all formal and structural devices are ideological, then, content notwithstanding, there seems scant prospect for the production of progressive—let alone neutral—mass art (or, for that matter, any form of progressive or neutral coherent discourse).

Proponents of the discourse-as-ideology view attempt to flesh out this contention with various analyses of the ways in which structural features of mass art operate to position subjects. Reviewing those hypotheses one at a time now would be too time-consuming, and, in any case, it has already been done elsewhere.[48] Suffice it to say that these explanations are often strained and *ad hoc*. The notion, for example, that coherent discursive structures somehow impart their own impression of unity to the social agent who, in consequence, misperceives himself as coherent and unified, seems to involve little more than the equivocal repetition of

---

[47] See David Bordwell, 'Contemporary Film Studies and the Vicissitudes of Grand Theory', in *Post-Theory*, ed. David Bordwell and Noël Carroll (Madison: University of Wisconsin Press, 1996).

[48] See, for example, my *Mystifying Movies*.

words like *coherent* and *unified*, applied in one sense to discursive structures and, then, once again, with an altogether different meaning, to human individuals.

On the discourse-as-ideology view, all coherent—or at least apparently unified—mass art is ideological, its overt content notwithstanding. Even mass art that might appear to be politically subversive is undermined by its structural elements, which work ideologically to reinforce the status quo.[49] That is, these elements position subjects. But since ideological critics themselves are dedicated to constructing autonomous agents for the purposes of justice, their endorsement of such a broad conception of ideology would appear to be self-defeating.

In short, a more constrained notion of ideology than that of ideology as discourse seems required for ideological analysis. Moreover, it would also appear profitable to think of the operation of ideology more specifically than globally identifying it with subject-positioning. Thus, instead of locating ideology in the putative subject-positioning operation of *all* discourse, I propose that we think as a matter of the *rhetorical* organization of *some* discourse.[50] Which discourse? The discourse that inclines audiences to take on ideological beliefs, concepts, ideational systems, emotions, desires, and so on; the discourse whose content can be identified as ideological in accordance with the theory advanced in the previous section.

That is, individual mass artworks employ rhetorical structures—several of which I will characterize in what follows—to advance ideological propositions, concepts, and systems. Neither all discourse nor all discursive structures are ideological; only some are. And, moreover, ideological discourse depends heavily on rhetoric. Ideology is not a function of

[49] See, for example, Mike Cormack's account of the way in which the familiar restrained stylistic devices in screwball comedies purportedly block the potentially subversive messages of these films. This is an example of how word play and *ad hoc*-ery figure in the ideology-as-discourse approach. From a description of the style in these films as non-disruptive, restrained, and predictable, Cormack goes on to suggest that it is conservative and reassuring (for the purposes of the status quo). Not only is this specimen of analysis incredibly mechanical and reductive; it also rides primarily on word association—leaping from the style's being non-disruptive to its being reassuring. Moreover, Cormack presupposes that the way in which the style is reassuring is relevant to its being reassuring for the purposes of the status quo, even if its content is radical. But there is a middle term missing here—how does one get from x is reassuring in that the style throws the audience no unexpected curves to its being reassuring in the sense that implies the content of the work is harmless?

By analogical reasoning, imagine the consequences of Cormack's approach for socialist writing. Irving Howe and Michael Harrington employed very limpid, non-disruptive writing styles. But, since they hadn't read Cormack, little did they know that their writing style utterly compromised their political analyses. Was it that audiences no longer realized their views were radical since their style was 'conservative'? Unlikely.

See Mike Cormack, 'Screwball Restraint: *The Awful Truth*', in his book *Ideology and Cinematography in Hollywood, 1930–39* (New York: St Martin's Press, 1994), 93–106.

[50] The notion that ideology is rhetorical can also be found in Pareto's discussion of what he calls derivations. See V. Pareto, *A Treatise on General Sociology* (New York: Dover, 1916).

discourse as such or discursive form as such. Not all mass artworks are necessarily ideological. It is a matter of the rhetorical organization of certain discourse, i.e., of certain works of mass art.

The idea that the locus of ideology in mass art resides in the way in which specific works articulate their stories and images rhetorically is fairly commensensical. Perhaps it would not seem to be worth dignifying by the title of 'an approach' were it not the case that many contemporary critics think that they have isolated a deeper level of ideological manipulation via the notion of discursive subject-positioning. But this view has the liability of being overly general in two ways: it makes all mass art ideological, if only in virtue of its generic structures, *and* it makes them all ideological in the same way, i.e., they all work to dispose audiences to misrecognize themselves as Cartesian subjects. Alternatively, the view that ideological beliefs are disseminated by mass artworks through their specific rhetorical organization allows both that some mass artworks may not be ideological—if they promote no ideological beliefs—and that there can be quite a wide range of ideological beliefs, including ones that may not pertain to issues of personal identity (Cartesian subjecthood).

To say that ideological beliefs are advanced by mass artworks by means of their rhetorical organization is obviously uninformative, unless we have some idea of what the notion of 'rhetorical organization' signifies. So, how are we to understand *rhetoric*, and how is it relevant to analysing the operation of ideology in mass art?

Rhetoric is a matter of attempting to influence thought—a matter of persuasion, as a consequence of presenting material in a way designed so that its structure operates to facilitate an audience's agreement with certain conclusions, or, at least, its favourable disposition toward those conclusions. Those conclusions may be stated outright by the orator, or the listener may be encouraged to embrace them in so far as they are strongly implied by, insinuated by, or presupposed by the rhetoric in question. Moreover, as we shall see, many of the techniques of oratory can be adapted to the processes of representation and narration employed in mass art so as to promote ideological beliefs or openness to ideological beliefs in audiences.[51]

Of course, rhetoric is not in and of itself ideological. The device of the rhetorical question, for example, can be employed in a physics demonstration that has no ideological implications. To suppose that rhetoric necessarily involves ideology would be an instance of a genetic conception of

---

[51] As in the previous two chapters, in this chapter I will restrict my discussion to the operation of ideology in narrative mass art.

ideology—a reversion to the view that certain ways of acquiring beliefs are tainted. I have already argued that we do not need a genetic component in our conception of ideology, since the work that such a component is supposed to do is already done by considering whether the cognitive content in question is epistemically defective and whether it has favourable implications for some practice of domination.

Thus, there is no reason necessarily to correlate ideology and rhetoric. Some uses of rhetoric are ideological and some are not, depending on the content of the messages for which the relevant rhetorical devices provide communicative vehicles. And whether that content is ideological can be determined by means of the conception of ideology presented in the last section.

However, even though rhetoric is not invariably a vehicle of ideology in mass art, rhetoric is in play in the great majority of cases where mass art purveys ideology. Thus, one gains a useful sense of the ways in which ideology is disseminated by mass-art narratives by looking at the recurring rhetorical structures employed in mass art for ideological ends. Thus, in the remainder of this section, I will explore certain of the most frequently recurring rhetorical devices for the dissemination of ideology in mass art, particularly in mass fictions and representations.[52]

That rhetorical strategies may be implemented by mass-art narratives should be fairly obvious. Aristotle, for example, pointed out that establishing one's good character is influential in securing a speaker's point of view.[53] Similarly, in mass-art narratives, an ideological perspective may be advanced by a character, and the persuasiveness of the view may hinge, in part, on portraying said fictional character as virtuous.[54]

Often in American mass art, these virtues—strength, fortitude, ingenuity, bravery, loyalty, etc.—are more frequently Greek than Christian.[55] However, quite often, a character is designated virtuous in terms of his or her courteous, respectful, and thoughtful treatment of supporting characters, especially ones who are poor, weak, old, lame, wrongfully ostracized or oppressed, children, and so forth. That is, the character

[52] Two caveats are in order here. First, I do not deny that these rhetorical devices are in evidence outside of mass art, but for reasons given earlier, I do not think that this is problematic. Second, the inventory of rhetorical devices to be explored here does not pretend to be exhaustive, nor are all the categories mutually exclusive. This section is more of the nature of an exploratory probe.

[53] Aristotle, *Rhetoric*, Bk. I, ss. 8 and 9.

[54] This is not only true of the mass art produced in capitalist countries, but is also a mark of Socialist Realism where Socialist heroes are presented as exemplary founts of virtue. Think of the famous *Maxim* film trilogy, produced in the former Soviet Union.

[55] For a further discussion of the use of pagan virtues in this way, see Noël Carroll, 'The Paradox of Suspense'.

curries the audience's allegiance by treating characters who might be thought of as his or her social 'inferiors' with consideration and dignity.

Whereas villains in mass fictions are apt to behave toward 'social inferiors' quite brutishly (kicking the dog, tormenting the retarded, misleading children, etc.), the protagonists in mass art generally evince a democratic courtesy to such characters. They are 'nice' (toward other 'nice' characters). They protect the weak. Obviously, given the aims of mass art, this tendency toward egalitarianism is predicated upon winning the mass audience over to the side of the protagonist. But it also functions to make the moral and political positions that the characters represent—which may be ideological—attractive. That the comic-book character Superman is such a fine fellow is apt to function rhetorically to help substantiate his pronouncements about truth, justice, and the American way.

In addition, Aristotle pointed out that a crucial form of rhetorical argument is the example, of which the fable or invented story is a major variation.[56] And clearly whole mass-art narratives can serve as rhetorical examples. André Bazin took Orson Welles' *Citizen Kane* as an example supporting the proposition that 'there is no profit in gaining the whole world if one has lost one's own childhood.'[57]

Moreover, where a mass-art narrative serves as an argumentative example for views that are epistemically defective and tenets in some practice of social domination, they are ideological. The episode of the TV series *The Waltons* entitled 'Prophecy' is a case in point. It begins with indications that Daddy is starting to feel his age, and that he is none too happy about this. Next a neighbour comes by to announce that there is to be a high school reunion, and that Daddy Walton is expected to play a large part in organizing it. He is very uncomfortable about this. Some of his fellow students have gone on to achieve wealth and status in the wide world. One is an advisor to FDR, and his name is mentioned often in the newspapers; another runs a lucrative salon in New York. Clearly Old Man Walton is worried that he will appear to be a failure next to all this.

But as the high-school graduates begin to gather, Daddy's life looks good in comparison to the lives of the others. He has love, contentment, and his family. At the reunion celebration, FDR's advisor recalls that Walton was voted 'most likely to succeed' by his classmates, and the New Dealer adds that, indeed, Walton has been the most successful. He has everything anyone could want—a loving wife, a family, and so on.

---

[56] Aristotle, *Rhetoric*, Bk. II, s. 20.

[57] André Bazin, *Orson Welles* (New York: Harper and Row, 1978), 66.

Everyone at the table agrees, and just to make sure that the audience doesn't miss the point, it is repeated in the coda—a recurring device in *The Waltons*–at the end of the episode by John Boy.

The ideological message of the playlet is obvious. Cultivate your own garden. Though you may not realize it, your own life is a success in terms of what counts—friends, family, and a place to call home. Those whom society regards as successes are in fact envious of people like you, people like the Waltons. Your apparently meagre life is really a triumph, if only you can learn to look at it in the right way. As a general prognosis, this is obviously epistemically defective, though it does have favourable implications for the status quo. It encourages average working people to have very exalted views of their place in society, in part by suggesting that the social élite are really envious of them. In this sense, it is related to the Poor Little Rich Girl (or Boy) motif that is perennially popular in mass art. Here, as in *The Waltons*, the rhetoric encourages social immobility in a way that has favourable implications for existing systems of social domination.

Clearly, through their dramatic construction, mass artworks may present mythologized examples of how the social structure of society works. One recurring picture of social arrangements in sixties' TV programmes in America involved the integration of younger professionals into the larger society through the agency of benevolent, older figures. For example, in *Dr. Kildare*, a young intern is counselled by the older and wiser Dr Gillespie about how to channel his idealism; in *The Defenders*, a young lawyer is taught similar lessons by his father; in *Ben Casey*, an even more ethnically marked and rebellious young doctor is tutored by Dr Zorba, while the same structure is repeated in *The Nurses*, and, with respect to high school, there is Mr Novak, in the series of the same name, and his worldly-wise principal.[58]

In all these cases, the suggestion is not only that society has a place for criticism, but that there are understanding superiors at the helm of the relevant social institutions who are prepared to sympathize with young rebels, to appreciate their worries about injustice, and to help them to realize their ideals. Rest assured, these programmes seemed to suggest, under the suggestive guidance of such learned, sometimes saintly elders, any problem can be handled by working within the system. This was not the case—as young TV viewers in the sixties were to learn in but a few years—but the recurring image certainly had favourable implications for the powers that be.

There is a persistent ideological prejudice in many western societies

---

[58] Perkinson, *Getting Better: Television and Moral Progress*, 247–8.

that the wealthy are morally superior to the poor.[59] This view is not only false, its currency has favourable implications for the rich, suggesting that they have a presumptive claim to the role of arbiters of justice. This prejudice is exemplified in countless mass fictions—from Edgar Wallace's best-selling *Four Just Men* to Batman comic books—in which unimaginably wealthy avengers are presented as naturally suited to mete out righteous punishment, perhaps precisely because their great riches render them disinterested. It is no accident that these super-talented heroes are also super-rich. They are the guardians or stewards of justice because they can afford to be. Wealth carries moral authority, and mass fictions that specialize in deliriously rich secret super-cops brazenly exemplify such transparently ideological notions.

Similarly, wealth is often promoted in our culture as a reward for natural talent. Thus, if one has money, ideologically speaking, that is because one deserves it. As Ariel Dorfman writes with reference to Donald Duck and his uncle Scrooge McDuck:

Donald can start with a million and end up with zero while McDuck can start with zero and regain all his vast wealth. The old geezer has rewritten the Horatio Alger story in just one episode. The fact that he loses and recovers his fortune in the face of adversaries or thieves, as usually happens in adventures where he is reduced to penury, once again legitimatizes its origins. Behind all that money there is clearly sweat, cunning, calculation and perseverance. Now. And in the past, too.[60]

That is, monetary success is presented simply as a function of real virtue, an empirically exaggerated proposition which nevertheless serves the ideology of the rich, not only by suggesting that their money is their moral birthright, but that the lack of money on the part of the poor is an intrinsic moral failing.

As Dorfman already indicates, the pulp fictions of Horatio Alger are argumentative fables to this effect. In *Ragged Dick*, the street urchin Richard Hunter, a struggling bootblack, is contrasted with his friend Johnny Nolan. Ragged Dick is enterprising, smart, honest, good natured, and self-reliant. His very looks are said to radiate virtue. Johnny is constitutionally lazy. Thus, it comes as no surprise that by the end of the book Dick is on his way to success. It is the natural reward for people like him, people of whom others can tell just by looking that they are going to make

---

[59] This way of thinking is discussed by George Lakoff in his book *Moral Politics: What Conservatives Know that Liberals Don't* (Chicago: University of Chicago Press, 1996), 83.

[60] Ariel Dorfman, 'Of Elephants and Ducks', in his book *The Empire's Old Clothes* (New York: Penguin, 1983), 61.

something of themselves. Thus, the narrative itself is a kind of argumentative example, showing that success is a reward for natural talent, while staying mired in poverty, as Johnny Nolan does, is one's own fault. Needless to say, there is no notion of structural impoverishment in Horatio Alger. Riches and poverty both are just deserts, a piece of economically dubious reasoning that certainly has favourable implications for social practices that discriminate against the impoverished.

Along with his discussion of the argumentative example as a rhetorical strategy of persuasion, Aristotle also emphasizes the importance of the enthymeme—the syllogism that leaves something out and that requires the audience to fill in the missing premiss.[61] Indeed, Aristotle thought that this form of rhetorical argument was the most effective one available. The advantage of this device for the rhetorician is that it engages the audience as participants in the process of argument in such a way that listeners, by what Arthur Danto calls 'an almost inevitable movement of the mind', supply what is needed for the argument to go through.[62] This enhances the credibility of the argument for the listener, since in so far as she has the impression of reaching the missing segment of the argument on her own, she may regard it as her own idea.

For example, rhetorical questions function as a means of bringing the listeners to certain conclusions before the orator states them outright. And, then, when the orator does state them outright, the listener greets them favourably as conclusions that she has already formed on her own. Similarly, with respect to the enthymeme, 'when the arguer suppresses one or more parts of a rhetorical syllogism, the arguer invites an audience to complete it, thereby contributing to its own persuasion and exhibiting its rationality in the process.'[63]

Mass-art fictions are not arguments. But, as we have seen in previous chapters, mass-art narratives often do presuppose ideas that the audience fills in in order for the narrative to be intelligible. Mass-art fictions, then, may be thought of as rhetorical, inasmuch as they are structured to lead the audience to fill in or to complete certain ideas—especially ideas about human conduct—in the process of rendering the story intelligible to themselves.

For instance, in James Whale's film *The Bride of Frankenstein*, there is a scene in which the monster is alone, raging through the forest. At one point, he hears offscreen music, issuing from an unseen fiddle. Suddenly, his demeanour changes from that of a rampaging beast to one marked by

[61] Aristotle, *Rhetoric*, Bk. II, ss. 22–5.

[62] Arthur Danto, *The Transfiguration of the Commonplace*, 170.

[63] Walter R. Fisher, *Human Communication as Narration* (Columbia: University of South Carolina Press, 1987), 28.

childlike yearning. In order for the scene to make sense to the viewer, one must realize what is missing and fill in what is being presupposed, namely a commonplace cliché about behaviour that goes something like 'music has charms that soothe the savage breast.'

That is, the narrative here is structured in such a way as to elicit this presupposition—which is of the order of a cultural commonplace—from the audience in its own process of making sense of the action. We may call this operation the narrative enthymeme. Though it is not the only rhetorical structure in mass fiction, it is a crucial one—one whose operation is in evidence throughout the history of mass art.

As discussed in the last chapter, narratives presuppose all sorts of vague generalizations as conditions of intelligibility. In order to follow the narrative, the audience is prompted to supply these missing presuppositions, just as it supplies the missing premises in oratorical enthymemes. That is, the audience makes sense of the structure of the narrative to itself by inferring the presuppositions that make the narrative cohere. Moreover, where the presuppositions that make the story cohere are ideological, the use of the narrative enthymeme is ideological.

For example, in D. W. Griffith's *The Birth of a Nation*, there is an underlying presupposition that white people are morally superior to black people. The black characters who are given sustained individual treatment—such as Lydia Brown, Silas Lynch, and the rapist Gus—are morally depraved, while the goodly black servants, though loyal to the Camerons, are portrayed as comically simple-minded. They are not full moral agents, but made to be led. Even when involved in heroic exploits, like the rescue of the elder Cameron, they are minstrel-like caricatures; the 'mammy' figure subdues Cameron's guards by comically crushing them under her great weight.

Of course, most of the black people in the film are not treated individualistically, but as members of riotous, drunken mobs. The black state assembly is represented as a travesty of legislative decorum, and black voters cast their ballots as a result of a mixture of bribery and confidence tricks. In all, the African-Americans in the film come off as either morally dissolute or incompetent, though occasionally well-meaning.

Whites, on the other hand, are another story. Most, especially the Southern whites, are paragons of virtue. One exception is the abolitionist Austin Stoneman, but he is portrayed as self-deceived. There are also white carpetbaggers and besotted white soldiers who are complicit with the blacks, but few of them wander into the dramatic limelight for very long.

The underlying argument of Griffith's film is that blacks are morally inferior and that, as a result, the correct social order is one in which they are dominated by whites, presumably for their own moral good. This proposition is not stated outright by the film. But it is, however, a premiss of the film that the audience is meant to fill in. The story makes sense in light of this premiss. The victorious feeling that is supposed to attend the concluding images of the Ku Klux Klan frightening black voters away from the polls is a function, where it takes hold, of the audience's filling in the presupposition that this is the morally right order of things.

Though today I think few would deny that it is entirely false to suppose that whites are by nature morally superior to African-Americans and that such beliefs have favourable implications for deeply unjust practices of racial domination, Griffith's idea was openly embraced by many white people at the time of the release of *The Birth of a Nation*. As we saw in our discussion of mass art and morality, typically mass artworks do not function as the source of new beliefs about human conduct, but mobilize pre-existing ones. Thus, the narrative enthymeme strives to activate audience preconceptions—often in the form of commonplace ideas—to fill in the narrative. The racist tenet that whites are morally superior to blacks was, of course, widely shared in the early decades of this century by audiences not only in America, but Europe, and quite possibly elsewhere. As a result, it was not hard for mass audiences, excepting blacks of course, to supply the missing premiss to Griffith's narrative enthymeme.

In *The Birth of a Nation*, the relevant missing premiss is not voiced explicitly in the intertitles. However, in many other mass artworks, like 'The Prophecy', it is stated in the text. Moreover, where the unstated generalizations that make sense of the story are made explicit, they have particular resonance, because the audience has already been prompted in their direction by the rhetorical structure of the narrative. Typical episodes of the eternally rerun TV series *Star Trek* (the first generation) exemplify this quite nicely. Very often, these programmes will conclude with a vaguely liberal observation by Captain Kirk—frequently an entry into his log—which takes the form of a generalization that comprehends the action of the episode in terms of an organizing moral that is virtually on the audience's lips already—precisely because the story has been structured in such a way as to elicit it from the viewer.[64]

As may be already evident from my examples, also crucial to the rhetorician for securing conviction from audiences is the manipulation of commonplaces, clichés, and what Aristotle calls maxims. The rhetorician exploits what is common or familiar in order to gain the assent of the

---

[64] In his *Rhetoric*, Aristotle treats the argumentative example and the enthymeme as distinct forms of oratorical persuasion; where they are both deployed in the same discourse, he advises that the enthymeme precede the example so that the force of the former not be diluted. However, with what I am calling the narrative enthymeme, it is frequently the case that the example and the ellipsis work in tandem.

audience. That is, the rhetorician uses what the audience is already likely to believe or to have cognitively available in order to encourage conviction, because it leaves the audience with the impression that what they've heard is what they already believe and that the conclusions the rhetorician reaches are, again, their own conclusions. For the rhetorician has elicited these conclusions from the audience by way of generally accepted commonplaces and, indeed, the conclusion—which the rhetorician ideally tries to inspire in the mind of the audience even before it is uttered (if it is even uttered)—is itself often couched in commonplaces. Of course, where the rhetorician has already inspired the commonplace in the minds of the audience before it is uttered, the ideal effect of uttering it will be that the audience may recognize (or misrecognize) the utterance as their own concurrent thinking on the matter.

The relevance of the role of commonplaces in oratory to what I have called the narrative enthymeme is, of course, that the presuppositions that the narrative prompts the audience to fill in are generally of the order of commonplaces, clichés, nostrums, platitudes, or maxims of a general sort currently widely abroad about the nature of human conduct and behaviour. The narrative functions to dispose the audience toward mobilizing these commonplace generalizations in the process of rendering the narrative intelligible to itself, thereby—ideally—reinforcing the audience's faith in them in virtue of the impression that the audience has reached these conclusions 'on its own'.

Given our arguments concerning moral education in the previous chapter, this is what we would expect, since ideological propositions and concepts are often a subset of moral propositions and concepts. In mass art, the moral address as well as the ideological address operate primarily on pre-existing beliefs that are widely distributed amongst mass audiences. Ideological rhetoric in mass art aims at bringing what the audience already 'knows' to the particularities of a story. And this 'knowledge' is generally of the nature of commonplaces, since the mass artwork must be accessible to large audiences. Of course, the mobilization of a commonplace is not automatically ideological. It will only count as ideology, by my lights, where the commonplaces themselves are ideological or are used ideologically (in ways to be discussed below).[65]

---

[65] Mass artworks may be rhetorical without being ideological. Mass artworks may propose genuinely moral (in the sense of upright) arguments by means of rhetoric. And, of course, the use of rhetoric in and of itself is not a sign of disvalue. The rhetorical operation of a mass fiction will only count as ideological if it meets the criteria laid down in the previous section of this chapter. At the same time, I am also claiming that ideology in mass art is primarily disseminated through rhetorical operations of which the narrative enthymeme, often employing commonplaces, is one of the most important.

In order to clarify the application of these points about the use of rhetoric for the purposes of ideology in mass art, a somewhat extended illustration will be useful. Consider the original version of the film *Back to the Future*. The point or theme of the film seems to be that anything can be altered by acts of individual will. This is the general principle or premiss that the film dramatizes, and, in order for the film to make sense to audiences, they must embrace, or, at least, entertain it.[66] That is, if the film is to appear as a coherent whole to them, they will have to see it in the light of this generalization. It is the moral, the point, or the theme of the narrative.

As well, this generalization is a commonplace of western individualist culture—a tenet of what in America is called positive thinking—and it is serviceable in a number of ways for upholding practices of social domination. For example, if someone finds himself in dire straits, such as homelessness, this is sometimes said to ultimately be his own fault—and not the product of social conditions—because he has failed to think himself positively out of his circumstances.

In *Back to the Future*, this commonplace is sown early in the film. Walking down the street with his girlfriend Jennifer, the leading protagonist, Marty, says that Doc says 'if you put your mind to it, you can accomplish anything.'[67] At this point in the film, this commonplace slogan is cited tentatively; it is quoted by Marty, but it is not yet a matter of conviction for him. But it is repeated on two subsequent occasions. Marty offers it as a piece of advice to George, his father. And then, at the end of the film, George—who has promised never to forget Marty's advice—repeats it when advance copies of his first novel arrive in the mail. By this time, the commonplace clearly expresses the viewpoint of the film. Moreover, the audience has been encouraged to see the events of the film under the aegis of this commonplace throughout, and it has been rewarded in adopting this generalization as a relevant presupposition about human behaviour, in so far as this generalization offers the most comprehensive explanation of the action in the film.

Obviously, the generalization applies to the exploits of the major character, Marty, who, among other things, is able to change the conditions of

---

[66] Or know that others in a given target audience believe it.

[67] There is a similar commonplace in *Back to the Future III* to the effect that your future is what you make it. This cliché is woven through the narrative in a way that is analogous to the example discussed above and, as well, it is literalized by the special features of time-travel, as is the maxim that we are considering.

Interestingly, the commonplace is relevant to a subsequent Michael J. Fox film—*Teen Wolf*—which also takes place in a high school setting. Perhaps *Back to the Future* served as a patent for *Teen Wolf*, a film that also deploys fantasy for the sake of ideology.

his own existence by putting his mind to it. This is achieved in large measure by changing his father George, whose transformation, in turn, is achieved in virtue of his acceptance of the principle that willing enables you to accomplish anything, whether it be decking the bully Biff or publishing a novel. Likewise, Goldie Wilson becomes the first African-American mayor of Hill Valley, due, the film implies, to his go-getter attitude—to his commitment to making something of himself and to standing tall; while Doc, himself, is moved from his despondency over his history of failed experiments to enthusiasm by the challenge of putting his mind to sending Marty 'back to the future'.

Rhetorically speaking, *Back to the Future* plants the idea in the audience's mind that 'if you put your mind to it, you can accomplish anything'—an idea that is already a cultural commonplace. The viability of this idea, furthermore, is enhanced at least in so far as the idea, as a presupposition of the plot, underwrites the narrative development of much of the action in the film. That is, this idea supplies a general principle that applies to a great deal of the action in the film, most notably to virtually all the successful activity in the film. The audience, in turn, comes to adopt it as its own hypothesis for the sake of comprehending the events in the film. And finally, when the commonplace is uttered for the last time—when George receives his copies of his novel—the film iterates the commonplace to an audience that is likely to endorse it as its own concurrent thought, in so far as it has already reached this view, if only as a generalization that best explains the events in the film.

Of course, this is not the only commonplace in the film. Another, made explicit by Goldie Wilson, is that one needs to stand up to bullies and not let them walk all over you. This is connected to the notion that you can do anything to which you put your mind, not only because it occurs in the context of Goldie's speech about making something of himself, but also because the road to George McFly's 'accomplishing anything' is bound up with confronting a bully, namely Biff. Bullies, that is, are defeatable by acts of will, and this commonplace is, in turn, a particular instance of 'If you put your mind to it, you can accomplish anything,' which includes defeating bullies.[68]

A further particularization of the nostrum of positive thinking that is crucial to the film concerns the importance of taking risks or of trying. This arises in several contexts, including: Marty's paralysing fear of rejection with respect to his music; and his father George's parallel fear about

---

[68] Though a recurring motif in mass fictions, this is a palpably false proposition, as any wimp, like myself, who has ever confronted a much larger football player, can attest.

showing his science fiction stories to anyone; and, of course, the importance of trying is also related to George's asking Marty's mother Lorraine for a date and, later, to his exercising his will in dealing with bullies like Biff and then the carrot-topped redhead at the dance.

When characters complain of their fears of rejection, the audience is apt to think that the character will never know whether he can succeed unless he puts himself on the line. We almost subvocalize: 'You'll never know unless you take a chance.' The conversations in which these anxieties are expressed function in a way that is analogous to rhetorical questions— given the culture that we inhabit, they tend to elicit from us an almost predictable answer to the character's plight. As well, this answer underwrites the narrative action as a general principle—i.e., the characters do succeed when they try—and, furthermore, it is connected to the overarching commonplace that structures the film. For resolving to try, to take a risk, or to take a stand is part of what is required by 'putting your mind to it.'[69]

If this analysis of the rhetoric of *Back to the Future* appears convincing, then it suggests that central to the film is the manipulation of commonplaces, often in concert with narrative enthymemes. Either these commonplaces are presented overtly to the audience, or they are elicited by contriving dramatic situations to which the audience is apt to respond associatively with a well-worn truism (like 'in order to succeed, you have to take risks'). Moreover, the audience uses these commonplaces to track the action which—in so far as these commonplaces have in fact structured

---

[69] Interestingly, the characterization of the ideological operation of *Back to the Future* that I am advancing may appear to correlate with the kind of ideological effect that I claimed proponents of the subject-positioning view find pervasive in mass art. That is, I have maintained that *Back to the Future* celebrates an exorbitant belief in personal agency and freedom. The question then arises as to how really distinct my analysis is from what might be the subject-positioning view of the same film. Here, I think that three differences are noteworthy.

First, the beliefs that I find proponed in *Back to the Future* are more of the nature of folk platitudes, which, contra proponents of the subject-positioning view, need not be thought to hook up necessarily to an entire ontology of the subject, nor can they be worked seamlessly into a theory of the subject that you could intelligibly label Cartesian, Husserlian, or even Idealist.

Second, if these propositions can be derived from *Back to the Future*, this is not—again, *pace* the subject-positioning approach—a function of the fact that the film is projected by an apparatus, that it employs pictorial verisimilitude, perspective, narrative, or continuity editing (including point-of-view editing). It is, rather, a matter of rhetoric—indeed, of the rhetorical/narrative organization of this specific film. This theme is not a function of the structure of mass fiction as such.

And finally, though *Back to the Future* appears to traffic in ideology in terms of personal freedom, the method used to isolate this commitment does not privilege themes of agency as *sine qua non* of ideology, and it allows that in other mass artworks there may be other sorts of ideological commitments, ones that may have nothing to do with personal efficacy, but which are conveyed by narrative enthymemes. On the other hand, I take it that the proponents of subject-positioning are committed to the view that any mass artwork that is also narratively coherent is not only always ideological, but is, at the very least, always involved in propagating an ideology of exorbitant personal agency.

the action—account for it quite expeditiously. So by the time the leading commonplace is delivered at the conclusion, the spectator is likely to recognize it as something that she has already thought, for she has already come to it herself, albeit as the result of rhetorical promptings.

So one crucial element in the rhetorical operation of the film is that it instils its conclusion in its spectators in such a way that the spectator's conviction is reinforced by his sense that the conclusion is a matter of something that the spectator is already disposed to embrace. Key to instilling this conviction is that the view in question be of the order of a commonplace *and* that this commonplace—as a generalization or principle of conduct—fit the events in the plot as the best way to make sense of them.

That is, the plot is rather like an example of the commonplace. The audience's acceptance of the commonplace is encouraged as it comes to recognize the story as an instance of the commonplace. This is in turn may have the net effect of reinforcing the commonplace—in so far as it appears successful in accounting for some behaviour, even if fictional—while also concretizing the commonplace in the audience's mind in terms of a paradigm case that may guide future applications of the commonplace.

How generalizable are these observations about what I have called the rhetorical organization of *Back to the Future*? My hunch is that they can be extended to quite a lot of mass artworks, and that adopting the notions of rhetoric, presupposition, and the use of commonplaces will provide a useful framework for isolating the ideological operation of a great many mass artworks. To support my hunch about commonplaces, two considerations come to mind. First, one notices that the titles of many mass artworks are themselves often commonplaces—*You Can't Take It With You*, *The Best Years of Our Lives*, *Cheaper by the Dozen*, *It's A Wonderful Life*, *Father Knows Best*, *The Life of Riley*, *Grace Under Fire*—and, in these cases at least, the role the clichés play in organizing the narrative seems to accord with our hypothesis about works like *Back to the Future* (where the commonplace is not featured in the title). Secondly, one would predict, on what might be called 'design grounds', that the presuppositions that are favoured in mass narratives would be something of the order of commonplaces and clichés, since they would have to be familiar enough for mass audiences to have access to them.

That mass fictions involve presuppositions that the audience fills in, I conjecture, is something that most ideological critics accept. However, several qualifications about the relevance of filling in presuppositions with respect to the operation of ideology in mass art need to be registered. First, I am not claiming that narrative presuppositions are always ideological; they are only ideological where they meet the criteria stated in the previous section of this chapter. Moreover, eliciting presuppositions from audiences is not the sole means of conveying ideology; mass artworks may have long speeches, as in the case of *Triumph of the Will*, that state their ideological position quite bluntly. Rather, my claim is that the use of presuppositions, in terms of the way in which it involves the audience 'finding the conclusion for itself' is a powerful rhetorical device for conveying ideology and a frequent one. Moreover, though sometimes the presuppositions may be found stated somewhere in the dialogue or the title of a mass artwork,[70] in other cases, the commonplace remains tacit.[71]

As we have seen, ideology in mass art often proceeds by presenting examples of commonplace maxims and concepts. Furthermore, inasmuch as ideology may operate by concretizing commonplaces and truisms, it is important to note that one way in which a mass artwork may secure its ideological effect is by falsely instantiating commonplace ideas—by instantiating them in a way that is epistemically defective, but that has favourable implications for some practice of domination. This is related to what we discussed as a potential grounds for moral defectiveness in the last chapter. That is, a mass artwork may exemplify a common precept or concept in a way that confuses the issue, and, where that confusion is ideological, it will have implications favourable to some tenet of domination.

I call this process tendentious instantiation. Provisionally, we can divide tendentious instantiations of commonplace ideas into two sorts—false positives and false negatives. A false positive occurs when a commonplace is given a misleading ideological spin that presents a case as a positive paradigm which has favourable implications for some practice of domination. For example, in the episode of *thirtysomething* in which Gary is denied tenure at the university, there is a great deal of talk, as well as dream and fantasy imagery, about what constitutes a hero.[72] A hero is said to be someone who is willing to acknowledge what he wants and to be willing to pursue it, come what may. This functions as a commonplace in the plot.

Moreover, Gary wants tenure. His friend Michael forces him to admit this and adds that if he really wants tenure, he must be prepared to do

---

[70] For example, in *Back to the Future*, Marty quotes Doc as saying that 'if you put your mind to it, you can accomplish anything'.

[71] For example, in the original film of *Invasion of the Body Snatchers*, part of the horror of the collectivist invaders is that they lack individuality. As vegetables, the pod people are alike—as alike as two peas in a pod, to recall a commonplace cliché. That is, a commonplace about vegetables is exploited for horrific as well as ideological effects, though it is never explicitly stated in the film. The effect is ideological, of course, since the metaphor is being applied to communists of some sort (intergalactic ones) in a way that redounds to the favour of American militarism.

[72] This episode aired on ABC on 31 May 1988. It does not have a title.

anything to get it, including grovelling to the chairman of his department. The episode ends with Gary—hat in hand, so to speak—repressing his pride and approaching his chairman, pleading for a second chance. This episode seems to me to present a false positive instantiation of the notion of a hero. It is positive, since it casts Gary's behaviour in a positive light. It is false, since it is a specious example of heroism. It is ideologically tendentious, since it has obviously favourable implications for practices of social domination. It suggests that one should waive one's principles and grovel for the purpose of securing one's ends in the face of institutional injustice. It completely confuses the notion of a hero by falsely instantiating it in tendentious manner that should brighten the hearts of those in power everywhere.

Similarly, the movie *Death Wish* falsely instantiates commonplace ideas of justice in the person of Paul Kersey, casting his vigilante activities in a positive light. In the context of American politics, this has favourable implications for reactionary forces who admire and endorse the use of extra-constitutional means for dealing with urban crime.

Likewise, Ariel Dorfman argues that the cartoon figure Babar the elephant is a misleading instantiation of the concept of the progressive colonial through the presentation of the ultimate assimilationist (Babar is an African elephant who dons European clothing) as the paradigm for Third World progress.[73]

And Henry Louis Gates has hypothesized that the character of Cliff Huxtable on *The Cosby Show* is a tendentious instantiation of the notion of the representative African-American, since Huxtable's affluence not only may mislead white viewers about the social status of typical black people, but because it has favourable implications for the commonplace myth of social mobility in America, which also has ramifications for socially unjust practices.[74]

Ideologically tendentious instantiation is of the nature of a false positive when it portrays the epistemically defective concretization of notions and propositions in a positive light, which, in turn, has favourable implications for practices of domination. But ideology also operates in mass art by false exemplifications that cast their objects in a negative light. We may call these false negative tendentious instantiations.

In the movie *Dirty Harry*, the criminal Zodiac is evil incarnate, a veritably mythological force. He instantiates the concept of a criminal in

---

[73] Ariel Dorfman, 'Of Elephants and Ducks', 39–41.

[74] Henry Lewis Gates, 'TV's Black World Turns—But Stays Unreal', *New York Times* (12 Nov. 1981), Arts and Leisure Section. Here Gates is speaking of the ideological significance of the show for white audiences. African-American audiences may see its significance differently. See Justin Lewis, *The Ideological Octopus: An Exploration of Television and its Audience* (New York: Routledge, 1991), 159–202.

the way that a powerful demon might. He presents such a danger that the extra-legal means employed by Dirty Harry may seem warranted in context. But few, if any, criminals are like Zodiac. Police behaviour need not be tailored to deal with creatures like Zodiac. But by offering Zodiac as a paradigm of the urban criminal, the film has favourable implications for authoritarian police practices.

Similarly, in the novel *The Man With The Golden Arm*, Ian Fleming represents the Cuban operative, Scaramanga, as nothing more than literally a gangster. James Bond is a patriot. The Queen thinks that he is worthy of knighthood. But his counterpart is nothing but a common criminal and an outrageously vicious one at that.[75] Within the context of the Cold War, this obviously served an ideological purpose, demeaning opposing secret agents in a way that had favourable implications for the espionage activities of NATO, since if Scaramanga (like Zodiac) is an example of what the Western powers were up against, any sort of retaliatory measures may appear acceptable.[76]

Though the rhetorical organization of a mass artwork in terms of argumentative fables, narrative enthymemes, presuppositions, commonplaces, and tendentious exemplifications may proffer ideological tenets to audiences, they do not, of course, guarantee their acceptance. For audiences who do not already accept the ideological propositions and concepts of a given mass artwork, and who realize that they do not accept them, the ideological address of the mass artwork, no matter how skilful rhetorically, is apt to seem unintelligible or ridiculous or distorting and, perhaps, worthy of indignation.[77] That is how many angry African-American viewers greeted the film *Fort Apache: The Bronx*, for example.

[75] As soon as we are introduced to him, he wantonly shoots the pet birds that belong to a barmaid that James Bond has befriended.

[76] If so far my examples have all hailed from the 'free world', it is important to note that the rhetoric of Socialist Realism frequently functioned in the same way for the purpose of casting the Soviet empire in a favourable light.

[77] One advantage of what I am calling the rhetorical approach to ideology in mass art, in contrast to the subject-positioning approach, is that whereas the subject-positioning view appears to present the ideological effect of a mass artwork as inevitable, the rhetorical approach allows that audiences may reject and resist the ideology proffered by a mass artwork. That is, on the subject-positioning model, if a mass artwork has a certain generic structure—like narrative closure—this will, so the theory entails, inexorably cause the audience member to misrecognize himself as a Cartesian ego. However, in my analysis of *Back to the Future*, there is no problem in acknowledging that a viewer may recognize the ideology of positive thinking that the film presupposes and still reject it. That viewers are quite often aware of—and ill-disposed toward—the ideological address of a mass artwork seems to me to be an indisputable fact. That the viewer is always duped, as the subject-positioning model suggests (at least in respect to Cartesian egohood), is just wrong. It is empirically the case that audiences can resist the importunings of ideology. Comparatively speaking, one strength, then, of the rhetorical approach to ideology in mass art is that it can explain how mass artworks dispose audiences to various ideological stances, while also admitting that audiences do not always succumb to them. For rhetoric, though often effective, is not omnipotent, whereas subject-positioning is presented as if it were ineluctable.

On the other hand, where audiences readily accept the ideological rhetoric of a mass artwork, they probably already accept the ideological commonplaces, propositions, and concepts, and the ideological operation of the mass fiction in such cases is probably best described as reinforcing existing ideology. As with the case of moral truisms, ideology in mass art would appear to work on what the audience already believes. Mass art, then, I would conjecture, contributes primarily to the reinforcement of ideology; it is not a major originating source of securing ideological commitment in the first instance.

Of course, some audiences may neither antecedently accept nor reject the ideological commonplaces, propositions, and concepts that the mass artwork elicits. What, we may ask, is the ideological effect of such a work on them? Here, we do not have enough empirical evidence to be certain. However, I would tentatively speculate that the rhetorical structures of the mass fictions in question may at least tilt them toward the relevant ideological premises by enhancing the viability of the commonplace in their cognitive stock of heuristics.[78]

That is, human beings are optimizers.[79] When confronted with situations, we will often grasp for whatever heuristics—such as commonplace generalizations and vivid paradigms—are available for the purpose of rendering the situation intelligible. That a mass artwork reinforces one of these heuristics with respect to some fictional behaviour, then, may have some spillover effect in the sense that when subsequently searching for a heuristic to apply to real circumstances, the heuristic in question is one whose availability is attractive because it has succeeded in the past in rendering some stretch of phenomenon, albeit fictional, intelligible.

Moreover, recent research in cognitive and social psychology indicates that vivid information is more likely to be stored, remembered, and accessed than is pallid information. Factors that contribute to vividness include the extent to which the information is, for example, emotionally interesting, concrete, and imagery-provoking.[80] Thus, heuristics wedded to mass artworks are apt to have a high degree of availability in the minds of audience members who are not already ill-disposed to the heuristics to begin with. In other words, the availability of said heuristics may incline

---

[78] For discussions of heuristics in human reasoning, see Amos Tversky and Daniel Kahneman, 'Judgment Under Uncertainty: Heuristics and Biases', *Science* (1974), 185; Amos Tversky and Daniel Kahneman, 'Availability: A Heuristic for Judging Frequency and Probability', *Cognitive Psychology*, 5 (1973); Daniel Kahneman, Paul Slovic, and Amos Tversky (eds.), *Judgments Under Uncertainty: Heuristics and Biases* (Cambridge: Cambridge University Press, 1982); and Richard Nisbet and Lee Ross, *Human Inference: Strategies and Shortcomings of Social Judgment* (Englewood Cliffs, NJ: Prentice Hall, Inc., 1980).

[79] Shelley E. Taylor, 'The availability bias in social perception and interaction', in *Judgment Under Uncertainty: Heuristics and Biases*, 190–1.　　[80] See Nisbet and Ross, *Human Inferences*, ch. 3.

viewers to mobilize and to apply them to an actual case.[81] And, of course, where the heuristic in question is ideological, a mass artwork's reinforcement of its availability contributes to its ideological effect.[82]

Where contemporary ideological critics attempt to locate the most important ideological dimensions of mass artworks in the formal structures of the work that putatively abet subject-positioning, I propose that we think in terms of the rhetorical organization of particular mass fictions—in light of such features as argumentative fables, narrative enthymemes, the manipulation of commonplaces, and tendentious instantiation. The work of the critic should involve him or her, for example, in examining the rhetorical deployment of presuppositions, often in the form of commonplaces, and tendentious examples in the service of attempting to elicit ideological tenets. The devices I have singled out are not the only relevant rhetorical levers in mass art; further research is certainly necessary. However, I hope that by calling attention to these examples I have at least made the rhetorical approach to studying the ideological operation of mass art appear feasible.

Thinking about ideology and mass art in terms of rhetoric has certain advantages over its contemporary rivals, especially the theory of subject-positioning. The rhetorical approach satisfies our intuition that not all mass art is necessarily ideological, and it matches the recognition that ideology in mass art can be more than a matter of supposedly causing people to conceive of themselves as Cartesian egos.[83]

Furthermore, the subject-positioning approach suggests that the ideological operation of mass art is virtually irresistible—that, through its formal discursive structures, mass art uniformly and unavoidably causes

[81] My usage of terminology above differs somewhat from that of cognitive psychologists. They call vividness itself an example of the availability heuristic, i.e., a heuristic that privileges a biased inference or interpretation because it is available. Nevertheless, despite our slightly different uses of terminology, I believe that our points amount to roughly the same thing.

[82] In many cases, an audience member may be unaware that the heuristic, commonplace, or the spin put on the commonplace by a given mass fiction is ideological. Such a viewer might even be opposed to the ideological message of the mass artwork, were the ideological implications of the message apparent. In such cases, the mass fiction may manage to contribute to the distortion of the audience's own understanding of his or her own beliefs.

[83] Since the ideological presuppositions and commonplaces that a mass fiction mobilizes may involve issues that don't raise questions of personal identity. Many mass fictions, like Horatio Alger's *Struggling Upward, or Luke Larkin's Luck*, imply that there is, as George Lakoff puts it, a ladder to success, 'that everyone has access to it, and that the only thing involved in becoming successful and being able to take care of oneself is putting out the energy to climb it. If you are not successful, then it is your fault. You just haven't tried hard enough.' A mass fiction that plays off this commonplace is surely ideological. But this specimen of ideology has nothing directly to do with conceiving yourself to be a Cartesian ego. One could endorse Hume's bundle theory of personal identity and still buy into this fragment of ideology.

See George Lakoff, *Moral Politics*, 203.

us to misrecognize ourselves as Cartesian egos. The subject-positioning model appears virtually fatalistic methodologically.

A final advantage, then, of the rhetorical approach is that, as indicated in the preceding paragraphs, it allows that the uptake of a mass fiction's ideology is variable, depending in large measure upon an audience's predispositions.

Concluding remarks

Because of the intense preoccupation with the relation of mass art to ideology in the humanities today, I have spent this chapter discussing ideology. This chapter also seems to follow quite naturally from the previous chapter on mass art and moral education. For ideology and the issue of moral education overlap in at least two ways. First, even though ideological propositions and concepts need not necessarily concern morality—the citation of I.Q. scores may serve the purposes of ideologues—the claims of ideology are often moral. And, second, even where ideological claims do not concern morality directly, the purposes of ideology, as I conceptualize it, raise moral issues, since they are necessarily connected with practices of social injustice. Thus, this chapter may be regarded as a continuation of the project initiated in the previous chapter.

In order to determine whether the propositions and concepts advanced by a mass artwork are ideological, one needs a theory of ideology. I have argued that this should not be a broad conception— one that identifies ideology with culture or with discourse (including all the formal/structural elements of discourse)—because such a conception of ideology defeats the purposes of contemporary critics of the ideological operation of mass art. It divests their discussion of ideology of its pejorative thrust by severing ideology from injustice, since neither culture in general nor discourse as such is necessarily implicated in practices of social domination. In so far as the contemporary criticism of ideology is motivated by a sense of injustice, it has seemed appropriate to me to incorporate that dimension into any concept of ideology that one hopes might serve the purposes of the contemporary criticism of ideology.

The first section of this chapter has been primarily conceptual, concerned with articulating and defending a conception of ideology. The concept of ideology that I have arrived at is a fairly conventional one, though I hope that the arguments on its behalf have been more thorough than is usually the case. Like many standard accounts of ideology, mine has a strongly cognitivist bent in that it characterizes ideology in terms of propositions, concepts, and systems of propositions and concepts. This sort of approach is often criticized for being oblivious to the affective dimensions of ideology, but I have tried to address reservations like this by explaining how, in virtue of its cognitive content, ideology addresses the emotions and desires. Moreover, this discussion of the relation of ideology to the emotions and desires expands the discussion of the affective dimensions of mass art initiatied in Chapter 4.

The second section of this chapter is somewhat more empirical. It has been an attempt to identify some of the most frequently recurring rhetorical strategies for disseminating ideology in mass art. My method here has admittedly been somewhat desultory; the list of rhetorical devices that I have proposed is not complete—far more research is required—and the items on the list are not necessarily mutually exclusive. My inventory of the rhetorical devices used by mass fictions to advance ideology is nothing but a first step. It is not proposed as the final word on the matter. However, I would hope that, as a first step, it appears fruitful enough to encourage further steps in a sympathetic direction by other researchers.

The emphasis that I have placed on the rhetorical manipulation of commonplaces in the service of ideology, moreover, links up suggestively with a number of the other themes that I have been developing about mass art throughout this book. With respect to mass art, not only does the use of commonplaces for the purposes of ideology parallel in certain respects the use of moral truisms for the purposes of moral education; but the use of both fits with the underlying conception of mass art that I have attempted to defend.

For on my account, which was articulated in Chapter 3, mass art properly so called gravitates toward what is accessible to large numbers of people. Thus, it should be predictable that if mass art is to act as a serviceable conduit of ideology, it will have to touch upon something that is intelligible to masses of people. It is no accident, then, that ideology in mass art frequently exploits widely held commonplaces, clichés, maxims, and so on, since were it otherwise, it would be unlikely to have a chance of securing uptake by large numbers of people.

Or, to put it differently, inasmuch as the rhetorical operation of mass art for ideological purposes often requires the audience to fill in the mass fiction, the presuppositions involved must be within the cognitive reach of masses of people. Thus, the way in which mass art gravitates toward the mobilization of commonplaces, clichés, and truistic maxims satisfies what we have called a design desideratum of mass art. Mass art must gravitate toward what is accessible to mass audiences. And, for the same reasons, the ideological address of mass artworks will also seek to sound a common chord in its audience.

Envoi

Now at the end of this foray into the philosophy of mass art, we are in a position to stand back and survey the damage. The first two chapters of this book were devoted to ground clearing. Many of the most important arguments for and against mass art were rehearsed and contested in order to make room for a classificatory theory of mass art. I proposed such a theory in the third chapter of this book, where I argued that mass art can be distinguished from other sorts of art along the dual axes of technology and accessibility. Moreover, my emphasis on accessibility highlighted the relation of mass art to its audience, and, thereby, to questions about its reception. And the theme of the reception of mass art, in turn, was followed up by considering the ways in which mass art addresses its audience emotionally, morally, and ideologically.

Admittedly, the theories of the various structures I developed in the last three chapters of the book apply to other kinds of art than merely mass art. However, throughout I have been at pains to stress that mass art's commitment to audience accessibility governs the ways in which these structures are deployed in mass art. That is, mass art addresses widely distributed emotions, invokes pervasive moral principles and concepts, and exploits ideological commonplaces because it is predicated on engaging mass audiences. Were mass art to address uncommon emotions, morals, and political convictions, it would not secure mass uptake. And mass art is, among other things, ideally designed for ease of accessibility by maximum numbers of audience members expending minimum effort. This is not the only kind of art on offer in the market-place today. It is one kind of art. It is mass art.

If there is any one theme that runs throughout this book, it may be the theme of audience participation. In the first chapter, we saw how audience participation, or the putative lack thereof, has been used to provide a grounds for castigating mass art. Mass art has been said to render audiences passive. Theorists like Benjamin and McLuhan attempted to short-circuit these charges of passivity by claiming that mass art possesses the capacity either to engender critical spectatorship (Benjamin) or to re-activate multi-dimensional tribal thinking (McLuhan).

But both these claims seem to me to be exorbitant as well as insufficiently motivated by the data. Instead, I tried to rebut passivity theorists like Greenberg by showing how routine, widely acknowledged audience responses to every kind of mass art presuppose participatory audiences involved in co-creating the mass artwork—at least in the special sense that mass artworks require readers, listeners, and viewers to fill them in through the various activities discussed in this book.[1]

For a mass artwork to be successful, these structures of engagement must be accessible to large numbers of people. Consequently, the mass artwork (at least ideally) gravitates toward structures that render it comprehensible—cognitively, emotively, and morally—to masses of people. But against theorists like Greenberg, I have argued that the commitment to accessibility does not preclude audience participation either logically or in fact.

The final three chapters of this book may be regarded as a further elaboration of the case against what I have called the passivity argument. They attempt to unearth some of the most important structures of engagement available to mass art for enlisting the audience's active emotional, moral, and political participation. For these structures to operate successfully in mass art, they must be deployed in a way that is accessible to large numbers of people. But, once again, accessibility does not amount to passivity, nor does it foreclose the possibility of active audience participation.

Recently the philosopher Deborah Knight has challenged my claims about audience participation in regard to mass fictions.[2] One of her objections is that the picture of audience participation that I invoke by alluding to the audience's activities of following and constructing ongoing narratives is not transgeneric enough. It may, she argues, pertain to mystery stories and stories with enigmas in them, but it does not apply to all mass fictions. She

---

[1] Perhaps it is unfair always to hold up Greenberg as the proponent of the passivity argument, as if he were the only one. So let the record show that others are also culpable. For example, Irving Howe says that movies are 'put together along strictly stereotyped patterns that permit us the pleasure of relapsing into passive spectators.' See Irving Howe, 'Notes on Mass Culture', *Politics*, 5 (1948), 123.

[2] Deborah Knight, 'Making Sense of Genre', *Film and Philosophy*, vol. ii (1995), 58–73.

concedes that this covers quite a lot of territory,[3] but she adds that it doesn't work across the board for all kinds of mass fictions.

Why not? First, because she misconstrues my view as claiming that the audience's response to a narrative amounts to nothing more than *guessing* (!?) what happens next, and she contends that there are many stories where neither is the audience involved in this sort of guessing, nor is it profitable for them to be so. At the same time, following Paul Ricoeur, she maintains that following a story is not merely a matter of prospection—guessing ahead—but is also a matter of retrospection, of grasping the unity of the story, of seeing how it hangs together and why. And, though she agrees that mysteries and stories with mysteries in them involve the play of prospection and retrospection, she denies that other sorts of mass fictions, like action-adventures, do. Thus, she concludes that I have failed to show that mass narratives in general are participatory in the way called for by my own argumentative agenda.

Let me rebuff her pincers one at a time. First, she reduces my picture of the audience's active response to mass narratives to a matter of guessing ahead. I will not quibble that what she calls guessing I would parse in terms of inferences, conjectures, and tracking what is going on within a framework of structured expectations. But still, I would not have thought that I had even so narrowly circumscribed the audience's readerly and spectatorial activities. Among the audience's activities, I also include filling in presuppositions, picking up on implications, interpreting narrative meaning—both in terms of what events signify and how they fit into larger causal explanations of the course of events in the story—as well as colligating events and characters under the rubric of themes, interpreting metaphors, detecting theses, and the gamut of other spectatorial and readerly activities enumerated throughout this text and earlier ones.[4] At least some of these activities are available in most mass fictions and, therefore, the case for the active participation of the audience to mass fictions does not lean upon so slender a reed as the one Knight deals me.[5]

---

[3] That is, puzzles saliently posed engage readers, viewers, and listeners in speculation very, very frequently in all sorts of mass fictions that are not strictly mysteries. In Petru Popescu's *Almost Adam*, a jungle cum evolution adventure, the reader is, for a time, occupied with suspicions about why Modibo has arrived on the scene and about who really sent him; while in George Gissing's *Eve's Ransom*, a romance, the reader plays with the question of what actually accounts for Eve's hesitancy with respect to Hilliard before it is explained. In other words, a mystery element is a feature of many, many mass fictions, not just the ones 'officially' designated as mysteries.

[4] Prof. Knight's article is a response to my 'Paradox of Junk Fiction'.

[5] See David Bordwell's *Narration in the Fiction Film* (Madison: University of Wisconsin Press, 1985) for further examples of the constructive activities of movie audiences above and beyond guessing ahead. For examples of the readerly activities of filling in with respect to comic books, see Will Eisner, *Comics and Sequential Art* (Tamarac, Florida: Poorhouse Press, 1985).

Second, let me address Knight's emphasis on retrospection. She thinks that if following a mass fiction were to be as decisive for the issue of audience participation as I make out, then it would have to involve what she calls retrospection, along with prospection. And she claims that, outside mystery stories, there is little retrospection with respect to mass fictions. This, of course, depends on what she means by retrospection. If she means, as I think she suggests, a process of seeing the parts of the narrative fall into place—of comprehending that the narrative is unified; of not simply grasping what happens next, but why it happens—then I think that she is wrong to suppose that mass fictions of all sorts do not encourage retrospection. Not only stories with mysteries do this. Every kind of mass fiction does.

Just before writing this envoi, I saw the movie *Escape from L.A.*. It is not a mystery. It is a fairly representative action film of the sort that Knight alleges provides no room for retrospection. The last shot involves the character Snake lighting a wooden match. That match not only brings together a number of important themes of the film—including a reassertion of freedom of choice (the right to smoke) and the need for humans to return to a less technologically regulated existence—it also reminds the viewer of the earlier scene in the film when Snake acquired his wooden matches. Since that was an occasion when he also came into possession of the other paraphernalia that he uses to overthrow two dictatorships, the lighting of the match brings the whole film before the mind's eye as a neatly structured ensemble. There can be no doubt that it provokes retrospection, though *Escape from L.A.* cannot be called a mystery.

But what does this one counter-example prove? Quite a lot, I think. Because the use of the match in this film is really an example of Scribe's Law—only instead of a gun, in this case, the match that appears in the first act is ignited in the last act. Such unifying structures are generic throughout mass fiction. And with them comes retrospection in what I understand to be Knight's sense of that concept.[6]

In the 'Author's Afterword' to *Coffey on the Mile*, the last instalment of the serial novel *The Green Mile*, Stephen King talks about how he needed to return to the theme of the mouse Mr Jingles and how he worked out the parallel between the characters of the orderly Dolan in the framing

---

[6] For example, at the end of Charles Willeford's pulp fiction *Pick-up*, the reader suddenly learns that the protagonist is black. This prompts the reader to reinterpret the significance of many of the previous scenes and actions in the novel. Upon reflection, many of the events in the story take on new layers of meaning. Surely this counts as retrospection. Moreover, inasmuch as this sort of 'hook' or 'trick' ending—remember O. Henry—is quite common in mass fiction, one must agree that retrospection is a customarily recurring feature of mass narrative.

story and Percy Wetmore in Coffey's story. Both these repetitions are quite apparent to the plain reader. King literally puts them out front where they are hard to miss. They do not require a degree in literary criticism to be detected. But once detected, as they are intended to be, they bring the coherence of the story before the reader's mind. They engender retrospection. And they are not unusual features for mass fictions to have. Thus, mass fictions other than mysteries can facilitate retrospection.[7] Indeed, this is quite common, unless Knight means something peculiar by retrospection.

Of course, I do not restrict audience participation in response to mass fictions to following or constructing the story. I also consider their moral and emotional responses. But Knight questions whether we really make moral and emotional judgements when reading, viewing, or listening to mass fictions. She writes: 'Here I must confess real skepticism. I think that it is far from obvious that moral judgments are *made*—i.e., deliberated over, reflected upon, contemplated—by viewers or readers of generic fictions. Rather, they are made for us by generic texts.'[8]

Here I want to make two points. First, as I have shown in earlier chapters, *sometimes* mass fictions do involve reflection of the rather sustained and protracted sort that Knight valorizes. But second, what are we to make of her metaphysically strange-sounding view that texts make judgements for us?

At best, it must be a metaphor. But a metaphor for what? I conjecture that Knight is actually talking about passivity. For Knight, we don't actively make moral and emotional judgements in response to texts; texts make the judgements for us. Yet, one wonders whether Knight is prepared to deny that the fast moral and emotional assessments that we frequently make in everyday life are active?

Similarly, one suspects that Knight thinks that when I speak of the audience following the narrative, of the audience's filling it in or tracking it, and of our construction of the story, these are not really active events, or

---

[7] Similarly, Mary Higgins Clark's *Moonlight Becomes You*, like several of her other novels, repeats the motif of a young woman who treats older women not as distant, alien creatures from another generation/race, but as interesting, lively intelligences, almost always worth engaging in conversation. This advances a theme of Clark's work—an idealized relationship between the young and the old—and this readily detectable, recurring theme gives the reader a sense of the novel's unity. This novel, of course, is a mystery; however, the aspect of the novel I am pointing to does not involve figuring out a mystery, but rather detecting a theme.

Moreover, few mass fictions are altogether bereft of themes like this, and, in so far as they are easily and intentionally within the ordinary reader's grasp, they supply another way in which readers of junk fiction can appreciate (retrospect?) the unity of mass novels.

With respect to Hollywood films, George Wilson has also provided many intriguing examples of the ways in which movies can enlist interpretative activity from audiences. See George Wilson, *Narration in Light* (Baltimore: Johns Hopkins Press, 1986).   [8] Knight, 'Making Sense of Genre', 70.

active enough for Knight's taste. They do not show that there is transactional value to be had from mass narratives, because the audience is not really participatory. They're really passive, despite the appearance of activity. So it's *déjà vu* Greenberg all over again.

But as I argued in Chapter 1, the burden of proof here actually lies with those who endorse the passivity argument. They must come up with a precise account of what they mean by *activity* and *passivity* when it comes to aesthetic responses. For there is a prima facie case for believing that the audiences of mass art are participatory. We can point to so many different things that they do in the process of processing mass art. If all this activity is supposed to be passive, we must ask them for a rigorous definition of what they mean by 'passivity' and for evidence to show that this concept really applies to the mass-art audience.

And while they are busy with that, we can occupy ourselves with other things, including the adumbration of further modes of what we may still call audience participation in response to mass art. And, of course, there are so many other topics yet untouched. By focusing on the reception side of things, we have said little about the production side of mass art, let alone the distribution side. There is so much more work to be done in terms of the philosophy of mass art.

But, in the words of that premier heroine of mass art, Scarlett O'Hara: 'Tomorrow is another day.'

Index

H: 847-475-9861

O 312-996-3029